ATLAS OF
BRITISH &
IRISH HISTORY

THE PENGUIN ATLAS OF BRITISH & IRISH HISTORY

Consultant Editors

Barry Cunliffe, Robert Bartlett, John Morrill, Asa Briggs, Joanna Bourke

PENGUIN BOOKS

Published by the Penguin Group
Penguin Books Ltd, 80 Strand, London WC2R 0RL, England
Penguin Putnam Inc., 375 Hudson Street, New York,
   New York 10014, USA
Penguin Books Australia Ltd, Ringwood, Victoria, Australia
Penguin Books Canada Ltd, 10 Alcorn Avenue, Toronto,
   Ontario, Canada M4V 3B2
Penguin Books India (P) Ltd, 11, Community Centre,
   Panchsheel Park, New Delhi – 110 017, India
Penguin Books (NZ) Ltd, Cnr Rosedale and Airborne Roads,
   Albany, Auckland, New Zealand
Penguin Books (South Africa) (Pty) Ltd, 5 Watkins Street,
   Denver Ext 4, Johannesburg 2094, South Africa

Penguin Books Ltd, Registered Offices:
80 Strand, London WC2R 0RL, England

On the World Wide Web at: www.penguin.com

First published 2001
First published in the USA 2002
1

Printed in Italy by L.E.G.O.
Cover printed by Concise
Colour Reproduction by Anglia Graphics Ltd, Bedford
Production controlled by Helen Eka

ISBN 0-140-29518-6
ISBN (US) 0-141-00915-2

Conceived and produced by John Haywood and Simon Hall
Designed by Darren Bennett
Edited by Elizabeth Tatham
Picture research by Veneta Bullen
Illustrations by Roger Hutchins
Cartography by Cosmographics/Haywood & Hall

...a Haywood & Hall production for Penguin Books

For Jo and Charlotte

CONTENTS

PART FOUR
19th-CENTURY BRITAIN & IRELAND

PART FIVE
MODERN BRITAIN & IRELAND

PREFACE

It is fully twenty years since the last major new historical atlas of the British Isles was published – at least, it is fully twenty years if we discount those illustrated books marketed as atlases that actually include very few maps. This length of time alone suggests that a new atlas is overdue, since an authoritative and up-to-date historical atlas remains both a vital reference tool and a uniquely fascinating visual introduction to the complexities of history. *The Penguin Atlas of British & Irish History* is that overdue and up-to-date guide.

In fact, the last twenty years have also seen perhaps the greatest revolution to date in the way the history of the British Isles is approached, studied and taught. The 'New British History' that has emerged in the course of this revolution is balanced and holistic where traditional British history was resolutely Anglocentric. Its starting-point is the recognition that the British Isles have always been home to a number of different nations and cultures, each with its own continuous and unbroken history – and that the history of the British Isles is the sum of all those histories. This new approach is most obvious in the case of the nations of Britain: where once the historical relationship between England and Scotland, or between England and Ireland, was studied primarily as one of conflict and conquest, it is now understood as a much more complex interaction, in which each nation was influenced in many different ways by the other, over a long period. But the New British History is not just a matter of nations. It also reflects a much wider change in the study of history in general, namely the recognition that the traditional history of rulers and major events is only a small part of a much wider and more exciting history of the whole of human experience. *The Penguin Atlas of British & Irish History* is the first major atlas of the New British History.

Here you will still be able to trace the story of England's gradual rise to political domination of the British Isles, but you will also encounter the attempt of Robert and Edward Bruce to extend the Scottish monarch's power over fourteenth-century Ireland, the lawless independence of the early modern Borders and the pivotal role of Ireland in the Civil Wars. You will find accounts of the Norman Conquest of England, the Reformation and the battle of the Atlantic – but also of the north–south divide in Roman Britain, the role of circulating schools in early modern Wales, the mushrooming of seaside resorts in Victorian England and the distribution of pirate radio stations and Beatles concert venues in 1960s Britain. You will also find yourself exploring the streets and landscapes of eight extraordinarily detailed artwork reconstructions of historical British cities, from Roman London and medieval Norwich to eighteenth-century Dublin and early industrial Manchester.

The atlas offers, we believe, not only an entirely new overview of the history of the

British Isles, but also many, many examples of historical data never before presented in map form for the general reader. In many cases, these innovations are a reflection of the continuing advance of historical research itself; two examples among many are the northernmost Agricolan marching camp shown in our map of Rome's Northern Frontier, which was uncovered by archaeologists only within the last few years, and the comparative data for the medieval economies of the British Isles, based on papal taxation returns that are still being examined by historians.

The atlas has a modular structure, with each subject self-contained in either one or two double-page spreads. Those modules that may be thought of as supplementary to the main story of British history are distinguished by a coloured background; these cover some of the most exciting thematic subjects in the atlas, or in some cases explore in more detail subjects touched on in the core modules. This modular approach and the large number of separate contributors mean that the atlas offers a variety of perspectives on British and Irish history, and that absolute consistency of coverage is impossible; we regard this as a positive reflection of the variety of history practised in Britain and Ireland today. All historical atlases involve a succession of compromises between scale and detail, and we have attempted, wherever possible, to keep such compromises to a minimum by complementing large-scale overview maps with smaller-scale maps showing the working out of historical developments at a more local, human scale. This, too, reflects a major – and admirable – preoccupation of exponents of the new history with explaining historical subjects by example rather than by generalisation.

Historical atlases are works of collaboration, perhaps more so than any other type of book. The list of collaborators on this atlas is a long one, and many others have provided support or encouragement. Our consultant editors were an enormous help in assembling the authorial teams as well as taking an expert oversight of their respective parts of the atlas. Many of our contributors made the time to engage with the project to a far greater extent than we could reasonably have expected, and all of them were generous in sharing their expert knowledge of their subjects. Alan Grimwade and Mark Eldridge of Cosmographics were a pleasure to work with. Our own core production team – Darren Bennett (design), Elizabeth Tatham (editorial) and Veneta Bullen (picture research) – displayed throughout the project a level of sheer publishing professionalism far higher than we had any right to request. John Swift provided expert assistance as a research editor at very short notice. Our illustrator, Roger Hutchins, exceeded even his own exceptional standards in his work on this project. Finally, our publisher, Nigel Wilcockson, ended up working as hard on the atlas as any of us – despite his numerous other responsibilities, and despite our promise that, this time, he really would be able to leave it all to us. We are very grateful to all of them, and are proud to work with them.

SIMON HALL
JOHN HAYWOOD

CONSULTANT EDITORS

Professor Robert Bartlett *University of St Andrews*

Professor Joanna Bourke *Birkbeck College, University of London*

Lord Briggs *formerly of Leeds, Sussex, Oxford and the Open universities*

Professor Barry Cunliffe *Institute of Archaeology, Oxford*

Professor John Morrill *Selwyn College, Cambridge*

CONTRIBUTORS

JA	Dr Joost Augusteijn *Leiden University*
BA	Mr Brian Ayers *Norfolk County Archaeologist*
SEB	Dr Sarah Barber *Lancaster University*
NB	Dr Nicholas Barton *Oxford University*
JMB	Professor Jeremy Black *University of Exeter*
JB	Professor Joanna Bourke *Birkbeck College, University of London*
RHB	Dr Roger Bowdler *English Heritage*
RB	Professor Richard Bradley *Reading University*
HB	Dr Huw Bowen *University of Leicester*
BMSC	Professer Bruce Campbell *Queen's University Belfast*
PPC	Dr Peter Catterall *University of London*
CC	Dr Caitriona Clear *National University of Ireland, Galway*
SC	Dr Stephen Constantine *Lancaster University*
BC	Professor Barry Cunliffe *Institute of Archaeology, Oxford*
AC	Dr Anne Curry *Reading University*
DD	Professor David Dickson *Trinity College Dublin*
STD	Dr Stephen Driscoll *University of Glasgow*
SD	Dr Seán Duffy *Trinity College Dublin*
SGE	Professor Steven Ellis *National University of Ireland, Galway*
HF	Ms Hazel Forsyth *Museum of London*
MF	Dr Michael Freeman *Oxford University*
AH	Dr Alasdair Hawkyard *Institute of Historical Research*
JH	Dr John Haywood *Lancaster University*
MH	Professor Martin Hewitt *Trinity and All Saints University College, Leeds*

DH	Dr Della Hooke *University of Birmingham*
RH	Dr Rosemary Horrox *Cambridge University*
CJ	Dr Clare Jackson *Cambridge University*
ATJ	Dr Andrew Jotischky *Lancaster University*
SDK	Professor Simon Keynes *Cambridge University*
DK	Professor David Killingray *Goldsmiths Gollege, University of London*
SL	Dr Shompa Lahiri *Queen Mary and Westfield College, University of London*
AM	Dr Alan Mackley *University of East Anglia*
JM	Professor John Mackenzie *Lancaster University*
RM	Dr Roger Middleton *Bristol University*
EOC	Dr Éamonn Ó Ciardha *University of Notre Dame*
WMO	Professor Mark Ormrod *University of York*
RDP	Dr Robert Pearce *St Martin's College, Lancaster*
RP	Dr Robert Penhallurick *University of Wales, Swansea*
GP	Professor Gordon Pirie *University of Salford*
CR	Dr Cathy Ross *Museum of London*
SR	Dr Sarah Richardson *University of Warwick*
RR	Professor Richard Rodger *University of Leicester*
DCAS	Dr David Shotter *Lancaster University*
JS	Dr John Swift *St Martin's College, Lancaster*
JGT	Dr Geoffrey Timmins *University of Central Lancashire*
JKW	Professor John Walton *University of Central Lancashire*
SW	Dr Sabine Wichert *Queen's University Belfast*
RW	Professor Richard Wilson *University of East Anglia*
NZ	Dr Nuala Zahedieh *University of Edinburgh*

The Atlas

PART ONE

ANCIENT BRITAIN & IRELAND

For the last 700,000 years, the land mass that has become Europe has experienced a succession of major oscillations in climate. The pattern is very complex, but in general terms it is possible to distinguish six periods of glaciation, interspersed by warmer periods. However, recent advances in the study of the palaeoclimate, using a wide range of scientific techniques, now suggest that there were no fewer than 19 different climatic events – an intense cold event alternating with a warm one. The last glaciation took place about 15,000 years ago. Since then, the temperature has been getting warmer, though not without fits and starts, and we have not yet reached the warmest part of our present 'interglacial'.

Humans were certainly living in what was to become southern Britain half a million years ago. At Boxgrove, near Chichester, a remarkable site, where Palaeolithic hunters camped, has been found. Amid the debris, archaeologists have recovered a few scraps of bone of an early species of human – *Homo heidelbergensis* – at present the earliest identifiable inhabitant of Britain. From that time until as recently as 10,000 years ago human groups came and went as the climate dictated, but from about 8000 BC the climate rapidly improved and Britain has since been continuously occupied.

One result of the retreat of the ice caps has been a change in sea level. The melting ice has raised the overall level of the water, but with the weight of ice removed, the land, previously depressed by the ice caps, has risen. For Britain and Ireland the overall effect has been a rise in sea level relative to the land, with Britain becoming an island for the first time around 7000 BC.

At this time the British Isles would have been largely covered by vast tracts of forest. The people, like their predecessors, were hunter–gatherers and relied entirely on wild foods. At first, meat was important, though wild fruits and plants were a necessary supplement, but as time went on and communities learnt to develop their local resources, more specialist regimes developed. Those living close to the seashore, for example, became heavily reliant on seafood, while others living on the lighter sandy soils created clearings by burning to encourage new growth, which attracted animals to browse.

Between 4000 and 3000 BC a trickle of new people from the Continent introduced domesticated cattle and sheep and cultivated wheat and barley, as well as the technology of pottery-making, into the two islands. The new innovations were quite quickly taken up and by about 3000 BC 'farming' had spread to most parts, and the open landscape familiar to us now began to take shape.

The last 3,500 years of the Ancient period (3000 BC–AD 500) can, most simply, be divided into three parts – a period of monument building, a period of intensive farming and a period of incipient industrialisation.

From about 3000 BC until just after 2000 BC the British and Irish landscapes were monumentalised. Enormous amounts of human effort were invested in building – communal enclosures (known as causewayed enclosures), great tomb monuments to proclaim the power of the ancestors, and a variety of ritual monuments variously called henges, stone circles and alignments by archaeologists. Taken as a whole, this 'age of monument building' demonstrated a growing cohesion in society, the act of construction calling for planned communal activity. The resulting structures were our first architecture. We will never know what the true motivation was behind the imperative to build, but perhaps, deep down, was the desire of the precarious Neolithic communities to demonstrate their control of nature, to reassure themselves by imposing visible signs of their history on the land.

Over the next 2,000 years the land was brought increasingly under control as farming regimes spread and became more permanently established and the earth was made to yield new resources – copper, tin and, later, iron, as well as other luxuries such as gold, amber, jet and shale for making ornaments. It is fair to say that by the first century AD the human control of the land had reached a level that was not surpassed until the sixteenth century.

The third period – that of the Roman occupation – saw the imposition of Mediterranean systems of urbanisation and low-scale industrialisation on southeastern Britain. It was premature and, with the collapse of the Roman administrative structure, the island's communities relaxed and reverted – at least for a time – to their traditional prehistoric modes.

BARRY CUNLIFFE

Although Britain is an island today, we should not forget that for the greater part of human prehistory it was joined to Europe by a land-bridge. That period overlaps with the Pleistocene Ice Ages, which began 1.6 million years ago, and was a time of major climatic fluctuation. During warmer stages, continental plant and animal species could migrate into Britain, while in colder times their geographic ranges shifted further south. Humans, like other large

about 200,000 years ago, when new stone toolkits characterised by implements made by flaking stone became more common. This Middle Palaeolithic flaking technique made more economical use of stone and permitted a wider range of tools to be manufactured. The new technique is usually attributed to the Neanderthals (*Homo neanderthalensis*).

THE NEANDERTHALS

The Neanderthals evolved in Europe and western Asia from the archaic human species such as *Homo heidelbergensis* that were already living there. The place of the Neanderthals in human evolution has been much debated, but the recent recovery of fossil Neanderthal DNA suggests that they were not ancestral to modern humans. Although the only site so far discovered with Neanderthal human remains on the British mainland is Pontnewydd Cave in Wales, typical Middle Palaeolithic flake tools have a widespread occurrence in England and Wales – so the Neanderthals must have been equally widespread. The grouping of Middle Palaeolithic sites in regional clusters supports the impression that the Neanderthals lived in isolated groups and did not range very far from their home bases. As yet, no artefacts of this period have been found in Ireland or Scotland, but the known presence in these areas of animals such as woolly rhinoceros, mammoth and reindeer, which formed part of the Neanderthal diet, suggests that one day we may find signs of Neanderthal human activity in these countries as well as in England and Wales.

EXTINCTION AND REPLACEMENT

The Neanderthals are regarded as the great survivors of the Ice Ages, and they appear to have had Europe to themselves until about 40,000 years ago, when they began to be replaced by people with very different ideas and cultural traditions. The newcomers were members of our own species, modern *Homo sapiens*, who brought with them a technology that we characterise as Upper Palaeolithic, encompassing a wide range of tool types, including slender flint blades for inserting into knife handles and spearshafts. Similarities in stoneworking techniques suggest that these first fully modern human inhabitants of Europe were migrants from the Middle East. Tools carved out of antler, ivory and bone are another feature of this phase.

Human fossils in Europe

- Homo erectus and Homo heidelbergensis, c.800,000 –300,000 years ago
- Pre-Neanderthals, 300,000–150,000 years ago
- Homo neanderthalensis, c.150,000–28,000 years ago
- Modern Homo sapiens
- → Conjectural spread of physically modern humans
- Glaciation 18,000 years ago
- Coastline 18,000 years ago

Early humans in Europe

The human colonisation of Europe took place in the Ice Age, a time of climatic fluctuation between intense cold and warm spells. The earliest human species to live in Europe, *Homo erectus*, arrived about 800,000 years ago. They were succeeded by *Homo heidelbergensis* and then by *Homo neanderthalensis*. Physically modern humans, *Homo sapiens*, arrived from Eurasia c.40,000 years ago.

mammals, migrated periodically in and out of the British peninsula; their presence is certainly recorded in southern England at sites like Boxgrove by about 500,000 years ago. At Boxgrove, fossil human teeth and bones of *Homo heidelbergensis*, flint implements known as handaxes, and the bones of animals such as rhinoceros and wild horse have been recovered. That these handaxes were used for butchery is clearly shown by wear traces on the edges of the tools and corresponding cut-marks at the animal bones. The range of animal body parts represented on such butchery sites also indicates that the animals were hunted rather than scavenged, and this in turn implies a high degree of social organisation and communal effort. It seems likely, therefore, that the earliest human visitors to Britain lived in sizeable human groups, and had language skills and the ability to think and plan ahead.

Lower Palaeolithic (Old Stone Age) assemblages similar to those at Boxgrove, with handaxes, occurring over a wide area of Europe, remained remarkably unchanged until

Britain's first humans

For most of the Ice Age, so much of the world's water was locked up in ice sheets that sea levels were at times over 100 metres (328 feet) lower than those of today, and Britain was linked to the Continent by a land-bridge. Britain's first human inhabitants, therefore, arrived on foot. The earliest evidence of human habitation dates to about 500,000 years ago, but there were long periods when Britain was made uninhabitable by Arctic conditions. Physically modern humans first reached Britain about 31,000 years ago, but they became widespread only towards the end of the last Ice Age, around 13,000 years ago. Sea levels raised by melting ice finally cut Britain and Ireland off from continental Europe around 5000 BC.

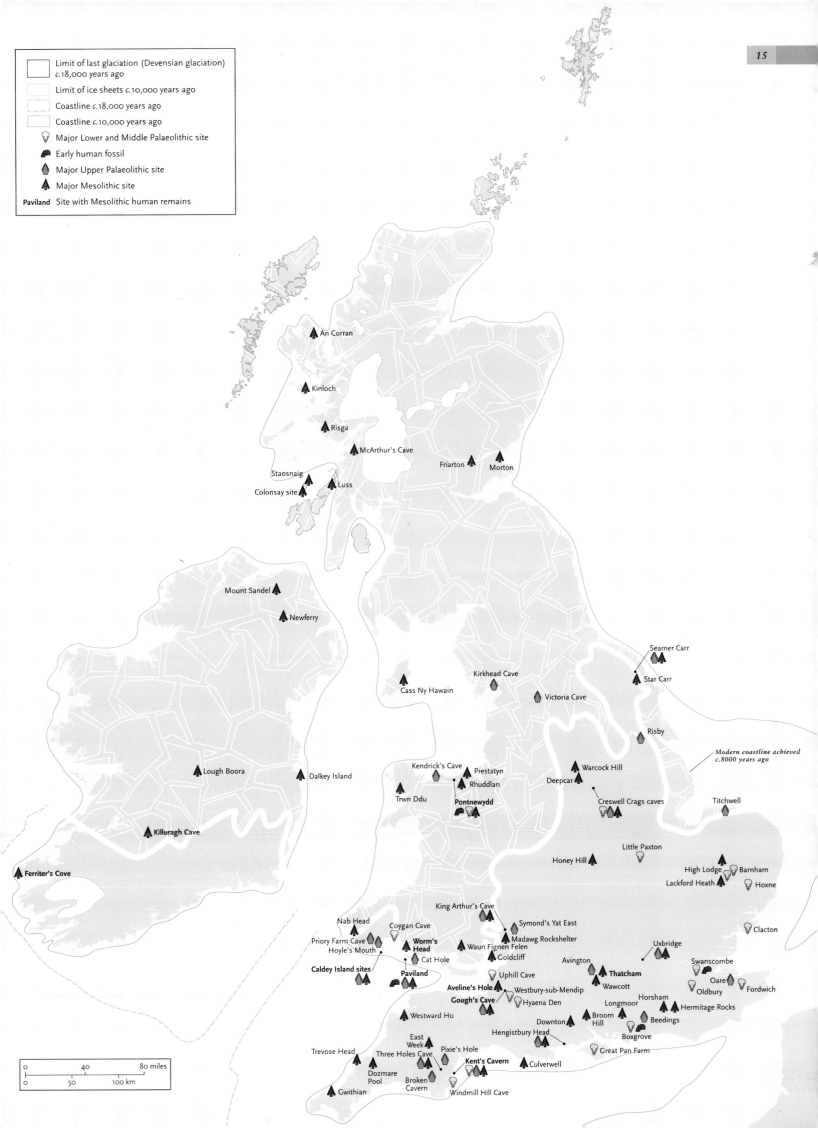

Limit of last glaciation (Devensian glaciation) c.18,000 years ago

Limit of ice sheets c.10,000 years ago

Coastline c.18,000 years ago

Coastline c.10,000 years ago

Major Lower and Middle Palaeolithic site

Early human fossil

Major Upper Palaeolithic site

Major Mesolithic site

Paviland Site with Mesolithic human remains

An Corran

Kinloch

Risga

McArthur's Cave

Staosnaig

Colonsay site

Luss

Friarton

Morton

Mount Sandel

Newferry

Seamer Carr

Kirkhead Cave

Star Carr

Cass Ny Hawain

Victoria Cave

Risby

Lough Boora

Dalkey Island

Modern coastline achieved c.8000 years ago

Kendrick's Cave

Prestatyn

Rhuddlan

Warcock Hill

Deepcar

Creswell Crags caves

Titchwell

Killuragh Cave

Trwn Ddu

Pontnewydd

Little Paxton

Ferriter's Cove

Honey Hill

High Lodge

Barnham

Lackford Heath

Hoxne

King Arthur's Cave

Clacton

Nab Head

Coygan Cave

Symond's Yat East

Priory Farm Cave

Worm's Head

Madawg Rockshelter

Uxbridge

Hoyle's Mouth

Cat Hole

Waun Fignen Felen

Swanscombe

Avington

Caldey Island sites

Paviland

Goldcliff

Thatcham

Oare

Uphill Cave

Wawcott

Oldbury

Fordwich

Aveline's Hole

Westbury-sub-Mendip

Longmoor

Horsham

Hermitage Rocks

Gough's Cave

Hyaena Den

Broom Hill

Beedings

Westward Ho

Downton

Boxgrove

Trevose Head

East Week

Pixie's Hole

Hengistbury Head

Great Pan Farm

Three Holes Cave

Kent's Cavern

Culverwell

Dozmare Pool

Gwithian

Broken Cavern

Windmill Hill Cave

0   40   80 miles

0   50   100 km

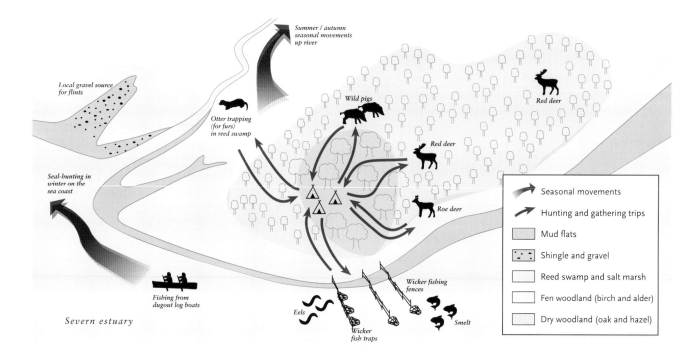

Summer / autumn
seasonal movements
up river

Local gravel source
for flints

Wild pigs

Red deer

Otter trapping
(for furs)
in reed swamp

Red deer

Roe deer

Seal-hunting in
winter on the
sea coast

Seasonal movements

Hunting and gathering trips

Mud flats

Shingle and gravel

Reed swamp and salt marsh

Fen woodland (birch and alder)

Dry woodland (oak and hazel)

Fishing from
dugout log boats

Eels

Wicker fishing
fences

Wicker
fish traps

Smelt

Severn estuary

Mesolithic Goldcliff

Goldcliff, on the Severn estuary in South Wales, is the site of an encampment of Mesolithic hunter–gatherers, occupied c.6,600 years ago. Goldcliff was then a wooded rise in an area of extensive coastal reed swamps. Bones of fish and land mammals, such as deer and wild pigs, found in archaeological excavations on the site, indicate that it was occupied only during winter and spring. During the summer, the inhabitants probably moved inland or further along the sea coast for seal-hunting.

The arrival of modern humans also witnessed a new sophistication in symbolic behaviour, revealed by the first appearance of cave paintings, musical instruments (bone flutes) and highly elaborate human burials in which the remains were decorated with red ochre and marine shell grave goods. These traditions spread extremely rapidly, suggesting the existence of long-distance social networks and complex modern language.

Such factors may have provided these humans with a competitive edge over the Neanderthals, but very little is known about the behavioural transition or the disappearance of the Neanderthals. Certainly, such advantages as the modern humans enjoyed cannot have been dramatic, because there was a long period of co-existence of the two

Horse engraved on bone

From Robin Hood's Cave, Creswell Crags, Derbyshire, late Upper Palaeolithic, c.12,500 years old. So far, this is the only piece of Upper Palaeolithic art showing an animal found in Britain.

species, and the Neanderthals did not become extinct in their last strongholds in Spain and the Balkans until about 28,000 years ago.

BRITAIN'S FIRST MODERN HUMANS

The earliest evidence of modern *Homo sapiens* in Britain comes from a jaw fragment from Kent's Cavern, Devon, dated to 31,000 years ago. A richly decorated adult male burial with red ochre and covered in ivory ornaments is known from a slightly later date at Paviland Cave in South Wales. Both of these human finds are associated with Early Upper Palaeolithic artefacts. Discoveries from this period are so far very rare, and this probably reflects low-level human activity. They include an example of a spear point of bone or antler from Uphill Cave near the Mendips. After a phase of major ice sheet expansion, followed by rewarming 13,000 years ago, more widespread occupation of the country is indicated by finds of Late Upper Palaeolithic type. Human settlement does not seem to have extended into Ireland at this time, but possible Late Upper Palaeolithic artefacts have been found in western Scotland. Among the best-known sites in England and Wales are those in caves and rock shelters, but large open-air sites like Hengistbury Head in Dorset hint at what might still await discovery. During this period, temperatures in Britain rose to levels similar to those of today, and red deer and wild horse came to dominate the native large mammal faunas, while tundra-dwelling species like mammoth disappeared.

The existence of widely shared cultural traditions and exchange networks spanning much of northwestern Europe can be verified by similarities in bone and antler equipment, including barbed points, ivory rods, perforated antler batons and bone eyed-needles. However, the paucity of figurative art (a solitary bone engraving of a horse's head from Robin Hood's Cave at Cresswell Crags) and stylistic differences in lithic tool types does suggest regional variability, perhaps reflecting lower population levels on the European periphery. A rare example of human burial from this period was found in Gough's Cave in Cheddar Gorge, where the corpses of several adults and children bear cut-marks inflicted by skinning and dismembering during the funerary ritual. About 11,000 years ago, climatic deterioration began and the return of arctic conditions led to another period of human abandonment, signalling the end of the Palaeolithic in Britain.

THE MESOLITHIC SETTLEMENT

In chronological terms, the Mesolithic (Middle Stone Age) immediately follows the Palaeolithic and covers the period from 10,000 to 5,500 years ago, after which farming was introduced to Britain. The beginning of the period was marked by rapid climatic warming, which made Britain once again attractive for human occupation. In the warmer conditions, tundra and open steppe gave way first to birch and pine woodland and then to thick deciduous forests of hazel, oak, elm and lime. The increase in temperatures also led to a rise in sea levels, which finally established the shorelines of Britain more or less as they are today. In addition to the very wide distribution of Mesolithic sites in England and Wales, certain evidence of human activities is recorded for the first time in Scotland and Ireland. Mesolithic sites like Mount Sandel are among the earliest in Ireland, suggesting that colonisers arrived by boat from southwestern Scotland.

The people of the Mesolithic, much like their predecessors, were hunter–gatherers. They relied on collecting edible wild plants, on fishing and on hunting animals such as red deer, roe deer and wild pig. The survival of hafted stone axes and bow hunting equipment suggests that they were adapted to the forested conditions that now prevailed. Finds of tiny retouched tools, or microliths, used in rows to form barbed arrowheads, are known from several sites, including Waun Fignen Felen in Wales and Seamer Carr in Yorkshire. The deadly effectiveness of such weaponry is demonstrated at Mother Grundy's Parlour, Creswell Crags, by a broken microlith lodged in an animal bone. Nor were microliths simply single-purpose tools: at Nab Head, Pembrokeshire, for example, microliths were used as drill bits for making stone beads, and elsewhere they were used as the blades of harvesting knives. The use of mastic for gluing stone tools into wooden hafts is attested by finds of plant resin on an artifact from Thatcham and by mastic 'cakes' at Lackford Heath, Suffolk and Star Carr, Yorkshire. Rare examples of barbed antler spearheads from Star Carr also show traces of mastic and birch bark bindings. Other tools found at Star Carr include perforated elk antler mattocks. Wear patterns on these indicate that they were used for digging, perhaps for edible roots near the lakeside.

Increased social complexity and sedentism (that is, a tendency to settle) are generally considered characteristic developments of the later Mesolithic. Evidence of these changes in Europe include the appearance of semi-permanent coastal villages, massive shell middens, food storage pits, territorial boundaries and large, planned cemeteries. But such indicators are seemingly absent in Britain and Ireland, where shell middens tend to be relatively small or dispersed and coastal sites, where preserved, are all on a fairly minor scale. Nor are large cemeteries found: burials are generally of single individuals, apart from the cave of Aveline's Hole, in the Mendips, where a cemetery of 70 or so individuals was recorded. At this site, a rare glimpse of the symbolic treatment of the dead is provided by human skeletons adorned with pig and red deer incisors and sprinkled with red ochre.

Smaller, temporary settlements with no obvious storage facilities are more typical of the British Mesolithic. At Goldcliff on the Severn estuary, for example, partly water-logged sediments preserve food residues of fish bones and land mammals which indicate that the site was occupied only during winter and spring. Rocks for tool-making all derive from the local beaches, while imported beach flint and marine shell beads occur at nearby inland sites like Madawg Rockshelter and King Arthur's Cave and at Three Holes Cave in Devon, showing how people moved up and down the main rivers, probably on a seasonal basis.

Recently, stable isotopic analysis of human bone has provided an insight into the Mesolithic diet. It shows that although plants were certainly consumed, meat was very important in the diet. Land mammals were the main source of protein – even, surprisingly, at seashore locations such as Paviland and Worm's Head, South Wales – further strengthening the idea that regular coastal–inland contacts were maintained. Where there is evidence for a high marine food component in the diet, as at Ferriter's Cove in Southwestern Ireland, Colonsay, and on Caldey Island, the sites are generally younger in age and may suggest a progressive shift in emphasis on coastal resources towards the end of the Mesolithic. **NB**

Handaxe
A Lower Palaeolithic flint handaxe from Oxfordshire. Handaxes were actually a kind of knife, probably used for butchering animals.

Upper Palaeolithic tools
A leaf-shaped flint projectile point (c.20,000 years old), a flint blade and an antler harpoon (both c.12,500 years old). Sophisticated tools such as these appeared in Europe at the same as the first physically modern humans.

Middle Palaeolithic tools
A handaxe (left) and side scraper, used for cleaning hides, both c.40,000 years old. These tools are typical of those manufactured by Neanderthals.

THE NEOLITHIC AGE

The meaning of the term 'Neolithic' has changed since it was first coined in the nineteenth century. It was originally intended to refer to particular ways of making stone tools, but was subsequently extended to include the adoption of domesticated plants and animals. The term has since been further expanded to embrace the earliest stone and earthwork monuments found in these islands, so that it is now used to describe all aspects of the period of prehistory from the beginning of farming through to the introduction of metal-working. These changes are not simply the results of the vagaries of fashion, but reflect the growing confidence of archaeologists in coming to terms with a period that lasted from around 4000 to 2500 BC. Although the evidence for farming has been re-examined in recent years, as has our knowledge of the prehistoric pattern of settlement, there is much about the Neolithic that remains an enigma. At present, more is known about the monumental architecture of the period than about the lives of the people who built it.

Despite these changes in perspective, certain points are uncontroversial. The first domesticated animals – especially sheep – must have been introduced by settlers from continental Europe, as their wild prototypes are not found in Britain or Ireland. It seems likely that these immigrants from the Continent lived alongside the indigenous population, who eventually embraced the new subsistence economy. Other innovations included wheat, barley, pottery and the principal forms of monument. Both islands adopted the new way of life at about the same time, but there were significant differences between developments in these two areas. In Ireland, recent excavation has unearthed a large number of rectangular houses belonging to this period, but in England and much of Scotland these are rare. It may be that only certain regions witnessed a sedentary pattern of settlement and in others cereal farming was not the mainstay of the economy until the Bronze Age. Before that time, more emphasis was placed on livestock, an interpretation supported by chemical analysis of human bones for evidence of diet.

During the Earlier Neolithic period (4000–3300 BC) settlement took place on the lighter soils, which would have been easier to farm, and involved the piecemeal clearance of the native woodland. Settlers may have avoided the main areas occupied by indigenous hunter–gatherers, but by the Later Neolithic (3300–2500 BC), that distinction had broken down and quite large parts of the landscape were in use,

West Kennet

Built c.3300 BC, West Kennet long barrow, Wiltshire, is one of the largest Neolithic tombs in Britain. The burial chamber, entered through an opening in the stone façade, contained the remains of 40 people. The skeletons were disarticulated and several skulls and long bones were missing, possibly removed for some ritual purpose.

some of them on a seasonal basis. The initial settlements were small and often short-lived, and few of them contained many buildings. The landscape may well have been rather similar to that found in parts of western Britain or Ireland today, with a network of dispersed farmsteads. Only in the Later Neolithic are there signs of the formation of small villages – evidence that at present is limited to Orkney, where the remains of houses are exceptionally well preserved.

MONUMENTS TO THE DEAD

Earlier Neolithic monuments were, like farming itself, of continental inspiration. There were numerous monuments to the dead, and these conformed to two very general traditions. One consisted of long mounds or cairns, whose distinctive form seems to have echoed that of the longhouses (buildings that incorporated accommodation for humans at one end and a byre for livestock at the other) occupied many generations earlier in regions such as the Rhineland. The same forms were created in earth and stone, and both were associated with the remains of the dead, whose bodies may have been exposed in order to allow their flesh to decompose before their remains were deposited at these monuments. Only a small part of the population seems to be represented here, and there is evidence that selected bones may have circulated as relics over a wider area.

The second tradition was the passage grave. Essentially an Atlantic phenomenon, it may have originated among indigenous communities along the coast of continental Europe. These monuments were especially prevalent in Ireland and the Northern and Western Isles and were often associated with circular cairns. Each had a corbelled chamber at its centre, approached by a low passage roofed with lintels. Some of the main tombs were decorated with abstract designs. These designs are a particular feature of the chambered tombs in the Boyne Valley north of Dublin, but they share a number of carved motifs with the open-air rock art found in northern Britain and Ireland.

CEREMONIAL CENTRES

Together with these monuments to the dead, we find enclosures that probably acted as ceremonial centres for a wider population. These are characteristically defined by one or

---

Neolithic monuments in Britain and Ireland 4000–2500 BC

The first farmers began to transform the landscape of the British Isles by clearing woodland and building monuments. Characteristic monuments of the Neolithic are tombs, such as earthen long barrows and cairns in eastern Britain, or passage graves in the West and in Ireland. Ritual earthwork enclosures, known as causewayed 'camps' were built throughout the Neolithic in much of southern Britain. In the later Neolithic (c.3300–2500 BC), circular earthwork enclosures called henges were built, often containing burials or circles of stones or timber posts, and linear earthworks, sometimes several kilometres long. In many parts of the British Isles the remains of Neolithic stone-mining can still be seen.

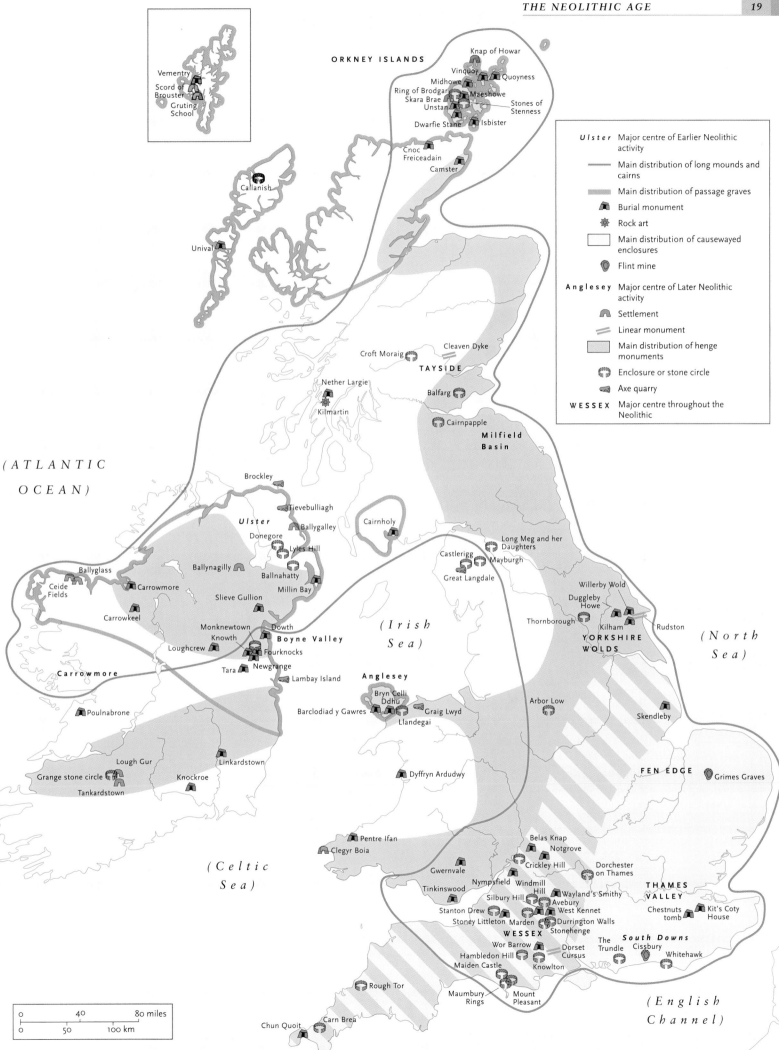

ORKNEY ISLANDS

Knap of Howar
Vinquoy
Midhowe
Quoyness
Ring of Brodgar
Skara Brae   Maeshowe
Unstan   Stones of Stenness
Dwarfie Stane   Isbister

Cnoc Freiceadain
Camster

Vementry
Scord of Brouster
Gruting School

Callanish

Unival

Ulster   Major centre of Earlier Neolithic activity

Main distribution of long mounds and cairns

Main distribution of passage graves

Burial monument

Rock art

Main distribution of causewayed enclosures

Flint mine

Anglesey   Major centre of Later Neolithic activity

Settlement

Linear monument

Main distribution of henge monuments

Enclosure or stone circle

Axe quarry

WESSEX   Major centre throughout the Neolithic

Croft Moraig   Cleaven Dyke
TAYSIDE
Nether Largie   Balfarg
Kilmartin
Cairnpapple

Milfield Basin

(ATLANTIC OCEAN)

Brockley
Tievebulliagh
Ulster   Ballygalley
Donegore   Cairnholy
Lyles Hill
Ballynagilly   Long Meg and her Daughters
Ballyglass   Ballnahatty   Castlerigg   Mayburgh
Ceide Fields   Carrowmore   Millin Bay   Great Langdale
Slieve Gullion   Willerby Wold
Carrowkeel   Duggleby Howe
Monknewtown   Dowth   Thornborough   Kilham   Rudston
Knowth   *Boyne Valley*   YORKSHIRE WOLDS
Loughcrew   Fourknocks   (North Sea)
Carrowmore   Tara   Newgrange
Lambay Island
Anglesey   Arbor Low
(Irish Sea)
Poulnabrone   Bryn Celli Ddhu   Skendleby
Barclodiad y Gawres   Graig Lwyd
Llandegai

Lough Gur   Linkardstown
Grange stone circle   Knockroe   Dyffryn Ardudwy   FEN EDGE
Tankardstown   Grimes Graves

(Celtic Sea)

Pentre Ifan
Clegyr Boia   Belas Knap
Notgrove
Gwernvale   Crickley Hill   Dorchester on Thames
Nympsfield   THAMES VALLEY
Tinkinswood   Windmill Hill   Wayland's Smithy
Silbury Hill   Avebury   Chestnuts tomb   Kit's Coty House
Stanton Drew   West Kennet   *South Downs*
Stoney Littleton   Marden   Durrington Walls   Cissbury
WESSEX   Stonehenge   Whitehawk
Wor Barrow   The Trundle
Hambledon Hill   Dorset Cursus
Maiden Castle   Knowlton
Rough Tor   Maumbury Rings   Mount Pleasant   (English Channel)

Chun Quoit   Carn Brea

0   40   80 miles
0   50   100 km

The Langdale site

The long scree slopes on the flanks of Pike O'Stickle in Langdale in the Lake District are waste from a Neolithic stone axe factory. Axes were 'roughed out' at the mining site before being carried down to be finished elsewhere.

more circuits of ditches interrupted at frequent intervals by causeways of unexcavated soil – hence their designation as 'causewayed' enclosures. This form of monument is also found on the Continent, where the earliest examples were associated with groups of domestic buildings. Few causewayed enclosures have been found in Ireland, Scotland and Wales, and the great majority of these earthworks have been identified in lowland England. None seems to have been used as a settlement, at least in its initial phases, and their main association is with feasting and the exchange of non-local artefacts. These places were also used to commemorate the dead, whose relics are often found there. They may have been among the places used for the exposure of human bodies before burial.

Few of these traditions continued much after 3300 BC. Instead, new linear monuments, which have few, if any, counterparts in mainland Europe, were built, suggesting that links with the Continent had become less important by this time. In Britain, one of the most widely distributed forms of linear monument was the cursus, so called because they were once compared with the form of the Roman racecourse. They were elongated rectangular earth-banked enclosures, thought to have been used for processions. Occasional examples lead between burial mounds and there are even sites that enclose a central mound, rather like an enormously extended long barrow. Few artefacts have been found at these monuments, but they appear to be later in date than the causewayed enclosures, as they occasionally cut through them. Like the ceremonial centres, cursuses can be associated with finds of human remains. Most of these

Stone axe factories in the Lake District

Miners at Pike O'Stickle exploited an outcrop of hard, fine-grained volcanic rock that could be flaked and polished to make high-quality axes. Neolithic prospectors identified several other suitable outcrops of the same rock for axe production.

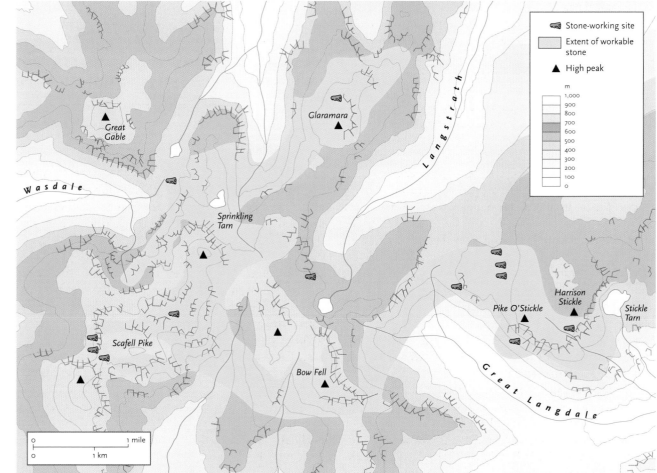

monuments are in England and Scotland, but recent work has identified a few examples in Ireland and Wales.

LATER NEOLITHIC ARCHITECTURE

The main tradition of Later Neolithic architecture had a quite different source: the Atlantic coast of Europe. Some of the best examples of this architecture can be seen in Orkney. Orkney has a major concentration of Neolithic passage graves, which continued to be built until about 3000 BC. These seem to have been associated with a new kind of settlement, typified by groups of stone houses and circular earthwork enclosures of the kind known as henge monuments. The two examples in Orkney both contained rings of monoliths. The same style of pottery has been linked with all these sites, suggesting that they were in use at the same time.

Between 3000 and 2500 BC the tradition of circular monuments was adopted much more widely, until their distribution extended into most regions of Britain and Ireland. There are numerous local variations: some of the henge monuments in southern England were exceptionally large, certain of these enclosures contained rings of wooden posts or upright stones, and recent work has identified a number of sites whose perimeter was defined by a massive palisade. Whatever the significance of these local variations, two basic points are clear: these were not settlements but ceremonial centres, and they were used by large numbers of people drawn from the surrounding area. A few were aligned on the movements of the sun and possibly the moon. Stonehenge, which gives its name to this class of monument, is related to this tradition but is not a typical example. It may have begun life as a causewayed enclosure and was then rebuilt as a palisaded enclosure, probably with a post circle at its centre. Finally, that structure was replaced by the monument we know today. The form of Stonehenge, with its uprights and lintels, was based on that of similar wooden structures known to have been constructed at about the same time.

As with causewayed enclosures, excavations of henges have revealed a wide variety of exotic artefacts, some of which may have been intended as offerings. These provide an important indication of long-distance contacts between different communities in Britain and Ireland, revealing the background to the widespread adoption of these styles of monument-building. The clearest indication of the wider pattern of communication comes from the production and exchange of stone axes.

Great Langdale

THE LANGDALE AXE FACTORY

Stone axes were made in two main areas: at the flint mines of lowland England, most of which functioned before about 3300 BC, and at a series of stone quarries in the highland zones, where production increased after that time. More is known about the products of the latter group because the sources of individual artefacts have been identified by geologists, so that it is possible to work out the distribution of the axes made at particular quarries. The largest source was in the central Lake District, around Great Langdale, and axes made in this area can be shown to have travelled to virtually every part of the British Isles. Excavation at the Langdale quarries has shown that the people who were making these artefacts deliberately chose to obtain the raw material they needed in the most dangerous and inaccessible parts of the site, suggesting that the products may have been imbued with special qualities. They served as work tools for clearing the landscape, but sometimes also as valuable items to be dedicated to the supernatural. This exemplifies the interplay between the practical and the spiritual sides of prehistoric life that characterises the Neolithic period as a whole.   RB

THE RITUAL LANDSCAPE

The term 'ritual landscape' was originally invented to describe some of the clusters of Neolithic and Early Bronze Age monuments on the chalk of southern England, in particular the great concentrations of earthworks around Stonehenge on Salisbury Plain and Avebury on the Marlborough Downs. The term was first devised to describe major groups of ritual or ceremonial monuments, some of which had histories extending over more than a thousand years – but it also came to be used to distinguish these particular landscapes from those that formed part of the everyday life of Neolithic and Bronze Age people. It was automatically assumed that 'ritual' landscapes were quite separate from the places where people lived and that these landscapes had developed according to a logic of their own.

Prehistorians soon began to extend this idea to sites in other regions, but in doing so they had to drop some of their original assumptions. There is no doubt that the term describes a real phenomenon: concentrations of specialised stone and earthwork monuments do indeed occur at intervals across Britain and Ireland. Nor is there any dispute that

> 'The monumental landscapes of the Neolithic are qualitatively different from the spatial orders which preceded and which then succeeded them.'
>
> Julian Thomas, *Understanding the Neolithic* (1999)

rituals were conducted at these sites. But the assumption that such places were necessarily uninhabited became harder and harder to sustain, and so did the idea that ritual in prehistory was entirely cut off from daily life. Fieldwork around Stonehenge and Avebury has yielded enormous numbers of surface finds, some of which might very well mark the positions of settlements. When the idea of ritual landscapes was extended to the equally rich archaeology of Orkney, the original formulation had to be significantly modified. While 'ritual landscape' might describe the group of monuments around the Stones of Stenness, it could not account for the discovery of an entire Neolithic village just outside that site. The ritual monuments of this period could no longer be thought of as existing in isolation.

This is not to say that all these structures were built in the heart of inhabited areas. In fact, there was considerable variation. Certain groups of monuments, including causewayed enclosures, may have been positioned on the margins of the settled land and could even have been concealed within areas of forest, while others, including henges and stone circles, were often constructed along natural routes across the terrain, where they would have been accessible to large numbers of people. This is hardly surprising when we consider the amount of labour that was needed to build them. Construction of the Dorset Cursus, for example, required roughly half a million worker hours; Avebury demanded twice as much effort. Such structures may not have been located in the midst of the inhabited area, but

practical considerations alone suggest that they would have been positioned so that a workforce from the wider region could be drawn on. Where environmental evidence is available, it seems clear that major constructions of this kind were in parts of the country that had already seen sustained clearance and exploitation. At the same time, such was the importance of these sites that people may have travelled over long distances in order to build them.

THE DISTRIBUTION OF MONUMENTS

Clusters of monuments often seem to have been spaced across the landscape at approximately equal intervals, as if to suggest that each served the occupants of a specific territory. This is most apparent in Wessex and the Thames Valley, but a similar pattern of distribution can be seen in the cemeteries of passage graves in Ireland, and in the positions of the largest chambered tombs in the Orkney Islands. It is not clear whether or not each of these centres functioned as an independent entity; there is a good deal of evidence to indicate that Neolithic and Bronze Age people may also have moved between them.

Not only were these groups of monuments particularly accessible, but they also contained a large number of artefacts that originate from outside the immediate area. This evidence is of two kinds: there are specific artefacts, like stone axes, which come from distant sources, and there are also close stylistic links between the decorated pottery

Stonehenge, Wiltshire

Stonehenge, built in several phases from the Late Neolithic to the Middle Bronze Age, is only the most imposing structure of a complex landscape of barrow cemeteries, henges, processional avenues and a cursus, a narrow 2,750 metre (3,000 yard) long earth-banked enclosure of unknown function.

Chambered tombs in Orkney

Possible Neolithic tribal territories in the Orkney Islands, based on the distribution of large, chambered tombs.

The Ring of Brodgar, Mainland, Orkney

A henge and stone circle at the centre of a complex of barrows and isolated standing stones. There are alignments between stones in the circle, surrounding hills and the positions of the sunrises and sunsets at the winter and summer solstices. The monument probably dates to the 3rd millennium BC.

Newgrange

One of several decorated kerb stones from the Newgrange passage grave, Meath, built around 3000 BC. The significance of the carving is unknown.

found in widely separated regions of Britain and Ireland. For instance, one vessel from a group of monuments near Oxford carries the same unusual motif as a chambered tomb in Orkney and a mace head from the Boyne Valley. In the same way, individual monuments may share architectural details over considerable distances. For example, one of the major henges in the Upper Thames is built in a distinctive style otherwise found only in North Yorkshire; another, in Cumbria, is more like earthworks in Ireland than other structures in the same region. The movement of artefacts and ideas suggests that certain beliefs were widely shared in Neolithic society and it may be that these links resulted from an institution rather like pilgrimage.

CONTINUITY OF USE

Once a particular monument was established in the Neolithic landscape, other structures were usually built around it. The original monument might well have continued in use, and many examples were maintained for hundreds of years before they were abandoned. At the same time, they may have been modified in accordance with changing beliefs. Thus, cursuses could be built across the sites of causewayed enclosures, and in their turn henge monuments could be established where cursus monuments already existed. Sites could be enlarged or embellished, or even change their form. Thus, timber circles were often replaced in stone and smaller enclosures might be built inside what had originally been open arenas. Monuments of similar form tended to duplicate themselves over time: two henges containing stone circles were built on either side of a narrow isthmus on the Mainland of Orkney; at Knowlton in Dorset, four henges were built in one small area, and in the Milfield Basin in north Northumberland there are even more of these monuments.

One very common pattern was for older monuments to be reused as the sites for deposits of human remains. Not only were graves dug inside older enclosures, but those

earthworks might themselves become the focus for an entire cemetery of burial mounds. Very often, these date from the Early Bronze Age but take an older, Neolithic monument as their point of departure. In other cases, older monuments might be brought back into commission after an interval of disuse. They might be rebuilt, like the successive structures at Stonehenge, or they might provide the focus for offerings of artefacts. Throughout these lengthy sequences individual monuments might also be aligned on one another, as if to form links between structures that had been built at different times. They might also be directed towards striking features of the natural topography or towards the positions of the sun and moon at specific times of year. The summer and winter solstices were especially important and account for the orientation of monuments in Wessex, the Thames Valley, Cumbria, Orkney and the Boyne Valley.

THE BOYNE RITUAL LANDSCAPE

The Boyne ritual landscape provides one of the finest examples of such a group of monuments anywhere in Europe. The most impressive structures are the passage graves of Newgrange, Knowth and Dowth, which have been described as the cathedrals of the megalithic religion. Each of these sites may have been accompanied by a cemetery of

smaller tombs, and at Newgrange there may also be the remains of a cursus. The passage graves were lavishly decorated and their mounds were probably covered in quartz. The passage at Newgrange is aligned on the midwinter sunrise, so that the burial chamber is illuminated on the shortest day of the year.

This group of monuments retained its importance even after passage graves had ceased to be built, and became the

The Boyne ritual landscape

This ritual landscape, in County Meath, Ireland, is one of the most complex in the British Isles. Three large passage graves at Knowth, Newgrange and Dowth, dating from the early 3rd millennium BC, are the focus of smaller graves, henges, artificial ponds, standing stones and wooden structures. The major monuments were built on a low ridge, dominating an open, mixed-farming landscape that had already lost most of its woodland.

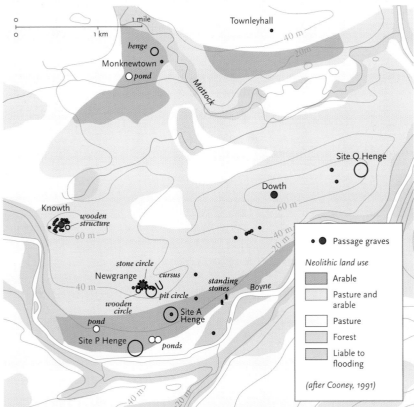

	Passage graves
Neolithic land use	
	Arable
	Pasture and arable
	Pasture
	Forest
	Liable to flooding

(after Cooney, 1991)

focus of new monuments. Excavation has shown that small wooden circles were built outside both Newgrange and Knowth, and in the wider landscape a number of large henge monuments as well as standing stones were erected. A number of artificially created ponds can also tentatively be assigned to this period, though their function remains unknown.

It is at Newgrange that the continuing significance of this landscape is most clearly seen. Some time after the great mound had been built, it seems to have lost its capping of quartz. The fallen material was bounded by a bank of clay in front of the entrance to the tomb and a series of hearths and other structures was established in this area. Enormous numbers of animal bones have been found around these hearths, apparently resulting from feasting. The remains of the mound were enclosed by a massive stone circle, and a

great ring of timber uprights was built just beyond the limits of the monument. The form of this ring suggests that it may be related in ritual function to the henges that are distributed across the surrounding area. The detailed layout of the monuments may have changed over time but, like other parts of Neolithic Britain and Ireland, this section of the Boyne Valley shows evidence of ritual activity extending over hundreds of years.   RB

Stones of Stenness

A massive standing stone at Stenness, Mainland, Orkney, one of three surviving from a circle of 12 standing stones built in the early 3rd millennium BC. A stone setting at the centre of the circle contained cremated bone, charcoal and pottery.

THE BRONZE AGE

The period traditionally called the Bronze Age spans some 17 centuries, from about 2400 BC to about 700 BC. It coincides with a period when temperatures were slightly higher than today's and, in the west of Britain at least, the rainfall was probably a little greater. This seems to have encouraged the development of peat in upland areas, but elsewhere the processes of forest clearance and regeneration continued much as before, creating different landscapes according to the size of the local populations and the fragility of the soils. In many areas, like the chalklands of Wessex, large tracts of open grassland would have begun to spread across the landscape.

The Bronze Age was a time of both continuity and change. The great ritual monuments created in the Neolithic period continued to dominate the land, and many of them remained in active use for some time, but by the early centuries of the second millennium, the old ancestral tombs had ceased to be used, a number of them having been deliberately and finally blocked: it was as though an era had come to an end.

The great henge monuments of Wessex saw limited refurbishment into the second millennium. At some there is evidence that settings of upright stones marked the last major stage of construction. The best-known example of this is Stonehenge, where the sarsen circle, and later the horseshoe setting inside it, had been set up within the old henge earthwork during the period from about 2800 to 2100 BC. The bluestone horseshoe and circle were erected inside them between 2200 and 1900 BC. In a final stage, dating to between 1900 and 1500 BC, new settings of stone-holes were dug to enclose the sarsen circle, presumably to accommodate the bluestones in their final repositioning, but the work was never completed. Stonehenge may be a unique and complex example, but it characterises the widespread enthusiasm for erecting stone circles that culminated in the early centuries of the second millennium and effectively marked the end of the long-lived Neolithic ritual tradition.

By this time, new belief systems were beginning to take root. Perhaps the most far-reaching change was the rapid spread of the practice of single burial, the dead body being laid in an individual grave, usually under a circular mound of earth. Often arranged together in linear cemeteries, these barrows or tumuli are a familiar feature of the landscape even today.

The sudden flowering of this new tradition, some time around 2400 BC, coincides with the appearance of distinctive beaker-shaped pots and a recurring range of personal equipment buried with the dead person. These sets may include copper knives, barbed and tanged arrowheads, stone bracers to protect the wrists from recoiling bow strings, V-perforated buttons and, more rarely, gold basket-shaped earrings. So similar were the beakers and grave sets over large areas of western and central Europe that archaeologists used to write of 'Beaker Folk' and their 'migrations'. Nowadays, while some degree of mobility must be assumed, it is more usual to think of the Beaker phenomenon as the spread of a belief system along the well-established routes that linked communities together.

NEW MATERIALS

That the adoption of the 'Beaker package' was so rapid and extensive may well have been due to intensification in

the exchange of raw materials at this time. The use of copper, and later its alloy bronze, was spreading, and with this came a demand for raw copper and tin. In southwestern Ireland, early copper-mining, dating to the period 2400–2000 BC, has been identified on Ross Island in Lough Leane. Later, between 1700 and 1500 BC, copper-mining was under way on a considerable scale on Mount Gabriel on the Mizen Peninsula. Copper was also to be had in Wales and Cornwall. Tin, from Cornwall, soon became a highly desirable product, while gold from the Wicklow Mountains of Ireland was always in demand. Soon other rare materials made their appearance in burials – amber from the coasts of Jutland, jet from Whitby in Yorkshire and shale from the cliffs of Kimmeridge in Dorset. It is in this period that the first artificial material – faience – was made by fusing sand and various ashes and minerals together at a very high temperature to create a bright blue glassy substance much favoured for beads.

Burial treasure

A gold bracelet (above right) and two gold-bound amber discs (right) from a barrow burial of the early Bronze Age Wessex Culture at Wilsford, Wiltshire. Gold was extremely scarce in the Wessex Culture: its possession was a mark of elite status, a status that could be preserved even in death by placing such precious objects in the burial.

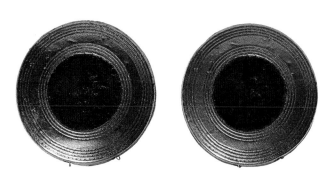

As the demand for these and many other materials increased, so the flow of commodities from one community to another intensified, bringing with it increased communication and a more rapid flow of ideas. It was in this way that belief systems and their accompanying behaviour patterns spread.

Some communities, by virtue of their favoured geographical position, seem to have benefited by being able to take a tithe of the prestige goods that passed through their lands. On the chalklands of Wessex, for example, which formed something of a natural hub to a series of radiating route-ways, the elite were interred with great wealth. The famous Bush Barrow chieftain was accompanied by two daggers, an axe and a mace, together with three gold plaques, while the female buried at Upton Lovell had an elaborate five-strand amber necklace as well as a gold-covered shale cone, two gold studs, eleven gold beads and a knife and an awl of bronze. These exceptionally elaborate burials clearly

Key

Distribution of stone circles

Distribution of Late Bronze Age regional metalworking traditions

Distribution of mineral resources

C Copper

  Gold

S Silver

T Tin

S Shale

J Jet

  Copper mine

Distribution of Early Bronze Age elite burials

Major Middle Bronze Age enclosure

Late Bronze Age circular enclosure

Other sites

Barrow or cairn

Stone circle

Chambered tomb

Wedge tomb

Fort

Other important site

Bronze Age Britain

The Bronze Age in Britain and Ireland covers the period from around 2400 BC to around 700 BC. Initially, there were strong elements of continuity with Neolithic traditions, with the ongoing use of stone circles and communal burials in chambered tombs. By the early second millennium, new traditions had arisen, including that of individual elite burials under cairns or barrows. Towards the end of the period, warfare became more important and the first hill-forts appeared. Because of the uneven distribution of metal ores, trade links were important in the Bronze Age, but these did not prevent the development of distinctive regional metalworking traditions.

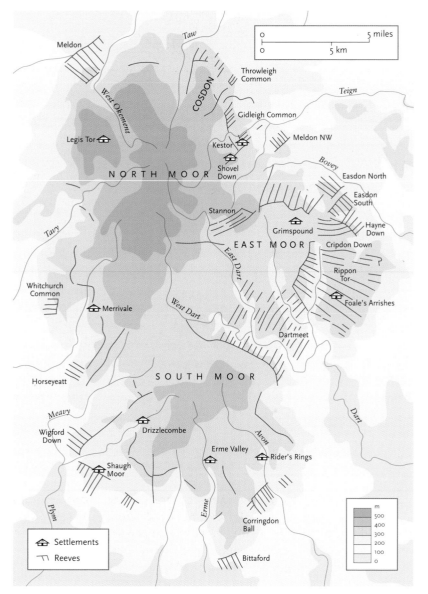

Settlements
Reeves

Formal enclosure and division of the land was an important feature of the later Bronze Age in Britain and Ireland, a response – perhaps – to increasingly dense settlement. The most impressive example of this can be found on Dartmoor, which was divided up into ten or more farming units by systems of stone banks known as 'reeves' (or 'reaves') sometime after 1500. Each unit, the largest of which, around Rippon Tor, covered some 3,300 hectares, included areas of good valley land, hill slopes and upland grazing. It is thought that this enormous feat of enclosure was carried out as a single planned enterprise.

In the second half of the second millennium, all this was to change. From about 1500 BC human communities began to enclose and divide the land on a rapidly increasing scale. Their settlements, usually comprising small clusters of timber buildings suitable for a single family, were often contained within roughly rectangular enclosures defined by banks and ditches, while all around were small, squarish fields edged by banks and scarps (called lynchets) created by the continuous ploughing of the same plot. In some parts of Wessex, it is still possible to see the very careful and ordered way in which huge tracts of land were divided into regular chequer-boards of small fields. Some of the large blocks were evidently laid out from long, straight ditches running along the crests of ridges. In other areas, like Dartmoor, parallel walls, or reeves, were built to divide up tracts of pasture land; linear ditches were also used to delineate territories on the York Moors. The latter half of the second millennium, then, saw the landscape of Britain totally transformed as communities everywhere began to impose a new structure on the land they were attempting to control.

In some areas, like the southern chalklands, the increased cereal productivity that resulted from newly organised fields led to further changes, most notably an increased awareness of fertility and of the importance of nurturing soil to maintain productivity. There is evidence that fields were marled and manured, and by the eighth century BC huge tips of midden refuse were being created in Wessex, though there may have been some ritual or religious imperative in these quite exceptional communal constructions.

It was also in the late Middle Bronze Age that grain storage pits began to be regularly used. These silos, dug down into the rock, were effective stores for seed corn so long as the pits were sealed and air-tight. The reason for putting the corn into the ground may have been to place it within the protection of the chthonic deities – deities who were believed to live within the earth – who would ensure its survival and fertility. Pit storage was to become increasingly common, particularly during the first millennium BC.

belonged to elite lineages capable of commanding enormous wealth and resources. Although these burials are concentrated in Wessex, similar wealth is found throughout the heavily populated areas of the British Isles.

SETTLEMENTS AND INDUSTRY

We know relatively little of the agrarian economy of the Early Bronze Age. Wheat and barley were grown, and cattle, sheep and pigs were reared, but these activities have left no lasting mark on the landscape. One possibility is that animal husbandry was dominant at this time, while the growing of cereals played a secondary part in the economy.

Bronze Age tools

A 'halberd pendant' (right), with a metal blade set in a gold-bound amber handle, from a barrow burial of the early Bronze Age Wessex Culture at Wilsford, Wiltshire. Far right: A bronze axe head of the Wessex Culture found in a barrow in Wiltshire.

While the productivity of the land ensured the survival of the populations, many other skills were developed to meet different needs. The skill most evident in the archaeological record is that of the bronze smith. His raw materials were simple: a basic tool kit, refractory clay, beeswax and bronze (an alloy of about 90 per cent copper and 10 per cent tin). At first, his products were relatively simple, consisting of flat knives and daggers and comparatively flat axes with splayed cutting blades, but as time went on, he began to display greater ingenuity. Complex three-dimensional axes, with loops, hafting flanges and eventually sockets, were cast using the lost-wax method. This involved modelling the item first in wax and investing it with clay. When fired, the clay would harden and the wax would melt, leaving a void to be replaced by molten metal. Another of the bronze smith's skills was sheet metalworking, creating fine repoussé-decorated shields and items like cauldrons.

The output of bronze weapons and implements was enormous in the 600 years of the Late Bronze Age (from about 1300 to 700 BC), but it is worth asking why so much of their work has survived to fill our museums. These were hardly casual losses or discards: in reality, most of the bronzes now surviving have come from hoards buried in the ground or from rivers or bogs into which the items were deliberately thrown. Both the hoards and the 'watery deposits' were probably motivated by the desire to placate the gods who were believed to reside in the earth or the water. The water claimed predominantly warrior gear – swords, shields, cauldrons and the like, while hoards buried on land were usually valued for their metal content, whether the items were whole or broken. Perhaps in this divide we may be glimpsing something of the complexity of the belief system and the hold that the gods had over the minds and deeds of mere mortals.

The Late Bronze Age (about 1300–700 BC) has the appearance of being a time of increased social stress, brought about, perhaps, by an overall increase in population. Weapons became more frequent, particularly long, slashing swords and spears. Shields would also have become more common. Most of these would have been of leather or perhaps wood, but a few of the more elaborate shields were of bronze or at least had bronze facings.

Another feature suggesting increased social stress is the appearance of enclosed, and sometimes strongly defended, settlements. In the east of Britain, a particular kind of circular enclosed site is known, probably representing the homesteads of the elite. This period also saw the construction of the first hill-forts, though at this stage it is unlikely that they were occupied on a continuous basis.   BC

Dartmoor settlement

A settlement of circular huts at Grimspound on Dartmoor. Deteriorating climatic conditions forced the abandonment of such upland settlements in the later Bronze Age.

Bronze Age dwellings

A modern reconstruction of a thatched round house. Round houses were the most common form of dwelling in Bronze Age Britain.

THE IRON AGE

Celtic Europe

Celtic languages emerged across a wide area of western Europe, probably sometime in the second millennium BC. In the 4th century, Celtic-speaking tribes from central Europe began a series of migrations into Italy, eastern Europe, Greece and eventually Asia Minor. By the 1st century AD the Celtic-speaking peoples of Europe had been conquered by the Romans and the Germans, and in Britain maintained their independence only in the far north and in Ireland.

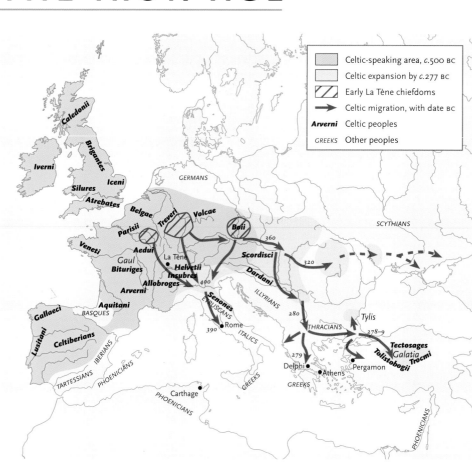

Legend:
- Celtic-speaking area, c.500 BC
- Celtic expansion by c.277 BC
- Early La Tène chiefdoms
- Celtic migration, with date BC
- **Arverni** Celtic peoples
- GREEKS Other peoples

The story of the Iron Age in Europe is the story of the inter-action between the 'civilised' states of the Mediterranean fringe (the Greeks, Etruscans, Phoenicians and Romans) and the 'barbarians' beyond, played out over a period of some 800 years. It begins in the eighth century BC, as the Greeks and Phoenicians were beginning to colonise the Mediterranean coasts. At this time, the local elites living in the favoured zone of temperate middle Europe, which spanned the upper valleys of the Rhône–Saône, Seine, Rhine and Danube, were displaying their power by indulging their dead with rich burial rituals involving the interment of elaborate funerary carts and a range of other valuable offerings. By about 600 BC, Greek luxury objects such as bronze vessels, Attic cups and Massaliot wine were being transshipped northwards to these communities. These imported luxuries were used in daily life in the hill-forts of the elite and in their burials to enhance the status of the dead.

By the fifth century BC, new centres of power were emerging further to the north, in an arc extending from the Loire valley to Bohemia, with major foci in the Marne and Moselle valleys. Known as the La Tène chieftains, these new leaders employed skilled craftsmen who, inspired at first by imported Etruscan metalwork, soon developed their own distinctive style of art (usually referred to as La Tène or Celtic art). It was in these centres of power that the famous 'Celtic migrations' described by classical writers were to originate. From here, large bands of people moved south, to settle in the Po valley (and later to attack Rome),

and eastwards, to settle along the Danube – from where an attack on the Greek sanctuary at Delphi was orchestrated. Some migrants settled as far afield as the centre of Anatolia.

There is no evidence to suggest that migrant groups spread westwards to Britain, Ireland and Iberia, as was once thought. However, by the time of the migrations in the fifth and fourth centuries, much of western Europe, including Britain and Ireland, was using dialects of a language group which, since the seventeenth century, has come to be known, somewhat confusingly, as 'Celtic'. Many would now argue that the 'Celtic' language probably developed in Atlantic Europe some time towards the end of the second millennium BC and was already ancient by the time the La Tène chieftains had begun to wield their power. In other words, there is no direct relationship between the extent of the Celtic languages and the La Tène culture of the middle European migrants.

CULTURAL ZONES

In Britain and Ireland, therefore, we cannot talk of 'Celtic immigrants', but this does not mean that the islands were isolated from continental developments. Far from it: the sea provided the means of contact, as it had done for

Bronze bucket

A bronze-covered wooden bucket, probably used for mixing wine, from Aylesford, Kent, late 1st century BC. Wine was a luxury for the rich and such buckets were often placed in high-status burials of the Aylesford-Swarling culture, along with other prestige goods.

ANCIENT BRITAIN & IRELAND

millennia. In reality, the links were various and determined by geography. Ireland and the west of Britain constituted an Atlantic zone that included the western seaboard of Europe. This is not to suggest that long-distance voyages between Iberia and Britain were the norm, but simply that the sea allowed adjacent communities to remain in contact, exchanging ideas and gifts and trading certain commodities, among them the metals in which the region was rich. A web of interconnecting short-haul contacts between neighbours bound the entire zone throughout the Iron Age. Other maritime contacts were maintained across the Channel and the southern North Sea and it was these links that were to ensure that Britain shared in the developing culture of the Continent. East-facing and west-facing Britain were very different lands, not only in terms of external contacts, but also with regard to geology, climate and resource potential – distinctions that are reflected in the types of settlements that developed and the economic strategies that supported the communities.

The Atlantic zone of Britain is characterised by many small but strongly defined homesteads scattered quite densely where the land is good. These homesteads would usually have supported a single extended family or perhaps a couple of families. In the southwest peninsula and southwest Wales, where they are called 'rounds' and 'raths' respectively, they were usually enclosed with earthworks. In the west and north of Scotland and the islands, homesteads were usually stone-built and are known as 'duns' and 'brochs'. The brochs were essentially large, round houses with immensely thick walls that were sometimes taken to considerable heights, making them look like towers. The duns were larger and less regular structures and seldom attained much height.

In southeastern Britain, settlements tended to be larger, some forming quite substantial villages, but there were also many single farmsteads scattered throughout the landscape. In the northeast, the farms were usually enclosed by protective banks and ditches. Another familiar feature of the Iron Age landscape were hill-forts – large, strongly defended enclosures occupying, as their name implies, prominent positions on hilltops. Building works of this size required the activity of quite a large community working with common purpose. Hill-forts are not found everywhere, but tend to be concentrated in a band extending through central southern Britain from North Wales to the south coast – the interface between the east-facing and west-facing settlement zones – perhaps representing a region of social instability.

In Ireland, Iron Age settlements are far more elusive, but a number of hilltop enclosures have been identified. Along the west coast there are many stone-built forts, some of which may well have started life in the Iron Age. The famous fort of Dun Aengus in the Aran Islands originated in the Late Bronze Age.

TRADE AND ART

By the beginning of the Iron Age, a balanced agricultural economy was well established in Britain and Ireland, wherever the environment was conducive. Wheat and barley were grown and the familiar farm animals reared in a carefully integrated arrangement that benefited both systems. Hunting was not widely practised, but coastal communities made good use of the additional resources of shellfish that were readily to hand. There were, of course, many regional variations. In Devon, for example, cattle were important, while on the Wessex chalkland the emphasis was on sheep and corn. Many regions would therefore have been able to provide some goods in surplus – corn, hides, wool, salt – for exchange. In this way, communities would have maintained networks of contact through which they distributed and acquired goods.

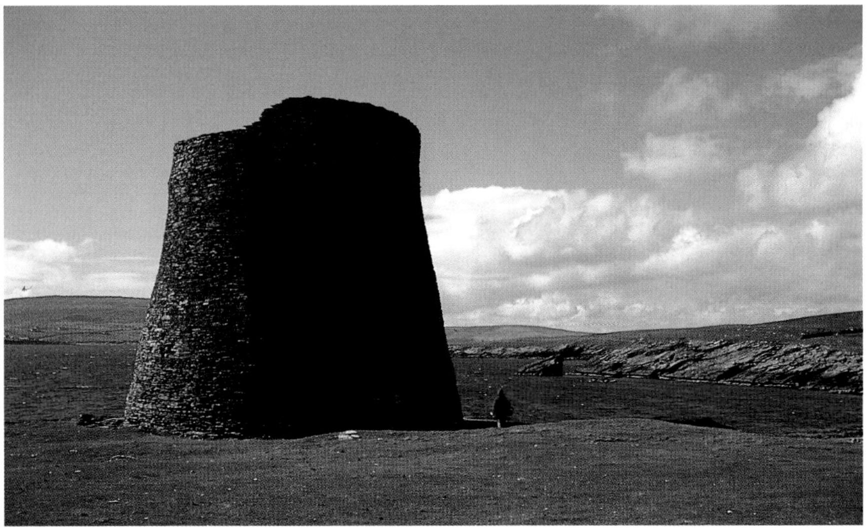

Mousa broch
Built in large numbers in northern Scotland in the last centuries BC, brochs were spectacular fortified family dwellings. Mousa broch, in Shetland, is the only one to survive nearly to its original height of over 13 metres (43 feet).

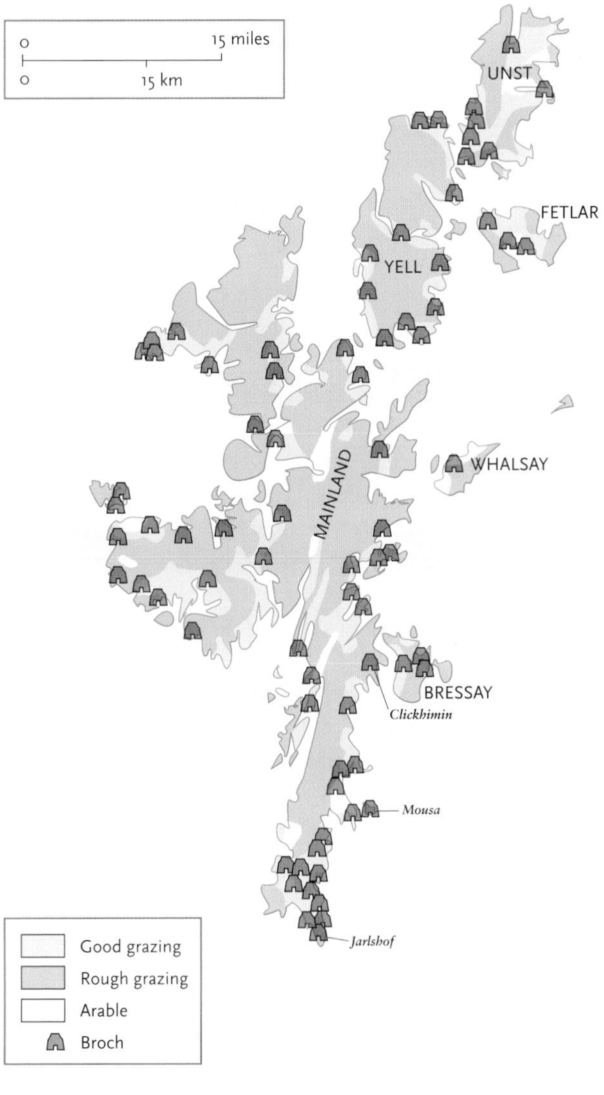
0
15 miles
0
15 km
UNST
FETLAR
YELL
WHALSAY
MAINLAND
BRESSAY
Clickhimin
Mousa
Jarlshof
Good grazing
Rough grazing
Arable
Broch

Shetland brochs
The distribution of brochs in Shetland is closely related to that of good grazing land, an indication of the importance of stock-rearing in the Iron Age economy of northern Britain.

Celtic ship

A gold model of a sailing ship from Broighter in Northern Ireland, late 1st century BC. The sea linked rather than divided the Iron Age communities of the Atlantic coasts.

tin – that were to be had in southern Ireland, southwestern Britain and Wales. Tin, an essential component of bronze, was in particular demand because of its rarity, and in the sixth and fifth centuries, British tin was reaching as far as the Mediterranean. Towards the end of the fourth century a Greek scientist, Pytheas, travelled from his native Massalia (Marseille) to the Bay of Biscay and, probably using local vessels, visited the British tin market in Cornwall before circumnavigating the island, stopping off at the amber-producing coasts of Denmark on his way back. The book he wrote on his return, *On the Ocean*, introduced the Mediterranean world to these remote Atlantic islands for the first time. Before his voyage there were only vague rumours of the mysterious 'tin islands'. After about 300 BC, contacts across the North Sea seem to have declined, but the Atlantic networks continued to develop and expand as the demand for tin intensified.

At the end of the second century BC, Rome firmly established its control of the Mediterranean coast of Gaul (France), and Italian entrepreneurs moved in. One of the effects of this was that Italian wine, produced in huge surplus, was made available to the native Gauls, who appear to have developed a particular love for the drink. The new commodity was drawn into the long-established trading networks and by about 100 BC amphorae of wine were being carried to Armorica (Brittany) and beyond to southern Britain. It was at this time that a trading port was established on Hengistbury Head overlooking the well-protected Christchurch Harbour. From here, corn, hides, metals and possibly slaves were exported, while wine, coloured glass and figs were among the imports. This last leg of a long-distance trading network was probably controlled by Armoricans from the north coastal region of Brittany, but it introduced the Britons, for the first time, to the luxuries of the Mediterranean world.

Throughout the Iron Age, the people of Ireland and the British Isles were able, selectively, to absorb new ideas from the Continent. In the seventh and sixth centuries BC, warrior equipment such as swords and horse gear (and probably the horses as well) arrived in the islands, most likely through systems of gift exchange, and were copied by local craftsmen. Other items imported at this time include bronze buckets, razors, bracelets and brooches, the last raising the possibility that women may also have been exchanged as wives to help bond relationships. It was in this way that later, in the fourth and third centuries, knowledge of La Tène art styles was introduced to Britain on imported metal goods such as swords, and was soon adopted and adapted by local craftsmen working in the courts of the elite in eastern Britain and in Ireland.

It was not only art styles that were adopted, but belief systems as well. In Yorkshire, for example, the local communities began to adopt burial practices, including the burial of a chariot, that were very similar to rituals carried out on the Continent, in what is now Belgium and northern France. In Britain, these communities form part of what is known among archaeologists as the Arras culture. While it is possible that such new practices were introduced by a limited influx of new people, it is equally possible that the rite was simply adopted by local elites familiar with the customs and beliefs of communities on the Continent – familiarity acquired through regular systems of trade and exchange.

While these trans-North Sea exchanges were in operation, the Atlantic seaways continued to flourish, inspired by the desire for the metals – copper, gold and

Votive offering

This superbly crafted 1st- or 2nd-century BC bronze shield was found in the river Thames at Battersea, where it had probably been deliberately deposited as a votive offering for the gods. The shield was made for show; it was too cumbersome for use in battle.

RENEWED CONTACTS

The first century BC was a time of renewed contacts. Close relationships were growing between the British communities on either side of the Thames estuary and their neighbours in northern Gaul. Gallo-Belgic coinage was being introduced to Britain and was widely copied under the authority of the local elite, who also adopted some of the burial rites and pottery styles of their neighbours. In Britain, this is usually referred to as the Aylesford–Swarling culture. It was also at about this time that a migrant group from Belgic Gaul arrived in Britain, probably landing in the Solent area, and settled in what is now Hampshire, West Sussex and Berkshire. In the midst of all this activity, Julius Caesar made his two exploratory expeditions to Britain, in 55 and 54 BC, establishing treaty relationships with certain tribes in Kent and Essex and introducing the Britons for the first time to the reality of Roman power.

The 90 years between the expeditions of Caesar and the conquest of Claudius, beginning in AD 43, saw rapid social and economic change in Britain. Coinage, and with it a coin-using economy, spread to much of the Southeast, and new market settlements (called *oppida*) developed at important route nodes. Some of these, like Calleva (Silchester), Verulamium (near St Albans) and Camulodunum (Colchester), became the capitals of local kingdoms and were sufficiently well established as economic centres to become towns under the new Roman administration.

While the Southeast developed rapidly after about 100 BC, much of the rest of Britain, and the whole of Ireland, was largely unaffected. Here, traditional ways of life continued, and settlements established many centuries earlier remained in uninterrupted use. The north–south divide was already in place.   **BC**

Late Iron Age Britain and Ireland

Contacts with the Continent made the Southeast politically and economically the most developed region in Iron Age Britain. By the late 1st century BC, tribal kingdoms were emerging, urbanisation was beginning as hill-forts were abandoned for more convenient lowland sites and a money-using economy was developing. Elsewhere, more traditional forms of society continued, centred on hill-forts or smaller fortifications. In Ireland, where fortifications were rare, great ritual assembly places developed.

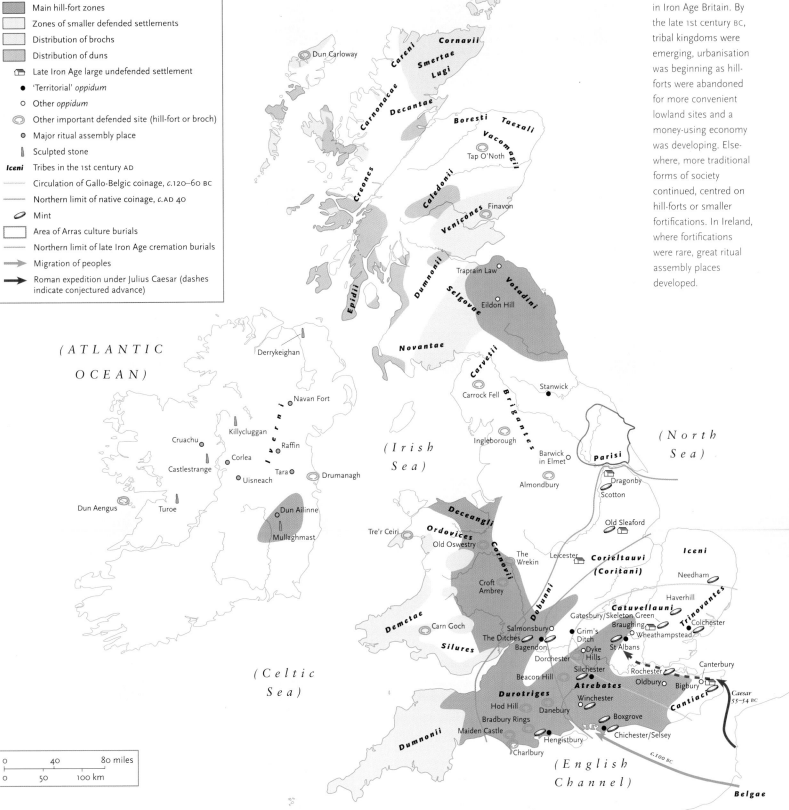

Legend:

- Main hill-fort zones
- Zones of smaller defended settlements
- Distribution of brochs
- Distribution of duns
- Late Iron Age large undefended settlement
- 'Territorial' *oppidum*
- ○ Other *oppidum*
- ◎ Other important defended site (hill-fort or broch)
- ◉ Major ritual assembly place
- Sculpted stone
- *Iceni* Tribes in the 1st century AD
- Circulation of Gallo-Belgic coinage, *c*.120–60 BC
- Northern limit of native coinage, *c*.AD 40
- Mint
- Area of Arras culture burials
- Northern limit of late Iron Age cremation burials
- Migration of peoples
- Roman expedition under Julius Caesar (dashes indicate conjectured advance)

Old Oswestry hill-fort
Hill-forts were built to protect livestock as well as people. At Old Oswestry, corrals were built between the outer and inner ramparts on both sides of the main entrance.

One of the most familiar aspects of Iron Age Britain is the many hill-forts that dominate the countryside, in particular the central southern part of the island, where they are concentrated in a broad band stretching from North Wales, through the Welsh borderlands and Cotswolds, to the chalk downs of Wessex and Sussex. The term 'hill-fort' covers a variety of different kinds of fortified site built and used in the period from about 800 BC until the Roman conquest in the first century AD.

The earliest hill-forts are the most varied in form. Some are roughly circular contour works of about 5 hectares (approximately 12 acres); others may be smaller and sited at the ends of spurs or ridges, while a few are very large, sometimes more than 10 hectares (approximately 25 acres), defined by quite slight banks and ditches. Such variety implies different functions. Excavations suggest that the ridge-end forts were quite densely occupied and were therefore probably high-status settlements, while the very large hilltop enclosures appear to have had very little inside them, apart from a few settings of four posts, which may be fodder racks. If so, it is possible that they served as stock enclosures for communal flocks and herds rounded up for culling and redistribution at varying times throughout the year.

From the sixth century BC, the contour fortifications of about 5 hectares (approximately 12 acres) become the norm. The sixth and fifth centuries saw the number of forts proliferate. Some early forts, like Danebury (Hampshire) and Chalbury (Dorset), seem to have been quite densely occupied, but others show far less evidence of internal activity. Around 300 BC a change is discernible: many of the early forts were abandoned, while a few continued to be used and became more strongly defended with massive banks and ditches, sometimes in multiple rows, and with elaborate entrances defined by outworks.

> *'I discovered that we were quite close to Cassivellaunus's oppidum…The British give the name* oppidum *to any densely wooded place they have fortified with a rampart and trench, and use as a refuge from the attacks of invaders.'*
>
> **Julius Caesar, *The Gallic War***

Well-known examples of these developed hill-forts include Maiden Castle and Hambledon Hill in Dorset and British Camp on the crest of the Malverns.

HILL-FORT DEFENCES

The defining characteristic of hill-forts is the defensive work that encloses them, usually comprising a rampart fronted by a ditch. There is much variation in construction technique, but in the early forts an attempt was usually made to create a vertical wall face to the rampart. This was often done using timbers set in palisade trenches or post-holes tied back with horizontals into the body of the rampart. Where stone was plentiful, the vertical face might be a drystone wall or a combination of stonework and timbering. When a vertical front wall was adopted, it was necessary to leave a space, or berm, between the wall and the ditch so that the erosion of the ditch did not subsequently undermine the wall. Even so, there was much instability, and by about 300 BC the old style was abandoned for a new type of defence known as a glacis, in which the rampart was given a sloping outer face continuous with the slope of the inner face of its fronting ditch. This produced a highly effective barrier that required little maintenance.

The gates were potentially the weakest parts of the system. In the early forts, there were usually two, at opposite sides of the enclosure, but in the later developed forts, one gate was the norm. This sometimes involved blocking one of the earlier gates, as is the case at Danebury, Uffington Castle and probably Beacon Hill. The later gates were often set at the ends of long, inturned passages and were usually defended by elaborate outworks, making a direct approach very difficult. The most elaborate example of complex gates of this kind are those of Maiden Castle.

FUNCTION

The amount of effort spent on the defences immediately raises questions about the functions of hill-forts. Yet there is no reason to suppose that their prime function was defence against attack. The act of enclosure could satisfy a number of needs, both social and ritual, while the massive defences and gates could have been designed to impress rather than to deter, proclaiming the status of the occupants. Evidence of attack has, however, been identified at a number of sites, in the form of layers of burning at gates and sometimes bodies, or parts of bodies, lying unburied. At the very least, these discoveries suggest that outright aggression was not entirely unknown.

Perhaps the most important question to be answered by archaeologists studying hill-forts is what went on inside. Over the years, many suggestions have been put forward – from refuges used only at times of stress to permanently occupied towns. The question is not easily addressed because few hill-forts have been excavated on an appropriate scale.

Danebury is one hill-fort that has undergone large-scale excavation. Over a 20-year period, more than half the interior area was totally excavated. Evidence recovered suggests that the site was occupied from the fifth to first centuries BC, though not necessarily continuously. The pattern of roads established early on seems to have been maintained during the life of the settlement, while the defences were restructured on a number of occasions. During one major reconstruction, one of the gates was blocked and the rampart was greatly enlarged in size.

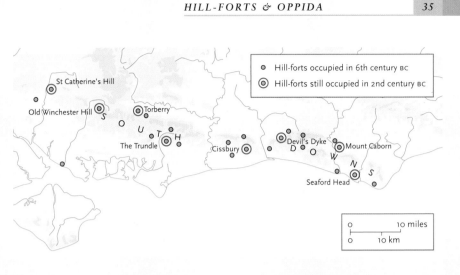

Internally, the arrangement was by no means haphazard. The circular houses were, for the most part, arranged around the periphery of the enclosure and were protected from the elements in the lee of the rampart. Pathways running from building to building could be traced and social units containing a variety of structures, some for storage

South Downs hill-forts

As in other areas of Britain, the number of occupied hill-forts in the South Downs declined in the later Iron Age, while those that remained in use became more heavily fortified. This probably reflects a process of political centralisation focused on a few pre-eminent centres.

Maiden Castle
The complex earthwork defences of Maiden Castle (Dorset) developed over a period of several centuries. At the time of the Roman invasion the fort was the capital of the Durotriges, one of the major Celtic peoples of southern Britain.

age, probably of seed corn, in silos dug into the chalk. In the centre of the site was a group of small rectangular buildings that might well have been shrines. Thus the overall impression is that Danebury was quite a large, thriving community engaged in a variety of crafts, as well as farming, and that the occupants were in permanent occupation. Excavations at a number of other forts like Maiden Castle, Croft Ambrey and South Cadbury have provided evidence that that they too housed similar permanent communities.

However, when Danebury is compared to other forts in the area, something of the complexity of the situation emerges. In the early period (c.600–300 BC), a number of forts were built, but only at Danebury was there clear evidence of internal occupation. The others – Woolbury, Figsbury, Quarley and Bury Hill – seem to have been largely devoid of extensive occupational activity, though some traces of sporadic use have been found. After about 300 BC, by which time Danebury was intensively occupied, the other forts seem to have been abandoned, but at the end of the period, about 100 BC, Bury Hill was totally refortified and settled, offering a rival to Danebury. The picture in this part of Hampshire is clearly quite complicated but it need by no means be abnormal: the Iron Age was a time of considerable social and economic change.

OPPIDA

In the first century BC, new types of nucleated settlements appear. These are generally classed together under the title of oppida – a term Caesar used, rather loosely, for large settlements in Gaul. The earliest of these found in the southeast of Britain are known as enclosed oppida, since they, like the hill-forts, were defended by massive banks and ditches. The main difference lies in their size (they are usually larger than hill-forts), and the fact that they were seldom built on hilltops but were usually sited to command route-ways, often at river crossings.

Good examples of this type are found at Winchester, commanding the crossing of the Itchen, and at Dorchester (Oxfordshire) on the Thames. Very little is known about these sites, but they appear to have been in use in the latter part of the first century BC, by which time the old hill-forts in the southeast were no longer in use.

The impetus for the appearance of these enclosed oppida may well have been the intensification of trade consequent upon the Roman presence just across the Channel in Gaul. The discovery of Roman wine amphorae at several of the oppida is an indication that trade was by this time well under way.

By the beginning of the first century AD, oppida were well established. Constructed enclosures seem no longer to have been favoured, but activities of varying kinds extended over quite considerable areas. At Camulodunum (Colchester), the main activity area was contained by a series of dykes that sliced across the landscape between river valleys. Within, there were areas set aside for occupation, cemeteries containing elite burials, and what appears

Danebury hill-fort

Danebury hill-fort in Hampshire was occupied from the 6th to the 1st century BC. It is one of only a few hill-forts to have been excavated on a large scale.

and cooking, associated with one large house for living in, could be recognised. The site was so well preserved that it was possible to show how the houses had been rebuilt on a number of successive occasions. The inner area seems to have been set aside for storage. In one zone, large timber-built granaries aligned along parallel streets were identified, while another zone appears to have been devoted to stor-

Danebury excavations

The inhabitants of the fort lived in circular huts, built close to the ramparts for shelter. The inner zone was occupied by granaries and storage pits and at the centre of the fort were four square structures identified as shrines.

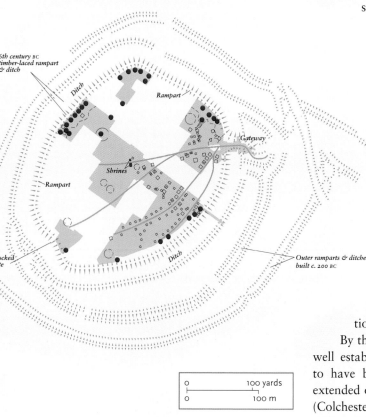

6th century BC timber-laced rampart & ditch

Ditch

Rampart

Rampart

Shrines

Gateway

Blocked gate

Ditch

Outer ramparts & ditches built c. 200 BC

	Excavated area
	Road
□	Granary
●	House
	Gully
- - -	Edge of quarry

0   100 yards
0   100 m

The Iron Age landscape of Danebury c.300 BC

Around 300 BC, Danebury lay at the heart of a network of satellite villages, field systems and larger enclosures for grazing; other hill-forts in the area had been abandoned – and in fact none of those in the immediate area have revealed signs of permanent occupation. Occupation at Danebury itself ended suddenly in about 100 BC, at about the same time that the nearby Bury Hill fort was reoccupied and re-fortified.

to be a large temple enclosure. At Verulamium, near St Albans, the earthworks are less massive and less extensive but again cemeteries and settlement zones can be identified, and in one area the debris of a mint has been discovered.

The sheer size of these late oppida means that it has been impossible to excavate them on a large enough scale to understand them fully, but information accumulates as excavations proceed. From what is now known, it is reasonable to regard them as the social, economic and religious centres of the main tribes. As such, they can fairly be called our first towns.

The oppida, in their various forms, were confined to the southeast of Britain and reflect a more sophisticated economic system than that still in force in the rest of the country – one in which trade and exchange were becoming centralised and coinage was coming more widely into use. In the West and North many hill-forts continued in use. In Dorset, for example, Maiden Castle and Hambledon Hill were occupied at the time of the Roman invasion in AD 43, and were probably among the more than 20 that Vespasian, then in command of the Second Legion, had to storm before he could gain control of the territory of the Durotriges. In remote regions of Wales and the far north some hill-forts continued to be used, even if sporadically, throughout the Roman period.

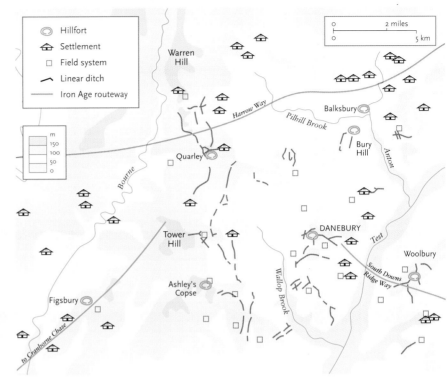

After Roman military forces were withdrawn, and Roman control finally broke down in the fifth century AD, a number of the old forts – places such as Cadbury Castle in Somerset – were brought back into use as the strongholds of the Romano-British warrior elite who now controlled the west of Britain. It was as if the Roman interlude had never happened. **BC**

Island fort

Dun Ardtrek, Skye, a small stone fort of the early Iron Age. Family-sized forts such as this are common in western Scotland.

THE ROMAN CONQUEST

Julius Caesar initiated the first formal contacts between Rome and Britain in 55–54 BC, although he was more concerned with keeping the tribal leaders of the Southeast from interfering in Gaul than he was with acquiring territory in Britain. His achievements appear to have been largely diplomatic; it has been said that if he had not written about his British campaigns in his account of the war in Gaul, there would be little evidence that they had taken place.

Nearly a century passed before Roman conquest was seriously undertaken. The delay suggests that treaties between Rome and British leaders such as Cunobelinus of the Catuvellauni and Verica had successfully reduced British involvement in Gaul; Rome had also established valuable trading links with parts of Britain.

Claudius's decision to invade in AD 43 stemmed mainly from his need to create a favourable public image for himself in Rome. Nonetheless, by 43, the tribes of southern Britain were beginning once more to pose problems: as the established leaders grew older, they may have found themselves overtaken by a new nationalism promoted by a younger generation. According to contemporary Roman observers, these new leaders were influenced by Druidic priests, who had become more of a force in Britain since the outlawry of the Druids in Gaul during the 20s. Typical of such young leaders was Cunobelinus's son Caratacus, who began to engage in an aggressive expansionism within

Roman might

The 1st-century tomb-stone of Flavinus, the standard-bearer of a Roman cavalry regiment, now in Hexham Abbey, Northumberland. Flavinus is shown riding triumphantly over a cowering, naked Briton.

southern Britain. The notorious activities of Caligula on the Gallic coast in AD 40, often seen as a failed attempt at invasion, were probably a deliberate military demonstration designed to encourage Rome's friends in Britain and to intimidate Caratacus and his fellow anti-Roman leaders.

INVASION

Three years later, Claudius initiated far more purposeful moves. His invasion force, which numbered approximately 50,000 men, landed at the site of modern Richborough in the kingdom of the Cantiaci (Kent) and probably also at other points on the south coast, such as Chichester harbour. The importance of the expedition is demonstrated by the fact that, after the initial military defeat of Caratacus and his brother, Claudius himself came to Britain to participate in the victory parade, which took place close to Cunobelinus's former capital at Camulodunum (Colchester), the site of the first legionary fortress in Britain. Yet there was still room for diplomacy in the initial arrangements: three friendly British leaders – Cogidubnus of the Atrebates (Regnenses), Prasutagus (Iceni) and Cartimandua (Brigantes) – were left with some control over their former territories.

The Roman army ranged rather more widely across the countryside than military maps sometimes suggest. A number of military sites large enough for substantial legionary detachments *(vexillationes)* have been located, indicating that legionary troops must have been flexibly used. However, three lines of Roman advance stand out: north from London to Lincoln, which later became Ermine Street, northwestward to Wroxeter and North Wales (Watling Street), and southwestward to Exeter (Stane Street).

Best documented is the advance into the West Country, the principal target of which was Caratacus himself. Substantial gains were made, including the surrender of two tribes (probably the Durotriges and Dobunni) and 20 hill-forts (two of which were certainly Hod Hill and Maiden Castle, where a hastily dug war cemetery provides an insight into the ferocity of the fighting), but Caratacus remained elusive, evidently escaping into Wales.

The attack on Wales was two-pronged: from the south (via modern Gloucester and Usk) and from the Midlands (via Wall and Wroxeter). By the late 40s, the new Roman province consisted of all the territory to the east of the Fosse Way – though this road should be seen as a line of lateral communication rather than as a frontier *(limes)*, for it was not intended that the advance would stop there.

Caratacus was eventually brought to battle in AD 50, at a site that cannot be positively identified, although the landscape features described by the Roman historian Tacitus match Llanymynech Mountain on the modern border between Wales and Shropshire. Following his defeat, Caratacus appealed to Queen Cartimandua of the Brigantes for sanctuary. In accordance with her treaty with the Romans, she rejected this request, though her decision led to factional squabbling among the Brigantes. Caratacus was captured and taken to Rome, where he was pardoned.

The removal of Caratacus allowed the fortification of Wales and the northwest Midlands to proceed: indeed, the

The Roman conquest of Britain

The Roman conquest of Britain took over 40 years and ultimately remained incomplete. The politically and economically advanced Southeast, which had been open to Romanising influences for nearly a century, was conquered quickly, though there were later rebellions, and a temporary frontier was established along the line of a road, the Fosse Way. This success was due to diplomacy as well as arms, the Romans benefiting from alliances with sympathetic native rulers who were given favoured client status. The less advanced West and North proved much harder to subdue. Three main lines of advance can be identified from the distribution of Roman forts and marching camps: north towards York and beyond; northwest towards Chester and North Wales; and west towards Exeter.

Legend

- ■ British *oppidum* (tribal centre)
- → Initial Roman invasion, AD 43
- → General lines of Roman advance
- ⇢ Roman naval support operation
- ▣ Roman legionary site
- XIV Area of activity of Roman legion and number of legion
- ⊞ Other Roman military site
- ⊗ Battle
- ☐ Extent of Roman conquest by AD 47

Roman client kingdoms, c.AD 47
- Kingdom of Cogidubnus
- Kingdom of Prasutagus
- Kingdom of Cartimandua

- 🔥 Place destroyed during Boudica's revolt, AD 60
- ☐ Extent of Roman conquest by AD 68
- □ Agricolan campaign camp, AD 83
- ☐ Maximum extent of Roman conquest by AD 83

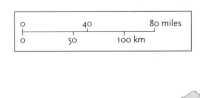

Fishbourne mosaic

This superb mosaic floor was part of the palatial villa built in about AD 75 at Fishbourne, Sussex. The villa may have been built for the British client-king Cogidubnus rather than for a Roman – the spread of Roman tastes in art and building was an important part of the Romanisation of Britannia.

intended to make this possible. After Caratacus's capture, however, Cartimandua's position among the Brigantes proved less than secure, not least because of anti-Roman sentiment stirred up by her husband Venutius. Rivalry between Cartimandua and Venutius forced Rome's hand: Roman military and naval forces began to intervene in the North in the 50s and 60s, operating from bases such as Viroconium (Wroxeter) and Deva (Chester).

Rome's difficulties in the North came to a head in 69, when Venutius took control of the Brigantes; Roman forces had to rescue Cartimandua from her stronghold, a hill-fort at modern Barwick-in-Elmet. The Roman response to Venutius's coup was otherwise severely hampered by the upheavals of the 'Year of Four Emperors' (68–9), an empire-wide political and military struggle between the rival successors to Nero in which the British legions were involved. The eventual victor was Vespasian, who established the Flavian dynasty that ruled from 69 to 96.

Vespasian was determined to renew the programme of conquest in Britain, evidently intending to bring all of the mainland into the Roman province. Venutius was dealt with by the governor, Marcus Vettius Bolanus, who thereby laid the foundations for substantial territorial gains, particularly under Quintus Petillius Cerialis (71–4) and Gnaeus Julius Agricola (77–83). Cerialis probably secured most of the territory up to Luguvalium (Carlisle) and Coriosopitum (Corbridge), establishing a legionary fortress at Eburacum (York), and then advanced into Scotland, perhaps as far north as the river Tava (Tay). A tactic favoured by Cerialis was the deliberate military and administrative separation of dangerous British tribes: for example, the Parisi of eastern Yorkshire and the Carvetii of northwest Cumbria from their Brigantian neighbours. In Scotland, Cerialis cultivated the Votadini, whose grain was of value to Rome, as a Roman client. He also separated the Venicones of Fifeshire from the Caledonian hillspeople by a line of forts and watchtowers now known as the Gask Ridge *limes*.

Romans were moving towards the demolition of Druidic centres on the isle of Mona (Anglesey) when, in 60, the province was rocked by a rebellion among the Iceni and the Trinovantes, led by Prasutagus's widow, Boudica. The causes of the rebellion were partly Boudica's own treatment at Roman hands after her husband's death, and partly resentment felt by the Trinovantes at the construction of a *colonia* (settlement of Roman army veterans) at Camulodunum. Although the Roman forces eventually prevailed, Boudica's troops won at least one major engagement, and caused widespread damage to Roman settlements and interests. It was clear that greater care would be necessary in handling British tribal sensibilities. In any case, such events had served to exacerbate pro- and anti-Roman sympathies among the Brigantes. The neutrality of that tribe was now under increasing strain.

CONQUEST OF THE NORTH

The original intention of the Roman commanders had been to delay the conquest of the North until the Midlands and Wales were subdued; the treaty with Cartimandua had been

Agricola's governorship is well recorded, thanks to a biography written by Tacitus, his son-in-law. However, the chief author of policy in any province was the emperor; during Agricola's governorship, three different men held this position: Vespasian (until mid-79), Titus (until late 81) and Domitian. Vespasian favoured total conquest, while Titus was more circumspect, perhaps preoccupied with unfolding problems on the Danube – which led to the removal of legionary troops from Britain in 80. Domitian permitted a resumption of the colonial advance, but perhaps with the limited objective of reducing the fighting power of the Caledonians in case further troop withdrawals should prove necessary.

Agricola may have had personal misgivings about Domitian's policy, but did his duty: at the battle of Mons Graupius in 83, he effectively committed genocide on the Caledonians. His campaign camps suggest that he provoked the battle by denying the Caledonians access to the coastal lowlands to their east and northeast, just as the Gask Ridge forts had blocked the glens through which they could reach the lowlands to their southeast.

It appears that Agricola continued his advance to the shores of Moray, and even to modern Inverness: recent excavations have revealed camps at Thomshill and Cawdor. He was recalled to Rome in 83; despite the suggestions of Tacitus, there was nothing sinister in this, as his tenure had already been extended to twice the norm. Agricola's depar-

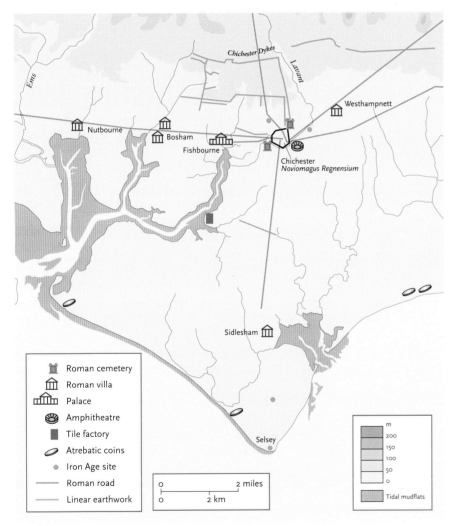

Roman cemetery
🏛 Roman villa
Palace
Amphitheatre
Tile factory
Atrebatic coins
Iron Age site
Roman road
Linear earthwork

least made it possible and relatively safe for Rome to halt its territorial expansion within Britain. The period of conquest was complete; the imperatives of consolidation and occupation had now taken over.

ROMANISATION

Excavation and chance discoveries around the city of Noviomagus Regnensium (Chichester), the Romanised tribal capital of the Atrebates (Regnenses), have not only revealed a major palace site at Fishbourne, but have also provided an insight into Rome's policies towards the British ruling classes in the earliest days of the invasion.

The Atrebates had a long history of good relations with Rome and readiness to trade with the Roman empire: the tribal leader, Verica, was a client of Rome whose discomfiture at the hands of Caratacus had provided one of the reasons for the Roman invasion of AD 43. The attitude of the Atrebatic leaders explains why their territory provided a secure base for the Roman army; pro-Roman sentiment is also hinted at in a dedication to the Roman gods Neptune and Minerva made by the obviously privileged local leader, Cogidubnus. His pre-Roman centre was at nearby Selsey, and he appears to have been left in charge of a semi-independent portion of the Atrebates with the descriptive name Regnenses ('people of the kingdom' – that is, those with their own king rather than under direct Roman rule).

The earliest buildings excavated at Fishbourne were military in nature – perhaps part of a depot for the campaigns in the South and Southwest of *Legio II Augusta* under Vespasian. The military phase at Fishbourne was short-lived, however, and military buildings were replaced first by civilian buildings of high status, and then, in Nero's reign (54–68), upgraded to what has been called a proto-palace. In about 75, this was in its turn replaced by a palatial villa constructed around a garden-courtyard, and well appointed internally with mosaics, wall paintings and statuary of Mediterranean origin. The owner was clearly a person of some consequence – although whether it was Cogidubnus himself or a senior Roman official remains a matter of speculation.

The villa retained its high status as a residence into the second century, although it subsequently suffered from subsidence and, in the later third century, a disastrous fire. By that time, rising sea levels may anyway have made the site less attractive, and it appears that the fire damage was not substantially repaired.   **DCAS**

Fishbourne Palace and its surroundings
West Sussex, part of the territory of the pro-Roman Atrebates, was one of the earliest areas of Britain to become Romanised. The old tribal centre at Selsey was abandoned in favour of a new town, with typical Roman amenities such as an amphitheatre. Many villas developed in the surrounding countryside, including one of palatial proportions at Fishbourne. This may have belonged to the local client king or a senior Roman official.

ture did not coincide with a Roman decision to abandon Scotland. Indeed, it is likely that the building of a new legionary fortress at Inchtuthil is attributable to his unknown successor as governor. Such a commitment implies an intention to remain in the area for some time.

By 87, however, the building of the new fortress had been abandoned, and one of the four British legions in Britain, *Legio II Adiutrix*, was in the process of transferring to the Continent, indicating that frontier problems in Europe were mounting. Britain did not take priority over these problems. However, by neutralising the last remaining enemy tribes in the British Isles, Agricola's victory at Mons Graupius at

Rome's frontier

After Agricola, the Romans withdrew to Hadrian's Wall. They briefly reoccupied the lowlands, but only Severus's campaigns finally brought security.

Until the early 80s AD, total conquest was the Roman goal in Britain. The frontiers *(limites)* were merely zones around fortified roads that temporarily separated friendly tribes from enemies. The governor Gnaeus Julius Agricola had seen his victory at Mons Graupius (83) as an opportunity to complete the conquest, but the emperor Domitian, with responsibility for the whole empire, had to reflect more circumspectly. With the empire under pressure on the Danube, Domitian began to withdraw troops from Britain, including a complete legion in 87. The Roman authorities therefore decided to relinquish most of the territory north of the line formed by the river Tinea and the estuary of the Ituna (the Tyne–Solway line), forming a frontier zone around the road now known as the Stanegate. This frontier eventually ran from Arbeia (South Shields) to Kirkbride, and consisted of the road itself, strengthened by a palisade and ditch, and forts (such as Vindolanda), fortlets and watchtowers. Our knowledge of this period is limited, but it seems that on the accession of Hadrian in 117, the western end of the Stanegate was under threat from tribes to its north.

THE TWO WALLS

By 119, stability had been restored, and it was probably then that the Romans began work on a turf wall from the Ituna (Irthing) to Maia (Bowness). In 122, however, Hadrian himself visited Britain with a new plan: to construct a stone wall from Pons Aelii (Newcastle) to join the turf wall at Willowford. This stone wall, which occupied the ridge to the north of the Stanegate, was intended to enhance the former frontier but actually superseded it, eventually becoming a much more elaborate military complex. In its final form, it consisted of a ditch to the north, the wall itself with forts, milecastles and watchtowers along it, and a military road with a *vallum* (ditch with embankments) to the south. Territory to the north was supervised, creating a substantial frontier zone. By the time of Hadrian's death (138), the turf wall had been rebuilt in stone, and the fortifications extended, mostly in turf, along the coast to Alauna (Maryport).

The purpose of these structures was given at the time as 'to separate barbarians from Romans'. They were certainly intended to facilitate the supervision of movement across the frontier and the collection of taxes from those crossing. Additionally, they allowed patrolling and other forms of intelligence-gathering. The wall's construction in stone also suggests that it was intended to provide a demonstration of Roman organisation and technology, and to serve as a monument to an emperor who well understood the connection between buildings and political power.

Within months of his accession (138), Antoninus Pius was planning to reoccupy territory up to the line from the river Clota to the Bodotria estuary (the Forth–Clyde isthmus), and the construction there of a new wall. This was built throughout of turf, although the existence of stone 'wings' on one fort (modern Balmuildy) suggests that a stone construction was originally anticipated. It

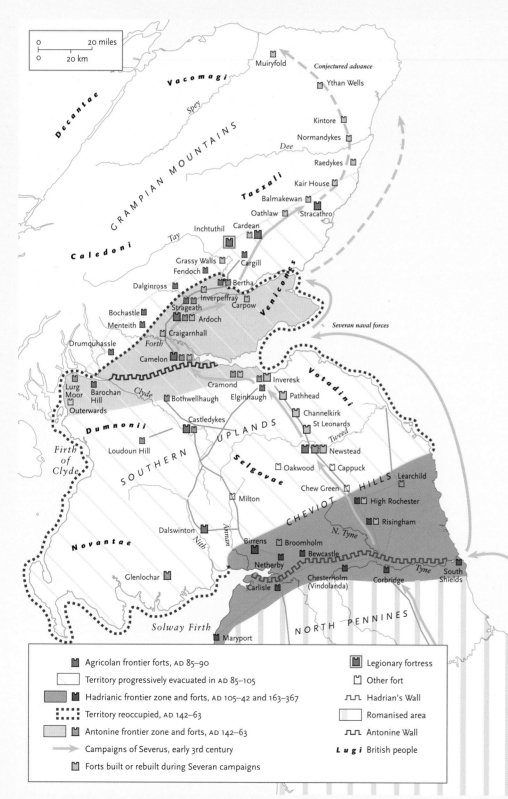

Legend:

- Agricolan frontier forts, AD 85–90
- Territory progressively evacuated in AD 85–105
- Hadrianic frontier zone and forts, AD 105–42 and 163–367
- Territory reoccupied, AD 142–63
- Antonine frontier zone and forts, AD 142–63
- Campaigns of Severus, early 3rd century
- Forts built or rebuilt during Severan campaigns
- Legionary fortress
- Other fort
- Hadrian's Wall
- Romanised area
- Antonine Wall
- *Lugi* British people

was probably intended to resemble Hadrian's Wall in form, but was subsequently modified in favour of a design with forts of varying size at much shorter intervals.

Little is known of what precipitated this advance, although the fact that disturbances continued intermittently through the second century among some of the tribes between the walls suggests that the objective may have been closer policing of these tribes. Similarly uncertain is the explanation for an apparent break in occupation in the mid 150s. However, under pressure of problems elsewhere in the empire, Marcus Aurelius decided in about 163 to abandon his predecessor's wall and reoccupy that of Hadrian.

THE SETTLED FRONTIER

Continuing tensions in the frontier zone were handled with a combination of military force, diplomacy and subsidies until early in the third century, when Septimius Severus, from bases at Coriosopitum (Corbridge) and Arbeia (South Shields), led a new and well-organised combined military and naval advance into northern Scotland, perhaps with genocide as his aim. A successful campaign (though apparently without pitched battles), followed up by diplomacy, finally brought to the northern frontier a stability that was to last for nearly a century.

The fourth century witnessed the emergence of new enemies beyond the frontier, principally the Picts and the Scots. On Hadrian's Wall, the individual forts probably became more important than the frontier's linear features because of the development of an empire-wide strategy of defence in depth. The area suffered from intermittent raiding, including at least one major incursion – the 'Conspiracy of the Barbarians' (367) – after which all sites north of the Wall were abandoned. It appears that in the later years of the fourth century, the forts housed communities of soldiers and civilians; these probably operated as semi-independent fortified villages, feeding and defending their own populations, until Roman order came to an end in Britain. **DCAS**

Hadrian's Wall

The highest section of Hadrian's Wall, at Cuddy's Crags near Housesteads, looking east. This part of the Wall follows the Whin Sill escarpment, allowing excellent views north (left).

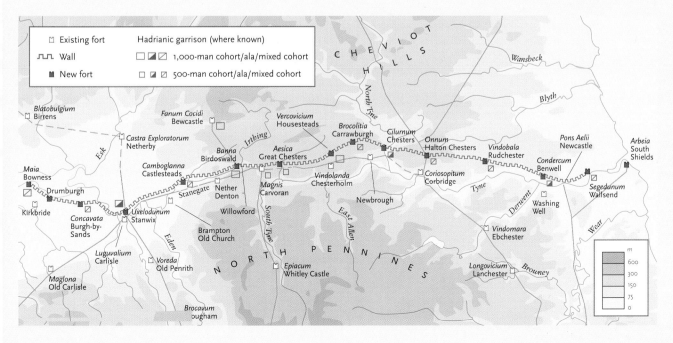

Hadrian's Wall as completed, mid-130s

The continued threat to the western end of the frontier in Hadrian's time is evident in the deployment of the auxiliary units that made up the Wall's first garrisons. The 1,000-man ('milliary') units – infantry cohorts, mixed cavalry and infantry cohorts, and cavalry alae – are concentrated in the west, and include the elite *Ala Petriana* at Stanwix.

Although the Romans rated military glory highly, conquest was not an end in itself. If a province was to be integrated into the empire, the willing cooperation of its people had to be guaranteed through a process of Romanisation. In Britain as elsewhere, conquest created the conditions in which this transformation could be achieved.

Archaeological evidence warns us not to over-emphasise the primitiveness of the British tribes before the conquest. Some had well-developed oligarchic systems of government – and Rome related well to oligarchies. In a few cases, existing British leaders were sufficiently highly regarded to be left in charge of their territories after the Roman conquest – temporarily, at least. This implies a degree of political sophistication and wealth among these tribes, which must have been acquired in part through contact with the Roman world. The Greek geographer Strabo, writing in about AD 14, records that the southern British tribes produced an exportable grain surplus and imported a variety of goods from the empire. Even in the north, deforestation was further advanced than modern observers once thought, and many Roman forts have been found to have been built on ploughed land. The rapid growth outside Roman forts of small towns (vici) shows that the army's need of support services provided wealth-generating opportunities that the local people were willing and able to take. In the countryside, too, the Roman need for food led to arrangements with tribes both inside and outside the province for the supply of grain. As Dio Cassius remarked of Roman Germany, people became 'different without knowing it'. For many, therefore, the 'peace that was a desolation', prophesied by the Caledonian chieftain Calgacus, was a far cry from the reality.

CITIES AND TOWNS

It suited Rome to rely on local leaders for local administration; as in Rome itself, such responsibility fell to the wealthy, as they were expected to contribute personal wealth as well as effort. The pre-Roman tribal leaders and their descendants became the core of the new administrative system. The Romanised tribes (civitates) did not necessarily correspond precisely in territorial terms with their predecessors, but they provided an important element of continuity.

Within these territories, sites were chosen for towns to act as the administrative centres. These were the successors of tribal meeting-places, though they did not usually occupy the same sites. They were more likely to be built on lower ground, and often developed from vici that had appeared early in the Roman occupation – and so were closely integrated into the system of communications. Corinium (Cirencester), for example,

established on the site of an early fort, succeeded the tribal centre of Bagendon as the administrative centre of the Romanised Dobunni, and became one of the most thriving towns of Roman Britain. Interestingly, Corinium generated a greater level of social and commercial activity than nearby Glevum (Gloucester), one of a number of *coloniae* or settlements created for legionary veterans. Corinium's success is a measure of the opportunities – commercial, industrial and agricultural – available to Romanised Britons.

The social and political rewards available to those who took on administrative responsibilities must have been considerable, for the financial burden was substantial: they had to pay for building and repair work in the towns, for local religious and secular ceremonials, and even for shortfalls in local tax payments – or be prepared to raise loans to cover these. A particularly heavy expense in the later years of Roman Britain arose from the walling of towns.

The towns of Roman Britain may not have enjoyed the magnificence of those in other parts of the empire, but they certainly had similar facilities: a forum (public square), baths, temples and places of entertainment. They were also places of work, and much industrial raw material and agricultural produce was taken into towns to be processed into saleable items. Such towns, both large and small, were lively places, full of noise and bustle.

THE COUNTRYSIDE

The links between urban and rural life were strong, especially since many of those who administered the *civitates* must have made their money from industry, which was dependent on raw materials from the local countryside, or from agriculture. In fact, the principal source of all income was agriculture; documents such as writing tablets from Vindolanda on Hadrian's Wall provide clear evidence of this.

Rural settlement patterns varied between the lowland and highland zones of Roman Britain. In the lowland areas south and east of a line from the Humber to the Severn, villas were a major feature of the landscape. These ranged from small, rectangular cottages to large country houses, according to the resources of their owners. Most were built on the profits of arable estates or stock-rearing.

To the north and west of this line, villas gradually decreased in frequency in the lowland areas of Yorkshire, the Cheshire gap and South Wales, and circular and rectilinear huts became more frequent. In the highland zones of the West Country, North Wales and the North, no villas at all have been found, and rural settlement consisted entirely of huts owned by local people and retired soldiers. Unprepossessing as many of their farms may seem, the economic opportunities they offered were no less significant than those of their richer counterparts in the south and east. Some *civitates* in the north – for example, the Brigantes and the Carvetii – grew considerably under Roman rule.

Traditional gods
A silver and gold figurine of Harpocrates, the Greco-Roman god of silence, found in the river Thames at London. Though the British aristocracy quickly adopted Roman cults, they did not abandon their tradional Celtic gods.

Imported glassware
An elegant amber-coloured glass flagon from Radnage, Buckinghamshire, 1st century AD. The flagon was imported from Italy, probably to grace the table of a Romanised British aristocrat.

Resources and industries

- Coal
- Copper
- Gold
- Iron
- Jet
- Lead
- Marble
- Oysters
- Pottery
- Salt
- Silver
- Tin
- Wool

Towns of Roman Britain

- ■ Provincial capital
- ■ Colonia
- □ Legionary fortress with settlement
- ● Civitas capital
- ○ Major town
- Port
- **ICENI** Civitas

Zones of villa development

- Principal area of villa development
- Area with fewer known villas

Important villas

- 1st–2nd century villa
- 2nd–4th century villa
- 3rd–4th century villa
- Known Roman road
- Land over 150 m (500 ft) above sea level

The economy of Roman Britain

Roman Britain was divided into two broad social and economic zones. In the fertile lowlands of the south and east a prosperous agricultural economy based on villas developed. Culturally, this area became the most Romanised area of the province; it also became the most urbanised area, though British towns remained small compared to those on the Continent. In the high country of the north and west, there were no villa estates; these areas were valued as much for their mineral resources as their agriculture. Both farming and settlement here showed greater continuity with Iron Age practices.

The traditional view of the British as sullen opponents of Rome has to be abandoned: the Romano-British benefited from a range of economic and social opportunities offered by Roman occupation. This helps to explain why, at the end of the fourth century, they competed with one another not in rediscovered tribalism, but over the most effective way of sustaining their Romanised culture. **DCAS**

LATE ROMAN BRITAIN

The 'end of Roman Britain' is a concept that has been much misunderstood in the past: we now see a Roman disengagement from Britain as a gradual process rather than as an event, and we appreciate better the degree to which many Britons regarded Roman culture as their own, and as something that they wished to defend.

The third and fourth centuries do not represent a period of uniform decline; indeed, although it cannot be denied that generally times were more fraught – militarily, politically and economically – some parts clearly prospered, at least in the first half of the century. In general, Britain appears to have been less acutely troubled than some other parts of the empire. Militarily, the northern frontier appears, as a result of the campaigns of Septimius Severus, to have been relatively free of disturbance until the later years of the third century, when the activities of Picts (from Scotland) and Scots (from Ireland) first appear in the classical sources. The Picts – their name means 'painted' or 'tattooed' people, and was probably a Roman term – were the same people as the Iron Age groups known to earlier Romans as Caledones and Maeate; their principal centres were in the area of the Moray Firth and Strathmore. The most celebrated of their artefacts were the metalwork dec-

orated with symbols (fourth century) and the 'symbol stones' of the fifth and sixth centuries. These years of the Picts' emergence saw some reconstruction of forts along Hadrian's Wall, although the wall as a linear feature appears to have had a diminishing role in a developing strategy of defence in depth.

However, new enemies became apparent: raiding from Europe gathered momentum, and people of Germanic stock – the later 'Anglo-Saxons' – may have been allowed to settle, especially in the east of Britain; it has been argued by some that they may have been granted land in return for their labour in the building of town walls. By the latter part of the third century, however, the east coast was witnessing new fortification in the form of the 'castle-like' forts of the 'Saxon Shore', stretching from the Wash to Southampton Water. There is little indication as to how such forts were manned, but their military personnel may have been few in number, defending their forts with pieces of heavy artillery mounted on bastions. These large forts may have also offered shelter to elements of the civilian population. Such forts, however, must have operated less like police stations and rather more like defended strong-points. Their chief characteristics, apart from the bastions on the walls, were the height and thickness of those walls (still dramatically obvious at sites such as Pevensey and Portchester), and the small number of access-points. There is little evidence, however, regarding the nature of internal structures.

A DIVIDED EMPIRE

Britain did not escape the political and economic problems that affected the empire: the virtual collapse of the coinage and the military and political anarchy of the mid-third century both manifested themselves in Britain. On two occasions, Britain became 'separated' from the empire – in the 'Independent Empire of the Gauls' (259–73), and again in the 'British' rebellion, which was headed by two Roman military leaders, Carausius and Allectus (286–96); these must have been periods in which all the debilitating effects of civil war were felt. Britain also, however, experienced the effects of the major administrative changes introduced by Diocletian from 294; the province, which had already been split into two by Severus – Britannia Superior (south) and Britannia Inferior (north) – was in the late third century divided into four. Further, military and administrative authority were separated for the first time, as Diocletian tried to secure his own position by fragmenting the power bases of potential rivals. The empire as a whole, too, was subdivided into four parts, Britain lying in that ruled by the 'junior emperor' (*caesar*), Constantius Chlorus; he was 'represented' in Britain by a new officer (*vicarius*), who was based in London. Although Constantine briefly reintroduced a unified control over the whole empire, fragmentation of imperial rule dominated the politics of the fourth century, against a background of increasing pressure on the frontiers. Britain was certainly embroiled in the rivalry between Constantine's sons in the 340s, and again in the rebellions of Magnentius in the early 350s and of Magnus Maximus in the 380s.

'But in Britain in the tenth consulship of Constantius [AD 360]... raids of the savage tribes of the Scots and the Picts, who had broken the negotiated peace, were laying waste the border regions, so that fear seized the provincials.'

**Ammianus Marcellinus,
History (mid-380s)**

The Mildenhall treasure

A 4th-century silver dish from the treasure hoard found at Mildenhall, Suffolk. The treasure was buried for safe keeping but its owners were never able to recover it – a sign of insecure times.

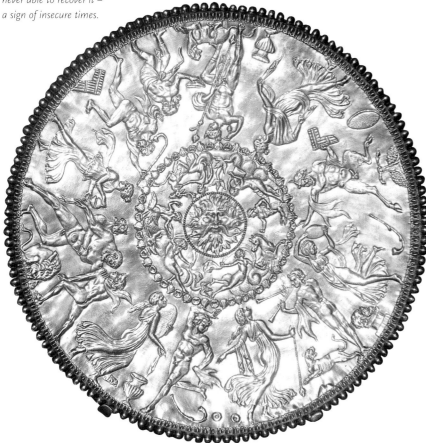

Legend

- Roman Empire
- Independent British tribes
- Diocletianic province
- ■ Provincial capital
- ○ Colonia
- Legionary fortress
- Other fort or fortress (with or without artillery bastions)
- Fort of the Saxon Shore command
- Watchtower
- ⊙ Walled town
- → Scotti (Irish) raids
- → Pictish raids
- → Saxon raids
- ✠ 4th-century site with evidence of Christian activity
- Treasure hoard

Map labels

Picts

Dumnonii

Votadini — Traprain Law

Selgovae

Novantae

Coleraine

UI NEILL

ULAID

Iverni (Scotti)

MEATH

LEINSTER

Oceanus Hibernicus

Hadrian's Wall — Backworth

Bowness-on-Solway

Maryport

Burrow Walls

Moresby

Luguvalium Carlisle — Vindolanda

Coriosopitum Corbridge — South Shields

Huntcliffe

Goldsborough

Ravenscar

Scarborough

Filey

Oceanus Germanicus

Glannoventa Ravenglass

BRITANNIA SECUNDA

Isurium Brigantum Aldborough

Lancaster

Eburacum York

Mamucium Manchester

Caer Gybi

Segontium Caernarfon

Deva Chester

Biddulph

Risley Park

Lindum Lincoln

FLAVIA CAESARIENSIS

Ermine Street

Branodunum Brancaster

Viroconium Wroxeter

Great Casterton

Ratae Leicester

Venta Icenorum Caistor-by-Norwich

Caister

Carmarthen

BRITANNIA PRIMA

Fosse Way

Watling Street

Durobrivae Water Newton

Thetford

Hoxne

Mildenhall

Icklingham

Gariannum Burgh Castle

MAXIMA CAESARIENSIS

Lydney

Glevum Gloucester

Venta Silurum Caerwent

Isca Caerleon

Cardiff

Uley

Corinium Cirencester

Verulamium St Albans

Camulodunum Colchester

Walton Castle

Othona Bradwell

Mucking

LONDINIUM LONDON

Wapping

Regulbium Reculver

Calleva Silchester

Durobrivae Rochester

Durovernum Canterbury

Rutupiae Richborough

Lullingstone

Venta Belgarum Winchester

Bitterne

Noviomagus Chichester

Anderitum Pevensey

Portus Lemanis Lympne

Dubris Dover

Lindinis Ilchester

Stoke Hill

Isca Exeter

Frampton

Poundbury

Durnovaria Dorchester

Carisbrooke

Portus Ardaoni Portchester

Highdown

Boulogne

Oceanus Britannicus

GAUL

Scale

0 — 40 — 80 miles

0 — 50 — 100 km

Late Roman Britain

As an island, Britain suffered less severely from barbarian invasion in the 3rd and 4th centuries than other areas of the empire, but it was vulnerable to raids by Germanic, Irish and Pictish pirates. Impressive forts, many of which still survive, were built along the Channel, North Sea and Irish Sea coasts in the later 3rd century. In the 4th century these were supplemented by watch-towers; there may have been many more of these than presently survive as there has been considerable erosion of the east coast since Roman times. Christianity began to become estab-lished in the 4th century but paganism remained vigorous.

Richborough Fort

The walls of the Saxon Shore fort at Richborough, Kent, one of several built by the Romans on Britain's south and east coasts in response to raids by Germanic pirates.

The Picts

The Picts dominated Britain north of the Forth–Clyde isthmus during the late Roman period and the early Middle Ages. However, the distribution of the most distinctive Pictish monuments, such as square barrow cemeteries, symbol stones and power centres – usually forts on steep craggy hills or coastal promontories – suggests that their heartlands were east of the Highlands.

Some of the divisiveness in the empire in the fourth century focused on the newly accepted Christianity; while there is certainly evidence of the faith in Britain – for example, in the fine mosaics and wall-paintings from the villas at Hinton St Mary (Dorset) and Lullingstone (Kent) – its spread is poorly understood because of the small amount and often contradictory nature of surviving structural and artefactual evidence. Recently, late buildings of a basilican type have been recognised at forts, such as Vindolanda and Birdoswald, and are thought by some to have been churches. While some 'Christian objects' are very mundane in character, others suggest considerable wealth, such as the collection of 'plate' found at Water Newton, and now in the British Museum. At the same time, however, the continuing strength of pagan cults suggests that Christianity may not immediately have appealed to the wealthier administrative classes. This is demonstrated by the extensive temple complex of the god Nodens at Lydney (Gloucestershire), none of which was constructed before the 360s.

It is too easy, however, to assume that everything in fourth-century Britain

manifested decline: although the walling of towns had undoubtedly imposed crippling financial burdens on *civitas* administrators, thus reducing their ability to engage in general refurbishment programmes, many towns at least offered safety, and some positively flourished – for example, Cirencester. The continued success of such towns is to be explained by the fact that in some areas, at least, agriculture remained vibrant. For some villas, the first half of the fourth century represented a heyday, with large estates centred on sites such as Chedworth, Turkdean, Woodchester (all in Gloucestershire), Bignor (Sussex) and Lullingstone. In the Cotswolds, at any rate, an explanation of this may lie in a concentration on sheep-farming. In other parts, too, there is some evidence of a reduction in arable in favour of pastoral farming. There may have been a climatic reason behind some of this.

THE 'CONSPIRACY OF THE BARBARIANS'

A turning-point came with the widespread attack in 367 by most of the enemies of Roman Britain, known as the 'Conspiracy of the Barbarians'; it was probably a climax rather than a sudden event. Considerable damage was done, although much of it was quickly repaired, and measures were taken to prevent a recurrence: a new system of watchtowers was put in place on the coast of northeast England, and the west coast, too, received some new forts of the 'Saxon Shore' type (as at Cardiff, Caer Gybi and Lancaster), and possibly watchtowers also. All of this shows that

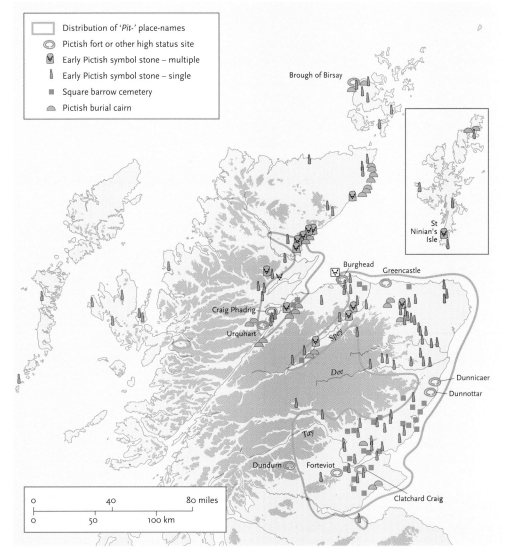

Distribution of '*Pit-*' place-names
Pictish fort or other high status site
Early Pictish symbol stone – multiple
Early Pictish symbol stone – single
Square barrow cemetery
Pictish burial cairn

Brough of Birsay

St Ninian's Isle

Burghead
Greencastle

Craig Phadrig

Urquhart

Spey

Dee

Dunnicaer
Dunnottar

Tay

Dundurn
Forteviot

Clatchard Craig

0   40   80 miles

0   50   100 km

both the Roman authorities and the Romano-British felt a continuing need to maintain Britain's place in the empire; this was probably due to the fact that its island status gave it relative security as a source of supplies and raw materials for the armies trying to defend Roman provinces on the Continent. This was dramatically demonstrated by the decision of Julian (in 359), following a disaster on the Rhine, to send 600 transport ships to Britain to requisition supplies with which to effect recovery.

Perhaps the most damaging development was a loosening of the communications system and the command-hierarchy that had been so characteristic of the Romanised province; as a result, many sites – forts and towns, especially – may have become isolated strong points, in which local militias (perhaps formed, in part at least, from elements of what had been the Roman army) defended and supported their homes and families. Recent work at Birdoswald and at other Hadrian's Wall forts has lent some support to this notion; to some degree, this changing picture may account for the new style of building in forts, which saw the so-called 'chalet barracks' replacing the very regular and orderly structures characteristic of earlier periods. Did the totally military forts gradually absorb a more mixed population, and come to resemble villages?

THE END OF ROMAN BRITAIN

The ability to sustain the status quo will have varied from place to place, and have depended on a number of local factors. It is clear, for example, that at Wroxeter and Carlisle elements of a Romanised lifestyle were maintained for a considerable period: at Wroxeter, work was clearly being undertaken at a very late stage to keep the baths and basilica in use, while at Carlisle there is evidence of renovation and use of buildings into at least the middle of the fifth century; indeed, Bede (in his *Life of St Cuthbert*) indicates that elements of the Romanised urban infrastructure still functioned as late as the seventh century. In other places, however, for a variety of reasons, the continued use of urban centres may have proved to be less feasible, precipitating in some cases a return to hill-forts as providing the best means of defence. This should not, however, be seen as evidence of a desire to break with the Romano-British past.

The somewhat confused source material relating to the later fourth and early fifth centuries (Zosimus, for example) has been taken as indicating that, while Romans tried to keep Britain within the empire, the British themselves wanted their independence, and that there were pro- and anti-Roman parties in Britain. Such evidence needs to be treated with caution: it is evidently the case that elements of field armies were being sent to Britain (under such generals as Stilicho) perhaps as late as AD 400, though it is less clear what they were trying to achieve. Inside Britain, however, it is now thought that different approaches were emerging regarding the most efficacious means of achieving what was evidently a common goal – that of retaining a Romanised culture in the face of the new invasive cultures that threatened it. Some, probably the remnants of the *civitas* leaderships, wanted to work for an institutional re-engagement with Rome – an aim still maintained beyond the middle of the fifth century. Others, on the other hand, local warlords of the type symbolised by such figures as Vortigern ('mighty king') and Arthur ('bearman'), who were more realistic and

independently minded, preferred to take their salvation into their own hands; it has been suggested that such leaders may have been influenced by the contemporary and similarly independently minded Christian heresy of Pelagianism – which also originated in Britain.

In the final analysis, however, the effect of outside invasions was to disturb the Romanised status quo beyond the point of recovery: it was, in other words, a lack of ability rather than a lack of will that determined the ending of Roman Britain – a gradual and uneven process, however, in which, once again, the British 'became different without knowing it'.

DCAS

Europa and the bull

A floor mosaic laid c.350, from Lullingstone villa in Kent, depicts the myth of Europa's abduction by Zeus disguised as a bull. The early 4th century was a 'golden age' for British villas but almost all had been abandoned by the end of the century.

ROMAN LONDON

Londinium

Roman London in the 2nd–3rd century AD, seen from the south-east. The entire city occupied roughly the area of the modern City of London, from the Fleet river in the far west to the site of the later Tower in the east.

The site of modern London had no great significance in the pre-Roman period; indeed, the river Thames itself was probably of greater consequence than any settlement – it appears to have served at different times as a commercial route and as a tribal frontier line.

It was not until the Romans established political unity in the south, and the Tamesis (Thames), as a commercial route, became important for communications with other parts of the empire, that a settlement at London made sense. The earliest activity that was associated with Londinium (London) was probably military in nature, connected with the crossing of the river established at Southwark. A Roman military settlement here must have included a headquarters for the governor and the financial procurator, since, even though we are told by Tacitus that the settlement did not enjoy an elevated legal status, it was of sufficient importance to have been targeted in 60 by Boudica's rebels.

The earliest settlement lay north of the Thames and to the east of the Walbrook, centring on a major east–west road (the standard *via decumana* of Roman military establishments). Development along this road swiftly crossed the Walbrook and extended westwards. Originally built largely of timber,

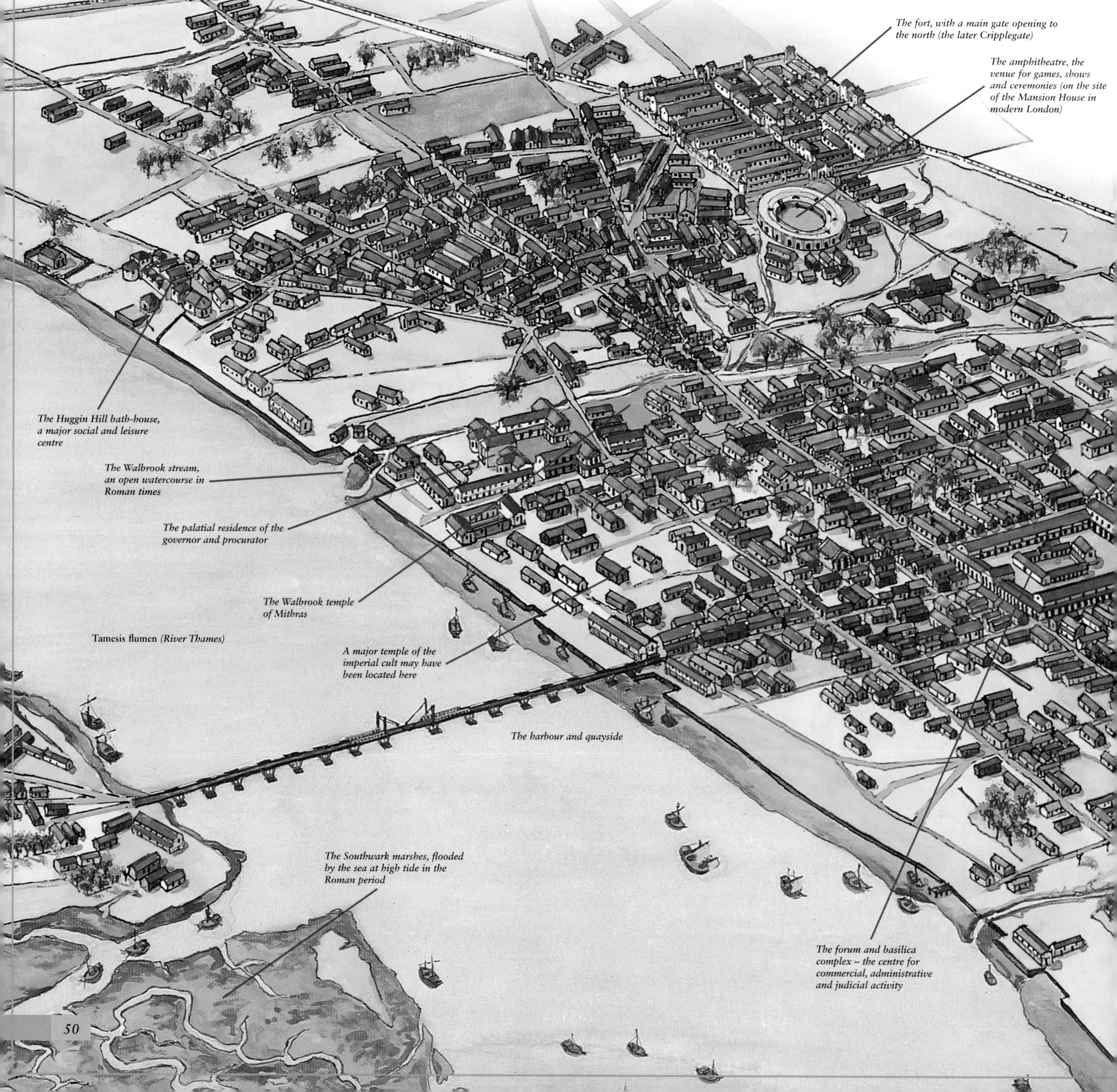

The fort, with a main gate opening to the north (the later Cripplegate)

The amphitheatre, the venue for games, shows and ceremonies (on the site of the Mansion House in modern London)

The Huggin Hill bath-house, a major social and leisure centre

The Walbrook stream, an open watercourse in Roman times

The palatial residence of the governor and procurator

The Walbrook temple of Mithras

Tamesis flumen (River Thames)

A major temple of the imperial cult may have been located here

The harbour and quayside

The Southwark marshes, flooded by the sea at high tide in the Roman period

The forum and basilica complex – the centre for commercial, administrative and judicial activity

the town was rebuilt after Boudica's rebellion, using timber for shops and private residences, but more durable stone and tile for public buildings.

The turn of the first century saw the construction of a 'palace' (*praetorium*) for the governor; it was evidently an impressive structure built around a garden-courtyard with extensive offices. Excavations have revealed other major structures, suggesting that officials such as the judicial officer (*legatus iuridicus*) and the procurator were officially housed nearby. Other official buildings included a fort (in the northwest corner of the settlement), which housed the governor's guard (*speculatores*), and an amphitheatre.

Londinium no doubt had a number of bath-houses, and some of these have been located: the most impressive was probably that at Huggin Hill. The most extensive public building, however, was the great forum and basilica, which formed one of the largest of its kind in western Europe. Such structures were the heart of administrative and commercial life in all major Romanised towns. Nonetheless, much of the city's space was taken up with small houses of craftsmen of various kinds, in crowded streets. Londinium profited from its site on the Thames, and housed thriving craft and merchant communities, like other major towns in Roman Britain.

A major fire in about 130 caused a notable interruption in the development of the city; much damage was done, and not all was repaired. In the aftermath, the most important changes during the second and early third centuries were the construction of an extensive timber waterfront and a complete wall-enclosure of the town's landward side, with gatehouses certainly at Ludgate, Newgate, Bishopsgate and Aldgate, in addition to the fort. It appears that these works were completed at the same time as new monumental structures, including a decorated arch at Blackfriars. The expense and effort involved contrasts clearly with the traditional perception of 'decline' in this period; whatever negative changes took place in the city (perhaps prompted by outbreaks of disease), commercial life remained vibrant.

Some of this work may have been stimulated by a visit to Britain in 209–11 of members of the Severan dynasty, though it is clear that, during the third century, there was also local demand for expensive works. A good example of evident wealth is provided by the sculptures found near the Temple of Mithras at Walbrook, which are of Italian origin. Another insight into third-century developments is provided by a signal tower down river at Shadwell, which was presumably similar in origin to the 'Saxon Shore' forts.

Londinium's importance in the fourth century was undeniable, and is confirmed by its acquisition of the title Augusta, and its role as the seat of the *vicarius* of the four British provinces. The building of a riverside wall and the equipping of the existing walls with bastions for artillery also suggest that the city was seen as important enough to be defended. In fact, surviving archaeological evidence indicates both the desire and the ability of local leaders, as at other centres, to sustain a Romanised lifestyle in Londinium until well into the fifth century.

DCAS

The city walls, complete with bastions for artillery

Grave offerings

A cremation urn and glass bottles from a cemetery in Roman London, 1st–2nd century AD. It was a Roman as well as a Celtic custom to give the dead food and drink for their journey to the otherworld.

God of commerce

A 2nd-century AD statue of Mercury, the god of commerce, holding a money bag. The statue was found in the Walbrook temple of the god Mithras, whose cult was popular with merchants.

PART TWO

MEDIEVAL BRITAIN & IRELAND

Once the Roman legions had withdrawn and imperial power within the British Isles had evaporated in the course of the fifth century, an older political pattern reasserted itself. Both in Britain and in Ireland the fundamental units of authority were the petty kingdoms, based upon the force of warrior bands sustained by booty and tribute. The Christian Church became a part of these societies only gradually. Already present in Roman Britain, Christianity continued in Wales, Cornwall and other areas where there was no sharp break with the Roman past. In Ireland and Scotland, which were never part of the Roman Empire, Christian missionaries introduced the new religion in the fifth, sixth and seventh centuries. At the same time, the Anglo-Saxon settlers, who had disembarked along the North Sea coasts during the fifth and sixth centuries, encountered missionary activity both from Ireland and from Rome. By the time of the Venerable Bede (died 735), the great historian of early medieval Britain, almost the whole of the British Isles had been incorporated into the Christian world.

This arrangement, of petty kingdoms of Germanic origin in the south and east and Celtic origin in the north and west, all marked by a strongly monastic strain of Christianity, was suddenly disrupted around the year 800 by the appearance of the Vikings – pagan Scandinavian raiders, traders and farmers, whose maritime mobility enabled them to appear more or less simultaneously in Orkney and Dorset. The long struggle against the Vikings left only two preponderant powers in Britain: the kingdoms of England and Scotland, which were to remain the largest and most powerful polities within the British Isles for the rest of the Middle Ages. In Wales and Ireland local dynasties survived, but these were fragmented and in constant competition. In Ireland the Vikings founded a series of towns, such as Dublin and Limerick, which were to play a major role in the political life of the region.

In the course of the ninth and tenth centuries, the resilient Anglo-Saxon kingdom of Wessex absorbed the remnants of the other English kingdoms and conquered the Viking territories of the north and east. A kingdom of England emerged. Meanwhile, most of the north of Britain fell under the control of the kings of the Scots. Large political units with increasingly sophisticated administrations were thus emerging. Peasant communities, squeezed for their scarce resources, were the foundation of powerful warrior systems headed by royal dynasties. In Wales and Ireland the warrior elites strove for such goals with less effect. By the time of the Norman Conquest in 1066 the political pattern of the British Isles was characterised by a sharp disjunction between the political centralisation of England and Scotland and the relatively small scale of the Welsh and Irish kingdoms.

The 250 years from 1100 to 1350 were marked by population growth, urbanisation, commercialisation and an increase in literacy. Money, in the shape of the English silver penny or the Scots penny modelled on it, circulated at all levels; markets and boroughs proliferated; more land was brought under the plough. This expansion in production and exchange was paralleled by a cultural efflorescence, with the building of hundreds of churches (monastic, mendicant and parochial) and the creation of scholastic centres in the new universities of Oxford and Cambridge. An assertive aristocracy also benefited from economic development, expressing its values of prowess and display in castles, tournaments and romances.

The Norman conquest of England in 1066 tied the fortunes of the British Isles tightly to those of France for the rest of the Middle Ages. By 1200 the Normans had established colonial lordships over half of Wales and Ireland and had settled, by invitation, many parts of Scotland, too. During these centuries a rich and populous England was increasingly able to impose its will on other parts of the British Isles, although the kingdom of Scots under the leadership of Wallace and Bruce secured its independence in prolonged warfare.

The Black Death of 1348–9 killed half the population, and its recurrence in subsequent generations meant that medieval population levels never returned to their pre-plague heights. Although this signified a general contraction of the economy, it benefited many peasant tenants and labourers, for land was now more available and wages were higher. For many aristocrats it represented a crisis and this perhaps explains the fierce struggle for the profits of war and office that characterised the later Middle Ages, with prolonged warfare in France (the Hundred Years War, 1337–1453), civil war in England (the Wars of the Roses, 1455–85) and bloody aristocratic feuding in Scotland and Ireland. Nonetheless, the internecine conflicts of the later medieval nobility were aimed not at destroying the complex state apparatus that had evolved, but at controlling it. It was more profitable to manipulate parliament, the law courts and the fiscal machinery than it was to wreck them.

ROBERT BARTLETT

THE MIGRATION PERIOD

Symbol stone

Pictish symbols on the reverse of a cross slab from Golspie in northern Scotland. The meaning of the symbols, which originated in the 4th century, is unknown. It is unlikely, however, that they had religious significance, as they continued in use after the Picts were converted to Christianity in the 5th–6th century, only to disappear soon after the Scots' take-over of Pictland in the 9th century. An inscription in the Irish ogham alphabet can be seen along the edges of the slab.

The collapse of the Roman province of Britannia created a vortex that drew Germanic migrants from across the Channel and propelled native peoples around the British Isles. Although in many respects the social and political consequences were felt most strongly in southern and eastern Britain, where Roman culture had been most entrenched, the upheaval affected all of the British Isles. Since the early Middle Ages the origins of the English nation have been identified with the first Anglo-Saxon settlers; from the perspective of the Celtic-speaking peoples, the arrival of the Anglo-Saxons initiated a period of struggle and decline. Naturally, in a period that saw mass migrations across the North and Irish seas and the creation of new political order, social unrest and warfare were endemic. This period of conflict provides the historical context for the heroic efforts of (the probably largely legendary) King Arthur to resist the Anglo-Saxon expansion into western Britain.

There can be little doubt that the long period of conflict heightened ethnic tensions and refined the competing identities. A new political landscape, consisting of small kingdoms that owed little to the Roman provincial structures, emerged, largely along ethno-linguistic lines. In many respects Celtic and Anglo-Saxon social organisation was similar, but there were profound linguistic and religious differences. By the time of the collapse of the Roman province, Christianity had a significant number of adherents in Britain, while the Saxon homelands remained resolutely pagan. Anglo-Saxons in Britain remained pagan until well into the seventh century.

Following the English settlement, there were three broad cultural zones: Britain was divided between the English-speaking Anglo-Saxon east and the Celtic north and west where the British (ancestral to Welsh) and Pictish languages persisted, while in Ireland and in enclaves in western Britain a different Celtic language, Gaelic, was spoken. These zones to some extent reinforced cultural distinctions established in the Roman period, and the most Romanised part of Britannia, where there had been towns and villas, broadly corresponds to the area occupied by the early Anglo-Saxon kingdoms. The zones, while not static, can be mapped through early medieval place-names.

COMMUNITIES OF BELIEF

In addition to the linguistic differences, different communities of religious belief are apparent from the range of the material culture left behind. From an archaeological perspective, the most pronounced differences relate to funerary practice. The British and Irish erected incised memorial stones, but their burials were neither clothed nor furnished. The British inscriptions, written in Latin, are undoubtedly Christian. The Irish examples, written in Gaelic using an indigenous ogham alphabet, are more ambiguous, but may be Christian. The so-called 'symbol stones' of Pictland represent a related tradition, though employing a pictorial rather than an alphabetic system.

The contrast with the Anglo-Saxon world is profound. Here there are no inscribed memorials, and burial practice followed traditions of continental origin. The scale of English settlement can be gauged from the widespread distribution of fifth-century Anglo-Saxon cemeteries. The earliest hint of Anglo-Saxon presence is seen in graves from late Roman cemeteries that contain belt-fittings and other metalwork regarded as stylistically Germanic. During the fifth and sixth centuries a wide range of burial rites developed, which included the elaborate use of clothing and equipment to signal social position and to mark out special individuals at burial or cremation. Important graves might be further dignified by the construction of a mound or barrow. Traditionally, such burials have been taken as reflecting pagan religious belief, but arguably they were to reinforce the social order or to express political aspiration. The pattern of burial rites within individual Anglo-Saxon cemeteries tends to be the same, but there is a huge range of minute ritual variation between cemeteries. This can best be interpreted as the means by which neighbouring settlements

The migration period
c.400–600

Archaeology has begun to shed some light on the 'Dark Ages', where documentary evidence is lacking. The distribution of pagan 5th-century Anglo-Saxon burials indicates the probable areas of earliest English settlement in Britain. The English advance continued throughout the period – though both English and British kingdoms fought as often amongst themselves as against each other. Inscriptions in the Irish ogham alphabet – also adopted by the Picts – point to areas of Irish settlement in southwest England, west Wales and southwest Scotland; Latin memorial stones reflect successful British campaigns to drive the Irish out. Meanwhile, British and then Irish missionaries spread Christianity throughout Ireland and among the Picts; by the end of the period Irish, continental and native English missionaries had also begun the conversion of the English.

Legend:

☐ Roman foundation
— Main Roman road
▨ Distribution of 5th-century Anglo-Saxon burials
➜ Anglo-Saxon expansion, 5th–8th centuries
➜ British migration, 5th century
➜ Irish expansion, 5th century
Ⓢ Ogham memorial stone
Ⓐ Memorial stone with Latin inscription

Peoples, c.600
☐ Picts
☐ Gaels
☐ Britons
☐ Anglo-Saxons

Christian missionary activity, with name of missionary
✠ British church
✞ Irish church
✟ English church
✠ Continental Roman church
♔ Major royal centre
⊗ Battle
▨ Main distribution of Pictish symbol stones
✝ Important church
● Other important site

Map labels:

Birsay
Freswick
Golspie
Udal
Burghead
Dun Cuier
PICTLAND
Columba (6th century)
Iona
Dunollie
FORTRIU
Dundurn
Forteviot
Abernethy
Clatchard Craig
MAEATAE
Dunadd
Dumbarton
Din Eidyn (Edinburgh)
GODODDIN
Kentigern (5th century)
Melrose
Bamburgh
Yeavering
BERNICIA
Aidan (7th century)
Degsastan 603
RHEGED
Mote of Mark
DAL RIATA
Ailech
Derry
Druim Cett
NORTHERN UÍ NÉILL
ULAID
Bangor
Carlisle
Clogher
Emain Macha
Armagh
Patrick (5th century)
Downpatrick
MANAW
Catterick c.600
DEIRA
Paulinus (7th century)
York
ELMET
CONNACHT
Cruachu
SOUTHERN UÍ NÉILL
Tara
Knowth
Lagore
Durrow
Naas
Kildare
Auxilius (5th century)
Oceanus Hibernicus
Deganwy Castle
Aberffraw
GWYNEDD
Dinas Emrys
Chester
LINDSEY
Lincoln
Oceanus Germanicus
Palladius (5th century)
LAIGIN
POWYS
Wroxeter
MERCIA
MIDDLE ANGLIA
EAST ANGLIA
Felix (7th century)
Sutton Hoo
MUNSTER
DÉISI
Cashel
Llanbadarn Fawr
Chad (7th century)
Garryduff
Garranes
David (Dewi) (6th century)
St David's
DYFED
Llangorse Crannog
Llangorse
ERCYNG
Gloucester
Cedd (7th century)
ESSEX
Fursa (7th century)
St Albans
Cirencester
Dorchester
GOWER
Illtud
Llandaff
GLYWYSING
Caerleon
Caerwent
GWENT
HWICCE
Dyrham 577
Bath
London
Rochester
Llancarfan
Dinas Powys
WESSEX
KENT
Canterbury
Winchester
Silchester
Augustine (late 6th century)
South Cadbury
Birinus (7th century)
Hamwih
SUSSEX
Wilfred (7th century)
Tintagel
DUMNONIA
Exeter
Castle Dore
Oceanus Britannicus
to Brittany

Scale:
0   40   80 miles
0   50   100 km

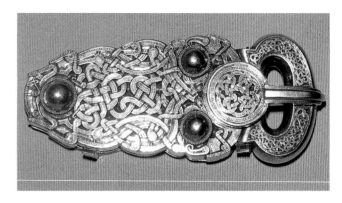

sought to strengthen group identity. Both elaboration and variation are indicative of the volatile social and political environment of the early Anglo-Saxons.

The artefacts recovered from Anglo-Saxon cemeteries reveal the technical accomplishments and material culture of the early English, but they also offer insights into the ideology of a society dominated by a warrior aristocracy. The prominence of weapons in male graves leaves little doubt as to the role of arms and warfare in defining social status. Clothing, jewellery and domestic objects formed the vocabulary of the female burial rite. Similarly, cremations show that objects were used to define social identity on the pyre, before the ashes were scooped into urns and buried.

POPULATION MOVEMENT

The arrival of the Anglo-Saxons coincided with a drastic decline in towns and a reorganisation of the landscape, partly as a result of large-scale population movement. London is probably the only place where urban life continued, and even here the centre shifted west, to an area outside the Roman walls. Elsewhere, towns were largely abandoned, some never to be reoccupied, others, like Winchester and Canterbury, eventually to be reborn as royal centres. A handful of new trade ports were established, as at Hamwih (Southampton) and Ipswich. In the North and West some Roman fortresses became local political centres, notably at York and Carlisle, but most were ignored.

Within the British zone, there is a far greater degree of continuity in the settlement record, particularly regarding centres of power. Edinburgh Castle stands on a hill that was first occupied in the Bronze Age and typifies a preference for prominent, defended strongholds. Some Dark Age hill-forts, like South Cadbury, were reused Iron Age hill-forts; others, like Dumbarton or Bamburgh, were newly built on strategic landmarks. In instances where the local setting can be reconstructed, the prehistoric ritual landscape seems to have played a part in the selection of the site. Despite this cultural continuity, British kingdoms started to appear at the same time as the earliest Anglo-Saxon ones.

In Ireland, too, this was an age of political reorganisation. Large provincial divisions came to overlie a network of smaller kingdoms, whose ruling elites began to appear in the sixth century. The preferred settlements of the Irish

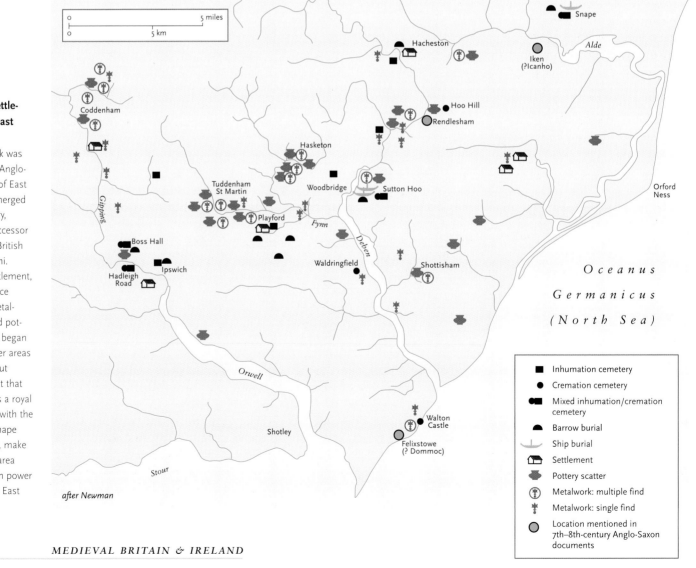

Anglo-Saxon settlement in southeast Suffolk

Southeast Suffolk was part of the early Anglo-Saxon kingdom of East Anglia, which emerged in the 6th century, possibly as a successor to the Romano-British *civitas* of the Iceni. Anglo-Saxon settlement, for which evidence (settlements, metalwork, burials and pottery) is plentiful, began later than in other areas of East Anglia, but Bede's statement that Rendlesham was a royal centre, together with the rich burials at Snape and Sutton Hoo, make it likely that the area became the main power base of the early East Anglian kings.

nobility were either elaborately defended homesteads (ring-forts) or artificial islands (crannogs). Links to the past remained strong, and some of the pre-eminent prehistoric religious complexes, notably Tara and Emain Macha, which were believed to have been the seats of mythological kings, as a result retained a great symbolic significance.

Only in one region – Northumbria – is there any significant evidence for cultural integration between incomers and natives. Here the level of Anglian settlement was lighter and a high degree of continuity can be seen in the landscape and social institutions of the kingdoms of Bernicia and Deira. By contrast, there was a much greater degree of social integration among the different Celtic peoples of western Britain and Ireland. For a time the kingdom of Dál Riata in western Britain spanned the North Channel; elsewhere, ogham inscriptions are a permanent record of a more ephemeral Irish presence. The Irish Sea served as the main conduit by which the Britons and Gaels maintained contact with the continental Christian heirs to Rome. Finds of pottery and glass provide evidence for a vigorous trade with the Mediterranean and western Gaul, in which wine was probably the most important import.

At the time, wine was the most prestigious alcoholic drink, but perhaps more importantly it was essential for the conduct of the Christian mass. If Christianity was not universal in Britannia before the end of the Roman province, it was becoming so by the end of the fifth century. By this time, the new faith was sufficiently vigorous to reach beyond the Roman frontiers. Patrick (active *c*.425–50) is only the most famous of several missionaries to Ireland and northern Britain who had a profound effect on the political as well as the religious landscape. Within a few generations, the Irish were bringing monastic Christianity back to Britain and the Continent. The most famous of the Irish foundations was Columba's monastery of Iona, established in 563. During the sixth and seventh centuries Iona emerged as the greatest Christian centre in northern Britain, with strong political links that extended its influence into Bernicia through the monastery of Lindisfarne.

Outside Northumbria, Celtic missionary activity did not extend to the English, so, in 597 (the year of Columba's death), the Pope dispatched a mission to the English, under Augustine. Evidently there was a sufficient Christian legacy in Canterbury to provide a platform to build an English church. The process of conversion was, not surprisingly, highly politicised, and during the course of the seventh century, there were repeated set-backs as the fortunes of Christian kings waxed and waned.

EARLY ANGLO-SAXON ROYALTY

Few places in Britain reveal as much about the nature of early medieval political power as Sutton Hoo. The site is a cemetery containing at least 17 barrows, the greatest concentration in England, and numerous flat graves and cremations. The largest barrow, Mound 1, was first excavated in 1939 and has proved to be by some margin the richest Anglo-Saxon burial ever found in England. It contained a ship and a huge collection of precious objects gathered from across Europe, some of which signal the burial's royal status. These finds include objects needed for a lavish feast

Parade-ground armour

A reconstructed ceremonial helmet from the early 7th-century ship burial at Sutton Hoo, tentatively identified as belonging to King Raedwald (died c.617–31). Decorative panels on the helmet, showing scenes from Norse mythology, have close affinities with the contemporary Vendel style of central Sweden. Helmets were associated with royal status in the early Anglo-Saxon kingdoms.

(drinking vessels of glass and horn, Byzantine silver plate, bronze hanging bowls decorated with enamel, a lyre) and splendid jewellery, armour, clothing and other accoutrements fit for a king. As was typical with high-status pagan Anglo-Saxon burials, objects symbolising warrior status were given great emphasis. The sword, shield and helmet are all richly decorated, to complement the even more spectacular golden jewellery (buckle, shoulder clasps and purse). In the purse was found a large collection of coins from throughout France, probably all minted before 625. On the basis of this date, the burial is widely regarded as that of Raedwald, a powerful king of East Anglia, and the cemetery as a royal burial ground of his dynasty.

Sutton Hoo is located on the upper reaches of the Deben, which gave access to the important river and maritime network of the East Angles, whose presence is reflected in the distributions of settlements, pottery, metalwork and cemeteries. The cemetery was also convenient for the royal residence of Rendlesham and the important trading centres of Felixstowe and Ipswich. Sutton Hoo offers a unique insight into Anglo-Saxon ceremonial rites, as an elite sought to create a kingdom and secure their rights to it.

Burial at Sutton Hoo probably began early in the seventh century. As time passed the kingdom grew in power and the graves increased in prestige. By the end of the seventh century, Christianity began to pose a serious challenge to traditional pagan belief. It may be that the lavish Mound 1 burial was intended as a conspicuous statement of pagan belief in the face of nascent Christianity.   **STD**

SAXONS & CELTS

Saxons and Celts

By c.700 the borders between the Anglo-Saxons and the Celtic peoples of Britain were beginning to stabilise. The Britons maintained their independence in Dumnonia, Wales and Strathclyde. The Picts successfully resisted Northumbrian attacks, but came increasingly under the influence of Dál Riata in the 8th century. Northumbria, the leading Anglo-Saxon kingdom in the 7th century, declined in the 8th and Mercia achieved a hegemony over southern Britain. Ireland, divided into seven over-kingdoms and dozens of sub-kingdoms, experienced a 'golden age' of monastic culture.

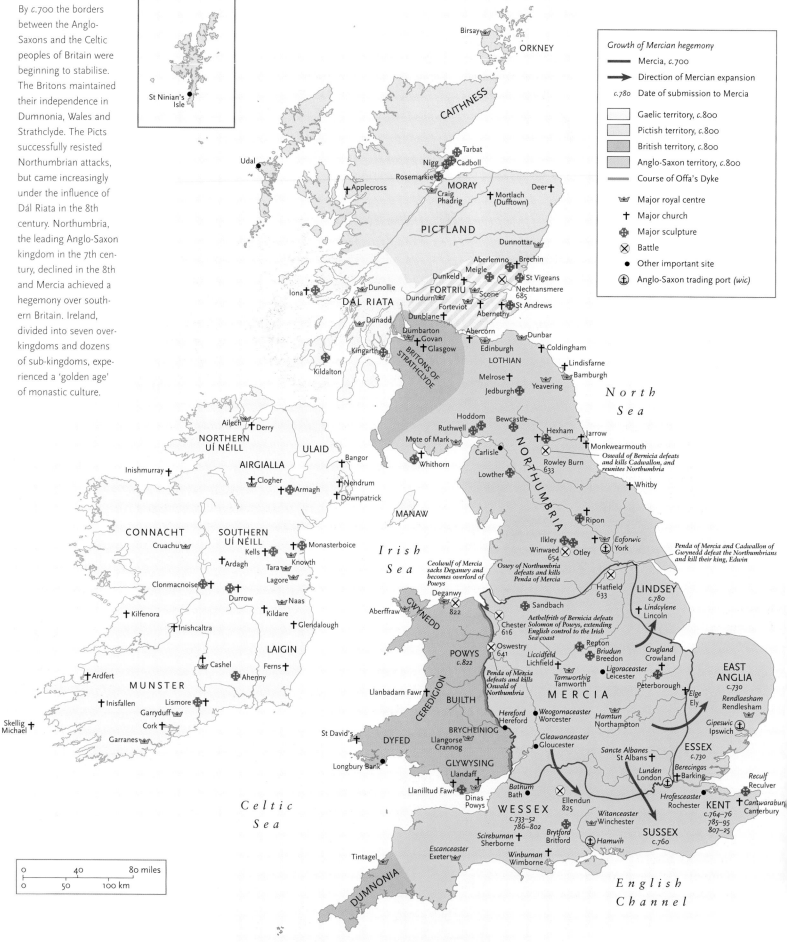

Growth of Mercian hegemony

——	Mercia, c.700
→	Direction of Mercian expansion
c.780	Date of submission to Mercia
	Gaelic territory, c.800
	Pictish territory, c.800
	British territory, c.800
	Anglo-Saxon territory, c.800
——	Course of Offa's Dyke
♛	Major royal centre
✝	Major church
✠	Major sculpture
✕	Battle
●	Other important site
⚓	Anglo-Saxon trading port (wic)

St Ninian's Isle

ORKNEY

Birsay

CAITHNESS

Udal

Tarbat
Nigg   Cadboll
Rosemarkie   MORAY   Deer
Applecross   Craig Phadrig   Mortlach (Dufftown)

PICTLAND

Dunnottar

Aberlemno   Brechin
Dunkeld   Meigle
Iona   Dunollie   FORTRIU   St Vigeans
Dunadd   Scone   Nechtansmere 685
DAL RIATA   Dundurn   Forteviot   St Andrews
Dunblane   Abernethy

Dumbarton   Abercorn   Dunbar
Govan   Coldingham
Kingarth   Glasgow   Edinburgh
BRITONS OF   LOTHIAN   Lindisfarne
Kildalton   STRATHCLYDE   Melrose   Bamburgh
Jedburgh   Yeavering

Ailech   Derry
NORTHERN   Hoddom   Bewcastle
UÍ NÉILL   ULAID   Ruthwell   Hexham   Jarrow
Inishmurray   Bangor   Mote of Mark   Carlisle   Monkwearmouth
AIRGIALLA   Clogher   Nendrum   Whithorn   Lowther   Rowley Burn 633
Armagh   Downpatrick   MANAW   Oswald of Bernicia defeats and kills Cadwallon, and reunites Northumbria
Whitby

NORTHUMBRIA   Ripon

CONNACHT   Irish Sea
Cruachu   SOUTHERN   Ilkley   Eoforwic
Kells   UÍ NÉILL   Monasterboice   Winwaed 654   Otley   York
Ardagh   Tara   Knowth   Penda of Mercia and Cadwallon of Gwynedd defeat the Northumbrians and kill their king, Edwin
Clonmacnoise   Lagore   Ceolwulf of Mercia sacks Deganwy and becomes overlord of Powys   Oswy of Northumbria defeats and kills Penda of Mercia
Durrow   Naas   Hatfield 633   LINDSEY c.780
Kilfenora   Kildare   Deganwy   Sandbach   Lindcylene Lincoln
Inishcaltra   Glendalough   Aberffraw   822   Aethelfrith of Bernicia defeats Solomon of Powys, extending English control to the Irish Sea coast
LAIGIN   GWYNEDD   Chester 616   Repton   Crugland
Cashel   Ferns   Oswestry 641   Liccidfeld   Breedon   Crowland
Ardfert   MUNSTER   Ahenny   POWYS c.822   Lichfield   Briudun   EAST ANGLIA
Inisfallen   Lismore   Llanbadarn Fawr   Penda of Mercia defeats and kills Oswald of Northumbria   Ligoraceaster   Rendlaesham
Skellig Michael   Garryduff   CEREDIGION   Tamworthig   Leicester   Rendlesham
Cork   BUILTH   Hereford   Tamworth   Peterborough   Elge
Garranes   St David's   BRYCHEINIOG   Hereford   Weogornaceaster   Hamtun   Ely
Llangorse Crannog   Worcester   MERCIA   Northampton   Gipeswic
DYFED   Gleawanceaster   Ipswich
Longbury Bank   GLYWYSING   Gloucester   Sancte Albanes   ESSEX c.730
Llandaff   St Albans   Berecingas   Reculf
Llanilltud Fawr   Dinas Powys   Bathum   Lunden   Barking   Reculver
Bath   Ellendun 825   London
Tintagel   Witanceaster   Hrofesceaster   Cantwarabur
Scireburnan   Brytford   Winchester   Rochester   KENT   Canterbury
Sherborne   Britford   WESSEX   Hamwih   c.764-76
Escanceaster   c.733-52   SUSSEX   785-95
Exeter   786-802   Winburnan   c.760   807-25
DUMNONIA   Wimborne

North Sea

Celtic Sea

English Channel

0   40   80 miles
0   50   100 km

Between the seventh and ninth centuries the various polities that had emerged in post-Roman Britain became increasingly state-like in their organisation and institutions. Successful kingdoms, such as Wessex, Mercia, Northumbria, Gwynedd, Fortriu and Dál Riata, fought wars to expand their territories into large regional hegemonies. In Ireland a less centralised political landscape evolved. There, as many as 300 small kingdoms (*tuatha*) existed. These were consolidated under the shifting control of overkings, but the rule of even the most successful of the provincial dynasties, the Uí Néill, was more contingent and fluid than its counterparts in Britain.

EXPANSIONIST KINGDOMS

In Britain the most northerly of the major kingdoms, Fortriu, grew to encompass most or all of southern Pictland. Fortriu's era of greatness was ushered in by the Pictish triumph over the expansionist Northumbrians at the battle of Nechtansmere in 685 and continued for most of the eighth century. A political and cultural high point was reached during the reign of Óengus I (died 761).

The British kingdoms in southern Scotland were ruled from imposing, rock-perched hill-forts: in the west, the most powerful British kingdom was ruled from Dumbarton, dominating the mouth of the Clyde; in the east, the British kings of Gododdin surveyed their lands from the equally dramatic Edinburgh Castle rock. The Clyde-based kingdom survived until the eleventh century, while, in the east, Edinburgh fell to the Northumbrians in 638. Lothian remained under Northumbrian control and became linguistically and culturally anglicised.

Over the course of the seventh century, Northumbria came to dominate its British neighbours through the aggressive energy of kings like Edwin (died 633). The small independent kingdoms of Rheged and Elmet disappeared as the Anglian kingdoms of Bernicia and Deira coalesced into a single, powerful unit capable of extending its authority west of the Pennines. Eventually, Northumbrian rule encompassed Whithorn in Galloway – and briefly stretched as far north as the Tay.

Also during the seventh century, Mercia emerged as the chief kingdom in the English Midlands, expanding westward to the Welsh marches and securing the area south of the Humber, under the rule of the pagan king Penda (died 655). Generally good relations with the British (Welsh) kingdoms to the west enabled the Mercians to campaign successfully against their English neighbours. The high watermark of Mercian hegemony came in the late eighth century under the rule of Offa (died 796), who aspired to rule all of England and dominated the South as far as Kent. The ascendancy of Mercia was abruptly ended following defeat by Egbert of Wessex (died 839) at Ellendun in 825.

Within Wales the post-Roman political landscape survived more intact. The series of earthworks known as Offa's Dyke defined the frontier between the British and Mercia. Topography (in the form of mountainous borders that deterred potential enemies) and political resilience allowed the kingdoms of Gwynedd and Powys in particular to consolidate their territories and develop into durable kingdoms that would last until the Norman Conquest of Wales in the twelfth century.

In southern England the Wessex kings came to overshadow their Kentish and South Saxon neighbours, while at the same time expanding ever further westwards into British territory. Throughout this period, London, still the largest port in Britain, remained the greatest political prize in England. Control of London was the source of extended conflict between Mercia and Wessex, which was ended only by the disruptions of the Viking wars.

In Ireland aggressive kings constructed elaborate structures of overlordship that allowed a few royal kindred groups to dominate whole provinces. These kindreds were large and complex, resulting in a great deal of internal competition for royal succession. Despite this inherent instability, exceptionally successful dynasties were able to construct and maintain large polities. The northern and southern branches of the Uí Néill effectively dominated most of the north and east Midlands, while the Eoganacht dynasty came to rule Munster.

Traditionally, the extension of the kingdom of Dál Riata from Antrim to Argyll has been explained as the consequence of Uí Néill pressure on the local dynasty from the west. However, an increasing body of archaeological evidence appears to suggest that Scottish Dál Riata was not so much a recent Irish colony as the eastern part of a Gaelic-speaking zone that straddled the North Channel. The physical proximity and maritime culture encouraged deep connections between western Scotland and Ireland, which persisted throughout the Middle Ages.

ROYAL CENTRES

The characteristic form of royal settlement in Celtic-speaking Britain was the hill-fort. Although sometimes built on the sites of Iron Age hill-forts, the early medieval hill-fort was a new phenomenon. It tended to occupy a craggy knoll, rather than towering heights, and its elaborate masonry or earthwork ramparts enclosed relatively small areas suitable for the residence of the king and his extended household. Although they are architecturally quite different from the later medieval castle, these fortified dwellings served a similar range of domestic, administrative and ceremonial functions. Where these have been excavated (for example,

'The glorious reign of Edwin over English and Briton alike lasted seventeen years, during the last six of which...he laboured for Christ.'

Bede, *Ecclesiastical History of the English People* (731)

St Martin's Cross
The 8th-century St Martin's Cross at Iona Abbey in the Hebrides is one of the earliest known wheel-headed crosses. Elaborately carved stone crosses, often erected as preaching stations, are the most distinctive early medieval monuments of the British Isles.

magnificent hall of Heorot in *Beowulf* may not be greatly exaggerated. Unlike the hill-forts, Anglo-Saxon royal centres appear not to have been the focus of either trade or manufacturing.

Nonetheless, the Anglo-Saxons did participate in a cross-Channel trade network, which encouraged the development of royal emporia and coinage. Newly established trading centres, such as Hamwih (Southampton) and Ipswich, quickly developed into significant towns, which became the commercial rivals of London.

LOCATIONS OF POWER

Early medieval kings were keen to legitimise their power by associating themselves with sites of ancient authority. This is well seen at Dunadd, the chief royal fortress of Dál Riata, which occupies an isolated rocky knoll overlooking the richest prehistoric ritual landscape in western Scotland. Since Neolithic times people have been coming to the Kilmartin valley to bury their dead, erect standing stones and create rock art on outcrops. These ancient associations cannot have been lost on the founders of Dunadd – and were arguably a primary motive for the site's selection.

The highest point of the Dunadd complex was occupied by a fortified dwelling, built in the local dry-stone tradition. Such dwellings, first known from the Iron Age, are ubiquitous in western Scotland and are taken to indicate the presence of free property-owners. At Dunadd, however, the building was enclosed within two additional ramparts, creating considerable additional space for the royal household. Within this area was a royal workshop where fine metalworkers made brooches and other jewellery. Large quantities of imported pottery and glass vessels have been excavated, which attest to regular trade with Gaul.

A remarkable series of carvings near the summit of Dunadd suggest that it also served as the inauguration place of the kings of Dál Riata. These carvings include a single-shod footprint, a rock-cut basin, an incised boar and an ogham inscription. The footprint echoes royal ceremonies documented in Ireland, with their symbols of the physical union between the king and the land, and is part of a broader phenomenon found throughout Britain and Ireland where royal authority sought to create links with the ancestral past through the re-use of ancient sacred places.

The growth and development of Dunadd is closely linked to the fate of Dál Riata. It was founded in the sixth century and grew into the most important royal site in Argyll during the seventh and eighth centuries. The complex survived sacking by the Picts in the mid-eighth century, only to be abandoned as the centre of Scottish power shifted east in the ninth century.

THE CHURCH

During these centuries the Church grew in influence, wealth and organisation. This development was closely intertwined with secular political developments, not least because the same aristocratic families dominated the Church and the Crown. Frequently, a particular saint became identified with a specific kingdom, which meant that the spread of saintly cults was strongly influenced by political concerns. In Ireland the cult of Patrick (and thereby Armagh's claims to primacy) were promoted by the Uí

Dunadd, Dumbarton, Dunollie, Dundurn, Edinburgh, Mote of Mark, Deganwy, Dinas Powys, Tintagel) they have produced similar kinds of evidence for the manufacturing of fine metalwork and the importation of pottery, glassware and, presumably, wine from the Continent via the Irish Sea.

By contrast, the Anglo-Saxons developed an elite architectural tradition that was more in keeping with post-Roman practices on the Continent. In some cases, Roman centres were reoccupied, as at Winchester and York, where the late Roman town walls may have provided a measure of security along with prestige. Bamburgh, Northumbria's royal seat, is the major exception to the rule. It is a former British hill-fort perched on a coastal crag – a clear indication of the native contribution to the social structure of Northumbria.

Conceptually, at the heart of the Anglo-Saxon royal complex was the hall, where the main ceremonial and administrative business of the lord was conducted. Excavations of royal halls, such as at Yeavering and Northampton, suggest that the descriptions of the

Néill. Northumbria's influence is reflected in the church dedications to Saints Oswald and Cuthbert. Nowhere is the relationship between cult and kingdom easier to appreciate than in Dál Riata, whose ruling dynasty looked to Saint Columba as patron and protector.

Iona, founded by Columba in 563, grew to become one of the greatest ecclesiastical centres in the British Isles and established an extensive network of associated monasteries, which spread from northern Britain to Kells and Durrow in the Irish midlands, to Derry in the north and Lindisfarne in Northumbria. These monasteries were places of scholarship and religious devotion, and were also repositories of great wealth. From the late eighth century the Argyll coast was ravaged by Vikings and Iona was repeatedly raided. More sustained Viking assaults in the east undermined the Pictish elite, allowing a new Gaelic dynasty, headed by Cináed mac Alpín ('Kenneth MacAlpin', died 858) to seize the kingship of the Picts. Columban relics were moved from Iona to Dunkeld and there was a great enthusiasm for dedications to Columba and other Iona saints. This eastern Gaelic kingdom, with its new ceremonial centre at Scone, provided the basis of the Scottish state, which survived throughout the Middle Ages.

By about 700 the conversion of the Anglo-Saxons to Christianity was largely complete and the Church was becoming increasingly political, not least because of its vast land-holdings. Nevertheless, religious authority was not effectively centralised in this period, despite the claims of Canterbury and York to authority beyond their local political boundaries. In terms of church art and architecture, the Anglo-Saxons invested far greater artistic energy in their buildings than in monumental sculpture, except in Northumbria. By contrast, an interest in monumentality in religious art continued unbroken in the Celtic regions in the post-Roman era – though styles evolved over time. Extremely fine, but distinct, sculptural traditions developed in Pictland, Argyll, Ireland and Wales – in some cases, the

presence of a collection of sculpture is all that now remains to provide evidence of the importance of a particular church.

THE COMING OF THE VIKINGS

By around 800 it is possible to identify five or six kingdoms within Britain with the social and administrative characteristics of a state, while in Ireland large regional polities were taking shape. However, we will never know how these kingdoms might have developed had they been left to their own devices. Viking raids and settlement led to cataclysmic upheavals and a transformation in the political landscape. Of the Anglo-Saxon kingdoms, only Wessex survived. In the north the Vikings were instrumental in the birth of the kingdom of Alba out of the dying ashes of the Pictish kingdom. In Ireland the effect of the Vikings was to derail attempts to create a unified Ireland until the eleventh century. Only Wales emerged little changed.   STD

Kilmartin valley

The Kilmartin valley in Argyll is the site of one of Scotland's richest archaeological landscapes, with a continuous series of monuments dating back to the Neolithic age. These monuments confirmed the valley as a site of power and were almost certainly one of the reasons why the Scots of Dál Riata chose the craggy hill of Dunadd as the site of their capital. The large royal fort they built there included a number of symbolic carvings probably associated with the annointment of kings. It was to take advantage of similar associations with past power that Anglo-Saxon rulers sometimes re-occupied ruined Roman sites.

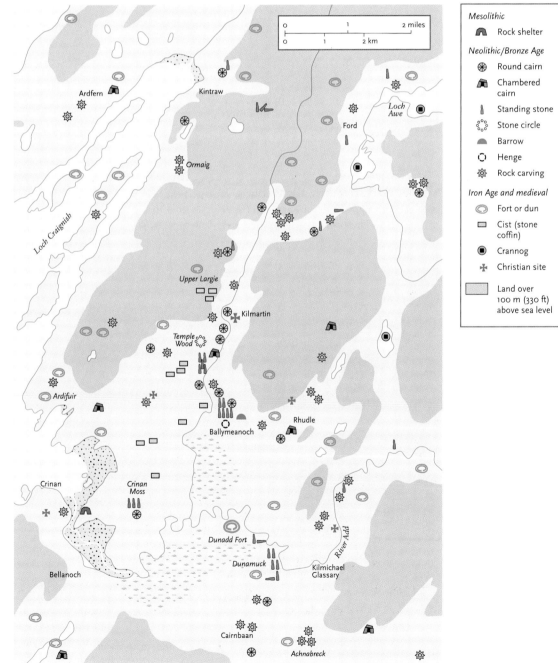

Mesolithic	
	Rock shelter
Neolithic/Bronze Age	
	Round cairn
	Chambered cairn
	Standing stone
	Stone circle
	Barrow
	Henge
	Rock carving
Iron Age and medieval	
	Fort or dun
	Cist (stone coffin)
	Crannog
	Christian site
	Land over 100 m (330 ft) above sea level

THE VIKING AGE

The Viking age in Britain and Ireland began with the killing by Norwegian pirates of a royal official at the port of Portland in Wessex, in or around 789. Within a few years, Danish and Norwegian Vikings – a 'Viking' was simply someone who went *i víking*, that is, plundering – had launched raids around the entire coastline of Britain and Ireland, as well as the Channel and Atlantic coasts of the Frankish empire. The Vikings' favoured targets were monasteries, such as those at Lindisfarne and Iona, sited on or near the coast or navigable rivers. Not only were monasteries rich, but they were also virtually defenceless and, being pagans, the Vikings were not deterred by the spiritual sanctions that protected the Church when Christians were at war. Exploiting the speed of their longships to the full, the Vikings could attack, plunder and be gone before the locals could organise a counter-attack.

The earliest Viking raids were carried out by small fleets of up to about a dozen ships, but the numbers recorded in contemporary annals began to increase in the 830s until, by the 850s, fleets of several hundred ships are reported. It was probably Ireland that suffered most severely during this phase of Viking activity. Ireland was divided into some half-dozen competing provincial kingdoms whose kings exercised a loose sway over dozens of quarrelsome tributary sub-kingdoms. This extremely decentralised power structure made any kind of coordinated defence difficult.

Beginning in 836, the Vikings began to build fortified bases, called *longphorts* by the Irish, in which they spent the winter so as to be able to make an early start to raiding come the spring. Most *longphorts* were occupied only briefly, but a few became permanent settlements, which in the tenth century developed into Ireland's first true towns. The most successful of these was Dublin, founded in 841, which probably owed its early growth to Viking slave-trading.

The Viking raids were shocking to their victims, not only for their violence and unpredictability. Early medieval Christians confidently believed in the power of the saints: that the saints had not intervened to protect their monasteries from impious pagans surely meant that the Viking raids were an expression of the wrath of God against a sinful people. The raids were in reality caused by social and political developments in Scandinavia itself. Eighth-century Scandinavia was experiencing the early stages of state formation, and competition for power had created a violent, predatory society. Initially at least, piracy was primarily a way for ambitious men to gain wealth, reputation and an armed following to pursue their ambitions at home. However, the ineffectiveness of the opposition soon persuaded some Vikings that it would be possible to seize land as well as plunder.

SETTLEMENT

The earliest substantial Viking settlement in Britain was probably in Shetland, Orkney and the Hebrides: the exact date is unknown but it was certainly under way by about 850. By the end of the ninth century, Orkney had become

> *Never before has such an atrocity been seen...The church of St Cuthbert is spattered with the blood of the priests of God, stripped of all its furnishings, exposed to the plundering of pagans – a place more sacred than any in Britain.*
>
> **Alcuin of York, 793**

Viking treasure

Part of the Cuerdale hoard, a huge collection of Viking treasure buried c.905. Weighing 40 kilograms (about 90 pounds), it contained 1,000 silver ingots, pieces of jewellery and 7,500 coins, some of them from as far afield as Spain and Afghanistan. The failure to recover such a valuable hoard suggests a bad end for all involved in its burial.

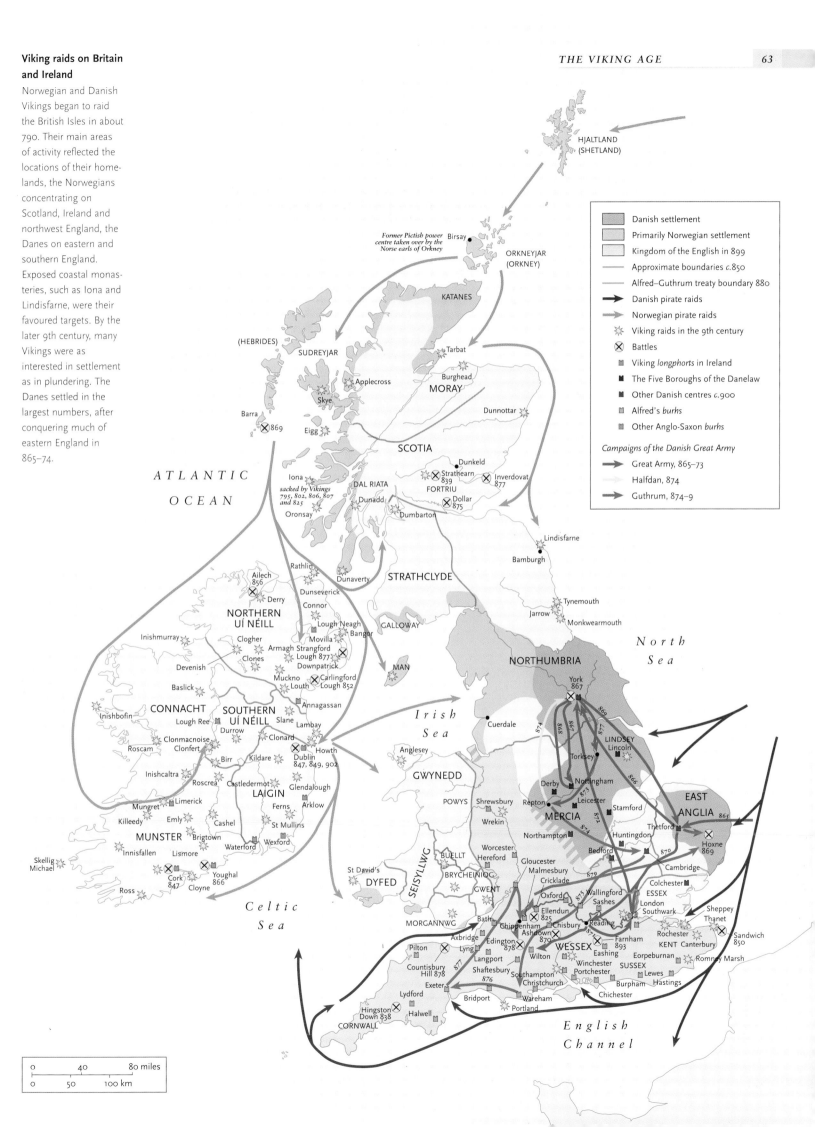

Viking raids on Britain and Ireland

Norwegian and Danish Vikings began to raid the British Isles in about 790. Their main areas of activity reflected the locations of their homelands, the Norwegians concentrating on Scotland, Ireland and northwest England, the Danes on eastern and southern England. Exposed coastal monasteries, such as Iona and Lindisfarne, were their favoured targets. By the later 9th century, many Vikings were as interested in settlement as in plundering. The Danes settled in the largest numbers, after conquering much of eastern England in 865–74.

	Danish settlement
	Primarily Norwegian settlement
	Kingdom of the English in 899
	Approximate boundaries c.850
	Alfred–Guthrum treaty boundary 880
	Danish pirate raids
	Norwegian pirate raids
	Viking raids in the 9th century
	Battles
	Viking *longphorts* in Ireland
	The Five Boroughs of the Danelaw
	Other Danish centres c.900
	Alfred's *burhs*
	Other Anglo-Saxon *burhs*

Campaigns of the Danish Great Army

Great Army, 865–73
Halfdan, 874
Guthrum, 874–9

HJALTLAND (SHETLAND)

Former Pictish power centre taken over by the Norse earls of Orkney • Birsay

ORKNEYJAR (ORKNEY)

KATANES

(HEBRIDES)

SUDREYJAR

Tarbat
Burghead
MORAY

Barra
Skye
Applecross

Dunnottar

Eigg
SCOTIA

Dunkeld

Iona
sacked by Vikings 795, 802, 806, 807 and 825
Oronsay

DAL RIATA
Dunadd

Strathearn 839
FORTRIU
Dollar 875
Dumbarton

Inverdovat 877

ATLANTIC OCEAN

869

Lindisfarne
Bamburgh

STRATHCLYDE

Rathlin
Ailech 856
Dunseverick
Derry
Connor
Lough Neagh
Bangor
NORTHERN UÍ NÉILL
Movilla
Clogher
Armagh Strangford
Lough 877
Downpatrick
Clones
Muckno
Louth
Carlingford Lough 852

GALLOWAY
Tynemouth
Jarrow
Monkwearmouth

Inishmurray
Clonard
Devenish
Baslick

MAN

North Sea

NORTHUMBRIA
York 867

Cuerdale

CONNACHT
Inishbofin
Lough Ree
Durrow
Roscam
Clonmacnoise
Clonfert
Inishcaltra
Roscrea
Birr
Kildare
Castledermot
Ferns
Arklow
LAIGIN
Glendalough

SOUTHERN UÍ NÉILL
Slane
Lambay
Clonard
Dublin 847, 849, 902
Howth

Annagassan

Irish Sea

Anglesey

GWYNEDD

LINDSEY
Lincoln

Torksey

Derby
Nottingham
Repton
Leicester
Stamford

MERCIA

POWYS
Shrewsbury
Wrekin

EAST ANGLIA
Thetford

Mungret
Limerick
Killeedy
Emly
Cashel
Brigtown
Innisfallen
Lismore
MUNSTER

St Mullins
Wexford
Waterford

Cork 847
Cloyne
Youghal 866

Skellig Michael
Ross

Celtic Sea

St David's
DYFED

SEISYLLWG
BUELLT
BRYCHEINIOG
GWENT

MORGANNWG

Worcester
Hereford
Gloucester
Malmesbury
Cricklade
Oxford
Wallingford
Sashes

Northampton
Bedford
Huntingdon

Hoxne 869
Cambridge
Colchester
ESSEX
London
Southwark

Bath
Chippenham
Ashdown
Ellendun 825
Chisbury
Reading
Farnham 893
Eashing
WESSEX
Wilton
Winchester
Portchester
SUSSEX
Lewes
Burpham
Hastings

Sheppey
Thanet
Rochester
KENT
Canterbury
Sandwich 850
Eorpeburnan
Romney Marsh

Axbridge
Lyng
Edington 878
Langport
Shaftesbury 876
Southampton
Christchurch
Chichester

Pilton
Countisbury Hill 878
Exeter
Bridport
Wareham
Portland

Lydford
Halwell

Hingston Down 838
CORNWALL

English Channel

0   40   80 miles
0   50   100 km

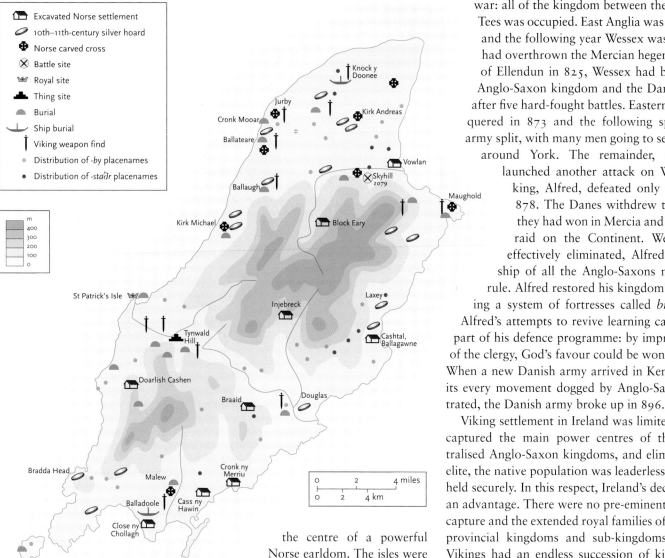

Legend

- Excavated Norse settlement
- 10th–11th-century silver hoard
- Norse carved cross
- Battle site
- Royal site
- Thing site
- Burial
- Ship burial
- Viking weapon find
- Distribution of -*by* placenames
- Distribution of -*staðr* placenames

m
400
300
200
100
0

Map labels: Knock y Doonee, Jurby, Cronk Mooar, Kirk Andreas, Ballateare, Vowlan, Ballaugh, Skyhill 1079, Maughold, Kirk Michael, Block Eary, St Patrick's Isle, Laxey, Injebreck, Tynwald Hill, Cashtal, Ballagawne, Doarlish Cashen, Braaid, Douglas, Bradda Head, Malew, Cronk ny Merriu, Balladoole, Cass ny Hawin, Close ny Chollagh

Scale: 0   2   4 miles / 0   2   4 km

Viking settlement in the Isle of Man

Its strategic position in the middle of the Irish Sea made the Isle of Man attractive for Viking settlement. Though the native population was not wiped out, the distribution of archaeological sites and Scandinavian place-names shows that the settlers seized the best land for themselves. The many silver hoards suggest that the island prospered by its proximity to the important Viking trading centre at Dublin.

---

war: all of the kingdom between the Humber and the Tees was occupied. East Anglia was conquered in 869 and the following year Wessex was invaded. Since it had overthrown the Mercian hegemony at the battle of Ellendun in 825, Wessex had been the strongest Anglo-Saxon kingdom and the Danes were repulsed after five hard-fought battles. Eastern Mercia was conquered in 873 and the following spring the Danish army split, with many men going to settle the rich lands around York. The remainder, under Guthrum, launched another attack on Wessex, which its king, Alfred, defeated only with difficulty in 878. The Danes withdrew to settle the lands they had won in Mercia and East Anglia, or to raid on the Continent. Wessex's old rivals effectively eliminated, Alfred assumed leadership of all the Anglo-Saxons not under Danish rule. Alfred restored his kingdom's defences, building a system of fortresses called *burhs*, and a fleet. Alfred's attempts to revive learning can also be seen as part of his defence programme: by improving the quality of the clergy, God's favour could be won for the kingdom. When a new Danish army arrived in Kent in 892 it found its every movement dogged by Anglo-Saxon forces. Frustrated, the Danish army broke up in 896.

Viking settlement in Ireland was limited. Once they had captured the main power centres of the relatively centralised Anglo-Saxon kingdoms, and eliminated the ruling elite, the native population was leaderless, so land could be held securely. In this respect, Ireland's decentralisation was an advantage. There were no pre-eminent power centres to capture and the extended royal families of each of the many provincial kingdoms and sub-kingdoms meant that the Vikings had an endless succession of kings to fight. The Vikings remained confined to their fortified coastal settlements and were even temporarily expelled by the Irish in 902. Many of the refugees settled in northwest England. The Viking impact was perhaps slightest on Wales. The coast suffered its fair share of raids, often launched by Irish-based Vikings, especially in the tenth century, but there were few Viking settlements and these had no discernible cultural or political influence.

ASSIMILATION

In most of Britain and Ireland, the Scandinavian settlers soon began to assimilate with the native populations through intermarriage and conversion to Christianity. Relatively few Viking burials and even fewer settlements have been identified, perhaps because the settlers quickly adopted the material culture and burial customs of the natives and so became archaeologically invisible, although waterlogged sites in Dublin and York have provided spectacular evidence of everyday life in Viking towns. Scandinavian influence on place-names is in fact the best guide to the areas of Viking settlement. In England, the process of assimilation was made easier, as the languages spoken by the Anglo-Saxons and the Danes were similar enough to be mutually intelligible with a little effort. Though it was the Danes who finished up speaking English, English vocabulary was greatly enriched by loan words from Danish, including 'sky', 'egg', 'sister' and 'skin'. The Danish-settled areas of England later became known as the

---

the centre of a powerful Norse earldom. The isles were convenient bases for raiding the mainland. These raids were certainly destructive but sometimes native leaders were able to benefit from them. Serious Viking attacks on the Picts in 839 paved the way for their take-over in 844 by Kenneth MacAlpin, king of the Scots of Dál Riata. Before the century was out, this new kingdom had become known as Scotia – 'Scotland' – and it was not long afterwards that the Picts, together with their language and most of their culture and traditions, disappeared from history. The British kingdom of Strathclyde was also weakened when the Dublin Vikings sacked their capital at Dumbarton in 870–1 and in the tenth century it too fell increasingly under the sway of the Scots. Thus the early growth of the Scottish kingdom was, in part at least, a consequence of the Vikings' disruption of the established power structures of northern Britain.

The impact of the Vikings on the Anglo-Saxon kingdoms was, if anything, even more dramatic. In 865, as recorded in the *Anglo-Saxon Chronicle*, a 'great heathen army' landed in East Anglia from Denmark. Its leaders had royal blood and from the start their object was conquest rather than plunder. By seizing horses from the East Anglians, the Danes enjoyed the same mobility on land as their longships had given them at sea. First to succumb was Northumbria, which had chosen this ill-starred moment to hold a civil

'Danelaw' because of Danish influence on legal customs there, which persisted until after the Norman Conquest. In the Hebrides and southwest Scotland a hybrid Gaelic-Norse population emerged, known to the Irish as 'Gall-Gaedhil' ('foreign Gael'), from which Galloway gets its name. It was not until the twelfth century, however, that the assimilation of the Viking settlers to the native Gaels was complete. It was only in Orkney and Shetland that the settlers escaped assimilation to the natives – here it was the native Picts who adopted Scandinavian ways and speech. Almost all place-names here are Scandinavian, suggesting a particularly dense Viking settlement. Norn, a Scandinavian dialect, continued to be spoken in the northern isles until the eighteenth century, when it was replaced by English.

The process of assimilation and coexistence between native and Viking is well seen in the Isle of Man. The evidence of pagan burials, containing weapons and sometimes ships and human sacrifices, indicates that substantial Viking settlement began in the later ninth century. The native Christian Gaelic-speaking population was not wiped out, but the distribution of typical Scandinavian place-name elements, such as *-by* ('village') and *-staðir* ('fields in meadowland'), shows that the settlers took the better,

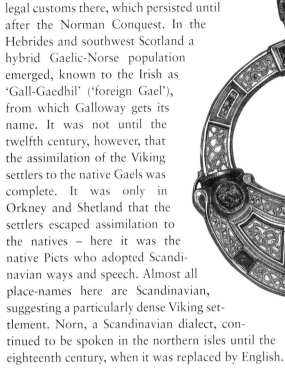

The Hunterston brooch

This brooch, found in Scotland, was made c.700 in Ireland. It later came into the possession of a Viking and has a Gaelic woman's name inscribed on the back in Scandinavian runes.

lower-lying land for themselves. After they adopted Christianity in the tenth century, the settlers erected a series of fine carved stone memorial crosses that incorporated Irish, northern English and Scandinavian decorative motifs and both Christian and pagan imagery. Inscriptions are always in Scandinavian runes, but several commemorate people with Celtic names, a sign of intermarriage between the two populations. One bilingual inscription, in Norse and Gaelic, is also known. Godred Crovan of Islay won control of the island at the battle of Skyhill in 1079 and made it the centre of a Norse kingdom that included all of the Hebrides. The kingdom survived under Norwegian sovereignty until 1266, when it was ceded to Scotland. By this time, the population had become once again primarily Gaelic in language and culture but Norse institutions such as the thing ('assembly') survived. The Manx parliament continues to meet annually in the open air to announce legislation at Tynwald (from Old Norse *Thingvöllur*, meaning 'thing plain'), the traditional assembly place of the Norse kingdom, as has been done for over 900 years.   JH

St Patrick's Isle at Peel, Isle of Man

An early Christian cemetery on the island was used for burials by pagan Viking settlers, a symbolic way for the newcomers to display their power over the Christian natives. The islet became a major political and ecclesiastical centre of the Norse kingdom of Man.

VIKING YORK

Silver penny
A high-quality silver penny from the reign of Olaf Guthfrithsson, king of York 939–41.

York originated as a Roman legionary fortress on the river Ouse in about AD 71. A thriving civilian settlement, which became a provincial capital soon after 200, developed on the opposite bank of the river. With the end of Roman rule, York, like other British towns, fell into decay, though the legionary headquarters building remained in use – perhaps first as the palace of the local British kings, and then of the Anglian kings who supplanted them – until destroyed by fire in the early seventh century. Despite the demise of

Micklegate, the 'Great Street'

The Roman colo of Eburacum wa centred on this a

The walls of the Roman colonia were falling into decay in the Viking period

St Mary Bishopshill Junior, the only church in York that displays visible Viking masonry

Anglian helmet
A restored Viking-age helmet of Anglian manufacture, found in the Coppergate excavations of Jorvik. It includes a nasal (nose guard) and a mail protective skirt for the wearer's neck.

its empire, Rome retained residual prestige as a symbol of authority, which may have ensured York's survival as a power centre, if not a functioning town.

York's revival as an urban centre of the Anglo-Saxon kingdom of Northumbria began with the growth of trade between Britain and the Continent in the seventh and eighth centuries. This stimulated the development of trading ports, or *wics*, on navigable waterways, including Hamwic (Southampton), Gipeswic (Ipswich), Lundenwic (London) and Eoforwic (York). At York, the site of the legionary fortress continued to be occupied as a royal and ecclesiastical centre with an international reputation for learning, but the main focus of settlement was to the south, on the banks of the Ouse and its tributary the Foss. Both archaeological and literary sources suggest that the town's main trade links were with Frisia and the lower Rhine.

York was first captured by Danish Vikings in 866, and made the capital of an important kingdom. By around 1000 the area of the old Roman colony was being resettled and the population had reached about 10,000 – making York ('Jorvik' to the Vikings) a large city by contemporary standards and, in the British Isles, second only to London in size. Though they were mostly pagans, the Scandinavian kings did not interfere with the Church, and they adopted other institutions of the Northumbrian kingdom, such as the mint, which went on to produce coins bearing a mixture of Christian and pagan symbols. York's Roman walls were refurbished, and evidence suggests effective urban planning and the laying out of parts of the city into regular tenement blocks and streets in the early tenth century.

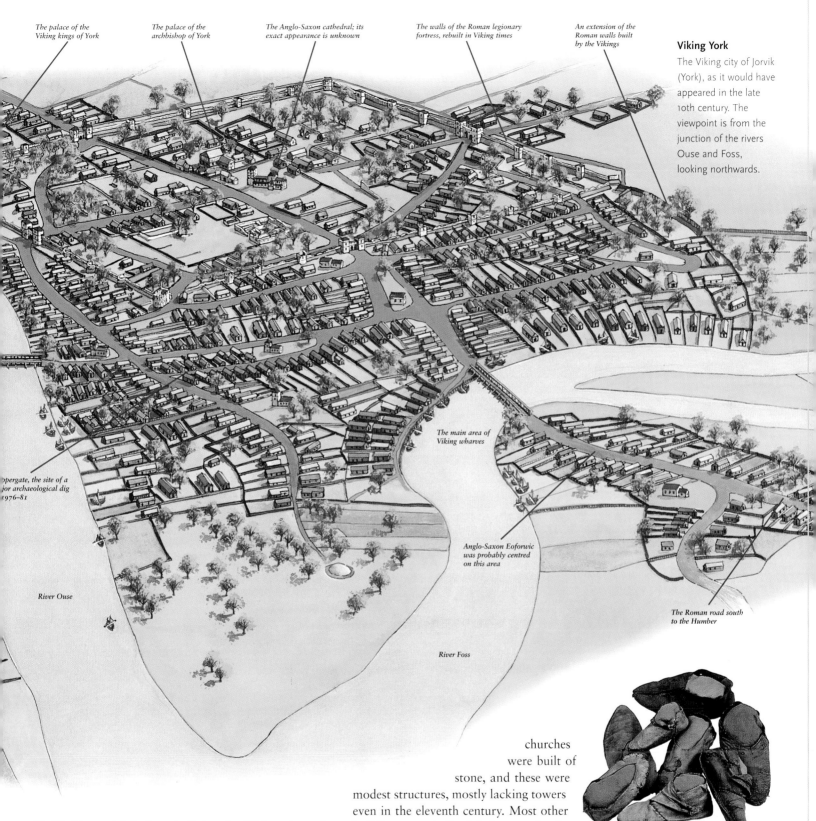

The palace of the
Viking kings of York

The palace of the
archbishop of York

The Anglo-Saxon cathedral; its
exact appearance is unknown

The walls of the Roman legionary
fortress, rebuilt in Viking times

An extension of the
Roman walls built
by the Vikings

Viking York

The Viking city of Jorvik
(York), as it would have
appeared in the late
10th century. The
viewpoint is from the
junction of the rivers
Ouse and Foss,
looking northwards.

oppergate, the site of a
jor archaeological dig
1976–81

The main area of
Viking wharves

Anglo-Saxon Eoforwic
was probably centred
on this area

River Ouse

The Roman road south
to the Humber

River Foss

To York's established trade links, the Vikings brought new connections with Ireland and Scandinavia. The city's Viking rulers actively encouraged trade, which they could tax to their own benefit; their success in stimulating commercial activity is demonstrated by the fact that the silver content of the city's coinage increased under Viking rule. Archaeological excavations have revealed a wide range of craft and industrial activities in the city, including glass-making, metallurgy, textile production and the manufacture of items in bone, antler, jet, wood and leather.

York would not have impressed visiting merchants from the more urbanised Mediterranean world. Only its

churches were built of stone, and these were modest structures, mostly lacking towers even in the eleventh century. Most other buildings were built of timber, wattle, clay and thatch. Life in the crowded waterfront areas was damp, muddy and unhygienic – latrines were often dug within feet of wells used for drinking water. Settlement elsewhere in the city was far less dense, allowing space for fields, vegetable gardens and orchards.

The end of Viking rule in 954 did not interrupt York's prosperity. The city's Scandinavian population was not expelled – it had anyway begun to assimilate with the native English through intermarriage and conversion to Christianity – and York retained an Anglo-Scandinavian character until after the Norman Conquest. **JH**

Leather footwear

Viking Jorvik was a major manufacturing centre; these restored shoes and boots from the Coppergate excavations confirm that leather-working was well established there.

The process of political development in the ninth and tenth centuries from the kingdom of the West Saxons to the kingdom of the English, coupled as it was with repeated claims to a kingship 'of the whole of Britain', must qualify as one of the grandest themes in the history of the British Isles. It is a tale that can be told in various ways, exposing a truth that it is still not fully understood; but while Anglocentric accounts of the period make good reading for the English, they do not have so much appeal for the Irish, Welsh or Scottish readers.

It is generally supposed that the process was driven from the outset by a determination on the part of successive rulers (and their advisers) to transform a concept of the unity of the English people from an aspiration to a political

'King of all Britain'

King Aethelstan (924–39) presents a copy of Bede's Life of St Cuthbert to the church of St Cuthbert at Chester-le-Street, near Durham. In 927 Aethelstan extended his rule over the Northumbrians, and thereby became the first ruler of all the English. He also aspired to be 'King of all Britain'.

reality. The concept itself is first attested in letters written by Pope Gregory the Great in connection with the mission of St Augustine in 597, but was given much wider currency when adopted by Bede as an organising principle of his *Ecclesiastical History of the English People*, completed in 731. The Mercians tried and failed to achieve Bede's purpose, in the later eighth and early ninth centuries, whereupon the Vikings simplified matters by conquering the kingdoms of East Anglia, Northumbria and Mercia, and by presenting themselves as a common enemy. Only the West Saxons stood firm, and soon seized the initiative. King Alfred the Great (871–99) saw clearly how Bede's vision legitimised his political aspirations, and how advantage was

to be gained from promoting a sense of 'Englishness' among all those whom he presumed to regard as his people. But he was ahead of his time, and on his death, Wessex and Mercia were still separate political entities. So it was Alfred's son Edward the Elder (899–924) who forcibly extended West Saxon control over the Danes of eastern England and the Mercians, and it was Alfred's grandson Aethelstan (924–39) who further extended West Saxon control over those who lived in the North.

THE MAKING OF ENGLAND

The main difficulty with this view of events is that it overlooks the existence of a complex succession of polities transitional between 'Wessex' and 'England', and thereby obscures the factors that determined movement from one stage in the process to the next. The kingdom of the West Saxons had expanded eastwards in the central decades of the ninth century to absorb Kent, Sussex, Surrey and Essex; and in Alfred's reign the process was taken a stage further when his kingdom was extended across the Thames into 'English' Mercia, thereby creating the distinctively Alfredian polity known to his contemporaries as the 'kingdom of the Anglo-Saxons'. This new polity, with its centres of power at Gloucester and Winchester but the source of its prosperity flowing down the Thames to the restored city of London, symbolised a working combination of Anglian and Saxon peoples. It arose not from Bede's vision of a unified 'English' people, but more directly from the complex political circumstances that drove the course of events in the late ninth century, and it would endure for nearly 50 years.

The new polity is implicit already in Alfred's treaty with Guthrum, the Danish king of East Anglia (c.880); and it was Alfred's rule over the Mercians, as much as his prowess in resisting the Danes, that prompted a Welsh admirer to address him as 'ruler of all the Christians of the island of Britain'. The Alfredian 'kingdom of the Anglo-Saxons' passed intact to Alfred's son Edward the Elder, and provided the political context in which Edward and his sister Aethelflaed conducted their spectacular campaign against the Danes who had settled or set up their strongholds in East Anglia and in the eastern Midlands. By 918 the frontier of Edward's extended kingdom reached down from Chester across the Midlands to the Fens. By 920 the fron-

---

The age of unification

The 10th and early 11th centuries saw the emergence of the kingdoms of England and Scotland in recognisable form. The ancient kingdom of the West Saxons had been transformed into a 'Kingdom of the Anglo-Saxons' by King Alfred the Great, and his successors in the 10th century extended their rule over the Danes and the Northumbrians. By about 900 the Scots had assimilated the Picts and by the 11th century they had annexed the British kingdom of Strathclyde and also won Lothian from England. Ireland, too, seemed to be moving towards greater political unity under the High King Brian Boru, but his hegemony collapsed after his death in battle against the Leinster–Viking coalition at Clontarf (1014). In Wales, it proved difficult for any king to establish any sort of lasting authority over the others.

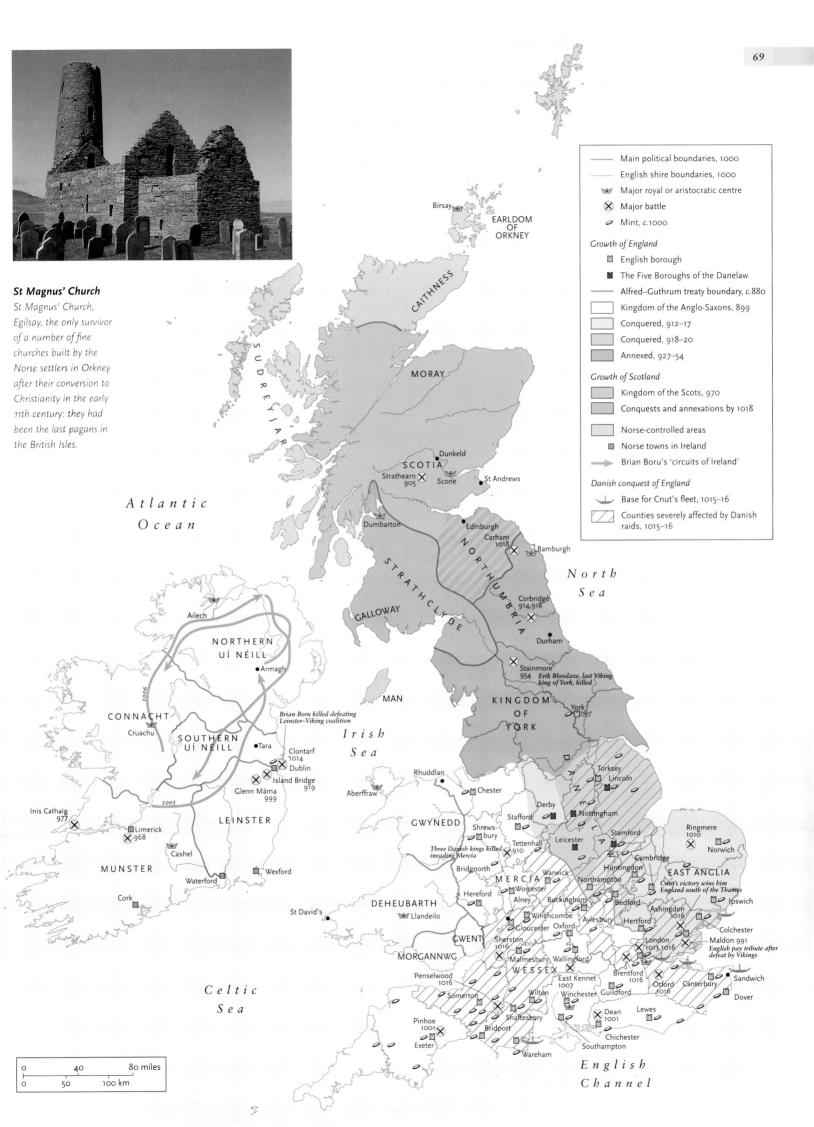

St Magnus' Church

St Magnus' Church, Egilsay, the only survivor of a number of fine churches built by the Norse settlers in Orkney after their conversion to Christianity in the early 11th century: they had been the last pagans in the British Isles.

Birsay

EARLDOM OF ORKNEY

CAITHNESS

Legend:

— Main political boundaries, 1000
— English shire boundaries, 1000
♛ Major royal or aristocratic centre
⊗ Major battle
⬭ Mint, c.1000

Growth of England
▣ English borough
■ The Five Boroughs of the Danelaw
— Alfred–Guthrum treaty boundary, c.880
☐ Kingdom of the Anglo-Saxons, 899
Conquered, 912–17
Conquered, 918–20
Annexed, 927–54

Growth of Scotland
Kingdom of the Scots, 970
Conquests and annexations by 1018
Norse-controlled areas
■ Norse towns in Ireland
➔ Brian Boru's 'circuits of Ireland'

Danish conquest of England
⌐ Base for Cnut's fleet, 1015–16
▨ Counties severely affected by Danish raids, 1015–16

MORAY

SCOTIA
Dunkeld
Stratheárn 905 ⊗
Scone
St Andrews

Atlantic Ocean

SUDREYJAR

Dumbarton

STRATHCLYDE

GALLOWAY

Edinburgh
Carham 1018
⊗ Bamburgh

NORTHUMBRIA

North Sea

Corbridge 914,918 ⊗

Durham

Stainmore 954 ⊗ *Erik Bloodaxe, last Viking king of York, killed*

KINGDOM OF YORK
York ♛

Ailech ♛

NORTHERN UÍ NÉILL

Armagh

CONNACHT
Cruachu

SOUTHERN UÍ NÉILL
Tara

MAN

1006
1005

Clontarf 1014
⊗ Dublin
Brian Boru killed defeating Leinster–Viking coalition
⊗ Island Bridge 919
Glenn Máma 999

Irish Sea

Inis Cathaig 977 ⊗

Limerick 968 ⊗

LEINSTER

Cashel ♛

MUNSTER

Waterford

Cork

Wexford

Rhuddlan

Aberffraw ♛

GWYNEDD

Chester ▣

Shrews-bury

Stafford

Derby ■

Nottingham ■

DANELAW

Leicester ■

Stamford ■

Torksey
Lincoln ■

Ringmere 1010 ⊗

Norwich

St David's

DEHEUBARTH
Llandeilo ♛

Hereford

Tettenhall 910 ⊗ *Three Danish kings killed invading Mercia*

Bridgnorth

MERCIA

Worcester

Alney

Winchcombe

Gloucester

Oxford

Warwick

Northampton

Buckingham

Aylesbury

Huntingdon

Bedford

Cambridge

EAST ANGLIA
Cnut's victory wins him England south of the Thames

Ipswich

Hertford

Colchester

Ashingdon 1016 ⊗

London 1013,1016 ⊗

Maldon 991 *English pay tribute after defeat by Vikings*

GWENT

MORGANNWG

Sherston 1016 ⊗

Malmesbury ⊗

Wallingford

WESSEX

East Kennet 1007

Brentford 1016 ⊗

Otford 1016 ⊗

Guildford

Canterbury

Dover

Sandwich

Penselwood 1016 ⊗

Somerton

Wilton

Winchester ♛

Dean 1001 ⊗

Lewes

Shaftesbury ⊗

Bridport

Chichester

Southampton

Pinhoe 1001 ⊗

Exeter

Wareham

Celtic Sea

English Channel

0   40   80 miles
0   50   100 km

Danish tombstone

A tombstone from St Paul's churchyard, London. The stone, originally painted in bright colours, is decorated in the extravagant 11th-century Ringerike style of Scandinavian relief carving.

ans accepted that their interests would be best served, and protected, by submission to the southern English king. It was thus not until the reign of King Edgar (959–75) that the unified kingdom of the English could be taken for granted, giving rise yet again to the expression of greater aspirations. Edgar's second coronation at Bath, in 973, was probably designed to celebrate his kingship throughout Britain, and was followed by a carefully staged ceremony at Chester, in which Edgar coxed an eight of 'British' kings along the river Dee.

THE CELTIC AREAS

The view of this period from Ireland, Wales or Scotland would naturally have been very different. The tenth century was indeed an age of the unifying principle, not only for the English but also for other peoples with agendas and aspirations of their own.

The Norse had been driven from Dublin in 902, leading to the establishment of fresh settlements in northwest England (with further impact on the Norse communities in Man and the Western Isles); but they returned to Ireland in 914, and from their bases at Limerick, Waterford, Wexford and Dublin, sought for some time thereafter to re-establish their political and commercial power on both sides of the Irish Sea. The Irish had plans of their own. The native rulers of Munster were soon in the ascendancy, eclipsing the power of the Southern Uí Néill; and in the person of Brian Boru (976–1014) they found someone whom they would come to regard as their saviour.

For their part, the Welsh rulers seem to have acknowledged English overlordship almost as a matter of routine. In 918 Hywel Dda and his brother Clydog (rulers of the south Welsh), Idwal (ruler of Gwynedd), 'and all the race of the Welsh' had sought Edward the Elder as their lord; Hywel Dda, styled 'King of the west Welsh', and Owain, king of the people of Gwent, were among those who submitted to Aethelstan in 927; and thereafter Hywel (died 950), Idwal (died 942) and Morgan ab Owain (died 974) were regular visitors to King Aethelstan's court. The true feelings of the Welsh towards the English may, however, be more accurately reflected in the mid-tenth-century poem *Armes Prydein Vawr* ('The Great Prophecy of Britain'), which foretold the day when the Welsh would free themselves from their English oppressors; and they never gave up hope.

In Scotland, Kenneth II (971–95) and Malcolm II (1005–34) were more successful than Constantine had been in holding their own against the English. Lothian (between the Tweed and the Forth) was ceded by Edgar to Kenneth in 973, doubtless for good political reasons, and Malcolm took rather more forceful possession of the region following his victory over the English at the battle of Carham in 1018. Not long afterwards, the kingdom of Strathclyde was absorbed more fully than before into the kingdom of the Scots. The position further north is less clear. The rulers of Moray, and the earls of Orkney, retained some degree of independence, but had little prospect of any lasting success against the kings of the Scots.

THE POLITICAL LEGACY

There was a tendency in the tenth century towards the consolidation or centralisation of political power in all parts of

> *'[King Edgar's] eight under-kings, that is: Kenneth, king of the Scots, Malcolm, king of the Cumbrians, Maccus, king of many islands, and five others...swore that they would be faithful to him and be his allies by land and sea. On a certain day he went on board a boat with them, and, with them at the oars, he took the helm and steered it skilfully on the River Dee.'*
>
> **Florence of Worcester (early 12th century) referring to 973**

tier had been taken up to the river Humber; and although the rulers of the Hiberno-Norse kingdom of York, and of the northern English beyond the Tyne, made their submission to King Edward, together with the rulers of Strathclyde and of the Scots, there the frontier remained on Edward's death in 924. The process was taken a stage further by Edward's son Aethelstan, who drove Guthfrith from York in 927, and to assert direct rule over Northumbria, thereby bringing a unified 'kingdom of the English' into existence.

A northern chronicler commented in this connection that Aethelstan brought under his rule 'all the kings who were in this island', and the king's agents began to project images of him that were commensurate with his new-found glory: 'King of the English, elevated by the right hand of the Almighty to the throne of the whole of Britain', or 'King of Albion', in his charters, and 'King of the English', or 'King of the whole of Britain', on his coins. Other rulers and peoples in the British Isles are more likely to have been provoked by, rather than to have acquiesced in, the expression of such grandiose pretensions. Aethelstan had occasion to ravage Scotland in 934, taking care to pay his respects to St Cuthbert on his way north past Chester-le-Street; and when his position was challenged again, three years later, by the Norse of Dublin acting in alliance with Constantine, king of the Scots, the confederates were resoundingly defeated at Brunanburh (a place that still defies identification). Yet on Aethelstan's death, in 939, the Dublin Norse were able to re-establish their links with York, and it was another 20 years before the Northumbri-

the British Isles, represented by the emergence of rulers with the ability to match their pretensions with actions. In retrospect, the tendency might be regarded as a form of progress, although there is no reason to suppose that it was seen in this way by contemporaries. Yet while there was no kingship of Britain in the tenth century, despite the extravagant claims entertained on behalf of Aethelstan, Edgar and others, few would deny that considerable progress was made during this period towards the establishment of a unified and well-regulated kingdom of England. The shire system, which had originated in Wessex, extended throughout the land; a uniform coinage was in circulation; and kings, through their agents, were resolute in maintaining law and order. Significantly, there was no thought of dividing Edgar's realm when the succession was disputed following his death in 975, and it was only under the severest kind of external threat, compounded by political faction of the most divisive kind, that the English eventually succumbed to Danish conquest in the early eleventh century. Cnut took over a well-formed and fully operational kingdom in 1016 and made it the centre of his so-called 'North Sea Empire' by extending his rule first over Denmark itself (following the death of his elder brother in 1018), then over Norway (after the expulsion of Olaf Haraldsson in 1028), and latterly, it seems, into parts of Sweden. The kingdom of England (but not the North Sea Empire) survived Cnut's death

Lands gained by Cnut:
- Oct 1016
- Nov 1016
- Dec 1018
- Dec 1028

Land under Cnut's influence by 1030

→ Cnut's journeys

✕ Battle

♕ Main royal centre

The empire of Cnut, 1016–35

Cnut's conquest of England in 1016 drew the kingdom closely into the Scandinavian world. Cnut spent most of his reign in England, ruling Denmark and Norway through regents. He initially rewarded his Scandinavian supporters with earldoms, but came increasingly to rely on the English, notably Earl Godwin. English influence in Scandinavia, especially on the Church, was great, and English merchants benefited from trade with the Baltic. But Cnut's empire broke up after his death in 1035. In 1042 the native dynasty was restored to power in England, in the person of Edward the Confessor, who had lived in exile in Normandy since 1013 with his uncle, Duke Richard II.

in 1035, but it remained to be seen what his successors would be able to make of the political complications his reign had created.

For all its institutional and economic strength, the kingdom of England was weakened in the eleventh century by regional and political faction. There was widespread loyalty to the king, and a pronounced sense of 'Englishness', which found expression in a natural hostility to anything perceived as 'foreign'; but the faction was the product of circumstances that reached deep into the past, and proved difficult to overcome. The political inheritance for Cnut's successors was a kingdom dominated by two earls (Godwin of Wessex and Leofric of Mercia), one representing the 'new nobles' of the Anglo-Danish regime and the other representing entrenched political interests north of the river Thames. The burning political issue remained the question of the succession to the English throne. Matters were made all the more complex, if always the more interesting, by the involvement of the redoubtable Queen Emma (wife of King Aethelred 'the Unready', 1002–16, and wife of King Cnut, 1017–35), acting on behalf of her sons (by each of her husbands) and more particularly on behalf of herself. In the event, it was her son Edward the Confessor (1042–66) who faced the consequences of all these complications, making friends and creating problems of his own.   **SDK**

Christian king

King Cnut and Queen Aelfgifu (Emma), receiving symbols of their power from Christ, present a cross to the New Minster at Winchester, from a manuscript written and decorated at Winchester in 1031. The double portrait acknowledges their importance to each other.

THE NORMANS

In the light of the previous half-century of Scandinavian intervention in England, the Norman invasion was neither unprecedented nor unexpected. The childless Edward the Confessor, educated in Normandy and a Francophile, perhaps wished to be succeeded by his mother's great-nephew, William, duke of Normandy, as early as the latter's visit to court in 1051. However, opposition to William's succession was formidable, especially from the House of Wessex under Earl Harold Godwinson. Godwinson may earlier have sworn to support the duke's claim, but King Edward, on his deathbed in 1066, acknowledged him as his successor and he was duly crowned. Harold's brother Tostig, exiled in 1065, was more intent on recovering his earldom of Northumbria than helping either Harold or William, and allied himself with the king of Scots and Harald Hardrada of Norway, who also claimed the English throne.

William's forces landed at Pevensey on 28 September and dug in at Hastings. When news reached Harold, he began a forced march south, with up to 6,000 men, to confront the heavy Norman cavalry, so memorably depicted in the Bayeux Tapestry. The most famous battle in English history took place on 14 October, and although Harold and his forces fought fiercely (he and his brothers were killed), by nightfall a Norman victory was secure. Wessex had a representative still in Edgar 'the Atheling', but he lacked William's powers of leadership. As the latter advanced on London, the Anglo-Saxon leaders submitted to 'the Conqueror', acknowledged him as lawful claimant to the throne, and attended his coronation in Westminster Abbey on Christmas Day.

THE TRANSFORMATION OF ENGLAND

William was at pains to point out that he, as lawful successor to the Confessor, would guarantee the rights of his new subjects. But by 1068 the harsh new Norman regime had led to native uprisings, and soon there were further revolts in the North, among the English supporters of the Atheling (now in Scotland at the court of King Malcolm Canmore), while a Danish fleet in the Humber stirred Wessex and Mercia into action. William's response was resolute. He came north, recaptured York, paid off the Danes, and spent the winter of 1069–70 laying waste all before him, until all resistance was ended. Although William experienced one other serious revolt, in 1075, its leaders were discontented Norman barons: the 'Harrying of the North' had put paid to any threat of a popular English uprising.

It had also taught William that he could not count on the support of the native aristocracy and had therefore to rely on his northern French followers. Even before the rebellions, he had given his half-brother, Odo of Bayeux, the earldom of Kent and a castle at Dover, from which to defend the Channel, while the Welsh marches were guarded by entrusting a vast new earldom of Hereford to his steward, William fitz Osbern, who also held Norwich in case of Danish attack. Now, in 1071, he gave Hugh d'Avranches the new earldom of Chester to secure the border with Gwynedd, and conquer it if possible. Hugh began by placing his cousin Robert in the new castle at Rhuddlan. By 1075 another of William's barons, Roger de Montgomery, now earl of Shrewsbury, was intent on expanding

The battle of Hastings
William the Conqueror rides into battle with his knights at Hastings, as portrayed in the Bayeux Tapestry. At Hastings, William's combination of armoured knights and archers, and their better discipline, triumphed over King Harold's axe-wielding infantry.

In the summer of 1066, therefore, England faced invasion on two fronts: the new King Harold stayed in the South, aware of Duke William's preparations for a landing, while defence of the North was left to earls Edwin of Mercia and Morcar of Northumbria. The earls proved no match for the combined forces of Hardrada and Tostig when they met at Fulford on 20 September. This Norse success prompted King Harold's finest hour: a four-day march north to their camp at Stamford Bridge on the Derwent, a surprise assault, a hard-fought battle and a clear victory for the English forces, resulting in the deaths of Hardrada and Tostig. But Harold was now 400 kilometres (about 250 miles) from the Channel, which Duke William's warships, with several thousand armoured knights, archers and infantry, were crossing, having set sail from St Valery-sur-Somme with papal blessing (thanks to a row between the pope and Harold over the archbishopric of Canterbury).

The Norman conquest of England, 1066–80

In summer 1066 England faced invasion on two fronts: by the Norwegian king, Harald Hardrada, and by William, duke of Normandy, both of whom claimed the throne. The English king, Harold, managed to defeat and kill Harald at Stamford Bridge, but his subsequent death in battle against William at Hastings left the English leaderless. William proceeded to ravage the Southeast, after which the English reluctantly accepted him as king. He was crowned in Westminster Abbey on Christmas Day 1066. There were widespread English rebellions, supported by the Danes, in 1068–70, but these were ruthlessly suppressed by William. The effects of his 'Harrying of the North' were particularly severe. Castle-building helped secure his position.

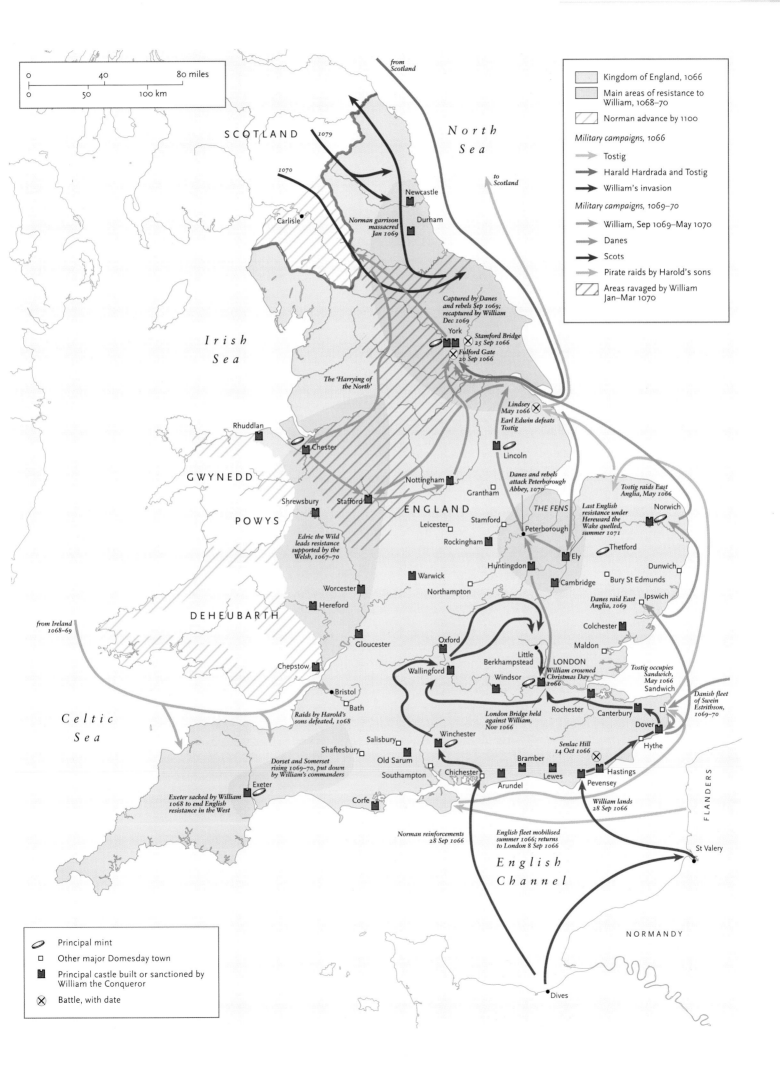

Principal mint

□ Other major Domesday town

■ Principal castle built or sanctioned by William the Conqueror

⊗ Battle, with date

Kingdom of England, 1066

Main areas of resistance to William, 1068–70

Norman advance by 1100

Military campaigns, 1066

Tostig

Harald Hardrada and Tostig

William's invasion

Military campaigns, 1069–70

William, Sep 1069–May 1070

Danes

Scots

Pirate raids by Harold's sons

Areas ravaged by William Jan–Mar 1070

SCOTLAND   *1079*

1070

Carlisle

Newcastle

Norman garrison massacred Jan 1069   Durham

from Scotland

to Scotland

North Sea

Irish Sea

Captured by Danes and rebels Sep 1069; recaptured by William Dec 1069

York   ⊗ Stamford Bridge 25 Sep 1066

⊗ Fulford Gate 20 Sep 1066

The 'Harrying of the North'

Lindsey May 1066 ⊗

Earl Edwin defeats Tostig

Rhuddlan

Chester

GWYNEDD

Nottingham

Grantham

Lincoln

Tostig raids East Anglia, May 1066

Norwich

POWYS

Shrewsbury

Stafford

ENGLAND

Leicester

Stamford

Danes and rebels attack Peterborough Abbey, 1070

THE FENS

Last English resistance under Hereward the Wake quelled, summer 1071

Edric the Wild leads resistance supported by the Welsh, 1067–70

Rockingham

Peterborough

Ely   Thetford

Dunwich

Huntingdon

Cambridge   Bury St Edmunds

Warwick

Ipswich

Worcester   Northampton

Danes raid East Anglia, 1069

DEHEUBARTH

Hereford

Colchester

from Ireland 1068–69

Gloucester

Oxford

Little Berkhampstead

Maldon

Chepstow

Wallingford

LONDON William crowned Christmas Day 1066

Windsor

Tostig occupies Sandwich, May 1066

Sandwich

Bristol

Raids by Harold's sons defeated, 1068

Bath

London Bridge held against William, Nov 1066

Rochester

Canterbury

Danish fleet of Swein Estrithson, 1069–70

Celtic Sea

Winchester

Dover

Shaftesbury

Salisbury

Hythe

Dorset and Somerset rising 1069–70, put down by William's commanders

Old Sarum

Senlac Hill 14 Oct 1066 ⊗

Southampton

Bramber

Chichester   Lewes

Hastings

Exeter sacked by William 1068 to end English resistance in the West

Exeter

Arundel

Pevensey

William lands 28 Sep 1066

FLANDERS

Corfe

Norman reinforcements 28 Sep 1066

English fleet mobilised summer 1066; returns to London 8 Sep 1066

English Channel

NORMANDY

St Valery

Dives

The Norman kings placed the security of the Welsh frontier in the hands of marcher barons who were given a free hand to conquer new lands in Wales. Conquests were secured, as in Gower in South Wales, by building castles and monasteries, granting manors to both Anglo-Norman and Welsh military tenants, by encouraging English settlement in the countryside and by creating new, defended, towns like Swansea. Place-names, such as Fernhill and Oxwich, indicate the main areas of English settlement.

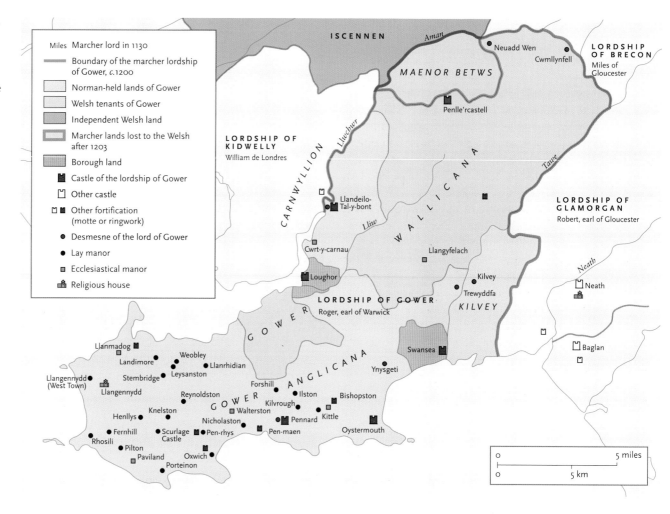

Map legend:

Miles Marcher lord in 1130
— Boundary of the marcher lordship of Gower, c.1200
Norman-held lands of Gower
Welsh tenants of Gower
Independent Welsh land
Marcher lands lost to the Welsh after 1203
Borough land
Castle of the lordship of Gower
Other castle
Other fortification (motte or ringwork)
Desmesne of the lord of Gower
Lay manor
Ecclesiastical manor
Religious house

'It is the habitation of strangers and the dominion of foreigners. There is today no Englishman who is either earl, bishop or abbot. The newcomers devour the riches and entrails of England, and there is no hope of the misery coming to an end.'

William of Malmesbury on England after the Conquest, early 12th century

into Powys. William himself visited St Davids in 1081, recognised its native ruler, Rhys ap Tewdwr, as his vassal in South Wales, while treating Robert of Rhuddlan effectively as lord of North Wales. William did not attempt to conquer Scotland, being content with establishing a loose overlordship. In 1072 he went north to Abernethy, where King Malcolm submitted to him and became his vassal, handing over his eldest son, Duncan, as a hostage. But the question of where the Anglo-Scottish border should be fixed was by no means settled and, when Malcolm invaded England in 1079, William's son Robert was sent north and built the 'New Castle' on the Tyne to help secure the frontier.

By the time of William's death in 1087, England had changed greatly. The Conquest was no mere change of leadership. To defend his new kingdom, William needed large numbers of loyal mounted knights, and continental-style castles. He also had to reward with estates those who had assisted him. Although Norman 'feudalism' was partly an adaptation of existing institutions and customs, it brought huge changes in land ownership in England. By 1086, the Domesday Book (a detailed survey of landholders and estates) revealed only four members of the Old English ruling class still in possession of their lands; over 4,000 pre-Conquest thegns had been dispossessed; England was now in the hands of fewer than 200 new barons. With papal support, William also reorganised the English Church, removing Englishmen from bishoprics and abbeys. In this he was ably assisted by his ecclesiastical adviser, the Italian-born Lanfranc of Bec, archbishop of Canterbury from 1070.

The culture of the Normans was French. The new regime was headed by a French-speaking elite, the focus of whose world was the European mainland, where they continued to hold land. William himself was an infrequent visitor to England after 1072, usually only when trouble arose: he was buried at Caen in Normandy. As duke of Normandy, he was a vassal of the king of France; English and French politics were thus inextricably entwined. William's enemies, including the king of France (who sought control of the Vexin, between Paris and Rouen) and the count of Anjou (who claimed Maine), exploited the restlessness of his eldest son, Robert Curthose, to undermine him from 1078 onwards.

THE DISPUTED SUCCESSION

When the Conqueror was mortally wounded attacking Mantes, in France, in July 1087, Robert Curthose was at the French court. Though he succeeded in pressing his claim to Normandy, his younger brother, William Rufus, claimed England: the Conqueror himself perhaps believed that the duchy, his by inheritance, should pass to the eldest son, while England, his by conquest, could go to a younger son.

This strategy was opposed by Anglo-Norman magnates with cross-Channel estates, who argued that they could not serve two masters, and rebelled against William II. He overcame both this and a later conspiracy in 1095, and shortly afterwards acquired Normandy from his brother when the latter went on the First Crusade. In England, Rufus succeeded in consolidating Norman control over the North, establishing a base at Carlisle, and exploited the death of Malcolm Canmore by installing as kings of Scots the latter's Normanising sons Duncan (1094) and Edgar (1097–1107). Edgar, in turn, was succeeded by his brothers Alexander (1107–24) and David (1124–53), each excelling his predecessor in opening Scotland to Anglo-Norman culture and colonisation. Rufus encouraged further expansion into Gwynedd and Powys, also from Hereford along the Usk and Wye valleys, and from Gloucester into Glamorgan. When Rhys ap Tewdwr was killed by the Normans in 1093, all Deheubarth was opened up and the Norman lordships of Gower, Kidwelly and Pembroke were established.

William II, except perhaps with regard to the Church (he had quarrelled with Anselm, the saintly archbishop of Canterbury), was enjoying considerable success when he was killed while hunting in the New Forest in 1100. His older brother Robert was journeying home from the Crusade, but a third brother, Henry 'Beauclerc', seized the advantage and

had himself made king. Robert retook Normandy and invaded England in 1101, but the brothers eventually compromised: Henry would hold England in return for £2,000 a year, and Normandy would be Robert's. Only when Henry defeated Robert at Tinchebrai in 1106 were duchy and kingdom reunited under one man, but Henry was to spend more than half his reign thereafter in Normandy, trying to keep at bay the French king and the count of Anjou. His absences and financial need help to explain the advances in the machinery of Anglo-Norman government that were a feature of his reign, including the emergence of professional administrators and an exchequer.

Henry I astutely married the daughter of Malcolm Canmore and Margaret, sister of the Atheling, so that his heirs had legitimacy in English eyes (while ensuring good relations with the Scots), but his only legitimate son, William the Atheling, was drowned in 1120, leaving his

daughter, the empress Matilda (wife of Henry V of the German empire), as heir. The last 15 years of his life were dominated by the succession. To bolster Matilda's position, Henry arranged her remarriage, after her husband's death, to Geoffrey Plantagenet, count of Anjou, but he did little else to ensure her succession. Hence, when Henry died in 1135, his nephew Stephen of Blois, count of Boulogne and holder of vast estates in the southeast of England, staked his claim: he sailed across the Channel, won the support of London, seized the royal treasury at Winchester, and persuaded the archbishop of Canterbury to anoint him king. The result of this was a prolonged civil war in England.

At first, Stephen reigned securely throughout the entire Anglo-Norman realm, but the Welsh, subdued under Henry I, now revolted, while David of Scotland seized Northumbria (despite defeat by an English army under the archbishop of York at the 'Battle of the Standard' in 1138). By then, Robert of Gloucester, Henry's illegitimate son, had joined his half-sister, providing Matilda with a base in the west of England, and standing by her when she landed in England in 1139. Now there were two rival courts in England, and stalemate ensued. Meanwhile, Matilda's husband, Geoffrey of Anjou, having overrun Normandy, was proclaimed its duke in 1144, and won papal and French support to pass the duchy to their son Henry in 1151. It looked as if the Anglo-Norman realm would be split permanently between the two camps, even after Henry invaded England the following year. It took the death of Eustace, Stephen's heir, to break the stalemate: by the treaty of Winchester (December 1153), Stephen acknowledged Henry as his heir and died within a year, bringing a protracted civil war to an agreed end, and securing for Henry Plantagenet the first undisputed succession to the English throne for more than a century.   SD

Norman architecture
The Norman church at Iffley, Oxfordshire, built in the continental Romanesque style. Norman churches were much larger and more imposing than those built before the Conquest.

The civil war between Stephen and Matilda, 1139–53
The civil war between King Stephen and his rival, the empress Matilda, saw much localised disorder but few major battles and campaigns: neither was able to impose their authority far outside their main power bases in the Southeast and the West Country, or prevent the Scots occupying much of northern England.

THE MEDIEVAL CHURCH

In medieval Britain, practically every aspect of life was guided by the Church. Acceptance of the structure of beliefs and practices of Christianity was, on the surface at least, almost universal. Except for the small urban communities of Jews, everyone was baptised soon after birth and became a member of the Catholic Church. Regular attendance at mass and confession was obligatory. The formalisation of marriage became an increasingly ecclesiastical affair from the twelfth century onwards, and burial in consecrated ground was granted to all except suicides, and excommunicates who had died without being reconciled to the Church. Few people can have lived far from a church or monastery, and the larger towns were dominated by church buildings. The routines of daily life were governed by church bells sounding the ecclesiastical offices, and the administrative systems of government and commerce followed calendar divisions marked by saints' days.

The material presence of saints was a key feature of popular Christianity. Saints were regarded as points of contact between heaven and earth, and thus as mediators between humans and God. Images from the lives of the saints decorated the walls, windows and interior furnishings of churches. Their virtues were celebrated on feast days. In the thirteenth century, model books of sermons came into use among priests, and many of these sermons were also inspired by stories from the saints' lives. Relics of the saints, usually bones, were treasured as sacred and powerful objects, capable of working miracles – and the practice of pilgrimage to the shrines in which they were housed became perhaps the most obvious sign of popular religious devotion. Throughout Britain and Ireland, sites that retained associations with the burial places of saints were visited by the faithful in search of healing and comfort, or offering gratitude for miracles performed. Celtic and Anglo-Saxon Christianity had abounded in local saints, but the spread of the Norman Church brought something of a rationalisation. In England, the most popular pilgrimage site after 1170 was Canterbury, site of the martyrdom of Thomas Becket, but York, Walsingham, Beverley and Chichester were also visited. In Scotland, St Andrews and Tain, and in Wales, St Asaph and Llandaff, drew the most visitors. These

The medieval church in the British Isles c.1300

The government of the Church in the British Isles was provided for by dozens of bishoprics grouped in seven archbishoprics. The Isle of Man (until the 14th century), the Hebrides, Orkney and Shetland were part of the archbishopric of Nidaros (modern Trondheim), reflecting their long history of Norwegian rule. In addition to cathedrals and parish churches, there were thousands of monasteries and religious houses, both in the countryside and the towns – some ancient, others founded in the waves of monastic reform that spread new orders of canons and monks across Europe in the Middle Ages. In the 13th century, towns proved a magnet for the new orders of friars. Most towns had at least one friary; many had several.

popular pilgrimage sites stimulated local economic activity on a scale similar to that of the great tourist attractions of today.

THE SECULAR CHURCH

The division of Britain and Ireland into bishoprics, each responsible for the provision of the ministry to lay people through parish churches, developed organically during the early Middle Ages. Considerable diversity of practice is noticeable in Scotland and Ireland, as opposed to Anglo-Saxon England, which had always been closer to the Roman model prevailing on the Continent. In Ireland, for example, 'bishop' might be an honorary title, not necessarily signifying the tenure of a ministerial office. Bishoprics in Anglo-Saxon England largely reflected administrative divisions of shires, and survived with only minor changes after the Norman Conquest (1066). Each bishopric had at its centre a cathedral church that functioned as the bishop's seat, which, even before the Conquest, might also be the governmental centre of a region. Bishops were valued by kings as local agents of government, partly because they were literate, but also because they were unable to found dynasties that might later threaten royal authority.

The parish was the basic unit of religious life. Every parish, in theory at least, had a resident priest whose responsibility it was to provide the sacraments of baptism, the eucharist, confession, marriage and extreme unction, to hold regular services and, so far as he was able, to instruct his parishioners in Christian doctrine. Since mass was in Latin, a language of which most lay people were ignorant, this latter function was especially important. In the early Middle Ages, however, many priests were poorly educated and unable to preach. The norm was for them to marry and have families, but from the eleventh century onward this practice was regarded by the Church as an abuse, and clerical celibacy became standard.

The parish priest also fulfilled a social function within the rural community: because his role as confessor gave him unrivalled access to information about relationships within the community, he could act as a mediator in quarrels, as confidant, and even as banker. The parish church, usually the only stone building in the village, was often a place of refuge during times of violence. Parishioners paid a tithe from their income – usually, in rural areas, in kind rather

Monk and lady
A monk and a lady in the stocks, from an early 14th-century English illuminated manuscript. Despite repeated legislation, the ideal of clerical celibacy was never fully achieved. Concubinage remained common among the lower clergy.

SHETLAND
(Part of the
Bishopic of Orkney)

ATLANTIC
OCEAN

The secular church
— Archdiocesan boundary
— Diocesan boundary
🏛 Archbishopric
🏛 Bishopric

The regular church (major houses)
🏛 Benedictine house
🏛 Nunnery
🏛 Cistercian, Carthusian or
other new order house
🏛 House of canons regular
(Augustinian canons)
✝ Town with three or more friaries
(Franciscan of Dominican)
✝ Major pilgrimage site
📖 University founded by 1500

Kirkwall
(ORKNEY)

(CAITHNESS)

(ROSS)
Dornoch
Tain *St Duthus*
Fortrose
Beauly
Elgin
Pluscarden
(MORAY)
Moneymusk
ABERDEEN
BRECHIN
DUNKELD
Lismore
(ARGYLL)
Iona
DUNBLANE
Elcho ST ANDREWS
Culross
Stirling Dunfermline
Manuel Haddington
Paisley Coldstream Berwick
GLASGOW Melrose Lindisfarne
Dryburgh Kelso
Jedburgh

Sweetheart Lanercost Newcastle
(GALLOWAY) Hexham Jarrow
Glenluce *St Ninian* CARLISLE
Whithorn Armathwaite DURHAM Whitby
Shap *St Cuthbert*
Cartmel Jervaulx Rievaulx
Coverham Fountains Byland
(SODOR & Bolton Bridlington
THE ISLES) St Germans Furness Ripon YORK Watton
Rushen Nun *St John* Meaux
Monkton Beverley

RAPHOE Macosquin
DERRY
Nendrum
(DOWN)
CONNOR Inch
ARMAGH Dromore
CLOGHER Downpatrick
KILLALA
ACHONRY Boyle
Clare Island ELPHIN
MAYO Mellifont
ARDAGH Kells (MEATH)
TUAM Athlone Kilbeggan Drogheda
ANNAGHDOWN CLONFERT Clonmacnoise Grace Dieu
KILMACDUAGH Kildare Irish
KILFENORA KILLALOE *St Patrick's DUBLIN Sea
KILLALOE Purgatory*
Ardaneer (OSSORY) LEIGHLIN
LIMERICK EMLY Kilkenny
ARDFERT CASHEL FERNS Glascarrig
Abbeydorney Monasteranenagh Jerpoint Begerin
Dingle Fermoy Inishlounaght Wexford
Innisallen LISMORE
CORK WATERFORD
CLOYNE Youghal
ROSS

North
Sea

Nun Cotham
Sixhills
St Winifred LINCOLN
Holywell *St Hugh*
ST ASAPH Hampole Boston *St Guthlac*
Norton Sempringham
Clynnog Fawr Vale Royal Crowland *Virgin Mary*
BANGOR Aberconwy Chester Garendon Walsingham
Bardsey Island Valle Stafford Leicester *Kings Lynn*
Crucis *St Chad* Stamford Marham
Beddgelert Llanllugan LICHFIELD Nuneaton NORWICH
Llanllugan Halesowen Sawtry Thetford Bungay
Wigmore Kenilworth ELY
Strata Florida HEREFORD Northampton Bury
WORCESTER Cambridge St Edmunds
St David Hailes Dunstable
ST DAVID'S Carmarthen Gloucester Godstow Markyate
Haverfordwest Cirencester St Albans Waltham
Kidwelly Monmouth Oxford Kilburn
St Teilo Tintern Malmesbury Reading LONDON
LLANDAFF Bermondsey *St Bartholomew's*
Margam Bristol Wells Waverley ROCHESTER *St Thomas*
(BATH & WELLS) SALISBURY WINCHESTER CANTERBURY
St Joseph Wilton CHICHESTER
Glastonbury Shaftesbury Romsey Lewes Battle
Taunton Forde
EXETER
Launceston Christchurch
Buckfast
Bodmin
St Michael St Germans
St Michael's Mount

Celtic
Sea

English
Channel

0   40   80 miles
0   50   100 km

Ely Cathedral

The unique lantern tower of Ely Cathedral, built of timber between 1322 and 1342. Britain's Gothic cathedrals were dedicated to the glory of God, but also served to demonstrate the wealth of the communities that built them.

than in money – for the upkeep of the church. Payment of marriage and burial fees also became standard practice. In addition, priests offered what rudimentary education was available in the village.

Education at a higher level remained largely within the oversight of the Church. Every cathedral was supposed to maintain a school, but the level of education offered varied widely. Most schools provided elementary teaching in Latin grammar. The school at Oxford, however, was sufficiently sophisticated to attract teachers and students from the new university at Paris in the early thirteenth century, and thus to become a university itself. Other universities were subsequently formed at Cambridge, St Andrews, Aberdeen and Glasgow. Despite attempts to free themselves from episcopal authority, universities remained under the overall control of the bishop of the relevant diocese throughout the medieval period.

From the thirteenth century, and especially after the great reforming Fourth Lateran Council (1215), priests were better educated, but abuses such as the holding of more than one office at a time, and thus absenteeism, continued to plague the secular church.

THE FRIARS

The greatest stimulus to the offering of a fuller ministry by priests from the 1220s onwards was competition from the new orders of mendicant friars, particularly the Franciscans and the Dominicans. The friars, whose function was to provide public preaching and teaching in Christian doctrine, filled a genuine gap in meeting lay spiritual needs – and as a consequence were highly regarded by the laity. Their institutionalised poverty, which contrasted markedly with the wealth of the great cathedrals and abbeys, was also seen as a sign of true spirituality. The friars concentrated their ministry in urban areas, where the building of new churches had often failed to keep pace with the growth of towns. By about 1350, most towns in England had a convent of one or other order of friars, and in the larger towns, such as London, York, Bristol and Norwich, all four orders were represented. The activities of the friars came to be resented by bishops, whose parishes lost income when lay people opted for burial in the churches of friars rather than in their own parish churches. Rural Britain was not as well served by the friars, although the two smaller orders, the Augustinian Hermits and the Carmelites, retained an element of solitude in their professions, and were drawn to remote areas. Thus, for example, we find Carmelite friars active in Scotland, which was less urbanised than England.

THE MONASTIC ORDERS

Throughout the medieval Christian world, a proportion of people found the ministry of the secular church an inadequate answer to their spiritual needs. For these people, life within a monastic community was the solution. The early British monasteries were of two types, one unique to the Celtic regions, and the other conforming to the continental pattern. Monasteries in Celtic Ireland were inspired by the early Christian ascetic tradition of Egypt and Palestine. They imposed a harsh code of self-denial on the monks, and their communities tended to be in locations that emphasised solitude and remoteness. Irish missionaries who founded the early monasteries in Scotland, such as that on Iona, brought these same ideals with them. Although the Celtic influence can also be found in northern England, English monasticism from the seventh century onwards tended to be based on the Benedictine Rule (written in about 550). The first purely Benedictine houses in Britain were Ripon and Hexham, founded by St Wilfrid of York in the late seventh century – but Benedictine ideas adopted from abbeys in France may already have been current in English religious communities by this time. The location of English monasteries, moreover, was determined more by association with local saints than by ideals of remoteness. Thus, monastic communities evolved at places such as St Albans and Bury St Edmunds, around the shrines of saints.

By the tenth century, monasticism in England had become so lax that a major reform initiative was required. A great wave of monastic reform spread throughout Europe from the abbey at Cluny, in Burgundy; it reached England in 1077, with the foundation of a Cluniac priory at Lewes. After the Norman Conquest, other new reforming ideas from the Continent passed easily into England, and huge numbers of new foundations were established in the twelfth century, many of them for women. One new order, the Gilbertines, founded by Gilbert of Sempringham, combined monks and nuns in 'double houses'. This new model of monasticism was a peculiarly British contribution to the reform movement.

The most enduring of the new orders were the Cistercians, founded at Cîteaux in Burgundy in 1098. From their

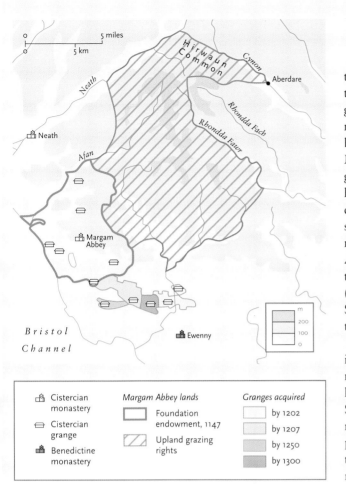

Cistercian monastery

Cistercian grange

Benedictine monastery

Margam Abbey lands

Foundation endowment, 1147

Upland grazing rights

Granges acquired

by 1202

by 1207

by 1250

by 1300

that it should be land that was wanted by no one else, and therefore unlikely to form part of a network of feudal obligations. The Cistercians exploited their far-flung estates by means of granges, which were model farms operated by *conversi*, or lay brothers, who supervised paid labourers. Most granges were established in the twelfth century, the great era of Cistercian expansion. Yorkshire, for example, had 46 granges by the year 1200. The size of a grange depended, naturally, on the type of farming it had to support, so that in Wales, where the land was mostly mountainous and barren, Aberconwy's grange comprised 4,856 hectares (12,000 acres), whereas the average size of the Meaux granges in eastern Yorkshire was 188 hectares (464 acres). The pattern of granges around Margam in South Wales provides a good example of the spatial relationship between the abbey and its outlying farms.

In rural districts, where parishes might be far apart and ill-equipped, monasteries had always provided a pastoral ministry. Scottish Cistercian monasteries such as Sweetheart and Glenluce operated a mission field in southwest Scotland. The Augustinian canons, founded at the beginning of the twelfth century, supplemented the work of parish priests by combining external ministry with the cloistered life. The main purpose of the monastery, however, remained the contemplation and worship of God within the abbey walls. Although most monasteries probably remained poor, and many began to suffer declining fortunes in the thirteenth century, the wealth of a few, particularly those, like Westminster, that enjoyed royal patronage, gave monasticism a bad image in the later Middle Ages. Friars, and the new urban gilds and confraternities, began to attract the patronage of the laity in the towns. Although some monasteries, such as the London Charterhouse, retained a reputation for piety into the sixteenth century, most had become, by the time of the Dissolution of the Monasteries in 1536, shadows of the spiritual fortresses of yesteryear. **ATJ**

first foundation at Waverley (1128), they quickly spread throughout Britain. Because they favoured remote and uncultivated sites, the Cistercians were attracted to Scotland, Wales and northern England. The Cistercian abbeys of Rievaulx, Fountains and Byland in North Yorkshire and Tintern in Wales are among the most celebrated of all surviving monastic sites in Britain.

The economy of Cistercian monasticism in Britain was based typically on sheep farming, to which the remoteness of their sites was particularly conducive. But Cistercians also farmed coastal marshlands or woodlands; the key was

Margam Abbey lands

The lands of Margam Abbey c.1300. The ideal of the Cistercian order was to seek seclusion from secular society, and many of their abbeys, such as Margam in South Wales, were sited in sparsely populated upland areas. Extensive upland grazing rights, granted to the abbey by its founders, were ideal for sheep farming. Wool provided a lucrative source of income, enabling the abbey to extend its lands still further.

Rievaulx Abbey

Rievaulx Abbey, North Yorkshire, was one of the earliest Cistercian houses to be founded in Britain, in 1131–2. Building the magnificent abbey church (right) and the equally impressive complex of cloisters, refectories, kitchens, infirmaries and dormitories, left the monastery deep in debt.

THE ANGEVIN EMPIRE

Although he was king for 34 years, Henry II, duke of Normandy, count of Anjou and duke of Aquitaine, spent only 13 years in England. More at home in the rich and cultured valleys of the Seine and the Loire (where he was buried, in the abbey of Fontevrault), it was in France that his real ambitions lay. By 1160 he was pressing from Aquitaine into Toulouse and from Normandy towards Paris, and later that decade his son Geoffrey became duke of Brittany. Geoffrey had two older brothers: Henry, who was intended to inherit England, Normandy and Anjou; and Richard, destined to get their mother's homeland, Aquitaine (the youngest brother, John 'Lackland', was given Ireland in 1177). The young Henry was even crowned king while 'old' King Henry was still alive, but the sons' desire for a taste of real power produced in 1173 a family rebellion in league with the Capetian king of France, Louis VII. Events were exacerbated by an opportunistic invasion of England by the then king of Scotland, William the Lion.

HENRY II'S ACHIEVEMENTS

Although Henry II eventually put down the rebellion, and imposed humiliating terms of submission on the captured Scots king, his plans continued to be thwarted by his rebellious sons, especially when the resolute Philip II Augustus ascended the French throne in 1180 and started to exploit the family's differences. Even after the deaths of young Henry (1183) and Geoffrey (1186), problems remained: Richard knew his father favoured John, and so he allied with the French against his father.

Henry II eventually died a defeated man in 1189. Still, the first of England's Plantagenet kings must by any standards be reckoned a great monarch. Having inherited a kingdom depleted by civil war, he quickly restored the stable government it had known under his grandfather, Henry I, while simultaneously ruling two-thirds of France. He extended royal power in England by reforming both civil and criminal law. The Assizes of Clarendon (1166) and Northampton (1176) established the grand jury system, whereby royal justices and sheriffs tried those suspected of serious offences, while civil writs such as 'novel disseisin' and 'mort d'ancestor', obtainable from the royal courts, secured speedy restoration of those dispossessed without due process. All in all, Henry's reign ranks as a milestone in the development of English Common Law.

Angevin tombs

The tombs of Richard I 'the Lionheart' (1157–99) and Henry II (1133–89) and his wife Eleanor of Aquitaine (c.1122–1204) at Fontevrault Abbey in Anjou; their choice of burial site reflects their French identity.

When Henry Plantagenet succeeded to the English throne in 1154 he could fairly claim to be the most powerful ruler in western Europe. His lands stretched from the Pennines to the Pyrenees, their focal point being Anjou, home of his forefathers. He held far more lands in France than its king (though the French king was his feudal overlord), while England's wealth let him outshine the German emperor.

Henry began his reign by seeking to consolidate his island kingdom. In 1155 he briefly contemplated invading Ireland, and, by proposing church reform there, obtained papal support for his plan. However, it was only when an Irish provincial king, Diarmait Mac Murchada, sought his help in 1166 that he actually took things forward. He encouraged his Norman-Welsh barons to go to Ireland to reinstate Diarmait, and so successful were they that in 1171 Henry felt compelled to take charge (his direct involvement at this point also enabled him to escape the papacy's wrath following the murder by Henry's men of the troublesome Archbishop Thomas Becket). Thus, Henry became the first English king to visit Ireland and to add it to his domain. He also took advantage of the weakness of Malcolm IV of Scotland to recover northern England, overrun during Stephen's reign by Malcolm's grandfather, King David. But he was less successful in Wales, where Owain of Gwynedd and Rhys of Deheubarth survived campaigns against them in 1157 and 1165. Gwynedd and Deheubarth both remained autonomous until Rhys's death in 1197, after which Gwynedd emerged as the paramount principality.

> 'In his laws he displayed great care for orphans, widows and the poor; and in many places he bestowed noble alms with an open hand...He never imposed any heavy tax on the realm of England, or on his possessions beyond the sea, until that last tax of a tenth for the purpose of an expedition to Jerusalem...yet in his own days he was unpopular with almost all men.'
>
> **William of Newburgh on Henry II, c.1200**

The Angevin empire, 1150–1215

By marriage, inheritance, diplomacy and, occasionally, war, Henry II built up one of the largest domains in western Europe, his sovereignty being recognised from Scotland and Ireland to the Pyrenees. Henry failed to give his empire any institutional unity, nor was he able to provide a satisfactory settlement for his ambitious and ultimately treacherous sons. Richard I held the empire together through his charisma and ability as a warrior, but it collapsed under his less able brother John who, diplomatically and militarily, was comprehensively outmanoeuvred by Philip II of France. At his death in 1216, John had lost all of the Angevins' continental lands except Gascony, and England itself had been invaded by the French.

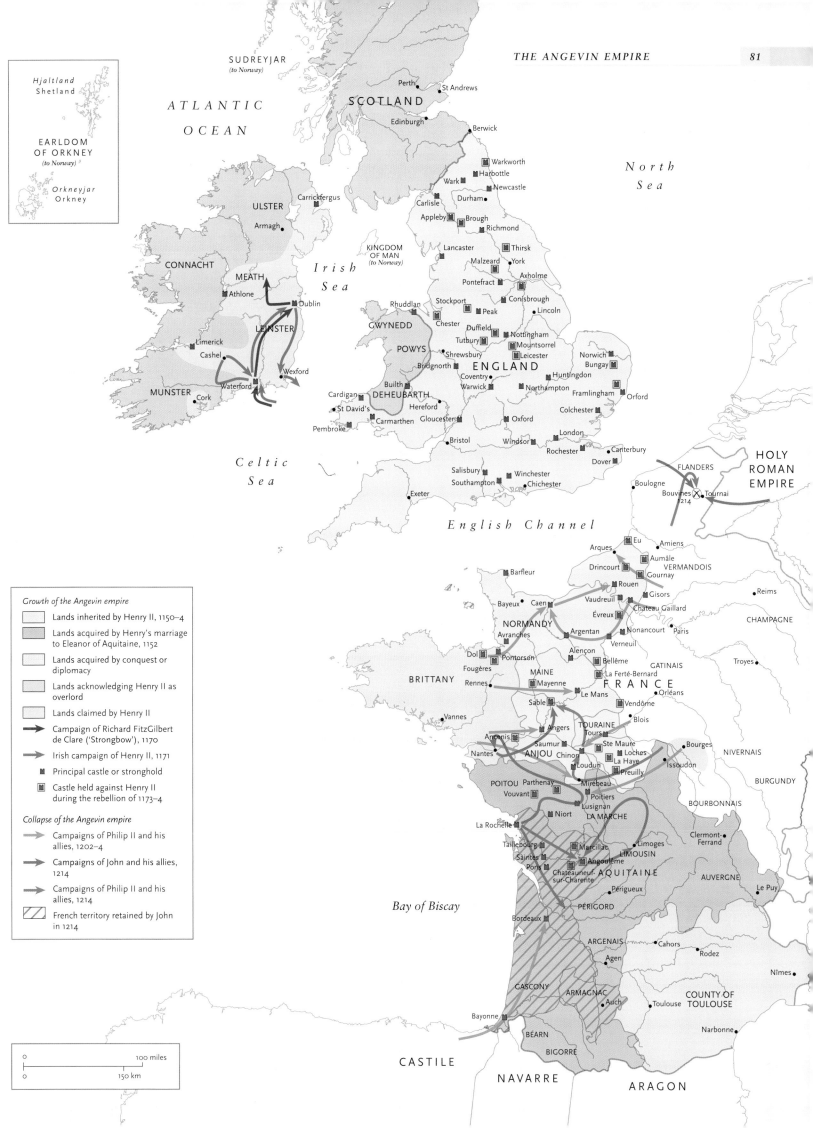

Map labels

SUDREYJAR
(to Norway)

ATLANTIC
OCEAN

Hjaltland
Shetland

EARLDOM
OF ORKNEY
(to Norway)

Orkneyjar
Orkney

SCOTLAND

Perth · St Andrews

Edinburgh

Berwick

North
Sea

Warkworth
Wark · Harbottle
Newcastle
Carlisle · Durham
Appleby · Brough
Richmond
Lancaster · Thirsk
Malzeard · York
Pontefract · Axholme
Stockport · Conisbrough
Peak · Lincoln
Chester · Duffield
Tutbury · Nottingham
Shrewsbury · Mountsorrel
Bridgnorth · Leicester · Norwich
Builth · Coventry · Bungay
Warwick · Northampton · Framlingham
Hereford · Huntingdon · Orford
Gloucester · Oxford · Colchester
Bristol · London
Windsor · Rochester · Canterbury
Dover
Salisbury · Winchester
Southampton · Chichester
Exeter

ULSTER
Carrickfergus
Armagh

CONNACHT
MEATH
Athlone · Dublin
LEINSTER
Limerick
Cashel · Wexford
Waterford
MUNSTER · Cork

Irish
Sea

KINGDOM
OF MAN
(to Norway)

GWYNEDD
Rhuddlan
POWYS
Cardigan
St David's
Carmarthen
Pembroke
DEHEUBARTH

ENGLAND

Celtic
Sea

English Channel

FLANDERS
Boulogne
Bouvines ⊗ Tournai
1214

HOLY
ROMAN
EMPIRE

North Sea

Barfleur
Arques · Eu · Amiens
Aumâle · VERMANDOIS
Drincourt · Gournay
Rouen · Gisors
Vaudreuil · Château Gaillard
Bayeux · Caen · Évreux · Reims
Argentan · Nonancourt · Paris
Avranches · Verneuil · CHAMPAGNE
NORMANDY
Dol · Pontorson · Alençon · Troyes
Fougères · MAINE · La Ferté-Bernard · GATINAIS
Rennes · Mayenne · Bellême
BRITTANY · Sablé · Le Mans · FRANCE
Vannes · Vendôme · Orléans
Angers · Blois
Ancenis · TOURAINE
Nantes · Saumur · Tours · Bourges
ANJOU · Chinon · Ste Maure · NIVERNAIS
Loudun · Loches
POITOU · Parthenay · La Haye · Issoudun
Vouvant · Mirebeau · Preuilly
Poitiers · BURGUNDY
La Rochelle · Lusignan · BOURBONNAIS
Niort · LA MARCHE
Clermont-Ferrand
Taillebourg · Marcillac · Limoges
Saintes · Angoulême · LIMOUSIN · AUVERGNE
Pons · Châteauneuf- · Le Puy
sur-Charente · AQUITAINE
Périgueux
PÉRIGORD
Bordeaux
ARGENAIS · Cahors
Agen · Rodez
GASCONY · Nîmes
ARMAGNAC · Auch
Toulouse · COUNTY OF
Bayonne · TOULOUSE
BÉARN · Narbonne
BIGORRE
CASTILE · NAVARRE · ARAGON

Bay of Biscay

Legend

Growth of the Angevin empire

▢ Lands inherited by Henry II, 1150–4

▢ Lands acquired by Henry's marriage to Eleanor of Aquitaine, 1152

▢ Lands acquired by conquest or diplomacy

▢ Lands acknowledging Henry II as overlord

▢ Lands claimed by Henry II

→ Campaign of Richard FitzGilbert de Clare ('Strongbow'), 1170

→ Irish campaign of Henry II, 1171

▣ Principal castle or stronghold

▣ Castle held against Henry II during the rebellion of 1173–4

Collapse of the Angevin empire

→ Campaigns of Philip II and his allies, 1202–4

→ Campaigns of John and his allies, 1214

→ Campaigns of Philip II and his allies, 1214

▨ French territory retained by John in 1214

Scale

0 · 100 miles
0 · 150 km

Murder in the cathedral

The murder of Archbishop Thomas Becket, from a 13th-century book of Psalms. Becket's murder was a short-term embarrass-ment to Henry II, and a long-term benefit to Canterbury, which became a major pilgrim-age centre as a result.

THE DEFENCE OF ANJOU

Henry's death cleared the path for the older of his surviving sons, Richard 'the Lionheart', backed by Philip Augustus. Both were committed to going on crusade, and Richard stayed in England only long enough to raise money to pay for his journey. In July 1190 the two kings set off for the Holy Land, where Richard earned a reputation for valour by his successes against Saladin. But he was captured on his journey home, and remained for over a year as a prisoner of his enemy, Henry VI of Germany. In his absence his younger brother John attempted a coup. It had collapsed by the time Richard arrived back in England in March 1194, but now the Capetians, with John's connivance, were threatening Normandy. Richard was forced to leave England immedi-ately, appointing as justiciar the gifted Hubert Walter, arch-bishop of Canterbury, who for the next five years supplied him with the men and money needed to fight Philip. In this contest Richard displayed such skills of military leadership and diplomacy that the French gains were pushed back and the fortunes of Richard's Angevin 'empire' restored. In April 1199, however, while besieging a castle in the Limou-sin, he was wounded by an arrow and died within days.

Historians have sometimes depicted Richard as a fine warrior but an irresponsible king, who ruled England for a decade but spent no more than six months there, neglecting

it in all respects except for the exaction of taxes to fund his adventures in France and the Holy Land. This is unfair. Par-ticipation in the Third Crusade was considered an obliga-tion on Christian princes, and Richard did his best to ensure England's stability during his absence. As for France, that is where his heart lay (literally, since he bequeathed it to Rouen Cathedral). Richard Cœur de Lion *was* French, as was his father, and he too was buried in Fontevrault Abbey in the duchy of his mother, Eleanor of Aquitaine. To fault him for not concentrating his efforts on England is to fault him for defending his Angevin inheritance.

THE END OF THE ANGEVIN EMPIRE

The death of Richard without legitimate sons caused a cri-sis. His late brother Geoffrey had a young son, Arthur of Brittany, for whom there was strong support in Anjou and elsewhere. But it was John who seized England and Normandy and, with the backing of Philip of France, the entire Angevin empire. Problems only arose when Philip Augustus abandoned John's cause and, as his feudal over-lord, declared his French lands forfeit. When John captured Arthur of Brittany in 1202 and had him murdered, he lost what few allies remained. Barons throughout the Angevin lands rebelled, and Philip set about the conquest of Nor-mandy. Throughout 1203 the two kings waged war, John living up to his new nickname 'Softsword'; by December he had withdrawn to England. When his mother, Eleanor of Aquitaine, died the following year, her duchy also fell to Philip. The Angevin empire lay in ruins.

After 1204, therefore, King John inevitably focused more attention on Britain and Ireland, and his enforced

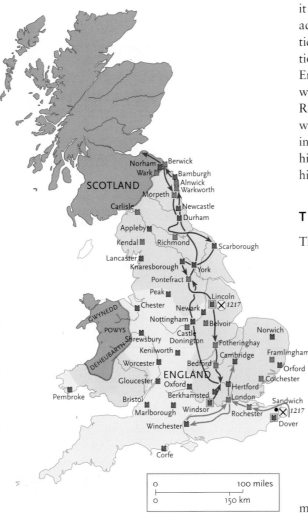

The civil war of John's reign

- ☐ Territory loyal to John, summer 1215
- ☐ Territory held by rebels, summer 1215
- ☐ Kingdoms opposed to John, summer 1215
- ☐ Territory occupied by the Welsh, summer 1215
- ◪ Royal stronghold
- ◪ Rebel stronghold
- ▣ Rebel siege
- ⊗ Battle, with date
- → John's northern campaign, Dec 1215–Mar 1216
- → Prince Louis' invasion, 1216

0   100 miles
0   150 km

Anglo-Norman settlement of the Hook, County Waterford

The Hook peninsula was one of the first areas of Ireland to experience Anglo-Norman colonisation, as it was at Bannow Island that the first major Anglo-Norman force landed in Ireland in 1169. As in the Welsh marches, defence was a major concern of the Anglo-Normans. Motte and bailey castles and other fortifications were widespread. Much land was granted to the military orders, who could help protect the area, and to two Cistercian abbeys. The native Irish were removed from around half of the district and replaced with English peasants settled in manorial villages and a defended town established at Clonmines.

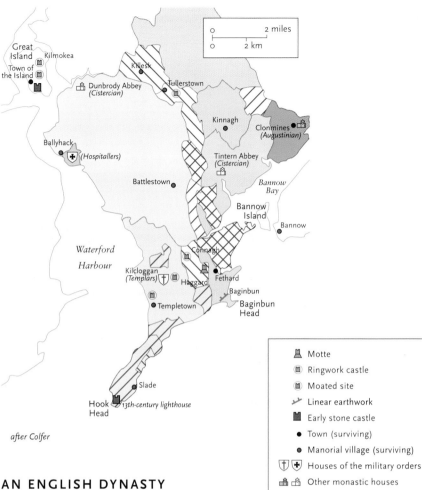

after Colfer

Legend:

- Motte
- Ringwork castle
- Moated site
- Linear earthwork
- Early stone castle
- Town (surviving)
- Manorial village (surviving)
- Houses of the military orders
- Other monastic houses

Landholding arrangements

- Knights Hospitallers
- Knights Templars
- Tintern Abbey
- Dunbrody Abbey
- Clonmines burghal lands
- Episcopal manors
- Knights' fees
- Free tenants
- Tenants-at-will

presence was not a pleasant experience for his subjects. Determined to win back his former continental possessions, he spared no effort in exploiting the taxable resources of England and Ireland – and this at a time of rampant price inflation. He even confiscated all church lands in response to an interdict imposed in 1208 by Pope Innocent III over a disputed election to the archbishopric of Canterbury. The quarrel was only healed in 1213, when John agreed to hold England as a papal fief. He also sought to extend his authority over King William of Scotland and the Welsh princes, particularly Llewelyn ab Iorwerth of Gwynedd: several major expeditions followed against the Scots and Welsh and, in 1210, against baronial opponents in Ireland.

John's problem was that he trusted no one, and, consequently, no one trusted him: prisoners in his custody had a habit of disappearing, and men raised by him from the dust sometimes ended up biting it. Moreover, to recover his continental lands, he bled his subjects dry. He might, however, have survived baronial opposition had not his great expedition to Poitou in 1214 ended in disaster at the battle of Bouvines. King John's strategy in tatters, his opponents now broke out in rebellion, and formulated a programme of reform, which, after much hard bargaining, produced Magna Carta ('Great Charter'), sealed by John at Runnymede in Berkshire in June 1215. It set in writing specific limitations on royal rights in order to prevent the king and his officials abusing vague unwritten customs, and it emphasised the primacy of 'the law of the land'.

King John had, however, only agreed to the Great Charter to buy time, and by September his failure to implement it led to civil war. The opposition sought a new king in France, offering the throne to King Philip's son Louis. When Louis entered London in May 1216, John retreated ignominiously before him. The rebels, even the new king of Scots, Alexander II, performed homage to Louis, and it looked as if the Norman and Angevin conquests of England would be followed by a Capetian one. But when King John died in October 1216, the rebels, who had offered the throne of England to the French prince because of hatred of John, not of the Plantagenet line, began to drift away from Louis, switching allegiance to John's young son, whom they hurriedly crowned as King Henry III. In battles on land and sea, at Lincoln and Sandwich, Louis's forces were defeated, and in September 1217 he withdrew from England and the Capetian invasion collapsed.

AN ENGLISH DYNASTY

England now had a nine-year-old Plantagenet king, but power lay in a regency council headed by the renowned William Marshal, which secured the reissue of Magna Carta. Henry's personal rule did not begin until 1232, after which point he ignored the new limitations on royal power, going his own way in matters of foreign policy and the appointment of royal ministers. This inevitably led to a crisis similar to that faced by his father: a baronial movement seeking radical reform grew up, led by Simon de Montfort. It surfaced in 1258 in the newly emerging institution of parliament, and the civil war that followed only ended with de Montfort's defeat at the battle of Evesham in 1265. The Barons' War was partly a response to Henry's many foreign policy failures, especially his inability to reassemble the Angevin empire. Henry III was no general, and in spite of his personal campaigns in France in 1230, 1242 and 1254, all the Angevin lands, Gascony excepted, stayed in French hands. By the treaty of Paris (1259) Louis IX accepted Henry's homage for Gascony, while Henry relinquished his ancestral claim to Normandy, Poitou and Anjou. When he died in 1272, Henry III was but an English king and the Plantagenets an English dynasty.

SD

Ducal seal

The seal of Henry II as duke of Normandy and count of Aquitaine. The Angevins ruled their French lands not as kings of England but as vassals of the kings of France. Seals were attached to documents as evidence of authenticity.

BRITAIN & THE CRUSADES

The military and religious movement now known as the Crusades began in 1095, with the call of Pope Urban II for a campaign to free the holy places of the Middle East from Muslim domination. Christian Europe mounted a series of military expeditions throughout the twelfth and thirteenth centuries, establishing four small Christian states in the Holy Land. The most visible and permanent sign of British involvement in the Crusades was the presence of the priories of the Hospitaller and Templar knights throughout Britain and Ireland. These military orders, whose headquarters lay in the Holy Land during the twelfth and thirteenth centuries, depended on their network of landed possessions in the West for income, supplies and military

personnel. Most British priories, staffed by only a few knights, were primarily administrative centres from which the estates could be managed. About one-third of their annual revenue was sent to the East.

Britain's involvement with crusading was at first modest. A twelfth-century English chronicler wrote that of the events in Asia, only a faint murmur crossed the Channel. The First Crusade was almost certainly preached in England in 1095, although we know very little about the circumstances. A few Anglo-Norman knights undoubtedly joined the contingent of Robert, duke of Normandy; in general, cross-channel family connections must have been the means by which most crusaders were recruited from

Crusading organisation in Britain and Ireland

The most visible aspect of crusading organisation in Britain and Ireland were the priories of the two military orders of warrior monks. The priories were administrative centres for the orders' estates, which provided supplies and money for the defence of the Holy Land. Organisation for the Third Crusade reached new levels of sophistication with the levying of a special tax, the Saladin Tithe, and preaching tours by leading churchmen.

English participation in the Crusades
England's greatest crusading effort was its contribution to the Third Crusade (1189–92), but Anglo-Norman and English soldiers and seamen participated in most of the major expeditions to the Holy Land. They also joined the German-led crusades against the pagans in the Baltic and contributed to the Christian *Reconquista* of Muslim Spain.

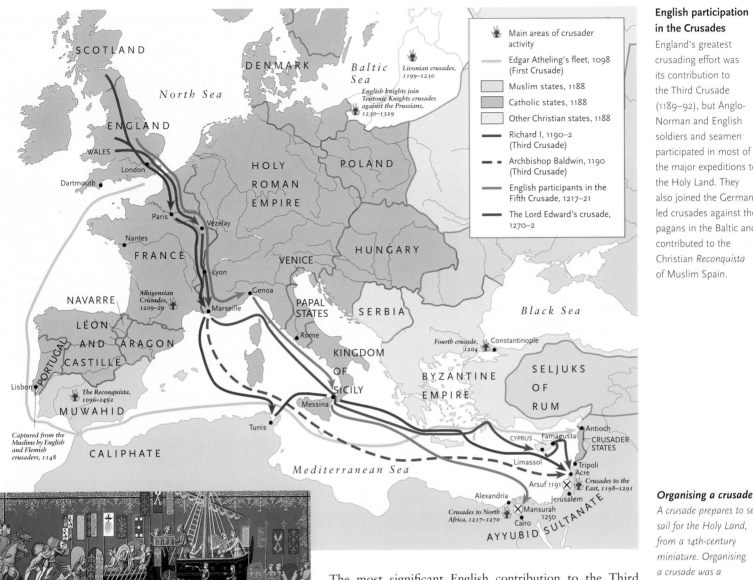

Legend:

- 👑 Main areas of crusader activity
- Edgar Atheling's fleet, 1098 (First Crusade)
- Muslim states, 1188
- Catholic states, 1188
- Other Christian states, 1188
- Richard I, 1190–2 (Third Crusade)
- Archbishop Baldwin, 1190 (Third Crusade)
- English participants in the Fifth Crusade, 1217–21
- The Lord Edward's crusade, 1270–2

Organising a crusade
A crusade prepares to set sail for the Holy Land, from a 14th-century miniature. Organising a crusade was a complex and hugely expensive enterprise.

Britain. One group of Englishmen, led by Edgar Atheling, distinguished itself in service to the Byzantine emperor on the crusade of 1101–2.

THE LATER CRUSADES

The conquest of the crusader kingdom of Jerusalem by Saladin in 1187 shocked the warring rulers of the West into taking the cross. Henry II of England and Philip II of France agreed to put aside their war in order to rescue Jerusalem from the Muslims. In the event, it was to Henry's son Richard the Lion Heart that the responsibility of fulfilling his vow devolved. Despite notable military successes against Saladin, Richard's crusade failed in its ultimate aim of restoring Jerusalem to Christian hands; nevertheless, his campaigns in 1191–2 laid the basis for the recovery of the crusader kingdom. Richard recruited heavily for his crusade from England, and some Scottish nobles also took the cross. Gerald of Wales has left us a description of the crusade-preaching undertaken by Archbishop Baldwin of Canterbury in Wales in 1188 – which seems to have been successful: some 3,000 Welshmen joined Richard's army.

The most significant English contribution to the Third Crusade, however, was financial. A special tax (the Saladin Tithe) was levied in 1188, and preaching, recruitment and vow-redemption payments were for the first time organised centrally by the Crown.

English knights, many in the entourage of Ranulf, earl of Chester, also served in the Fifth Crusade (1217–21). The crusade provided an opportunity for barons who had fought against the Crown in the civil war (1214–17) to remove themselves from the tense atmosphere of domestic politics and gain a reputation for chivalry overseas. In 1270–2 the Lord Edward recruited for his crusade from among those who had rebelled against the Crown in 1264–5 in order to foster reconciliation with the baronage.

The influence of crusading ideas was also felt in the domestic arena. In 1066 the Crusading concept of the 'just war' could be seen in the papal banner that accompanied William the Conqueror's army. In 1170 Henry II tried to have his invasion of Ireland preached as a crusade, on the grounds that the Irish were barbarians and the Irish church was unreformed. The defence of England by those loyal to the Angevin crown in 1217 was seen as a crusade, and crosses were worn by the royalist sailors at Sandwich. In contrast, Simon de Montfort's army wore crosses at Lewes (1264) and Evesham (1265) to signal the justice of their rebellion against the Crown.   **ATJ**

encircled with fences. An outer enclosure (the bailey) might be linked to the motte, and the whole complex defended by a moat or ditch. William the Conqueror imported stone from Caen to build the White Tower in London, and from the 1080s onward the towers (keeps) were increasingly built in stone. Castle design changed little until the later twelfth century, when the improving technology of siege warfare required greater sophistication in defence. Castles were always individual affairs, however, and the design depended on the particular site chosen, the specific military purpose of the castle and the budget available. Improved techniques learned in the crusader states came to influence castle design in Britain in the thirteenth century, and round towers began to replace the traditional square keep from the 1220s, as they were more resistant to undermining. Edward I encountered eastern castles during his crusade (1270–2), and it may have been as a result of this experience that he introduced the concentric castle into Britain in the 1280s. The concentric castle relied on a symmetrically arranged ring of walls and towers around an open bailey, dominated by a strengthened gatehouse. Edward I's Welsh castles, notably Conwy, Caernarfon and Harlech, are good examples of this new design.

The increasing sophistication of castle design in the thirteenth century meant an escalation in the costs of castle-building. Edward I was almost bank-rupted by the cost of his

Orford Castle, Suffolk

Built by Henry II between 1165 and 1173, Orford Castle has an unusual polygonal keep, which was easier to defend than the square keeps favoured by the Normans.

Major castles of Britain and Ireland

The most common castles were earth and timber motte and bailey castles built in the 11th and 12th centuries, and stone tower houses of the Anglo-Scottish borders and Ireland, built in the later Middle Ages. Major castles were expensive, and thus the prerogative of kings and leading barons.

A form of fortification for settlements, probably based on surviving Roman walls and known as the burh, was developed by the Anglo-Saxons. The fortified private residence of a lord that we know as the castle, however, was introduced by the Normans after 1066. The *Anglo-Saxon Chronicle* mentions the Norman castle as an innovation unknown in England. The castle had been developed in tenth-century France, initially as a means of defending lands against external threat, but it had proven equally useful as a means of control. The first castles in Britain provided a series of strongpoints that enabled the Normans to subdue a hostile population.

The first castles consisted of square wooden towers raised on mounds (mottes)

🏰	11th century
🏰	12th century
🏰	13th century
🏰	14th–15th centuries

Urquhart
Glamis
Rothesay
Stirling
Tantallon
Bothwell
Bamburgh
Dunstanburgh
Hermitage
Warkworth
Dunluce
Caerlaverock
Raby
Carrickfergus
Brough
Castle Bolton
Richmond
Ballymote
Skipton
Middleham
Lancaster
York
Trim
Clitheroe
Pontefract
Athenry
Beaumaris
Conisborough
Conwy
Beeston
Tattershall
Caernarfon
Harlech
Belvoir
Norwich
Castle Rising
Cahir
Grannagh
Clun
Thetford
Ludlow
Kenilworth
Orford
Warwick
Kidwelly
Hedingham
Raglan
Pleshey
Caerphilly
Berkeley
Colchester
Pembroke
White Tower,
London
Nunney
Rochester
Leeds
Bodiam
Dover
Tiverton
Old Sarum
Herstmonceux
Restormel
Corfe

eight castles in Wales. His castle-builder, the Savoyard Master James of St George, commanded high fees and employed hundreds of masons for building projects that might take over 10 years to complete. Castle-building had always been the prerogative of the Crown, and barons had to be licensed to 'crenellate' – in other words, to erect a fortification with battlements. Illegal, or 'adulterine', castles could be confiscated by the king. High building and maintenance costs, however, made it increasingly impractical for anyone but the king to build castles, particularly in the thirteenth century, a period in which inflation was high and agricultural returns low.

Castles also provided a means of colonising newly conquered regions. Conwy, for example, which was built on the site of Aberconwy Abbey, encompassed a new town. A castle functioned as a centre of administration and political life for a region, as well as a defensive outpost.

LIFE IN THE CASTLE

A large castle might house a population of a few hundred people, of whom many were not under arms. The castle needed to have space for storage of food and fuel, especially over the winter, while also providing living quarters for the lord's family, household, servants and craftsmen, and stables for horses. In a concentric castle, the garrison itself would be concentrated in the gatehouse. Smaller castles had functions more closely related to the administration of local estates, though they might also form part of a network of defensive outposts, as, for example, in the complex of Clun, in the Welsh marches. Clun itself, held by John Fitz Alan, formed the southern apex of a triangle of castles, with the bishop of Hereford's castle to the north, and the outpost of Bryn Amlwg in Welsh-held territory to the west. Knights whose fiefs lay within a radius of about 30 kilometres (approximately 20 miles) owed military service in the form of castle guard at Clun.

Such castles were unlikely to have been served by garrisons of more than a few dozen men at a time, and living conditions were probably primitive. A great lord's castle, however, was also a social centre. Recreation had to be provided for the bachelor household knights, who served the lord for wages, and the ladies of the household, who might be the daughters of the lord's tenants. Courtly culture was based on group entertainment in the form of recitals of songs by professional minstrels, with feasting and dancing. Cramped quarters, communal eating and a lack of private domestic space enforced on the castle's inhabitants a style of life in which social skills were paramount.

Castles continued to be built in the fourteenth century, but the development of cannon and other changes in the practice of warfare meant that they became increasingly impractical for strategic defence. By the end of the fourteenth century, brick was already being used in some British castles in place of stone, a sign that the castle was seen primarily as living accommodation rather than as a place of protection. Fifteenth-century castles such as Leeds in Kent and Herstmonceux in Sussex already prefigure the palaces of early modern Europe.

ATJ

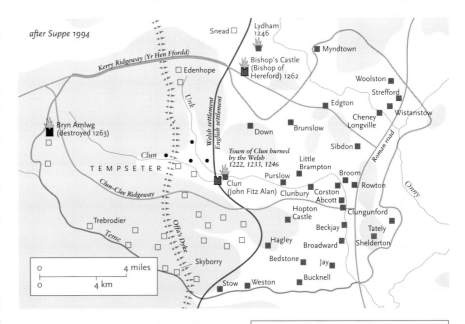

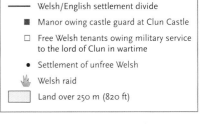

- ▪ Castle
- ▪ Castle not permanently garrisoned
- —— Welsh/English settlement divide
- ▪ Manor owing castle guard at Clun Castle
- ☐ Free Welsh tenants owing military service to the lord of Clun in wartime
- • Settlement of unfree Welsh
- ⚜ Welsh raid
- ▭ Land over 250 m (820 ft)

Clun in 1272

Clun Castle, in Shropshire, was built to block two ridge routes used in Welsh raids on the Midlands. It was garrisoned by knights holding manors in the English part of the castlery, supplemented by free Welsh tenants.

Kidwelly Castle, Dyfed

The defences of major castles could be updated several times during their lifetimes: Kidwelly began as a walled enclosure in the 12th century, to which round towers and an outer wall were added in the 13th and, finally, a large gatehouse after 1300.

The late thirteenth century witnessed an extraordinary bout of empire-building within the British Isles: the English crown, which had already claimed the lordship of Ireland under Henry II, now in effect declared its sovereignty over the whole of Britain. It is tempting to interpret this as part of a grand strategy on the part of Edward I, who was eager to re-establish the Plantagenet monarchy after the loss of many of his family's continental lands during the previous century and the civil war of his father's reign. In fact, Edward's interventions were merely opportunistic, and ran alongside, but did not replace, the revival of English claims in France.

Wales, in the thirteenth century, consisted of two political zones: the marcher lordships earlier established by the Anglo-Norman aristocracy; and the native princedoms – Gwynedd, Deheubarth, Powys – whose own jostling for power became a cause for increasing concern to the English crown. In 1267 Henry III had recognised Llewelyn ap Gruffudd of Gwynedd as 'prince of Wales' (that is, overlord of the native princedoms beyond the march), but Llewelyn proved reluctant to fulfil his side of the bargain and accept the feudal overlordship of the Plantagenets. Llewelyn had taken advantage of Henry's problems with his barons, which culminated in civil war in 1264–5, to expand his territories at the expense of both rival Welsh princes and the English marcher barons: his success made him overconfident and needlessly provocative. In 1277 Edward I undertook a campaign designed to bring Llewelyn to heel. Proceeding via Chester, Flint and Rhuddlan to Deganwy, he cowed Llewelyn into a negotiated settlement. The terms were harsh for the Welsh prince: he was forced to surrender the area known as the 'Four Cantrefs', between Chester and the river Conwy, which Edward then used to create a new series of powerful marcher lordships. The English also imposed a potentially crippling war indemnity of £50,000. It is hard to see how Llewelyn could ever have raised such a sum, and the waiving of the demand was one means by which Edward I demonstrated the control that he now enjoyed over the prince of Wales.

In 1282 Llewelyn's brother Daffydd launched a revolt against the English. Ironically, he had been an ally of Edward I, but felt aggrieved at the lack of reward for his former services to the crown of England. Edward's response was to launch a full-scale war of conquest. Proceeding along the north coast of Wales, as he had done in 1277, his forces successfully took Anglesey and pushed Llewelyn back into the fastnesses of Snowdonia. Llewelyn attempted to move south, but was ambushed and killed in November 1282 at Irfon Bridge, near Builth. Thereafter, Edward's forces made steady progress, proceeding into Gwynedd and eventually capturing Prince Daffydd (possibly through the treachery of his own remaining forces) in June 1283.

The most striking memorial to the conquest of Wales is the remarkable string of castles built or rebuilt by Edward I – at Flint, Rhuddlan, Conwy, Beaumaris, Caernarfon, Criccieth, Harlech, Conwy and Aberystwyth – to stand both as bastions and as symbols of Plantagenet rule. But the military occupation of the north and west was also followed up with constitutional settlement, and in 1284 Edward I imposed the Statute of Wales, by which the former principality was placed under the direct jurisdiction of the English crown and English law. Further revolts, in 1287 and 1294, were ruthlessly suppressed; in 1295 the earl of Warwick defeated the North Welsh rebel leader, Madog ap Llewelyn, at Maes Moydog, in an engagement whose tactics presaged the famous 'mixed formation' of archers and dismounted men-at-arms used to such effect during the Hundred Years War. The king himself then undertook a great circular march through Wales to reinforce his authority. The creation of his eldest surviving son as prince of Wales in 1301 was no act of conciliation, but a powerful reminder that the days of the native princes were over.

SCOTLAND'S SUCCESSION CRISIS

The crown of Scotland had undergone a process of consolidation rather similar to that of Gwynedd in the thirteenth century. But whereas the ruler of Gwynedd enjoyed his authority largely at the will of the English crown, the rulers of Scotland undertook their relations with the English and the other states as independent, sovereign rulers. Thus, for example, in the treaty of Perth (1266), the king of Norway ceded to Scottish control the lordship of Man and the Western Isles. When Alexander III of Scotland died in 1286, leaving only an infant granddaughter as heir, Edward I seemed prepared to honour the integrity of the Scottish

> '...the king's host came upon Llewelyn ap Gruffudd and slew him and many of his host...And then all Wales was cast to the ground.'
>
> **The Kings of the Saxons (1283)**

Harlech Castle, Gwynedd

The castle was built by Edward I in 1285–90 for the then enormous sum of £8000. Harlech, which featured the latest concentric defences, was one of a series of castles built by Edward to isolate Gwynedd from the rest of Wales.

crown. By the treaty of Birgham (1290), Princess Margaret would marry the English king's heir, Prince Edward, and thus finally establish one ruler over two otherwise independent kingdoms.

The death of Margaret, however, created a succession crisis in Scotland, during which Edward I chose – indeed, was invited – to intervene and act as arbitrator. His favoured candidate, John Balliol, the lord of Galloway, was crowned in 1292, but was required to pay liege homage to the English crown. When the Scottish council resisted Edward I's overlordship, the latter took direct action, entering the kingdom with force in 1296. He marched via Edinburgh, Perth and Aberdeen as far north as Elgin, removing the stone of destiny from Scone, forcing Balliol to resign his throne, and reducing Scotland to the status of a dependent 'land'. It seemed that the kingdom of Scotland had simply been subsumed into the rampantly expansionist Plantagenet empire.

THE WAR

In the event, Edward I and his successor were to face much more deep-seated and sustained resistance than had ever been encountered in Wales. The English king misjudged the situation in Scotland at the end of the campaign of 1296, believing the region to be thoroughly subdued, and turned his attention to a war with France provoked by Philip IV's seizure of Edward's duchy of Aquitaine. During his absence, a Scottish army under William Wallace, then a relatively unknown minor lord, inflicted a decisive defeat on an English force led by the Earl Warenne at Stirling Bridge in September 1297. The Scots immediately followed up their victory by breaching the border and launching raids into northern England.

Edward quickly responded to the demands of his own subjects for restitution, returning home to deal with the emergency, moving his administration to York in the spring of 1298, and beginning what became a series of annual military campaigns lasting for the rest of his reign. The capture and execution of Wallace in 1305 symbolised the apparent success of this considerable investment of time and resources. In the same year, Edward issued an ordinance for the government of Scotland, allowing much of the existing system of administration and law to remain intact, but subordinating the territory to his own sovereignty. The conquest of Scotland was not, however, accompanied by a programme of castle-building. Although English garrisons were established in a series of Lowland border strongholds from Berwick to Dumfries, it proved impossible fully to protect the northern English counties from the continued

impact of the Scottish raids.

The stalemate in Scotland was transformed by the emergence of Robert Bruce, the earl of Carrick. His assumption of the vacant throne in 1306, followed soon afterwards by the death of Edward I in 1307, turned the advantage decisively towards the Scots. Any king would have found it hard to live up to the reputation of Edward I, and Edward II was hobbled from the start in possessing none of his father's military or administrative abilities: an inheritance of huge debts, the legacy of Edward I's wars, was a further handicap. Edward II's efforts to re-establish order in Scotland were faltering: a number of campaigns were abandoned, allowing the Scots valuable breathing space, and Edward's defeat by Bruce at Bannockburn in 1314, while not of great strategic significance, proved very publicly that English armies were not invincible and that English sovereignty was now more token than real. The Declaration of Arbroath of 1320, while primarily intended as a means of securing papal recognition for Bruce's kingship, demonstrates the deep sense of political and cultural identity established among the Scots during this sustained resistance to English rule.

Edward I and II both used the entire resources of their empire to fight the Scots, and money, men and victuals were transferred to the war zone from their various dependencies

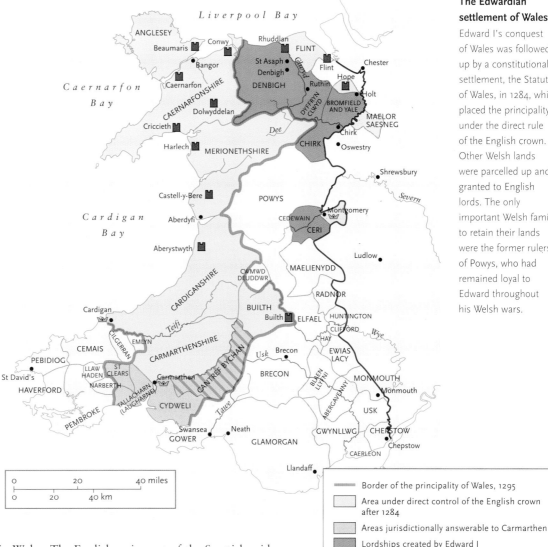

The Edwardian settlement of Wales
Edward I's conquest of Wales was followed up by a constitutional settlement, the Statute of Wales, in 1284, which placed the principality under the direct rule of the English crown. Other Welsh lands were parcelled up and granted to English lords. The only important Welsh family to retain their lands were the former rulers of Powys, who had remained loyal to Edward throughout his Welsh wars.

Map legend:
- Border of the principality of Wales, 1295
- Area under direct control of the English crown after 1284
- Areas jurisdictionally answerable to Carmarthen
- Lordships created by Edward I and granted to English families
- Limit of marcher lordships
- Castles built or rebuilt by Edward I
- Other royal centres

Scale: 0 — 20 — 40 miles / 0 — 20 — 40 km

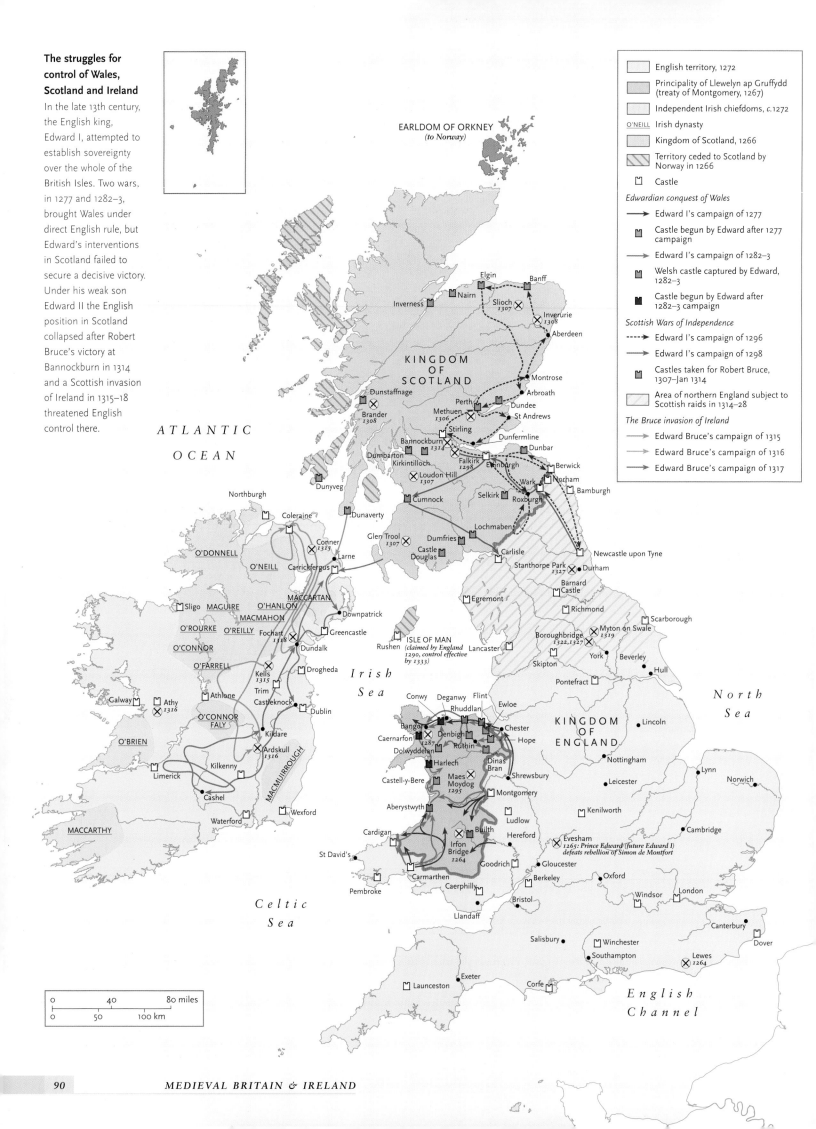

The struggles for control of Wales, Scotland and Ireland

In the late 13th century, the English king, Edward I, attempted to establish sovereignty over the whole of the British Isles. Two wars, in 1277 and 1282–3, brought Wales under direct English rule, but Edward's interventions in Scotland failed to secure a decisive victory. Under his weak son Edward II the English position in Scotland collapsed after Robert Bruce's victory at Bannockburn in 1314 and a Scottish invasion of Ireland in 1315–18 threatened English control there.

Legend

- English territory, 1272
- Principality of Llewelyn ap Gruffydd (treaty of Montgomery, 1267)
- Independent Irish chiefdoms, c.1272
- O'NEILL Irish dynasty
- Kingdom of Scotland, 1266
- Territory ceded to Scotland by Norway in 1266
- Castle

Edwardian conquest of Wales
- Edward I's campaign of 1277
- Castle begun by Edward after 1277 campaign
- Edward I's campaign of 1282–3
- Welsh castle captured by Edward, 1282–3
- Castle begun by Edward after 1282–3 campaign

Scottish Wars of Independence
- Edward I's campaign of 1296
- Edward I's campaign of 1298
- Castles taken for Robert Bruce, 1307–Jan 1314
- Area of northern England subject to Scottish raids in 1314–28

The Bruce invasion of Ireland
- Edward Bruce's campaign of 1315
- Edward Bruce's campaign of 1316
- Edward Bruce's campaign of 1317

EARLDOM OF ORKNEY (to Norway)

ATLANTIC OCEAN

KINGDOM OF SCOTLAND

Elgin · Banff · Inverness · Nairn · Slioch 1307 · Inverurie 1308 · Aberdeen · Montrose · Arbroath · Dunstaffnage · Brander 1308 · Perth · Methuen 1306 · Dundee · St Andrews · Stirling · Bannockburn 1314 · Dunfermline · Dumbarton · Kirkintilloch · Falkirk 1298 · Edinburgh · Dunbar · Dunyveg · Loudon Hill 1307 · Wark · Berwick · Norham · Cumnock · Selkirk · Roxburgh · Bamburgh · Glen Trool 1307 · Dumfries · Lochmaben · Castle Douglas · Carlisle · Newcastle upon Tyne · Stanthorpe Park 1327 · Durham · Barnard Castle · Egremont · Richmond · Scarborough · Myton on Swale 1319 · Boroughbridge 1322, 1327 · York · Beverley · Hull · Skipton · Lancaster · Pontefract

Northburgh · Coleraine · Conner 1315 · Larne · Carrickfergus · Downpatrick · Greencastle · Rushen · ISLE OF MAN (claimed by England 1290, control effective by 1333)

O'DONNELL · O'NEILL · Sligo · MAGUIRE · O'HANLON · MACMAHON · MACCARTAN · O'ROURKE · O'REILLY · Fochart 1318 · Dundalk · O'CONNOR · Kells 1315 · Drogheda · O'FARRELL · Athlone · Trim · Castleknock · Galway · Athy 1316 · O'CONNOR FALY · Kildare · Dublin · O'BRIEN · Ardskull 1316 · MACMURROUGH · Limerick · Kilkenny · Cashel · Wexford · Waterford · MACCARTHY

Irish Sea · Celtic Sea · North Sea · English Channel

KINGDOM OF ENGLAND

Conwy · Deganwy · Flint · Rhuddlan · Ewloe · Bangor · Chester · Caernarfon 1287 · Denbigh · Hope · Dolwyddelan · Ruthin · Harlech · Dinas Bran · Shrewsbury · Castell-y-Bere · Maes Moydog 1295 · Montgomery · Aberystwyth · Ludlow · Cardigan · Builth · Kenilworth · St David's · Irfon Bridge 1264 · Hereford · Evesham 1265: Prince Edward (future Edward I) defeats rebellion of Simon de Montfort · Goodrich · Gloucester · Carmarthen · Caerphilly · Berkeley · Oxford · Pembroke · Bristol · Windsor · London · Llandaff · Lincoln · Nottingham · Leicester · Lynn · Norwich · Cambridge · Salisbury · Winchester · Southampton · Lewes 1264 · Canterbury · Dover · Exeter · Corfe · Launceston

0   40   80 miles
0   50   100 km

in 1318, Robert Bruce's forces raided far into English terri-tory, penetrating the Vale of York and moving rapidly across the Pennines into a devastating raid on Lancashire. In 1319 the city of York itself came under threat, when a Yorkshire scratch force largely of clerics and peasants was routed by Scots raiders at Myton on Swale. The sense of panic and the considerable material hardships suffered as a result of these raids caused some of Edward II's own sub-jects to question his authority in the north of the kingdom. Andrew Harcla, earl of Carlisle, was merely the most cele-brated of a number of northerners who threw in their lot with the Scots. The situation was exacerbated when an inheritance dispute over the lands of the earl of Gloucester – one of the casualties of Bannockburn – led to the outbreak of civil war in England in 1321: Edward's victory over his cousin Thomas of Lancaster at Boroughbridge in 1322 may have marked the end of that dispute, but it did nothing to quell the sense of frustration and alienation felt in the North. When Edward established a truce with Robert Bruce in 1323, he effectively created a no-man's land of the whole area between the Humber and the Tweed.

The deposition of Edward II in 1327 – itself an unprece-dented act in post-Conquest English history – was account-ed for by contemporaries in no small measure by the king's failure to maintain his father's ambitions and achievements in Scotland. It also allowed Bruce to re-open hostilities. In an action typical of his strategy, Robert cleverly avoided a direct engagement with the English at Stanhope Park, caus-ing the young Edward III to weep tears of frustration, and continued his campaign of raids. In 1328 the English crown did the unthinkable: by the treaty of Edinburgh, it acknowl-edged Bruce as king of the Scots. Although Edward III was to challenge the treaty in his relations with Robert's son, David II, the prospect of direct English rule in Scotland effectively ended in 1328. **WMO**

John Balliol and Edward I

John Balliol, made king of Scotland in 1292, swears fealty to Edward I of England. John's removal from power by discontented nobles in 1295 precipitated Edward I's ultimately disastrous Scottish wars.

in England, Wales, Ireland and France. It was partly to cut off the particularly important supply route from Ireland that, in 1315, Robert Bruce's brother Edward launched an invasion of the lordship. Proclaiming himself king of Ire-land in 1316, he defeated the Anglo-Irish magnates at Athy in the Midlands and returned northwards to take the great Ulster fortress of Carrickfergus. In 1317 he was joined by his brother Robert, and the Bruces' force marched on Dublin. It was only the timely appointment of Roger Mor-timer as English lieutenant of Ireland that provided an effective defence, and in 1318 Edward Bruce was defeated and killed at Fochart near Dundalk.

SCOTLAND'S INDEPENDENCE

Meanwhile, however, the situation in the north of England was becoming increasingly desperate. After taking Berwick

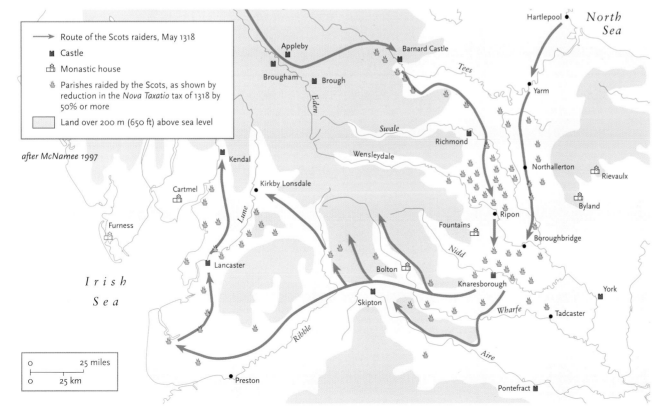

The Scottish raid of May 1318

Robert Bruce attempted to force the English government to recognise him as king of Scotland by repeatedly raiding the north of England. Records of grants of tax relief and repairs to monastic buildings show both the route and the scale of damage caused by the major raid of May 1318.

MEDIEVAL LANDSCAPES

A deserted medieval village

Although the timber buildings have decayed long ago, the pattern of fields, house plots and lanes of this abandoned village near Gagingwell, Oxfordshire, can still be seen as irregularities in the ground.

Nucleated settlement

Nucleated settlement in the Thames valley in the mid-19th century. Settlement is concentrated in villages, and the surrounding countryside is unpopulated except for a few isolated farms. This pattern is characteristic of much of lowland Britain.

The pattern of settlement in medieval Britain and Ireland is closely related to developments in agriculture from the prehistoric period onwards. Although the extent of land under arable in England, at least, was probably already enormous in prehistoric times, much of this land subsequently went out of cultivation. High moorland and mountain regions experienced peat deposition during the Iron Age, owing to soil deterioration after clearance and climatic change to cooler, wetter conditions. Areas such as the southern downlands, which had been intensively cropped when vast supplies of food were required for the armies and towns of the Roman period, were allowed to revert to pasture under the Anglo-Saxons. The Anglo-Saxon economy also favoured woodlands as areas of valuable wood-pasture (especially for pigs) and for hunting, and many were extended as royal sport and game reserves under the Norman kings. Many once-open areas such as the Weald had reverted to woodland and pockets of pasture long before the Norman Conquest. There were other areas, however, where cultivation remained extensive throughout prehistoric, Roman and early medieval times, and it was in these regions that open-field farming, associated with the emergence of nucleated settlement in villages, appears to have become dominant from about the ninth century.

The open-field system eventually dominated a swathe of countryside from Dorset to Northumberland. As the system spread, farms were relocated into a central village core, and outlying farms were gradually abandoned, in a slow process of nucleation that continued long after the Norman Conquest. By the medieval period these villages lay amid a number of large, open fields in which villagers held strips of ploughland and also enjoyed rights in the common meadows and remaining waste. In the so-called 'Midland system' of openfield agriculture, an individual farmer's strips would be scattered more or less evenly through three or four large common fields, but would not be enclosed by any hedge or wall. Each peasant farmer would be responsible for cultivating his own strips only between sowing and harvest, and after that the land would become once more part of the common field, available for pasture until ploughed by the shared plough teams in the early spring. Crop rotation helped to maintain fertility, cereals alternating with pulses (peas and beans) – but every few years part of each field, at least, would be left fallow, again providing valuable pasture for domestic stock. The hay meadows along streams and rivers were the source of winter fodder; each year, lots would be drawn for temporary ownership of the strips or 'doles' and stock excluded until after mowing in summer. Beyond the open fields of a township, any remaining waste would supply grazing for the township's stock, shepherded by the village herdsman.

Many woods and groves were appropriated by manorial lords by the Middle Ages, but the remaining waste was often at least partially wooded, providing firewood and timber for building and fencing. The use of the township resources obviously required strict regulation and was managed by the manor court, which every peasant farmer had a duty to attend and, indeed, to help run. The system was not

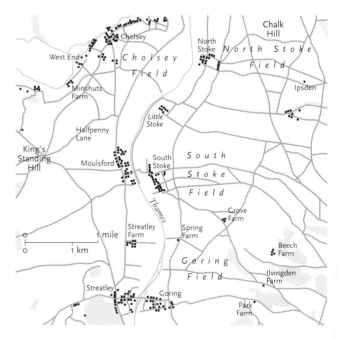

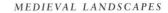

inefficient, but as population levels rose before the Black Death, pasture supplies became seriously diminished; in heavily populated regions most of the land fell under the plough, requiring even closer organisation of the township's resources.

Although open fields were to be found across much of England in the Middle Ages, less regular field patterns prevailed outside the area of the Midland system, with considerable regional variations. In the Welsh borderland, for instance, there were often dozens of small, scattered patches of open field within a township, closely related to hamlet settlements. Here, population pressure was less and nucleated village settlement was limited to such areas as the central plain to the north of Hereford. Population density was not always the decisive factor, however, since irregular systems also characterised most of eastern England where population levels were high. In areas of light soils, chalk, limestone or sandy heath, as in the Cotswolds or in parts of

East Anglia, fertility could only be maintained by a 'sheep-corn' system in which sheep would graze heaths and sheep-walks by day, but be moved at night to the arable fields to fertilise them with their dung. Here, farmers often held strips close to their own farms, but strict regulation of stock movement remained essential.

NUCLEATED VILLAGES

Most villages began to develop as estate centres in the later Anglo-Saxon period, as open-field farming was introduced. Village settlement could take many forms. Some villages grew organi-

	Village settlement with hamlets and dispersed farms
	Hamlet settlement with occasional villages and many dispersed farms
	Dispersed homesteads with occasional villages and hamlets
	Area of 'Midland' open fields

cally, while others were laid out along roads, often with a back lane separating the village crofts from the fields beyond; some, especially in Durham and the Home Counties, incorporated a village green. Some might shift as they spread along a road or incorporated a market area. Most began as clusters of small farming units around a manor house (or manor farm, if there was no resident lord) and church, though in certain parts of the country villages might have special functions – such as fishing villages in Cornwall. It was only in later centuries that farms left the village itself. Indeed, many remain, especially at Laxton in Nottinghamshire, where an open-field system has been fossilised to this day. Politics also influenced settlement patterns. In the Welsh borders, many villages grew up around a Norman motte or castle, tiny copies of grander fortified towns. After the Anglo-Norman invasion

Dispersed settlement
This map shows an area of the Devon–Somerset border in the mid-19th century. There are few villages and the countryside is densely scattered with farms and small hamlets. This pattern is typical of much of western Britain and Ireland.

Late medieval settlement patterns
Here the relationship of nucleated settlement and open-field agriculture is clear. In most of Britain, this pattern survives to the present day, but it was disrupted in the Highlands by the 19th-century Clearances, and in Ireland by the 17th-century Plantations.

Open fields
Medieval ridge and furrow marks near Guisborough, North Yorkshire, preserve the pattern of medieval open fields. Open fields were divided into narrow strips; centuries of up and down ploughing threw soil to the middle of the strips, building them up into ridges.

Wharram Percy

A reconstruction of the deserted medieval village at Wharram Percy in the Yorkshire Wolds, with the lord's manor in the foreground. Each peasant house has a small yard surrounding it, called a toft or a croft, which served as a small, intensively cultivated garden to supply the family with vegetables. Open fields surround the village.

Building types

Vernacular building traditions in Britain and Ireland are broadly divided into upland and lowland zones. In the wealthier lowland zone, building in durable materials was common by the 15th century; in the highland zone, it did not begin until the end of the 17th century. Longhouses – buildings combining accommodation for both people and livestock – were widespread in the British Isles in the Middle Ages, but the tradition persisted longest in the far west.

of Ireland in the twelfth century, deliberately created centres in eastern Ireland varied from small nucleated villages to towns, occupied mostly by colonists, all enjoying special rights and freedoms. Again, these are often associated with the mottes of early castles, and outlying settlements on the periphery of the Anglo-Norman areas were often moated.

DISPERSED SETTLEMENT

Much of Britain is characterised by a landscape not of villages but of scattered hamlets and farms. This is an ancient settlement pattern, but has not been without change. Farms were often smaller and more numerous in the past, and some single farms today were once small hamlets. In those parts of the countryside with more woodland and waste, pastoral farming remained more important than arable and was more easily carried out from scattered farms set among their own fields. Throughout medieval times, the practice of woodland clearance was carried out anew, with assarts (cleared and enclosed fields) nibbling into the woodland edge. The edges of the common waste also provided a place for landless labourers and others to establish their dwellings. In Wales the tradition of the *ty unnos* cottage survived, in which custom sanctioned the building of a cottage on waste land, provided its construction could be completed by daybreak; such encroachment cottages are a common feature of many parts of Britain.

Upland building zone

Longhouse zone

(after Aalen, 1997)

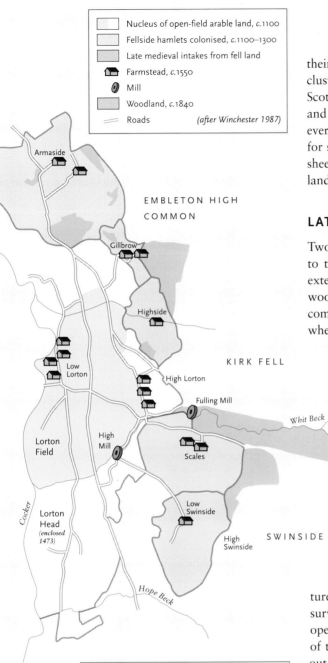

Nucleus of open-field arable land, *c.*1100
Fellside hamlets colonised, *c.*1100–1300
Late medieval intakes from fell land
Farmstead, *c.*1550
Mill
Woodland, *c.*1840
Roads   *(after Winchester 1987)*

Armaside

EMBLETON HIGH COMMON

Gillbrow

Highside

KIRK FELL

Low Lorton

High Lorton

Fulling Mill

Whit Beck

Lorton Field

High Mill

Scales

Scawgill

Cocker

Lorton Head (*enclosed* 1473)

Low Swinside

High Swinside   SWINSIDE

Hope Beck

```
0          ½              1 mile
0       ½         1 km
```

Throughout western Britain, from Cornwall through Ireland to the Scottish Highlands, this largely dispersed settlement pattern included hamlets (*baile* in Ireland), often occupied by family or kin groups. They farmed the surrounding common 'infield', in which strips radiated out from the settlement, and grazed the surrounding marginal land, parts of which might be intermittently cropped as 'outfield'. In Ireland such a system of farming was known as 'rundale' and it was also a feature of medieval Scotland, where it was known as 'run-rig', joint-tenants holding land from the laird. In Scotland, these clusters of tenanted farms formed the 'fermtoun', sometimes sharing a mill and church. In Wales, the Edwardian conquest of the late thirteenth century largely destroyed the clustered hamlets of native settlement as both Welsh and English landowners built up their estates and established new small tenanted farms, mostly set within their own land, in their place.

In the Middle Ages, transhumance was still practised in much of upland Britain, members of the community moving to higher or more remote pastures in early summer with

their stock, often producing dairy products there. Their clusters of seasonal dwellings were known as 'shielings' in Scotland, 'booley houses' in Ireland and *hafodydd* in Wales, and usually lay close to streams. In medieval times, however, increasingly large tracts of upland, formerly available for summer pasture, were taken up by the monasteries for sheep pasture, especially in the southern uplands of Scotland and the uplands of northern England.

LATER CHANGES

Two trends are apparent in medieval landscapes. First, up to the time of the Black Death, farmland was gradually extended, with new farms and enclosed fields edging into woodland or heath or biting into the fringes of the upland commons. Second, in the aftermath of the Black Death, when an inadequate labour force remained in many areas to sustain the established manorial arable economy, and stock-rearing became economically more rewarding, the open fields in many areas were gradually turned over to pasture and enclosed for more efficient grazing management. In areas such as the White Peak, newly built stone walls fossilised the ancient strip pattern to produce a distinctive pattern of enclosed narrow fields. In some Midland regions, in particular, enclosure seems to have begun in the fourteenth and fifteenth centuries and was more drastic, with whole villages deserted, and their fields laid down to pasture and broken up with hedges. Most medieval villages survived, however, to become today's villages. In the core open-field regions it was not until the organised enclosure of the eighteenth or nineteenth century that farms moved out of the surviving villages into the surrounding fields.

The settlement patterns of Highland Britain were also not without later change. Many of the villages of Ireland, especially in the Midlands, were destroyed in the seventeenth century by post-Cromwellian social engineering, when pastoralism replaced labour-intensive tillage. A population explosion in western Ireland in the eighteenth and nineteenth centuries was accompanied by colonisation of more difficult marginal lands, with new hamlets known as *clachans*, a process that could not be sustained after the potato blight of the mid-nineteenth century. Famine followed, and in a desperate attempt at redress, whole landscapes were remodelled into patterns of consolidated ladder holdings with new farmhouses superimposed over earlier rundale landscapes. Livestock farming increased in importance, especially in central and eastern Ireland, where tenanted farms were held from landlord graziers. In the Highlands of Scotland, after similar population expansion, the run-rig system was replaced by crofting, and common arable was divided between joint tenants into separate crofts. In the nineteenth century, however, many landlords evicted whole townships in the 'clearances' to make room for sheep. Thus the wilderness of the Highlands is actually of quite recent origin. **DH**

The Vale of Lorton
The medieval settlement of the Vale of Lorton, Cumbria. From an open-field nucleus, *c.*1100, cultivation spread progressively along the valley floor and on to marginal lands on the edges of the surrounding fells. Expansion ceased at the end of the Middle Ages, when pastoral farming increased in importance.

THE HUNDRED YEARS WAR

An English victory
The battle of Crécy, 1346, from a late 14th-century copy of Froissart's Chronicles. The English archers and dismounted men-at-arms won a spectacular victory over the French cavalry, enabling Edward III to go on to besiege and take Calais.

Although the term 'Hundred Years War' as a description for the Anglo-French wars of 1337 to 1453 was invented only in the mid-nineteenth century, there is no doubt that contemporaries were well aware of the long-drawn-out and seemingly insoluble nature of Anglo-French conflict.

Essentially, the war was fought over the claim of Edward III and his successors to the French crown. But Anglo-French conflict had erupted on several occasions before 1337, caused by the lands that the English kings held in France. Although in the early thirteenth century most of these lands – Normandy, Anjou, Maine and Poitou – had been lost, English kings took their remaining territorial rights seriously. They continued to hold Gascony, which provided England with most of its wine. Bordeaux, with 30,000 inhabitants in the early fourteenth century, was second only to London as the largest urban centre under the rule of the English king. In 1259 Henry III accepted his obligation to pay homage to Louis IX for Gascony and other lands in southwest France. While Henry's successors might jib at this obligation, they found it impossible to avoid, all the more so from 1279, when the county of Ponthieu came to the English through the inheritance of Edward I's wife, Eleanor of Castile.

The awkwardness of one king being the vassal of the other, in a period when notions of royal sovereignty were ever expanding, led to two wars between England and France, in 1294–7 and 1324–7. Meanwhile, the English kings attempted to extend their own lordship by demanding homage from the kings of Scotland. Edward I's request that his nominee as king of Scotland, John Balliol, provide troops for the French war led to a Scottish alliance with France in 1295. England thus found itself with enemies on both its northern and its southern frontiers.

In 1328 Charles IV of France died without a direct male heir. Edward III had a claim to the French throne through his mother, Isabella, who was Charles's sister. However, the crown fell to Philip of Valois, Charles's cousin. Over the next 10 years Anglo-French hostility grew considerably. This was fanned by Edward III's actions against the Scots, whose king, David II, sought safety in France in 1334. War between England and France broke out in 1337 when Philip confiscated Edward's French lands. England's south coast was now subjected to French raids. Southampton was sacked in October 1338. Edward immediately issued instructions for defensive walls to be built, especially on the undefended quayside. In January 1340 he declared himself king of France in Ghent (he hoped to find allies in Flanders), and in June removed much of the maritime threat to England by a victory over the French fleet at Sluys.

ENGLISH VICTORIES

After intervening in a Breton succession war in the early 1340s, Edward invaded Normandy in 1346, almost reaching Paris before moving northwards across the Somme into Ponthieu and defeating the over-confident French at Crécy on 26 August. The Scots invaded England in support of their French ally, but met with defeat at Nevilles Cross near Durham on 17 October 1346. In the following year, Edward took Calais, which was developed into an English base and not retaken by the French until 1558. Nearer home, Edward celebrated his victories, and cemented relations with his nobility – one of his major sources of military manpower – by founding the Order of the Garter.

In the mid-1350s the war escalated again, with raids by the Black Prince, Edward's eldest son, first from Bordeaux almost to the Mediterranean in 1355, and in the following year towards the Loire. The French intercepted his army at Poitiers, but were dealt a crushing defeat; their king, John II, was captured. Negotiations followed, and by the treaty of Brétigny of May 1360, Edward gained a large ransom for King John, and full sovereign control of Calais, Ponthieu, Poitou and an enlarged duchy of Aquitaine. Although he agreed to give up his French title and his conquests in the

'They came into Southampton harbour one Sunday morning when the people were at mass...they pillaged and looted, killing many people and raping a number of women, which was a deplorable thing, and loaded their vessels with the great plunder they found in the town, which was rich and well stocked.'

Froissart, Chronicles, on the events of 5 October 1338

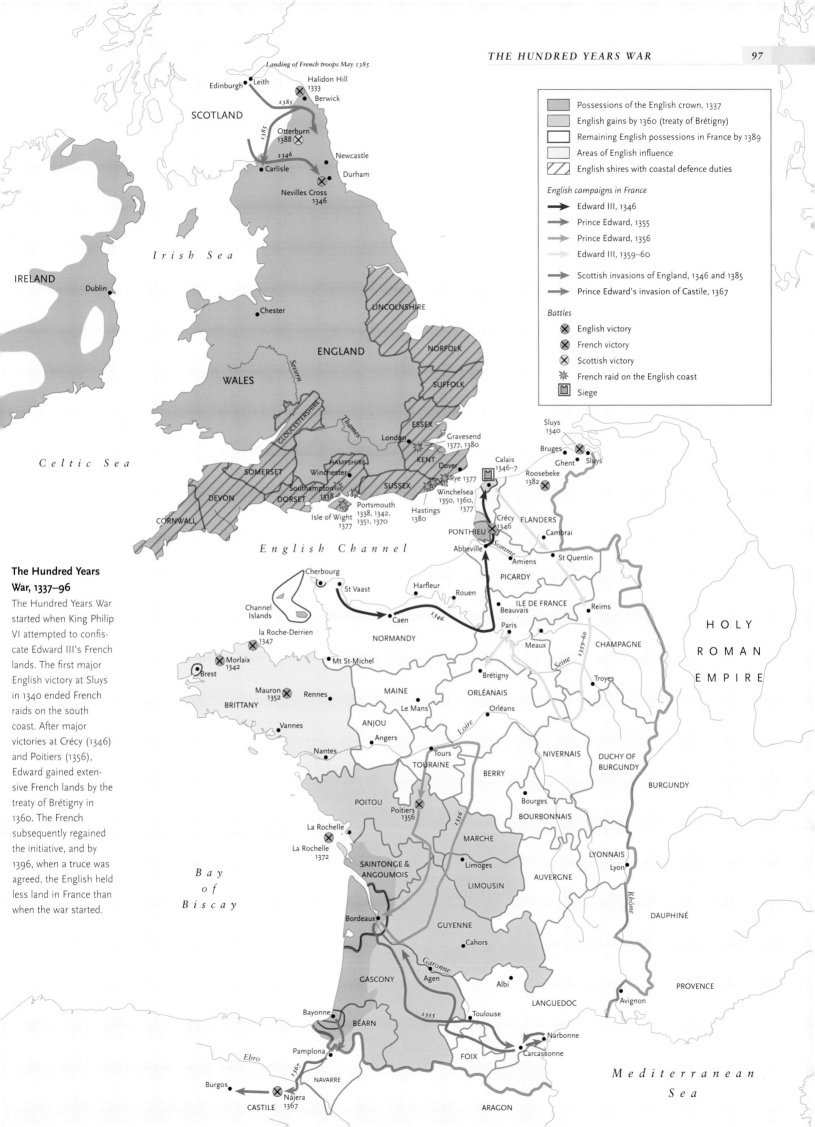

The Hundred Years War, 1337–96

The Hundred Years War started when King Philip VI attempted to confiscate Edward III's French lands. The first major English victory at Sluys in 1340 ended French raids on the south coast. After major victories at Crécy (1346) and Poitiers (1356), Edward gained extensive French lands by the treaty of Brétigny in 1360. The French subsequently regained the initiative, and by 1396, when a truce was agreed, the English held less land in France than when the war started.

Legend:

- Possessions of the English crown, 1337
- English gains by 1360 (treaty of Brétigny)
- Remaining English possessions in France by 1389
- Areas of English influence
- English shires with coastal defence duties

English campaigns in France

→ Edward III, 1346
→ Prince Edward, 1355
→ Prince Edward, 1356
→ Edward III, 1359–60

→ Scottish invasions of England, 1346 and 1385
→ Prince Edward's invasion of Castile, 1367

Battles

⊗ English victory
⊗ French victory
⊗ Scottish victory
✳ French raid on the English coast
⌂ Siege

Rival archers

The battle of Agincourt, 1415, as portrayed in a 15th-century French manuscript. At Agincourt, English archers inflicted appalling casualties on a much larger French army; their victory opened the way for Henry V's conquest of Normandy.

north, there can be no doubt this was the peak not only of his personal success, but also of English ascendancy. In 1363 the Commons thanked their king for delivering them from servitude to other lands and from the costs sustained by them in the past – wars were not cheap, and the Commons had been reluctant to pay for the war until Edward's success. Peace was agreed with the Scots, and imports of Gascon wine began to recover from the blow they had been dealt by the war. But the underlying issues of the Anglo-French and Anglo-Scottish conflicts persisted; hopes of a permanent end to the war proved illusory.

THE LATER STAGES OF THE WAR

The uneasy peace that followed the treaty of Brétigny was shattered when Charles V reclaimed sovereignty over the English king's continental possessions in 1369. The gains that Edward III had made were lost with great rapidity, so that the English found themselves in much the same position as they had been in 1337, save for their bridgehead at Calais. Several campaigns were waged between 1369 and 1389, mostly *chevauchées* (mounted long-distance raids) through French territory. There was much action at sea, where the English now found themselves at a disadvantage, for the French had built up a naval base at Rouen as well as drawing on the fleet of their Castilian allies. English coasts were thus vulnerable. In 1377 the French laid siege to Carisbroke Castle and left the Isle of Wight only after a substantial ransom had been levied. Further invasion scares followed in 1385 and 1386, with fears of Franco-Scottish coordination. The Commons and the population at large grew increasingly reluctant to pay high war taxes – a factor in the Peasants' Revolt of 1381.

The issues remained insoluble, and were further complicated by the Papal Schism (1378–1418), when the French and English supported opposing popes. Yet the French were never strong enough to drive the English from France completely. The growing insanity of their king, Charles VI, led to a long truce with Richard II in 1396, intended to last until 1426. After Richard's deposition by his Lancastrian cousin Henry IV, in 1399, hostilities reopened. The French sent aid to Owain Glyndwr's Welsh revolt and began to threaten Calais and Gascony and to harry English shipping. But the tide began to turn in favour of the English when civil war in France escalated between the Burgundian and Armagnac (or Orleanist) factions for control of the ever-madder Charles VI. Henry V was prompted to launch a major invasion in 1415, when he succeeded in taking Harfleur. Despite being severely outnumbered and weakened on the march homewards via Calais, the English won an emphatic victory at Agincourt. Henry followed up his brilliant generalship with a second campaign (1417–19) devoted to a systematic conquest of Normandy by sieges, the first time in the Hundred Years War that the English had attempted this strategy on a major scale. After the fall of Rouen in January 1419, the duchy was effectively in Henry's hands and he began to march towards Paris.

THE FINAL YEARS

Instead of uniting in the face of English success, the French grew more divided. On 10 September 1419 the duke of Burgundy was assassinated by the supporters of the Dauphin Charles, who now led the Armagnac group. In the panic that followed, the new duke of Burgundy, Philip, allied with the English. Henry V thus had to be accepted by Charles VI as heir and regent of France by the treaty of Troyes in May 1420. It looked as though the English had at last won. Although Henry's early demise in 1422 was a major blow as his heir was only nine months old, the English were able, under the sound command of the duke of Bedford and earl of Salisbury, to extend their control almost to the Loire. With a Burgundian ally in support on the eastern and northern frontiers (the dukes of Burgundy having acquired Flanders in the 1380s), an ally in the duke of

Brittany, and continuing tenure of Gascony, the extent of English domination in France had never been greater. The Scottish threat had also been minimised by the capture of the future James I in 1406 and by English victories at Cravant (1423) and Verneuil (1424) against Franco-Scottish armies. English soldiers and administrators were given lands in Normandy; merchants enjoyed renewed trade opportunities with Flanders and northern France as well as Gascony; the English people were free from raids and were able to rejoice in their pre-eminence over their ancient enemies, onto whom the burden of war taxation now fell.

This favourable position was to be short-lived. Plans to expand south of the Loire foundered when the French, inspired by the religious visionary Joan of Arc, raised the siege of Orléans. Henry VI was crowned king of France at Paris on 16 December 1431 – the only king of England to realise the claim put forward almost a century earlier – but it was too late. The Dauphin had himself been crowned at Reims in July 1429. The Burgundians defected in 1435, and soon afterwards Paris, Harfleur and much of Upper Normandy fell to the French. Although Harfleur was recovered

in 1440, the English could do no more than maintain an increasingly expensive defensive position. Henry VI showed no inclination to play a part in the war. In 1444 a truce was agreed, accompanied by the king's marriage to Margaret of Anjou. Defences in Normandy were scaled down to save money, leaving them as easy pickings for Charles when he invaded with Breton help in 1449. What was left of English Normandy fell within a year, Gascony following suit in 1451. A rebellion against the French in Bordeaux encouraged the English to send an army under the veteran John, Lord Talbot, but both he and the English war effort met their end at Castillon on 17 July 1453. Only Calais remained an English toe-hold in France, and English coasts were once more vulnerable. England fell into civil war, while the French monarchs, able now to tap all of their kingdom's resources, grew stronger. English kings clung to their French royal title until 1801, but it was meaningless without lands in France.   **AC**

Legend:
- English controlled lands, 1429
- Burgundian territories, 1429
- French controlled lands, 1429
- Area of shifting allegiance
- Henry V's campaign, 1415
- Joan of Arc's campaign, 1429
- Boundary of kingdom of France, 1429

Battles
- ⊗ English victory
- ⊗ French victory
- 🏰 Siege

The Hundred Years War, 1399–1453

The truce agreed in 1396 lasted only three years, but there was little fighting until Henry V invaded Normandy in 1415. Henry's victory at Agincourt turned the war dramatically in England's favour and an alliance with Burgundy in 1419 further strengthened the English position. Henry was accepted as heir to the French throne in 1420, but his early death, the revival of French resistance by Joan of Arc, and the end of the Burgundian alliance led to the complete collapse of the English position by 1453.

THE MEDIEVAL ECONOMY

Sheep in a fold

Medieval Britain and Ireland supported well over 13 million sheep. As well as producing wool for the export trade, they also manured the arable and supplied milk for making cheese, as shown here.

In the twelfth and thirteenth centuries the economies of England, Wales, Scotland and Ireland were much less advanced than those of Flanders and Italy, the leading European economies of the day. All four were predominantly agrarian. Primary raw materials – wool in great quantity but also hides, grain, tin, lead and coal – dominated exports, while manufactured goods, wine and luxury commodities obtained through long-distance trade were the principal imports. England had once supported a thriving urban cloth industry but by the end of the thirteenth century this was in decline as rising costs drove English cloth out of export markets. Not only was little value added to exported goods but the bulk of overseas trade was carried in foreign-owned ships for foreign merchants.

No British or Irish port handled more overseas trade than London – over a third of all English trade by 1300. Its international trading links were wider than those of any other port. Here, for example, the leading Baltic and Italian merchant companies had their British headquarters. In the early fourteenth century the German Hanse trading league established their 'Steelyard' just upstream of London Bridge and it was in the heart of the city, in Cheap and Langbourn, that the wealthiest of the Italian super-companies – the Cerchi Bianchi, Peruzzi, Spini, Bardi and Chiarenti – were located. The financial and mercantile interests of many of these companies embraced England, Wales, Scotland and Ireland. Already the British Isles were integrated into an international commercial economy, even though the core of that economy remained located in the Mediterranean.

If the British Isles were peripheral to the European commercial economy, within the British Isles that peripherality increased towards the north and west, as distance heightened the risks and costs of long-distance commerce. A marked economic gradient existed from southeast to northwest, with the most developed parts of eastern England and Scotland sharing more in common with those parts of the Continent with which they were commercially connected than with Wales, Ireland and Highland Scotland. In this period the latter derived next to no economic advantage from their Atlantic-edge location. Rather, it was the Channel and especially the North Sea that offered the greatest commercial opportunities. Far more trade flowed east than west, so the leading towns, ports and international fairs were largely concentrated down the eastern side of Britain. Here, too, levels of taxable wealth as recorded by the Pope Nicholas IV taxation of 1291–2 and lay subsidy of 1334 attained their maximum.

MARKETS AND TRADE

Commercial penetration of the English, Scottish and, to a lesser extent, Welsh and Irish economies was facilitated by a dense, if uneven, network of chartered trading places – markets, fairs and boroughs – where trade took place at designated times and often on privileged terms. Kings and lords were largely responsible for the creation of this infrastructure. Their aim was to stimulate and profit from trade. Almost everything had a price and a resale value. Although many people lived at little better than a subsistence level, most satisfied at least some of their needs by participating in the market economy. Peasants went to market to sell their surpluses, obtain cash, and purchase seed corn, replacement livestock and essential household goods from the range of textiles, pottery and ironware produced by specialised workers. Those with surplus labour hired it out. Wives and widows brewed and sold ale for profit. Others purveyed pies, pastries and puddings. Lords and their agents bought and sold on an even grander scale, and managed their wide estates to yield both provisions and cash. Commercial confidence was boosted by a sustained but moderate rate of inflation and the increasingly ample supply of sound silver coinage maintained by the English and Scottish kings. In both England and Scotland the money supply grew faster than the population during the thirteenth century and in the same century a monetised economy was introduced to the English Lordship of Ireland. By the 1280s the estimated money supplies of Ireland, Scotland and England were £60,000, £130,000–£180,000 and £674,000 respectively, equivalent to perhaps a shilling a head in Ireland, three shillings a head in England, and possibly as much as four shillings a head in Scotland.

Economy, population and wealth in medieval Britain and Ireland

Economic activity in the British Isles in the medieval period was overwhelmingly dominated by agriculture. Mineral extraction was important but very small-scale, while manufacturing was almost entirely on a local, craft-based level. The influence of trading links with Europe drew trade – and prosperity – towards the Southeast, where busy ports handled bulk goods shipped from the interior by river. International trade fairs and urban centres of the cloth trade were also concentrated in the Southeast, as were the main population centres.

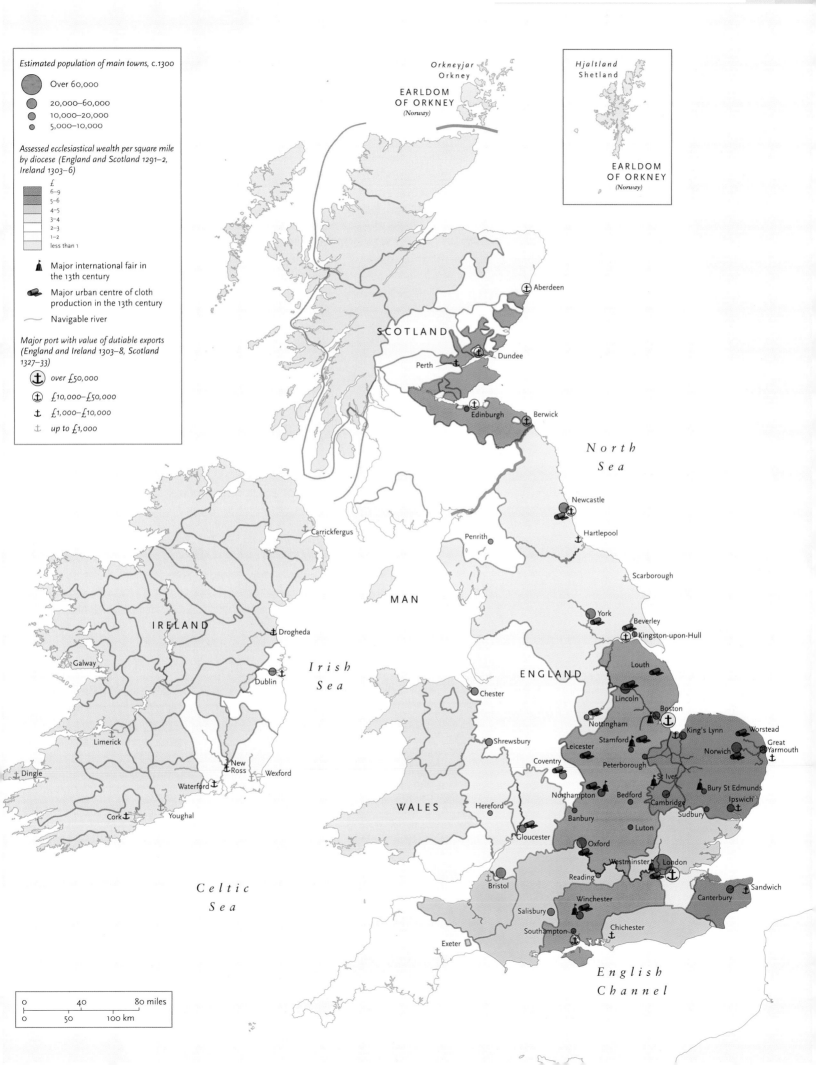

Estimated population of main towns, c.1300

- Over 60,000
- 20,000–60,000
- 10,000–20,000
- 5,000–10,000

Assessed ecclesiastical wealth per square mile by diocese (England and Scotland 1291–2, Ireland 1303–6)

£
- 6–9
- 5–6
- 4–5
- 3–4
- 2–3
- 1–2
- less than 1

Major international fair in the 13th century

Major urban centre of cloth production in the 13th century

Navigable river

Major port with value of dutiable exports (England and Ireland 1303–8, Scotland 1327–33)

- over £50,000
- £10,000–£50,000
- £1,000–£10,000
- up to £1,000

Orkneyjar Orkney

EARLDOM OF ORKNEY (Norway)

Hjaltland Shetland

EARLDOM OF ORKNEY (Norway)

Aberdeen

SCOTLAND

Dundee

Perth

Edinburgh

Berwick

North Sea

Newcastle

Carrickfergus

Penrith

Hartlepool

Scarborough

MAN

York

Beverley

Kingston-upon-Hull

IRELAND

Drogheda

Galway

Dublin

Irish Sea

Chester

ENGLAND

Louth

Lincoln

Boston

Nottingham

King's Lynn

Worstead

Shrewsbury

Stamford

Norwich

Great Yarmouth

Leicester

Limerick

New Ross

Wexford

Coventry

Peterborough

St Ives

Bury St Edmunds

Ipswich

WALES

Hereford

Northampton

Bedford

Cambridge

Sudbury

Dingle

Waterford

Banbury

Luton

Cork

Youghal

Gloucester

Oxford

Westminster

London

Bristol

Reading

Sandwich

Celtic Sea

Winchester

Canterbury

Salisbury

Southampton

Chichester

Exeter

English Channel

0   40   80 miles

0   50   100 km

Expanding trade and commerce presupposed that people and goods were mobile. Monarchs and magnates with their retinues and households; merchants, mongers and hucksters with their wares; armies; prelates, priests and pilgrims; packmen, carters and drovers on land and boatmen and sailors on river and sea were all actively on the move in the twelfth and thirteenth centuries. Even bonded villeins regularly took to the road to transport their lords' produce to market or estate headquarters. Progressively, the horse was replacing the slower ox for haulage. The roads, many inherited from the Romans, were in better shape than in centuries to come when traffic would be heavier. Most major rivers were bridged or provided with ferries; tolls helped repay the investment.

Information and instructions travelled fast. Bulk goods travelled more slowly and did so most cheaply by water. Major navigable rivers, especially those flowing east, were busy. Boats of varying capacities were readily available for hire, as were warehouses and granaries in the principal riverine and coastal ports. This trade interconnected with an equally busy seaborne commerce, nowhere more so than in London, the greatest entrepôt in the land. With a population of approximately 75,000 in 1300, it was also the single largest concentration of demand. Via the Thames

London was able to tap a wide hinterland. Queenhithe, just upsteam of London Bridge, was the principal wharf for bulk goods moving downstream, just as Billingsgate was for provisions brought upstream. Henley in Oxfordshire and Faversham in Kent were the main grain entrepôts for London cornmongers upstream and downstream of the city. Marlow was much frequented by London woodmongers, while hay to support the capital's huge population of draught animals was delivered down the river Lea from commercial meadows that bordered it. Livestock, on the other hand, could be walked to market. On occasion beef cattle for the king's table at Westminster were obtained from as far afield as Lancashire. London woolmongers also ranged widely for their supplies; by the early fourteenth century wool from the Welsh border – the finest in England – was being delivered to London for shipment overseas.

Throughout this period ships increased in number and in capacity as overseas commerce grew in importance. Ship design also advanced, resulting in the gradual development of the cog, which became the characteristic merchant vessel of the age. Cogs were eminently seaworthy, could carry large cargoes at low cost, and with their fore and stern castles could be effectively defended against pirates. Moreover, by 1300 the compass – first mentioned about 1180 – had

The London region

London's domination of Britain's trade in the Middle Ages meant that its economic influence spread far across the southeast of England. Its position on the Thames made it the natural centre for bulk exports across the North Sea to Europe, while large parts of the surrounding countryside profited from supplying the city with grain, meat and wood. The region as a whole had a high density of markets in towns and chartered boroughs. In the Southeast, as in Britain as a whole, concentrations of taxable wealth tended to occur in areas where navigable rivers allowed extensive trading activity to flourish.

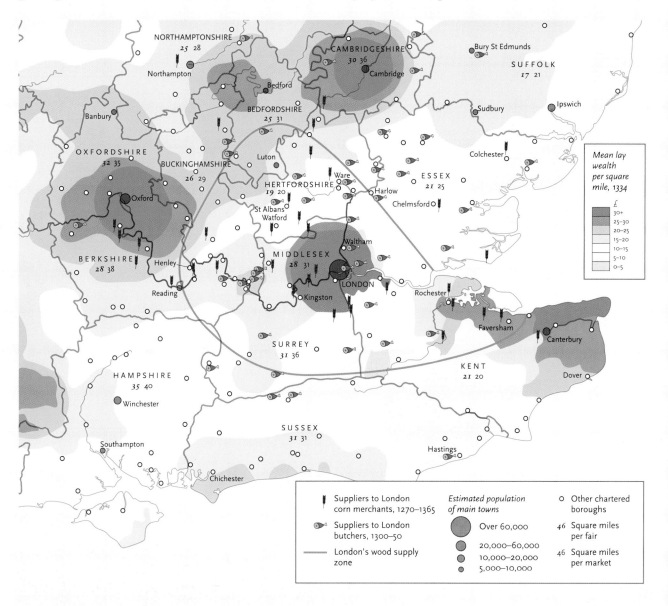

become sufficiently improved to become a key navigational aid to sailors. Flanders, the northern terminus of the great overland trade route to Italy and the Mediterranean, was the focus of most English, Scottish and Irish sea-borne trade and its great cloth-working towns the destination for the bulk of the wool that dominated exports. Possibly 1 million sheep in Ireland were producing wool for export, 2 million in Scotland, and 8–10 million in England at the opening of the fourteenth century when the wool trade was at its peak. Additional numbers of sheep were, of course, producing an unknown quantity of wool for domestic consumption. Although the largest flocks were maintained by lords and monasteries, the vast majority of sheep were managed by lesser producers using the 'sheep-corn' system in which stock manured the arable fields by night.

AGRICULTURE AND WEALTH

Agriculture was the single largest sector of the economy whether measured in terms of the value of its output, its contribution to exports, or the amount of employment that it generated. Moreover, although pastoral products in the form of wool and hides dominated exports, arable products probably accounted for two-thirds to three-quarters of all agricultural production by value. Grain production and processing provided more employment than any other single activity. This was because grain – for bread, pottage and ale – dominated diets. By the close of the thirteenth century at least three-quarters of the population lived and worked on the land and landed wealth was the foundation of social status and political power. By this date primary production of crops, animals, wood and minerals probably accounted for at least two-thirds of the combined gross domestic product of Britain and Ireland. The remainder was contributed by the value added to these commodities by processing them, transforming them into manufactures, trading them, and supplying a range of services to those who produced them. It was these activities that gave employment to the 10 to 20 per cent of the population who lived in towns.

By 1300, on the threshold of a half century of war, famine and human and animal disease, the British Isles supported a population of perhaps 7 to 8 million, of whom 4 to 5 million lived in England. Assessments of ecclesiastical income – from glebe (priest's) lands, tithes, donations and land property – made for the Pope Nicholas Taxation of 1291–2 for Britain and 1303–6 for Ireland indicate that per square mile Wales was twice as wealthy as Ireland, Scotland was 50 per cent more wealthy than Wales, and England was three times wealthier than Scotland. The poorest dioceses in the Highlands and islands of Scotland and western Ulster and Connacht in Ireland were assessed at less than 4 shillings per square mile, in contrast to the

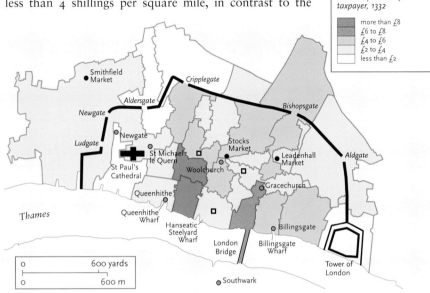

Main cornmarket
Other foodmarket
Ward where major foreign companies were based

Mean lay wealth per taxpayer, 1332

more than £8
£6 to £8
£4 to £6
£2 to £4
less than £2

richest – Norwich, Ely and Canterbury in England – which were assessed at well over £6 per square mile. The lay subsidy of 1334 – a tax on lay movable goods – confirms the superior taxable wealth of Norfolk and the east Midlands of England and highlights those areas in Cambridgeshire, Bedfordshire, Oxfordshire and Kent where the tax yield was exceptionally high. Nevertheless, nowhere could match the wealth of London. Here were both the greatest concentration of taxpayers and the greatest concentration of wealthy taxpayers in the land. This was the magnet that drew both native and foreign traders to the city. During the thirteenth century London had probably grown faster than either the population or the economy. It is thus the principal monument of this commercialising age.   **BMSC**

London's wealth

Medieval London was by far the greatest trading port in Britain and Ireland. Its richest wards were Cordwainer and Vintry, while the German and Italian merchant companies were based around the Steelyard and in Cheap and Langbourn wards in the heart of the city.

Medieval barn

A surviving medieval great barn at Cressing Temple, Essex. The size of the barn and sophistication of its construction give some idea of the importance of agriculture in the medieval economy.

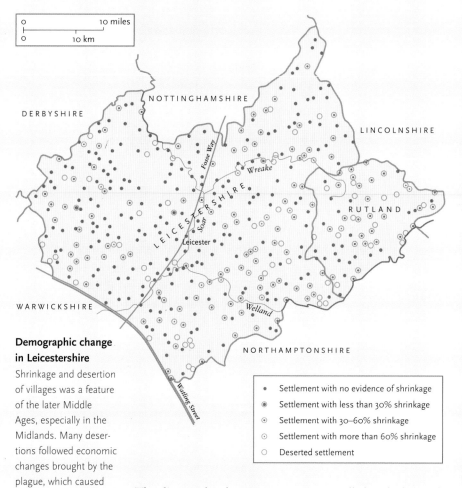

Demographic change in Leicestershire

Shrinkage and desertion of villages was a feature of the later Middle Ages, especially in the Midlands. Many desertions followed economic changes brought by the plague, which caused landlords to restructure estates.

Scale: 0 — 10 miles / 0 — 10 km

Legend:
- Settlement with no evidence of shrinkage
- Settlement with less than 30% shrinkage
- Settlement with 30–60% shrinkage
- Settlement with more than 60% shrinkage
- Deserted settlement

Plague graffito

A graffito in Ashwell church, Hertfordshire, records an outbreak of plague in apocalyptic terms: '1350, pitiful, savage and violent, the dregs of people remaining at last become witness to a tempest'.

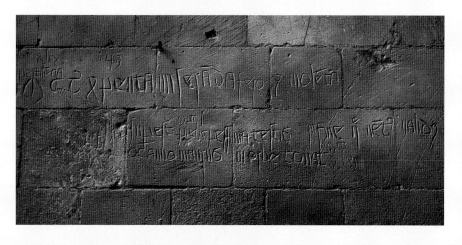

The disease that later writers were to call the Black Death spread from Central Asia along trade routes in the mid-fourteenth century, reaching Italy in 1347. From the Mediterranean it spread throughout Europe and the Middle East, arriving on the south coast of England in the summer of 1348, and probably just a few weeks later on the east coast of Ireland. Its spread, though inexorable, was erratic. The southwest of Britain seems not to have been affected until the following year, for instance, and although the plague was reported in London by September 1348, Kent escaped until the following spring. By Christmas 1349 the plague was thought to be over in England and Wales, and the archbishop of Canterbury commanded survivors to offer prayers of thanksgiving; Scotland was spared until the following year.

Most modern commentators agree that the disease was bubonic plague and its variant, pneumonic plague, caused by the bacillus *Yersinia pestis* and initially transmitted from its usual rodent hosts into the human population by the bites of fleas. It is clear from medieval accounts, however, that the disease did not behave exactly like its nineteenth- and twentieth-century counterpart. It was far more virulent, and spread much more readily through the human population than it does today. In the 18 months or so that the plague was active in England, just under half the population died. The figures become even more striking when it is remembered that in any given town or region, the plague usually lasted only two or three months, and that a mortality rate as high as 60 per cent or even 70 per cent was reached in some places in a matter of weeks.

This was a human tragedy of unimaginable proportions. Fear of the plague cut across almost all normal human behaviour. The sick were left to die like animals; the survivors could barely keep pace with the need to bury the dead, and resorted to mass burials. The social and economic dislocation was dramatic. The sheer number of deaths caused an enormous shortage of labour, creating an inflationary spiral of wages. Landlords had to offer improved terms to find tenants for vacant holdings. The English government resorted to legislation in an effort to peg wages and prices at their pre-plague levels. The first attempt, the Ordinance of Labourers in 1349, was by all accounts a failure, but the revised Statute of Labourers two years later was strongly enforced and does seem to have pulled cash wages back to their former level – although employers desperate for labour may well have offered hidden extras like food to be sure of keeping their workers.

THE AFTERMATH OF THE PLAGUE

By the early 1350s, empty land had been largely re-tenanted, and wages, at least on the face of it, were under control. One of the most intriguing questions raised by the plague is whether, if the outbreak of 1348–50 had been the only outbreak, it would have come to seem a mere blip, with rapid demographic recovery restoring the earlier balance of economic power. Some contemporary writers suggest that the plague was followed by a baby boom, but others contradict them, claiming that women found it harder to conceive and that miscarriages were frequent. The question is impossible to answer, because the plague returned. There was another major outbreak in 1361, and again in 1369, and further outbreaks more or less every decade thereafter. These were generally less severe than the first plague, which had hit a population with no natural immunity – although Scotland, which seems to have escaped more lightly than England in 1350, may have suffered much more badly in the 1360s. But these later outbreaks tended to kill children – particularly, perhaps, male children. The result was to hold back the population from recovery, and it is not until the second half of the fifteenth century that it is possible to glimpse signs of an upward turn in the population.

After the plague, the population of England probably bottomed out at about 2.5 million, compared with over 4.5 million before the plague. The results of this long-term demographic slump were profound and, for contemporary commentators, deeply depressing. Put simply, the economic balance of power had tilted in favour of employees and tenants against employers and landlords. With wages moving steadily upwards, workers found themselves with more spending power and, if they chose, more leisure time. To late-medieval moralists, this was evidence of a world upside down, and of greedy and lazy workers. The post-plague world saw a new hostility to the able-bodied poor – the 'sturdy beggars' who were to be the bogeymen of subsequent centuries.

Modern commentators tend to see things differently and more positively. The late Middle Ages are often characterised as an 'age of ambition', with individuals enjoying more autonomy. Tenurial unfreedom eroded, and standards of living tended to rise. But there was a darker side. In the imagery surrounding Western Christians, death was increasingly personified as an attacking corpse, striking down individuals in the midst of life. The plague may have brought good things for the survivors, but the cost had been fearsome.   **RH**

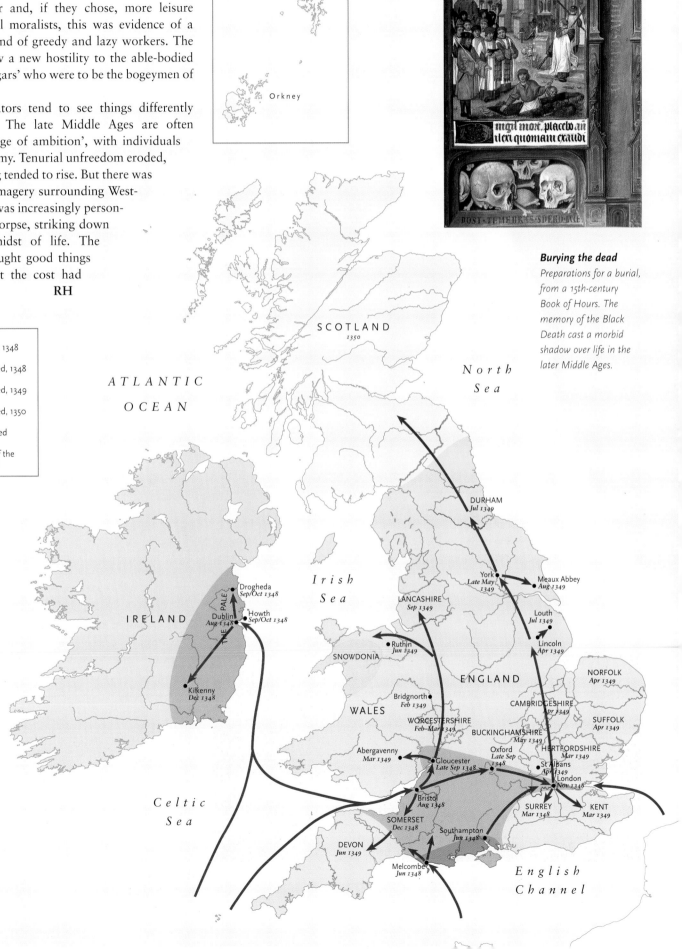

Burying the dead
Preparations for a burial, from a 15th-century Book of Hours. The memory of the Black Death cast a morbid shadow over life in the later Middle Ages.

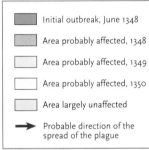

	Initial outbreak, June 1348
	Area probably affected, 1348
	Area probably affected, 1349
	Area probably affected, 1350
	Area largely unaffected
→	Probable direction of the spread of the plague

The spread of the Black Death, 1348–50

The Black Death reached ports on the south coast of England from the Continent in June 1348. Other early outbreaks of the plague were in ports – Dublin and Bristol in August and London in the autumn. The progress of the plague was unpredictable and some areas, such as the Gaelic areas of Ireland, escaped relatively unaffected.

The Peasants' Revolt

Wat Tyler, the leader of the Peasants' Revolt in 1381, is killed by the Lord Mayor of London while the young king, Richard II, parleys with the rebels. With the death of its leader, the revolt collapsed.

The Lordship of the Isles

Weak royal authority in the Highlands permitted the growth of the powerful Gaelic Lordship of the Isles in the 14th century. It began when Angus Og MacDonald became lord of Islay in 1307. His son, John of Islay, greatly expanded his inheritance and in 1354 adopted the title 'Lord of the Isles'. The lordship was most extensive when Alexander, the third lord, inherited the earldom of Ross in 1424. The lords overstretched themselves in the 15th century by allying with the English; in 1493 James II of Scotland abolished the lordship.

Traditionally, the period after the Black Death was seen as the death throes of the Middle Ages – a time of instability and conflict. This view has largely been abandoned, with scholars now stressing that the period's various political and social upheavals were not cataclysmic.

The year 1381 saw a major rising in southeast England, usually called 'The Peasants' Revolt', although this does not do justice to the social range of the rebels, and in particular to the significant urban involvement. The rising was triggered in Essex by government attempts to collect underpayment of the third poll tax, a new form of national taxation introduced in 1377. But underlying it was widespread frustration at the attempts of landlords and employers to block the potential economic benefits to tenants and workers of the demographic collapse caused by recurrent outbreaks of plague, and the rising spread rapidly through the Home Counties. Accompanied by the murder of leading officials of Church and State, it terrified the elite, but the rebels dispersed when ordered to do so by the young King Richard II, and none of their demands was met. But the fall in population meant that change came anyway, bringing the erosion of serfdom, and higher wages and more autonomy for workers.

Some contemporaries, without much evidence, linked the rising with the growth of religious dissent in England. That dissent, which came to be known as Lollardy, had roots in popular criticism of the wealth of the Church and in the experience of more personal forms of piety, but gained a higher profile through the writings of the Oxford don John Wyclif. As long as Wyclif's views were purely a matter of academic debate within the university, they gen-

erated little concern, but once they began to spread through preaching and writing in English, the Church became alarmed and moved to suppress what it regarded as heresy. The dividing line between this and the more intense forms of private spirituality which, while theologically orthodox, could at times be critical or dismissive of the institutional Church was, however, blurred and the term 'Lollard' covered a wide spectrum of opinion. The insistence of leading clergy that religious dissent meant social and political subversion, apparently confirmed by the Lollard rising of 1414, helped to marginalise the movement, and it never spread much beyond England's Southeast and Midlands.

POLITICAL CONFLICT

In both England and Scotland, the fifteenth century brought political conflict, although recent historians have modified the traditional picture of societies torn by uncontrolled violence. In Scotland the problem was that after the death of Robert III in 1406, no king was succeeded by an adult heir, and the resulting minority governments were marked by factional power struggles. In England the situation was rather different. There was one long minority, that of Henry VI, but it passed relatively smoothly. The problem was rather a new element of dynastic uncertainty, introduced with the deposition of the capricious Richard II by his cousin Henry of Lancaster in 1399. Richard had no children, and although Henry was his male heir, there was another possible claimant to the throne,

▨	Lands of Angus Og, 1307
☐	Granted to Angus Og by Robert I, 1314
▨	Added by John of Islay, first Lord of the Isles, 1346–76
▨	Added by John II, 1424
—	Maximum extent of the Lordship of the Isles, 1424
▪	Castles of the lordship
▪	Other castles

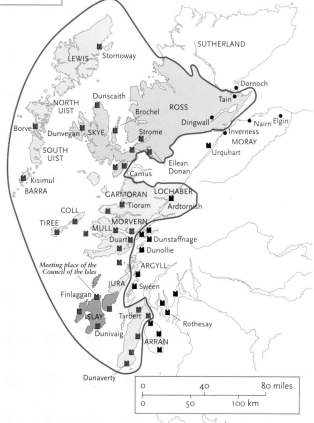

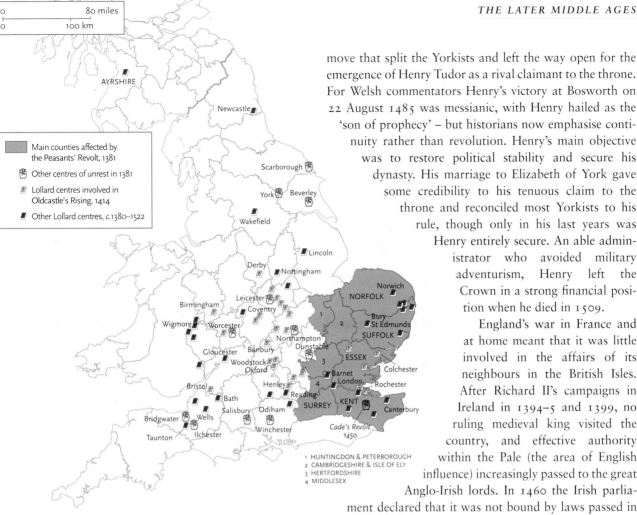

Main counties affected by the Peasants' Revolt, 1381

Other centres of unrest in 1381

Lollard centres involved in Oldcastle's Rising, 1414

Other Lollard centres, c.1380–1522

1 HUNTINGDON & PETERBOROUGH
2 CAMBRIDGESHIRE & ISLE OF ELY
3 HERTFORDSHIRE
4 MIDDLESEX

move that split the Yorkists and left the way open for the emergence of Henry Tudor as a rival claimant to the throne. For Welsh commentators Henry's victory at Bosworth on 22 August 1485 was messianic, with Henry hailed as the 'son of prophecy' – but historians now emphasise continuity rather than revolution. Henry's main objective was to restore political stability and secure his dynasty. His marriage to Elizabeth of York gave some credibility to his tenuous claim to the throne and reconciled most Yorkists to his rule, though only in his last years was Henry entirely secure. An able administrator who avoided military adventurism, Henry left the Crown in a strong financial position when he died in 1509.

England's war in France and at home meant that it was little involved in the affairs of its neighbours in the British Isles. After Richard II's campaigns in Ireland in 1394–5 and 1399, no ruling medieval king visited the country, and effective authority within the Pale (the area of English influence) increasingly passed to the great Anglo-Irish lords. In 1460 the Irish parliament declared that it was not bound by laws passed in the English parliament unless it passed them too, and it was only in 1494 that the primacy of the English parliament was reasserted. In the greater part of the country, Gaelic lords ruled in complete independence. Relations with Scotland were also relatively quiet until Edward IV's last years. Scottish kings were more expansionist. James III's marriage brought Orkney and Shetland to the Scottish crown, and kings throughout the period sought to draw the Highlands more firmly into the orbit of royal authority, in 1493 finally destroying the semi-independent Gaelic Lordship of the Isles, which had dominated the Hebrides for over a century.

Popular unrest

Attempts by government and landlords to prevent others from benefiting from the changed economic situation after the Black Death caused popular discontent in England. The imposition of a poll tax led to the outbreak of the Peasants' Revolt of 1381. The revolt was concentrated in the most market-orientated farming counties in the Southeast. Criticism of the Church was voiced by the Lollards, but the movement had little impact, especially after it was associated with a rising in 1414.

in the shape of Edmund Mortimer, whose nephew and heir Richard, duke of York, was to challenge Henry VI in the 1450s. Meanwhile, the new king, Henry IV, faced significant unrest, in both England and Wales, the latter in the form of the rising of Owain Glyndwr, who sought to re-establish an independent Principality of Wales. But he weathered the opposition to die in his bed, and the military victories of his son Henry V, most famously at Agincourt, seemed to complete the securing of the dynasty.

THE DYNASTIC STRUGGLE

In 1420 Henry V was recognised as heir to the throne of France, which committed his successor to the impossible task of making English control a reality throughout France. The war dominated the following 30 years, and emphasised the incompetence of the third Lancastrian, Henry VI. His disastrous reign reopened the dynastic issue. His chief critic, his cousin Richard, duke of York, found himself increasingly isolated politically, particularly after his name had been linked with Jack Cade's rising of 1450, directed against the circle of advisers around the king. As England collapsed into civil war, York reclaimed the moral high ground by asserting that he was the rightful heir to the throne; a claim made good when York's son, Edward, defeated the Lancastrians at Towton in March 1461 to become Edward IV. Although the new king proved a success, his dynasty did not long survive his death in 1483. Its collapse was triggered by the deposition of Edward's son, Edward V, by his uncle Richard, duke of Gloucester – a

THE NORTH IN THE WARS OF THE ROSES

The north of England has often been seen as beyond the full control of the medieval kings of England. This was not just a matter of its distance from Westminster. It was also a border zone – by the late Middle Ages, England's only land boundary with another realm. The noblemen who held the office of warden of the Scottish march were, uniquely, expected to maintain their own armies (at Crown expense) for the protection of the region against Scottish incursions. The region thus seemed to conform to the stereotypical view of the Middle Ages as a world of over-mighty subjects, wielding quasi-regal power in their own regions. The great families of the region, the Nevilles and the Percys, became a byword for aristocratic power.

In truth, royal authority did reach to the North, although two counties, Durham and Lancashire, were palatinates, where the bishop of Durham and the duke of Lancaster wielded the administrative authority that would elsewhere

belong to the king. But as royal authority weakened in the 1450s, tensions and rivalries in the region began to flare into violence, which, as the families concerned looked for more powerful backing, inevitably came to parallel the developing dynastic struggle between the houses of York and Lancaster. Both dynasties had their territorial roots in the North. The ruling House of Lancaster, headed by the inept Henry VI, were lords not only of Lancashire itself, but of extensive lands east of the Pennines and large parts of the north Midlands. The northern lands of the duchy of York were less extensive, concentrated in south Yorkshire.

Of the great northern families, the Percys (made earls of Northumberland by Richard II in 1377) and the Cliffords emerged as committed supporters of Lancaster, both losing family members in the king's service at St Albans in 1455. The first 'battle' of the Wars of the Roses, St Albans was in fact little more than a skirmish in which the Yorkists picked off their opponents, and it generated something close to a blood feud between the families concerned. The other great northern family, the Nevilles, were internally divided. Ralph Neville of Raby, first earl of Westmorland, had married twice. His son by his first wife inherited the earldom, but much of the family land went to Richard Neville, earl of Salisbury, the eldest son of the second marriage. It was this junior line that was to provide much of the political support for Richard, duke of York in the late 1450s. Salisbury died with York at the battle of Wakefield in 1460, but his son, Richard Neville, earl of Warwick, 'the Kingmaker', became the chief political ally of York's heir, the new King Edward IV.

The death of Northumberland at Towton, and the confiscation of his land, left the junior Nevilles unrivalled in the North. Warwick's younger brothers, John and George, became, respectively, earl of Northumberland and archbishop of York. But, by the late 1460s, relations between Edward and Warwick were cool-

ing, and in 1470 the earl brought about the restoration of Henry VI. This lasted only a few months, and the defeat and death of Warwick and his brother John in 1471 at the hands of the victorious Edward IV prompted a rethinking of power in the North. Edward had already restored Henry Percy to his family's earldom, but he was to be eclipsed in the 1470s by Edward's brother Richard, duke of Gloucester. The duke was granted Warwick's northern lands (later augmented) and also held major office within the duchy of Lancaster in the North. Other northern figures, including the Percys and the senior Neville line, were drawn into his orbit, with only the Stanleys in the Northwest remaining beyond his influence. In the early 1480s Gloucester's power base became the springboard for English attacks on Scotland, which captured Berwick for the English crown but were also designed to benefit Gloucester himself, with the duke promised hereditary possession of any Scottish land he was able to conquer in the West March.

When in 1483 Gloucester took the throne as Richard III, some southern critics saw it as the triumph of the North,

with the new king's allies lavishly rewarded with confiscated land in the South. But Richard's accession also drew the North more fully under direct royal control, since he allowed no northern nobleman to take over the role he had himself enjoyed under Edward IV – a decision that may well have alienated the earl of Northumberland, who saw himself as the natural candidate for such a role. The earl contributed to Richard's defeat at Bosworth by withholding his support, and it was another northern family, the Stanleys, resentful of Richard's interference in the Northwest, who delivered the coup de grâce by throwing in their troops against the king. If the North had helped Richard to the throne, it also helped him to lose it 26 months later. **RH**

Battlefield execution

Execution of the Lancastrian duke of Somerset by King Edward IV after the battle of Tewkesbury in 1471. Rough justice was handed out by both sides to prominent opponents during the Wars of the Roses.

The battle of Barnet

Edward IV's victory over Warwick 'the Kingmaker' at Barnet in 1471 restored him to the throne after a short exile. After this battle, and the subsequent defeat of the Lancastrians at Tewkesbury, Edward faced little serious opposition.

'...the world, I assure you, is right queasy, as you shall know within this month. The people here feareth it sore.'

John Paston II to his mother Margaret, April 1471

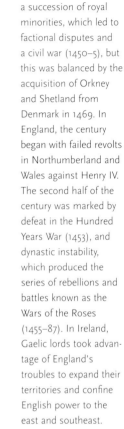

SHETLAND
to Scotland (from Denmark) 1469

Legend

Bolingbroke's usurpation, 1399
- ➡ Bolingbroke (Henry IV)
- ➡ Richard II

Political allegiances
- England
- Principality of Wales
- English Pale in Ireland, 1488
- Independent Irish and Anglo-Irish lordships
- Scotland
- Lordship of the Isles, 1424

Battles
- ⊗ Yorkist victory
- ⊗ Lancastrian victory
- ⊗ Tudor victory
- ⊗ Other battle
- ▣ Castle besieged by the Welsh during Owain Glyndwr's Revolt, 1400–8

Power centres of noble families
- ▪ Lancaster
- ▫ York
- ▪ Percy
- ▪ Neville
- ▪ MacDonald
- ▪ Butler
- ▪ Fitzgerald
- ▫ Douglas

O'BRIEN Independent Irish dynasty

➡ Henry Tudor's invasion, 1485

15th-century Britain and Ireland

Scotland and England both had their share of troubles in the 15th century. Scotland had a succession of royal minorities, which led to factional disputes and a civil war (1450–5), but this was balanced by the acquisition of Orkney and Shetland from Denmark in 1469. In England, the century began with failed revolts in Northumberland and Wales against Henry IV. The second half of the century was marked by defeat in the Hundred Years War (1453), and dynastic instability, which produced the series of rebellions and battles known as the Wars of the Roses (1455–87). In Ireland, Gaelic lords took advantage of England's troubles to expand their territories and confine English power to the east and southeast.

0   40   80 miles
0   50   100 km

MEDIEVAL NORWICH

Norwich Cathedral

A 14th-century roof boss from the cloisters of Norwich Cathedral. It depicts a 'green man', a popular folklore figure of obscure origins.

institutions, including the great royal castle (established about 1068), the cathedral with its attendant Benedictine Priory (1094), Carrow Priory (about 1146), four large friaries (from 1226), and the Great Hospital (1249). In the thirteenth century, there were over 60 parish churches, although by around 1500, a number of these had closed, leaving some 50 or so.

The walls of the city were constructed between 1297 and 1344 and encircled an area that extended on both sides of the river Wensum. In the wall, there were 12 gates and some 40 towers, with the river forming the defences to the east, where defences were also

By area, Norwich was the largest city of any settlement in medieval England, greater even than London in size. It was the dominant city of the east of England, one of the richest agricultural areas of the country.

By the late Middle Ages, Norwich had acquired all its major

Carrow Priory, a nunnery established in about 1146

The Music House, a 12th-century house owned by Isaac, a Jewish financier (died 1235)

St Julian, a parish church with a hermit's cell that was home to St Julian of Norwich (died c.1432)

Dragon Hall, a cloth merchant's warehouse, built 1422

An Augustinian friary, established in 1290

Bishop Bridge

Bishop Bridge over the river Wensum, the last survivor of Norwich's medieval bridges. The bridge was gated at the town end for security.

provided by the precinct wall of the Cathedral Close, a timber palisade and a free-standing artillery tower built in 1398–9 at the bend of the river. The defended area incorporated a considerable amount of open ground, such as the river meadows east of the cathedral. The sweep of the walls was an effective control for the city's trade, but would have been ineffective against any sustained attack. Their construction, however, enabled Norwich to promote its urban identity, an important consideration when almost all the land outside the walls was controlled by ecclesiastical institutions.

The river was crossed by five bridges, one of which, Bishop Bridge, was fortified. Water mills were built astride the river in 1410 as a corporate initiative, with other such initiatives being the provision of a Cloth Seld to regulate the sale of cloth (1384) and the building of a Guildhall (from 1407), both at the north end of the market place.

The cloth trade was the single most important industry in late medieval Norwich, although over 120 different crafts and trades are recorded in medieval documentation. Much cloth was manufactured in the surrounding countryside and then finished and marketed in Norwich. Dyers, bleachers, fullers and shearmen were concentrated in the riverside areas on the western side of the city, close to the Maddermarket (a subsidiary market for dyestuffs) and the tenting grounds (for drying the dyed cloth). A large cloth-merchant's warehouse, now known as Dragon Hall, was

30,000 people before the Black Death of 1349). Its location ensured that it could exploit the diverse and extensive agricultural area of East Anglia around it, itself one of the most densely populated rural areas of the medieval kingdom of England, providing a market for produce and a commercial outlet for goods to the East Coast and to northern Europe.   **BA**

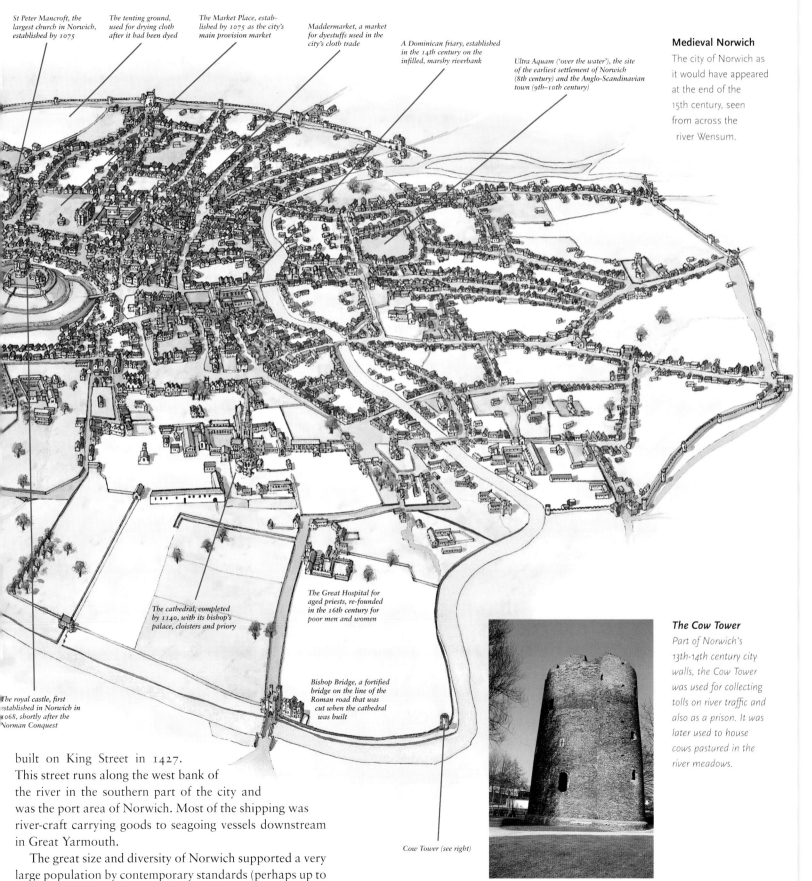

St Peter Mancroft, the largest church in Norwich, established by 1075

The tenting ground, used for drying cloth after it had been dyed

The Market Place, established by 1075 as the city's main provision market

Maddermarket, a market for dyestuffs used in the city's cloth trade

A Dominican friary, established in the 14th century on the infilled, marshy riverbank

Ultra Aquam ('over the water'), the site of the earliest settlement of Norwich (8th century) and the Anglo-Scandinavian town (9th–10th century)

Medieval Norwich

The city of Norwich as it would have appeared at the end of the 15th century, seen from across the river Wensum.

The cathedral, completed by 1140, with its bishop's palace, cloisters and priory

The Great Hospital for aged priests, re-founded in the 16th century for poor men and women

The royal castle, first established in Norwich in 1068, shortly after the Norman Conquest

Bishop Bridge, a fortified bridge on the line of the Roman road that was cut when the cathedral was built

Cow Tower (see right)

The Cow Tower

Part of Norwich's 13th-14th century city walls, the Cow Tower was used for collecting tolls on river traffic and also as a prison. It was later used to house cows pastured in the river meadows.

built on King Street in 1427. This street runs along the west bank of the river in the southern part of the city and was the port area of Norwich. Most of the shipping was river-craft carrying goods to seagoing vessels downstream in Great Yarmouth.

The great size and diversity of Norwich supported a very large population by contemporary standards (perhaps up to

PART THREE

EARLY MODERN BRITAIN & IRELAND

The reign of Henry VIII was to cast a longer shadow than any since that of William the Conqueror. It began a process that redefined the frontiers of the English monarchy; it launched the English Reformation, which transformed the religious and cultural experience of the peoples of Britain and Ireland; and it coincided with the beginning of a long period of economic and social change predicated on a steady growth in the population.

For many centuries the ambitions of the English monarchy had been focused on Europe rather than on the upland regions of Britain and Ireland: at Henry's accession, his authority, English law and the English language extended to less than half the land area of Britain and Ireland. The early modern period saw this situation transformed.

First, the ambition to build an Anglo-Norman state straddling the English Channel was abandoned. A decade after Henry's death Calais was lost and with it the dream of a trans-Channel empire. Dynastic roulette – compounded by the barrenness of Henry's children – led to the unification of English and Scottish crowns in 1603. Henry's schism from Rome and dynastic uncertainty created insecurities that made him assert his authority first in those parts of England that were only loosely under his control, then in Wales, and finally in Ireland. This policy was a success in all but the last, where heavy-handedness led to resentment, then to resistance, rebellion and a new Hundred Years War, ended only by Cromwell's ruthlessness and the brutality of others in the 1650s. By the time of the Hanoverian succession in 1715, the English language had become *the* language of a majority, and *a* language of the vast majority of those living in Britain and Ireland. Anglo-Norman law had everywhere displaced Celtic. There was a state system for the whole archipelago, if not a single state: a single parliament for Britain, but a subordinate one for Ireland; a single court and executive authority for Britain, but with a viceregal court and some devolution of authority to Dublin; yet a legal system in Scotland sealed off from the English, and a totally different religious system. And if, formally, the Church of Ireland had the same rights and privileges as the Church of England, in reality Irish 'Anglicans' represented barely 10 per cent of the population of Ireland (albeit the 10 per cent that owned nearly 90 per cent of the land), whereas Catholics constituted 80 per cent. It was an unstable mix. Indeed, the period 1689–1746 can reasonably be seen as the War of the Two Dynasties, as the House of Stuart sought to overturn throughout Britain and Ireland the usurpations of 1689 and 1715.

The Reformation brought about a not especially United Kingdom; and it dis-united the peoples of its constituent parts. But it everywhere changed the landscape. The greatest buildings of medieval England, apart from the royal castles, were abbeys and (many of them monastic) cathedrals. In the last 10 years of Henry VIII's reign, the abbeys and monasteries were torn down and their vast land holdings were transferred to the laity. The magnate class – which had rarely exceeded 70 families in number – was reinforced by a much larger group benefiting from economic opportunity and the growth of governance. They, and those farmers who exploited high prices and low wage costs as the population grew faster than food supply, invested in bricks and mortar. Now it was the gentry houses and the substantial farms that dominated the landscapes.

The new geopolitics helped to further the development of a more fully integrated national economy. Towns grew in size, if not – until the eighteenth century – in number, and it was towns on the coast or navigable rivers that expanded the most. Bristol, Norwich and Newcastle emerged as the biggest towns other than London by 1650. Yet London dominated England in a way matched by no other capital. Paris was three times as big as French regional capitals; London was 20 times the size of Bristol. It dominated politics, government, export and distributive trades in a unique way. And gradually, there emerged a single economic system for all of Britain and Ireland.

The special character of the English, Scottish, Welsh and Irish peoples was a crucial dimension of the state system that was not a state. But it allowed for integration at many levels: intermarriage among the elites, the full participation of all the Protestant peoples in the new expansion across the Atlantic, Indian and (eventually) Pacific oceans, and a greater cultural extroversion. The later parts of this section explore the economic, social and cultural consequences of the hardening of people by centuries of insecurity and redefinition – a mongrel people with a more porous social structure and a more developed sense of its destiny than could be found elsewhere. This was a society with a limited sense of egalitarianism but that was intellectually and culturally more open and libertarian than its rivals. It was on the brink of becoming not the great continental power of the Plantagenet imagination, but the great world power of Victorian reality.

JOHN MORRILL

The Spanish Armada
Logistical difficulties and severe weather did as much to defeat the Spanish Armada in 1588 as the English fireships launched at them off Gravelines, as shown here. To the English, however, victory was evidence that God favoured their cause.

The sixteenth century witnessed a remarkable series of changes backwards and forwards in the public faith and private devotion of the English, Welsh, Irish and Scots. During that time the British Isles ceased to be part of the Universal, or Catholic, Church that had dominated Western Europe for over a thousand years. This disintegration went hand in hand with a revived sense of nationalism and the reassertion of the ancient idea that subjects should unquestioningly accept and adopt the religious beliefs and practices currently preferred by their ruler. Not to do so effectively placed an individual outside Christian society and its fundamental personal safeguards, even if the whims of a ruler were contradictory and inconsistent, or if successive rulers subscribed to different beliefs. Failure to comply was the crime for which believers of very different persuasions died. These were as diverse as Bishop Fisher (beheaded 1535), the London Carthusians (hanged 1535), Archbishop Cranmer (burnt 1554) and Edmund Campion (hanged 1581). Conscience, upon which later generations have placed so much emphasis, counted for little, except for certain religious oddballs like Sir Thomas More (beheaded 1535). The majority, faced with fluctuations of royal mood and policy, believed what they were told. In return, the monarch did not pry into an individual's actual convictions unless these were politically threatening. Queen Elizabeth famously desisted from making 'windows into men's souls'. The Reformation and Counter-Reformation were government-driven, and their success, or failure, a yardstick of political success.

An aptitude for self-preservation should not be interpreted as evidence for lack of faith. The Church on the eve of the Reformation, notwithstanding the reservations of Erasmus and humanist theologians, was a vital and vigorous body which provided for the spiritual, physical and educative needs of society. The strength of the faith of the majority is demonstrated by the observation of ancient rituals as much as the growing enthusiasm for scriptural study among the urban and working classes. Only the monastic houses had outlived their original purpose. However, since the late Middle Ages, moribund monasteries had been suppressed on a regular basis, and their endowments redistributed to fund more worthy projects. Cardinal Wolsey undertook such a reallocation in the 1520s. Only in Ireland and the outer Scottish Islands, long the cause of religious embarrassment to the Papacy, was the unreformed Church in poor shape, mainly on the grounds of poverty.

The catalyst for change in England was Henry VIII's need for a male heir. A smooth succession was a guarantee of continuing peace and order. The reluctance of Pope Clement VII to grant him a divorce from Catherine of Aragon precipitated a rupture between the pope and the king, barely a decade earlier designated *Fidei Defensor* (Defender of the Faith) for his defence of Catholicism against Protestantism. In 1534 Henry VIII was named supreme head of the Church in England, thereby asserting and confirming the break with Rome. From this assumption of authority over the English Church sprang a series of administrative changes and theological reappraisals that steadily moved the kingdom towards 'Godly faith', that is, Protestantism. As part of his policy of anglicisation of Ireland, where he was lord until 1541 and king thereafter, Henry ensured that the changes enforced in England and Wales were introduced there also. However, the process of dissolving the Irish monasteries was barely half completed by the time of his death in 1547 and the new faith had not put down secure roots among either Ireland's English or Gaelic inhabitants.

Henry's break with Rome was not accompanied by major doctrinal changes; he was essentially a religious conservative. Protestant reformers saw their chance in the short reign of Henry's son Edward VI (reigned 1547–53) and most vestiges of the old faith were suppressed. Edward's early death opened the way for a Counter-Reformation under his Catholic elder sister Mary (reigned 1553–8), but she soon followed him to the grave and it was left to their

> *There never was a merry world since the fairies left dancing, and the priest conjuring.*
>
> **John Selden *Table Talk* (1689)**

The age of the Reformation in the British Isles

The 16th century was a period of religious upheaval in the British Isles as elsewhere in Europe. Spurred by dynastic necessity rather than religious conviction, Henry VIII broke with the Church of Rome and introduced Protestantism into England and Wales. Scotland followed suit, while the Irish clung to Catholicism to protect their national identity from the English.

Resistance to change was muted. Such religious revolts as there were, though alarming, proved no real threat to the Crown, and while some individuals were willing to die for their faith, most were prepared to conform. Catholic Spain, Europe's greatest power, made various attempts to intervene, including the ill-fated Armada in 1588: all came to nought.

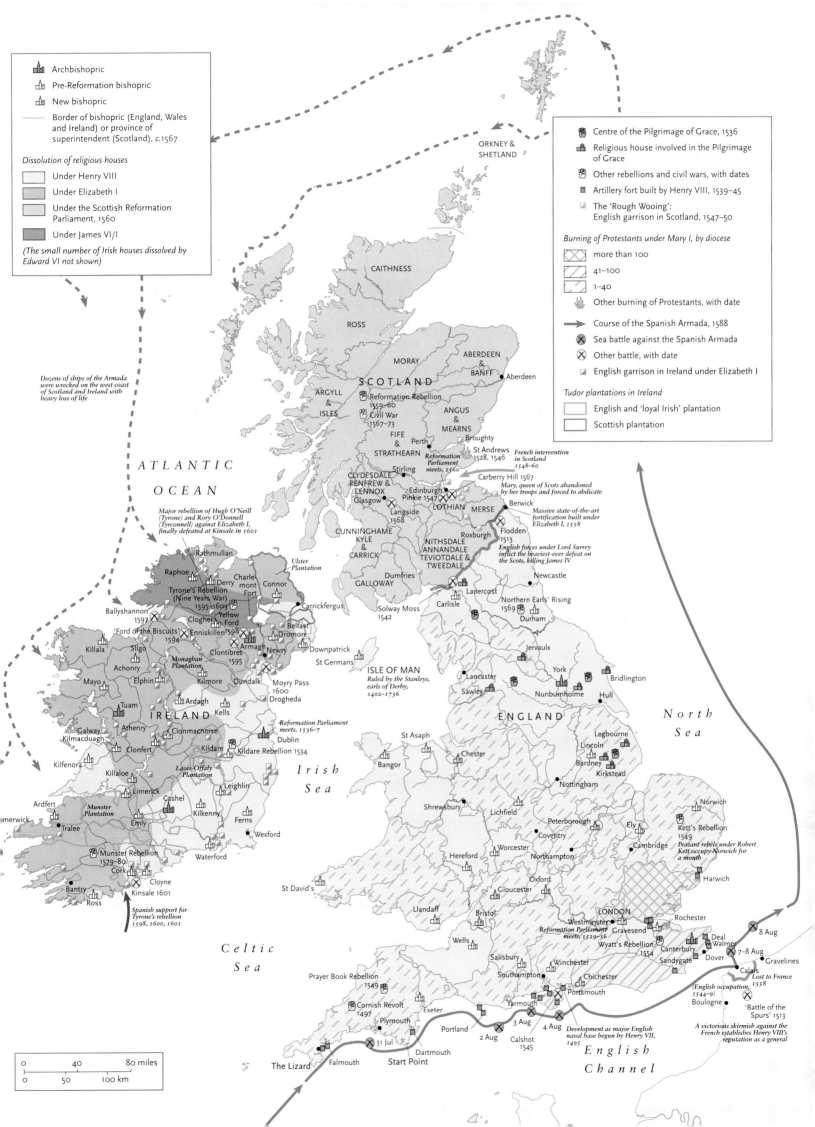

Legend (top left):

- Archbishopric
- Pre-Reformation bishopric
- New bishopric
- Border of bishopric (England, Wales and Ireland) or province of superintendent (Scotland), c.1567

Dissolution of religious houses
- Under Henry VIII
- Under Elizabeth I
- Under the Scottish Reformation Parliament, 1560
- Under James VI/I

(The small number of Irish houses dissolved by Edward VI not shown)

Legend (right):

- Centre of the Pilgrimage of Grace, 1536
- Religious house involved in the Pilgrimage of Grace
- Other rebellions and civil wars, with dates
- Artillery fort built by Henry VIII, 1539–45
- The 'Rough Wooing': English garrison in Scotland, 1547–50

Burning of Protestants under Mary I, by diocese
- more than 100
- 41–100
- 1–40
- Other burning of Protestants, with date

- Course of the Spanish Armada, 1588
- Sea battle against the Spanish Armada
- Other battle, with date
- English garrison in Ireland under Elizabeth I

Tudor plantations in Ireland
- English and 'loyal Irish' plantation
- Scottish plantation

Map labels:

ORKNEY & SHETLAND

Dozens of ships of the Armada were wrecked on the west coast of Scotland and Ireland with heavy loss of life

ATLANTIC OCEAN

CAITHNESS

ROSS

MORAY

ARGYLL & ISLES

SCOTLAND

ABERDEEN & BANFF — Aberdeen

Reformation Rebellion 1559–60
Civil War 1567–73

ANGUS & MEARNS

FIFE & STRATHEARN

Perth — Broughty

St Andrews 1528, 1546

French intervention in Scotland 1548–60

Stirling

Reformation Parliament meets, 1560

CLYDESDALE RENFREW & LENNOX

Glasgow — Edinburgh — Pinkie 1547 — LOTHIAN

Carberry Hill 1567

Mary, queen of Scots abandoned by her troops and forced to abdicate

Berwick — MERSE

Massive state-of-the-art fortification built under Elizabeth I, 1558

Langside 1568

CUNNINGHAME KYLE & CARRICK

Flodden 1513
Roxburgh

NITHSDALE ANNANDALE TEVIOTDALE & TWEEDALE

English forces under Lord Surrey inflict the heaviest-ever defeat on the Scots, killing James IV

Dumfries

GALLOWAY

Newcastle

Solway Moss 1542

Lanercost

Carlisle — Northern Earls' Rising 1569 — Durham

Major rebellion of Hugh O'Neill (Tyrone) and Rory O'Donnell (Tyrconnell) against Elizabeth I, finally defeated at Kinsale in 1601

Rathmullan
Raphoe — Derry — Charlemont Fort — Connor

Ulster Plantation

Tyrone's Rebellion (Nine Years War) 1595–1603

Ballyshannon 1597 — Clogher — Yellow Ford

Carrickfergus

'Ford of the Biscuits' 1594 — Enniskillen 1598 — Belfast — Dromore

Killala — Sligo — Clontibret 1595 — Armagh — Newry — Downpatrick — St Germans

Achonry — Monaghan Plantation — Kilmore — Dundalk

Mayo — Elphin — Moyry Pass 1600 — Drogheda

Tuam — Ardagh — Kells

IRELAND

Athenry — Clonmacnoise — *Reformation Parliament meets, 1536–7*

Galway — Kilmacduagh — Kildare — Kildare Rebellion 1534

Clonfert — Dublin

Kilfenora — Laois-Offaly Plantation

Killaloe — Leighlin

Limerick — Cashel — Kilkenny — Ferns

Ardfert — Munster Plantation — Emly — Wexford

merwick — Tralee — Waterford

Munster Rebellion 1579–80 — Cork

Bantry — Ross — Cloyne — Kinsale 1601

Spanish support for Tyrone's rebellion 1598, 1600, 1601

Irish Sea

ISLE OF MAN
Ruled by the Stanleys, earls of Derby, 1402–1736

ENGLAND

Lancaster — York — Bridlington

Jervaulx — Nunburnholme — Hull

Sawley

North Sea

St Asaph — Chester — Lincoln — Legbourne

Bangor — Bardney — Kirkstead

Nottingham

Shrewsbury — Lichfield — Peterborough — Ely — Norwich

Coventry — Cambridge — Kett's Rebellion 1549

Peasant rebels under Robert Kett occupy Norwich for a month

Hereford — Worcester — Northampton

Oxford — Harwich

Gloucester

St David's — Llandaff — Bristol — LONDON — Rochester

Reformation Parliament meets, 1529–36

Westminster — Gravesend — Deal — Walmer — 8 Aug

Wells — Wyatt's Rebellion 1554 — Canterbury — Dover — 7–8 Aug

Salisbury — Sandygate — Calais — Gravelines

Winchester — Chichester — *Lost to France 1558*

Prayer Book Rebellion 1549 — Southampton — Portsmouth

Cornish Revolt 1497 — Yarmouth

Exeter — *Development as major English naval base begun by Henry VII, 1495*

Plymouth — Portland — Calshot 1545 — Boulogne

(*English occupation, 1544–9*)

'Battle of the Spurs' 1513

A victorious skirmish against the French establishes Henry VIII's reputation as a general

Celtic Sea

The Lizard — Falmouth — Start Point — 31 Jul — 2 Aug — 3 Aug — 4 Aug

Dartmouth

English Channel

2 Aug · 3 Aug · 4 Aug

Scale bar:
0 — 40 — 80 miles
0 — 50 — 100 km

The Pilgrimage of Grace, 1536

The north of England was a Catholic stronghold, and the dissolution of the monasteries was resented. The rebellion of 1536 was encouraged by powerful families like the Percys, but it was quickly ended – by promises which Henry VIII promptly broke.

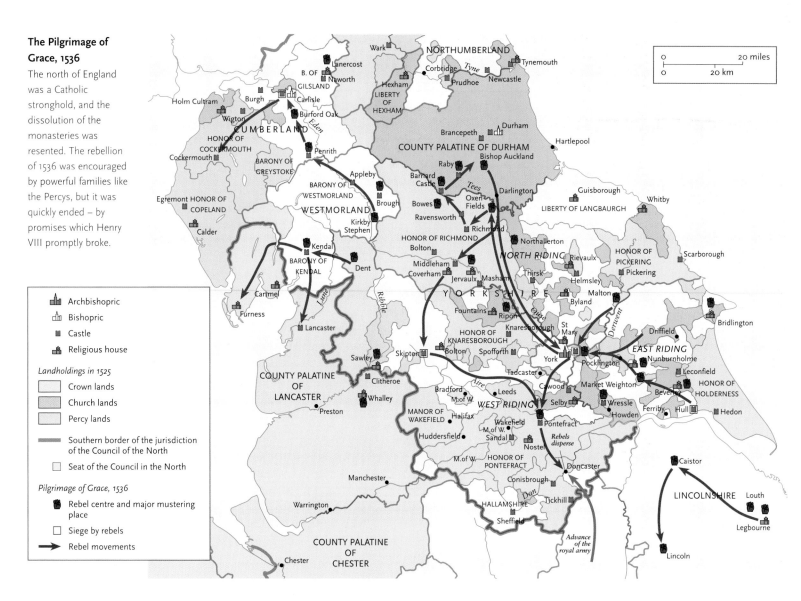

Legend:

- 🏛 Archbishopric
- ⛪ Bishopric
- ▪ Castle
- ⛪ Religious house

Landholdings in 1525
- Crown lands
- Church lands
- Percy lands

— Southern border of the jurisdiction of the Council of the North

☐ Seat of the Council in the North

Pilgrimage of Grace, 1536
- ✊ Rebel centre and major mustering place
- ☐ Siege by rebels
- → Rebel movements

sister Elizabeth to find a comprehensive religious settlement for England. Resisting pressure from Calvinistic Protestants, later known as Puritans, to purge all traces of Catholicism, Elizabeth's settlement was essentially a compromise and, as much as her father's break with Rome, represents the true foundation of the Anglican Church.

The Dissolution of the Monasteries in England had come to an end in March 1540 with the surrender of Waltham Abbey in Essex. The heads of three Benedictine houses, Colchester, Reading and Glastonbury, were executed for displaying 'cantankerous and traitorous hearts'. Although many houses were demolished for their building materials, some, like Lacock, Nostell and Woburn, were converted to domestic dwellings. The friaries were also suppressed, as in the years that followed were collegiate churches, chantries (for the saying of prayers to expedite the passage of souls into heaven), hospitals, almshouses and schools, which until then had largely been run by the Church. The disruption to the nation's basic welfare services necessitated a large programme of re-endowment from mid-century onwards. The re-allocation of much of the land which had passed into crown ownership at the Dissolution confirmed the ruling elite in its control of government, and did much to temper the extent of the Counter-Reformation under Mary when these families made plain their opposition to returning ecclesiastical property to the Catholic Church.

The course of the Reformation in Scotland was somewhat different. The long minorities of James V (1513–42), Mary, queen of Scots (1542–67) and James VI (1567–1625) resulted in an overall lack of direction in government, susceptibility to English and continental religious ideas and untrammelled envy of the English in their acquisition of church property. In these conditions, Protestantism became widespread, especially among the nobility, even while the country's rulers remained Catholic. Religious repression by Mary's regent, her militant Catholic French mother Mary of Guise, caused a Protestant rebellion in 1559, followed by an English-supported Reformation the following year. Partly through the firebrand preaching of John Knox, Calvinism won a large popular following and, after a century of often violent struggle, it became the established church in Scotland in 1690. Scotland's monasteries, already deliberately run down by James V (1513–42), who milked their revenues, or laid waste, like the great border abbeys of Jedburgh, Kelso and Melrose, by the English army in 1547, were pillaged during the general disorder of the Reformation and their lands confiscated. James VI, reared as a Protestant, and the Scottish parliament ensured the triumph of the reformed faith in Scotland when they guaranteed the new owners in their titles to appropriated church lands.

Catholic grandeur gave way to Protestant austerity, and the Mass was replaced by the Eucharist, or Communion, available to all celebrants. More significantly, the adoption of the vernacular (intelligible to all) in preference to Latin (understood only by an educated minority) made Chris-

Anti-Catholic propaganda

John Foxe's Acts and Monuments (1563), better known as the Book of Martyrs, *was a graphic account of those who had died for Protestantism – in this case, Sir John Oldcastle, a Lollard, in 1417. Foxe's book helped to fuel hostility towards Catholicism for at least 100 years.*

ry the English came to see their country as 'a precious stone set in a silver sea', a fortress protected by Nature and God from their enemies. A shared Protestantism helped heal ancient divisions between England and Scotland (epitomised by the 'Rough Wooing', Henry VIII's misguidedly brutal attempt to bully the Scots into a marriage between the infant Mary and his son Edward). Their inhabitants came to view any national disloyalty with suspicion. This was the origin of intolerance towards Roman Catholicism which was to become such a hallmark of later British history. Fortresses protecting national boundaries, such as those at Berwick-upon-Tweed and Carlisle, became redundant, though forts in Ireland lingered on to protect English rule there.

tianity more immediate and accessible than it had hitherto been. From 1539 Bibles in English were authorised in every parish church; from the mid-1540s collections of psalms were available; and from 1549 a series of Prayer Books. Statutory enforcement of their use did not ensure acquiescence. In 1549, in the Southwest, where Cornish was still spoken, texts in English were no more readily intelligible than those in Latin (which at least had the advantage of being customary), and the region rose in rebellion.

A FORTRESS OF PROTESTANTISM

General acceptance of superimposed change could not be taken for granted. This became evident during the Pilgrimage of Grace in 1536 when many in the North voiced their objections. From then onwards, uprisings increasingly espoused religious stances at variance with successive regimes, whether in England, Ireland or Scotland. Thus, Mary, queen of Scots, during her captivity in England (1568–87), reverted to the Catholicism in which she had been reared in the hope of securing Roman Catholic support for her claim to the throne. Under Elizabeth, the Howard dukes of Norfolk similarly returned to the Catholic fold. In Ireland, a country not previously known for its piety, opponents of the Elizabethan regime increasingly turned to Catholicism as an expression of dissent. This is why the advent of seminary priests and Jesuit missionaries from Catholic Europe was viewed so seriously by the government, and why those involved, like John Gerard and William Weston, were hunted down. It also led the Elizabethan regime to turn to a policy of plantation, to replace disloyal Catholic subjects in Ireland with loyal English settlers. Just as foreign powers supported attempts to reclaim the British Isles for Catholicism (the Spanish sending troops to Kinsale and elsewhere in Ireland), so the English crown endeavoured to promote 'God's cause' from the 1540s, by sending money, preachers and troops to Scotland, Normandy and the Netherlands. Philip II's most serious attempt to overthrow Elizabeth, transported by the Armada in 1588, came to nothing: *Flavit et dissipati sunt* ('He [God] blew and they were scattered'). In the late sixteenth centu-

The way to James VI's accession to the English throne in 1603 may have been smoothed by his unimpeachable Protestantism but the resistance of the English parliament ensured that the union of the Scottish and English crowns was not followed by the full political union that the king desired. The Scottish parliament had worked in a very different way to the English parliament, which was able to act with greater independence under James than it had under Elizabeth. James's son, Charles I, would decide that he could rule without this uncooperative body, with consequences that were ultimately fatal.   AH

The people, generally devout, are as I am informed, northward and by the west popishly affected, which other parts are zealous Protestants.

Thomas Fuller, *The Holy State and the Profane State* (1642)

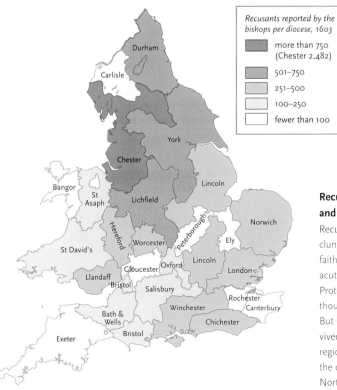

Recusants reported by the bishops per diocese, 1603

- more than 750 (Chester 2,482)
- 501–750
- 251–500
- 100–250
- fewer than 100

Durham, Carlisle, York, Chester, Bangor, St Asaph, Lichfield, Lincoln, Hereford, Worcester, Peterborough, Norwich, Ely, St David's, Gloucester, Oxford, Lincoln, London, Llandaff, Bristol, Salisbury, Rochester, Winchester, Canterbury, Bath & Wells, Chichester, Exeter, Bristol

Recusancy in England and Wales, 1603

Recusants – those who clung to their Catholic faith – were a source of acute anxiety to many Protestants, who thought them traitors. But Catholicism survived, especially in regions furthest from the capital, notably the North and Northwest.

WALES AFTER THE UNION

Early modern Wales

After the Act of Union in 1536, the marcher lordships were abolished and Wales was made subject to the same legal system as England, divided into English-style counties and given parliamentary representation. English became the language of administration but the majority of the people remained monoglot Welsh-speakers. The Protestant Reformation took root in Wales but Nonconformity and Methodism became more popular than Anglicanism.

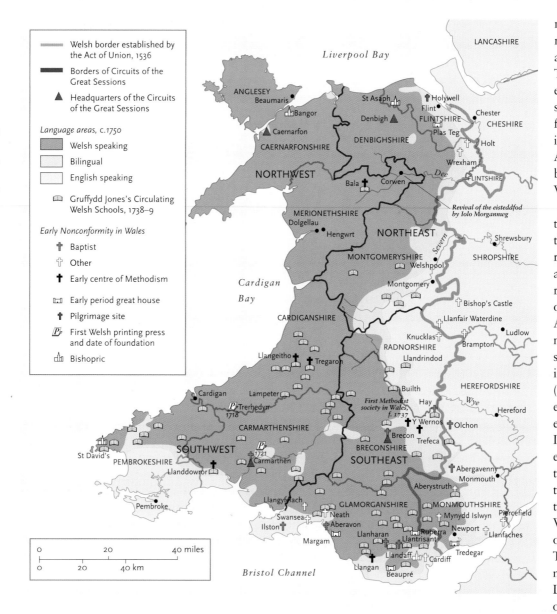

Key:

- ▬ Welsh border established by the Act of Union, 1536
- ▬ Borders of Circuits of the Great Sessions
- ▲ Headquarters of the Circuits of the Great Sessions

Language areas, c.1750
- ■ Welsh speaking
- ▨ Bilingual
- □ English speaking

- 📖 Gruffydd Jones's Circulating Welsh Schools, 1738–9

Early Nonconformity in Wales
- ✝ Baptist
- ✝ Other
- ✝ Early centre of Methodism

- 🏛 Early period great house
- ✝ Pilgrimage site
- ℗ First Welsh printing press and date of foundation
- 🏛 Bishopric

A Renaissance house

Plas Teg, near Mold, Flintshire, the earliest Renaissance-style house in Wales, built c.1610 for Sir John Trevor, a senior figure in naval administration.

The Act of Union of 1536 completed the long process of the absorption of Wales, with its marches, into the English kingdom. It rendered superfluous the castles that until then had held the region in subjugation. The marcher lordships were abolished and the region was subsequently administered as a corporate element of the same realm, divided into shires, subject to the same laws, and enjoying parliamentary representation. Shrewsbury, situated in the Welsh marches, remained in all but name the capital of the region, with the Council in the Marches, responsible for maintaining law and order in Wales and the English border shires, located there until its abolition in the 1640s. Though a consequence of these changes was that the language of the ruling classes became predominantly English, they at least ensured for the Welsh that justices of the peace and the men running the shires on behalf of the Crown were 'magistrates of their own nation', thereby guaranteeing that Wales would not come to be regarded simply as a part of England. This was the case even in Monmouthshire, which was fully incorporated into England by the Act of Union, and became part of Wales only in 1972.

At the same time that its administration was being remodelled, Wales also suffered the religious upheaval of the Reformation. At first, the Reformation merely substituted one barely intelligible tongue (Latin) with another (English). However, in contrast to Ireland, where little effort was made to make religious texts available in the native language, Welsh translations of the Creed, the Ten Commandments and the Lord's Prayer came out early as 1547, and these were soon followed by translations of the Prayer Book and the Scriptures. As a result, the Welsh people enthusiastically embraced Protestantism (and later

Nonconformity). A measure of Catholicism did survive, and St Winifred's Well at Holywell has remained a centre for pilgrimage until today.

LITERACY AND CULTURE

Though it was excluded from administration, the position Welsh gained as the language of religion did much to ensure its survival. Grammar school education was exclusively in English but basic literacy in Welsh became widespread in the eighteenth century, thanks to the efforts of the Society for the Propagation of Christian Knowledge, Gruffydd Jones and others to ensure that the poor could read the Bible for themselves. A growing market for Welsh language books led to the establishment of the first presses in Wales in the early eighteenth century. The survival of Welsh as a living tongue compensated for the collapse of the medieval bardic tradition with its characteristic prophesyings. Another Celtic tradition that sank into disfavour was the use of patronymics, by which a person's second name identified him or her clearly as the child of a known parent: this was superseded by the use of surnames, in the English manner, handed down from one generation to another. Many traditional Welsh Christian names also fell out of fashion in this period.

Wales did not become a Celtic backwater. The Welsh adopted Jesus College in Oxford (founded in 1571) and the Inns of Court in London to complete their education. The Welsh elite took enthusiastically to the Renaissance, building houses and art collections comparable with collections anywhere else in Europe. Against this cosmopolitanism should be set the achievement of Sir John Price in defending the Arthurian tradition against general scepticism, and the work of Gruffydd Done, in the sixteenth century, and of Robert Vaughan of Hengwrt, in the seventeenth century, who both collected and preserved medieval Welsh texts. Their example was emulated by others.

Welsh intellectual activity was not simply antiquarian. Scholarship extended to historical and topographical studies, among the glories of which was Edward Lhuyd's *Archaeologia   Britannica*

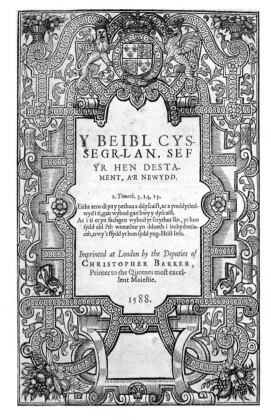

Y BEIBL CYS-SEGR-LAN. SEF YR HEN DESTA-MENT, A'R NEWYDD.

Imprinted at London by the Deputies of CHRISTOPHER BARKER, Printer to the Queenes most excellent Maiestie. 1588.

(1707), the first methodical study of the Celtic languages. Lhuyd's work was a major contribution to a Europe-wide rediscovery of the ancient Celtic past, which led to a fashionable 'Celtomania' in the later eighteenth century. Celtomania had particular resonance in Wales: identification with the Celtic past became an important way for the Welsh to assert their different identity from the English. Interest in the bardic tradition was reawakened in the late eighteenth century and, under the direction of Iolo Morganwg, *eisteddfodau* re-emerged as vehicles for regional and national cultural activities. Druidism (by then extinct) was 'revived' through colourful but largely invented ceremonies. Celtomania also went some way to persuade the English that the Welsh were not simply quaint.

Throughout the early modern period Wales remained predominantly agrarian, specialising in cattle production (rather than sheep-grazing), dairy products and, until the Industrial Revolution, cloth-manufacture. The countryside underwent gradual enclosure and deforestation. Settlements remained small and scattered, farmers maintaining upland summer homes and lowland winter houses. Towns were not an important feature in the landscape until the eighteenth century, and then restricted largely to Glamorgan. Neither coal-mining nor iron-casting were as important as they were later to become.   **AH**

The Bible in Welsh
Frontispiece of the first full translation of the Bible into Welsh, published in 1588. The early translation of the scriptures into Welsh helped Protestantism become accepted in Wales and contributed greatly to the survival of the Welsh language.

Methodism and literacy

There was a close relationship between literacy in Wales and Methodism in the late 18th century. In Caernarfonshire, those areas with the highest attendance at Gruffydd Jones's schools (which taught people to read the Bible in Welsh) also had the most Methodist chapels by 1800.

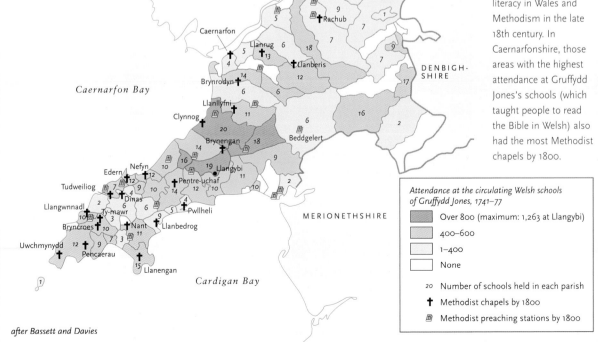

after Bassett and Davies

Attendance at the circulating Welsh schools of Gruffydd Jones, 1741–77

Over 800 (maximum: 1,263 at Llangybi)

400–600

1–400

None

20   Number of schools held in each parish

✝   Methodist chapels by 1800

▦   Methodist preaching stations by 1800

THE ANGLO-SCOTTISH BORDER

The Anglo-Scottish border 1500–1603

The balance of political and military power in the British Isles swung heavily in England's favour in the 16th century, with disastrous Scottish defeats on the battlefield at Flodden and Solway Moss. Paradoxically, in the border region, the chief result of this shift was an erosion of royal authority and the rise of the lawless reiver families. Only with the Union of Crowns in 1603 were the Borders finally brought back under royal control.

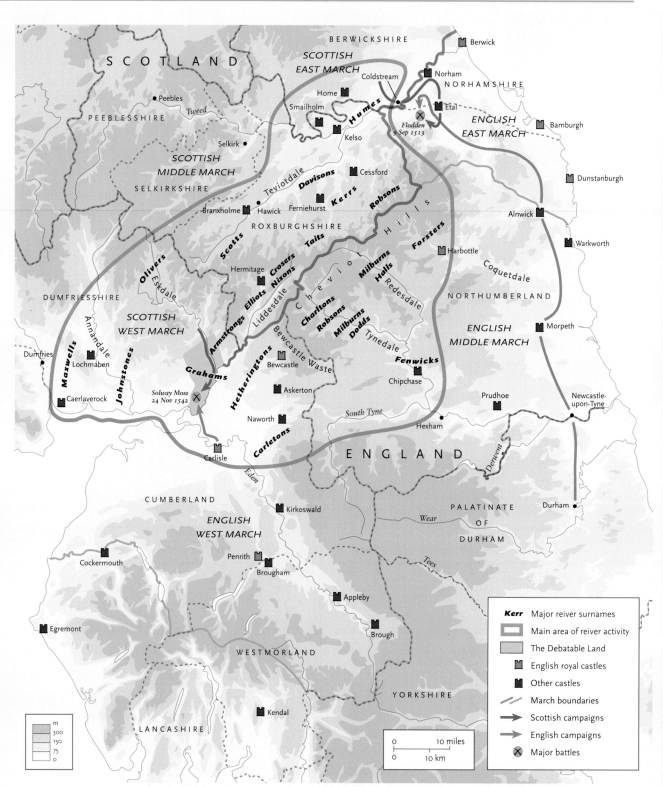

The Anglo-Scottish border region remained essentially a military frontier in the sixteenth century, with a society characterised by strong ties of kinship, the political ascendancy of Marcher lords with compact landholdings and warlike tenantry, and special administrative structures geared chiefly to defence. The actual border was comparatively stable and well defined: the treaty of York of 1237 had established the familiar Tweed–Solway line, and by 1500 there were only six small disputed areas, of which the

largest, the 'Debatable Land' north of Carlisle, was finally divided between the two kingdoms in 1552. All English attempts to alter this border unilaterally (for instance, by planting English garrisons on the Scottish side in 1548–50, following the so-called 'Rough Wooing' of the infant Princess Mary of Scotland on behalf of Henry VIII's son Edward) were unsuccessful. Nonetheless, constant warfare and petty raiding affected the entire region throughout the century.

Apart from several periods of open warfare between the two kingdoms – the last of which occurred between 1558 and 1560 – the chief cause of this turbulence was the borderers themselves. Frontier conditions had fostered the

development of the border 'surnames' (the earliest recorded use of the term occurred in 1498). These 'surnames' were quasi-autonomous kinship groups inhabiting parts of the frontier region, particularly in the poorer west and middle marches. They lived largely by reiving – that is, by raiding their neighbours – with little regard for the power politics of either kingdom. The Liddesdale surnames on the Scottish side were the most troublesome on the whole border, while the Tynedale and Redesdale surnames were the worst offenders on the English side. The inhabitants of the border districts had long suffered the more or less indiscriminate ravaging of armies from both sides during the wars between the two kingdoms, and the reivers therefore paid little regard to national loyalties. The Liddesdale men, in particular, were always ready to seize any opportunity provided by English raids on Scotland, and distinguished themselves in 1542 by mercilessly plundering the defeated Scots army on its way home from defeat at Solway Moss.

CONTROLLING THE REIVERS

The two royal governments maintained similar structures for border administration, aimed at securing the national frontiers, but also at controlling reiver activity – or at least channelling it against the opposing kingdom. Within each march, the respective crowns appointed special wardens to organise defence, liaise with the opposing warden, and enforce the special legal code (march law) that regulated the border. The duties of these wardens were complicated by the topography of the region, which inhibited east–west communications. In addition, good rule was hindered by the continued existence of numerous feudal franchises (known as liberties or regalities), from which royal sheriffs were excluded and in which the local lord exercised judicial powers. Underlying problems, however, were the Scottish crown's weakness in the face of English military pressure and, south of the border, the deliberate weakening of the region's traditional power structures by Tudor policy.

Since neither crown could afford a standing army, the most effective means of control and defence was to appoint as wardens regional magnates whose local connection and numerous tenantry provided them with an extensive feudal following. Under the Tudors, the Dacres and Cliffords dominated the English wardenships; in Scotland, the Maxwells, Humes and Kerrs of Cessford were favoured, although

these Scottish barons were less powerful than their English counterparts. The disadvantage of this system was that the authority of these locally connected wardens was often compromised by a real or perceived lack of impartiality in dealing with the reivers – and sometimes even by overt involvement of the warden in reiver politics.

THE 'DECAY OF THE BORDERS'

These difficulties were made worse, for much of the sixteenth century, by the non-residence of leading landowners, so precipitating a crisis of lordship. The Maxwells and Humes generally resided in Edinburgh, and after 1536 the Tudors themselves were leading absentees, having acquired extensive lands from the Percy family and the Church. The Tudors were distrustful of over-mighty subjects, particularly in sensitive military posts like the wardenries. Henry Tudor (Henry VII) had sharply reduced the traditional salaries by which the wardens had retained the leading gentry, and had begun to appoint separate constables for the major royal castles (those at Berwick-on-Tweed and Carlisle), and also to employ lesser landowners as wardens. Inflation and other economic pressures forced landlords to raise rents and other charges, so further undermining traditional ties between landlords and tenants. The result was a continuing decline of border service and a growth of reiving. From 1542, English officials instituted numerous inquiries into this 'decay of the borders', but with no significant result.

From the 1560s, the problems of controlling the border region began to change. The advance of the Reformation in both countries encouraged Protestant solidarity and cooperation between London and Edinburgh, so alleviating defensive problems, but the adherence of many borderers to the old religion served to create new security fears. These are exemplified by the dangerous 1569 Northern Rebellion of Catholics in England. The military frontier finally disappeared only with the Union of the Crowns in 1603, when the Anglo-Scottish borders were gradually transformed into the Middle Shires.   **SGE**

Hermitage Castle

Sited in a small valley off Liddesdale, the grim Hermitage was a base for the Keeper of Liddesdale, an officer of the Scottish Middle March charged with policing the most lawless area in the Borders.

Coquet Head

Upper Coquetdale reveals a typical Borders landscape of the 16th century. This was a poor, largely upland region of hill and forest, high pasture and moor-land waste, with a scanty population and few towns.

Between the fifteenth and nineteenth centuries, parliament was the political forum where, under the Crown, the ruling elite met to discuss their grievances and promote remedies in the form of law. It also met to grant money to fund the routine business of the monarch and the royal household, the administration of the realm, and the defence of the nation. For the elite, there was no consent to taxation unless parliament addressed current political and social issues. The Lords, which met separately for England and Wales, were the most powerful magnates of the realm. The rest of the governing classes – the Commons – elected their own representatives. These were leading members of the local elite, largely landed gentry, with a steadily growing proportion of professional men, especially lawyers. In short, all were from a very similar social background. They tended to see themselves as representatives of the nation rather than of particular constituencies. They did not, however, neglect local issues; in fact, they actively promoted them: the need to live amicably with their neighbours and to be re-elected ensured this.

The right to vote was restricted to the relatively well-to-do. The counties each elected two members, the vote being based on the '40-shilling freehold' – a measure of income intended to ensure that only independent yeoman farmers and their richer social superiors had the franchise. The majority of members were returned by boroughs, which also returned two members each. The franchise in the boroughs, however, varied considerably, reflecting the nature of local government in each place. Whatever the form of franchise, the vote remained firmly in the hands of independent and prosperous men.

The function of parliament evolved considerably over time. Initially, it was summoned simply to grant the monarch new taxes and to enact government legislation. Members presented their current grievances – for example, on the question of religious tolerance – to the monarch for consideration. The monarch, however, remained firmly in control. But parliament made steadily increasing attempts to win from the Crown acknowledgement for their rights and privileges. By the end of the seventeenth century, as a result of a mixture of political manoeuvring and open warfare, parliament had secured for itself a central position in government, and had a decisive voice in all major fields of state policy.

INSTITUTIONAL VARIATION

The form of parliament could vary somewhat. In Ireland the English model was closely followed. In Scotland, however, the Estates were the nobility, the Commons and the judiciary, which met in a single building with spaces clearly defined for each Estate. Until the Protestant Reformation, the different Houses of Lords included the abbots of the leading monasteries. In England bishops continued to sit in the Lords after the Reformation, but in Scotland they were excluded after 1638. To prevent the Lords from being swamped by Scottish peers after the Act of Union in 1707, a system was adopted whereby the Scottish peers chose a limited number of representatives from among their ranks. Other institutional changes also occurred. Initially, parliament met wherever the monarch found it convenient. First London, then Edinburgh, and finally Dublin acquired purpose-built parliament houses. The preference for the capital as a permanent venue was an important stage in the increasing bureaucratisation of parliament. This reflected its burgeoning importance in the constitution. Rules on procedure, which had previously been transmitted by word of mouth, were by the mid-sixteenth century being regularised and written down in books. This process elevated the respect generally accorded the institution. In the long term, it was this growing esteem that enabled parliament – which until the sixteenth century had largely done as it was told by the monarch and his council – to pursue an independent course of action.

> '...the liberties, franchises, privileges and jurisdictions of parliament are the ancient and undoubted birthright and inheritance of the subjects of England.'
>
> **Declaration accepted by the Commons, 1621**

Chairing the member

In this painting by Hogarth, a newly elected member is carried triumphantly around his constituency, buying ale for his supporters. Venality, if not outright corruption, was common in English elections before the 19th-century Reform Acts. 'Rotten Boroughs', declining towns with tiny electorates, such as Old Sarum, were particularly vulnerable to manipulation by landowners or non-resident monied interests who could effectively buy seats for themselves or their allies.

Seats of parliaments

The English parliament in 1584
- County returning 2 MPs
- County returning 1 MP
- No MPs

Residence of borough MPs in 1584
- Resident in the borough
- Resident in the county
- Not resident in either the borough or county
- Residence not known

The Irish parliament in 1586
- Counties returning 2 MPs
- Counties not represented
- Boroughs returning 2 MPs

The Scottish Reformation parliament in 1560
- Seats of nobles in parliament
- Areas from which lairds attended parliament
- Boroughs represented in parliament
- Bishops in parliament
- Other churchmen in parliament

50 Glamis
51 Byresers
52 Invermay
53 Alloa
54 Leslie
55 Inverkeithing
56 Haddington
57 Elphinstone
58 Saltoun
59 Dalkeith
60 Torphichen

Parliaments in the 16th century

The English parliament consisted of two chambers, the House of Lords, made up of the nobility, and the House of Commons, made up of elected representatives from the shires and main towns (the parliamentary boroughs). The Irish parliament was modelled on the English, though counties not under the effective control of the English government were unrepresented. The Scottish parliament had a single chamber for representatives of the Four Estates – the Lords, the Church, the Lairds (minor landowners) and the boroughs. The Manx parliament, the Tynwald, was self-chosen.

1 Penryn
2 St Mawes
3 Tregony
4 Fowey
5 Grampound
6 Mitchell
7 Lostwithiel
8 Camelford

9 Liskeard
10 Callington
11 West Looe
12 East Looe
13 St Germans
14 Saltash
15 Plympton
16 Melcombe Regis

17 Wareham
18 Christchurch
19 Yarmouth
20 Newtown
21 Newport
22 Wilton
23 Downton
24 Heytesbury

25 Old Sarum
26 Ludgershall
27 Great Bedwin
28 Calne
29 Wootton Bassett
30 Cricklade
31 Wallingford
32 Marlborough

33 Stockbridge
34 Whitchurch
35 Petersfield
36 Guildford
37 Haslemere
38 Midhurst
39 Chichester
40 Arundel

41 Steyning
42 Shoreham
43 Lewes
44 Bramber
45 Horsham
46 Reigate
47 Southwark
48 Westminster
49 London

0   40   80 miles
0   50   100 km

Cornwall in the 16th century

Cornwall's strategically important harbours, its vulnerability to seaborne attack, and its tin industry, were all reasons for Tudor monarchs to ensure that the county was well represented in parliament: the number of Cornish MPs at Westminster tripled in the 16th century. Though Cornwall declined in strategic and industrial importance in the 17th century, parliament refused to allow any boroughs to be disenfranchised, ultimately making it the most over-represented shire by the 18th century.

Over the years, the regional parliaments disappeared as political power became concentrated in London, which gradually became the base of a specifically British parliament. There, the House of Commons underwent considerable evolution. In 1542 members from Wales (hitherto rarely invited to assemblies) entered the English parliament on a permanent basis. Union with Scotland in 1707, and with Ireland in 1801, completed this process. The Commonwealth and Protectorate (1649–60) saw less successful constitutional experiments. During that period separate national assemblies were suspended, and parliament convened only at Westminster. In 1653 the profession of 'Godly faith' – in other words, extreme Protestantism – qualified only 100 members for election. This religious qualification was soon superseded. In the next five years the number of representatives allocated to each constituency directly reflected the size of the electorate. The House of Lords was abolished. Oliver Cromwell, as Lord Protector, antagonised many groups by reviving an upper house, but this proved to be only a temporary expedient. Yet in 1660, after his death, but before the Restoration of the Monarchy, the Convention Parliament included an upper as well as a lower house. There was a strong urge nationally to have done with constitutional experimentation and return to the 'normality' of pre-Civil War days.

CORRUPTION AND REFORM

England's union with Ireland and Scotland resulted in the peripheries of Britain being relatively over-represented. This inherent failing was exacerbated by a reluctance to strip constituencies of their right to elect members when they declined in population, and by a general opposition to the enfranchisement of new boroughs. As a result, the eighteenth-century House of Commons was more susceptible to the intrusion of government nominees than it had previously been, and electoral corruption was rife, particularly in the Scottish constituencies. A single great landowner could so dominate a borough as virtually to own the seats in parliament. Bribery of electors was standard practice and could take several forms, including supplying alcohol or offering generous subsidies to the local poor, which would ease the burden on all local ratepayers. It also allowed certain families to put their sons into parliament, not only to perpetuate their social and political status – and membership of the Commons did carry considerable prestige – but also to advance their careers.

As parliament evolved it met more often, and for longer periods. The acquisition of premises intended only for its use from 1500 allowed it to remain sitting for longer and to reassemble over a number of years. The prolonged existence over 17 years of the Cavalier Parliament, which originally opened in 1661, was rated excessive. To prevent any repetition, the Triennial Act of 1694 and the Septennial Act of 1716 respectively stipulated that future assemblies could not last longer than three, and later seven, years without a general election. This prevented stagnation and ensured that parliament continued to reflect changing public opinion outside its walls.

Another important change took place in what was expected of a member of parliament. Throughout, his duty remained the preservation and promotion of the common weal, or common good. Decisions taken in parliament were binding on the entire nation. Constituents, not surprisingly, expected their parliamentary representatives to obey instructions concerning their understanding of what contributed to the general good of themselves and others. But in November 1774 Edmund Burke explained to the voters at Bristol the constitutional position of a member: 'He owes you,' Burke argued, 'not his industry only; but his judgement; and he betrays instead of serving you if he sacrifices it to your opinion.'

REPRESENTATION IN PRACTICE

Cornwall has the unfortunate reputation of being the county most heavily over-represented in parliament before the Reform Act of 1832. Cornish voters were, accordingly, susceptible to the blandishments of carpetbaggers anxious to find a place in the House of Commons to further their careers, or simply to evade their creditors. They were highly amenable to the exercise of parliamentary patronage by local and national bigwigs.

At the opening of the sixteenth century, Cornwall's parliamentary representation consisted of two knights of the shire sitting for the county and 12 burgesses for six towns. However, in barely five decades, the number of boroughs multiplied over three times to 21. Callington was the last to be enfranchised, in 1584. This extraordinary growth reflected a number of considerations. Tin production, albeit in decline, continued to be important. Cornwall was extremely vulnerable to invasion, and a series of highly sophisticated fortifications was built to defend its coastline. Cornish engineers made significant contributions in campaigns abroad, notably at Boulogne in 1544. Foreign privateers did considerable harm to local trade and fishing. All these considerations, signs of the area's relative importance, contributed to the enfranchisement of ever more boroughs. Conceivably, this expansion was not at the time seen as permanent, but the House of Commons under James I, and subsequently, refused to allow the disenfranchisement of boroughs. The duchy of Cornwall (held by the heir apparent to the throne) did provide the Crown some powers of parliamentary patronage, but it was only active in a handful of boroughs. Thus the Cornish boroughs were rarely susceptible to Crown interference or intrusion, even if they were as vulnerable to common corrupt practices as anywhere else.

Cornish boroughs reflected the full range of electoral diversity to be found elsewhere in England and Wales. In various boroughs members of local corporations, freemen, household residents, or the tenants of certain institutions, might exercise the franchise. The franchise tended to fluctuate. As elsewhere, over the period, the size of the electorate declined. Although modest in size, the number of electors empowered to vote outstripped important commercial centres such as Bristol, Coventry and Norwich, most of which had restricted franchises until the Civil War. In other words, members from the Cornish boroughs were often more democratically elected than those for the rest of the country. Still, disputes over the precise nature of the franchise resulted in rival groups returning different men, particularly from the Restoration onwards; these problems had to be sorted out at the opening of parliament. Also, a number of members, anxious at any cost to procure a place in the House, took the precaution of obtaining election there as a failsafe should they not be returned elsewhere. **AH**

> *'I mean for your helps and assistance of voices when occasion shall require in the choice of the knights of the shire... Wherein I desire your best furtherance... especially for the public good which I prefer before mine own.'*
>
> **John Arundell of Trerice, 1625**

Pendennis Castle

Pendennis Castle was one of several specially designed artillery forts built by Henry VIII to defend important harbours on the south coast after his breach with the Roman Catholic Church in 1534 left England diplomatically isolated. The Crown's substantial investment in the county's defence was one reason for its rapid increase in parliamentary representation in the 16th century.

TUDOR LONDON

The first real map-views of London began to be published from the middle of the sixteenth century, perhaps reflecting the burgeoning confidence of the city in Tudor times. By this period, London was the largest city in England; it had grown from a medium-sized medieval urban centre with about 33,000 inhabitants into one of the five greatest cities in Europe, with a population of some 200,000. This prodigious growth was largely due to London's pre-eminent position as the centre of trade and commerce, which attracted a steady influx of migrants from the countryside and abroad.

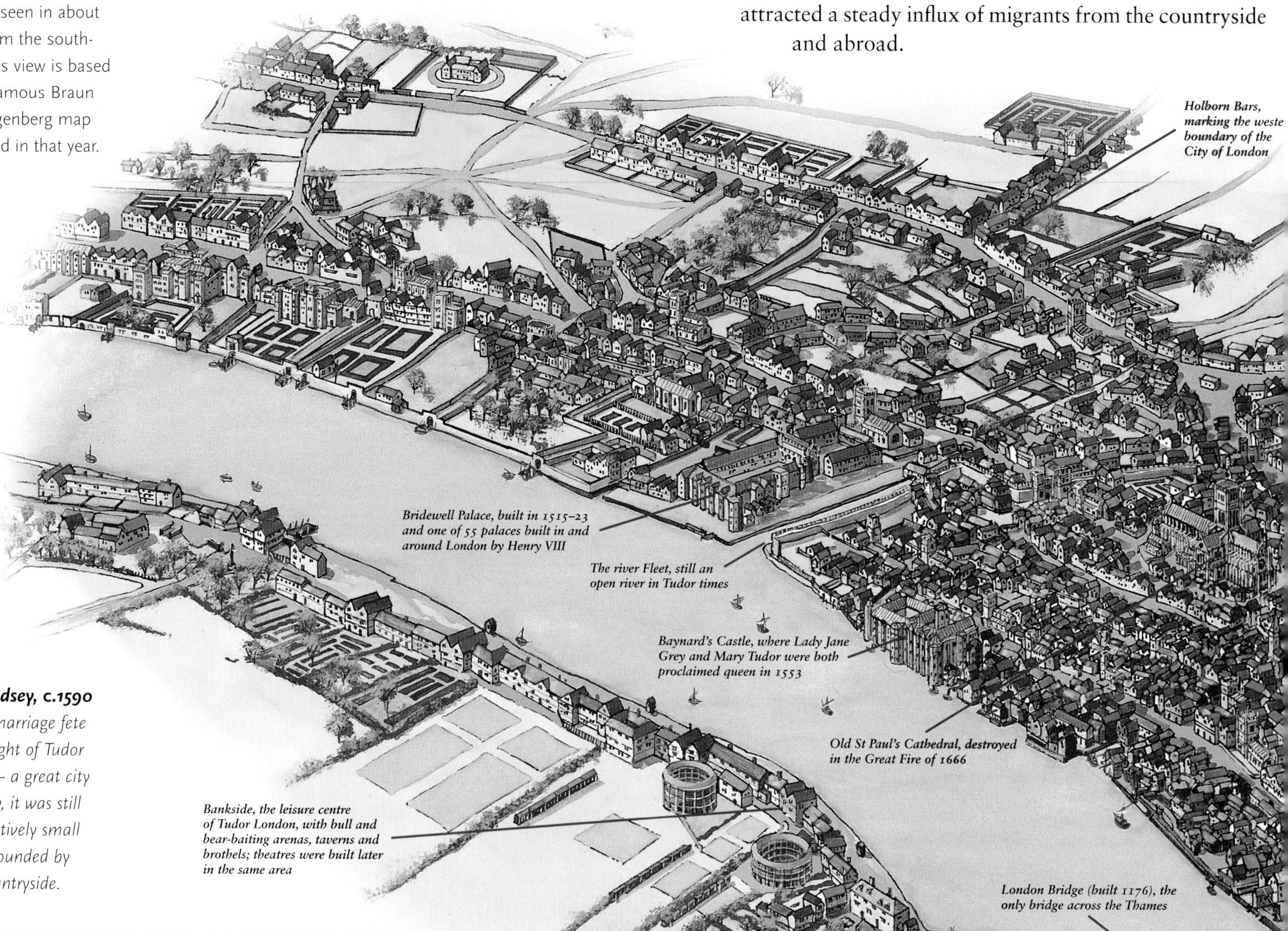

Tudor London

London seen in about 1572, from the south-east. This view is based on the famous Braun and Hogenberg map published in that year.

Holborn Bars, marking the weste boundary of the City of London

Bridewell Palace, built in 1515–23 and one of 55 palaces built in and around London by Henry VIII

The river Fleet, still an open river in Tudor times

Baynard's Castle, where Lady Jane Grey and Mary Tudor were both proclaimed queen in 1553

Old St Paul's Cathedral, destroyed in the Great Fire of 1666

Bankside, the leisure centre of Tudor London, with bull and bear-baiting arenas, taverns and brothels; theatres were built later in the same area

London Bridge (built 1176), the only bridge across the Thames

Bermondsey, c.1590

A rural marriage fete within sight of Tudor London – a great city of its day, it was still comparatively small and surrounded by open countryside.

EARLY MODERN BRITAIN & IRELAND

The metropolitan area was divided into three distinct urban communities: the City of London, the area within the medieval wall; Southwark, on the south bank; and, further to the west, Westminster. Suburbs were beginning to spread along the major axial routes and, during the course of the century, the marshy 'Moor Fields' to the immediate north of the wall were gradually drained and reclaimed for housing. To the west, conveniently sited midway between Westminster (the seat of government and the court) and the City of London (the commercial centre), were the luxury residences of the nobility, with gardens stretching down to the Thames. Nonetheless, the people of Tudor London were much less socially segregated than those of most other European cities: traders, craft workers and the poor jostled shoulder to shoulder with the powerful and the wealthy, in a maze of narrow, noisy alleys and lanes.

The river was the principal thoroughfare. Since there was only one bridge across the Thames, the services of some 2,000 watermen were in great demand. The 19 piers or 'starlings' supporting the bridge restricted the tidal flow, making river journeys up or down stream under the bridge extremely hazardous. In severe winters the Thames froze solid, allowing Londoners to walk and play games on the ice – in some years 'Frost Fairs' with stalls and booths were held on the frozen river. **HF**

Tenterfields, for the drying of dyed woollen cloths

Moorgate, the last city gate to be built, in 1415

Court of Wards and Liveries, c.1598
This feudal revenue-raising body was one of the many government institutions that added to the importance of Tudor London.

The Moor Fields, a marshy area being reclaimed in the Tudor period

River Thames

The Tower, a state prison, but also a popular tourist venue in the 16th century

ROYAL PALACES

Nonsuch Palace, Surrey, in 1568

One of Henry VIII's favourite building projects, Nonsuch cost considerably more than Hampton Court. Charles II subsequently gave it to his ex-mistress Barbara Villiers, who demolished it and broke up its parks in 1682.

In both England and Scotland, the monarchies inherited a remarkable stock of royal houses from the Middle Ages. These buildings were mostly fortresses dominating their localities, such as the Tower of London, Windsor Castle, Edinburgh Castle and Stirling Castle. In the sixteenth century, technological innovations in gunnery and military engineering made up-to-date castles less desirable as residences, and thus widened the potential choice of site for royal accommodation. The Protestant Reformation dissolved the abbeys and friaries in both kingdoms, and secularised their sites – making a new stock of grand buildings available to the monarchs and so leading to an increase in the number of royal palaces.

In both England and Scotland, the monarch conspicuously lacked a major residence in the capital. The Tower of London was cramped and defied improvement in an increasingly ostentatious and luxurious period, and Henry VIII never took to the new palace he had built at Bridewell in London; Edinburgh Castle, like the Tower, was intractable. In both kingdoms, proximity to the mercantile and industrial classes (who had little or no say in government), and to the volatile mob, incited by rabble-rousers, made the capitals unattractive places to the Crown.

Henry VIII possessed a series of houses that outshone those of all his contemporaries on the Continent, and his nephew James V of Scotland emulated his example. Henry's houses had all the main rooms situated on one level, an innovatory feature and one universally adopted elsewhere in Europe. Unlike European palaces, English and Scottish

Kensington Palace in the early 18th century

Disliking the damp riverside air at Whitehall Palace, William III bought Nottingham House in 1689. Christopher Wren and William Kent reconstructed it as Kensington Palace, which is still in use as a royal residence.

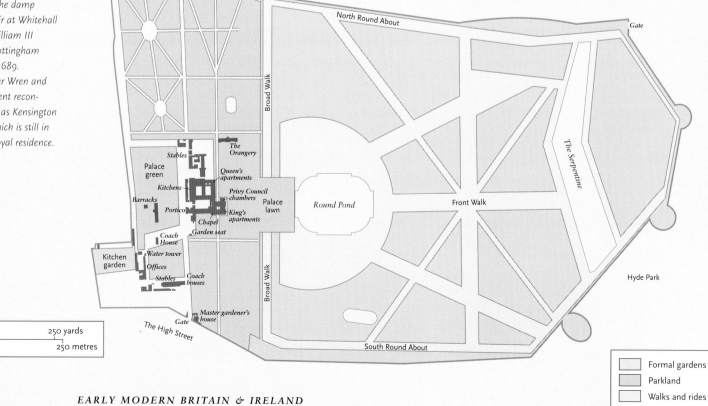

North Round About

Gate

Broad Walk

The Serpentine

The Orangery

Stables

Palace green

Queen's apartments

Kitchens

Privy Council chambers

Palace lawn

Barracks

Portico

King's apartments

Round Pond

Front Walk

Chapel

Garden seat

Coach House

Water tower

Kitchen garden

Offices

Stables

Coach houses

Broad Walk

Hyde Park

Master gardener's house

The High Street

Gate

South Round About

| | 250 yards |
| | 250 metres |

Formal gardens

Parkland

Walks and rides

royal houses were not created as architectural entities, but were characterised by a picturesque disposition of mass and blocks. Over time, they accommodated every change of fashion from mannerism to Palladianism to the baroque. Spectacular gardens were a feature from the reign of Henry VIII onwards; William III was an avid gardener. Park and gardens at Richmond, a Tudor palace, survived to become in the eighteenth century the nucleus of a house at Kew, now the Royal Botanic Gardens. As on the Continent, royal palaces under Charles I became treasure houses filled with magnificent pictures and sculpture.

The main houses were situated in the agriculturally rich parts of the kingdoms. In England they were restricted to the Thames valley, stretching from Woodstock in Oxfordshire via Windsor Castle, Richmond, Hampton Court and Whitehall to Greenwich. In Scotland they were largely confined to the neck of land between the Firth of Forth on the east and the river Clyde on the west. There were none in Wales. Transport by river eased movement otherwise cumbersome by road – over 500 carts were used by Henry VIII on his progresses from palace to palace.

THE DECLINE OF COURT AND PALACE

The main houses fell into two types: those used in the winter months, with the full court in attendance, and those used in the summer, with fewer courtiers present. Palaces were not only residences, but also political centres, so in addition to household officials, leading government officials also had to be accommodated. Only the more important houses had specific rooms for the Privy Council to meet, and it was these that survived in regular use. The development of better metalled roads enabled Charles II to start building a palace at Winchester, but in fact better communications and therefore speedier conveyance of provisions to feed the monarch and his court ended the necessity of moving at regular intervals once foodstuffs in an area had been exhausted. This growing tendency for the court to become settled resulted in a reduction of the number of royal houses, as those no longer needed were sold off. Another, related, factor tending to reduce the number of palaces was the union of crowns in 1603. As the Stuart kings turned their backs on their Scottish kingdom, most of the royal palaces there were let or sold off.

The Civil War also depleted the stock of royal houses. Several (Holdenby, Richmond and Theobalds) were demolished; Woodstock was sold by the Parliamentary Commission. Charles II undertook a programme of refurbishment, particularly at Whitehall, Windsor, Greenwich and Holyrood. But economic retrenchment obliged him to cut down on the diets (that is, the daily food allowances for courtiers), and then to abolish them. Further stringent economies led to the reversion to their original owners of ostentatious houses such as Audley End (a palace for over 30 years), which had proved too expensive to maintain. Fire destroyed the main palace at Whitehall (in the sixteenth century the largest in Europe) in 1698. Wars against Louis XIV's France left little spare cash for building.

All this resulted in a reduction in the size of the British court. Surplus building stock at Chelsea and Greenwich was transformed into hospital facilities for the war-wounded. Somerset House became government offices. (The process of disposing of unwanted palaces dated back to the

Royal palaces

British monarchs possessed a large number of residences, but their distribution is well reflected in the locations of the main palaces. There were comparatively few outside the Scottish Lowlands and the southeast of England. From the 17th century many became redundant and were converted to other uses.

mid-Tudor period when Edward VI had transferred Bridewell to the City of London to serve as a house of correction for social and sexual deviants.) The regular absence of William III in The Netherlands (where he was Stadholder) and of the Hanoverian kings in Germany (where they were electors of Hanover) made a profusion of palaces superfluous. This was in accord with the political climate after the Glorious Revolution, which in 1688–9 transformed the constitution. With the single exception of Hampton Court (disliked by the Hanoverian monarchy), British palaces of the eighteenth century – St James's and Kensington – were comparatively unpretentious and modest, in contrast to their continental counterparts. Even so, George III and his wife Charlotte preferred the domestic bliss of nearby Buckingham House (now Buckingham Palace, and much enlarged). **AH**

THE FIRST CIVIL WAR

Though they are usually known simply as the English Civil Wars, the civil wars of the 1640s are more accurately described by the name used by generations of Irish historians – the Wars of the Three Kingdoms. No part of the British Isles was unaffected by the struggle and the general population suffered far more severely in Scotland and Ireland than it did in England. If it is true that the outcome of the wars in Scotland and Ireland was largely determined by that of the war in England, it is also the case that King Charles I repeatedly looked to Scotland and Ireland to shore up his position in England.

Charles's difficulties began almost immediately on his accession in 1625. He offended his Scottish subjects by seeking to renegotiate the terms on which Crown and Church lands had been handed over to them in the previous century and by giving the bishops a prominent role in government. This was deeply resented by Scotland's Presbyterian majority, who were utterly opposed to the episcopal church. Charles also quickly fell out with the English parliament over taxation, and determined to rule without parliament if necessary. Many English Puritans were deeply suspicious of the king's apparent Catholic sympathies. Ireland, too, was simmering with discontent. Many Catholics, especially in Ulster, had been dispossessed of their lands and replaced by Scots and English Protestant settlers. Charles had promised the Catholic 'Old English' families limited religious freedom in return for a payment of £120,000, but had never confirmed their privileges.

The drift to war began in 1638, when Charles tried to impose a version of the English prayer book on Scotland – leading the Scottish Presbyterians to form the National Covenant and call for an end to English-style bishops. The king responded by raising an army in England, but when it was confronted by a large Scots force at Berwick on Tweed in 1639, he backed down. The following year Charles raised another army to invade Scotland but the Scots acted first, marching into England, winning an easy victory at Newburn and occupying Newcastle. These humiliating little 'Bishops Wars' strained the king's finances and forced him to call a parliament to pay off the Scots and confirm his concessions to them. The price parliament demanded for its cooperation – reforms that would limit the king's power – was unacceptable to Charles.

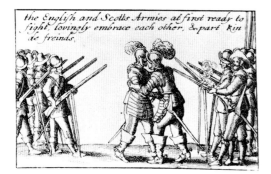

The Bishops Wars
This contemporary engraving gives some indication of the unwillingness of the English and Scottish soldiers to fight in the king's war.

Charles's position became critical late in 1641 when a Catholic rebellion broke out around Dublin and in Ulster. Of the 30–40,000 Protestant settlers there, perhaps 3,000 were massacred and around a third fled from their homes. Many died of their privations, but many more reached England to testify to their sufferings. In desperation, Charles attempted to break the deadlock with the English parliament by a coup in January 1642. When the attempt failed, he was forced to leave the capital for York, and both king and parliament began to gather military forces.

The English people were reluctant to take up arms: most shires were deeply divided in their loyalties, and civil war would literally set neighbour against neighbour. But fighting between parliamentary and royalist supporters broke out at Manchester in July 1642. Most shires saw early skirmishes (and sometimes larger battles) as the opposing factions fought for local control. By the end of 1642 these local actions had produced reasonably clear areas of parliamentary and royal control across the country. Support for parliament was strongest in London, the Southeast, East Anglia and in the port towns that traded with London. The king recruited heavily wherever he appeared in person, initially in the Midlands and western counties, later in the Southwest and Wales. Parliament prospered wherever the cloth industry and Puritanism were strong; the king prospered over less compact and less economically developed regions. This was costly to him in the long run.

THE WIDENING WAR

The king recognised this weakness in his position, and prepared a swift advance on London. He was met by a parliamentary army at Edgehill in Oxfordshire on 23 October. The two inexperienced armies fought each other to a standstill, but it was the parliamentarians who withdrew during the night. Charles pressed on towards London, but was checked by the re-formed parliamentary forces a few miles short of his objective, at Turnham Green (Brentford). His attempt to capture London came to nothing. Nonetheless, as a greater proportion of his commanders had gained significant military experience in the Thirty Years War in Europe, the war generally progressed in the king's favour; by late 1643 royalist control had been extended from the West Country over much of Wiltshire, Hampshire and Berkshire.

The First Civil War, 1639–47

In the First Civil War (opposite), the economically dominant landowners and merchants of southeast England mostly opposed the king, while royalist support was strongest in the poorer, more peripheral west and north. The Scots initially remained neutral, then took the field against the king in 1644. Ireland saw a three-way division between the Protestant towns under royalist control, Scottish Ulster, and the rebel Catholic countryside.

Three separate struggles against the Stuarts became fatally interlinked by Charles I's strategy of using Irish forces (both royalists and rebels after his 1643 truce with the Kilkenny Confederation) and Montrose's royalist Scots to try to retrieve his fortunes in England.

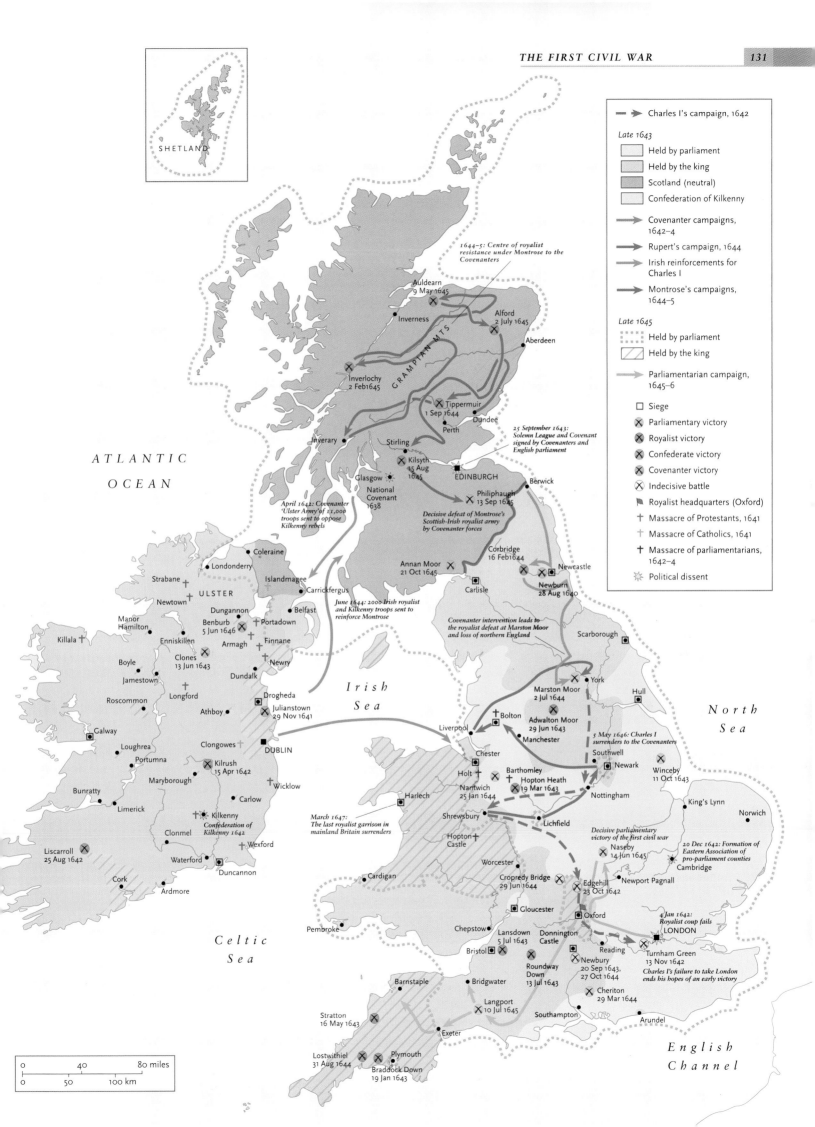

SHETLAND

ATLANTIC OCEAN

Legend:

- — ➤ Charles I's campaign, 1642

Late 1643
- Held by parliament
- Held by the king
- Scotland (neutral)
- Confederation of Kilkenny

- ⇢ Covenanter campaigns, 1642–4
- ➤ Rupert's campaign, 1644
- ➤ Irish reinforcements for Charles I
- ➤ Montrose's campaigns, 1644–5

Late 1645
- ⸬ Held by parliament
- ⫽ Held by the king

- ➤ Parliamentarian campaign, 1645–6

- ☐ Siege
- ⊗ Parliamentary victory
- ⊗ Royalist victory
- ⊗ Confederate victory
- ⊗ Covenanter victory
- ⊗ Indecisive battle
- ⚑ Royalist headquarters (Oxford)
- ✝ Massacre of Protestants, 1641
- ✝ Massacre of Catholics, 1641
- ✝ Massacre of parliamentarians, 1642–4
- ✳ Political dissent

1644–5: Centre of royalist resistance under Montrose to the Covenanters

Auldearn 9 May 1645
Inverness
Alford 2 July 1645
Aberdeen
Inverlochy 2 Feb 1645
GRAMPIAN MTS
Tippermuir 1 Sep 1644
Dundee
Inverary
Perth
Stirling
25 September 1643: Solemn League and Covenant signed by Covenanters and English parliament
Glasgow
Kilsyth 15 Aug 1645
National Covenant 1638
EDINBURGH
Philiphaugh 13 Sep 1645
Berwick
Decisive defeat of Montrose's Scottish-Irish royalist army by Covenanter forces

April 1642: Covenanter 'Ulster Army' of 11,000 troops sent to oppose Kilkenny rebels

Annan Moor 21 Oct 1645
Corbridge 16 Feb 1644
Newcastle
Carlisle
Newburn 28 Aug 1640

Coleraine
Londonderry
Strabane
Islandmagee
Carrickfergus
ULSTER
Newtown
Dungannon
Belfast
Manor Hamilton
Benburb 5 Jun 1646
Portadown
Finnane
June 1644: 2000 Irish royalist and Kilkenny troops sent to reinforce Montrose
Killala
Enniskillen
Armagh
Clones 13 Jun 1643
Newry
Covenanter intervention leads to the royalist defeat at Marston Moor and loss of northern England
Scarborough
Boyle
Dundalk
Jamestown
Longford
Roscommon
Athboy
Drogheda
Julianstown 29 Nov 1641
Irish Sea
York
Marston Moor 2 Jul 1644
Hull
Galway
Clongowes
DUBLIN
Liverpool
Bolton
Adwalton Moor 29 Jun 1643
North Sea
Loughrea
Portumna
Clonmel
Kilrush 15 Apr 1642
Manchester
Chester
5 May 1646: Charles I surrenders to the Covenanters
Southwell
Bunratty
Maryborough
Holt
Nantwich 25 Jan 1644
Barthomley
Hopton Heath 19 Mar 1643
Newark
Winceby 11 Oct 1643
Limerick
Wicklow
Harlech
Shrewsbury
Lichfield
Nottingham
King's Lynn
Norwich
Liscarroll 25 Aug 1642
Carlow
Hopton Castle
March 1647: The last royalist garrison in mainland Britain surrenders
Worcester
Naseby 14 Jun 1645
20 Dec 1642: Formation of Eastern Association of pro-parliament counties
Cambridge
Kilkenny *Confederation of Kilkenny 1642*
Wexford
Cardigan
Cropredy Bridge 29 Jun 1644
Edgehill 23 Oct 1642
Newport Pagnall
Clonmel
Waterford
Duncannon
Pembroke
Chepstow
Gloucester
Oxford
4 Jan 1642: Royalist coup fails LONDON
Cork
Ardmore
Lansdown 5 Jul 1643
Donnington Castle
Reading
Turnham Green 13 Nov 1642
Bristol
Newbury 20 Sep 1643, 27 Oct 1644
Charles I's failure to take London ends his hopes of an early victory
Barnstaple
Bridgwater
Roundway Down 13 Jul 1643
Cheriton 29 Mar 1644
Stratton 16 May 1643
Langport 10 Jul 1645
Southampton
Arundel
Exeter
Lostwithiel 31 Aug 1644
Plymouth
Braddock Down 19 Jan 1643

Irish Sea
Celtic Sea
English Channel

0   40   80 miles
0   50   100 km

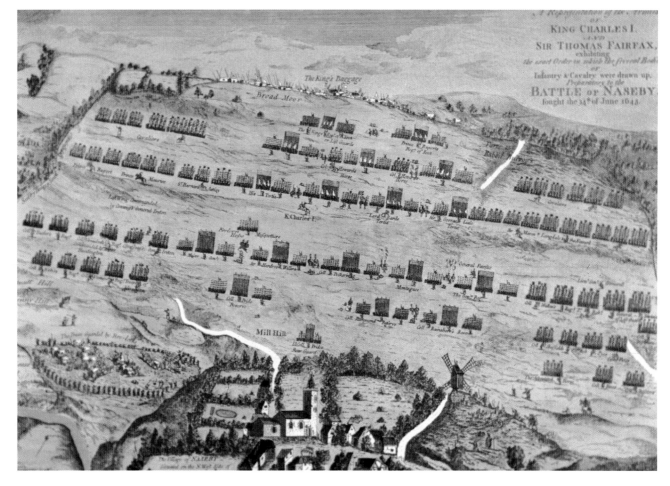

The battle of Naseby

A contemporary picture showing the two armies facing one another. At Naseby the greater resources available to parliament, as well as superior discipline, proved decisive. With his last army routed, Charles had lost the war.

'The world turn'd upside down'

The title page of an anti-radical tract. Moderates, horrified by the extremism engendered by the war, struggled to make their voices heard.

Charles looked to Ireland for troops to bring the war to a decision. The Catholic rebellion in 1641 had spread quickly, and most of Ireland had fallen into rebel hands within a few months. In April 1642 the Scots had sent an army of 11,000 men under Sir Robert Munro to Ulster to support the Protestants, and had succeeded in clearing much of the east of the province of rebels. Dublin and much of the Pale, together with many smaller enclaves, remained under the control of English commanders loyal to the king. The rebels were poorly organised and equipped, and could not take the remaining Protestant strongholds, but neither the royalist English nor the Scots were capable of mounting a sustained counter-offensive once hostilities had broken out in England. Charles had begun negotiations in June 1643 with the rebel Confederation of Kilkenny, seeking troops for the royalist cause in return for religious concessions. A one-year cease-fire was agreed in September, and a force of royalist troops freed from the fighting was sent to Cheshire. They laid siege to the parliamentary stronghold of Nantwich, but were routed on 25 January 1644 by a parliamentary army that had crossed from Yorkshire. Charles sought further reinforcements from Ireland – but their military value was slight, given the damage that his willingness to ally with Catholics did to his standing in England and Scotland.

In autumn 1643 Scotland's leaders saw that a victory for Charles in England would doom their Presbyterian revolution, so they abandoned their neutrality in favour of an alliance with the English parliament in January 1644. Reinforced by Scottish forces under Alexander Leslie, the Yorkshire army of Sir Thomas Fairfax and the Eastern Association cavalry commanded by Oliver Cromwell decisively defeated the main royalist army under the king's cousin Prince Rupert and the earl of Newcastle at Marston Moor on 2 July. The royalist position in the North collapsed, but an attempt by parliamentarian forces under the earl of Essex to capitalise on this success by invading the West Country was heavily defeated at Lostwithiel in Cornwall in August.

Charles attempted to retrieve his fortunes in Scotland, and to relieve the pressure in England, through a series of campaigns led by James Graham, the marquis of Montrose. Montrose was a resourceful commander, but the royalist position in Scotland was a microcosm of that in England. Royalist support was strongest in the largely Catholic Highlands, but this was also the poorest part of the country; the richer and more populous Presbyterian Lowlands remained committed to the Covenanter alliance with the English parliament. Reinforcements from Ireland never arrived in sufficient numbers (some 2,000 troops sent in June 1644 were the only significant contribution) and, after a string of victories, Montrose was at last crushed by the Covenanters under David Leslie at Philiphaugh in September 1645.

After Marston Moor, fighting in England tended to be concentrated around the royalist strongholds of Newark, Chester, Exeter and Oxford. Newark controlled a major bridge over the Trent and was a strategic base from which raiders could threaten parliament's north–south communications. Chester was the port Charles hoped to use to land further reinforcements from Ireland. Oxford was the king's headquarters; its garrison dominated the main routes to the

West Country. Large parliamentary forces were committed to besieging these centres, while the king prepared a new offensive. In spring 1645 Prince Rupert invaded the east Midlands, forcing parliament to lift its siege of Oxford. The two armies met on 14 June at Naseby: the royalists were resoundingly defeated and Charles was never again able to put a large army in the field. After the victory, parliament captured Oxford and swept into the West Country. All hope of victory lost, Charles surrendered to the Scots at Newark in May 1646, effectively ending the war.

The king's surrender did little to clarify matters in Ireland. The royalist governor of Dublin surrendered the city to parliament in July 1647 and the Scots expanded their enclave in Ulster at the expense of both the Confederates and the royalists. But the Confederates continued to control most of the countryside and royalist garrisons most of the towns. Parliament had more pressing problems, so Ireland was, for the time being, left to itself.

GLOUCESTERSHIRE IN THE CIVIL WAR

Study of the war in a single county helps illustrate the variety of national and local issues that determined loyalties. At the outbreak of the Civil War, Gloucestershire was deeply divided. As in other parts of the country, religious persuasion played an important part in deciding allegiances. The Anglican Cotswolds and Catholic Forest of Dean naturally inclined towards the Crown, while the Puritan vales were strongholds of parliamentary support. Parliamentary support was strong in the towns, especially Gloucester itself. Accounts from the port of Bristol of atrocities committed by the rebels in Ireland reinforced anti-Catholic prejudices to the benefit of the parliamentary cause. Anti-royalist sentiment in the north of the county was also fed by the king's attempts in the 1630s to destroy the local tobacco-growing industry to protect the interests of planters on Crown lands in Virginia.

Though a majority of the county gentry supported the Crown, Gloucestershire had few great landowners; the county therefore lacked obvious leaders, and both sides were slow to organise for war. The parliamentary leaders finally proved more able than the royalists, who allowed personal rivalries to interfere with their war effort. The parliamentarians were able to recover from serious reverses early in the war, while the royalists failed to capitalise on their advantages.

For a short time after the king seized Bristol in July 1643, Gloucestershire was the key theatre of the war. Urged by his generals to exploit parliament's disarray and advance on London, Charles instead turned aside to eliminate the last parliamentary garrison in the county, at Gloucester. Enthusiastically supported by the townsfolk, the garrison held out for six weeks until relieved by the earl of Essex, possibly costing Charles an opportunity to end the war quickly. For the next two years, Gloucester remained a parliamentary enclave in royalist territory. The royalists failed to prevent the Gloucester garrison raiding far and wide under its energetic commander Edward Massey; he slowly expanded the parliamentary enclave until, after Naseby, royalist support in the county collapsed.   **JH**

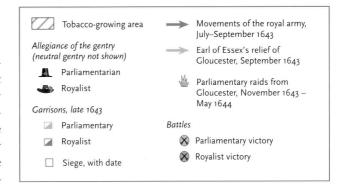

Tobacco-growing area

Allegiance of the gentry (neutral gentry not shown)

Parliamentarian

Royalist

Garrisons, late 1643

Parliamentary

Royalist

Siege, with date

Movements of the royal army, July–September 1643

Earl of Essex's relief of Gloucester, September 1643

Parliamentary raids from Gloucester, November 1643 – May 1644

Battles

Parliamentary victory

Royalist victory

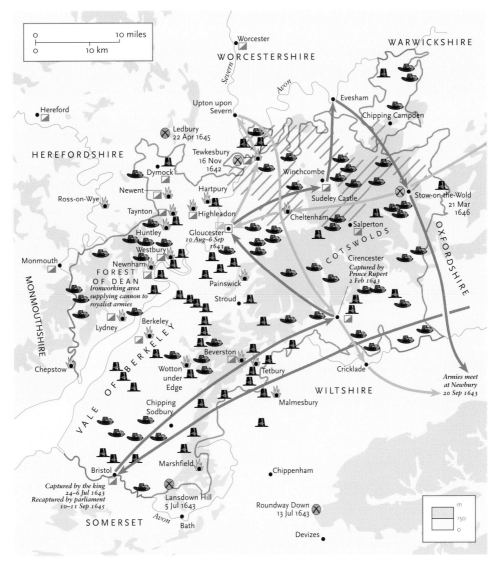

Gloucestershire and the Civil War

Gloucestershire was deeply divided during the Civil War – between royalists, parliamentarians and those who wanted nothing to do with the fight. Lacking great landed magnates to give leadership, and with Gloucester firmly in parliamentary hands, the royalists proved ineffective. Gradually the better organised parliamentarians gained control of the county.

The surrender of Charles I in 1646 brought no solution to the issues that had started the civil wars in any of the three kingdoms. Negotiations between the royalists and the parliamentary commissioners of England and Scotland dragged on as rifts opened between the victors. The English parliament had agreed to introduce Presbyterianism in England and Ireland in return for Scottish support during the Civil War. The Scots had kept their side of the bargain, but now that the war was over the English parliament seemed to have lost its enthusiasm for Presbyterianism. Many of the MPs were suspicious of the Scots; they believed that the defeat of the royalists made a political settlement possible in England without Scottish involvement, so they were unwilling to compromise. Charles, meanwhile, refused to make any concessions at all to parliament, since all concessions would reduce his prerogative powers.

The officers of the English parliament's New Model Army sought to break the deadlock by proposing their own peace terms, known as the 'Heads of Proposals'. Charles kept all sides at arm's length, at the same time holding secret negotiations with the duke of Hamilton, his former advisor on Scottish affairs who was now spokesman for a faction of discontented Scottish peers. While unrest continued south of the

> 'Oliver Cromwell, Captain-General of the forces of England, Scotland and Ireland, shall be, and is hereby declared to be, Lord Protector of the Commonwealth of England, Scotland, and Ireland and the dominions thereto belonging, for his life.'
>
> **Instrument of Government, Clause 33 (1653)**

The British Republic

The defeat of the king in 1646 did little to provide Britain with stability. The English parliamentary and Scottish victors were soon at loggerheads, leading to an attempted royalist invasion of England and a vigorous counter-campaign in Scotland by Cromwell. The Irish rebellion was finally put down, with the whole of Ireland forcibly united with England for the first time in its history. However, sporadic royalist risings continued, even after the execution of Charles I, while the new regime's efforts to find a constitutional settlement for the whole of the British Isles became increasingly dictatorial and unpopular.

border with uprisings in Wales, Kent and Essex, Hamilton attempted to raise Scottish support for a royalist–Presbyterian rebellion. Parliament placed England back on a war footing, and localised fighting in spring 1648 initiated the Second Civil War. Hamilton's Scottish army did not cross into England until July, and was caught in dispersed order by Cromwell's tough veterans at Preston in August. The parliamentary victory was crushing, and it ended the war at a stroke.

There were many aspects to the new negotiations that followed this second war. The moderate 'Presbyterians' in the English parliament still believed that compromise with the king was possible. The more radical 'Independents', including the Levellers, a popular movement, pressed for sweeping changes not only to the political system, but to society at large. Believing that a judgement of God had been delivered on Charles, many of the Independents sought vengeance for the blood spilled in the wars.

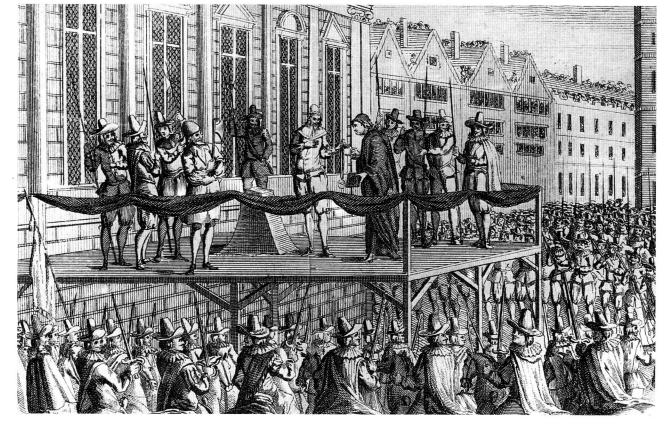

Execution of Charles I

Charles I faces execution, January 1649. Regicide horrified moderates and foreign powers alike. Diplomatic isolation did little to help the new republic establish itself.

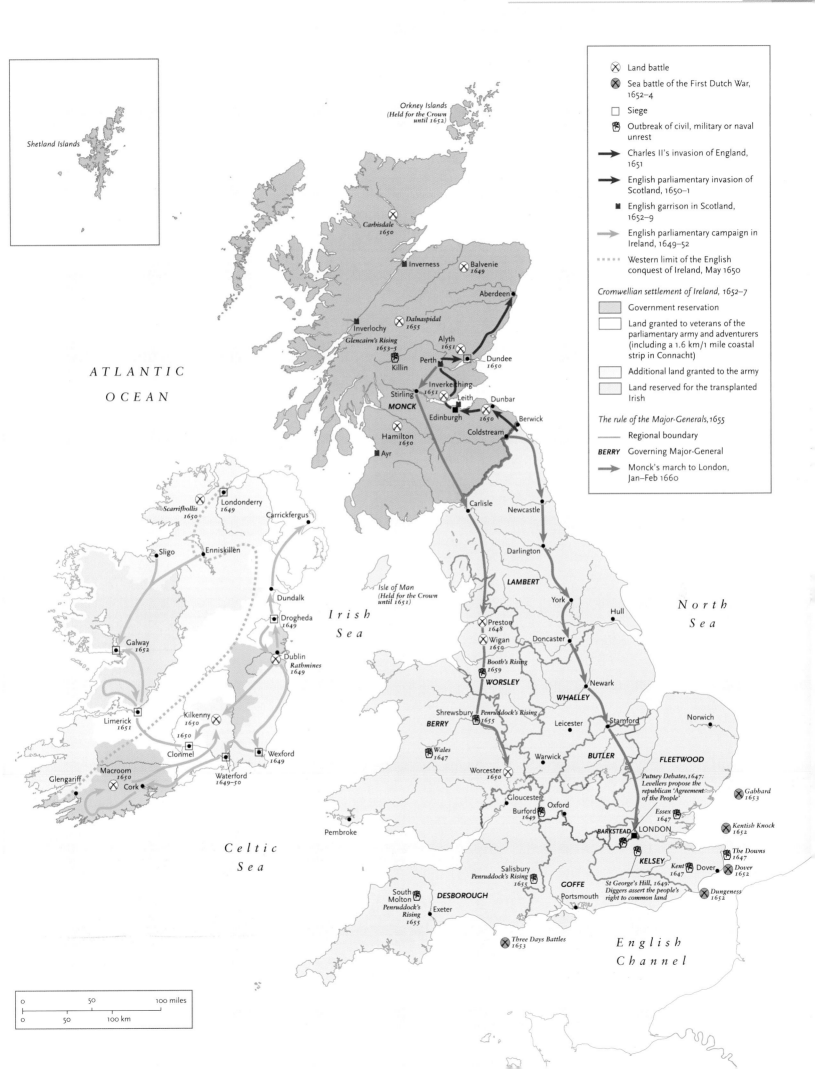

Shetland Islands

Orkney Islands
(Held for the Crown
until 1652)

Legend

⊗ Land battle

⊗ Sea battle of the First Dutch War, 1652–4

□ Siege

✊ Outbreak of civil, military or naval unrest

→ Charles II's invasion of England, 1651

→ English parliamentary invasion of Scotland, 1650–1

■ English garrison in Scotland, 1652–9

→ English parliamentary campaign in Ireland, 1649–52

····· Western limit of the English conquest of Ireland, May 1650

Cromwellian settlement of Ireland, 1652–7

▨ Government reservation

▢ Land granted to veterans of the parliamentary army and adventurers (including a 1.6 km/1 mile coastal strip in Connacht)

▨ Additional land granted to the army

▨ Land reserved for the transplanted Irish

The rule of the Major-Generals, 1655

— Regional boundary

BERRY Governing Major-General

→ Monck's march to London, Jan–Feb 1660

ATLANTIC OCEAN

Carbisdale 1650

■ Inverness   ⊗ *Balvenie 1649*

Aberdeen

■ Inverlochy   ⊗ *Dalnaspidal 1655*

Glencairn's Rising 1653–5   *Alyth 1651*

✊ Killin   Perth   ⊗   *Dundee 1650*

Inverkeithing 1651   Leith   Dunbar

Stirling   ⊗ Edinburgh   ⊗ *1650*

MONCK   Berwick

⊗ *Hamilton 1650*   Coldstream

■ Ayr

Carlisle   Newcastle

Scarriffhollis 1650   ⊗   Londonderry *1649*

Carrickfergus

Sligo   Enniskillen

Darlington

LAMBERT

Isle of Man (Held for the Crown until 1651)

York   Hull

North Sea

Dundalk

□ *Drogheda 1649*

Irish Sea

□ *Galway 1652*

□ *Dublin Rathmines 1649*

⊗ *Preston 1648*

⊗ *Wigan 1651*   Doncaster

Booth's Rising 1659 ✊

WORSLEY   Newark

□ *Limerick 1651*   *Kilkenny 1650*   ⊗

1650   Clonmel   □ *Wexford 1649*

WHALLEY

Shrewsbury   *Penruddock's Rising 1655* ✊   Leicester   Stamford   Norwich

BERRY

□ Macroom *1650*   Waterford *1649–50*

Glengariff   ⊗ Cork

Celtic Sea

Pembroke

Wales 1647 ✊

⊗ *Worcester 1650*   Warwick   **BUTLER**   **FLEETWOOD**

Putney Debates, 1647: Levellers propose the republican 'Agreement of the People'   ⊗ *Gabbard 1653*

Gloucester   Oxford

Burford 1649 □   *Essex 1647* ✊   ⊗ *Kentish Knock 1652*

BARKSTEAD ✊   LONDON   ✊

Salisbury   *Penruddock's Rising 1655* ✊   *Kent 1647* ✊ Dover   *The Downs 1647* ✊   ⊗ *Dover 1652*

GOFFE   **KELSEY**

South Molton   **DESBOROUGH**   Portsmouth   *St George's Hill, 1649: Diggers assert the people's right to common land*   ⊗ *Dungeness 1652*

Penruddock's Rising 1655 ✊   Exeter

⊗ *Three Days Battles 1653*

English Channel

0   50   100 miles
0   50   100 km

The moderates held sway in both Houses of the English parliament, and on 5 December 1648 they used their majority to force through a vote to continue negotiations with the king. Radicals in the Commons and the army resolved to force a settlement: the following day, Lord Grey of Groby identified the pro-negotiation MPs, and Colonel Thomas Pride's soldiers barred their entry to the Commons, arresting their leaders. The purged House, known later as the Rump, put Charles on trial for making war against his people; he was executed on 30 January 1649.

A series of radical acts followed: the Commons declared themselves the sovereign power, the monarchy and House of Lords were abolished (March 1649) and England was declared a Commonwealth (May 1649) – making its government a republic. An executive Council of State dealt with day-to-day business and an oath – the Engagement – was required of all seeking status in law and politics.

THE COMMONWEALTH

The early years of the Commonwealth revealed its international isolation. The immediate response of the Scots to the news of Charles I's execution was to proclaim his son, Charles II, king of all Britain. Ireland had still to be pacified, despite a major parliamentary victory at Rathmines, just south of Dublin, in August 1649. The means by which the Commonwealth came to power, its decision to create a Council of State and the slow pace of reform all also earned the opprobrium of potential allies like the Levellers. Soldiers tired of war mutinied in response to moves to send them to Ireland. The failure of a much-trumpeted Protestant republican confederation with the United Provinces of the Netherlands resulted in a counter-policy of antagonism toward the Dutch. The Navigation Act of 1651 tied English commercial goods to English shipping and English ports, provoking the first Anglo-Dutch war, of 1652–4.

Siege of Drogheda

Cromwell's suppression of Irish resistance was swift and effective. The notorious massacre that occurred at Drogheda remains a hugely emotive and controversial issue in Irish history.

Cromwell was sent with troops to Ireland in August 1649 and, after his success there, to Scotland in July 1650. He defeated the main Scots army at Dunbar in September and occupied Edinburgh, but resistance continued north of the Forth, where Charles II was raising forces.

In August 1651 Charles invaded England in an attempt to raise a royalist rebellion. He received little support, and his decisive defeat by Cromwell at Worcester on 3 Septem-

ber 1651 finished royalism as a military threat to the Commonwealth. The last royalist outposts in the Isle of Man and the Channel Islands surrendered before the end of the same year. The English troops in Ireland mopped up Irish resistance and in the Act of Settlement of 1652 Parliament decided to solve the Irish problem by transplanting the majority of Catholic Irish to Connacht; the remaining three-quarters of the country was to be granted to parliamentary veterans and other Protestant settlers. In the event, the settlement could not be implemented fully as few veterans took up the land allotted to them. The Catholic Irish remained on the land, but as the tenants of a class of Protestant landowners. Scotland's resistance had also been broken by 1652. Its factional politics – Highland Catholics, Stuart loyalists, Covenanters and anti-monarchists – left Scotland prey, eventually, to the Cromwellian forces. For the first time in their history, all of the British Isles were under the control of a single government.

THE PROTECTORATE

Cromwell's patience with the republican experiment ran out in April 1653, as a result of the slow pace of English reform and dissatisfaction with the Irish settlement. He accused the MPs of lacking the personal morality to rule, and forcibly removed them from the House. In place of the Commonwealth, a body of 144 men was chosen by the

Army Council, many being drawn from the recommendations of gathered congregations around the country. It was a mixture of religious enthusiasts from a variety of churches but mainly from gentry backgrounds. It lasted only five months, disrupted by the more radical religious dissenters. It volunteered up its power, and by the 'Instrument of Government' Oliver Cromwell was established as the first Lord Protector in December 1653. In September 1654 he called his first parliament, which contained 400 members from England and Wales, and 30 each from Scotland and Ireland. The new parliament failed to ratify the Instrument, and wrangling over the Protector's powers led to a purge and its early dissolution.

In 1655 Cromwell overreacted to a feeble set of royalist uprisings by setting up 11 military governors (the 'Major-Generals') in England and Scotland, to raise taxation from former royalists, to maintain local militias and to oversee a programme of godly reformation. Reaction against

The battle of Worcester

The defeat of Charles II at Worcester seemed to dash the last hopes of the Stuarts of ever regaining the throne. Charles was forced to flee to exile in France.

Cromwell's high-handedness led the second Protectorate parliament to try to circumscribe his powers, paradoxically by turning him into a constitutional monarch. He refused to accept the crown.

Cromwell died on 3 September 1658 and his son Richard succeeded him as Protector. The younger Cromwell proved unable to contain a revival of political radicalism in the army, which recalled the Rump parliament and put an end to the Protectorate.

In October 1659 an army coup led by John Lambert dispersed the Rump and installed a military junta. Dissidents restored the Rump, but neither it nor the army any longer enjoyed much popular support.

In January 1660, the army of occupation in Scotland, under the command of General George Monck, began to march towards London. On his journey south, Monck received petitions calling for free elections to parliament. These elections produced the moderate Convention parliament that proclaimed Charles II king on 8 May 1660.

FROM WAR TO PEACE

The transition from civil war to peace was not an easy one, especially in areas which had been bitterly fought over, such as Oxfordshire, where the king had had his headquarters, and neighbouring Berkshire. With the war over, here, as elsewhere in the country, the land of the Crown, the Church, and certain categories of royalist (such as 'Papists in arms', or those who, like Sir Edward Hyde, joined Charles II in exile) was confiscated and sold off. Sequestered lands were granted to prominent parliamentary supporters such as Henry Marten, who gained lands at Eynsham to add to his estates in the area between Shrivenham and Longworth, and the brothers John and William Lenthall, who increased their land holdings around Burford. These circumstances offered great opportunities for speculators such as the Leveller John Wildman, a lawyer, who used his knowledge of the land market and his connections with leading figures in government to accumulate large land holdings in northwest Berkshire, as well as in other counties around the country.

There was much to be done in restoring stability and prosperity to the area. As a region that had been at the centre of the fighting, Oxfordshire and Berkshire had much wasted land; landowners were heavily taxed, and in many cases their tenants had failed to pay their rents for some years. The new government provided an opportunity for petitions for redress. For example, the citizens of Oxford petitioned parliament for help to restore the damage done to the city during the siege and fire of 1644.

Others rebuilt their estates in a different way. The Loder family, based around Kintbury and Harwell, Berkshire, were keen to experiment in the most modern farming and land-management techniques. They were at the forefront of those progressive landlords who sought agreement to enclose land and to manage and divert water courses in order to improve the quality, productivity and profitability of their lands.

The region remained strategically important, as it lay between London and the west coast ports from which troops were to embark for the continuing (and unpopular) war in Ireland. Signs of dissent, such as the army mutiny at Burford in 1649 over pay and lack of motivation amongst those selected for the intended Irish campaign, remained a major concern for successive governments. The area also contained pockets of religious enthusiasm; Abingdon was particularly known as a centre of both religious radicalism and civil unrest.

In the 1650s both Oxfordshire and Berkshire were regarded as strongholds of opposition to the government, from committed royalists and also sectarians and radical politicians committed to opposition to Cromwell's Protectorate. In 1654–5, Cromwell's secretary John Thurloe believed that an alliance of royalists and republicans had been fomented by the earl of Berkshire, Henry Marten and John Wildman and his Leveller allies. No major threat to the government emerged from this cooperation, however.

At the Restoration, sequestered land throughout the country reverted to its previous owners; the most prominent republicans in Oxfordshire and Berkshire, Marten and Wildman, forfeited all their lands for their activities against the king.   **SEB**

Oxfordshire and Berkshire

Areas such as Oxfordshire and Berkshire, which had seen heavy fighting during the First Civil War, urgently needed to restore prosperity and stability. This was no easy matter, with royalist estates sequestered, or their owners paying heavy fines for opposing parliament. Nor was the continuing political controversy of any help, as radicals in both counties remained dissatisfied with successive governments and army loyalties wavered.

RESTORATION & UNION

On 29 May 1660, King Charles II rode into London, celebrating both his thirtieth birthday and the restoration of the Stuart monarchy. Greeted with near-universal enthusiasm, his return to power was predicated upon the moderate manifesto set out in the Declaration of Breda, which sought to 'heal and settle' political divisions and offered amnesty to all but a few individual regicides. Despite these stated aspirations of reconstruction and recovery, however, peace and stability remained elusive during the Restoration. The politics of Protestantism proved divisive as Episcopalians and Presbyterians competed for ecclesiastical superiority, while James VII and II's accession in 1685 brought a destabilising attempt to re-Catholicise the populace. Then, amid the dramatic events of the 'Glorious Revolution', the principle of indefeasible hereditary succession was fatally undermined when William and Mary were crowned joint sovereigns in 1689. During the 1690s, the Stuart multiple monarchy became increasingly involved in continental warfare, while endemic problems of dynastic insecurity and economic dislocation induced the Anglo-Scottish Union of 1707.

Charles II's restoration in 1660 was accompanied by a legislative attempt to erase memories of the civil wars. The ancient institutions of crown government were revived and separate legislatures restored in Westminster, Edinburgh and Dublin. In England the monarchy returned to its pre-1641 status, while in Scotland all legislation passed since 1633 was revoked. The characteristic spirit of political reconciliation was, however, undermined by a pervasive religious intolerance. A narrow form of Anglicanism was imposed in England by the so-called 'Clarendon Code' which ended the diversity of religious practice that had flourished under Cromwell and sought to make religious nonconformity synonymous with political disloyalty. After the widespread outbreak of bubonic plague in England in 1665, the devastation of the Great Fire of London in September 1666 was interpreted by many as divine retribution for national sins that included widespread moral laxity and Catholic conspiracy. In Scotland, the re-imposition of bishops on a largely Presbyterian population was received with hostility and erupted into violence during the Pentland Rising of 1666. The rising led to a series of coercive measures to enforce religious conformity, including the so-called 'Clanking Act' of 1670 which made preaching at unlicensed Presbyterian services a capital offence.

THE SUCCESSION CRISIS

Despite Charles II's personal aim of promoting religious toleration, fears of a crypto-Catholic court conspiracy were generated when details of the 'Secret' Treaty of Dover (1670) emerged. This revealed Charles's willingness to accept financial subsidies from Louis XIV of France in return for a commitment to improve the status of English Catholics. Anxieties increased when Charles's younger brother and heir, James, duke of York, converted to Catholicism and married the Catholic princess Mary of Modena as his second wife in 1673. The staging of ritual pope-burnings in England and Scotland reflected the increasingly obsessive anti-Catholicism permeating political and popular society alike. Frenzied hysteria was generated in 1678 when a Jesuit informer, Titus Oates, disclosed details of a 'Popish Plot' to murder Charles II and install his brother on the throne. Sectarian violence also continued in Scotland, where the archbishop of St Andrews, James Sharp, was brutally murdered on 3 May 1679 by Presbyterian extremists, who allegedly sang psalms as they thrust their swords into his body, convinced that their actions were divinely inspired. As civil unrest escalated, the Scottish authorities responded with ruthless and bloody repression; the era was later immortalised as the 'Killing Times' in Presbyterian martyrology.

Meanwhile, in England, a series of parliamentary attempts was made to bar James from accession to the throne on account of his Catholicism. Such endeavours failed when Charles II prorogued the third 'Exclusionist' parliament that had been summoned in the staunchly royalist city of Oxford in March 1681. To remove him from the

> 'If the general distraction and confusion which is spread over the whole kingdom doth not awaken all men to a desire and longing that those wounds which have so many years together been kept bleeding may be bound up, all we can say will be to no purpose.'
>
> **Charles II, Declaration of Breda, 1660**

Titus Oates on the pillory for perjury

The allegations of the 'Popish Plot', spread by Oates and his associate Israel Tonge, whipped up anti-Catholic hysteria in England in the late 1670s. After a number of high-profile Catholics had been executed, Oates was convicted of perjury in 1684 and imprisoned for life. He was released in 1688, but was not cleared of the charge.

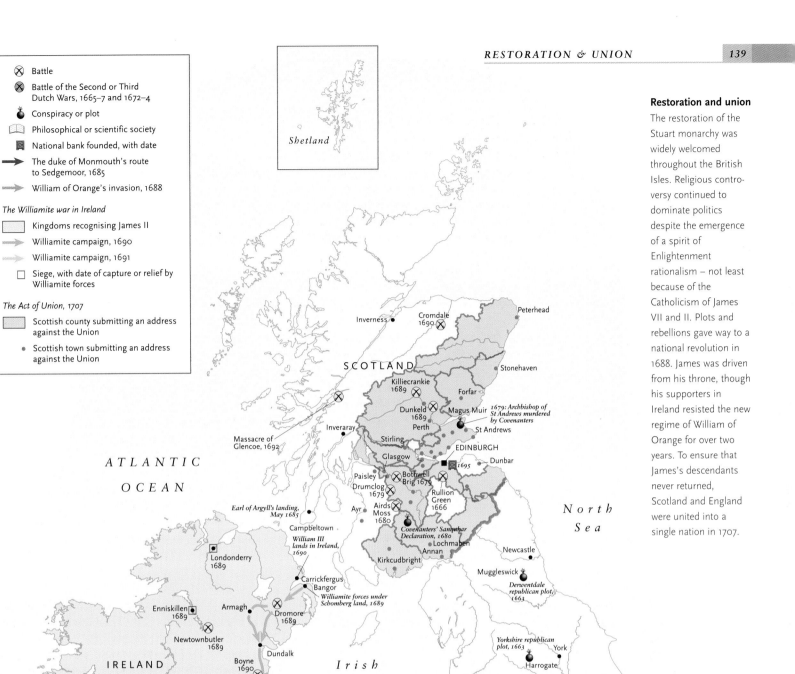

Key

⊗ Battle

⊗ Battle of the Second or Third
   Dutch Wars, 1665–7 and 1672–4

💣 Conspiracy or plot

📖 Philosophical or scientific society

🏦 National bank founded, with date

→ The duke of Monmouth's route
   to Sedgemoor, 1685

→ William of Orange's invasion, 1688

The Williamite war in Ireland

☐ Kingdoms recognising James II

→ Williamite campaign, 1690

→ Williamite campaign, 1691

☐ Siege, with date of capture or relief by
   Williamite forces

The Act of Union, 1707

☐ Scottish county submitting an address
   against the Union

• Scottish town submitting an address
   against the Union

Restoration and union

The restoration of the Stuart monarchy was widely welcomed throughout the British Isles. Religious controversy continued to dominate politics despite the emergence of a spirit of Enlightenment rationalism – not least because of the Catholicism of James VII and II. Plots and rebellions gave way to a national revolution in 1688. James was driven from his throne, though his supporters in Ireland resisted the new regime of William of Orange for over two years. To ensure that James's descendants never returned, Scotland and England were united into a single nation in 1707.

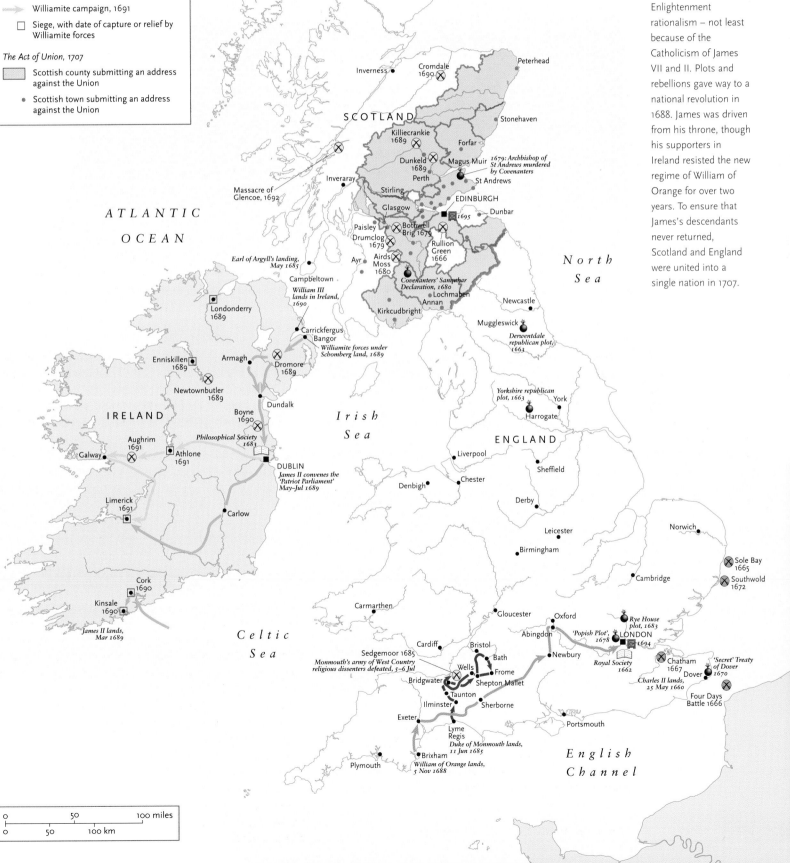

Shetland

ATLANTIC OCEAN

SCOTLAND

Inverness
Cromdale 1690 ⊗
Peterhead

Killiecrankie 1689 ⊗
Forfar
Stonehaven

Dunkeld 1689 ⊗   Magus Muir ⊗
   1679: Archbishop of St Andrews murdered by Covenanters
Perth   St Andrews

Inveraray
Stirling
Glasgow   EDINBURGH 🏦 *1695*   Dunbar

Massacre of Glencoe, 1692

Paisley   Bothwell Brig 1679 ⊗
Drumclog 1679 ⊗
Ayr   Rullion Green 1666 ⊗
Airds Moss 1680 ⊗

Covenanters' Sanquhar Declaration, 1680
Lochmaben
Annan

Kirkcudbright

Earl of Argyll's landing, May 1685
Campbeltown

William III lands in Ireland, 1690

North Sea

Newcastle

Muggleswick 💣
Derwentdale republican plot, 1663

Londonderry 1689 ☐
Carrickfergus
Bangor
Williamite forces under Schomberg land, 1689

Enniskillen 1689 ☐
Armagh
Dromore 1689 ⊗

Newtownbutler 1689 ⊗

IRELAND

Boyne 1690 ⊗
Dundalk

Aughrim 1691 ⊗
Athlone 1691 ☐
Galway

Philosophical Society 1683 📖

DUBLIN 🏦
James II convenes the 'Patriot Parliament' May–Jul 1689

Limerick 1691 ☐

Carlow

Cork 1690 ☐

Kinsale 1690 ☐

James II lands, Mar 1689

Irish Sea

ENGLAND

Yorkshire republican plot, 1663 💣
York

Harrogate ⊗

Liverpool

Sheffield

Denbigh
Chester

Derby

Leicester

Birmingham

Norwich

Cambridge

Sole Bay 1665 ⊗
Southwold 1672 ⊗

Celtic Sea

Carmarthen

Gloucester   Oxford
Abingdon

Cardiff
Bristol   Bath   Newbury
Sedgemoor 1685
Monmouth's army of West Country religious dissenters defeated, 5–6 Jul
Wells ⊗   Frome
Bridgwater   Shepton Mallet
Taunton
Ilminster   Sherborne
Exeter

Lyme Regis
Duke of Monmouth lands, 11 Jun 1685

Brixham
Plymouth   *William of Orange lands, 5 Nov 1688*

Rye House plot, 1683 💣
'Popish Plot', 1678 💣   LONDON 🏦 *1694*
Royal Society 1662 📖

Chatham 1667 ⊗   *'Secret' Treaty of Dover 1670*
Dover
Charles II lands, 25 May 1660
Four Days Battle 1666 ⊗

Portsmouth

English Channel

0 ——— 50 ——— 100 miles
0 ——— 50 ——— 100 km

volatile political atmosphere, Charles sent James to Edinburgh. Here James directed the Scottish parliament to pass a separate Succession Act in August 1681, endorsing his status as lawful heir to the Scottish crown. The crisis did, however, bequeath a permanent constitutional legacy in that it confirmed divisions between the 'Whig' party which had sought to exclude James and the resolutely loyalist 'Tory' party. After suffering defeat over Exclusion, the Whig Party was effectively proscribed in 1683 when its leaders were implicated in the 'Rye House Plot' which revealed a desperate scheme to assassinate both Charles II and his brother in order to place Charles's eldest illegitimate son, the Protestant duke of Monmouth, on the throne. A Tory reaction swiftly followed. Charles refused to summon parliament again, having secured the Crown's financial independence through enhanced excise revenues. The Anglican hierarchy cooperated in the vigorous persecution of religious dissenters, and the early 1680s witnessed the high point of Stuart loyalism as principles of divine right, hereditary succession and absolute monarchy were reiterated with unprecedented zeal.

After Charles's sudden death in February 1685, a wave of popular royalism accompanied James VII and II's accession. Rebellions by the earl of Argyll in western Scotland and by the duke of Monmouth in the West Country were quickly suppressed and their leaders executed. Yet James's initial popularity waned when, mindful that the next in line for the Crown was his Protestant daughter Mary, he immediately sought to obtain civil equality and religious freedom for his fellow Catholics. The mass conversions he had expected failed to materialise, although enthusiasm for James's Catholicising policies was, unsurprisingly, more extensive in Ireland, where Catholics were speedily promoted within the civil and military establishment.

THE 'GLORIOUS REVOLUTION'

The birth of a son to James in June 1688 changed the political landscape entirely by heralding the prospect of a Catholic succession. Five Whig and two Tory politicians, known as the 'Immortal Seven', responded by inviting James's son-in-law, the Protestant Stadholder of Holland, William of Orange, to intervene and restore England's 'ancient laws and liberties'. William quickly complied, eager to incorporate England in his anti-French coalition as well as to defend his wife Mary's hereditary title, after allegations challenging the legitimacy of James's baby son.

On 5 November 1688, William's Dutch fleet landed at Brixham in an operation four times the size of the Spanish Armada a century earlier. As his support evaporated, James fled to France the following month and a power vacuum resulted. Meanwhile, William's troops advanced towards London, encountering little opposition from a civilian population primarily concerned to avoid a repeat of the 'effusion of blood' that had convulsed the nation in the 1640s. In February 1689, the 'Convention Parliament' determined that since both the English and Irish thrones had been left vacant by James's 'abdication', they could be offered to William and Mary, who were duly crowned as joint sovereigns in April. When William and Mary accepted the Scottish crown in May, a more radical constitutional interpretation of events was devised: James was deemed to have forfeited the Scottish throne on account of his misgovernment.

The first steps were taken to re-establish Presbyterianism, but hopes that the Scottish revolution might remain bloodless were quickly dispelled when an army of Jacobite supporters inflicted a defeat on William's forces at Killiecrankie in July, before finally capitulating at Cromdale in May 1690. Two years later, another particularly poignant legacy was left by the massacre of Glencoe on 13 February 1692, when official attempts to enforce allegiance to the Williamite regime degenerated into a bloodbath; 38 members of the pro-Jacobite clan MacDonald were slain by members of the rival clan Campbell, acting under orders from the Scottish Secretary, Sir John Dalrymple.

Events in Ireland were even more dramatic. In March 1689, James set about attempting to regain his thrones by

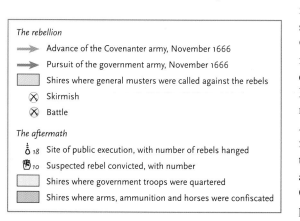

The rebellion

→ Advance of the Covenanter army, November 1666

→ Pursuit of the government army, November 1666

▨ Shires where general musters were called against the rebels

✕ Skirmish

✕ Battle

The aftermath

𐦥₁₈ Site of public execution, with number of rebels hanged

✊₁₀ Suspected rebel convicted, with number

▢ Shires where government troops were quartered

▨ Shires where arms, ammunition and horses were confiscated

The Pentland Rising, 1666

Post-Restoration attempts to re-impose episcopacy on Scotland were widely resented and led to a Covenanter rebellion in 1666 in the southwest. Around 1,100 rebels marched on Edinburgh while the bulk of royal army was preoccupied with the Second Dutch War, causing much alarm. Support for the rebellion was limited, however, and a government victory at Rullion Green was followed by (largely unsuccessful) efforts to pacify the region.

THE
Proteſtant Triumph :

OR,
The ſignal Victory of K. *William* over the *French* and *Iriſh*,
Chaſing them from Hill to Hill, taking their Arms and Ammunitions lſo ; the
Surrender of *Drogheda*, and the King's entring the City of *Dublin* ; to the un-
ſpeakable Joy and Satisfaction of all True Proteſtants.

This Victory was obtain'd on Tueſday the Firſt of July 1690.

To the Tune of The Spinning-wheel.   Licenſed according to Order.

DUBLIN.

The Protestant triumph

A broadsheet celebrating King William's victories in Ireland in 1690. With the defeat of the Jacobites, the triumph of the 'Glorious Revolution' was secured.

law Anne. In 1701 the English parliament passed the Act of Settlement, requiring all future English monarchs to be in communion with the Anglican Church. When James VII and II died in Paris later that same year, however, Louis XIV provocatively recognised his son (known among Jacobites as James VIII and III) as legitimate heir to the English throne. Anglo-Scottish relations were thereafter destabilised by issues of dynastic uncertainty and strategic insecurity. In 1698, concerned to preserve an international policy of pro-Spanish, anti-French diplomacy, William's administration had deliberately sacrificed a Scottish attempt to colonise the isthmus of Darien in the Spanish American empire. Since the Darien venture had absorbed around a quarter of Scotland's financial capital, its disastrous outcome exacerbated the devastating economic impact of a series of poor harvests between 1692 and 1698, known as the 'Seven Ill Years'.

> '...as no quarters could be had for such a number, they were forced to stand with their arms without in the field. And a great snow coming like to discourage the company.'
>
> **William Veitch's description of the Pentland rebels, 1666**

landing with a French force at Kinsale before proceeding to summon the 'Patriot Parliament' in Dublin. No English monarch had set foot in Ireland since Richard II, but the 'war of the two kings' subsequently erupted when William dispatched a large army of continental soldiers under Marshal Schomberg to land at Bangor, before joining them in person near Belfast in June 1690. Following 'King Billy's' decisive victories at the Boyne in July 1690 and at Aughrim in September 1691, the treaty of Limerick ended the war in October 1691. It also laid the foundations for a series of anti-Catholic penal laws enacted during the 1690s.

In England, a Bill of Rights was passed in December 1689. This represented a substantial shift in the balance of political power between parliamentary and monarchical supremacy. Parliament thereafter became a permanent institution, meeting at least annually; the significance of cabinet government also increased during William's frequent Continental absences.

Britain's involvement in both the Nine Years War (1689–97) and the War of the Spanish Succession (1702–13) indicated an intensification of foreign policy commitments. An overhaul of fiscal machinery strengthened the nation's state finances, and the English army became an increasingly formidable presence in Europe, recording major victories at Blenheim (1704) and Ramillies (1706) under John Churchill, duke of Marlborough.

After Mary's death from smallpox in 1694, William ruled as sole sovereign until a riding accident brought about his own demise in 1702. He was succeeded by his sister-in-

THE ACT OF UNION

Although the Irish House of Commons specifically requested an Anglo-Irish union in 1703, English attention remained focused on preventing Scotland from embracing the Jacobites. Taking advantage of the fact that over half of Scottish exports were destined for English markets, the English parliament passed the so-called 'Alien Act' of 1705, decreeing that all Anglo-Scottish trading opportunities would henceforth cease were the regal union to be broken. When commissioners were appointed to negotiate an incorporating union between the two kingdoms, the Scots' preoccupation with restoring their nation's prosperity was reflected in the fact that 15 of the 25 Articles of Union finally drawn up related to commercial and financial provisions. Separate legislation preserved the established status of the Presbyterian Church within Scotland as well as the independent integrity of the Scottish legal system. By the union of England and Scotland on 1 May 1707, a united Kingdom of Great Britain was thus created, encompassing a single coinage, system of weights and measures, peerage and bicameral parliament at Westminster. Although a quarter of the shires and a third of the burghs across Scotland submitted anti-union petitions, the surrender of parliamentary independence in return for economic viability was ultimately deemed acceptable by those such as the earl of Cromarty, who expressed the hope that henceforth 'may wee be Brittains and down goe old ignominious names of Scotland and England'.   CJ

Britain came late to Europe's imperial project. During the fifteenth and sixteenth centuries, while Spain and Portugal founded great empires spanning America, Africa and Asia, Britain's rulers watched from the sidelines. John Cabot, Martin Frobisher and others with English sponsorship, in search of a northwest passage to the Indies, played a part in mapping what became Canada and helped open up abundant new fishing grounds in Newfoundland and the North Atlantic; further south, raiders and traders such as John Hawkins, Walter Raleigh and Francis Drake attacked the rich Spanish Indies. The extension of territories in Ireland and the settlement of plantations in Ulster did provide the English with practical experience in the business of colonisation, but on the death of Elizabeth I in 1603, Britain had no permanent settlements outside Europe. In the following century England made a major and exceptional investment in overseas empire.

At the end of the sixteenth century, various pressures combined to arouse new interest in overseas expansion. War in Europe disrupted the trade networks that supplied profitable Eastern goods, and English merchants took an increased interest in securing direct access to Asian markets. The East India Company was chartered in 1600 to pursue this aim. Initially, the Company had two theatres of operation: Indonesia and India. Driven from the Spice Islands (the Moluccas) by the Dutch, the Company increasingly concentrated on India, where it established a number of trading posts, securing supplies of pepper, indigo and a range of other such exotic commodities. The Company at last achieved long-term profitability through trade in cheap, lightweight and colourful Indian cotton cloths, which proved hugely popular in Europe – and stimulated vigorous efforts at import substitution.

Expansion in the West took a more innovative turn than the policy of trading posts in the East. In the late sixteenth century, the writer and exponent of exploration Richard Hakluyt and others viewed an increas-

ingly commercial England, in which landownership was becoming more concentrated and agricultural production more geared to the market. This left many of the rising population landless and jobless: greater agricultural efficiency meant they were no longer needed or wanted on the land. It was argued that the surplus population should be sent to the abundant lands in America to produce valuable primary products for sale in England. These products would be exchanged for goods manufactured in Britain, providing a new market for domestic industry, which was facing stagnant or declining demand in Europe. The trade would also employ large numbers of English ships and seamen (vital for the defence of the nation) and generate a spiralling improvement in national wealth, health and security.

The establishment of the tobacco trade in Virginia by the 1620s proved the feasibility of this 'mercantilist' project,

Colonial expansion to 1707

In the 17th century England began to build an empire. The East India Company sought profit in the Far East, and established the first footholds in India. Colonies were established in the Americas, some in North America founded by those seeking to escape religious persecution. The West Indies gained most settlers. Many who moved there hoped for quick wealth through raiding Spanish America. Others became involved in the highly profitable slave plantation economy that developed there and in parts of North America. Large-scale emigration began, and the sheer volume of settlers crossing the Atlantic proved crucial to the growth of empire.

■	English territory, c.1600
□	Scottish territory, c.1600
→	Route of English or English-sponsored explorer
□	Failed English colony, with dates of occupation
■	Failed Scottish colony, with dates of occupation
■	English colony or trading post, c.1700
─	Main East India Company trade route
■	Other European colonial territory or claim, c.1700
JAMAICA 20,000	Destination and number of English emigrants, 1650–1700

Map labels: Hudson 1610; Rupert's Land (Hudson's Bay Company chartered territory) 1670; Newfoundland 1610; Quebec (Fr); MIDDLE COLONIES 25,000; Louisiana (Fr); Pennsylvania; CHESAPEAKE BAY COLONIES 1681 58,000; New York 1664; New England 1620; NEW ENGLAND 13,000; Maryland 1632; Virginia 1607; Roanoke 1584–90; Carolina 1663 CAROLINA 13,000; Bermuda 1609; NORTH ATLANTIC OCEAN; Florida (Sp); Bahamas 1648; Cuba (Sp); Hispaniola (Sp); OTHER CARIBBEAN 30,000; Grand Cayman 1655; Jamaica 1655 JAMAICA 20,000; Nevis 1628; St Kitts 1624; Antigua 1632; Montserrat 1632; Barbados 1625 BARBADOS 43,000; Providence Is 1629–41; Guyana (Neths); Cayenne (Fr); New Caledonia (Darien) 1698–9; Surinam 1630 1650–67; SPANISH AMERICAN EMPIRE; PACIFIC OCEAN; BRAZIL (Port); Drake 1577–80

and unleashed a wave of emigration to New World territories. More than half the migrants were indentured servants who mortgaged their labour for a term of years in return for payment of their passage. Most moved to the West Indies, where tobacco production could be combined with more predatory activities targeted against the Spanish empire, but where the disease environment ensured high mortality. A minority (around 40,000), inspired by less material ambitions but alienated by developments in the Anglican Church before the Civil War, moved to New England, where they

Roanoke, 1584–90

Roanoke, England's first colony in the Americas, failed – in part because the Armada war between England and Spain made voyages by support expeditions impossible. The settlers were evacuated and resettled once, but when a relief ship arrived in 1590 it found no trace of them. A number of early settlements were plagued by inadequate resources.

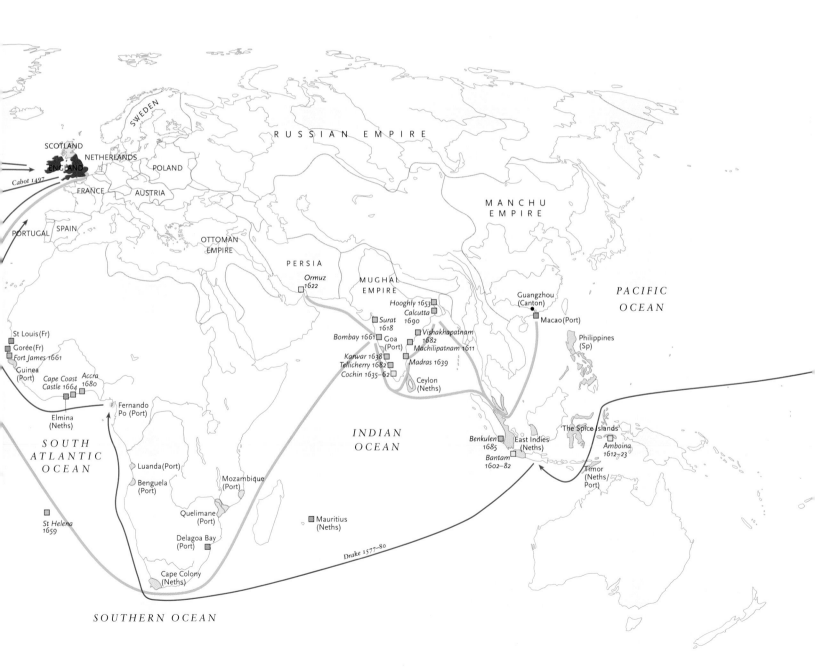

attempted to found Godly settlements in the wilderness. A relatively disease-free environment promoted successful settlement, but the colonists were unable to develop a profitable cash crop.

The Port Royal earthquake, 1692

A contemporary account of the earthquake, in Port Royal, Jamaica, viewed by many as divine retribution for the city's wickedness. Much of Port Royal sank beneath the harbour.

By the 1640s the output of tobacco from the southern colonies had expanded to levels where, despite greatly increased consumption in Europe, supply exceeded demand, and prices collapsed. Meanwhile, the introduction of sugar into Barbados in the 1640s, and the phenomenally high profits earned from it, opened up the prospects of great wealth to those who could command a sufficient labour supply. The move towards a slave plantation system followed swiftly. English colonial commerce took two important new turns. The first was the formation of the Royal African Company in 1662. This heralded wholehearted entry into the African slave trade, which England dominated by the end of the century. The second new development was the provision of a lifeline for the struggling settlements in the North American mainland: although they did not find a profitable cash crop, they were now able to earn export credits by providing food, timber and shipping services to the plantations. These were used to pay for imported goods from England.

Demand for sugar, more than tobacco, proved insatiable. As the production of sugar increased and the price fell, what had been a luxury available to a few became a luxury available to all, albeit only in small quantities. More and more people used more and more sugar, in more and more ways. From soon after its introduction in Barbados until the end of the eighteenth century, sugar accounted for over half the value of plantation imports. Sugar raised the stakes in the imperial project, with the English state and its European rivals all anxious to tap the profits and paying new attention to colonisation, which had, in England, initially been left to private enterprise. The English Navigation Act of 1651, directed above all at Dutch competitors, attempted to reserve the colonial carrying trade for English and colonial ships (the Scots were excluded) and to develop the English entrepôt. The legislation was refined and improved after the Restoration and remained in place until 1859, with other European colonial powers pursuing similar mercantilist strategies. Resentment at exclusion was a major factor in encouraging the ill-fated Scottish attempt at settlement in Darien (a swampy region of the Panama isthmus within easy reach of Spanish trade routes) in the 1690s. This resentment also played an important role in the lobby for Union in the years before 1707, as economic advantages to Scotland vied with wounded national pride.

In the decades after the Restoration, England's empire was consolidated and expanded. By 1700 England had settled 17 colonies in America (with a narrow strip of continuous settlement along the coast of North America from Maine to South Carolina and six islands in the Caribbean), alongside France's eight and the Dutch Republic's three. As territory expanded, the English population of America grew, increasing threefold between the Restoration and 1700 to reach around 400,000: a substantial addition to the population of 5 million at home. Meanwhile, France, with a population approaching 20 million in 1700, had a mere 70,000 colonial subjects. Trade with Europe became less important as England's involvement with the world beyond increased and, by the end of the seventeenth century, trade with the plantations and India accounted for over 30 per cent of imports and 15 per cent of exports. England had acquired a major stake in Europe's imperial project, which was to bear full fruit in the eighteenth century.

FROM COSTLY PRIZE TO PROSPERITY

The struggle to turn a territory acquired through adventure into a profitable colony is well illustrated by Jamaica, England's first state-sponsored colonial venture. In 1654 Oliver Cromwell dispatched a great fleet to 'gain an interest' in the Spanish Indies and, after a humiliating defeat at Hispaniola, the leaders turned on the thinly settled, and ill-defended, island of Jamaica as a consolation prize. The ease of the initial seizure proved deceptive. Runaway Spanish slaves in the mountainous interior sustained years of guerrilla war with Spanish support which, together with disease, took a heavy toll on the army, in terms of both lives and morale. At the Restoration, peace was made with Spain and it was widely expected that Charles II would return Cromwell's prize. In fact, the king decided to retain Jamaica and established a civil government designed to encourage private investors and secure the island's future.

Jamaica was ten times the combined size of the other English islands in the Caribbean and promised to provide a valuable extension to the sugar and slave system developed in Barbados. But the English inherited little from the Spanish. As one early settler remarked, 'The Spaniard doth call it the garden of the Indies. But this I will say: the Gardeners have been verie bad for here is verie little more than that which groweth naturallie.' Clearing the land and planting cash crops required time and great capital investment which, despite the king's hopes, were not forthcoming from outsiders. Although the first settlers took out patents for vast tracts of land, it was many years before the resources necessary to convert Jamaica into a thriving plantation economy were accumulated.

Meanwhile, the colonists exploited the island's strategic location. Unlike the earlier successful English settlements, Jamaica was in the heart of the Spanish Indies, well placed for both plunder and trade, with the additional advantage of a superb natural harbour protected by a long sand spit, at the end of which the English built the town of Port Royal. Privateering required little capital and provided the funds needed to ensure the infant colony's survival. In the long run, peaceful contraband trade (especially a slave re-export trade), which also got under way in the 1660s, proved more important and more rewarding. However, despite the treaty of Madrid of 1670, which promised peace and friendship between England and Spain in the Indies, privateers continued to refit their ships and sell their prizes at Port Royal throughout the late seventeenth century. The town, home of Henry Morgan and other famous adventurers, and notorious for its rowdy, dissolute, high-spending social life, acquired the reputation of being the wickedest city on earth. In 1692 a dramatic earthquake plunged most of its buildings under water. Many saw the disaster as well-deserved punishment from God.

As Port Royal prospered, the island merchants who profited from trade and plunder accumulated the capital to purchase a slave labour force (which increased from 10,000 in 1673 to 45,000 in 1703) and plant cash crops in the interior. Cocoa dominated in the 1660s, but was destroyed by

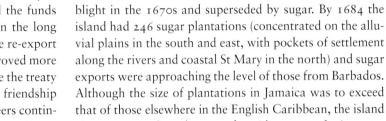

English traders and American Indians
This engraving shows English traders giving beads and knives to Indians. Early contacts between the English and the native Americans were based on trade and in many cases were quite amicable.

blight in the 1670s and superseded by sugar. By 1684 the island had 246 sugar plantations (concentrated on the alluvial plains in the south and east, with pockets of settlement along the rivers and coastal St Mary in the north) and sugar exports were approaching the level of those from Barbados. Although the size of plantations in Jamaica was to exceed that of those elsewhere in the English Caribbean, the island also maintained production of a wider range of minor staples than the smaller islands (including indigo, cotton, ginger and pimento) and a small-holding sector geared to the internal exchange of food and cattle. The earthquake of 1692, the ensuing disease and the war of the 1690s, during which Jamaica was invaded by the French, took a heavy toll on the island's population, trade and prosperity. The rapid progress made in the 1670s and 1680s was halted, and even reversed, with the white population declining from around 9,000 to 7,000 between 1680 and 1700. The lost ground was regained in the eighteenth century, however, when Jamaica became the brightest jewel in Britain's imperial crown.   NZ

Jamaica in 1685
Jamaica became an English possession almost by accident, yet in the 18th century it was to be Britain's most valuable colony. Privateering was initially its main source of income, but slowly, as resources were accumulated, a plantation economy based on slavery developed alongside a small-holding sector that produced food. The slave population, however, expanded far more rapidly than did the number of white settlers in the late 17th century.

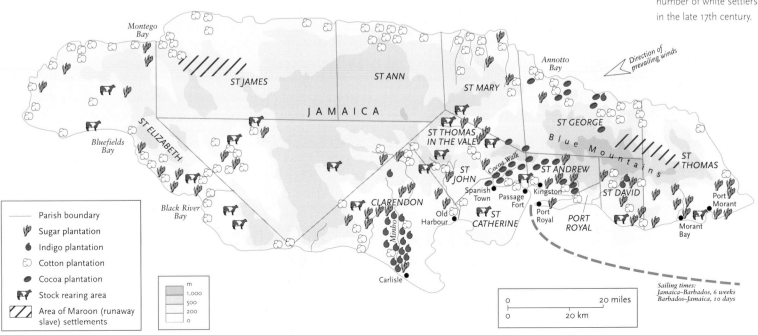

Parish boundary
Sugar plantation
Indigo plantation
Cotton plantation
Cocoa plantation
Stock rearing area
Area of Maroon (runaway slave) settlements

Sailing times:
Jamaica–Barbados, 6 weeks
Barbados–Jamaica, 10 days

18th-CENTURY DUBLIN

In the late seventeenth century, Dublin was a large and bustling town, the centre of English government in Ireland for almost 500 years and now the chief port for the island. But by the mid-eighteenth century, Dublin had been transformed in scale and had become the second largest city in the English-speaking world after London, with a population well in excess of 100,000 people. Brick-fronted façades and new speculative terraces were eclipsing the timber-framed and densely packed housing stock of the early modern town. The well-watered southwest of the city had developed a strongly industrial character, built around woollen and silk manufacture, while upper-class residential development was pushing eastwards on both sides of the river Liffey. Church spires, most of them recent, dominated the skyline.

Already by 1714, when the writer and cleric Jonathan Swift returned, embittered, from England to the city of his birth, institutional building had dramatically redefined the edges of the city: the first secular workhouse had been erected on the western approaches, and beyond it the spectacular Royal Hospital at Kilmainham, built for veterans of the army and modelled on Les Invalides in Paris, was now complete. North of the river, the new Royal Barracks separated the growing city from the great expanse of the Phoenix

A state ball, c.1730 (below)

Held at Dublin Castle, this was one of many extravagant social events that served to underline the power and wealth of the Protestant landed elite.

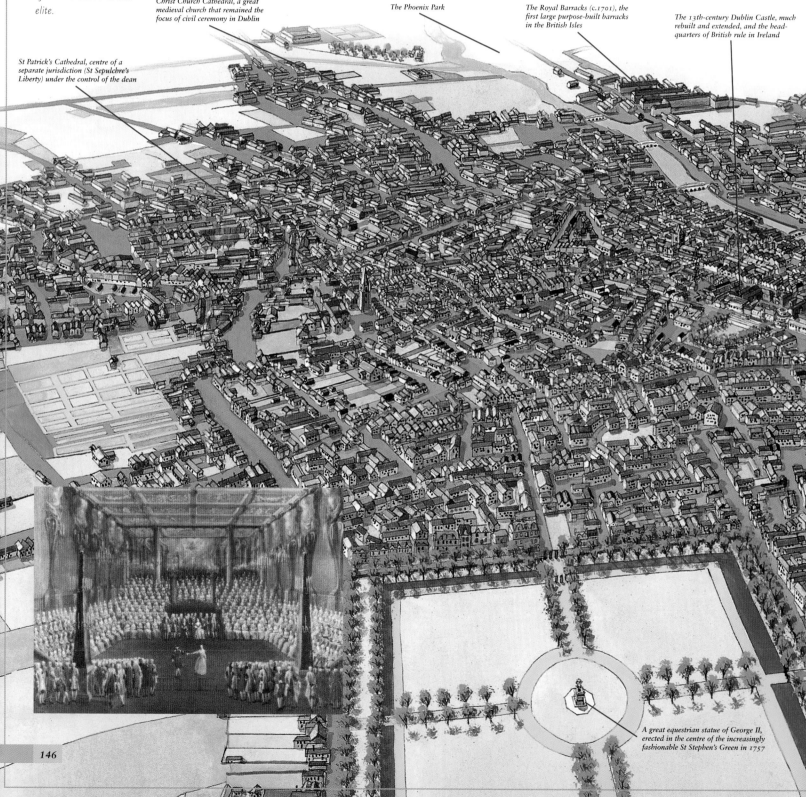

St Patrick's Cathedral, centre of a separate jurisdiction (St Sepulchre's Liberty) under the control of the dean

Christ Church Cathedral, a great medieval church that remained the focus of civil ceremony in Dublin

The Phoenix Park

The Royal Barracks (c.1701), the first large purpose-built barracks in the British Isles

The 13th-century Dublin Castle, much rebuilt and extended, and the headquarters of British rule in Ireland

A great equestrian statue of George II, erected in the centre of the increasingly fashionable St Stephen's Green in 1757

Park; to the east, work was beginning on the Great Library that was soon to tower over the campus of Swift's alma mater, Trinity College.

Dublin's rapid growth in the late seventeenth and early eighteenth centuries arose from a conjunction of factors: its commercial and financial pre-eminence in Ireland since the early seventeenth century; its monopoly of certain professional services – higher education and the high courts of law; the presence every second winter of a viceregal court at Dublin Castle, and of MPs attending biannual parliamentary sessions; and the social imperative that brought the Irish landed gentry to Dublin every winter to lobby and to litigate, to play, and to plan their daughters' marriages. Their deep purses and long credit-lines brought into existence a huge variety of luxury retail and craft businesses, from goldsmiths to soap manufacturers; the greatest development came with the textile and clothing trades which, in employment terms, outnumbered the rest.

The role of immigrants in this process was crucial: English and Dutch settlers had been important in the first half of the seventeenth century, but now it was the Huguenot 'asylum seekers' who brought new technologies and fashions to the city, notably to the streets of the Liberties quarter, adjacent to Swift's St Patrick's Cathedral. The dean had little regard for the nouveaux riches who dominated the Hanoverian Irish parliament, but he was comfortable in his role as champion of the 'drapiers' and journeymen of the crowded streets around him.

It was still a predominantly Protestant city, but by midcentury Catholic migrants from the city's historic hinterland were the main source of new Dubliners. By the time of the neoclassical rebuilding of the city core in the late eighteenth century, and of its striking embellishment with James Gandon's great set pieces (the Custom House, the Four Courts, the House of Lords), Dublin was once again a Catholic-dominated city, albeit with its governance still firmly in Protestant hands. The handicraft industries were being undermined by the Industrial Revolution, but few of the victims were worshippers in Swift's cathedral.   DD

18th-century Dublin

In the 18th century, Dublin underwent a rapid transformation from a town of densely packed timber-framed houses into an expansive city of brick-fronted terraces, parks and impressive Classical-styled public buildings. Politically, the city remained dominated by the Protestant elite, but a steady influx of rural migrants, attracted by the city's expanding commerce and industry, meant that Dublin had a Catholic majority by the end of the century.

The Custom House (c.1707) on Essex Quay, the epicentre of commercial Dublin in the 18th century

The Irish Parliament House, rebuilt c.1729–32 to the designs of Edward Lovett Pearce

Trinity College (founded 1592) expanded continuously in this period – the Library was completed in the 1730s

The Dublin Lying-In Hospital (1745) moved here, north of the Sackville Street Mall, in 1757

THE JACOBITE REBELLIONS

Jacobitism (from Jacobus, the Latin for 'James') relates to the followers of King James II and his Stuart dynasty, which lost the crowns of England, Scotland and Ireland after the so-called 'Glorious Revolution' of 1688. The resultant movement and ideology emerged as a major factor in domestic and European politics in the late seventeenth and eighteenth centuries, which manifested itself in both military rebellion and a vibrant literary and ballad tradition in English and in Irish and Scots Gaelic.

The birth of a son to James and his second wife, Mary of Modena, a Catholic, in June 1688 focused English Protestant minds on the prospect of a Catholic succession. Distaste at James's flirtations with Nonconformists and Catholics precipitated an invasion by his Protestant son-in-law William, Prince of Orange, Stadholder of Holland. William landed unopposed and James fled to France. Parliament declared that James had abdicated and bestowed the Crown jointly on William and his wife Mary, James's elder, Protestant, daughter.

English Whigs and Tories alike acquiesced in the Glorious Revolution and not a shot was fired in support of James in his English kingdom. However, the small group of Eng-

Battle of Glenshiel

This painting by Peter Tillemans depicts the rout by government troops of a force of Spanish infantry and Scottish Jacobites at the battle of Glenshiel in 1719. The Spanish had expected a popular uprising, but they received little local support.

lish Jacobites who refused to break their solemn oaths to James would be joined in the 1690s and early eighteenth century by a whole host of disgruntled Tories and Whig patriots, aristocrats, gentry, country squires, artisans, labourers, demobilised soldiers, robbers and highwaymen, who trumpeted the 'illegitimacy' of the new regime from printing-press and parlour to the tavern and gibbet. Many were appalled by the fact that the 'Protestant Champion' William and his eventual successor George I, elector of Hanover, put the interests of Holland and Hanover above those of England and squandered national wealth on futile European wars. Scottish national pride and solidarity with

their hereditary monarch was undermined by political, religious and clan rivalries, and such military resistance as there was to the Williamite regime in Scotland was effectively ended by the death of the charismatic John Graham of Claverhouse at the battle of Killiecrankie in July 1689. However, the massacre of the MacDonalds of Glencoe in 1692, the famines of the 1690s, the disastrous failure of the attempt to colonise Darien, and the hated Act of Union of 1707, would stoke the eighteenth-century fires of Scottish Jacobitism, when the Highlands would assume a particular importance for the Jacobite cause. The Highland clan system, in which tenants owed military service to the clan chiefs, meant that this was the one region of Britain and Ireland where substantial bodies of armed men could easily be raised to oppose the government.

THE WAR IN IRELAND

Irish loyalty to the House of Stuart had been established with James VI and I's accession to the English throne in 1603, and it survived the trauma of the wars of the 1640s and 50s. On the accession of James II in 1685, many Irishmen looked to him to restore lands that they had lost fighting for his father and brother (Charles II) against Oliver Cromwell and the English parliament. Others wished to reverse the political dominance of Protestantism, rehabilitate the Roman Catholic Church and reverse the anglicisation of Ireland. 'Fighting Dick' Talbot, James II's lord deputy in Ireland, had catholicised the Irish army and judiciary in the mid-1680s. Assured by Louis XIV, at war with England since William III's accession, of substantial French financial and military aid, he chose to defy the new regime in Whitehall.

Encouraged by Irish defiance, Louis XIV urged James to repair to Ireland. James landed in Kinsale in March 1689 but, following his subsequent failure to capture Derry and his defeat by William III on the river Boyne in July 1690, fled back to France, leaving the Irish Jacobites to continue the war with French support. The future duke of Marlborough's amphibious assault on the Southeast and the Williamite victory at the battle of Aughrim in July 1691 finally forced the Irish Jacobites to the negotiating table. They concluded the favourable treaty of Limerick, which guaranteed freedom of conscience for Irish Catholics and allowed the Jacobite General Patrick Sarsfield to take an Irish army into exile to continue the struggle on the European mainland. This would be the forerunner of the Na Géanna Fiáine (the 'Wild Geese'), the famous Irish Brigades in the service of France and Spain. They were perceived by friend and foe alike as a Jacobite army-in-waiting, which could be employed to devastating effect in the event of a Jacobite invasion.

Although the treaty of Limerick had terminated the Irish war, nobody on either side of the Irish Sea considered the Jacobite cause to be lost. Between 1692 and the death of James II in 1701, planning for a French and Jacobite invasion of Britain continued. In the spring of 1692, some 30,000 men, half from the Irish Brigades, were assembled at Brest to accompany James to England, but the invasion was

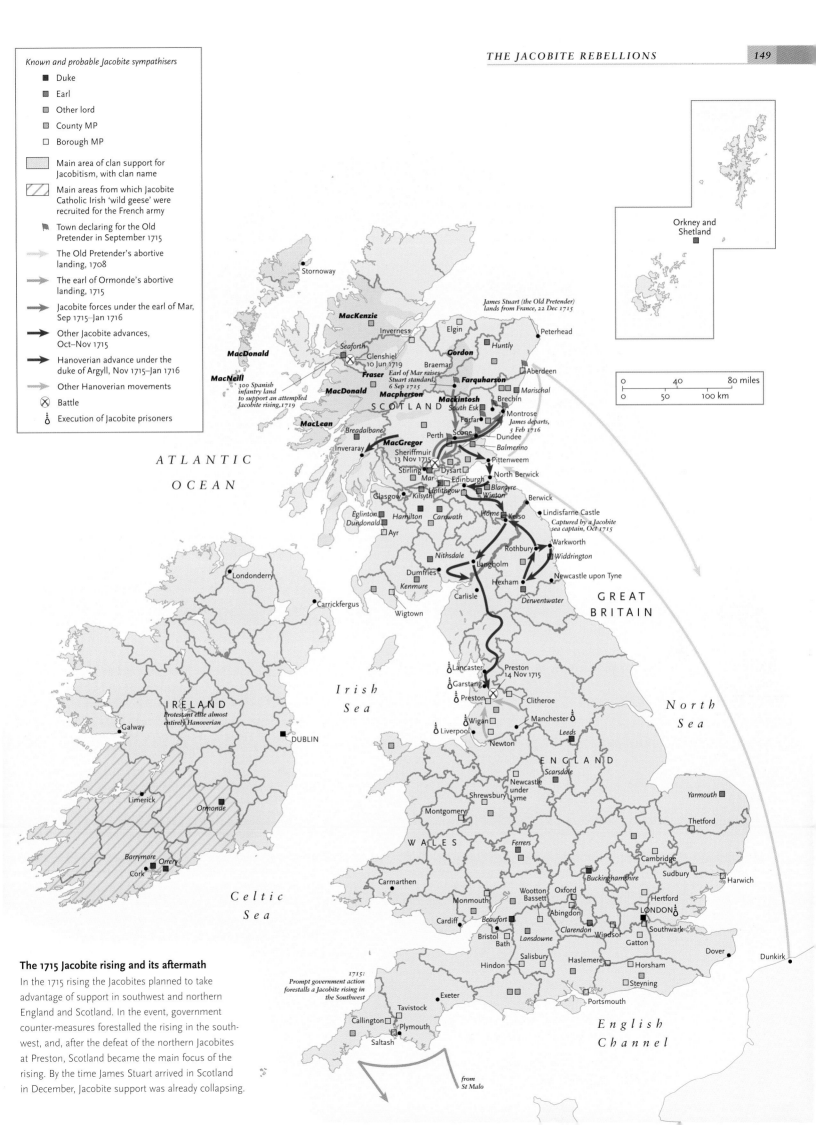

Known and probable Jacobite sympathisers

■ Duke
■ Earl
■ Other lord
□ County MP
□ Borough MP

▨ Main area of clan support for Jacobitism, with clan name

▨ Main areas from which Jacobite Catholic Irish 'wild geese' were recruited for the French army

⚑ Town declaring for the Old Pretender in September 1715

➤ The Old Pretender's abortive landing, 1708

➤ The earl of Ormonde's abortive landing, 1715

➤ Jacobite forces under the earl of Mar, Sep 1715–Jan 1716

➤ Other Jacobite advances, Oct–Nov 1715

➤ Hanoverian advance under the duke of Argyll, Nov 1715–Jan 1716

➤ Other Hanoverian movements

⊗ Battle

ᛉ Execution of Jacobite prisoners

Orkney and Shetland

James Stuart (the Old Pretender) lands from France, 22 Dec 1715

ATLANTIC OCEAN

MacKenzie
Stornoway
Inverness
Elgin
Huntly
Peterhead
Seaforth
Glenshiel 10 Jun 1719
MacDonald
Gordon
Braemar
Aberdeen
MacNeill
300 Spanish infantry land to support an attempted Jacobite rising, 1719
Fraser
Earl of Mar raises Stuart standard, 6 Sep 1715
Farquharson
Marischal
MacDonald
Macpherson
Mackintosh
Brechin
SCOTLAND
South Esk
Montrose
James departs, 5 Feb 1716
Forfar
MacLean
Breadalbane
Perth
Scone
Dundee
Balmerino
Inveraray
MacGregor
Sheriffmuir 13 Nov 1715
Pittenweem
Stirling
Mar
Dysart
North Berwick
Mar
Edinburgh
Blantyre
Glasgow
Kilsyth
Linlithgow
Winton
Berwick
Eglinton
Home
Kelso
Lindisfarne Castle
Dundonald
Hamilton
Carnwath
Captured by a Jacobite sea captain, Oct 1715
Ayr
Warkworth
Nithsdale
Rothbury
Widdrington
GREAT
Dumfries
Langholm
Newcastle upon Tyne
BRITAIN
Kenmure
Hexham
Carlisle
Derwentwater

Londonderry
Carrickfergus
Wigtown

Irish Sea

NORTH
Sea

Lancaster
Preston 14 Nov 1715
Garstang
Preston
Clitheroe
IRELAND
Protestant élite almost entirely Hanoverian
Galway
Wigan
Manchester
DUBLIN
Liverpool
Leeds
Newton
ENGLAND
Scarsdale
Newcastle under Lyme
Yarmouth
Shrewsbury
Montgomery
Thetford
WALES
Ferrers
Cambridge
Sudbury
Harwich
Limerick
Ormonde
Barrymore
Orrery
Carmarthen
Wootton Bassett
Oxford
Buckinghamshire
Cork
Monmouth
Abingdon
Hertford
LONDON
Cardiff
Beaufort
Clarendon
Southwark
Celtic Sea
Bristol
Lansdowne
Windsor
Gatton
Bath
Hindon
Salisbury
Haslemere
Horsham
Dover
Dunkirk
1715: Prompt government action forestalls a Jacobite rising in the Southwest
Callington
Tavistock
Exeter
Portsmouth
Steyning
Plymouth
English Channel
Saltash
from St Malo

The 1715 Jacobite rising and its aftermath

In the 1715 rising the Jacobites planned to take advantage of support in southwest and northern England and Scotland. In the event, government counter-measures forestalled the rising in the south-west, and, after the defeat of the northern Jacobites at Preston, Scotland became the main focus of the rising. By the time James Stuart arrived in Scotland in December, Jacobite support was already collapsing.

The failure of the 1715 rising broke English Jacobitism, forcing Charles Edward Stuart to rely on Scottish – mainly Highland – support in 1745. Despite impressive early victories over government forces and an unopposed march into England, which caused panic in London, the rising failed through lack of popular support and was finally crushed at Culloden in April 1746. The widespread lack of enthusiasm for the Hanoverians in both lowland Scotland and England did not result in a willingness to see a Stuart restoration.

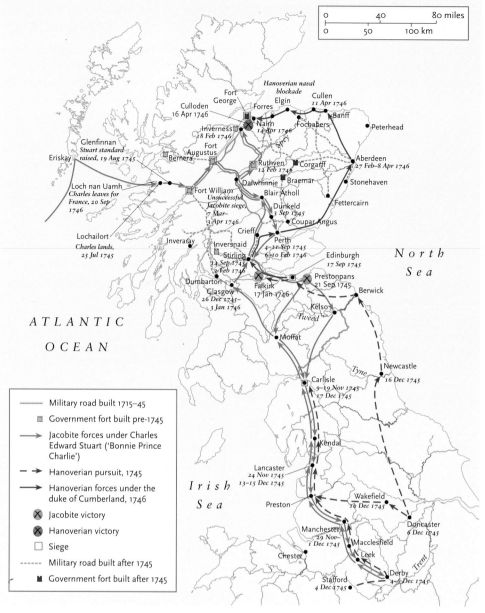

combined strength of Europe, France once again looked to Jacobitism as a means of neutralising Britain. At the beginning of 1705, Scottish Jacobites promised to raise 30,000 men if the French king provided them with 18,000 infantry soldiers, additional arms and a high-ranking general acceptable to James II's son James Francis Edward Stuart ('James III', the 'Old Pretender'). After the Act of Union between Scotland and England in 1707, the French finally decided to organise an expedition for the following year. James sailed from Dunkirk for Scotland in March 1708. Hampered by adverse weather conditions, the flotilla reached the Scottish coast, but failed to make contact with the assembled Jacobites at Leith. Deaf to James's entreaties, the French admiral refused to allow him to disembark and they returned to Dunkirk.

THE '15'

The death of Queen Anne in August 1714 and the proclamation of George I, the elector of Hanover, as king of Britain and Ireland presented the Jacobites with another opportunity to attempt a restoration of the Stuarts. Although prevented from waging war on behalf of James, and deterred from directly helping the Jacobites by the terms of the treaty of Utrecht (1713), the ailing Louis XIV again undertook to aid the Jacobite cause. He promised substantial unofficial aid, and authorised French half-pay officers and Irish volunteers to support a Stuart invasion of Scotland. He also encouraged his grandson Philip V of Spain, the duke of Lorraine and the Pope to provide substantial financial help. The Jacobites planned a three-pronged attack, in which the duke of Ormonde and James would lead an assault on the southwest of England with the object of marching on London. John Erskine, earl of Mar, would raise the clans in the Highlands to converge on Glasgow and Edinburgh; Jacobites on the English–Scottish borders would join the rebellion. However, the authorities were well informed of Jacobite invasion plans and they moved to arrest the chief insurgents. Ormonde reached the coast of Cornwall in the autumn but quickly returned to France.

After this fiasco, Scotland emerged as the main focus of rebellion. Mar raised King James's standard at Braemar on 6 September. He seized Perth, gathered a force of 12,000

called off after the Royal Navy destroyed their transport fleet at the battle of La Hogue. Jacobite optimism and French desperation at recent military reversals spawned another invasion scheme in 1695–6, to support a planned rebellion by a group of English Jacobites, led by the earls of Arran and Sunderland. In February 1696 James II joined 18 battalions of infantry and 30 squadrons of cavalry that had been assembled for the invasion at Calais. However, this plot foundered on mutual distrust between the French king and the English Jacobites. Louis XIV was not prepared to support a rising until it had actually broken out, and the English Jacobites refused to revolt openly until the French king showed his hand.

CONTINUED FRENCH INVOLVEMENT

Although Louis XIV was finally forced to accept William III as king of England, Scotland and Ireland by the terms of the treaty of Ryswick of 1697, he refused to banish James II from his dominions. The outbreak of the War of the Spanish Succession in 1702 again propelled the Jacobite cause to the forefront of the European political agenda. Facing the

men, and proclaimed James III as king in Aberdeen, Dunkeld, Perth, Montrose, Dundee and Inverness. A combination of chronic indecision and strategic incompetence on Mar's part allowed the loyalist duke of Argyll to overcome the numerical superiority of the Jacobite army and force a draw in the battle of Sheriffmuir on 13 November 1715. The following day, an army of Scottish and northern English Jacobites surrendered at Preston. This, and the government repression that followed, effectively ended Jacobitism as a force in England. By the time the Stuart king landed at Peterhead on 22 December, the initiative had been lost, Jacobite sympathisers had dispersed, and the rebellion was over.

After the death of Louis XIV in 1715, France concluded an anti-Spanish alliance with Britain. With a stroke of the pen, the Jacobites lost their most powerful prospective ally (France) but gained the friendship of Spain. Fired by the ambition of Philip V, the Spanish invaded Savoy and seized Sardinia and Sicily in 1717. When this naked aggression led to the outbreak of war with Britain, the Spanish fell back on the traditional idea of an armada. In February 1719 Philip V published a manifesto in favour of the House of Stuart. A considerable military force, mostly Irish, was allocated for James's service, and a detachment of Spanish infantry, accompanied by several prominent Scottish noblemen and Irish officers, set sail for Scotland in early March. They landed near Glenshiel, in Scotland, to await the arrival of Ormonde at the head of a large fleet, which had left from Cadiz. However, the fleet was dispersed by a storm off Cape Finisterre and Ormonde abandoned the enterprise.

BONNIE PRINCE CHARLIE

The renewal of Anglo-French hostilities in the War of the Austrian Succession provided new opportunities for the Jacobites. Britain and Ireland again became the focus of a Franco-Jacobite invasion plan, until the scheme was thwarted by the ever-dependable 'Protestant winds'. This, and French unwillingness to invest fully in the Stuart cause, prompted Charles Edward Stuart (the 'Young Pretender' or 'Bonnie Prince Charlie'), the eldest son of the Old Pretender and the great hope of the Jacobites, to make a descent on Scotland. Landing on the Isle of Eriskay on 23 July 1745, Charles Edward raised many of the Jacobite clans and conquered most of Scotland. His forces also succeeded in inflicting humiliating defeats on successive Hanoverian armies and in exposing the shaky foundations of the Hanoverian dynasty. A phenomenally successful invasion of England – largely masterminded by Lord George Murray, the most skilled by far

of the Young Pretender's generals – brought the Jacobites unopposed to within 200 kilometres (about 120 miles) of London. However, when it became clear that the expected rising of English Jacobites would not materialise, Charles's army retreated to Scotland in the face of superior Hanoverian forces, amid indecision, dissension and recrimination. They were finally destroyed by the duke of Cumberland at the battle of Culloden, near Nairn, on 16 April 1746. The clan system was one of the casualties of the genocidal government repression of the Highlands that followed.

THE END OF JACOBITISM

French defeat in the War of the Austrian Succession, the death of the Old Pretender in January 1766 and the steady decline of Charles Edward into alcoholism and political oblivion hastened the final demise of Jacobitism as a political force in European politics. A final attempt by the French to restore the Stuart dynasty during the Seven Years War was abandoned after the Royal Navy destroyed the French fleet at Quiberon Bay in 1759. The Irish Jacobite literary tradition smouldered on until it was transformed by the emergence of republican nationalism from the 1790s onwards, but it is fair to say that the Stuarts had become a sentimental irrelevance in English and Scottish politics and literature by the 1770s. This process was aided by the succession of the English-born 'patriot king' George III, the political rehabilitation of the Scottish Jacobites and their absorption into the British war machine. This would come to its final fruition in the 'Balmoralisation' of the British Royal family, under the influence of the novelist Sir Walter Scott. EOC

Defence of London
The March of the Guards to Finchley, *by Hogarth, presents an unflattering view of the troops sent to defend the approaches to London during the 1745 rising. Until Culloden, the performance of Hanoverian armies against the less well-supplied and armed Jacobites was unimpressive.*

Gaelic texts

Two closely related varieties of Gaelic, Manx (right) and Irish (left), appear very different in written form, as printed Manx adopted English-style spelling.

In 1500, six languages were commonly spoken in the British Isles: English, Welsh, Cornish, Gaelic, Norn and Norman French. By 1800, two of these, Cornish and Norn, had all but disappeared. Cornish, a Celtic language akin to Breton and Welsh that had been spoken across southwest England, was already confined to west Cornwall by the sixteenth century. Norn, a Norse dialect, was spoken in Orkney and Shetland (under Danish rule until 1468–9), and in Caithness. Yet after the Reformation the authorities did not consider it worthwhile publishing Cornish or Norn translations of the Bible or prayer books. The abrogation of Norse law in 1611 further undermined Norn's status, and both languages died out in about 1780. Norman French survived in the Channel Isles – the last outpost of England's medieval French empire – but its status was much reduced. Once the language of the court and aristocracy, it had disappeared as a spoken language in early fifteenth-century England, and its erstwhile status as a language of government was by 1500 largely reduced to an attenuated position in common law where 'law French' survived into the 1680s.

The decline of these languages reflected the advance of English and Scots dialects, the forerunners of modern English. Throughout this period, English also gained ground as a spoken and written language at the expense of the two remaining Celtic languages, Gaelic and Welsh. In 1500 about half the British Isles was still Celtic-speaking, although, since English-speaking areas were more densely populated, about two-thirds of the population spoke English. Medieval migration and settlement had established English in parts of Ireland and Wales, and also consolidated its position in lowland Scotland, where 'Scots', a derivative of the Northumbrian dialect spoken in Lothian, which became part of Scotland in the tenth century, had long been the language of the court and Lowlands. Bilingualism became more prevalent in Celtic-speaking areas: in Scotland, linguistic boundaries remained fairly stable at the Highland line, but in Ireland and Wales the 'Englishries' (small, predominantly lowland, enclaves of English settlement) gradually expanded.

The influence of the prestigious culture of the royal court and the advent of printing meant that English spelling was becoming more standardised by 1500, though in speech the distinct English dialects still inhibited easy communication between regions. Scots spelling differed, but perhaps better reflected northern English speech, too. Dialectal differences were one reason for the persistence of Latin as a written language of government, and English officials commonly communicated with Gaelic chiefs in a form of 'dog Latin'. Latin was also the language of the Church. The main influence on linguistic usage stemmed from the impact of the Reformation and the reformers' efforts to promote literacy in the vernacular. English translations of the Bible and the *Book of Common Prayer* were printed for use throughout the Tudor territories, and since the grammar and spelling of these translations reflected London–Midland English practice, the result was to consolidate these forms as the written standard and perhaps also to influence indirectly the spoken standard then emerging in aristocratic circles. In Scotland, moreover, the reformers used English texts: books and pamphlets aimed specifically at Scottish audiences were produced by London printers in accordance with English conventions, so that by 1600 a common Anglo-Scottish Protestant print culture had developed. Not only was there no literature in Scots, but Scottish pronunciation was subjected to strong anglicising pressures, particularly after the 1603 Union of Crowns.

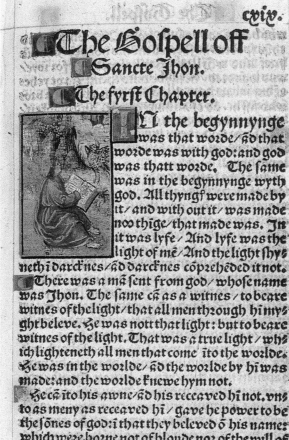

Tyndale New Testament, c.1526

William Tyndale's translation of the Bible into vernacular English became the basis of most subsequent English translations. Works such as this helped the language become more widely used and more standardised.

THE CELTIC LANGUAGES

The surviving medieval bardic traditions of the Celtic-speaking areas set a standard for written Welsh and Gaelic. But the Reformation presented the authorities with a dilemma. English officials had long regarded Celtic culture as innately primitive and savage, but they believed it 'plainly repugnant' to God's word to conduct services 'in a tongue not understood of the people'. In Wales, scholars like William Salesbury and William Morgan produced Welsh translations of the Prayer Book (1567) and the Bible (1588), so making the key religious texts available to Welsh Protestants, who were still predominantly monoglot in 1750. A literate Welsh tradition also developed among Welsh gentry, while, from 1735, the growth of Methodism promoted popular literacy in Welsh.

The promotion of literacy in Gaelic was more problematic. Elizabethan officials in Ireland believed that Gaelic bred sedition. Thus, Gaelic translations of the New Testament (1603) and the Prayer Book (1608) appeared only after the Tudor conquest, by which time the Reformation had won little support among the Gaelic learned classes. Things were a little different in Scotland, where *Foirm na n-Urrnuidheadh*, a Gaelic translation of Knox's *Book of Common Order*, appeared in 1567, and a Gaelic Protestant tradition soon developed, despite ambiguous official attitudes. But religious divisions between Catholic Irish and Protestant Scottish Gaeldom hastened the decline of the bardic tradition and the standard literary language, classical common Gaelic. Without this common link, the Gaelic dialects of Ireland, Scotland and the Isle of Man began to drift apart. By 1688, extensive revisions were needed when 'Irish' Bibles were reprinted for use in Scotland. And when publications in Manx Gaelic first appeared, in the eighteenth century, it was with English-style spelling, which rendered the language more or less unintelligible to speakers of the other Gaelic languages. By 1800, Irish Gaelic was predominantly the language of the illiterate Catholic peasantry, still spoken by perhaps a third of the island's people. A stronger Gaelic literary tradition had developed in Scotland, where the Highlands were still predominantly Gaelic-speaking, although there, too, English was increasingly understood. Even so, the position of English as the predominant literary language of the British Isles was assured, and spoken English was also increasingly familiar in the traditional Celtic heartlands.   **SGE**

Language areas in 1500

- English: Northumbrian dialects
- English: Midland dialects
- Norn
- Gaelic ⎫
- Welsh   ⎬ Celtic languages
- Cornish ⎭
- French

Areas of English language advance, 1500–1800

Language changes, 1500–1800

Between 1500 and 1800 English became increasingly the dominant language of the British Isles and, in both its spoken and written forms, became ever more standardised. Of the other languages, Norn and Cornish disappeared, while Welsh and Gaelic were progressively marginalised, and became the main languages of the least prosperous and isolated areas.

AGRICULTURAL CHANGE

In the eighteenth century, Britain experienced very rapid population growth. This population had to be fed, but the opportunities for increasing the area under cultivation were limited. Some expansion was possible through draining wetland areas such as the lough shores of Ulster, the peat mosses of southwest Scotland and northwest England, and in the Lincolnshire Fens, but most of what could be readily farmed was already being farmed. Changes in the organisation of farming and crops grown in the eighteenth century helped greatly to improve the capacity of British agriculture; it is these changes that are referred to by the term 'Agricultural Revolution'.

These improvements, which increased the productivity both of the land and of the agricultural labour force, permitted the feeding of most of Britain's population and accelerated the drift of population from the countryside, where it could no longer be usefully employed, to the industrialising towns where demand for labour was increasing. Crucial though these changes were to Britain's economic development, the term 'Agricultural Revolution' is itself something of a misnomer. Many of the developments that most characterise the period were simply applications on a larger scale of practices that had begun in the preceding two centuries. At the same time, what is arguably the greatest revolution in British agriculture – mechanisation – did not begin until the later nineteenth century.

ENCLOSURE

The major organisational change was the enclosure of medieval common fields. The first attempts at enclosure, in

'Mr Healey's Sheep'
The ability to breed prize animals was a matter of great prestige. It was not uncommon for those responsible to pay for portraits of their animals, as in this early 19th-century painting.

the sixteenth century, had met with widespread opposition from both Church and State. However, this opposition had begun to break down by the 1630s, and enclosure by mutu-

al agreement between landowners and tenants became fairly common up to the 1740s. This consensual arrangement changed dramatically in 1750, when the first of over 4,000 parliamentary Acts of Enclosure was passed. During the next 80 years, about 21 per cent of England was affected by enclosure acts; by the end of the nineteenth century, all but a handful of England's common fields had been enclosed. Enclosure was also a feature of Scottish agriculture, though to a lesser extent than in England.

Enclosure entailed either the consolidation of fragmented holdings or the subdivision of former common pastures and wastes. It was often accompanied by revision in tenure, by the replacement of tithes by land or grain rents, and by a series of expensive changes, including improved land drainage, construction of farm buildings and roads, and new agricultural methods. Property owners supported enclosure because they made possible a major rise in rents, and because landlords valued the increased control that resulted from the end of open-field farming, with its communal rights and obligations; the new control was reflected in the rectilinear shape of the new plots, straight-edged fields and straight roads.

CROPS AND MACHINERY

The eighteenth century also saw an increase in the use of fodder crops. 'Artificial grasses', including sainfoin and coleseed, were used to improve grazing. Nitrogen-fixing plants, such as the legumes, clover and trefoil, were also used to enhance soil fertility, as well as improve grazing. Charles, 2nd Viscount Townshend, a leading Norfolk landowner known as 'Turnip Townshend', popularised the idea of incorporating turnips in the 1730s. Grown for centuries for human consumption, these provided nutritious winter fodder for livestock. But improvements in agricultural productivity were not solely a matter of new crops. There were also important improvements to the soil, particularly in marling and under-draining. By changing the chemical and physical structure of the soil, these processes improved its productivity, although they required much labour. These developments made fallow unnecessary and increased the capacity of the rural economy to rear animals, because more fodder allowed heavier stocking. These animals were the source of manure, then the most important fertiliser for arable farming. They also provided capital: animals were the most significant 'cash crop' in the economy. They provided both the 'roast beef of old England' and the wool that was woven into cloth. The spread of convertible or 'up and down' husbandry, in which land alternated between pasture and arable, was also beneficial as it resulted in increased yields when the land was cultivated, and in improved grass at other times.

Agricultural machinery also improved during this period, although this factor was less important than it became over the following two centuries. Though its use did not become widespread until the 1780s, Jethro Tull, a Berkshire landowner, produced the first effective mechanical seed drill for sowing in about 1701, and a horse hoe in 1714. Furthermore, he published *Horse-Hoeing Husbandry* in 1733,

The 'Agricultural Revolution'

The 18th century saw widespread changes in agriculture. Common lands were enclosed and farms consolidated into more efficient units – a process resisted in Ireland, and in the Highlands, until after the 1745 rebellion. New crops, systems of crop rotation and technology were more widely used. As a result, the nation became more urbanised, and labour became available for developing industries.

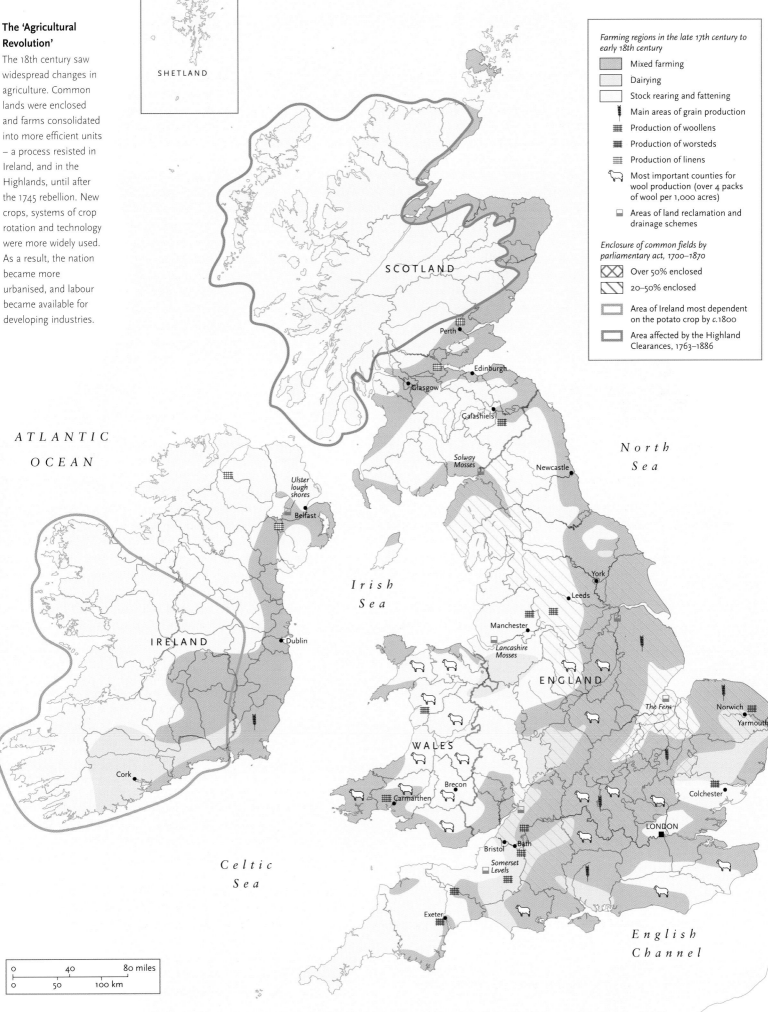

SHETLAND

Farming regions in the late 17th century to early 18th century

- Mixed farming
- Dairying
- Stock rearing and fattening
- Main areas of grain production
- Production of woollens
- Production of worsteds
- Production of linens
- Most important counties for wool production (over 4 packs of wool per 1,000 acres)
- Areas of land reclamation and drainage schemes

Enclosure of common fields by parliamentary act, 1700–1870

- Over 50% enclosed
- 20–50% enclosed
- Area of Ireland most dependent on the potato crop by c.1800
- Area affected by the Highland Clearances, 1763–1886

SCOTLAND

Perth

Edinburgh

Glasgow

Galashiels

Solway Mosses

Newcastle

ATLANTIC OCEAN

North Sea

Ulster lough shores

Belfast

Irish Sea

York

Leeds

IRELAND

Dublin

Manchester

Lancashire Mosses

ENGLAND

WALES

The Fens

Norwich

Yarmouth

Cork

Brecon

Carmarthen

Colchester

LONDON

Bristol   Bath

Somerset Levels

Celtic Sea

Exeter

English Channel

perhaps the best known of a flood of books on agriculture which shows how the culture of print could provide information on new techniques. Dozens of local agricultural societies were set up in the eighteenth century to promote better agricultural practices.

MARKET ECONOMIES

In Scotland, where common land was rarer and enclosure therefore less important a development, the rotation of crops helped to raise agricultural productivity. Scottish improvers such as William Cullen, Sir Archibald Grant of Monymusk and Alexander Murray, advocated sowing grass seeds to improve grazing and growing root crops. The area of Scotland most affected by changes in agricultural practice was the Highlands. In the aftermath of the '45 Jacobite rebellion, government authority was finally made effective across the Highlands. Clan chiefs, who were now forbidden to maintain the private armies they had traditionally raised from their tenants, began to restructure their estates. From the 1760s on, farming tenants were resettled in coastal villages, where they were expected to live by crofting, fishing and kelping (making fertiliser out of seaweed), or were helped to emigrate, while the hills were given over to more profitable sheep grazing.

In Ireland, dairy and livestock production expanded in the eighteenth century in response to external demands, with, for example, substantial exports of beef and butter to England, and of salted pork to British colonies such as Newfoundland. The hundreds of classical mansions and landscaped parks built by the country's Protestant landowning elite are eloquent testimony to wealth generated by market-oriented agriculture. Ireland's most valuable export, however, was linen cloth, produced mainly in Ulster, from flax grown on tiny plots by thousands of weaver–farmers. Like Britain, Ireland experienced rapid population growth in the eighteenth century. Much of the country's rising population was accommodated by the progressive subdivision of rented farms until many tenants had barely enough land for subsistence. Starvation was averted only by increasing reliance on the potato, large-scale cultivation of which had begun earlier in the century for its value as a soil-improving rotational crop. An economic downturn in the early nineteenth century showed that most of these tiny farms were not economically viable but, though evictions did increase, the high level of solidarity among the Irish tenantry prevented landowners from implementing any major restructuring of agriculture.

The continued growth and integration of the market economy in the British Isles, as transport links improved

The enclosure of Heapham, Lincolnshire

These two maps show the distribution of land before (above) and after (below) the enclosure of 1776. The enclosure of common land was often imposed by parliament after 1750. Communal rights and obligations gave way to individual responsibilities, which could encourage innovation and investment in, for example, drainage, roads and farm buildings. The improvements in efficiency that resulted, in turn provided for much increased profits for landlords.

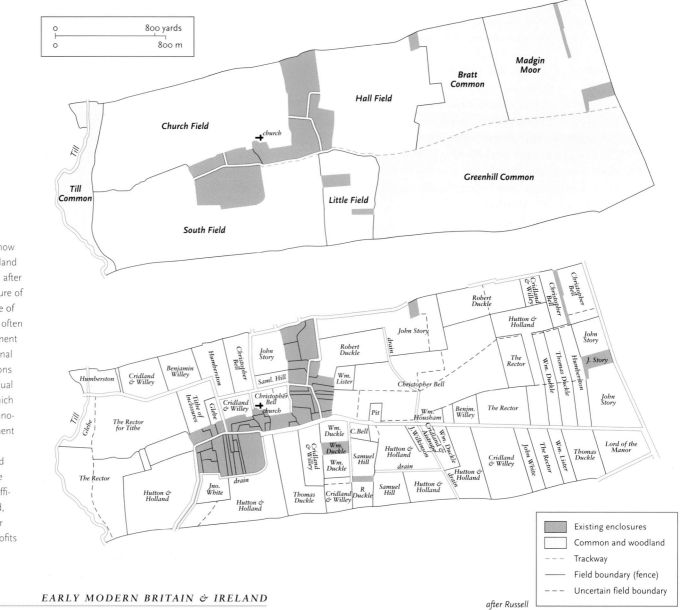

EARLY MODERN BRITAIN & IRELAND

after Russell

and the growth in population fostered demand, helped to encourage change. As national markets developed, so the relative importance of local consumption declined, and regional variations in price became less pronounced. The pattern of production and market was a complex one, but its overall development was dynamic, especially once the population started to increase. Manufacturing and mining areas, where there was substantial immigration and only limited agricultural production, were of growing importance as markets. For example, the linen manufacturing area of east Ulster provided a market for the barley and oatmeal of neighbouring counties, such as Monaghan, and for the young stock reared on nearby hills. This importance of markets suggests that agricultural change was not so much an external force, provoking and making possible other changes in society and the economy, but part of a more complex interactive system.

REVOLUTION OR CONTINUITY?

Yet it is also appropriate, as with industrial development, to consider how revolutionary changes were. Enclosure, and the opportunities and discontent it could create, were not new: there had been much unrest over agricultural change in the sixteenth century. Some 'revolutionary' changes were in fact long-term developments, particularly in regions at the forefront of new techniques, such as Norfolk. There, some of the changes commonly associated with the eighteenth century, such as the introduction of fodder crops, had actually occurred during the Middle Ages. On the other hand, the proportion of Norfolk and Suffolk farmers growing turnips or clover rose dramatically from the 1660s to the 1720s: probate inventories suggest a rise in the percentage of farmers growing turnips from 1.6 per cent to 52.7 per cent. The Norfolk four-course rotation, of wheat, turnips, barley and clover, was established on many farms by the middle of the century.

Continuity in change can also be emphasised for less 'advanced' regions, such as Aberdeenshire. There, many of the measures taken by the agricultural improvers of the mid-eighteenth century had already been tried in the seventeenth. These included attempts to encourage tenants to plant trees and to sow legumes. Similarly, organisational changes, such as the reduction of multiple tenancies and the commutation of rents in kind, had begun in the seventeenth century and accelerated in the eighteenth.

Just as the time span over which agricultural improvements took place was longer than the term 'revolution' might suggest, so the scale of change should not be exaggerated. Many areas showed only limited signs of agricultural improvement. Cornish agriculture, for example, remained largely stagnant until about 1780, although the earlier spread of potato cultivation was a sign of change. In North Yorkshire, Arthur Young praised Charles Turner who, on his estate at Kirkleatham, had created compact farms, constructed new farm buildings, and introduced cabbages, clover and improved breeds of cattle. However, most North Yorkshire farmers did not use clover, and Young criticised the failure to reclaim much of the moorland. Across the country as a whole, extensive commons persisted into the nineteenth century, and a major wave of enclosures took place in 1793–1815, during the French Revolutionary and Napoleonic Wars.

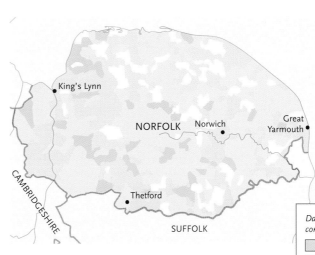

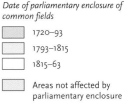

Land enclosure in Norfolk

The term 'Agricultural Revolution' can obscure the fact that changes were often gradual and patchy. In Norfolk only a comparatively small proportion of the land had been enclosed by parliament by 1793.

Date of parliamentary enclosure of common fields

	1720–93
	1793–1815
	1815–63
	Areas not affected by parliamentary enclosure

More generally, the demands of the market were critical in agricultural improvement. Price movements did not reward the improvers until after 1760, while local urban markets were often too small to act as a spur for specialised agriculture. Many farms were small, and the legacy of established practice pressed hard. It was not easy to alter the size, shape or nature of fields, nor the farm buildings and yards. Most British small farmers lacked the necessary capital and willingness to accept risk for a programme of improvement. Illiteracy also limited receptiveness to agricultural innovations. These factors help explain the limited impact of the new techniques before the middle of the eighteenth century.

Ultimately, increases in agricultural productivity did fail to keep pace with population growth and by 1815 there was a shortfall of 5 per cent in the nation's food supply. Britain relied mainly on imports from Europe to meet the demand, until the development of refrigeration, tins and the steam-powered iron ship in the late nineteenth century opened up new food sources in North America, Argentina and Australasia.   **JMB**

Rural workers

An agricultural worker and his family outside their home, in about 1857. The changes in agriculture in the 18th and 19th centuries resulted in great hardship for many poorer workers.

COUNTRY ESTATES

Stourhead, Wiltshire

Stourhead was built for the banker Henry Hoare in the 1720s, with a portico and flanking pavilions added later. Its famous gardens were on the route of every genteel tourist in Georgian England.

The countryside of Britain and Ireland in the period 1660–1880 was dominated by the estates of the gentry and nobility. Estates varied enormously in size, from the lower limit of 1,000 acres (405 hectares), usually thought to be the minimum size necessary to allow owners gentry status from the rental income of their land, to the 1,358,545 acres (about 550,000 hectares), mostly consisting of the poorest Scottish moors, of the Victorian dukes of Sutherland. Some landowners, usually the grandest peers, were among the richest in Europe; at the other end of the spectrum, others struggled on the margins of gentility between landowner and yeoman farmer. Some counties were more dominated by large landowners than others; England and Wales possessed a higher proportion of land owned by small owners than did Ireland and Scotland.

There is only one statistically reliable fixed point in any discussion of the landed estate between the Restoration and World War I, the series of parliamentary papers, known as the 'New Domesday', published between 1872 and 1876, which recorded the owners and gross annual values of estates of one or more acres of land in the United Kingdom. The results of the parliamentary papers, when analysed, have in equal measure fascinated and appalled contemporaries and historians ever since. They reveal that in 1873 fewer than 11,000 owners held 66 per cent of the United Kingdom's total land area.

How had this situation come about? It is generally believed that the New Domesday, undertaken on the eve of the great depression in agriculture, which ran almost unchecked from the late 1870s to the late 1930s, marked the zenith of the great estate. How precisely the picture differed from two centuries earlier it is impossible to determine. But it is certain that estates did grow in size between 1660 and 1870. They did so for three principal reasons: the use of the strict settlement or entail, allowing estates to be passed from one generation to another largely intact (somewhere between a half and two-thirds of land owned by landowners was settled); the negotiation of marriage settlements; and the increased reliance upon mortgages and borrowing to fund the purchase of more land, family settlements and estate debt generally. Manipulation of these three features was common to the ambitions of all landed families after 1660. It led to the evolution of the great landed estates of 3,000 acres (about 1,200 hectares) plus, which were such a marked feature of British life in the eighteenth and nineteenth centuries. Of course, there were other factors underpinning the successful realisation of these strategies: political stability and internal peace after the upheavals of the seventeenth century, low interest rates, mounting pros-

---

☐	Formal gardens, lawns etc
☐	Plantations, hedges etc

Stowe House, Buckinghamshire

Changing fashions in landscape gardening can be seen at Stowe. The first garden (left) was laid out with geometrical precision by Charles Bridgeman in 1739. Capability Brown remodelled the garden in 1780 (right) to reflect a new taste for 'natural' landscapes.

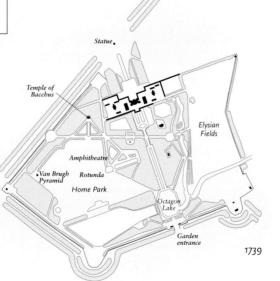

Statue

Temple of Bacchus

Elysian Fields

Amphitheatre

Van Brugh Pyramid   Rotunda

Home Park

Octagon Lake

Garden entrance

1739

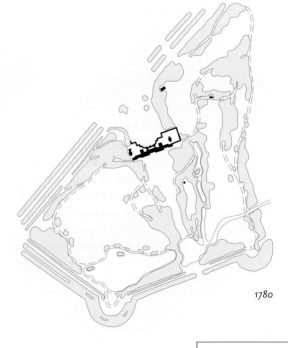

1780

0	200 yards
0	200 metres

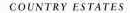

The map shows the
distribution of great
estates (those of over
3,000 acres – about
1,200 hectares) in
England and Wales,
based on the evidence
of the 'New Domesday'
survey of the 1870s. It
reflects the culmination
of the extension of
estates over the
centuries by purchase,
inheritance and mar-
riage. In some parts of
the country, mostly
those remote from
London or including
areas where large
estates never pre-
dominated, the smaller
landowner and squire
survived.

*Number of estates
of 3000+ acres
per 100,000 acres*

more than 9
8–9
7–8
6–7
5–6
4–5
3–4
2–3

ous eighteenth century and reaching its peak in the nineteenth. Tudor houses were replaced with mansions built in
Classical and, from the late eighteenth century, mock-Goth-
ic styles. Building a country house was an enormous financial and organisational undertaking, but the costs could be
justified by its importance as a statement of the owner's
social, political and economic status.

DECLINE OF THE GREAT ESTATE

This world, so confidently constructed in the two centuries
after 1660, began slowly to fall apart after the 1880s. Agriculture collapsed with the import of cheap grain and
other foodstuffs to an unprotected market;
rentals and the price of land, especially in
the arable counties, fell sharply. Landowners, especially those with smaller acreages
and without other forms of income,
became exposed. Sales of land and possessions were often necessary to stave off insol-
vency, or at least to pay the exactions of death
duties after 1894 and increasing taxation generally. Moreover, there was a broader attack
on landownership as Britain democratised.
The political influence of the aristocracy and
gentry visibly contracted as the 1884 Reform
Act and subsequent redistribution of parliamentary
constituencies removed one of their traditional buttresses.
The reform of local government in the late 1880s and 1890s
and the emasculation of the House of Lords in 1911
allowed the landed edifice to subside further. There was, in
addition, a mounting corpus of anti-landlord legislation, in
Ireland especially, but also in Scotland, England and Wales.
Tenants were granted unprecedented rights. The decline of
the aristocracy and the landed estate, some would argue by
no means complete at the millennium, proceeded at an
increasing pace at least to the late 1950s. Certainly, the pre-
eminence of the landed estate revealed in the pages of the
New Domesday was appreciably eroded.   **RGW/ALM**

perity in agriculture reflected in increased rentals, the
rewards of political office and, for some landowners, the
benefits of urban rentals in the growing towns, mineral
rights and wayleaves (payments to secure access).

Although estates became larger after the 1660s, and conditions, politically, economically and legally, favoured the
landowner, the land market was never completely closed.
And although there is debate among historians as to the
extent of its openness, newcomers, who had made great fortunes in trade, finance and industry, were admitted – most
often at the lower rungs – to the ladder of large landownership. Then they enjoyed the benefits of landed society in its
golden age, the security of rental incomes from farming
tenants and the pleasures of country life. According to taste
and means, they could indulge their interests in county and
national politics, in horse-racing, hunting and shooting, in
county administration as justices of the peace (the office
came almost automatically with estate ownership) and officers in the militia, and, above all, as agricultural improvers,
as builders, collectors and landscape gardeners. Thus a few
thousand owners created the most notable feature of the
British landscape, the large landed estate, with all the sym-
bolism of social and political power that it conferred.

The centrepiece of any estate was the country house.
Before the Restoration, most country houses were modest
affairs, though a very few, such as Longleat and Burghley,
were virtual palaces. A period of ambitious rebuilding
began with the Restoration, gathering pace in the prosper-

***Wollaton Hall,
Nottinghamshire***
*Wollaton Hall was
built by the famous
Elizabethan architect
Robert Smythson in the
1580s. By the 19th
century its owner Lord
Middleton had chosen to
retreat from encroaching
Nottingham to his other
estates in rural east
Yorkshire and remote
northern Scotland.*

ENLIGHTENMENT EDINBURGH

Edinburgh is internationally renowned in architectural circles for its classical 'New Town'. This area, physically separated from the medieval or Old Town by a stretch of water called the 'Nor Loch', was developed in the century following the royal approval in 1767 of James Craig's 'Plan of the New Streets and Squares intended for the Capital of North Britain'.

The use of the phrase 'Capital of North Britain' appealed to an emerging Scottish identity within the developing British nation state, yet carefully positioned Edinburgh as supportive of the Hanoverians just 20 years after the defeat of the Stuart cause at Culloden in 1746. Indeed, the street names – Hanover, Frederick, Princes (referring to the male heirs) and George Street – reflected the deference shown by

two directions, showing deference towards the British monarchy and prompting an increasingly confident Scottish national identity.

The building of the New Town proceeded relatively quickly from east to west along the quadrilateral defined by St Andrew's Square, Princes Street, Charlotte Square and Queen Street, so that by 1820 much of the area was completed, or at least under way. Further extensions, to east, west and north, took another 50 years to complete and formed no part of the original conception of James Craig. Though many commentators have claimed that the New Town was an early form of town planning and thus a decisive move away from the irregular forms of medieval and

Charlotte Square (built 1795–1820), the only section of the New Town built as a unified scheme

George Street

Queen Street Gardens

Princes Street

Frederick Street

Nor Loch: draining of the 'noxious lake' began in 1759, but was only completed 60 years later

St Cuthbert's Parish Church, built 1127 or earlier and much altered 1772–90

Edinburgh Castle, a fortified site from before recorded history, used as a barracks from 1650

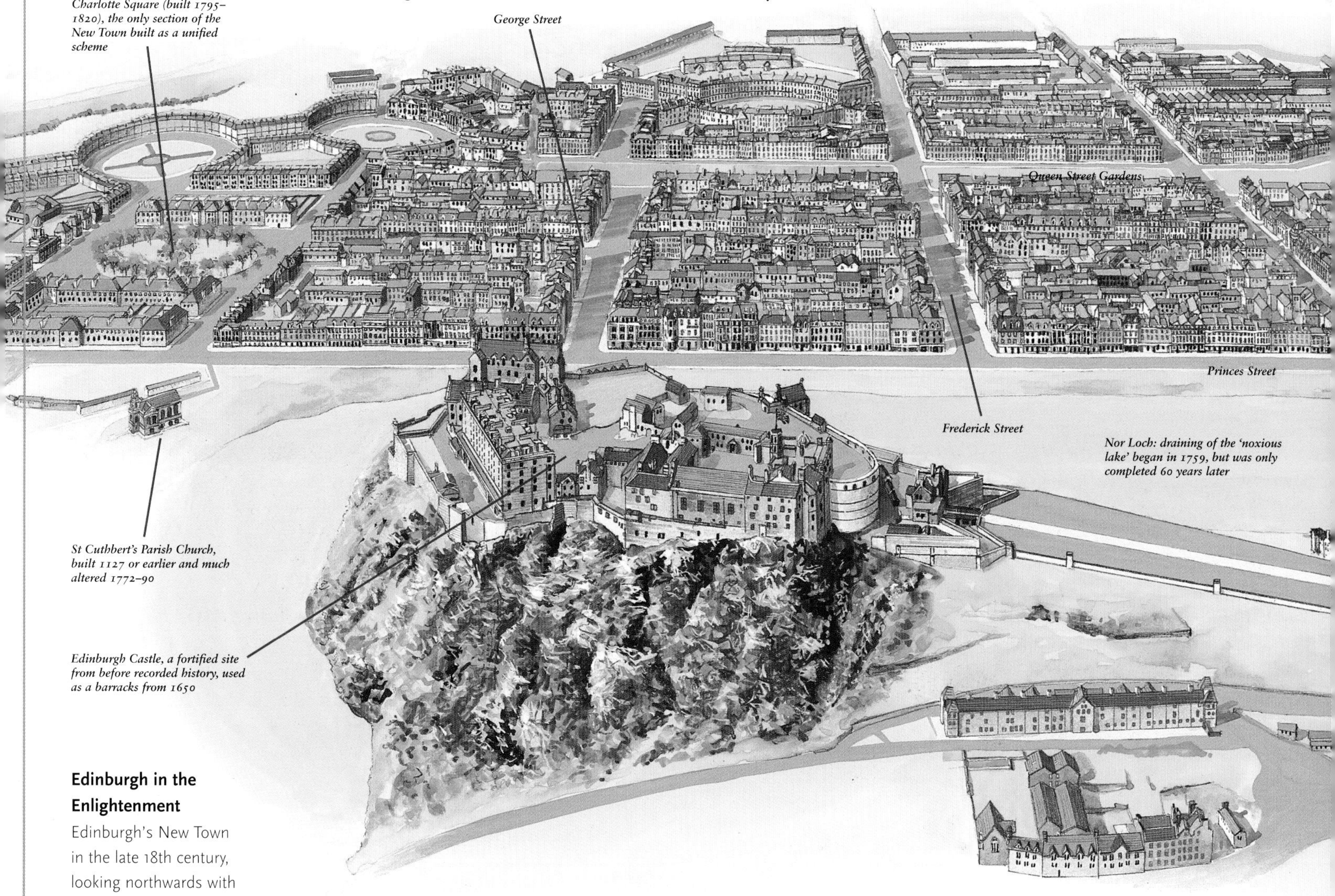

Edinburgh in the Enlightenment

Edinburgh's New Town in the late 18th century, looking northwards with the Castle and the Old Town in the foreground. The straight streets and neoclassical buildings of the New Town contrasted markedly with the congested, medieval Old Town.

Craig and the Edinburgh Town Council to the Hanoverian succession, and naming streets Rose and Thistle linked the English and Scottish national emblems. Many other New Town street names were also English – London, York, Northumberland, Albany and Cumberland – the latter a name particularly reviled among supporters of the Stuart cause. Jamaica and India Streets connected Edinburgh to the British empire. Cleverly, the New Town faced in

early modern street layouts, this is an oversimplified view. In fact, the geometric forms described by the streets owed more to the strict enforcement of clauses in legal documents governing building development in Scotland, and to the associated potential for capital accumulation.

The architectural contrast between the Old Town, with its narrow closes and wynds, steep gradients associated with the strategic position of the initial settlement, and high-rise tenements of seven or even 10 storeys, contrasted starkly with the architectural characteristics of the New Town. Here, the neoclassical proportions of the Georgian

EARLY MODERN BRITAIN & IRELAND

landscape provided expressions of order and rationality. The geometrical shapes of squares and crescents represented a distinct break with previous building styles and forms. In the Old Town, social classes had co-existed in the high-rise tenements; in the New Town, a more homogeneous middle- and upper-middle-class suburb was created.

The Edinburgh New Town plan was inscribed 'To His Sacred Majesty King George III. The Magnificent Patron of Every Polite and Liberal Art.' However, the New Town plan was much more than an astute political document. It also reflected the confident European credentials of Edinburgh as the centre of a semi-autonomous country with distinct judicial, financial, ecclesiastical and educational systems. Located at the epicentre of the Scottish Enlightenment, Edinburgh experienced two separate though related strands of cultural development. One was the refined development in artistic and literary endeavours that also found expres-

View from Calton Hill

Edinburgh in the early 19th century, looking westwards from Calton Hill.

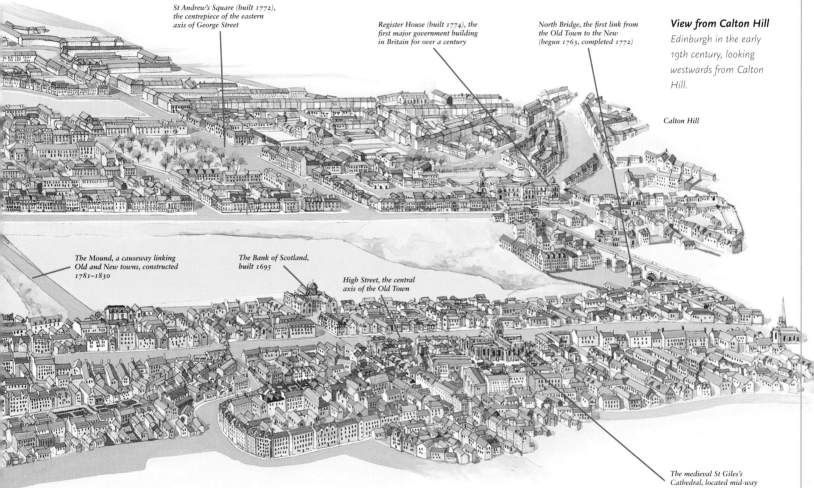

St Andrew's Square (built 1772), the centrepiece of the eastern axis of George Street

Register House (built 1774), the first major government building in Britain for over a century

North Bridge, the first link from the Old Town to the New (begun 1763, completed 1772)

Calton Hill

The Mound, a causeway linking Old and New towns, constructed 1781–1830

The Bank of Scotland, built 1695

High Street, the central axis of the Old Town

The medieval St Giles's Cathedral, located mid-way along the High Street

sion throughout Europe where 'polite' and 'liberal' became synonyms for all that was considered cultured, educated, intellectual and tolerant of alternative ideas. Just as architectural forms were rendered to simple, clean and logical lines, as in the Edinburgh New Town, rationality was developed in practical arenas – science, medicine and political economy. The status quo was also challenged in a second, related characteristic, an intense rejuvenation not just in poetry, prose, ballads and painting, but also in engineering and applied science. Scottish artists and inventors revelled in the local and the particular, and extolled the virtue

of a distinctively national identity. Confidently, and through different media, Scots expressed their identity through local history, song, poems and philosophy, and this was reflected in a welter of publications. On average, 165 books were published annually in Scotland in the years 1750–90; between 1790 and 1810 this figure had risen to 265 per annum, and by 1815 to 565 titles.

Ideas that challenged the status quo were increasingly embraced in Scotland, and in particular in Edinburgh. Pluralism was acceptable, in government, in the arts, and in architecture. The contrast between the ancient skyline of the Old Town, with its appeal to the Scottish vernacular, and the modernity of the New Town embodied these core values.   **RR**

THE 18th-CENTURY EMPIRE

The main focus of British attention remained in the Atlantic region, where migration and interlocking patterns of trade helped to define the growth of an empire of settlement and commerce. Underpinned by the slave trade with West Africa (until abolition in 1807), and reinforced by the commercial and maritime regulations embodied in the Navigation Acts, Britain's Atlantic empire was of great importance to the domestic economy. Sugar, tobacco, coffee, rice and timber were supplied to Britain in steadily increasing quantities, and demand from expanding overseas populations provided an important outlet for British manufactured products and re-exported goods derived from other parts of the world. Although the loss of the American colonies interrupted commercial expansion, it did not prove ultimately to be the economic catastrophe that contemporaries feared, and indeed trade with the United States of America rapidly exceeded the levels of pre-independence days. The Atlantic empire, which contained around 1.5 million inhabitants

The death of General James Wolfe

Victory in the battle of Quebec in 1759, even at the cost of Wolfe's life, effectively ended any French challenge to Britain in North America. The 1750s saw British military triumphs around the globe.

The British empire in the 18th century

During the 18th century Britain became a major imperial power. In the western hemisphere, the conquest of Canada added vast new territories. Even the loss of the American colonies did little serious harm to British power. In Asia the East India Company was steadily adding to its domains through conquest. New possessions in Africa and Australasia indicated new directions of imperial expansion.

The eighteenth century marked the full emergence of Britain as an imperial nation. There was a spectacular growth in all forms of overseas activity and, with power and influence being increasingly deployed on a worldwide scale, more territory and trade was brought under British control. This was by no means an uncontested or uninterrupted advance, as the loss of the 13 American colonies was so graphically to demonstrate in 1783, but by 1815 Britain had firmly secured a global empire upon which the sun never set. This had a profound effect not only on British perceptions of the world, but also on the making of Britain itself. Overseas activity was tightly woven into the economic, social and cultural fabric of Britain, and it served to shape the attitudes and identities that made the British an imperial people.

Britain's eighteenth-century empire was built upon the rather insubstantial overseas foundations that had been laid in North America, the Caribbean and Asia since 1600. Consequently, several long-run continuities can be discerned.

		British empire in 1707
		New territories 1701–1815, with date of acquisition
		British territorial claims in 1815
		Territories and possessions lost
		Territories occupied temporarily by Britain in time of war
		Other European colonial territories or claims

(settlers and slaves) in 1800, always had close links with Britain and, as colonies matured beyond the first stages of settlement, the white population or 'brethren overseas' often displayed many of the social and cultural characteristics of those in the home country.

THE EASTERN EMPIRE

Yet, for all the enduring significance of Britain's Atlantic possessions and connections, the most striking eighteenth-century overseas advances were made in South Asia. The monopolist trading organisation, the East India Company, transformed its original narrowly commercial presence in Bengal, Bombay and Madras by deploying its increasingly large and effective private army against rival European companies and local powers, thereby enabling it to establish political and military control over large parts of India. This process, which had its origins in the 1740s, gathered momentum after 1756, and by 1800 well over 30 million Indians had been brought under Company rule. Based upon conquest, the collection of revenue, and the government of alien peoples, this was a new and quite different form of empire, and it initially caused considerable anxiety among those in Britain who were concerned about the Company's exercise of unregulated power.

In the East, the British were also active beyond India. An important foothold was established at Penang on the Malay Peninsula in 1786, and British private traders were deeply involved in the intra-Asian or 'country' trade that played a key role in stimulating the growth of the East India Company's lucrative tea trade with China. James Cook's exploration of the Pacific between 1768 and 1778 helped to open new spheres of operation, and after 1787 colonies were established in New South Wales and Van Diemen's Land. Historians still debate whether, or to what extent, this represented a 'swing to the east' in British interests after 1763,

> 'The British Empire is arrived at that height of Power and Glory, to which none of the States and Monarchies upon Earth could ever lay the like claim.'
>
> **The Reverend John Entick,** *The Present State of the British Empire* (1774)

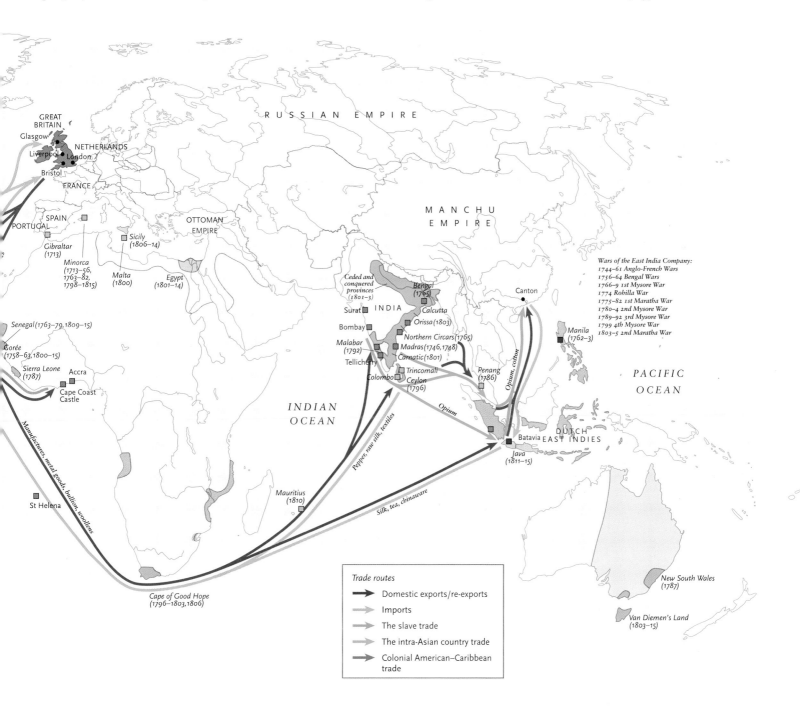

Wars of the East India Company:
1744–61 Anglo-French Wars
1756–64 Bengal Wars
1766–9 1st Mysore War
1774 Rohilla War
1775–82 1st Maratha War
1780–4 2nd Mysore War
1789–92 3rd Mysore War
1799 4th Mysore War
1803–5 2nd Maratha War

Trade routes
➡ Domestic exports/re-exports
➡ Imports
➡ The slave trade
➡ The intra-Asian country trade
➡ Colonial American–Caribbean trade

18th-century Bristol

In the late 17th and early 18th centuries, west-coast ports such as Bristol benefited greatly from the expanding transatlantic trade in slaves, sugar and tobacco. Beginning with the laying out of Queen Square in 1699, Bristol far outgrew its medieval boundaries to become the second largest city in Britain after London. However, the large tidal range of the river Avon was a disadvantage and, despite building a new merchant dock down-river in 1762, Bristol by 1800 had been over-taken by Liverpool, which had deep-water access for ships and had invested more heavily in new dock facilities.

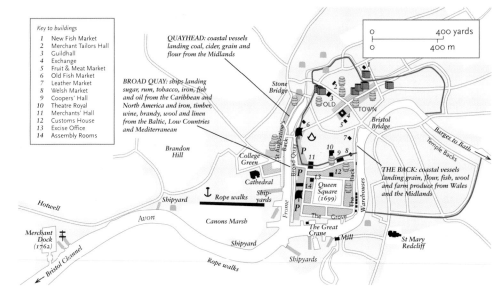

Key to buildings
1 New Fish Market
2 Merchant Tailors Hall
3 Guildhall
4 Exchange
5 Fruit & Meat Market
6 Old Fish Market
7 Leather Market
8 Welsh Market
9 Coopers' Hall
10 Theatre Royal
11 Merchants' Hall
12 Customs House
13 Excise Office
14 Assembly Rooms

QUAYHEAD: coastal vessels landing coal, cider, grain and flour from the Midlands

BROAD QUAY: ships landing sugar, rum, tobacco, iron, fish and oil from the Caribbean and North America and iron, timber, wine, brandy, wool and linen from the Baltic, Low Countries and Mediterranean

THE BACK: coastal vessels landing grain, flour, fish, wool and farm produce from Wales and the Midlands

Dry docks
Main mercantile districts
Extent of city c.1770
Medieval city walls
Sugar house
Mast maker
Anchor smith
Pump maker
Navigational instrument maker
Sail maker
Tea merchant
Wine merchant

but it cannot be denied that Britain's global empire of 1815 was quite different in composition to the empire of a century earlier.

Overseas expansion was driven by Britain's capacity to deploy financial, military and naval resources in the wider world, and the growth of the empire must, at least in part, be linked to the strengthening of the British state and the City of London that occurred during the eighteenth century. While many examples can be found of private enterprise serving to pave the way for the extension of overseas influence, national concerns and the affairs of state also dictated that the empire played a part in furthering British power and wealth. This was especially so in the light of successive worldwide campaigns fought against Spain and, in particular, France. Every major European war of the period was keenly contested in overseas theatres and, as a result, the fortunes of war were reflected in the colonial possessions and territories that changed hands in the peace treaties that ended every bout of hostilities. By the time of the Congress of Vienna in 1815, an almost unbroken sequence of wartime successes, together with the ultimate triumph over Napoleonic France, not only consolidated a global empire, but also ensured that Britain had secured a position of unrivalled supremacy among the European powers.

THE IMPERIAL IMPACT: CALCUTTA IN THE EIGHTEENTH CENTURY

The causes of British imperial expansion in the East are clearly illustrated in Bengal. The growth of British power and influence in India as a whole was founded upon events in Bengal between 1757 and 1765, when the East India Company responded forcefully and decisively to the loss of its Calcutta headquarters to the local ruler Siraj-ud-daula in

1756. Under the leadership of Robert Clive, Company forces first recaptured Calcutta and then, in the Bengal 'revolution' of 1757, defeated and deposed the Nawab, who was replaced by a British nominee, Mir Jafar. Further conflicts with Indian powers followed, and after successful campaigns in 1763 and 1764 the Mughal emperor, Shah Alam II, granted Clive the *diwani* of Bengal at the treaty of Allahabad (1765). This gave the Company the right to collect the territorial revenues of the Mughal provinces of Bengal, Bihar and Orissa, and thus acknowledged the Company as ruler of the region.

In microcosm, the extraordinary transformation of the East India Company's fortunes was reflected in the development and expansion of the city of Calcutta. By 1800 a small East India Company trading station or factory had become the second city of the British Empire and the capital of British India. As this happened, the British gave increasingly confident architectural expression to their presence, and wider patterns of urbanisation helped to define the broad outline of imperial relationships.

The East India Company's position in late seventeenth-century Bengal had been extremely vulnerable. In 1690, however, the decision to establish a new and secure commercial foothold led to the selection by Job Charnock of a safe landing place on the river Hooghly at a location which, although unhealthy because of the close proximity of

Colonial domesticity

A British colonial family – probably that of the East India Company administrator and general Robert Clive – with an Indian ayah, or nurse. Company officials lived a life of considerable luxury in India in the 18th century.

marshes and salt lakes, was easily defensible and served by good communications. Charnock chose a site based upon three existing settlements, the villages of Sutanuti, Gobindapur and Kalikata, which became incorporated in the town of Calcutta that grew up around the newly built factory and Fort William. The growth of the town was rapid, and by 1750 it had attracted over 100,000 inhabitants, although probably no more than 500 were British.

Company personnel and free merchants were clustered tightly around the fort and Tank Square, and a clearly defined European or 'white' town emerged. To the north, beyond groups of Portuguese and Armenians, was the 'black' town containing Indian bazaars, or markets, and distinct localities dominated by Bengalis, but arranged according to caste or occupation. This in turn gave way to numerous small villages of makeshift huts inhabited by labourers and weavers, and in these outlying parts of Calcutta the social mores of rural Bengal remained very strong indeed. By the end of the eighteenth century, however, a cosmopolitan zone had begun to appear between the white and black towns, and here were to be found many Eurasians, Indians, poor Europeans, and members of ethnic groups such as the Chinese and Parsis. This added a further dimension to the increasingly fluid patterns of zoning and organisation that were evident beyond the white town.

Calcutta itself was profoundly affected by the tumultuous military and political events of mid-century. The sacking of the white town by Siraj-ud-daula in 1756 was a humiliating defeat for the Company, and it responded by reorganising and relocating its fortifications. A massive new military base – Fort William – was built to the south of the old fort. Costing the enormous sum of £2 million, this ambitious 20-year construction project had a considerable economic impact on the city by giving employment to thousands of skilled labourers and coolies.

After the British had secured control of Bengal, Calcutta was nominated as capital of the province in place of Murshidabad. The administrative importance of the city was further elevated in 1773, when it became the seat of the Governors General, who were given authority over all of the Company's settlements in India. Consequently, it became necessary to build more of the offices and courts needed for the exercise of imperial rule, and this formed part of a much wider process of improvement that saw the white town acquire many of the classical architectural features associated with towns and cities in Britain.

The rapid construction of new public build-

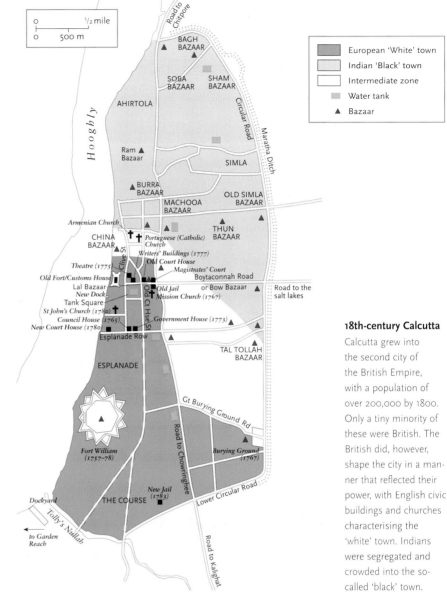

18th-century Calcutta
Calcutta grew into the second city of the British Empire, with a population of over 200,000 by 1800. Only a tiny minority of these were British. The British did, however, shape the city in a manner that reflected their power, with English civic buildings and churches characterising the 'white' town. Indians were segregated and crowded into the so-called 'black' town.

ings, social amenities, spacious private dwellings and garden house retreats after 1760 reflected a desire on the part of the wealthy British to create an urban setting in which they could, as far as circumstances allowed, enjoy genteel and 'civilised' lifestyles similar to those followed by their contemporaries in Britain and other parts of the empire. This process was unplanned but it served only to reinforce the distinctiveness and separation of the white town from the rest of the city. Although there was no strict racial segregation, little other than official or commercial business was conducted between the majority of the British and Indian inhabitants.

By 1800 the population of Calcutta stood at well over 200,000 people, yet the permanent British residents of the city remained a tiny minority of little more than 1,000. They may have been hugely outnumbered by the Indian inhabitants, but their power and wealth had nevertheless found unambiguous expression in the city that had grown up around them.   HVB

'This revolution [of 1757], effected in one day by a mere handful of men, but more important in its consequences than most of the protracted wars which have convulsed Europe...'

David Macpherson,
The History of the European Commerce with India (1812)

TURNPIKES & CANALS

Until the early eighteenth century, Britain was almost entirely dependent on natural features for inland carriage. While people could walk or ride, the movement of bulky goods was all but impossible. Coastal waters were therefore the most important conduit for trade, supplemented by a

The Great Dover Road turnpike

There were 16 turnpikes between London and Dover, where travellers were required to pay tolls. Although tolls were disliked, transport costs were actually reduced by turnpiking.

river system of varying navigability. Of those roads that existed, most were little more than the trackways carved by centuries of localised movement of carts and waggons, whether for agriculture, mining or early manufacture.

Before 1700, the responsibility for road maintenance had been unambiguously local. Under Tudor legislation, the parish was responsible for ensuring that roads remained passable. Parishioners were charged with the task of providing horses, carts, labour and tools for annual repairs. While road traffic remained localised and there were able bodies and horse teams for the purpose, the system

---

The turnpike system

The turnpike system, by requiring travellers rather than local parishioners to pay for road maintenance, resulted in the establishment of an elaborate road network, and a drastic reduction in journey times.

---

worked, to a degree. But as circulation increased, traffic grew in volume and journeys grew longer, it was necessary to find a new mechanism for maintaining roads.

THE TURNPIKE SYSTEM

The spread of the turnpike after 1700 shifted the burden from local parishioners to road users. Traffic that was not local was charged a toll, which was then applied to road upkeep. Turnpike trusts became the institutions responsible for this administrative innovation and, from the early eighteenth century onwards, were a central enabling force in economic expansion – in agriculture and in manufacturing. They facilitated the growth of markets, the movement and exchange of certain kinds of raw materials, and the speedier transmission of news and information. As early as 1770, England and Wales boasted 24,140 kilometres (15,000 miles) of turnpiked roads. By the early nineteenth century, the turnpike gate had become commonplace throughout England, Wales, lowland Scotland and parts of Ireland.

Although the trusts replaced parishes in the task of road maintenance, roads remained largely local endeavours, usually overseen by interested landowners and industrialists who subscribed loan funds for improvements to the roads under trust jurisdiction. An inevitable outcome of this was that there was no uniform standard for the

——	Turnpikes
——	Military roads

Stagecoach journey times from London (hours)

84 in 1750
30 in 1820

The canal system in about 1830

Canal construction reached its peak in the 'canal mania' of the 1790s. By the 1830s, some 4,023 kilometres (2,500 miles) of canal, including navigable rivers, had spread across the country.

basins rarely occurred where they were most needed to suit the transport needs of an economy increasingly based on inorganic resources like coal. The solution came in the making of 'deadwater' cuts, or canals. The first canals were fundamentally coal canals – short stretches of waterway linking coalfields with ports or navigable water, or with major industrial consumers. They were often promoted by local entrepreneurs, who had the most to gain from a speedier circulation of goods and lowered transport costs. Canal shares became a vital investor currency and, far more so than turnpikes, locked into free-market capitalism – as was powerfully demonstrated by the speculative canal mania of the 1790s. By then, canals were being promoted far and wide. Engineers were carrying them across major watersheds like the Pennines; in the southern farming districts of England, they were offered as lifelines to the rural poor, not least in the supply of cheap winter coal. In Ireland they were launched as a route to economic salvation in an otherwise depressed and backward economy.

A FRAGMENTED NETWORK

All told, Britain had gained some 4,023 kilometres (2,500 miles) of canal – including navigable rivers – by the 1830s. There was never a true national system, as fragmented ownership and the existence in England of broad and narrow canals (defined by lock widths) – the latter concentrated in the Midlands – limited integrated operation. Canal ventures also displayed great variation in financial performance. Some lost money steadily – either because traffic volumes failed to meet expectations or because they were plagued by engineering problems. A few, like the Loughborough Navigation, proved wildly lucrative for their investors. In industrial towns like Birmingham, they became vital arteries of commerce and much sought-after for industrial sites.   **MF**

quality of turnpikes. They varied as much as their underlying geology, which was often the most important arbiter of the stability of road surfaces. However, even a cursory glance at the remarkable reduction in journey times by stagecoach from London between 1750 and 1830 bears eloquent testimony to the impact of the turnpike trusts.

THE DEVELOPMENT OF CANALS

For traffic that was bulky or heavy, turnpikes remained inadequate as transport arteries. Materials like coal and ore were carried by water, which was more practicable and infinitely cheaper. In the seventeenth and early eighteenth centuries, a determined effort was made to 'improve' the courses of natural rivers, avoiding shoals, rapids and other restrictions to regular navigation. Ultimately, though, river

Bridgewater Canal

An aqueduct carrying the Bridgewater Canal over the river Irwell. Though the canals revolutionised the transportation of bulk cargoes, the engineering difficulties faced during their construction were often considerable.

Stocking-making, 18th century

The knitter sits at the frame, while his wife winds the silk on to bobbins. As industrialisation progressed, machinery became more complex and was concentrated in factories.

'...*the immense number of factories...each vomiting forth clouds of smoke, which collect in dense masses, and poison the surrounding atmosphere...I counted the factory chimneys in sight to near one hundred.*'

Description of industrial Leeds by William Dodd, in *The Factory System Illustrated* **(1842)**

Historians have long disagreed about the extent to which social and economic change occurred in Britain between about 1760 and 1840 – the period conventionally regarded as that of the Industrial Revolution. Some have viewed the period as one of profound change, associated particularly with the rise of powered machinery and factory production. Others have argued that the period in fact saw rather more limited change. They suggest not only that the nature and degree of industrial development at the time can easily be exaggerated – for example, relatively few people nationwide worked in factories even by 1850 – but also that too little attention is usually paid to important industrial advances that actually occurred before the late eighteenth century – such as the smelting of iron using coke.

Historians have also differed about the causes of the Industrial Revolution. Attempts to emphasise particular developments, such as advances in technology, have proven controversial. Moreover, many historians have tended to highlight changes that stimulated the supply of goods and services – the growing availability of labour and capital, technological change and so on – at the expense of changes in the demand for products. Though recent discussion has gone some way towards rectifying this lack of balance, discussion of the demand for consumer goods bought by households (pots, clothes, furniture and so on) has still tended to feature more strongly than that of producer goods purchased by businesses (such as machines and tools).

What must be stressed, however, is that a whole range of social, economic and political changes promoted Britain's industrialisation – and that the interrelationship between these changes is extremely complex.

It is also the case that an understanding of the social and economic changes that took place during the Industrial Revolution in Britain can only be gained by taking a regional approach. This is partly because industrialisation emerged far more strongly in some parts of the country than others, and also because the nature of industrial change differed considerably at regional level, not only in terms of the major industries that developed, but also in terms of the methods and organisation of production.

INDUSTRY AND THE REGIONS

Occupational data taken from census returns can be used to demonstrate the regional nature of industrialisation. The earliest available for this purpose were collected in 1841 and were subsequently printed in classified form, giving the numbers of both males and females employed in various occupational groups. For each county, these groups can be used to work out the proportions of the total labour force employed in mining, in manufacturing and in commerce (industry and commerce). It is therefore possible to map the main areas of industrialisation that had emerged by the end of the Industrial Revolution period, showing where 45 per cent or more of the labour force were engaged in industry and commerce. The figure of 45 per cent is slightly higher than the national average.

The picture that emerges should not be taken too literally. First, there is some doubt as to how accurate and full a record of occupations was made at the time – especially of female occupations – and how well constructed the original classifications were. Second, the fact that the original data were compiled at county level means that they give no indication of the extent to which regional concentrations of industrial activity arose within counties, since, in fact, only parts of counties became heavily industrialised. Third, it has to be remembered that the importance of industrial regions changed with time; for instance, the West Riding rose to prominence in the manufacture of woollens in the course of the eighteenth century, at the expense of East Anglia and the West Country. Finally, industrial activity was by no means absent in other counties, though it was usually much less prominent than agriculture: Cornwall, Middlesex (including London), Worcestershire and Edinburgh all had figures for industrial and commercial employment of just below 45 per cent.

The Industrial Revolution, 1800–40

The growth of industry during the Industrial Revolution period was concentrated in particular regions of the country, though industrial activity was widespread. In most of the industrial districts, manufacturing activity predominated, and particular industries became strongly localised within them – for example, the production of pottery became concentrated in Stafford- shire. The growing use of steam power reinforced the advantages of coalfield locations, though by no means all industries made extensive use of powered equipment by the mid-19th century. Those regions experiencing industrialisation saw rapid population growth and urbanisation. Canal-building and turnpike roads provided the transport links that made industrialisation possible.

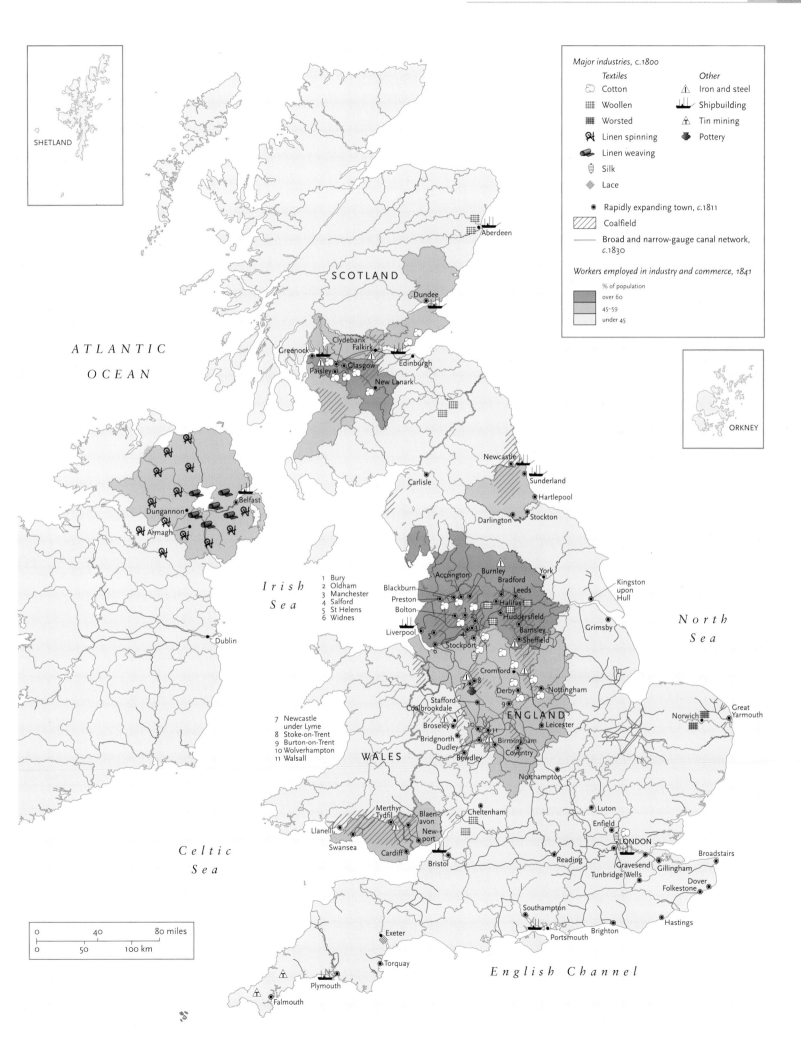

Major industries, c.1800

Textiles
- Cotton
- Woollen
- Worsted
- Linen spinning
- Linen weaving
- Silk
- Lace

Other
- Iron and steel
- Shipbuilding
- Tin mining
- Pottery

- Rapidly expanding town, c.1811
- Coalfield
- Broad and narrow-gauge canal network, c.1830

Workers employed in industry and commerce, 1841
% of population
- over 60
- 45–59
- under 45

SHETLAND

ORKNEY

ATLANTIC OCEAN

SCOTLAND

Aberdeen

Dundee

Greenock
Clydebank Falkirk
Paisley Glasgow
Edinburgh
New Lanark

Irish Sea

Belfast
Dungannon
Armagh

Dublin

Newcastle
Carlisle
Sunderland
Hartlepool
Darlington Stockton

Kingston upon Hull

North Sea

1 Bury
2 Oldham
3 Manchester
4 Salford
5 St Helens
6 Widnes

Accrington Burnley Bradford York
Blackburn Leeds
Preston Halifax
Bolton Huddersfield
Liverpool Barnsley Grimsby
Stockport Sheffield

Cromford

7 Newcastle under Lyme
8 Stoke-on-Trent
9 Burton-on-Trent
10 Wolverhampton
11 Walsall

Stafford
Coalbrookdale Derby Nottingham
ENGLAND
Broseley Leicester
Bridgnorth Norwich Great Yarmouth
Dudley Birmingham
Bewdley Coventry
WALES Northampton

Merthyr Tydfil
Blaen-avon Cheltenham Luton
Newport Enfield
Llanelli LONDON
Swansea Reading Broadstairs
Cardiff Gravesend Gillingham
Bristol Tunbridge Wells Dover
Folkestone
Hastings

Celtic Sea

Southampton
Exeter Brighton
Portsmouth

English Channel

Torquay

Plymouth
Falmouth

0 40 80 miles
0 50 100 km

Irish linen industry, 1791

A new warping mill and weaving loom in an Irish linen factory. The predominance of cotton and Lancashire in Britain's industrial history can obscure the fact that Irish linen and Yorkshire woollen industries were also important and underwent their own transformations.

THE NATURE OF INDUSTRIAL REGIONS

By the early Victorian period, some counties, or parts of them, had clearly experienced far more intense industrialisation than others. Renfrew, the West Riding, Lancashire and Lanark showed the strongest concentrations; the industrial and commercial labour forces in these counties was from 64 to 68 per cent of the total. Closely following were Forfar, Fife and Stafford, the corresponding figures being between 57 and 59 per cent. In parts of these counties, industrialisation had plainly become highly developed. Furthermore, as steam power rose to prominence, industrial activity in these regions became increasingly concentrated in urban areas, so that industrialists no longer had to depend on water-powered sites in country districts.

Apart from varying in the intensity of industrialisation, the industrial regions differed in character. In general, manufacturing dominated economic activity, but in several counties, including Durham and Glamorgan, mining – principally of coal – occupied a relatively high proportion of the labour forces. As might be expected, the agricultur-

al sectors in most industrialised counties came to occupy comparatively small proportions of the total labour force, the figures being as low as 7 per cent in Lancashire and Lanarkshire, and seldom above 20 per cent. Nonetheless, such figures do not indicate an actual decline in agriculture in these counties; in fact local farmers benefited from the rising incomes available to industrial workers. In Ireland, by contrast, the proportions of agricultural labour in the most industrialised counties remained relatively high, standing at 30 per cent in Antrim, 38 per cent in Down and more than 40 per cent in the others.

The distinctive nature of the industrial regions is also evident in the specialisms that arose within manufacturing activity, sometimes with sub-regional differences. In the West Riding, for example, worsted production became strongly localised in Bradford and Halifax and in the district to the north and west; woollen production became concentrated around Leeds, Dewsbury and Halifax; and steel-making was chiefly confined to the Sheffield area. Such concentrations were facilitated by natural and man-made advantages in the locations concerned. Amongst the former, the ready availability of coal was of general importance as steam-power grew to prominence; a strong link between regional concentrations of industry and coalfield locations is clear, with Ireland the notable exception. Amongst the latter, improvements in water and land transport played a vital role, with the main industrial districts being well served by canals and, in several instances, by navigable rivers.

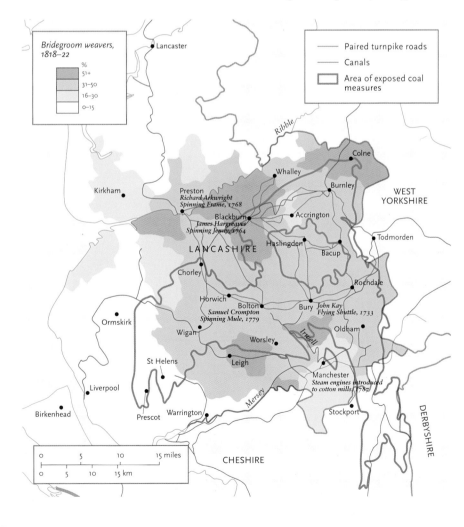

Bridegroom weavers, 1818–22

%
51+
31–50
16–30
0–15

Paired turnpike roads
Canals
Area of exposed coal measures

Lancaster
Ribble
Kirkham
Colne
Whalley
Burnley
Preston
Richard Arkwright Spinning Frame, 1768
Blackburn
James Hargreaves Spinning Jenny, 1764
Accrington
Todmorden
WEST YORKSHIRE
LANCASHIRE
Haslingden
Bacup
Chorley
Rochdale
Horwich
Bury
John Kay Flying Shuttle, 1733
Bolton
Samuel Crompton Spinning Mule, 1779
Oldham
Ormskirk
Wigan
Worsley
Irwell
St Helens
Leigh
Manchester
Steam engines introduced to cotton mills, 1782
Liverpool
Mersey
Stockport
Birkenhead
Prescot
Warrington
DERBYSHIRE
CHESHIRE

0   5   10   15 miles
0   5   10   15 km

Industrialising Lancashire

Anglican parish registers are a valuable source of information about employment patterns, as they often record the occupations of bridegrooms and fathers. Here the evidence from such registers shows the varying importance of handloom weaving in Lancashire in the early 19th century. At this time, the industry was at its height and was strongly concentrated in eastern and central parts of the county. In several parishes, handloom weavers formed more than half the bridegrooms and commonly more than a third. Other industrial concentrations centred on St Helens, Prescot and Warrington, where glass-making, chemicals and metal-working predominated. In the west and north of the county, agriculture generally remained dominant.

The emergence of specialised industrial regions excited great interest amongst contemporaries, often provoking them into highly critical comment about the changes they experienced or observed. Many contemporary observers, for example, complained about the employment of young children in textile mills, noting particularly the long working hours these children endured and the dangers they faced from exposure to unfenced machinery. Indeed, many gruesome tales were told of horrendous injuries that both child and adult factory workers received, including fatal injuries or the loss of limbs. And there was even concern about the immorality that was thought to arise when many young people were congregated together in factories. Nevertheless, other contemporary commentators strongly supported the factory system, even if they admitted to its drawbacks. They made great play of how easy factory work was because, they said, it substituted machinery for muscle, even though long working hours were required. Additionally, they provided impressive statistics on the massive increases in output that could be achieved when powered machines were used instead of hand-driven machines.

THE INDUSTRIAL REVOLUTION IN LANCASHIRE

Lancashire, where cotton manufacturing outpaced all other industries, has become synonymous with the Industrial Revolution. The marked upsurge in raw cotton imports into Britain during the 1780s and 1790s, which facilitated much higher levels of long-term production in the industry, was accompanied by a substantial move towards factory-based production as powered machinery, especially the mule – a hybrid combining elements of Hargreaves's Spinning Jenny and Arkwright's Frame – gained ground. And the expansion of cotton manufacturing encouraged, and benefited from, the more rapid growth of a wide range of other local industries, engineering and coal mining being prominent amongst them. In both urban and rural areas, these developments helped to extend appreciably the county's built environment, and to alter significantly its appearance. As a result, fundamental changes occurred in living and working conditions, with families and individuals having to make adjustments to their lifestyles in ways that they did not always find to their liking.

Yet the extent of such changes should not be exaggerated. First, textile production was heavily concentrated in central and eastern parts of the county, to the south of the river Ribble. Further west, and to the north of the Ribble, agriculture, stimulated by growing local demand for its products, generally remained dominant, though in south-west Lancashire, centred on St Helens, Warrington and Liverpool, a range of industrial activity emerged, including metal-working, glass-making and chemical manufacture. Second, even within the more heavily industrialised zone, the pace of industrial change varied. Thus, in cotton textiles, weaving transferred much more slowly from handloom production in cottages to mechanised production in factories than did spinning. Indeed, the main job losses for domestic handloom weavers did not occur until the 1840s – and even at mid-century well over 50,000 handloom weavers were still at work in the county, a sizeable proportion of them being young people. A key factor in this slow transition was that early powerlooms proved harsh in oper-

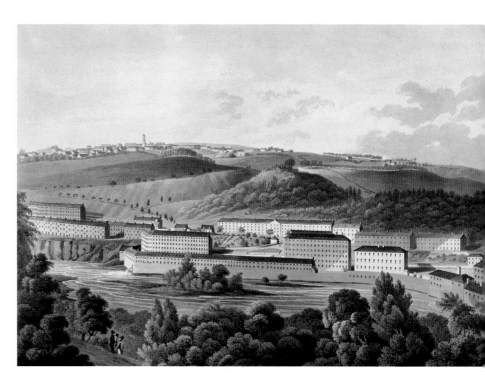

New Lanark mills and housing

Founded by David Dale in 1783, the New Lanark mills took advantage of an abundant water supply from the river Clyde. Blocks of one- and two-roomed tenement houses shown in the background were provided for the workers.

ation – leading to frequent yarn breakages, especially when weaving finer fabrics. The attraction of working at home as opposed to working in a factory was also important for many in the industry, not least because it gave them the choice of when to work. It is also a fact that, well before the Industrial Revolution, textile production was already employing a high proportion of the available labour force, albeit as domestic rather than factory workers. As a rule, the men wove while the women and children spun and wound the yarn that the weaver needed for his shuttle, an arrangement that persisted until men became spinners in factories and women turned to handloom weaving as the trade expanded without mechanising.

Explanations of Lancashire's Industrial Revolution have given much consideration to the county's natural advantages, including a humid climate that favoured the processing of vegetable fibres – and to its acquired advantages, amongst which were an extensive transport network and increasing supplies of capital and labour. In the case of transport, historians have made a great deal of the early construction of the county's canal system, though improved roads also played a key part. These roads not only facilitated the regular stagecoach journeys that numerous local businessmen had to make to and from Manchester – by the mid-1820s, well over a thousand of them were visiting the town regularly to transact business – they also met the transport needs of those industrial districts in the county without canal links, including the Rossendale valley in east Lancashire. Indeed, Lancashire towns that were not joined directly by canal often became joined by two generations of turnpike roads, the newer roads substituting for canal links.

'Manchester...the metropolis of the cotton manufacture...It is essentially a place of business, where pleasure is unknown as a pursuit, and amusements scarcely rank as secondary considerations.'

W. Cooke Taylor,
Notes of a Tour in the Manufacturing Districts of Lancashire (1842)

JGT

The war in America

The Seven Years War left Britain with an empire in North America, but attempts to make the American colonists contribute towards the defence of that empire aroused opposition and ultimately revolution. British forces were more than a match for the colonial militia, but were unable to secure a decisive victory. They evacuated New England and defeated an American advance on Quebec, but were unable to make progress in campaigns in the north, in Pennsylvania or in the southern colonies. The French naval victory at Chesapeake Capes in 1781 forced the supporting Royal Navy to withdraw to the West Indies, and the isolated army under Cornwallis surrendered to the Americans at Yorktown.

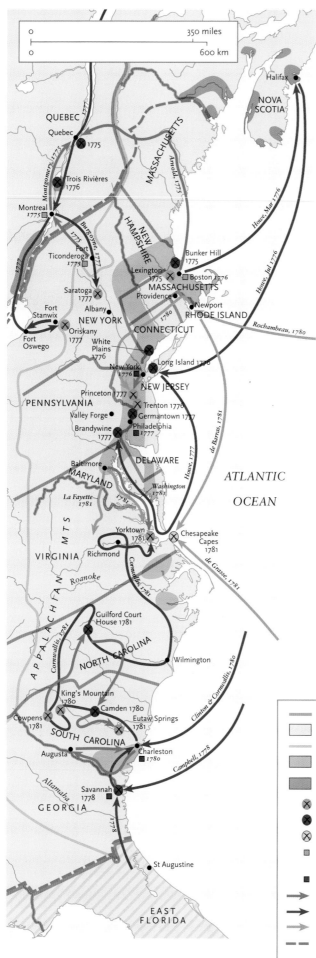

Legend:
- Colonial border, 1763
- British territory, 1763
- British Proclamation Line of 1763
- Area of significant loyalist support
- Area of loyalist settlement in Canada after 1782
- American victory
- British victory
- French victory
- American capture of fort or settlement
- British capture of fort or settlement
- American campaign
- British campaign
- French campaign
- Border of United States territory, 1783
- Spanish gains, 1783

In 1763 Britain secured huge gains from the Seven Years War. The war (1756–63) had been a Europe-wide struggle, in which Britain, allied with Prussia, fought a coalition of France, Austria and Russia. It had also been conducted on a worldwide scale, as Britain wrested colonial territory away from France. As a result, Britain ceased to be a mere colonial power: it became an imperial power. The problem now was to protect this new empire. Nowhere was the problem more acute than in North America. The vast areas controlled by the Thirteen Colonies had to be defended. In addition, a long and continually advancing frontier needed to be policed. This was no simple matter. An unimpressive performance by American militia troops during the war indicated that regular British troops were going to be necessary for the task. All of this amounted to a very costly burden, deeply resented by British taxpayers, who were already alarmed at the rapid growth of the national debt during the war. British efforts to limit this burden, and to shift part of it onto the colonists, was to lead to trouble.

Real difficulties resulted from attempts to impose a more effective tax regime on the colonies. Britain had hitherto been relatively lax in enforcing taxation in America; smuggling was rife. The Americans had become accustomed to this state of affairs. They were outraged when it became clear that the British were now serious about making them pay some of the costs of governing and defending them. The resistance to new taxes was both determined and on such a scale that the British government was stunned. Indeed, the colonists began to challenge Britain's right to tax them. They were, after all, not represented in the parliament that enacted these new taxes. The cry of 'no taxation without representation' was one the British understood – it was a principle the British held dear.

Unfortunately, however, the British government was not prepared to compromise: another principle they held dear was that parliament alone must control state finances. If they allowed a source of revenue to escape that control, there was a risk that the king would gain control of it. That would be dangerous: a financially independent king might be tempted to rule without parliament. The British therefore retreated in the face of determined opposition to new taxes and were willing to back down over the form of taxation – but they refused to accept the colonists' constitutional case, insisting that they had the right to impose whatever taxes they chose over their colonies.

Their successful resistance encouraged further defiance on the part of the colonists, while British intransigence on the matter of principle led to a hardening of attitudes. Relations deteriorated to the point that, when the British authorities attempted to confiscate colonists' arms at Concord in

April 1775, a confrontation between colonists and British troops developed at nearby Lexington, which resulted in the opening shots of the War of Independence.

A WORLD WAR

Many British observers expected a quick victory, not believing that the colonists could withstand regular troops. Only a few recognised the problems: the territory was vast, and the lines of supply so long, that there was no realistic possibility of a British victory. The Americans had sufficient resources and manpower (2 million people, one quarter of Britain's population), to make their land unconquerable. British forces floundered; they could make British rule effective wherever they stood, but only for as long as they remained there. They could and did win battles, but could not exploit them; they simply did not have the manpower. By 1778, it was clear that they were not winning. But they were also not losing – there seemed little chance of the Americans actually expelling them.

Events in Europe, however, were to prove decisive. In preceding years Britain had become dangerously isolated, lacking a single major ally. The temptation for France and Spain to take advantage of the situation and regain territory lost to Britain proved too strong. The Netherlands chal-

lenged Britain's right to blockade neutral vessels. Indeed, the hostility towards Britain of the League of Armed Neutrality, led by Russia and including Portugal, Prussia and Austria, amounted almost to war. America's war became a world war: the Dutch fought in the North Sea; France fought in Africa and the Caribbean; France, Mysore and the Marathas fought in India, and France and Spain fought in the Mediterranean and the Channel. Even the powerful Royal Navy was unable to maintain its control of the sea. British forces in America were isolated, which proved disastrous for Charles, Lord Cornwallis, at Yorktown. Without trading partners, and a merchant shipping fleet trapped in port by privateers, Britain faced ruin. By 1782 Britain was ready to give up America to buy peace.   **JMB**

The Boston Tea Party
One of the most famous acts of defiance against Britain's attempts to tax America occurred in December 1773, when about 60 Boston men, thinly disguised as Mohawk Indians and cheered on by a large crowd, destroyed tea worth £18,000.

The worldwide war

The American War was a salutary lesson to Britain, demonstrating the dangers of becoming isolated in Europe. Former enemies, such as France and Spain, were quick to seize the chance to avenge recent defeats. Former allies and neutral states had nothing to gain from assisting Britain; on the contrary, they knew that there were markets and colonial territories that might be won. Britain ended up fighting a world war. Naval victories in European waters, the West Indies and India preserved Britain's empire – but the cost was the loss of most of North America.

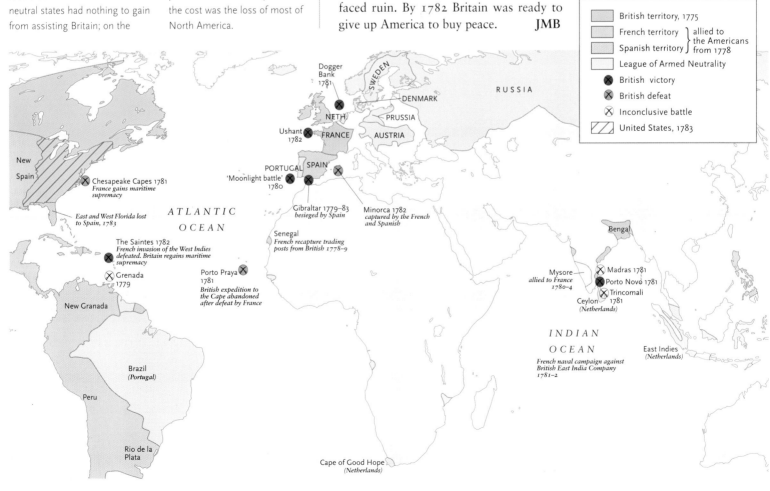

British territory, 1775

French territory ⎤ allied to
Spanish territory ⎦ the Americans from 1778

League of Armed Neutrality

⊗ British victory

⊗ British defeat

⊗ Inconclusive battle

United States, 1783

New Spain

Chesapeake Capes 1781
France gains maritime supremacy

East and West Florida lost to Spain, 1783

ATLANTIC OCEAN

The Saintes 1782
French invasion of the West Indies defeated. Britain regains maritime supremacy

Grenada 1779

New Granada

Peru

Brazil *(Portugal)*

Rio de la Plata

Porto Praya 1781
British expedition to the Cape abandoned after defeat by France

Dogger Bank 1781

SWEDEN

DENMARK

RUSSIA

NETH

PRUSSIA

Ushant 1782   FRANCE   AUSTRIA

PORTUGAL SPAIN

'Moonlight battle' 1780

Gibraltar 1779–83 *besieged by Spain*

Minorca 1782 *captured by the French and Spanish*

Senegal
French recapture trading posts from British 1778–9

Bengal

Mysore *allied to France 1780–4*

Madras 1781

Porto Novo 1781

Trincomali 1781

Ceylon *(Netherlands)*

INDIAN OCEAN

French naval campaign against British East India Company 1781–2

East Indies *(Netherlands)*

Cape of Good Hope *(Netherlands)*

PART FOUR

19th-CENTURY BRITAIN & IRELAND

The geography of Britain changed profoundly in the nineteenth century, largely as a result of the impact of industrialisation, urbanisation and a new railway system, but it had already been altered significantly during the last decades of the eighteenth century by agricultural enclosure and the building of canals. But it was not only the landscape that was transformed. The sense of place and the sense of time of the British and Irish people were transformed too. So, also, was their sense of scale. A rise in population, unequally distributed, with shifts in location, was essential to this process. In the second half of the nineteenth century, the total population of the British Isles almost doubled, increasing at a faster rate than that of France, Germany or Russia.

The human experience of living through unprecedented changes needs to be studied at different levels, beginning with the family and ending with the empire. Comparative history is necessary. Quantitative history, based on far more than census returns, has to be investigated, too, not only by economic but by political, social and cultural historians. Historians now pay more attention to literary and art history than their predecessors did. Visual evidence now often receives as much attention as verbal.

Maps are as much a part of the visual evidence as photographs. The Ordnance Survey, which raises every question of scale, was established in the 1790s to prepare up-to-date maps of the maritime counties of southeast England, not for economic reasons but as a preparation for repelling possible French invasion. After the wars against Napoleon ended in 1815, survey work continued and gradually extended to the rest of the country. For local historians, what the surveys reveal remains essential evidence. Likewise, for historians of empire, maps also provide crucial evidence. A growing proportion of the world was coloured red – the conventional colour for the British empire – on nineteenth-century world maps. These were often pinned to school walls.

Both Ordnance Survey maps and world maps demonstrate the continuing importance in the nineteenth century of military and naval history. In Europe, a largely peaceful century from 1815 ended in World War I, but as far as Britain was concerned, there had been many 'little wars' during the nineteenth century at the frontiers of empire. The nineteenth century proper ended for Britain with wars in South Africa that challenged British institutions, social structures and the British ways of life.

It is impossible to generalise confidently about Britain. Not only were there economic, social and cultural differences between England, Scotland and Wales, but inside each of them there were sharp social divisions. These were identified largely by geographers during the first two decades of the twentieth century. It was, however, a nineteenth-century sociologist, Patrick Geddes, lecturing at Edinburgh University, who, in addition, first used the word 'conurbation'. Describing south Lancashire – transformed in the nineteenth century – as a human region largely of towns and 'factory districts', he added that 'constellations' or 'agglomerations' were inadequate descriptions and asked, 'Cannot we call them conurbations?'

Ireland had a demographic history that was radically different from that of England, Scotland and Wales, like its politics. Yet all four countries were governed from London, and London, in the late nineteenth century, was not only a city of empire but a 'world city', with an equally distinctive Victorian history of its own.

During the late nineteenth century geographers made a substantial contribution to the study of history. The phrase 'geography behind history', an apt description of the content of any atlas, does not do justice to the range of the research. Like historians, geographers have to concern themselves with large spans of time as well as with centuries or shorter periods.

The nineteenth century, long or short, was the century in which the idea of the 'modern' began to be widely taken up. Its shape looks very different if it is approached from a pre-nineteenth-century vantage point rather than from a twentieth- or twenty-first-century perspective. There was much that was still 'traditional' in the Victorian age as well as much that was new or controversial.

Nineteenth-century Britain had a female sovereign from 1837 to 1901, who gave her name not only to an adjective – 'Victorian' – applied to a long 'age', sometimes called an 'epoch', but also to an 'ism' – 'Victorianism' – and, despite the researches of both historians and geographers, it is an age or epoch that is still often caricatured and misunderstood. Yet it was an age of extraordinary vitality and achievement throughout the British Isles.

ASA BRIGGS

Martello towers

A number of small fortifications, known as Martello towers, were built to defend the British coast during the Napoleonic wars. This example, in Orkney, was intended to prevent enemy privateers from raiding assembling convoys.

Defeat in the American War of Independence in 1783 had been a painful experience for Britain. A prolonged period of peace was deemed essential to allow for economic recovery. The 1780s, however, saw the first real surge of economic growth of the Industrial Revolution and fears for the future of British trade with North America proved unfounded: recovery came much more quickly than had been expected. Nonetheless, there remained great reluctance in Britain for any involvement in continental affairs. Even the outbreak of revolution in France in 1789, it was considered, did not warrant intervention. This, however, did not mean that the British government was indifferent to the dramatic events unfolding there. While the revolution thrilled radicals and romantics, conservatives watched in horror as the traditional social order was overthrown. Fearing the spread of revolutionary politics to Britain – the popularity of *The Rights of Man* (1791) by Thomas Paine, previously one of the most articulate advocates of American independence, was a source of particular concern – the government cracked down on radicalism and, in 1794, suspended habeas corpus.

Despite these concerns, it was only when the French threatened the Netherlands in 1793 that Britain was prepared to enter a conflict that was to embroil the entire continent for over two decades. The war was also to encourage a major expansion of British colonial possessions. Some of these gains, such as Ceylon and the Seychelles, were achieved at the expense of other European powers. Others, such as the annexation of much of southern India, were gains at the expense of non-European rulers. Britain would also fight an unsought war against the USA – very much an irritating sideshow, in which British policy was to seek as rapid a peace as possible.

BRITAIN'S STRATEGIC DILEMMA

Naval power had allowed Britain to dominate the world's seas in the late eighteenth century. It rested on a sophisticated and well-financed administrative structure, and on a large fleet drawing on the manpower of the world's leading merchant marine (although there were never enough sailors). It also depended on qualities of seamanship and gunnery (British gunners achieved consistently higher rates of fire than their opponents), a skilled and determined corps of captains, and able leadership. This was true not only of actual command at sea, as was to be demonstrated by Admiral Horatio Nelson's innovative tactics and ability to inspire his captains, but also of effective

Carving out dominions

In a contemporary cartoon, Prime Minister William Pitt and Napoleon carve up the world in the form of a plum pudding. To many satirists, the imperial ambitions of both nations were entirely too similar.

leadership of the navy as an institution. Britain was able to maintain not only the largest battle fleet in the world, but also the large number of smaller warships needed for blockade, convoying and amphibious operations.

The British Army, on the other hand, had been woefully neglected since 1783 – its prestige, morale and training had all suffered badly. Rapid expansion, which occurred once war had broken out, did little to improve matters. There was a serious shortage of able officers, and major deficiencies in planning and supply. The army was recruited from a smaller population than that of France, and without the French system of universal conscription. It was required to provide home defence, but also to win and garrison new colonial territories. Military resources were inadequate for a direct challenge to the mass armies of France and its allies.

Britain's economic base had also changed since the American War of Independence. Worldwide exports of British manufactured goods were replacing the re-export of colonial products to Europe as the mainstay of the economy. This meant that British trade, while it might be hurt by the loss of European markets, would not be crippled.

The combination of naval and economic strength with relative military weakness meant that, as in previous wars, Britain's strategy had to be to use naval power to strike at the periphery of the French empire. Local victories might be won and, if matters went awry, irreplaceable troops could always be evacuated. Such a low-risk policy was sensible –

The Napoleonic Wars in Europe 1793–1815

Naval power was to prove crucial in the wars against France (1793–1815). At sea, the Royal Navy was able to secure a string of crushing victories, which kept the nation safe from invasion, as well as securing the sea-lanes. On land, Britain was weaker, and subsidised a series of coalitions against France, thus leaving the brunt of the fighting to others. Britain fought actively only on the periphery of French power, with strictly limited forces. These became increasingly effective under Wellington in Spain, and made a significant contribution to the defeat of Napoleon.

Scale:
0 ——— 100 miles
0 ——— 150 km

North Sea

Stockholm

SWEDEN

DENMARK–NORWAY
Allied to France, 1801–13

Copenhagen · Battle of Copenhagen 1801; Bombardment of Copenhagen 1807

1801–7

1807

HELIGOLAND

Hamburg

Danzig

Eylau 1807

PRUSSIA
Allied to France, 1807–13

GRAND DUCHY OF WARSAW

Berlin

Lough Swilly 1798

Oct 1798

Sep 1798

Edinburgh

Aug 1798

Ballinamuck 1798

Castlebar 1798

Dublin

Vinegar Hill 1798

Bantry

Fishguard

1797

1797

Ilfracombe

Plymouth

1796

GREAT BRITAIN

London
Portsmouth · Medway · The Nore
Spithead · Boulogne

WALCHEREN

1809

Camperdown 1797

Amsterdam

HOLLAND

Brussels

Waterloo 1815 · Ligny 1815

Amiens

Paris

Valmy 1792

Leipzig 1813

Jena-Auerstädt 1806

Prague

CONFEDERATION OF THE RHINE

Austerlitz 1805

Vienna

AUSTRIAN EMPIRE
Allied to France, 1809–13

'Glorious First of June' 1794

Brest

Lorient

Île de Groix 1795

La Rochelle

Bay of Biscay

FRANCE

Basel

HELVETIA

Lyon

Munich

Salzburg

Turin

Marengo 1800

Milan

Genoa

ITALY

Venice

ILLYRIA

1808

1809

Ferrol

La Coruña 1809

1809

Vitoria 1813

1813

1814

Toulouse 1814

Marseille

1795

Toulon · Isles d'Hyères 1795

TUSCANY

ELBA
Occupied by Britain 1794–6

CORSICA

PAPAL STATES

Rome

OTTOMAN EMPIRE

NAPLES

Busaco 1810

1809

1809

1808

1812

1808

1809

Salamanca 1812

Madrid

Talavera de la Reina 1809

SPAIN

Barcelona

KINGDOM OF SARDINIA
Under British protection

Naples

Palermo

Maida 1806

CALABRIA

1806

Vimeiro 1808

Lisbon

Albuera 1811

PORTUGAL

Cape St Vincent 1797

Trafalgar 1805

Cadiz

Gibraltar

Algeciras 1801

Ceuta

Melilla

MOROCCO

BALEARIC ISLANDS

Mediterranean Sea

Algiers

Tunis

ALGIERS

TUNIS

KINGDOM OF SICILY
Under British protection

MALTA · Malta 1800

Legend:

- State dependent on Britain
- French empire
- State dependent on France
- French ally, 1812
- Area of support for the United Irishmen's rebellion, 1798

British campaigns
→ Moore
→ Wellington
→ Other

Battles
⊗ British victory
⊗ British defeat
⊗ Inconclusive battle
⊗ Other battle

Naval bases
⚓ British
⚓ French
⚓ Spanish

🚢🚢 British naval blockade
✊ Royal Navy mutiny, 1797
→ French invasion
▬ Coast fortified with Martello towers

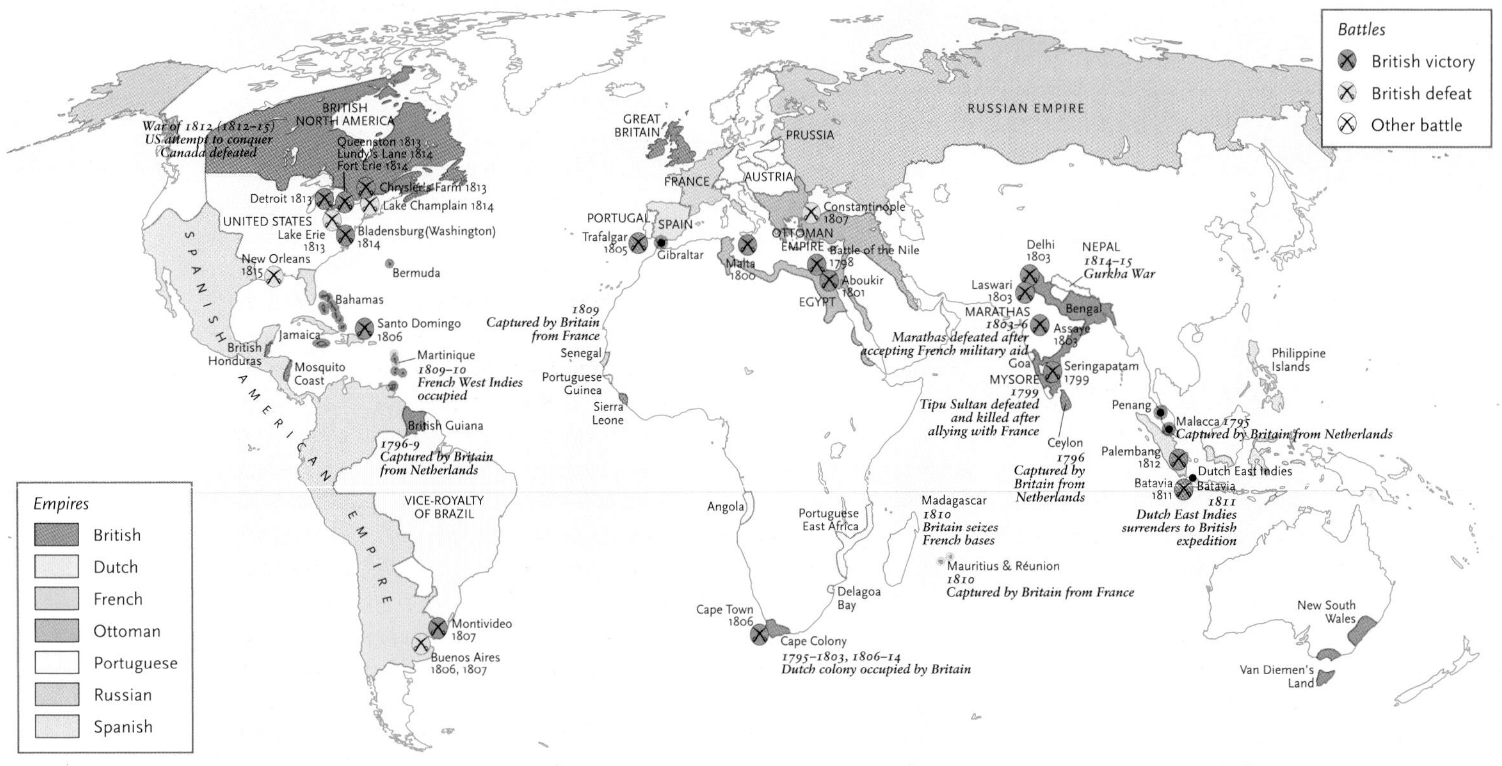
Battles
British victory
British defeat
Other battle
Empires
British
Dutch
French
Ottoman
Portuguese
Russian
Spanish
War of 1812 (1812–15)
US attempt to conquer Canada defeated
BRITISH NORTH AMERICA
Queenston 1813
Lundy's Lane 1814
Fort Erie 1814
Chrysler's Farm 1813
Lake Champlain 1814
Detroit 1813
UNITED STATES
Lake Erie 1813
Bladensburg (Washington) 1814
New Orleans 1815
Bermuda
Bahamas
Santo Domingo 1806
Jamaica
British Honduras
Mosquito Coast
Martinique
1809–10
French West Indies occupied
SPANISH AMERICAN EMPIRE
British Guiana
1796-9
Captured by Britain from Netherlands
VICE-ROYALTY OF BRAZIL
Montivideo 1807
Buenos Aires 1806, 1807
GREAT BRITAIN
FRANCE
PRUSSIA
AUSTRIA
RUSSIAN EMPIRE
PORTUGAL
SPAIN
Trafalgar 1805
Gibraltar
Malta 1800
Constantinople 1807
OTTOMAN EMPIRE
Battle of the Nile 1798
Aboukir 1801
EGYPT
1809
Captured by Britain from France
Senegal
Portuguese Guinea
Sierra Leone
Angola
Portuguese East Africa
Delagoa Bay
Cape Town 1806
Cape Colony
1795–1803, 1806–14
Dutch colony occupied by Britain
Madagascar
1810
Britain seizes French bases
Mauritius & Réunion
1810
Captured by Britain from France
Delhi 1803
NEPAL
1814–15
Gurkha War
Laswari 1803
MARATHAS
1803–6
Marathas defeated after accepting French military aid
Bengal
Assaye 1803
Goa
Seringapatam 1799
MYSORE
1799
Tipu Sultan defeated and killed after allying with France
Ceylon
1796
Captured by Britain from Netherlands
Philippine Islands
Penang
Malacca 1795
Captured by Britain from Netherlands
Palembang 1812
Dutch East Indies
Batavia 1811
Batavia
1811
Dutch East Indies surrenders to British expedition
New South Wales
Van Diemen's Land

The wider war

Naval strength allowed Britain to project its power worldwide and seize valuable colonial territories from France and others. But that power was not limitless: there were, for example, embarrassing failures in Argentina. Against the USA, a final defeat at New Orleans obscured considerable successes in raids on the American coastline.

but it was not a war-winning strategy. As had been the case in previous wars, therefore, British diplomacy was directed toward seeking and financing coalition partners whose military resources might match the French armies.

The first military actions of the new war against France painfully highlighted the army's weaknesses. Initial British campaigns were conducted in the area in which previous wars with France had been fought: the Low Countries. In 1793 a British force advanced from Flanders to besiege Dunkirk. It failed utterly, and the following year had to be hurriedly evacuated in the face of a full French invasion of the Netherlands. French control of the Low Countries thereafter remained secure until 1814, the longest period in British history in which the region was controlled by a hostile power. A renewed British attempt to intervene in the Netherlands in 1799 was equally unsuccessful. It seemed as though, having failed in North American warfare in 1775–83, the British army was now demonstrating its inadequacies in European conflict. There were also fears about the loyalty of the rank and file, and in 1798 a major programme of barracks-building was begun, so that soldiers could be isolated from civil radicalism.

> *'...composed of the scum of the earth...fellows who have enlisted for drink – that is the plain fact'.*
>
> **Wellington's view of his army**

Diplomatic efforts were disappointing, too. Successive coalitions proved fragile, and initially their armies were no match for the French. The First Coalition included Spain, Naples, Portugal, Sardinia, Prussia and Austria; it fell apart in 1795. A Second Coalition including Russia and Austria did the same in 1801. Temporarily at least, the British government was ready to acknowledge that it could not defeat France. In the peace of 1802–3, Britain accepted French control of the Low Countries – and concentrated on securing new colonial gains.

Control of the seas remained firmly in British hands. The threat of French invasion was to cause intense anxiety at times, and considerable resources had to committed to home defence, but a tight blockade was maintained on French ports, and the huge continental armies built by Napoleon Bonaparte simply could not reach Britain's shores. A series of naval actions, including the 'Glorious First of June' (1794), Cape St Vincent and Camperdown (both 1797), the Nile (1798) and Copenhagen (1801), destroyed the fleets of France and its allies. The French were unable to take advantage of serious Royal Navy mutinies in 1797, or even to exploit rebellion in Ireland in 1798.

The contrasting deficiencies of the army should not, however, be exaggerated. Rapid expansion meant that some problems were only to be expected, and these were addressed. The duke of York, commander-in-chief from 1795, did much to improve training and to improve the quality of the officer corps. The fighting ability of the army was revealed in the Egyptian campaign of 1801, where Ralph Abercromby's victory owed much to his careful training of the infantry. These improvements contributed greatly to later victories, including that at Maida in southern Italy in 1806, and the subsequent campaigns in Spain. Indeed, the duke of Wellington's qualities in command in Portugal and Spain would have been of scant value without troops used to withstanding very difficult circumstances.

THE RENEWED WAR

The peace did not last long, but the deadlock remained. Nelson's stunning victory at Trafalgar in 1805 destroyed the Franco-Spanish fleet, and no coalition built by Napoleon was able again to assemble a naval force that threatened British power at sea. Britain was secure from invasion, and was not going to be defeated economically. But how was the war actually to be won?

Only when Napoleon rashly imposed his own brother on the Spanish throne was it possible for Britain to establish a

permanent military presence on the Continent. Again, it was at the periphery of French power. It depended on a generally friendly population and a vicious guerrilla war against the French in Spain. Sir John Moore was warned in 1808 that the 32,000 troops he was taking to the Iberian Peninsula represented the whole of the disposable forces available to Britain. The expedition seemed fated to end in another disaster when Moore was forced into a gruelling retreat and finally killed at Corunna in 1809, but the army held out. Under Moore's successor, Wellington, about 60,000 British troops fought in Portugal and Spain, and eventually in France (about one-tenth the size of the force Napoleon was to take into Russia). It is noteworthy, however, that at least one-fifth of this 'British' force was a multi-national mix of French royalists, Greeks, Germans, Italians, Africans and others, raised wherever Britain could find manpower. It nonetheless evolved into a tough and experienced force, capable of sustaining the fight when the situation appeared in collapse, as at Talavera (1809) and Albuera (1811), and of inflicting severe defeats on the French. Wellington was to become a national hero through its exploits.

Wellington's achievements appear all the more striking against the background of British military failures elsewhere in 1805–15, notably in Argentina in 1806 and 1807 and in Egypt in 1807. A renewed effort to intervene in the Low Countries through a campaign in the Scheldt estuary in 1809 was short-lived and humiliatingly unsuccessful. Bad planning, bad leadership and bad weather defeated the expedition: out of a force of 44,000 troops, some 15,000 fell ill, and 4,000 died, mostly of malaria. An inept American attempt to conquer Canada in the war of 1812–15 was easily defeated and British amphibious operations, one of which burned Washington in 1814, demonstrated the Americans' defensive weakness, but here too, poor leadership contributed to a major defeat at New Orleans in 1815. There was no necessary superiority in British troops or tactics, and there was nothing inevitable about British victory.

Wellington's army fought a long, hard campaign, which eventually ejected the French from Spain and pursued them into France. The titanic events of Napoleon's campaign in Russia in 1812–13 were ultimately the decisive element in his downfall, and the war in Spain remained something of a sideshow in French eyes. Nonetheless, the coalition that destroyed Napoleon's empire was an alliance not only masterminded but also in large part financed by Britain, and the value of the British military contribution to the war was confirmed by the key role played by British forces in the final victory. For all the failings of the French emperor and several of his generals on the day, the French at Waterloo on 18 June 1815 were still a formidable army, and their defeat was a major achievement for Wellington, his troops and their allies. Napoleon was crushed, and the war was ended beyond any hope that events or Allied disagreements would rescue him.   **JMB**

The battle of the Nile
Napoleon's ambitions to open a route to India, and challenge British power there, led to his invasion of Egypt in 1798. His plans were shattered when Nelson destroyed his fleet at Aboukir Bay, near the mouth of the Nile.

Wellington at Waterloo
In 1815 Napoleon escaped from exile and sought to rebuild his empire. The stand of the British forces at Waterloo was a vital contribution to his defeat.

THE AGE OF REFORM

The expansion of the franchise in nineteenth-century Britain has generally been portrayed as a relentless forward march of democratic principles, but parliamentary reform actually occurred in a more hesitant and patchy fashion. The competing conservative and liberal philosophies on the franchise that underpinned a succession of Reform Acts considered factors other than increasing popular participation. The reformed electorate of the nineteenth century retained many features of the unreformed franchise system, and each Reform Act supplemented rather than replaced the previous system. As a result, the electoral system throughout the nineteenth century remained rooted in custom and privilege rather than there being a simple transfer to democracy.

The origins of the franchise in England and Wales date back to the birth of parliament in the thirteenth century. Initially, the electorate was wide, but a landmark piece of

legislation in 1430 introduced a uniform county franchise 'to exclude people of small substance and of no value' by restricting the vote to those possessing freeholds worth 40 shillings a year or more. Though this remained in place until the late nineteenth century, there was an inevitable tendency for the franchise to widen because of inflation. Borough franchises in England and Wales were never uniform and were based on a variety of principles, including residence, property ownership, payment of taxation, possession of freeman status, membership of a borough corporation, or a combination of these. The universities of Oxford and Cambridge also returned members of parliament. The wide variety of borough franchises and the addition of local, customary practices mean that it is impossible to define a 'typical' borough voter. In some constituencies, for example Preston, every adult male was entitled to vote; in others, the electorate was restricted to members of the town's corporation. The fact that there had been very little redistribution

of constituencies since the thirteenth century meant that some tiny communities returned members, including Gatton, where there were only 10 houses left in the borough.

The confused nature of the unreformed electoral system can be further demonstrated by the uncertainty over the status of women and the franchise. The sex of voters was not determined by law until 1832 and the fact that many borough and all county franchises were based on property ownership resulted in a measure of ambiguity surrounding women's – especially widows' – participation. There are instances of women turning up to claim their right to vote in elections, although customary practice was usually invoked to disqualify their votes. In the eighteenth century a practice developed of widows transferring their right to vote in some boroughs to a nominated male.

In Scotland and Ireland the franchise was generally more restrictive. Although Scotland was incorporated into the English parliament after 1707, the electorate remained based on the earlier franchises for the parliament of Scotland. In Scottish counties the electorate was restricted to those possessing land 'of old extent', that is, estates dating from the Middle Ages. In practice, this included only substantial landowners and there was no Scottish county where the electorate exceeded 200. With the exception of Edinburgh, Scottish burghs were combined in groups of four or five to elect one MP. The burgh electorates were very limited, with only 33 men selecting the member for Edinburgh, for example.

Ireland possessed a separate parliament before the Act of Union of 1800 and the electoral system was modelled closely on that of England. The county franchise used the 40-shilling freehold qualification and there were freeman, corporation, potwalloper (householders controlling their own front door and cooking facilities), freehold and university franchises for the boroughs. Catholics were barred from voting for county representatives until 1793 and continued to be largely excluded from the electorate until the Catholic Emancipation Act of 1829.

CALLS FOR REFORM

From the late eighteenth century onwards, demands for reform of the British electoral system became more insistent and widespread, particularly from the growing and increasingly self-confident urban middle classes. The debates centred on those arguing for a simple extension of the franchise and those who opposed any widening of the franchise as an invitation to mob rule but who nevertheless accepted that limited reforms were needed to make government more responsive and efficient. By the 1830s changing political circumstances finally pushed constitutional reform to the front of the parliamentary agenda. Popular pressure from the London Radical Association and the Birmingham Political Union was growing, while the death of the conservative King George IV in 1830, the fall in the same year of the duke of Wellington's Tory government and its replacement by the reformist Whig administration of Earl Grey, removed final obstacles to electoral reform. The 1832 Reform Act demonstrated both the extent and the limitations of the

Four views of reform, 1831

Whig, Tory, Liberal and Radical views of the reform debate. Their opinions range from the Tory, who feels that reform is tantamount to revolution, to the Radical, who threatens real revolution if reform is not forthcoming.

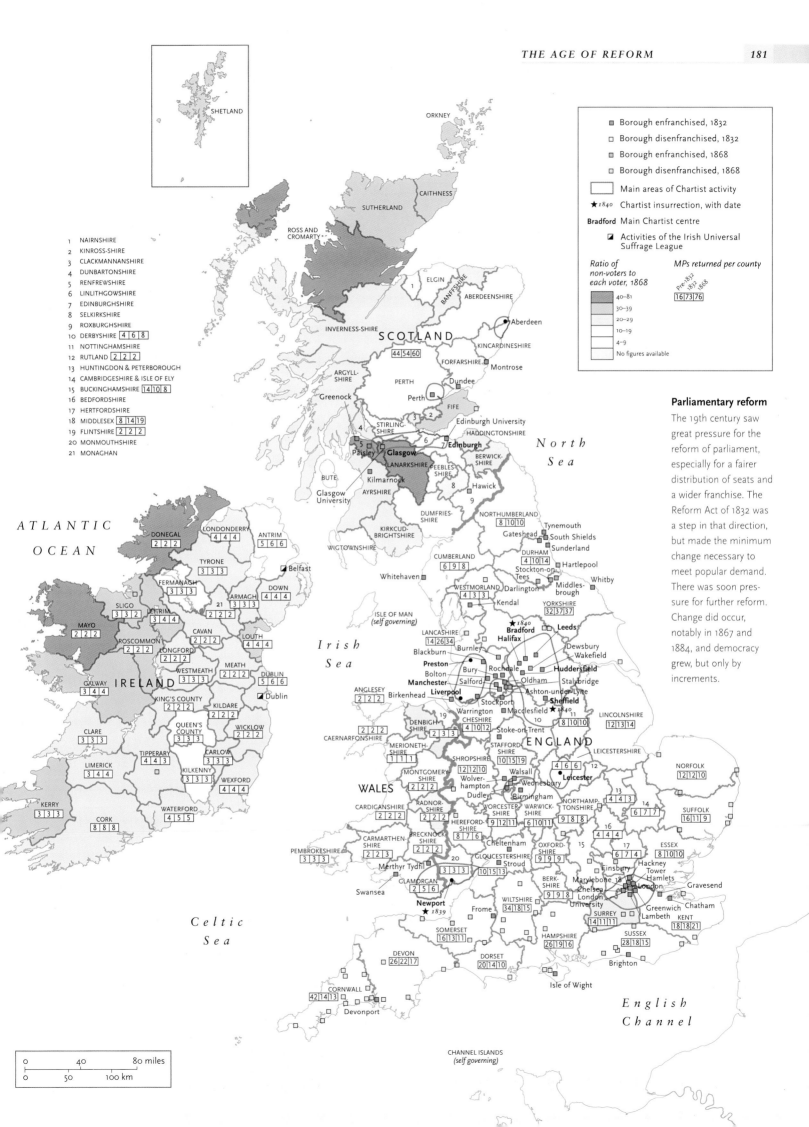

Legend

- ■ Borough enfranchised, 1832
- □ Borough disenfranchised, 1832
- ■ Borough enfranchised, 1868
- □ Borough disenfranchised, 1868
- ▭ Main areas of Chartist activity
- ★1840 Chartist insurrection, with date
- **Bradford** Main Chartist centre
- ◪ Activities of the Irish Universal Suffrage League

Ratio of non-voters to each voter, 1868
- 40–81
- 30–39
- 20–29
- 10–19
- 4–9
- No figures available

MPs returned per county
Pre-1832 / 1832 / 1868
16 | 73 | 76

Parliamentary reform

The 19th century saw great pressure for the reform of parliament, especially for a fairer distribution of seats and a wider franchise. The Reform Act of 1832 was a step in that direction, but made the minimum change necessary to meet popular demand. There was soon pressure for further reform. Change did occur, notably in 1867 and 1884, and democracy grew, but only by increments.

County index

1 NAIRNSHIRE
2 KINROSS-SHIRE
3 CLACKMANNANSHIRE
4 DUNBARTONSHIRE
5 RENFREWSHIRE
6 LINLITHGOWSHIRE
7 EDINBURGHSHIRE
8 SELKIRKSHIRE
9 ROXBURGHSHIRE
10 DERBYSHIRE 4 6 8
11 NOTTINGHAMSHIRE
12 RUTLAND 2 2 2
13 HUNTINGDON & PETERBOROUGH
14 CAMBRIDGESHIRE & ISLE OF ELY
15 BUCKINGHAMSHIRE 14 10 8
16 BEDFORDSHIRE
17 HERTFORDSHIRE
18 MIDDLESEX 8 14 19
19 FLINTSHIRE 2 2 2
20 MONMOUTHSHIRE
21 MONAGHAN

SHETLAND

ORKNEY

CAITHNESS
SUTHERLAND
ROSS AND CROMARTY
INVERNESS-SHIRE
ELGIN
BANFFSHIRE
ABERDEENSHIRE
● Aberdeen
KINCARDINESHIRE
FORFARSHIRE ■ Montrose
SCOTLAND
ARGYLL-SHIRE
PERTH
Perth
● Dundee
FIFE
44 54 60
Greenock
STIRLING-SHIRE
4
5 Paisley
Kilmarnock
● Glasgow LANARKSHIRE
Glasgow University
BUTE
AYRSHIRE
PEEBLES-SHIRE
Edinburgh University
HADDINGTONSHIRE
6 7 ■Edinburgh
BERWICK-SHIRE
8 ● Hawick
9
DUMFRIES-SHIRE
KIRKCUD-BRIGHTSHIRE
WIGTOWNSHIRE

North Sea

Atlantic Ocean

DONEGAL 2 2 2
LONDONDERRY 4 4 4
ANTRIM 5 6 6
■ Belfast
TYRONE 3 3 3
FERMANAGH 3 3 3
DOWN 4 4 4
SLIGO 3 3 2
ARMAGH 3 3 3
21 2 2 2
LEITRIM 3 4 4
MAYO 2 2 2
ROSCOMMON 2 2 2
LONGFORD 2 2 2
CAVAN 2 2 2
LOUTH 4 4 4
WESTMEATH 3 3 3
MEATH 3 3 3
DUBLIN 5 6 6
IRELAND
GALWAY 3 4 4
KING'S COUNTY 2 2 2
KILDARE 2 2 2
◪ Dublin
QUEEN'S COUNTY 3 3 3
WICKLOW 2 2 2
CLARE 3 3 3
TIPPERARY 4 4 3
CARLOW 2 2 2
KILKENNY 3 3 3
WEXFORD 4 4 4
LIMERICK 3 4 4
WATERFORD 4 5 5
KERRY 3 3 3
CORK 8 8 8

Irish Sea

Celtic Sea

NORTHUMBERLAND 8 10 10
Tynemouth
Gateshead
South Shields
Sunderland
DURHAM 4 10 14
Hartlepool
Stockton-on-Tees
Darlington
Middles-brough
Whitby
CUMBERLAND 6 9 8
Whitehaven
WESTMORLAND 4 3 3
Kendal
ISLE OF MAN (self governing)
YORKSHIRE 32 37 37
★1840 Bradford ■ Leeds
LANCASHIRE 14 26 34
Halifax
Dewsbury
Wakefield
Blackburn
Burnley
Preston
Rochdale
Huddersfield
Bury
Bolton
Oldham
Manchester Salford
Stalybridge
Liverpool
Ashton-under-Lyne
Birkenhead
Stockport
Sheffield
Warrington
Macclesfield ★1840
11
ENGLAND
ANGLESEY 2 2 2
19
DENBIGH-SHIRE 2 3 3
CHESHIRE 4 10 12
Stoke-on-Trent
LINCOLNSHIRE 12 13 14
CAERNARFONSHIRE
MERIONETH-SHIRE 1 1 1
STAFFORD-SHIRE 10 15 19
LEICESTERSHIRE 4 6 6 12
MONTGOMERY-SHIRE
SHROPSHIRE 12 15 10
Walsall
Wednesbury
Wolver-hampton
Dudley
Birmingham
WARWICK-SHIRE 6 10 11
● Leicester
NORTHAMP-TONSHIRE 9 8 8
NORFOLK 12 12 10
13
WALES
CARDIGANSHIRE 2 2 2
RADNOR-SHIRE 2 2 2
WORCESTER-SHIRE 9 12 11
4 4 3
14 6 7 7
SUFFOLK 16 11 9
HEREFORD-SHIRE 8 7 6
Cheltenham
OXFORD-SHIRE 9 9 9
15
16 4 4 4
17 6 7 4
ESSEX 8 10 10
CARMARTHEN-SHIRE 2 2 3
BRECKNOCK-SHIRE 2 2 2
20 3 3 3
GLOUCESTERSHIRE 10 15 13
Stroud
BERK-SHIRE 9 9 8
Finsbury
Marylebone 18
Chelsea
London University
Hackney
Tower Hamlets
● London
Gravesend
PEMBROKESHIRE 3 3 3
Merthyr Tydfil
GLAMORGAN 2 5 6
Swansea
Frome
WILTSHIRE 34 18 15
SURREY 14 11 11
Greenwich
Lambeth
Chatham
KENT 18 18 21
Newport
★1839
SOMERSET 16 13 11
DORSET 20 14 10
HAMPSHIRE 26 19 16
SUSSEX 28 18 15
Isle of Wight
Brighton

North Sea

English Channel

DEVON 26 22 17
Devonport
CORNWALL 42 14 13

CHANNEL ISLANDS (self governing)

0   40   80 miles
0   50   100 km

influence of the contemporary debates on the nature of the constitution. Ideas of responsible citizenship were accepted, but concepts of natural, universal rights were rejected in favour of the status quo. The reform had to be extensive enough to satisfy at least a proportion of public opinion, but was to be based upon property and existing franchises to appease the vested interests in parliament. Even so, the Bill had a hazardous journey through parliament and was only enacted after a turbulent general election in 1831.

The redistribution of seats rather than the extension of the franchise was the major feature of the Reform Act. Fifty-six borough constituencies were abolished and a further 30 were reduced from two members to one. The seats were redistributed, roughly equally, between new borough and county constituencies. New seats were also created in Wales, Scotland and Ireland. The 40-shilling freehold was retained as the qualification in county constituencies and a uniform borough franchise of £10 was introduced for England and Wales. However, the situation was complicated by the fact that 'ancient rights' customary voters remained in borough electorates and that the Chandos clause introduced voting rights for some tenants and leaseholders in counties.

The Act resulted in an increase in the number of electors of about 45 per cent. Thus, in England and Wales, around 18 per cent of adult males now possessed the vote. The effect was more dramatic in Scotland. Over 18 times as many voters existed after 1832, although a smaller proportion of the population could vote than in England and

Wales. The average burgh electorate comprised over 1,000 voters. Two members were returned for Edinburgh and Glasgow; one each for Aberdeen, Paisley, Dundee, Greenock and Perth and the remaining 14 members from 14 districts of burghs (this complexity has made it impossible to map the changes in Scotland to county level). In Ireland, the Reform Act had less impact than the Catholic Emancipation Act, which had increased the number of voters dramatically. In 1829 the county franchise had been increased to £10 because of the fear that Catholic voters were swamping the electorate. The Reform Act added a £10 leaseholder franchise in the counties, which increased the electorate slightly.

Calls for further reform began as soon as the statute was passed. The reform of local government provided one focus, but a more sustained challenge came from the mainly working-class Chartist movement, which demanded universal manhood suffrage and the secret ballot. Parliament refused even to consider Chartist petitions in 1840 and 1842, and militants who threatened an armed rising were deported. In 1848 the government, alarmed by the wave of revolutions sweeping Europe in that year, threatened the use of military force against the Chartists if a planned demonstration in support of a third petition went ahead. Chartism thereafter declined as a political force, but in the 1850s the front benches of the two major parties began to contemplate the possibilities for further reform and serious consideration was given to the incorporation of working men into the electorate. William Gladstone's Reform Bill of 1866 aimed to bring the franchise to urban male householders, in an attempt to unite the working men and middle classes. His Bill failed because of opposition from Conservatives and even some Liberals, who argued that men did not possess a natural right to the franchise, and must prove their fitness to vote. The rejection of Gladstone's Bill mobilised popular opinion in the same way as the Lords' rebuff to reform in 1831 had led to mass agitation. This pressure ensured that Benjamin Disraeli's minority government was compelled to introduce some measure of reform. The Second Reform Act of 1867 therefore reflected political pragmatism rather than commitment to any philosophical or ideological principle for extending the electorate. After much negotiation, four main franchises were established in the boroughs: a £10 occupational qualification; rate-paying male householders; a £10 lodger franchise; and the 'ancient rights' voters. In counties, the electorate was increased to a lesser extent by a £12-pound occupational franchise and a reduction in the lease and copyholder qualification from £10 to £5. The Reform Act for Scotland closely resembled that of England and Wales. In Ireland, the county franchise had already been

The West Riding in the 1830s

The West Riding shows how idiosyncratic Britain's political development was. Industrialisation made the area one of the most populous in England, yet it was represented by only eight MPs. The first Reform Act improved the situation, but not to everyone's satisfaction, and great landowners retained significant influence.

Substantial landlord influence

🏛 Whig (W)

🏛 Tory (T)

1 Sir E. Vavasour (W)

2 F. Fawkes (W)

3 Earl of Harewood (T)

4 G. Lane-Fox (T)

5 R. Davison-Bland (T)

6 Sir E. Dodsworth (T)

7 Sir J. Ramsden (W)

8 Sir G. Armytage (W)

9 H. Beaumont (T)

10 Lord Hawke (T)

11 Earl of Dartmouth (T)

12 T.W. Beaumont (W)

13 Sir F. Wood (W)

14 Lord Wharncliffe (T)

15 Earl Fitzwilliam (W)

16 Earl of Scarborough (W)

17 Duke of Leeds (T)

	Whig (60% or more)
	Tory (60% or more)
	No dominant party
■	Parliamentary constituency with date of enfranchisement
(1837: 67%)	Turnout in contested election

Ripon
1553
(1832: 97%)

Boroughbridge
1553–1832

Aldborough
1558–1832

Knaresborough
1553

Leeds
1832 (2 members)
(1841: 91%)

Bradford
1832
(1837: 82%)

Halifax
1832 (2 members)
(1837: 92%)

Huddersfield
1832 (1 member)
(1837: 94%)

Pontefract
1621

Wakefield
1832 (1 member)
(1837: 82%)

Sheffield
1832
(1837: 67%)

0 — 10 — 20 miles
0 — 10 — 20 km

each from Aldborough, Borough-bridge, Knaresborough, Pontefract and Ripon, all of them much reduced in importance since they were originally enfranchised in the Middle Ages. This was less than a fifth of the number of members returned by Cornwall, which had only a third of the population of the West Riding. The West Riding bene-fited greatly from the 1832 Reform Act, its representation increasing to a total of 18 MPs: two for the new 'county' constituency of the West Riding; two each for the boroughs of Bradford, Halifax, Knaresbor-ough, Leeds, Pontefract, Ripon and Sheffield; and one each for Huddersfield and Wakefield (Aldborough and Bor-oughbridge having been disenfranchised). The hopes and desires of the rapidly enlarging populations of the newly enfranchised boroughs were placed alongside the fresh expectations (if tinged with a certain weary cynicism) of the boroughs that had sent MPs to parliament in the decades before 1832. Factory politics, the aspirations of the radical dissenters, the hopes of the middle class and the political ambitions of the labouring poor all found a place in West Riding politics in the years after 1832. The county electorate, at around 20,000 voters, was one of the largest in the country. However, the territorial influence of aristo-cratic landowners remained significant, demonstrating that a simple increase in the numbers of voters could not of itself necessarily challenge the power of the traditional governing elites. **SR**

The Peterloo Massacre, 1819

Even peaceful demonstrations for political reform could be met with violence. At St Peter's Field the Manchester Yeomanry left 11 dead and 500 wounded. The name 'Peterloo' was given to the event as an ironical reference to the battle of Waterloo in 1815.

doubled by an Act of 1850. The Irish Reform Act of 1868, reluctantly introduced by Disraeli, reduced the borough qualification from £8 to £4, enfranchising most borough ratepayers though still excluding the very poorest (largely Catholic) men.

Further reform came in 1872 with the introduction of the secret ballot, which freed voters from employer and landlord influence. The first complete remodelling of the electoral system took place between 1883 and 1885, and for the first time was taken on the basis of the whole Unit-ed Kingdom. In 1883 some corrupt practices and electoral abuses were tackled. The Third Reform Act of 1884 assim-ilated the county and borough franchises so that all male householders now possessed the vote, whether they lived in borough or in county constituencies. The following year, a series of one-member constituencies was introduced and the principle of constituencies representing numbers of voters rather than particular interests was accepted. Therefore, for the first time, populous areas of England achieved a rea-sonably fair share of the representation. The effect of the legislation of 1884–5 was almost to double the electorate, from around 3 million to over 5 million.

The electoral system in the late nineteenth century was still a restrictive one, with only 60 per cent of adult males possessing the vote. The unenfranchised were domestic ser-vants, sons living with parents, soldiers living in barracks, those receiving poor relief, those not on the register, those in mobile occupations and those incapable of voting. Nev-ertheless, with the majority of men now enfranchised it became harder to justify the exclusion of women. By 1900 many MPs recognised that a further extension of the fran-chise was desirable.

THE WEST RIDING

A study of the parliamentary representation of the West Riding in the 1830s gives an indication of the idiosyncrasies of the political development of England as a whole during the nineteenth century. The West Riding was one of those areas which was most under-represented in parliament by the 1830s. The rapid growth of the West Riding's industri-al towns in the previous century had turned it into one of the most densely populated and prosperous areas of the country. Yet it returned only 10 MPs to parliament: two

Reform demonstration in London, 1884

Tories, especially in the House of Lords, feared that extending the fran-chise to more working-class men in the counties would result in a loss of Tory influence. Their opposition aroused a wave of protest that helped to force through further reform.

INDUSTRIAL MANCHESTER

In the 1770s Manchester was an unremarkable, if thriving, textile centre – which had capitalised on its position adjacent to the Pennine slopes, with their ideal conditions for cotton-spinning and weaving – and it had about 25,000 inhabitants. Thirty years later, the population had almost tripled, and visitors to the city were beginning to sense unprecedented transformations. By the early 1840s,

Industrial Manchester

More perhaps than any other city, Manchester epitomised the Industrial Revolution. In the 19th century it experienced massive expansion, as well as pioneering cultural innovation.

Victoria Station, built 1844, on the Manchester and Leeds Railway

Manchester Cathedral, formerly the Collegiate Church

The Royal Exchange, commercial centre of the cotton trade

Manchester's transformation sprang from the revolution in cotton manufacture. Large six- and seven-storey buildings sprang up along the rivers and new canals, initially for spinning raw cotton, and then from the 1820s for weaving cloth. But Manchester was never merely a factory town. It was also the commercial centre of the textile trade, and the factories were

Manchester had become the symbol of a new form of social organisation, a 'modern Athens' to Benjamin Disraeli. Visitors flocked in, and for 20 years or so it was the 'shock city' that announced to contemporaries the dawn of the industrial age.

quickly outnumbered by warehouses and, from the 1840s, by salesrooms for the finished cloth. The typical Manchester worker was not a factory hand, but a carter, porter, packer or labourer, and the social gulf between rich and poor that worried contemporaries was in fact filled with clerks, shopkeepers and members of the emerging professions.

The demands of the new factories encouraged the huge expansion of other manufacturing and service industries. By the 1830s, the city's rivers were open sewers, lined with tanneries, dye-works, foundries and abattoirs, and clogged with human and industrial waste. Railway lines isolated ghettos, such as the infamous 'Little Ireland'. Chimneys dominated the skyline and the city was shrouded in smoke, which blackened buildings and killed vegetation. Contaminated water supplies and the accumulation of waste in the streets and alleys contributed to a life expectancy for working-class inhabitants less than half that for the healthiest agricultural districts. As the old town crumbled under the strain of the increased population, new districts of working-class housing sprang up to the east and south, engulfing existing residences and driving the middle classes out into the neighbouring villages.

Yet, as a new form of society, Manchester pioneered new institutions and ways of thinking. The Literary and Philosophical Society (1781), the *Manchester Guardian* (1821), the Manchester Statistical Society (1832), the municipal parks and sanitary reforms of the 1840s, the first rate-supported lending library of 1851, the Anti-Corn-Law League, and early campaigns for non-sectarian education, all marked Manchester as a cultural as well as an urban pioneer. Only after 1853, when Manchester was granted the status of a city, did the political and cultural centre of gravity of urban England begin to shift elsewhere.   **MH**

The Royal Mill
The Royal Mill, built in 1797, and the Rochdale Canal at Ancoats in Manchester.

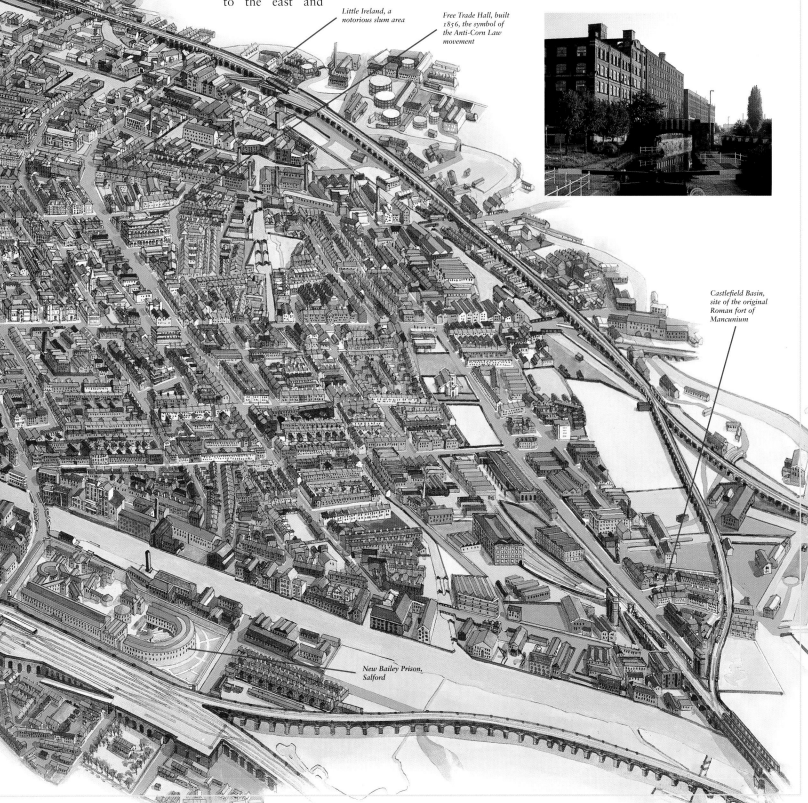

Little Ireland, a notorious slum area

Free Trade Hall, built 1856, the symbol of the Anti-Corn Law movement

Castlefield Basin, site of the original Roman fort of Mancunium

New Bailey Prison, Salford

THE 19th-CENTURY EMPIRE

Victory in the Napoleonic wars left Britain with the leading empire in the world. Within a century, this was to be enhanced both by subsequent expansion and by the collapse of the only empire of a comparable size: the Spanish Empire in Latin America. In the second half of the century, the British fought wars across the globe as never before. Britain's role was part of the wider story of European imperialism, but was greater than that of any other state, because of the country's limited involvement in power politics on the continent of Europe (which left Britain free to devote its resources to the empire), its unequalled naval and commercial strength, and the already extensive character of the empire. As a consequence, empire was more central to British history than to that of France or Germany. By the end of the century, Britain ruled a quarter of the world's population and a fifth of the land surface.

What is less clear is why this expansion occurred. There never was a plan for imperial expansion. Nor was there universal support for empire.

Supporters of free trade, such as the politician Richard Cobden, were highly critical. American independence seemed to show that the end of British colonial rule did not necessarily harm British trade: Cobden therefore called for the abolition of the costly burden of empire. Such opinions had little impact in the government, but even the government had little desire to take on the expensive responsibilities of new conquests. As long as the British were able to trade freely, and British traders and property protected, there seemed little need actually to conquer more territory.

Yet imperial expansion took place, for many reasons. Financial interests in the City, whose investments around the globe might be threatened by local events, could exert influence over the government, arguing that their own interests and the national interests coincided. The nationalist riots in Egypt in 1882, which led to British occupation, are an example of this. Local colonial officials, whose isolation allowed them considerable autonomy, could also take the

Citizens of empire

The propaganda of empire often stressed the idea of an imperial 'family', shown graphically in this Victorian postcard.

The British empire in the 19th century

Britain acquired the largest empire in history without any specific plan for imperial expansion. The empire's rulers were keenly aware of potential threats from other European powers, (notably Russia and France), of the difficulties of communication before the development of the telegraph, and of the small numbers of British troops available to defend the colonies.

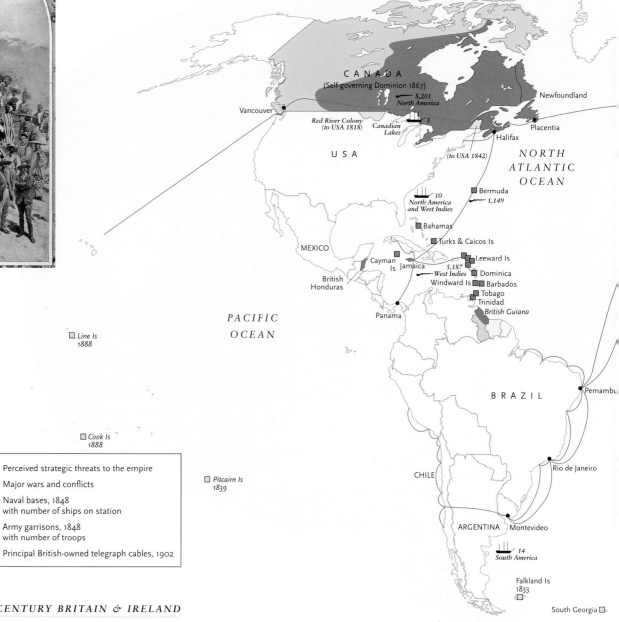

Perceived strategic threats to the empire

Major wars and conflicts

Naval bases, 1848
with number of ships on station

Army garrisons, 1848
with number of troops

Principal British-owned telegraph cables, 1902

initiative. There appears to have been considerable anxiety among such officials about unsettled frontiers: a fear that instability in neighbouring territories might spread into British possessions. This could lead to intervention to protect British interests. However, where the presence of the British themselves was destabilising the frontier, this was a never-ending process. A great deal of expansion into India can be interpreted in this way. Also, as in the so-called 'Scramble for Africa', Britain might respond to the actions of imperial rivals. British absorption of Uganda and Kenya was a response to German intervention in Tanganyika. Britain had no intention of allowing Germany to dominate the region.

EMPIRE AND DOMINION

The empire grew throughout the nineteenth century. It also evolved politically, at least in some territories. After a rebellion in Canada in 1837, Lord Durham, sent to investigate the affair, recommended the introduction of representative self-government. This was the origin of dominion status, under which domestic affairs were left to local elected governments, while foreign relations remained the concern of Britain. In the 1850s this was extended to the Australian colonies and to New Zealand, and in 1872 to the Cape Colony. This process was to lead to the development of separate colonies in Canada and Australia into distinct states whose people developed a fierce sense of nationalism. It was, however, no move to prepare colonies for independence or foreshadow the break-up of the empire. Rather it was seen as strengthening the empire by removing responsibility for local problems out of London's hands. It was also a method of reducing the costs of governing the empire to the British taxpayer. Dominion status was also restricted to 'settlement colonies', especially the so-called 'white dominions', which were dominated by Europeans. Colonies dominated by other races were not deemed ready for such government. Though

'I contend that we are the first race of the world and the more of the world we inhabit the better it is for the human race.'

Cecil Rhodes, 1877

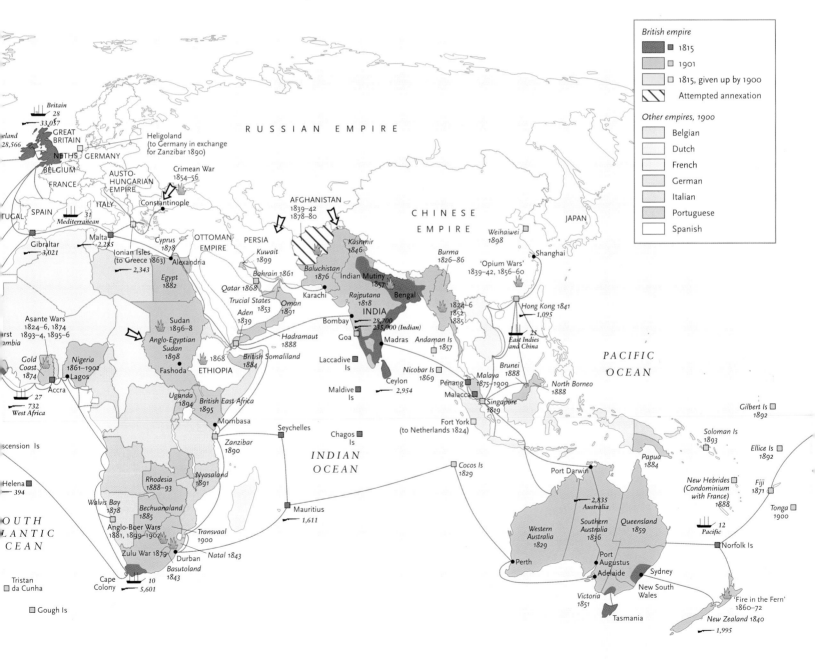

Social gatherings

*The Lieutenant-General
of the Punjab with his
guests. Such gatherings
reassured the Indian
princes of British
support, but also
reminded them where
the real power lay.*

'*What comparisons suggest
themselves between the
condition of the Pacific
region in the time of Cook
and now? What was then
held by illiterate savages
now constitutes the rising
communities of New South
Wales.*'

Missionary James Wyld, 1851

notions of trusteeship were sometimes aired (the argument that Britain's imperial mission was to prepare 'lesser races' for dominion status), little was done to achieve this in the nineteenth century. Racism remained institutionalised throughout the empire.

It was firmly and widely believed that Britain had a civilising mission. It was a matter of considerable pride to the British that their empire was the first to abolish slavery, in 1833. This was seen as proof of Britain's moral superiority. That the compensation paid saved the owners of sugar plantations from ruination from foreign competition, and that, for the slaves, one form of bondage was replaced by another based on poverty, poor education and racial prejudice, passed unnoticed.

Missionaries undertook their own 'civilising' task. Men such as David Livingstone became national heroes. While many did work hard to protect their congregations from white exploitation, their influence was not always beneficial. The 'Indian Mutiny' (1857–8) was a rebellion by part of the British Indian Army against foreign domination of India, cultural as well as economic and political. Insulted religious sensibilities were a major factor.

The negative aspects of empire – Africans dispossessed of their lands, Indian craftsmen ruined by British textile imports they were forbidden to exclude by tariffs, widespread and often brutal exploitation – generally received very little attention in Britain. The empire was popular, particularly among the upper and middle classes, for whom it provided prestigious military and administrative careers. There appear also to have been concerted efforts by imperialists to instil enthusiasm for empire among Britain's working class. This was reflected in the jingoistic strains of popular culture, such as the images depicted in advertisements for mass-produced goods, or the often militarist ballads of the music-hall. Songs such as George Lashwood's *The Death or Glory Boys* and *The Gallant Twenty-First*, in the 1880s, reflect this. How effective these efforts were is difficult to judge. Much of the working class appears to have remained apathetic about imperialism. Nonetheless, episodes such as the relief of Mafeking during the Anglo-Boer War were widely celebrated. Many Liberal politicians, including William Gladstone, the Prime Minister, were critical of jingoism and of imperial expansion for its own sake. But the Conservative Party tried with some success to identify itself with the empire, and it won an election under Disraeli in 1874. The empire became for many a part of British identity. The Golden and Diamond jubilees of Queen Victoria, in 1887 and 1897 respectively, were popu-

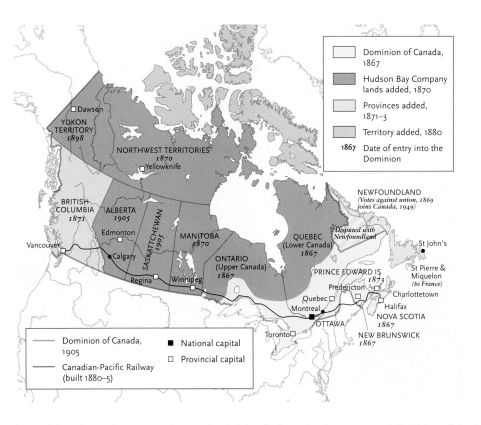

Legend:
- Dominion of Canada, 1867
- Hudson Bay Company lands added, 1870
- Provinces added, 1871–3
- Territory added, 1880
- **1867** Date of entry into the Dominion

- Dominion of Canada, 1905
- Canadian-Pacific Railway (built 1880–5)
- ■ National capital
- □ Provincial capital

humiliating defeats, and Britain had to spend £250 million and deploy 450,000 troops to defeat 100,000 farmers. A ruthless policy was followed to suppress a determined guerrilla war, forcing Afrikaner civilians into concentration camps in which 20,000 died. This aroused revulsion at home and international condemnation. It was also a blow for British self-confidence. Rather than following the tenets of the 'new imperialism', Britain began to seek European allies.

It is easy to present the empire as doomed to failure. British rule, in fact, encouraged the emergence of a British-educated middle class among colonised peoples, who were to form a new, anti-British political elite. Though Britain did not compare badly with others as an imperial power, there were certainly enough injustices in the empire to arouse nationalist hostility. Towards the end of the century, opposition to imperial rule appeared, although it was limited in scope. In 1885, the Indian National Congress was formed; in 1897, the Egyptian National Party. In the next century, Britain was going to have to find a way to accommodate their demands, or be defeated by them.   **JMB**

lar celebrations. In 1896, the earl of Meath launched Empire Day on 24 May, Queen Victoria's birthday.

THE NEW IMPERIALISM

Empire provided the stimulus for a new concept of exemplary masculinity, focusing on soldier heroes; men such as Charles Gordon, hero of Khartoum, were presented as national icons in a fusion of military prowess, Protestant zeal and moral manhood. Imperial clashes were re-enacted in open-air spectacles in Britain: the tableau and pageant became art forms. The ideology of empire was taken to new heights towards the end of the century as other European nations sought to emulate British success. Uneasy that Britain's domination of world trade was eroding and influenced by ideas of social Darwinism, which suggested that the survival of the fittest was as valid for nations as for species, men like Lord Milner began to bring forward theories that became known as the 'new imperialism'. They suggested that Britain urgently needed to prepare for the challenges of the future. These would come from European powers who would attempt to wrest the empire from Britain, and from emerging nationalist sentiment among colonised peoples, who would try to free themselves from British rule. Britain, it was held, needed to prepare by becoming a more militarised, disciplined nation. Demands for universal conscription were put forward. So were arguments for social reform, simply to create healthier soldiers.

There was little widespread enthusiasm for such ideas, but they were not without influence. Lord Milner was himself to play a leading role in the outbreak of the Anglo-Boer War, when Britain decided to end the independence of the Afrikaner (Dutch) republics of southern Africa, the Orange Free State and Transvaal. The government seems to have assumed that no fighting would be necessary, since few moves were taken to strengthen British forces in the region. The Afrikaners inflicted a series of

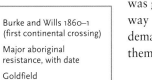

- → Burke and Wills 1860–1 (first continental crossing)
- Major aboriginal resistance, with date
- Goldfield

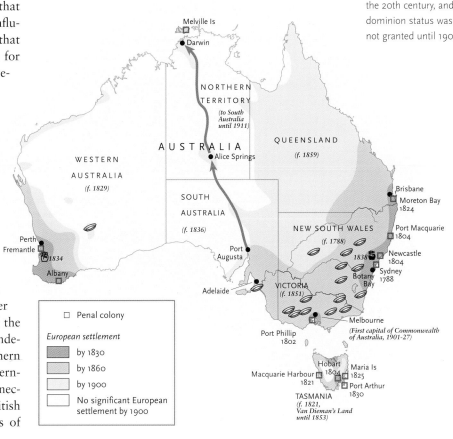

- □ Penal colony

European settlement
- by 1830
- by 1860
- by 1900
- No significant European settlement by 1900

THE RAILWAY AGE

Whereas turnpikes and canals were a response to the practical difficulties of inland transport, the railway revolution of the 1830s and 1840s has to be understood as an idea. Railways caught the imagination. The Liverpool and Manchester Railway, opened in September 1830, quickly became a new wonder of the world. The speed of its trains astonished contemporaries at home and abroad, as did the vast scale of its engineering. Attracted by its scope for huge profits, entrepreneurs and 'money men' clamoured to promote lines in many parts of Britain and Ireland. The accumulated profits of Lancashire's industrial magnates were soon underwriting trunk railways into London; within 20 years the country had acquired a national railway system extending nearly 10,000 kilometres (approximately 6,200 miles).

RAILWAY MANIA

The railway boom gave birth to a new kind of capitalist. Share markets opened up in cities up and down the land as individuals of almost all classes sought out 'railway scrip', a part paid-up share in a new venture. Travel by rail soon began to work other remarkable social transformations. Scientists travelling by rail to British Association annual meetings in the 1840s, for example, spoke of 'magical' transfers from place to place. Artists drew and painted the new wonder of the age. Publishers of children's books constructed new alphabets around it. In London and other big cities, railway construction swept all before it. Where clocks had hitherto been set to local time, the railway brought a truly national concept of 'railway time': as Charles Dickens remarked, it was as if the sun had given in.

Speculative booms rarely last, however. The first railway bubble of 1836 had burst by 1837, and the second, of 1844, by 1847, leaving a trail of lost fortunes, debt and litigation. Nonetheless, by the 1860s, the railway had become an indelible part of the social fabric, not to mention a growing economic force in Victorian industrial expansion. By 1901, the year of Queen Victoria's death, the network extended to over 30,000 kilometres (nearly 50,000 miles). By 1905, the Great Western Railway alone carried more freight tonnage than all the inland waterways of Britain put together. By 1910, the country's railways as a whole had clocked up a total of some 270 million passenger train miles.

Early livestock train
A train carrying livestock on the Liverpool and Manchester Railway in 1831. As early as the 1830s, the railway was beginning to transform agriculture as well as industry.

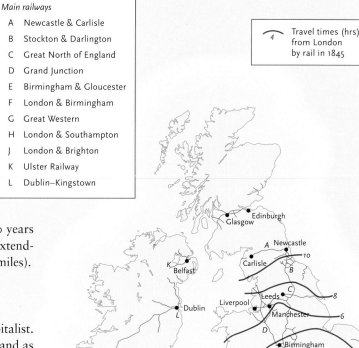

Main railways
A Newcastle & Carlisle
B Stockton & Darlington
C Great North of England
D Grand Junction
E Birmingham & Gloucester
F London & Birmingham
G Great Western
H London & Southampton
J London & Brighton
K Ulster Railway
L Dublin–Kingstown

4 Travel times (hrs) from London by rail in 1845

0 ——— 100 miles
0 ——— 150 km

The railway network in about 1840

The outline of a national railway system was already clear after the first wave of construction in 1837. The opening of the Liverpool and Manchester Railway (1825) was soon followed by that of the London and Birmingham Railway and the Grand Junction Railway (1838–9) linking the capital with the main industrial areas.

For the coal and metal industries, the railways became pulsating arteries, helping to transform the scale and reach of both internal and external markets. Equally, the general merchandise trade found in the railway a means of offering next-day deliveries across the land. Railway construction itself was a voracious consumer of materials and labour, and at the height of the boom of the 1840s, the 'navvy' population had grown to form mobile armies of men on a scale not seen since the Civil War. When British construction slowed, the railway engineers and their contractors took to building railways overseas. As a consequence, British engineering companies came to supply the world with locomotives and rolling stock.

THE SOCIAL IMPACT

The investment dramas of the 1840s prompted the government to investigate the need for state regulation of railway construction. But throughout the Victorian age, the railway in Britain remained a project of private business. Capitalist competition soon led to the control of the lion's share of the railway system by a small group of companies – largely through absorption and amalgamation. Indeed, companies like the Great Western and the London and North Western became forerunners of the modern business corporation. As early as 1858, these two companies had capitalisations of £43 and £28 million respectively.

By 1900, there was hardly an aspect of day-to-day life that remained untouched by the railway. Railway journeys made for 'captive reading time', and there was a vast multiplication in the number of cheap novels and other kinds of reading matter sold at bookstalls in stations. The modern preoccupation with being 'on time' was a creation of the early railway age, with its interlocking timetables. Ownership of pocket watches mushroomed. Catching trains invoked a litany of haste and anxiety in the minds of travellers. In the suburbs served by commuter trains, arrival and departure times became pivots of diurnal rhythms within the home. More widely, as railway passengers peered through their carriage windows, they could see revealed in great cuttings like that at Blisworth in Northamptonshire an entire new history of the earth – the layers of compacted sediments, often rich in fossils, bearing witness to millions of years of prehistory, confounding the familiar biblical account of Creation. Extinct monsters were constantly being disinterred by railway excavation. So as the speed of the railway notionally shrank the country to one-sixth of its size, giving 'a new celerity to time', according to the author Samuel Smiles, the origins of time in the accepted historical sense were becoming lost in an unfathomable abyss. **MF**

The railway network in about 1910

The railway system was largely complete by the 1870s; a third wave of building in 1863–6 had filled in the branch and suburban lines. Projects such as the Severn tunnel (1886) reduced specific journey times, and by 1910 the system had reached its full capacity.

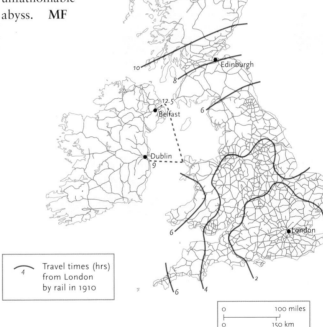

Travel times (hrs) from London by rail in 1910

0   100 miles
0   150 km

Launch of the SS Great Britain

Designed by one of the greatest engineers of the day, Isambard Kingdom Brunel, and launched at Bristol in 1843, the Great Britain was the first screw-driven iron ship to cross the Atlantic. It was a symbol of Victorian Britain's commercial and technological might.

The reign of Queen Victoria (1837–1901) was one of the most extraordinary periods of transformation in British history. At the beginning of the era, Britain was the sole mechanised industrial society of the world, embarking on a period of free trade that would help for a time to sustain its position. By the end, the country was in comparative industrial decline, facing major competition from the USA and Germany. Moreover, by the end of the nineteenth century, landed and farming interests had been through a period of crisis (partly as a result of competition from other food sources, which had become available through free trade), which produced significant changes on the land.

Yet other indices appear to have moved in the opposite direction: the British financial services sector, for example, which has remained important to the present day, had fully emerged, greatly helped by the globalising tendencies of new technology, by the scale of British overseas investment, and by the strength of British shipping and commerce. In 1837 the British rail network was only in its infancy; by

1901 the British Isles had one of the most extensive grids of lines in the world, encompassing even the remote Scottish Highlands. British shipbuilding and the merchant marine ruled the commerce of the globe. All manner of new technologies had come into play, including advanced triple and quadruple expansion marine engines, the steam turbine, the undersea telegraph cable, the telephone, modern bicycles, and the earliest internal combustion engines. The beginning of photography had coincided with the start of Victoria's reign, and by its end, cameras and photographic images were available almost to all. The cinema was becoming established (though not yet in dedicated buildings) and the queen herself, who seems to have been fascinated by all aspects of new technology, was captured on moving film. The phonograph was another major source of interest, and the voices of celebrities such as W. E. Gladstone and Florence Nightingale were recorded for posterity. Steel-framed buildings had made their appearance and prefabricated units had become relatively commonplace. In other words, many aspects of the modern world appeared in Victoria's time.

SOCIETY AND POLITICS

Equally significant changes took place in social and political life. Cities grew dramatically: Glasgow expanded from 200,000 people to 760,000, while Middlesbrough, a small rural community in 1837, was a major industrial centre of 100,000 by 1901. The population of England and Wales more than doubled, while that of Scotland grew by 70 per cent, despite considerable outward migration. This dramatic growth led to major health and other problems in the urban slums. By late Victorian times, social surveys, housing renewal, youth and temperance movements, and a certain amount of religious revivalism had developed, aimed at the alleviation of these problems. Municipal socialism, in the provision of fresh water supplies (Manchester's, for example, from Thirlmere in the Lake District, Glasgow's from Loch Katrine in the Trossachs), gas, public transport and other services (Birmingham has long been regarded as the forerunner), was becoming the order of the day. Successive Factory Acts (1847 and 1874) improved the working hours and the lot of workers, while eliminating some child and also female labour. Museums and public libraries, provided under legislation of 1845 and after, were everywhere available to enhance the opportunities for the 'rational recreation' of urban populations. Newspapers, which at the start of the Victorian period were subject to paper taxes and stamp duties and could be bought only by the wealthiest in

Queen Victoria enters Brighton, 1837

Brighton's Triumphal Arch Amphitheatre was splendidly decorated for Queen Victoria in her coronation year. Victoria soon turned her back on Britain's leading seaside resort, even though it had been popular with royalty earlier in the century, and chose instead the privacy of Balmoral.

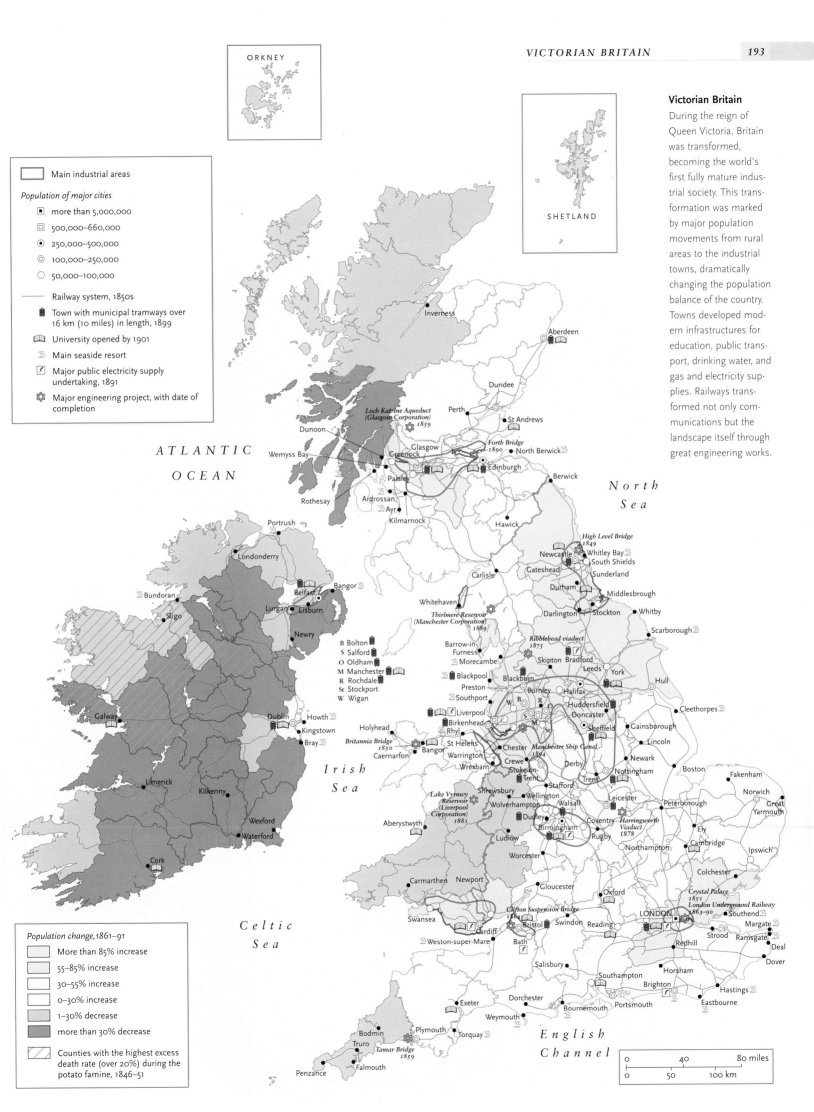

Victorian Britain

During the reign of Queen Victoria, Britain was transformed, becoming the world's first fully mature industrial society. This transformation was marked by major population movements from rural areas to the industrial towns, dramatically changing the population balance of the country. Towns developed modern infrastructures for education, public transport, drinking water, and gas and electricity supplies. Railways transformed not only communications but the landscape itself through great engineering works.

Main industrial areas

Population of major cities

- ■ more than 5,000,000
- ▣ 500,000–660,000
- ◉ 250,000–500,000
- ◎ 100,000–250,000
- ○ 50,000–100,000

— Railway system, 1850s

Town with municipal tramways over 16 km (10 miles) in length, 1899

University opened by 1901

Main seaside resort

Major public electricity supply undertaking, 1891

Major engineering project, with date of completion

Population change, 1861–91

- More than 85% increase
- 55–85% increase
- 30–55% increase
- 0–30% increase
- 1–30% decrease
- more than 30% decrease

Counties with the highest excess death rate (over 20%) during the potato famine, 1846–51

ORKNEY

SHETLAND

society (supposedly to prevent revolution), were available to all by the end of the century. The political party system progressively emerged as the franchise was extended in the Reform Acts of 1867 and 1884. By the latter, almost full male adult suffrage was achieved. The secret ballot was introduced in 1872. The Conservative and Liberal parties were the major players on the political scene, particularly as symbolised by the celebrated (though relatively brief) rivalry between Benjamin Disraeli and William Ewart Gladstone. Disraeli fostered a combination of romantic imperialism and domestic intervention that helped to develop a tradition of working-class Tory voting, greatly encouraged by the foundation of the Primrose League in his memory in 1883. The Liberal Party, by contrast, stood for free trade, fiscal frugality, and the 'rolling back of the frontiers of the state'.

The other question that distinguished the two parties was the matter of Ireland. The Irish potato famine of the 1840s caused the death of more than a million people and stimulated the mass emigration of Irish people across the Atlantic and elsewhere. Irish nationalism became a significant political force and the Fenian movement developed a policy of violent resistance, resulting in the assassina-

tion of the Chief Secretary of Ireland (1882). Gladstone's response was to attempt to develop a degree of devolution within the United Kingdom. The Scots secured their own Scottish Office and Secretary of State (1884), while Ireland was to be granted a degree of internal self-government in the Home Rule Bill of 1885. Many, however, recognised Ireland as essentially an imperial issue, and held that such a concession would be tantamount to preparing for the dissolution of the empire, at least the empire of white settlement. Gladstone's liberals split, with the Liberal Unionists (such as the radical imperialist Joseph Chamberlain) ultimately moving into coalition with the Conservatives. The Irish problem continued to haunt British politics throughout the twentieth century.

THE RISE OF THE MIDDLE CLASS

The ascendancy of Disraeli and Gladstone in the politics of the 1870s and 1880s represented the emergence of the middle class as a major force in British politics. It is true that the aristocracy maintained its grip on many of the leading organs of the state, including the ministries, and was to return to the prime ministership in the shape of the marquis of Salisbury and the earl of Rosebery, but more middle-class businessmen (Chamberlain was a classic example) and professionals now also aspired to political office. This mirrored the emergence of the middle class as a dominant class in British society, partially replacing the rural gentry. Britain's built environment is full of the homes they made for themselves. The wealthier echelons of the middle class, whose fortunes were usually made in the industry and commerce of the towns, also set out to secure country estates in order to gentrify themselves, although whether this served to dilute their entrepreneurial spirit remains a matter of controversy. The professional classes, including lawyers, doctors, academics and teachers, also grew tremendously during this period. New colleges, soon to be elevated to the status of universities, were founded in all the major industrial cities (joining the two ancient English and four Scottish Universities, together with Durham, University College, London, and Trinity College, Dublin), offering a more accessible tertiary education to many. Although standards of literacy had been relatively high before the Education Act of 1870, the emergence of compulsory primary education under that legislation produced one of the best-educated and most literate populations in Europe. The so-called public schools were reformed and became a model for a new wave of private schools as well as the grammar schools and high schools (sometimes based on ancient foundations) that emerged in every city and town.

The hand of the middle class was everywhere – in local government and national politics, in the churches, in local societies and pressure groups, on the magistrates' bench, and in governing trusts, foundations, schools and colleges. Middle-class women also exercised influence within society. They became involved in philanthropy, all manner of pressure groups, and the churches. By the end of the century, they dominated nursing and teaching (particularly in the primary sector), featured strongly among the ranks of artists and actors, and were graduating as doctors (212 doctors and 140 dentists were women in 1901) and going overseas as missionaries. By legislation of 1870, 1878 and 1882, women secured more legal freedoms in respect of property

Birmingham in 1885

Birmingham's diverse industrial base made it a serious rival to Manchester as England's second city in the later 19th century. Birmingham gained a reputation for municipal enterprise for its public works, including one of the country's most extensive urban tramway systems. Cheap and efficient public transport systems, based on horse-drawn omnibuses and trams, proved to be an effective way of dispersing the industrial working class from overcrowded and disease-ridden city-centre slums.

Birmingham's transport system in 1885

●—— Railways and stations

- - - Tramways constructed or in course of construction

····· Tramways authorised but not yet constructed

- - - - Horse-drawn omnibus routes

▢ Parks

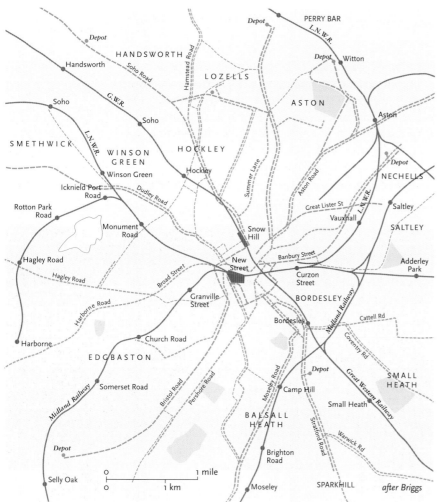

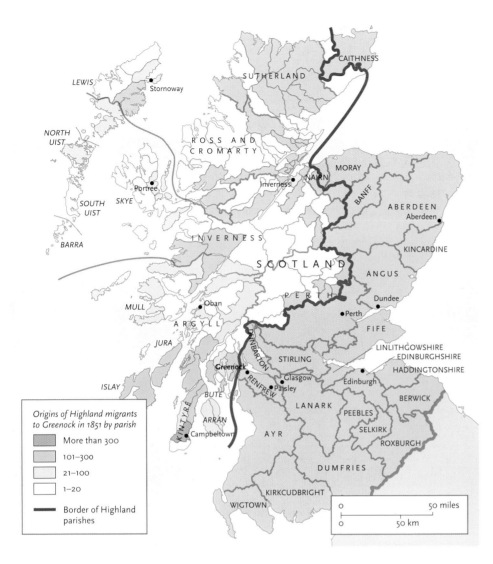

Origins of Highland migrants
to Greenock in 1851 by parish

- More than 300
- 101–300
- 21–100
- 1–20
- ── Border of Highland parishes

might secure some success in the relatively near future. But by the time of her Diamond Jubilee in 1897, Victoria had established herself relatively unassailably in the sentiments of the British people, and patriotic imperialism had come to act, to a certain extent, as an emollient for class conflict.

After 1868, the military was modernised under the reforms of Edward Cardwell, Gladstone's secretary of state for war, and the officer corps became more open to men of ability from different social backgrounds. In this period, the military became much more associated with colonial wars, and their exploits (together with those of explorers and missionaries) were celebrated in the adventure tales and books of heroes that became so popular. The military also contributed to urban spectacle, in ceremonies, band performances and the like. Indeed, spectacle was one of the characteristics of the Victorian era, represented particularly by the great exhibitions, the most notable being that held in the Crystal Palace in Hyde Park in 1851, with many more taking place, almost on an annual basis, throughout the country. Yet some of the self-confidence of the Victorian era was beginning to decline by its end, and apprehension of social disorder, epidemics, the Asiatic 'yellow peril' and European foreign enemies was beginning to develop.   **JM**

Highland migration to Greenock

Depopulation in the Highlands was more severe than in most parts of rural Britain because, to the positive lure of urban job opportunities, was added the compulsory clearance of farming tenants by landowners keen to create sheep-farming or sporting estates. Most migrants moved to the industrial towns of the central lowlands, generally settling as close as possible to their home districts. Though Greenock, for example, attracted migrants from across the Highlands, the vast majority came from Kintyre, Bute, Islay and Jura, which all had good sea communications with the Clyde.

Squerryes Court, c.1860

At luxurious houses such as this elegant manor at Westerham, the elite of Victorian England could enjoy the lifestyle they felt their class and status required. Women were expected to be decorous, modest and idle.

and divorce, though working-class women continued to act as a reservoir of cheap labour in factories, domestic service and the retail trades. In the last few decades of the nineteenth century, the working class, particularly those dubbed as 'respectable', had more disposable income, and this manifested itself in a number of important developments. While the rough sports of the early part of the reign (such as cockfighting) were banned or became less fashionable, sports such as soccer and rugby league were codified and secured large numbers of spectators. Cricket also achieved a wider following and an imperial context that pulled in the colonies of white settlement. The tradition of the annual holiday at a seaside resort became more widespread, and theatres, particularly those offering music-hall entertainment, flourished. At the same time, new forms of radicalism emerged among the working classes, including modern-style trade unions (the Trade Union Congress emerged in the late 1860s) and extensive strikes (for example, the London dockers' strike of 1890). Working-class radicalism culminated in a number of socialist movements – notably the Independent Labour Party, founded in 1893. Nevertheless, radicalism was not as potent a force as it had been in the early part of Victoria's reign, in the era of the Chartists and of the 1848 revolutions in Europe. Republicanism, however, was in evidence in the 1870s and some influential politicians thought that it

EDUCATION & LITERACY

For most of the nineteenth century, state interest in education was minimal. Educational provision therefore varied considerably from region to region. Literacy figures based on the numbers of brides and grooms who signed the marriage register with their names give only a crude impression of the level of education among the population. But they do indicate steadily rising literacy rates of roughly 50 per cent in 1754, 61 per cent in 1851 and 97 per cent by 1900. There was a clear connection between low literacy levels and the highly populated, industrial areas of Lancashire and Yorkshire. To some extent, this reflected rapid population growth and urbanisation, which outstripped the supply of schools. Free education depended upon generally inadequate charitable provision, so illiteracy was higher in areas of poverty. Child labour further interfered with education. Many parents saw little benefit from education, while the impoverished needed the extra income from children at work. Such problems were not limited to industrial areas. In fishing villages in Scotland and Cornwall, illiteracy rates remained high throughout the nineteenth century – education simply seemed to have no relevance to people's lives.

There were significant gender differences. Girls were less likely to attend school than boys. They were also less likely to learn to write. Sewing was deemed more important for girls whose main careers would be as servants, or who would remain in the domestic environment. From the 1850s, however, girls' literacy rates began to improve dramatically. There were several reasons for this, including the fact that employers of domestic servants preferred girls educated at voluntary or charity schools, who were reputed to be more obedient – that they were more literate was incidental. In some areas, such as East Anglia, female literacy levels eventually exceeded male rates.

The education census of 1851 identified the flagrant regional disparities in educational provision, in particular the poor facilities of large industrial and commercial towns.

The chief providers of elementary education for most of the nineteenth century were the voluntary bodies that, from the 1830s, received Treasury grants. Some among the middle classes supported universal education for philanthropic reasons, or to prevent crime and immorality, or as an insurance against social unrest. Others were alarmed at the growth of Catholicism and Nonconformism, and saw an Anglican education system as a defence against this. There was opposition, however, from those who feared that educating the working class would lead to higher taxes and labour costs, if not the spread of radical political ideas. Thus Nottinghamshire farmers reputedly discouraged education among their labourers' children, not wanting to lose their supply of cheap labour. In successive Education Acts from 1870, governments took steps to fill the most obvious gaps in education provision, and – much more controversially – made it universal and compulsory until the

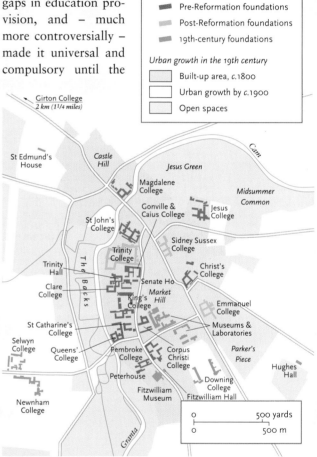

Growth of the university
- ■ Pre-Reformation foundations
- ■ Post-Reformation foundations
- ■ 19th-century foundations

Urban growth in the 19th century
- ☐ Built-up area, c.1800
- ☐ Urban growth by c.1900
- ☐ Open spaces

age of 10, though several loopholes existed. The act provided only religious and moral education and basic literacy and numeracy for most, though the curriculum was gradually widened.

National differences in education and literacy were marked. Levels of literacy were especially high in Scotland, where favourable attitudes to an educated population were supported by a network of parochial schools. In Wales, Nonconformists, and in Ireland, Catholics opposed state funding of education, fearing Anglican propaganda. The Welsh also feared that the established Church sought to extinguish the Welsh language by providing English-only schools. This strategy was undermined by the chapel-provided Sunday schools, in which Welsh was the medium of

Cambridge in the 19th century

Between the Reformation and the 19th century, only limited change was seen in Cambridge. But during the Victorian period the growth in university provision was as marked there as it was with the new university towns. This in turn encouraged rapid population and urban growth, and the development of modern Cambridge.

Newlyn School, Cornwall, 1889

During the 19th century even isolated fishing communities, such as Newlyn, experienced a growth in education provision, which was extended to girls as well as boys.

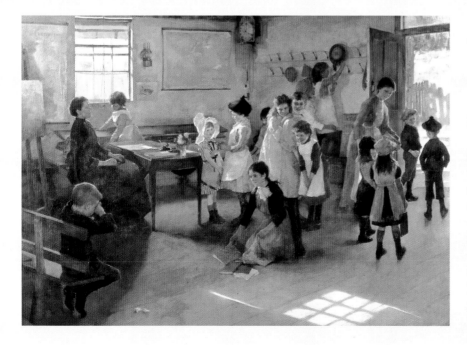

instruction. Nonetheless, there was overall an inadequate educational provision for the Welsh.

In Ireland, the government set up a national education system in 1831, funding schools irrespective of their religious affiliation, which vastly increased the scope of education throughout the country. Schools were initially concentrated in urban areas and the north, and illiteracy levels continued to be high in the rural south. The situation was further complicated by the fact that early in the century Irish continued to be the main language of the rural population outside Ulster; regional differences were thus more marked in Ireland than elsewhere in Great Britain.

University education slowly expanded in the nine-

teenth century, as it became clear that the ancient foundations could no longer meet the economic and intellectual demands of the country. In 1825 radicals including Jeremy Bentham and James Mill were influential in the establishment of University College London, and in 1845 the Queen's Colleges (Ireland) Act provided colleges at Belfast, Cork and Galway. By the end of the century, universities had been established in the main urban centres of England. In 1878 the University of London became the first institution to admit women students, and by 1900 women were attending all universities – though with some restrictions. The number of women achieving degrees was limited, and Oxford and Cambridge resisted awarding degrees to female students until well into the twentieth century. **SR**

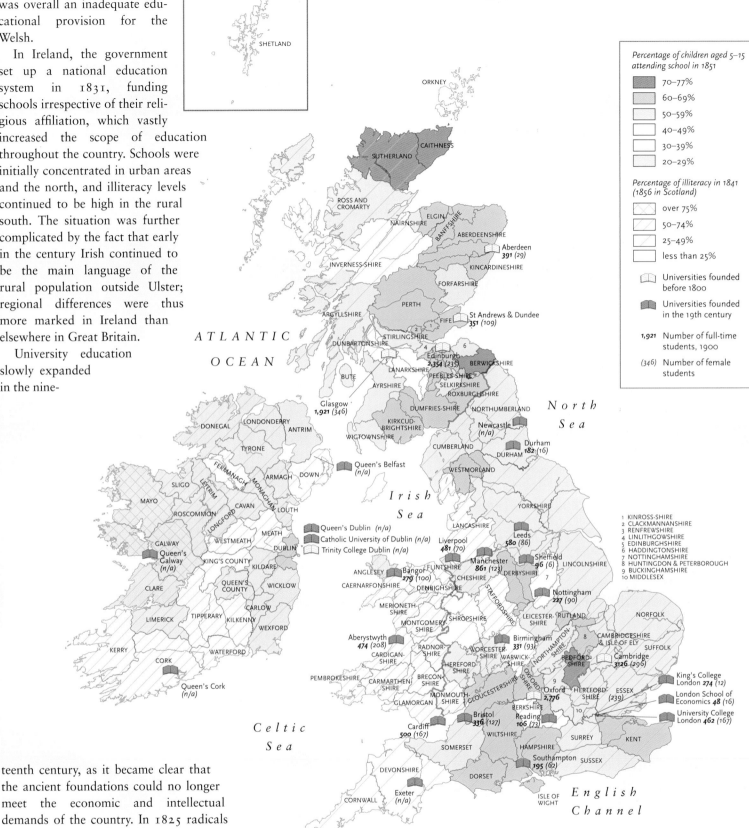

19th-century education and literacy

In the mid-19th century levels of illiteracy were generally high, though they varied from area to area: they were lowest in Scotland, highest in Ireland, and higher among girls than boys. Levels of school attendance were also generally poor. Education provision did, however, improve. The government introduced universal, compulsory primary education. University provision also became more widespread and began to include women.

PUBLIC LEISURE: SPORT

A cricket match c.1830

The Leicester match against Nottingham typically took place on a field with few facilities. Permanent cricket grounds appeared later.

national competitions with recognised governing bodies and standardised rules, and the emergence of a broad spectrum of new activities, transformed the sporting scene in lasting ways that visibly and directly prefigured most of the developments of the twentieth century.

The developments that took place in competitive sport during the nineteenth century tended to make it compatible with an industrialised society, confining it to specific locations, protecting property and commerce from disruption, imposing time-limits on contests (and thereby making them available to spectators with limited leisure time), reducing the risk of serious injury to participants, and organising regular performances that were susceptible to commercial exploitation. The changes were usually imposed from above, often to an agenda of encouraging 'muscular Christianity', the pursuit of the ideal of a healthy mind in a healthy body, and the ethos of fair play and playing the game for the game's sake, as encouraged by Evangelicals in the public schools and universities. When the industrial working class responded positively to the opportunity to participate, however, they (and their employers) often subverted these ideals to meet their own needs and preferences, playing competitively to win, seeking payment for participation at the highest levels, ignoring the religious agenda, and sometimes betting on the outcome. Among the spectators, football hooliganism was emphatically a Victorian invention; and it should be added that the middle and upper classes did not always practise what they preached. The cheating and nest-feathering attributed to the great Victorian cricketer Dr W. G. Grace is one example, and the very high expenses charged by football's Corinthians, supposedly the epitome of the amateur ethos, is another.

Competitive sport, whether involving horses and riders, the men of rival villages (or opposing groups within the same village) arrayed in mass conflict, challenge matches between teams hired and selected by noblemen, or bearers of the pride of towns or whole counties, was popular and well established in eighteenth-century England. However, it was not until the Victorian years that the development of

Rugby and cricket

Sport became more organised during the 19th century, with recognised governing bodies and rules. The original ethos of sportsmanship encouraged by public schools and universities gave way to competitiveness, professionalism and commercialism.

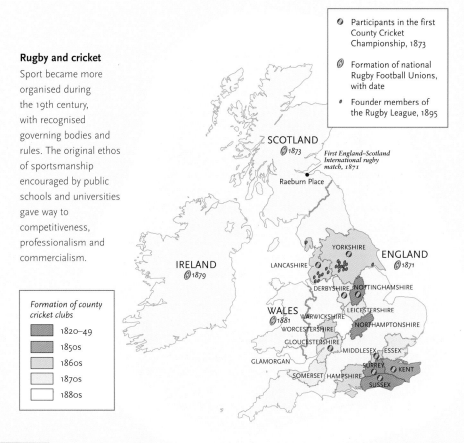

- ⊘ Participants in the first County Cricket Championship, 1873
- ⊘ Formation of national Rugby Football Unions, with date
- • Founder members of the Rugby League, 1895

SCOTLAND ⊘1873

First England–Scotland International rugby match, 1871

Raeburn Place

IRELAND ⊘1879

YORKSHIRE

LANCASHIRE

ENGLAND ⊘1871

DERBYSHIRE NOTTINGHAMSHIRE

LEICESTERSHIRE

WALES ⊘1881 WARWICKSHIRE

NORTHAMPTONSHIRE

WORCESTERSHIRE

GLOUCESTERSHIRE

MIDDLESEX ESSEX

GLAMORGAN

SURREY KENT

SOMERSET HAMPSHIRE

SUSSEX

Formation of county cricket clubs

▨	1820–49
▨	1850s
▨	1860s
□	1870s
□	1880s

TEAM GAMES

The most conspicuous development during this period was the rise of Association football as the most popular spectator sport. It emerged from the public schools as a distinct game during the 1860s and 1870s, with the Football Association (founded in 1863) as its national governing body, and the FA Cup, from the 1871–2 season, as the first national competition. In 1877 a national set of rules, combining ideas from London and Sheffield, was agreed, winning universal acceptance in 1882. At about this time, the centre of gravity in terms of density of clubs and number of spectators jumped northwards, from the Old Boys' and regimental teams associated with the Home Counties, to the industrial districts of the North and the Midlands. The first northern and predominantly working-class team to win the FA Cup was Blackburn Olympic in 1883, and this presaged a shift to professionalism that was pioneered in the relatively prosperous cotton-weaving district of east Lancashire, where fiercely competitive clubs were especially thick on the ground. When the Football League was established in 1888, five of the 12 founder clubs came from Lancashire cotton towns, and by the 1892–3 season, when there were two divisions, 10 of the 28 clubs were from Lancashire, with the rest ranging across the Midlands from Birmingham to Sheffield and Grimsby, with an outpost at Sunderland. Professional football in the South developed later and on a smaller scale, with the rival Southern League recruiting its early support from the metropolis and its immediate surroundings. Big crowds, and sporting success, became predominantly northern; but the picture was complicated by the development of what became Rugby Union, a middle-class sport (except in South Wales) that became powerful (although less well supported) across the south and west of England, and its northern variant Rugby League, which broke away as the Northern Union in 1895 to allow 'broken time' payments for working-class players, and then embraced full professionalism. At the end of the nineteenth century this was the dominant spectator sport in those parts of Lancashire and Yorkshire in which the Association game had not taken hold, especially in the mining and heavy-industry districts of south Lancashire and west Yorkshire. Meanwhile, the original so-called 'folk' form of the game, which might involve hundreds on either side, survived here and there, as at Ashbourne and Workington; in the latter it became a spectator sport in its own right, drawing crowds of rail excursionists every Easter.

Cricket's geographical trajectory was in some ways similar to that of football, as it also moved northwards from southern origins; and despite the hold that Lord's cricket ground in London's St John's Wood kept on its organisation, and the continuing importance of the southern counties and the public schools, the North (or at least Yorkshire and Lancashire) became a popular stronghold of the game. This applies even more strongly if we look below the County Championship which, from the 1870s, became the premier national competition, and emphasise the highly competitive leagues that emerged in the late nineteenth century: town was pitted against nearby town on

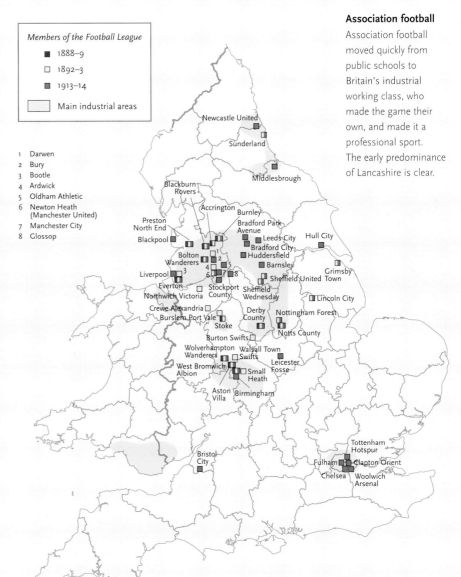

Members of the Football League
- ■ 1888–9
- □ 1892–3
- ▣ 1913–14
- ▒ Main industrial areas

1 Darwen
2 Bury
3 Bootle
4 Ardwick
5 Oldham Athletic
6 Newton Heath (Manchester United)
7 Manchester City
8 Glossop

Association football
Association football moved quickly from public schools to Britain's industrial working class, who made the game their own, and made it a professional sport. The early predominance of Lancashire is clear.

summer Saturday afternoons, with the local talent supplemented by imported professionals. This popular spectator sport contrasted with the predominant southern version, involving public schools, great houses and village friendlies, and it illustrates further that the key identities around which team sports rallied support were local, and increasingly revolved around a popular version of civic pride. Before the Land Wars of the 1880s and the rise of the Gaelic Athletic Associations politicised sport, Ireland was also a stronghold of the southern version of cricket. Thereafter, one's choice of sport became a political statement, as it still is to some extent in Northern Ireland.

These were the dominant team games of late Victorian England. The middle-class, essentially individual or family-oriented sports like golf (imported from Scotland and strongly identified with sand dunes and middle-class seaside holidays) or tennis (a mid-Victorian invention), had very different geographies based on leafy, lawned suburbs and leisure towns, and attempts to take over common land for golf courses were prolific generators of fierce conflict. But what stands out about the historical geography of organised sport in this period is the growing pull of its popular manifestations towards the industrial towns of the North and Midlands.   **JKW**

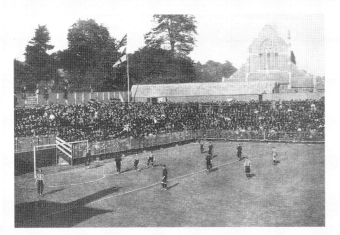

A Victorian football match
Southampton vs Brighton, September 1898: the first game played at The Dell. Purpose-built football stadia, designed to contain huge crowds, reflected not only the popularity but also the commercial success of the game.

SEASIDE RESORTS

The seaside holiday was an English invention of the eighteenth century, developed and democratised in the nineteenth. It was extended both geographically and down the social scale by the railways, which cut the cost of travel in time as well as money, and by rising working-class living standards and longer holidays in the last quarter of the nineteenth century. Paid holidays remained the preserve of a small minority (especially railway workers) below white-collar level, and the working-class seaside holiday was a regional phenomenon, concentrated into the Lancashire cotton towns (especially) and other factory (as opposed to

had grown over the period. The pace of growth really quickened during the second half of the century. But it is worth emphasising that most resorts had pre-railway origins (Brighton, for example, already had over 40,000 residents when the railway arrived from London in 1840) and only a handful were consciously created from scratch by railway companies as a matter of policy (Silloth). Some brought new life to declining or stagnating fishing ports (Brighton itself, Hastings, Scarborough), others were promoted by landowning families (Eastbourne, Southport, Llandudno), and still others grew rapidly from small begin-

Scarborough seafront in 1913

This once-stagnating fishing port became a very popular holiday destination. The promenade along the seafront was just one activity that made the seaside a favourite among Victorian and Edwardian holiday-makers.

mining) districts of the North and the Midlands, although the better-paid London workers formed a significant proportion. People saved through the year with holiday clubs in order to be able to afford seaside visits at the traditional Wakes and Feasts, making it worthwhile for entrepreneurs to invest in popular amusements and cheap accommodation at the resorts by spreading demand through the summer: August Bank Holiday, introduced in 1871, was of very limited importance outside London. What this demonstrated was that growing numbers of people had not only the money, time and transport facilities to spend a few days or a week at the coast, but they also chose to spend surplus income here rather than on fairs, music-halls or more basic domestic needs at home. So the desirability of the seaside as a destination, and the capacity of that distinctive category of town, the seaside resort, to appeal to a variety of markets, was crucial to this process.

Seaside resorts were prominent among the fastest-growing kinds of nineteenth-century town, and the sheer scale of their population growth and visitor capacity was breathtaking. The 1851 census report actually picked them out as the category of town that grew most rapidly in the first half of the nineteenth century, as they left cotton, hardware and mining centres (among others) trailing in their wake. This was misleading, because the calculation was based on a few of the largest resorts of 1851, and the percentages were inflated by the small beginnings from which these towns

nings because they were close to population centres and able to adapt to popular tastes (Blackpool, Southend, Cleethorpes). But every coastline developed its own system of seaside resorts, which competed with one another but also developed contrasting characteristics that attracted different markets and ensured that the seaside offered something for everyone – from bathing, dabbling in rock-pools, and promenading on the pier or along the shore and listening to the band, to the more commercial popular pleasures of music-halls, fairgrounds, boisterous outdoor dancing and the great entertainment centres of the largest resorts. Lancashire's Fylde coast, for example, in close proximity to industrial Lancashire and the West Riding of Yorkshire, and within easy reach of the West Midlands, was dominated by Blackpool, arguably the world's first predominantly working-class seaside resort, with an off-season population of just over 47,000 and well over 3 million visitors per year in 1901; but Blackpool itself had quieter, middle-class commuter and retirement enclaves within its boundaries, while nearby St Anne's (built by a land company) catered more for middle-class families, and Lytham (the fiefdom of the Clifton family) and Bispham (on the northern cliffs) attracted the more comfortable middle classes. All, however, could sample Blackpool's unique spectrum of entertainments, from opera singers (occasionally) to beach chiropodists, whenever they chose.

This was a particularly popular, dynamic and well-developed coastline. Even more so, perhaps, were the Sussex and Kent coasts, which were studded at ever-shortening intervals with resorts of all sizes, catering for all tastes, and benefiting from the huge reservoir of demand that London created. Essex was not far behind, with Southend prominent among the leading popular resorts (and 'marine suburbs' for London commuters), while Bournemouth was particularly dynamic, drawing as it did on the Midlands and the North as well as on London. The North Wales coast had a string of resorts following the Crewe–Holyhead railway line, and increasing in social aspiration with distance from Liverpool and the industrial towns, while another resort system followed the Clyde estuary down from Glasgow. Belfast, Derry and Dublin also grew their own resort systems for industrial workers. The more distant coastlines, where railways were tentatively unfurling their ultimate tentacles, were still the preserve of the artistic, adventurous and informal, as in Cornwall, north Norfolk and west Wales. But all this added up to impressive numbers, although the statistics of holiday-making themselves are too 'soft' to trust. Well over a million people lived in over 100

substantial resorts along the English and Welsh coastlines, according to the April census of 1901. The populations of most of these would double or treble at the crest of the season in August, and 65 of them had invested in that classic icon of the Victorian seaside, the pleasure pier. For all but the poorest, the seaside was becoming a national institution, if only as an experience to aspire to and occasionally taste for a fugitive day. These were important industrial towns, selling intangible but important wares involving pleasure, health and fashion, and employing extensive capitals and workforces in the process. **JKW**

Southsea in the 1890s

South coast resorts like Southsea (near Portsmouth) were within an easy railway journey of London, and were popular with the capital's relatively affluent working class. Children, especially, would find plentiful diversions on the beach as well as the sea front.

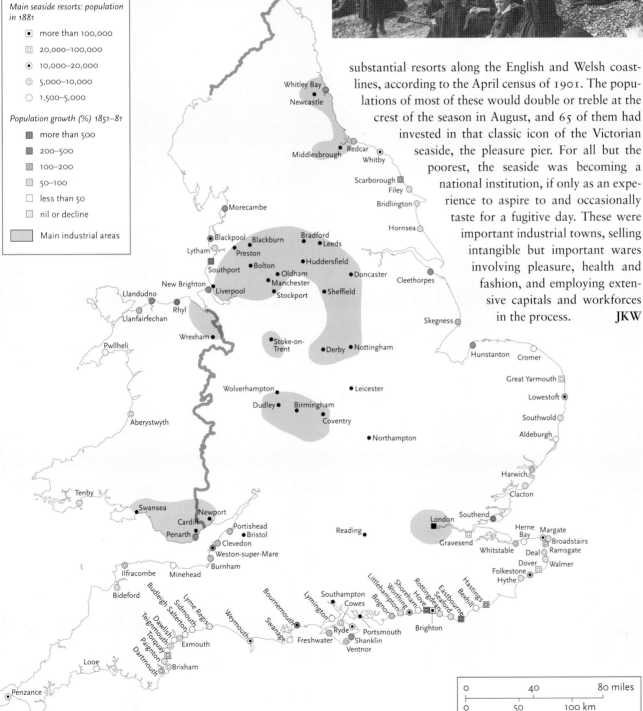

Main seaside resorts: population in 1881

- ■ more than 100,000
- ◪ 20,000–100,000
- ⊙ 10,000–20,000
- ◎ 5,000–10,000
- ○ 1,500–5,000

Population growth (%) 1851–81

- more than 500
- 200–500
- 100–200
- 50–100
- less than 50
- nil or decline
- Main industrial areas

0   40   80 miles
0   50   100 km

English seaside resorts

Seaside resorts were initially the preserve of the well-to-do, but the development of railways and growing working-class affluence in the later 19th century made them available to a much wider range of visitors. A week or even a day at the seaside was worth saving for. Their popularity transformed the economies of coastal towns within reach of the main industrial areas.

MIGRATION & EMIGRATION

Between 1821 and 1911 the total population of England, Wales, Scotland and Ireland grew from 20.9 million to 45.2 million. At the same time, the populations of what have been described as English-speaking neo-Europes, especially the USA, Canada, Southern Africa, Australia and New Zealand, also grew rapidly. These phenomena are connected: a significant proportion of the growing population of Great Britain emigrated, and these emigrants accounted over the century for a substantial part of the population growth of a number of states overseas.

Emigration from the United Kingdom must not be detached from migration within. Many Irish fled Ireland to settle in the west of Scotland, northern England and South Wales. Many Scots, too, moved south into England. The population of England and Wales increased with exceptional rapidity between 1821 and 1911, from 12.0 to 36.1 million, a 300 per cent increase overall. The population of Scotland also grew, but less quickly, by 227 per cent – from 2.1 to 4.8 million. Meanwhile, the population of Ireland rose from 6.8 million in 1821 to a peak of 8.2 million in 1841 and thereafter fell in every subsequent decade, reaching 4.4 million by 1911 – an overall decrease of 35 per cent.

These contrasting national experiences are only partly explained by different rates of natural increase (the excess of births over deaths). Even the dreadful mortality of the Great Famine, which caused a collapse in the Irish population in the 1840s, does not account for the sustained leakage of population through the rest of the century. Differential rates of emigration from the component parts of the United Kingdom were also involved. The exodus was very high as a proportion of the Irish-born population, substantial from Scotland, and least as a percentage from England and Wales. Much of this movement was internal.

For some migrants, external emigration was an alternative to, or an extension of, internal movement. The continuing fall in the population of Ireland and the restricted growth of that in Scotland certainly resulted from external emigration. It might even be argued that the population of England and Wales would have grown still faster had many of its native-born not emigrated. Official figures for external emigration in the nineteenth century are not very reliable, particularly for the first half of the century. Only those leaving for non-European destinations were counted; no distinction was drawn before 1913 between emigrants (those intending to settle abroad for a year or more) and other ship passengers; cabin-class passengers were rarely

'*I am working in a large rail road shop at the machine business. We have 86 locomotive engins to keep in repair & four hundred miles of road to keep open. Our formen are nearly all English & Scotch men & many of the men allso.*'

Extract from a letter written by David Laing from Logansport, Indiana, 19 February 1873

British emigration in the 19th century

Between 1821 and 1911 nearly 17 million people emigrated from the British Isles. Some sought to escape poverty – for example, the rural Irish. More, especially English urban-dwellers, hoped for new economic opportunities.

Preferred destinations were Europeanised territories in North America, South Africa, Australia and New Zealand, where cultural differences would be minimal and economic possibilities attractive.

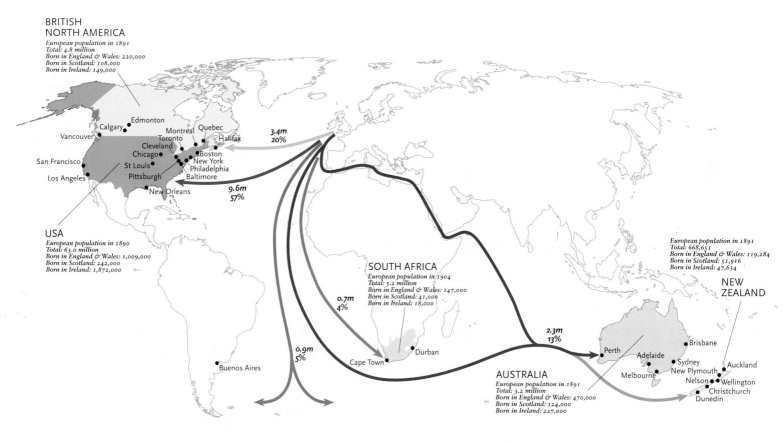

BRITISH NORTH AMERICA
European population in 1891
Total: 4.8 million
Born in England & Wales: 220,000
Born in Scotland: 108,000
Born in Ireland: 149,000

USA
European population in 1890
Total: 63.0 million
Born in England & Wales: 1,009,000
Born in Scotland: 242,000
Born in Ireland: 1,872,000

SOUTH AFRICA
European population in 1904
Total: 5.2 million
Born in England & Wales: 147,000
Born in Scotland: 41,000
Born in Ireland: 18,000

AUSTRALIA
European population in 1891
Total: 3.2 million
Born in England & Wales: 470,000
Born in Scotland: 124,000
Born in Ireland: 227,000

NEW ZEALAND
European population in 1891
Total: 668,651
Born in England & Wales: 119,284
Born in Scotland: 51,916
Born in Ireland: 47,634

3.4m 20%
9.6m 57%
0.7m 4%
0.9m 5%
2.3m 13%

Edmonton, Calgary, Vancouver, Montreal, Quebec, Toronto, Halifax, Cleveland, Chicago, Boston, San Francisco, St Louis, New York, Philadelphia, Pittsburgh, Baltimore, Los Angeles, New Orleans, Buenos Aires, Cape Town, Durban, Perth, Adelaide, Brisbane, Melbourne, Sydney, New Plymouth, Nelson, Auckland, Wellington, Christchurch, Dunedin

counted before 1863; and until 1853 no distinction was drawn between United Kingdom citizens and other nationals (and the latter included those from elsewhere in Europe who found it convenient to travel through Britain en route to overseas destinations). Nevertheless, a total emigration figure of nearly 17 million is real enough. A generally rising trend early in the century was lifted by a surge in emigration, especially from Ireland in the 1840s, a marked increase again in the 1880s, and a final late burst from 1901. Emigration after World War I was substantial; thereafter, it never again took place on the same scale.

MOTIVES AND DESTINATIONS

During the nineteenth century, those born in Britain and Ireland could be found in virtually all parts of the world. Overwhelmingly, emigrants were attracted to temperate regions, but some settled in the environmentally challenging tropical territories of Asia and Africa. What is striking is that there was a shift in destinations. Before the middle of the century, settlers in South America, Southern Africa, New Zealand and the Australian colonies were few (in spite of the 160,000 or so forcibly transported as convicts to Australia between 1788 and 1868). Initially, most set off for British North America (later Canada) or the USA. In fact, in most decades until 1900, about two-thirds of British and Irish emigrants went to the USA. From 1901, however, the numbers going to the USA each year, although remaining fairly constant, formed a smaller percentage of emigrants. A far greater share of the rising volume headed for empire destinations in Southern Africa, Australia, New Zealand and, especially, Canada.

Convention suggests that it was poverty that motivated early nineteenth-century migrants to move. In rural areas, population growth, fierce competition for land, low wages and industrialisation (as industry concentrated in towns) did indeed push many to migrate. Other factors included the decision of some landowners, in the Scottish Highlands, for example, to clear their lands of crofters to make room for sheep. Disease, notoriously the potato blight, which affected much of Ireland and parts of Scotland in the 1840s, was another push, as was famine. In spite of pressure on wages and poor living conditions, however, such compulsion in rural areas had become less severe by the later nineteenth century. Nevertheless, a significant drift from the rural areas of the United Kingdom continued.

Most migrants from rural counties did not leave the country, but settled in the expanding towns of the United Kingdom, attracted by the better-paid employment opportunities in industry and the services, and indeed by the social appeal of urban living – in Belfast, central Scotland, south Lancashire, the West Riding, the industrial Midlands and London. One consequence was the relocation of Irish people in, for example, Glasgow, Liverpool, Manchester and the East End of London. But other migrants went further. Indeed, some were engaged in so-called step migration, from rural areas to temporary settlement in towns and then on to distant places overseas. The men were mainly miners, agricultural workers and sometimes farmers; the women were usually farm workers or domestic servants. In the USA, Canada, Australia and New Zealand, and to a lesser extent in southern Africa (where black labour was exploited instead), they cleared land for farming, opened up the gold, silver, iron ore and coal mines, helped build the railways, created towns – and produced children.

Contrary to received wisdom, most nineteenth-century migrants – certainly the English, less so the others – were born in towns. Many were general labourers (more so late in the century), but others, including some women, had industrial or service-sector skills, as artisans, builders, mechanics, engineers, textile workers and, increasingly, shopkeepers, clerks and professional people. They may have felt anxious about their economic and social prospects in the United Kingdom, but they were also positively attracted by the greater opportunities that were emerging in the neo-Europes. They settled not on rural frontiers but in places like Pittsburgh, Toronto, Cape Town, Sydney and Wellington. Booming economic conditions, especially across the Atlantic, at a time when circumstances were less propitious at home, prompted surges in emigration. This also helps explain why the more rapid development of modernising and urbanising Canada and other parts of the British Empire around the turn of the century prompted increased flows in those directions.

Mid-19th-century emigrants embarking

Emigrating was a major step. The costs and emotional wrench (and, until the age of steamships, the dangers) could be considerable. It took severe conditions at home or attractive opportunities overseas to motivate migrants.

Emigrants depart for the USA, 1880

In spite of the political motives for emigration implied in this piece of US propaganda, most people who left the British Isles were looking for better economic and social opportunities.

Most migrants were young, male and single. However, many single Irish women emigrated to the USA throughout the century, and the proportion of women migrants in general increased as overseas settlements became more established. There was also a flow of single female emigrants for whom employment and indeed marriage prospects appeared better than at home. When married couples migrated, the husband sometimes went ahead to 'set up', with the wife and children following later – sometimes a considerable length of time afterwards. Later in the century, philanthropists like Dr Barnardo were responsible for dispatching children in their care to places like Canada, effectively as cheap labour – and sometimes in conditions of near slavery.

Adult migrants at least knew where they were going, and why. Usually, in a process know as chain migration, they were responding to information about opportunities relayed to them in letters by family or friends already over-seas, or in conversation with those who had been there and returned. For many, such sources determined not only whether to go, but also where and when.

THE EMIGRATION TRADE

Emigrants also responded in some instances to propaganda. Much propaganda was put out by overseas businesses seeking to attract labour, by pressure groups presenting emigration as a solution to social problems at home, by the governments of colonies, especially those of Australia and New Zealand, trying to boost the supply of labour and capital to their distant territories, and by shipping companies who had a vested interest in filling their vessels with human cargo. Initially, almost every port in Britain, especially on the west coast, dispatched emigrants – sometimes in dangerously fragile vessels and often in insanitary conditions. But by mid-century the development of steamships and government regulations had speeded up journey times, reduced costs, and increased safety margins. Such improvements alone encouraged more traffic. Moreover, because of the greater size and capital cost of modern vessels, the emigrant trade came to be handled mainly by large companies like Cunard, White Star, Anchor and P&O, operating out of large ports like Glasgow, Liverpool, Southampton and London. The first stage of the emigration journey of many Irish migrants was across the Irish Sea to connect with the big steamers heading across the Atlantic.

RETURN MIGRATION

The increasing ease and relative affordability of transport also allowed many more emigrants to return to Great Britain. Some of those who came back had failed to make good, but for others return had always been part of the prospect. They had responded at particular moments to perceived economic and social opportunities overseas by emigration, and returned when they had achieved their objectives or when the balance of advantage swung the other way. They were part of a mobile international labour force. The net balance between immigration and emigration was strongly outward, but the inward movement of returning migrants underlines the rational calculation that largely underpinned migration decisions.

FROM WARWICKSHIRE TO TARANAKI

New Zealand had become a British colony in 1840, but emigration from Great Britain was made difficult by the long, expensive and uncomfortable sea journey and the still raw nature of most settlements. Anxious to overcome these disadvantages, the New Zealand government in the 1870s offered subsidised (and, from 1873, free) passages, especially to agricultural labourers and their families. This policy coincided with the formation in England of the National Agricultural Labourers

Internal migration

The majority of migrants tended to travel relatively short distances. The cost of migration was, after all, considerable. Those seeking to escape the poor wages and limited opportunities of rural regions could find far better conditions within urban Britain. The industrial regions of Lowland Scotland, Belfast, South Wales and England offered plentiful opportunities for improved incomes and lifestyles.

SCOTLAND
Population in 1891
Total: 4.0 million
Born in England & Wales: 111,000
Born in Ireland: 195,000

IRELAND
Population in 1891
Total: 4.7 million
Born in England & Wales: 75,000
Born in Scotland: 27,000

ENGLAND AND WALES
Population in 1891
Total: 29.0 million
Born in Scotland: 282,000
Born in Ireland: 458,000

ATLANTIC OCEAN

North Sea

Irish Sea

Celtic Sea

English Channel

● Emigration ports

0   40   80 miles
0   50   100 km

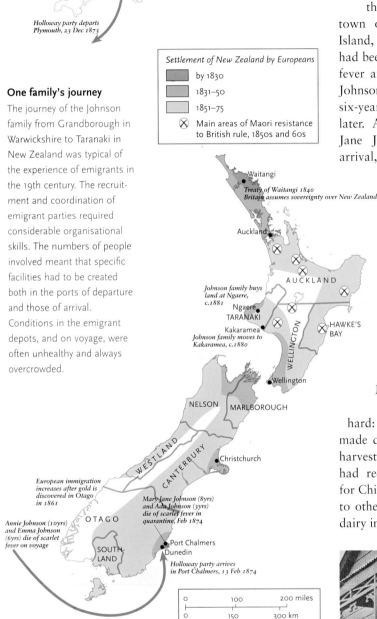

One family's journey

The journey of the Johnson family from Grandborough in Warwickshire to Taranaki in New Zealand was typical of the experience of emigrants in the 19th century. The recruitment and coordination of emigrant parties required considerable organisational skills. The numbers of people involved meant that specific facilities had to be created both in the ports of departure and those of arrival. Conditions in the emigrant depots, and on voyage, were often unhealthy and always overcrowded.

stage, via Didcot and Plymouth, of a very long journey. They sailed on 23 December, on the steamer *Mongol*, which had 313 emigrants on board. After a record journey of only 51 days, they arrived at Port Chalmers, the main port of the fast-growing town of Dunedin, in Otago, South Island, on 13 February 1874. But there had been deaths on board, from scarlet fever and measles. Ten-year-old Annie Johnson died on 29 January, and her six-year-old sister Emma three days later. Another of the children, Mary Jane Johnson, aged eight, died on arrival, followed by Ada, who was only three. Of the five Johnson children, the baby Ellen alone survived.

Joseph and Louisa, however, created a new home and indeed a new family, producing four more daughters and two sons. Initially, they settled in Otago, and then in 1880 moved to Taranaki in the North Island, living first on the coast at Kakaramea and then inland on land they had been able to buy at Ngaere, beneath Mount Egmont.

The Johnson family prospered because they worked hard: Joseph tended sheep and cleared bush land; Louisa made dresses; they cooked for a sheep station; and they harvested cocksfoot seed and an edible fungus (which had recently been developed as an export commodity for China). Prosperity eventually came to the Johnsons and to other settlers in the area with the rise of the Taranaki dairy industry.

SC

'We were pleased to hear that you were getting on so well at the chapel, and to hear good news of all our old friends...Joe...is going sixty miles in a steamboat today, up the country, shearing. I shall feel lonely while he is away, but I do not mind if he gets along well; he has plenty of work...He earned £2.15s. last week, and said he had worked harder in the old country for 15s. If you want to come out of bondage into liberty come out here.'

Extract from a letter written by Louisa Johnson from Careys Bay, Otago Harbour, New Zealand, 28 October 1874

Union and rural protest against low wages and poor employment conditions in the Midlands and the south of England, especially in Warwickshire, Oxfordshire, Cornwall and Kent.

With the backing of the Union, many families decided to emigrate. Between 1871 and 1880, the New Zealand government provided 100,679 immigrants with assisted passages. Among them, from Grandborough near Leamington, were Joseph Johnson, shepherd, aged 37, his wife Louisa, and their five young daughters. In the early morning of Saturday 13 December 1873, they joined the emigrant party assembled at Leamington's GWR station to begin the first

Emigrant family
Joseph and Louisa Johnson pictured with their family outside their farm in Taranaki, New Zealand, in 1897. Their experience of personal tragedy and hard work before they were established in their new life was typical of many emigrants from Britain.

IRISH NATIONALISM

Percentage increase in
death rate, 1846–51

%
20–33
10–19
1–9
Population increase

Poor Law Unions in receipt of the largest soup rations in 1847

The Great Famine

In 1845 an outbreak of potato blight caused immense distress in parts of northern Europe. In Ireland it led to a national catastrophe of appalling proportions. The over-dependence of small-hold-ers on the potato had been recognised as danger-ous; but when disaster arrived government response was woe-fully inadequate. Perhaps one million people died, mostly among the poor cottier class in the west. The legacy of bitterness was long-lasting. Britain's right, indeed Britain's competence, to rule Ireland was now questioned.

Nineteenth-century Ireland saw nationalistic feeling expressed in two ways. There was the constitutional or par-liamentary strain, which appeared to have succeeded con-clusively by 1900, when it seemed certain that the Irish parliament, abolished in 1801, would be restored. Home Rule was the main aim: the re-established Irish parliament would settle its domestic policies, while foreign and defence policies would be decided at Westminster. There was also the republican/revolutionary tendency, which challenged it successfully in the second decade of the twen-tieth century. These two tendencies were interconnected: constitutional leaders like Daniel O'Connell and Charles Stewart Parnell often invoked revolution in an attempt to win concessions, and revolutionaries like the Fenians some-times supported constitutional politics. British responses to Irish nationalism also influenced the forms it took.

Daniel O'Connell's first mass political campaign led to the Catholic Emancipation Act of 1829, which allowed Catholics to sit in the Westminster parliament. O'Connell was one of the first generation of Catholic lawyers after the Penal Laws, introduced in the late seventeenth century to exclude Catholics from politics, landholding, education and the professions, were relaxed in the late eighteenth cen-tury. He was also a firm opponent of the Act of Union of 1800, which abolished the Irish parliament. O'Connell's Catholic Association, at its height between 1825 and 1829, mobilised popular support and drew many working-class and small farming people into parliamentary politics.

O'Connell himself forswore violence and sectarianism, but the fact that he went on, after 1829, to run a campaign for Repeal of the Union strengthened the identification of Catholic with nationalist in popular perceptions. The Repeal campaign ran aground in 1843 when the govern-ment banned a proposed 'monster meeting' at Clontarf. O'Connell, who had always stressed his loyalty to the Crown, acquiesced in this. A breakaway group called the Irish Confederation, or Young Ireland, saw this as a betray-al, and staged an unsuccessful revolt in 1848, the year of political and social revolution all over Europe.

FAMINE AND LAND REFORM

It was also in 1848 that the mortality rate from the Great Famine, which had begun in 1845–6, began to taper off, though devastation and starvation were still in evidence. Government relief policy was inadequate because of the conviction that too-generous relief would 'demoralise' a class of cottiers, labourers and small farmers already viewed as over-dependent and idle. The Poor Inquiry Com-mission of 1836 had estimated that some 2 million of the population hovered on the brink of destitution and had pleaded in vain for public works, assisted emigration and other reforms to offset the dangers of a large-scale failure of the potato. The commission was proved tragically right as starvation, famine fever and panic mass emigration reduced the Irish population from 3.5 to 2 million in these years.

The fact that the famine victims were almost all rural-dwellers brought renewed attention to the conditions under which rural people lived. The overwhelming majority of farmers, labourers and cottiers, from the 200-acre grazier to the one-acre cottier, paid rent to a landlord. While con-ditions varied from one estate to another, leases in general were insecure, and tenants' rights to improve or to sell their interest in the property were limited. Following the exam-ple of Young Irelander James Fintan Lalor, several Irish MPs over the succeeding decades demanded the introduc-tion of 'tenant right' – the crucial element in agrarian reform. Meanwhile, rising agricultural prices in the 1850s and 60s brought a rise in the standard of living for all but the poorest farmers, while the coming of the railways and consequent development of towns and retailing forged links between the farmers and the town-dwellers that would prove to their mutual political benefit in 1879.

The Fenians, or Irish Republican Brotherhood, founded in 1858, took little interest in agrarian matters, but their revolutionary activities drew such attention to Irish grievances in general that one of William Gladstone's first statements on becoming Prime Minister in 1868 concerned his intention to 'pacify Ireland.' His Land Act of 1870 was later criticised for not going far enough, but at the time it constituted an unprecedented interference with landlord power. By responding to a separatist demand with an agrarian concession, Gladstone helped to set the nationalist agenda for the next two decades, when Fenians and constitutionalists alike turned their attention to land reform.

THE HOME RULE PARTY

From the 1830s, almost all of nationalist Ireland supported the Liberals (or O'Connellite variations); the 1868 map outlines clearly the loyalties of the Irish electorate before the founding of the Home Rule League in 1873. Irish MPs who supported the restoration of the Dublin parliament and demanded legislative independence for Ireland within the empire formed a vocal, though loosely disciplined, 'Irish' or 'Home Rule' Party.

It was the 'land war' (1879–82) that established this party as the leaders of nationalist Ireland. A succession of poor hay and turf harvests combined with economic depression to produce an agricultural and social crisis in 1879. Near-famine conditions in the West and unusual hardship even among the bigger farmers in the South and East united tenants of all sizes against the one burden they had in common – the obligation to pay rent in a land-holding system that was at best insecure, and at worst oppressive. They were supported by many townspeople. Charles Stewart Parnell, a nationalist MP, assumed presidency of

A Home Rule meeting
By 1886 Home Rule was arousing strong emotions. Here, the police are shown protecting a government reporter who is observing Charles Stewart Parnell's followers.

the League, and shortly afterwards of the Home Rule party. Significant concessions were wrung from a Liberal government – land courts were set up, and eventually, in 1882, the government agreed to pay rent in arrears on behalf of impoverished tenants, bringing the 'land war' to a close. When the Land League was transformed into the Irish National League in the same year, Parnell's party had a ready-made constituency organisation. Gladstone's conversion to the Home Rule cause followed, in 1885–6, and thereafter, as can be seen from the electoral maps, in all but two constituencies in the northeast, support for the Liberals meant support for Home Rule.

The Liberal Alliance gave Gladstone considerable authority in defining Irish parliamentary nationalism. The 'Union of Hearts', as the alliance was known, was only strengthened by the exposure in 1889 of the perhaps unwitting complicity of *The Times* in the publication of forged documents linking Parnell with nationalist violence. However, the illusion of equality between Parnell and Gladstone was shattered in 1890–1, when Gladstone demanded that the Home Rule party replace Parnell as leader following his involvement in a highly-publicised divorce case in 1890. Parnell's popularity had already been damaged in agrarian circles in Ireland, when he distanced himself from the 'Plan of Campaign' (1886–91), a well-publicised movement for rent reduction. The party split in 1890–1, and a slender majority of Home Rule MPs voted to depose Parnell – but the Second Home Rule Bill passed the House of Commons in 1893. In 1900 the Home Rule party was reunited under the leadership of John Redmond. The electoral map for that year shows the triumph of the party in all but a small corner of Ireland.

Irish Politics in 1868
In 1868 the new Liberal Prime Minister, William Gladstone, determined to address Ireland's grievances. He had little choice, for Irish votes and support were vital to his party. In the event, however, he was never able to go far enough or fast enough to satisfy Irish nationalists.

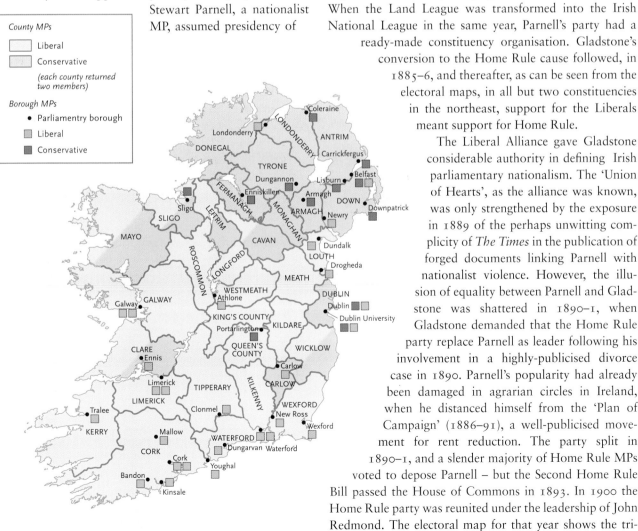

County MPs
☐ Liberal
☐ Conservative
(each county returned two members)

Borough MPs
● Parliamentry borough
☐ Liberal
☐ Conservative

Map labels: Coleraine, Londonderry, LONDONDERRY, ANTRIM, DONEGAL, Carrickfergus, TYRONE, Dungannon, Lisburn, Belfast, Enniskillen, FERMANAGH, Armagh, DOWN, Sligo, LEITRIM, MONAGHAN, ARMAGH, Downpatrick, SLIGO, Newry, MAYO, CAVAN, Dundalk, ROSCOMMON, LONGFORD, LOUTH, Drogheda, MEATH, WESTMEATH, Athlone, DUBLIN, Galway, GALWAY, Dublin, KING'S COUNTY, Dublin University, Portarlington, KILDARE, QUEEN'S COUNTY, WICKLOW, CLARE, Ennis, Carlow, Limerick, CARLOW, TIPPERARY, KILKENNY, LIMERICK, Clonmel, WEXFORD, Tralee, New Ross, KERRY, Mallow, Wexford, WATERFORD, CORK, Dungarvan, Waterford, Cork, Youghal, Bandon, Kinsale

A cartoon by George Morrow from the newspaper The Republic *in 1906 sums up Irish attitudes to British rule from the late 19th century onwards. Even moderate nationalists and the uncommitted felt that John Bull – the 'Stranger' here – had overstayed his welcome in Ireland.*

Unionist Ulster had maintained a vocal and effective opposition to Home Rule since 1885, in alliance with the Conservatives. The predominantly Protestant population in the four northeastern counties of Ulster feared domination by Catholics and a decline of their industrial prosperity, which was heavily dependent upon the imperial connection, if Home Rule were granted. Nationalists saw unionist opposition to Home Rule as the manipulation of misguided Irish people by cynical Conservatives, and underestimated it right up to 1922. The Conservatives, in government more or less continuously from 1885 to 1906, tried to neutralise support for Home Rule by a vigorous programme of reform. One land act after another in the 1880s and 1890s made it easier for tenants to buy their holdings, until the eventual introduction of compulsory purchase and abolition of the landlord system in 1903. Conservatives also invested in the poverty-stricken west, and brought in local government reforms. Nonetheless, nationalism survived; Conservative policies, with their emphasis on economic and social self-determination, may even have strengthened the cultural nationalism of the last two decades of the century.

The so-called 'Gaelic revival' of these years drew many into a self-conscious, self-confident expression of nationalism. The two biggest organisations attracted members of all classes, in town and country, women as well as men, and offered 'something for everyone' – sport, Irish language classes, the publication of Irish literature, the staging of *feiseanna* (competitions of Irish singing, dancing and music). The Gaelic Athletic Association

The STRANGER in the house

(GAA), founded in 1884, revived and codified hurling, Gaelic football and other native sports, fostering local and national loyalties. Royal Irish Constabulary men and members of the British forces were barred from membership, which made explicit the nationalist aims of the organisation. The Gaelic League, founded by Douglas Hyde in 1893, was not specifically nationalist at all, and included unionists who shared an interest in the revival of the Irish language and traditions. Many of those involved in the 1916–22 revolution, however, traced their emergent consciousness back to involvement in the League, the GAA, or similar organisations. The centenary commemorations of the 1798 rebellion used the language of cultural nationalism rather than republicanism, but protests against the visit of Queen Victoria in 1900 suggested that nationalists might not be content to remain within the empire; Arthur Griffith's Cumann na nGaedheal (later called Sinn Féin) was founded in the same year. The title, if not the founding principles, of this organisation, which was committed to dual monarchy (along Austro-Hungarian lines), non-violence and economic nationalism, would become a rallying point for all non-Home Rule nationalists, including socialists and republicans, after the 1916 Rising.

Irish politics in 1900

By 1900 the greater part of Ireland was solidly behind Home Rule. Political support for Home Rule was underpinned by a self-confident revival in Irish culture, fostered by organisations such as the Gaelic Athletics Association and the Gaelic League. In the northeast, opposition to any degree of Home Rule was becoming increasingly vocal and intransigent. The determination of the Protestant majority here to avoid domination in a Catholic state was continually underestimated by nationalist leaders.

Rural constituency MPs

☐ Unionist

☐ Nationalist

☐ Liberal Unionist

Urban constituency MPs

◼ Unionist

◼ Nationalist

◼ Liberal Unionist

All constituencies, urban or rural, returned a single MP

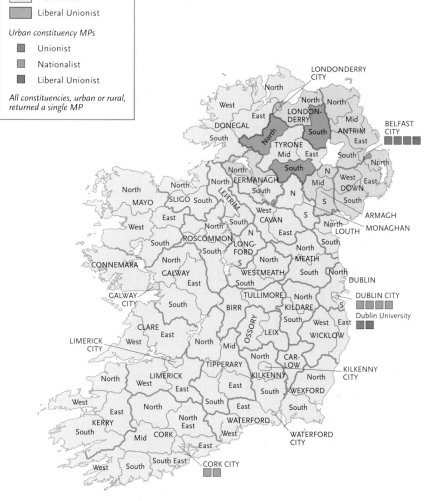

'Hell is not hot enough, nor eternity long enough, to punish these miscreants,' declared Bishop Moriarty of Kerry of the Fenians. Though numbers are notoriously hard to gauge, it seems that about 40,000 or 60,000 people, mainly lower-middle-class and working-class Catholics, ignored this condemnation. The Irish Republican Brotherhood, or 'Fenian Brotherhood', was founded simultaneously in Ireland and the USA in 1858 by James Stephens, Michael Doheny, John O'Mahony and Jeremiah O'Donovan Rossa. The involvement of Irish Americans was crucial from the start, not just for their contribution to propaganda and fund-raising, but also because they could supply arms and military experience; support was strong among Union veterans of the American Civil War. In Ireland, the Fenians were an oath-bound secret society on the model of continental organisations; it is possible that relatively few members seriously expected to participate in an armed rebellion.

The greatest impact of the Fenians on mainstream Irish politics was, arguably, after their failed rebellion of 1867. The execution of the 'Manchester Martyrs' William Allen, Michael Larkin and Michael O'Brien, and the large-scale imprisonment of Fenian suspects, focused the attention of British Liberals on Irish grievances, and also aroused sympathy among constitutional nationalists. In 1879 the Fenians decided to suspend armed revolution and to ally with the dynamic, Parnell-led wing of the fledgling Home Rule Party; Michael Davitt, who had been imprisoned in England for Fenian activities, shared the leadership of the land agitation. The Fenians were always more powerful in memory than they were in actuality, and the oral and written Fenian tradition was an important element in the develop-

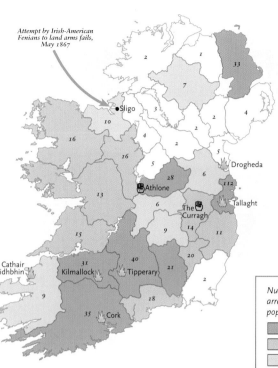

ment of alternatives to parliamentary nationalism in the closing years of the nineteenth century. The Fenians, or IRB as they were more commonly known by this date, played a key role in the 1916 Rising.　　CC

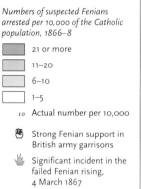

Numbers of suspected Fenians arrested per 10,000 of the Catholic population, 1866–8

- 21 or more
- 11–20
- 6–10
- 1–5
- *10* Actual number per 10,000
- Strong Fenian support in British army garrisons
- Significant incident in the failed Fenian rising, 4 March 1867

The Fenians

The Irish Republican Brotherhood, or Fenians, were founded in 1858. Despite Irish-American support, their attempt to launch a rebellion in 1867 proved no threat to British power. The fact that they kept republicanism alive as an alternative to Home Rule, however, came to have considerable importance later – during and after the 1916 Rising.

A Fenian attack

A contemporary depiction of a dynamite attack on Scotland Yard, London, in 1884. Such acts of terrorism tended to alienate British support for Irish reforms, but they did serve to keep the spirit of Irish republicanism alive.

THE LABOUR/CO-OP MOVEMENTS

The Rochdale Pioneers
Founding the first modern cooperative in Rochdale in 1844, with their first shop in Toad Lane, the Pioneers established the principles of consumer cooperation.

Cooperatives and trade unions

Working-class self-help or self-protection organisations grew rapidly in the 19th century. Many workers felt the need to make provision to avoid the much-feared Poor Law; skilled workers sought to combine together to defend their livelihoods in an era of rapid technological development. The relaxation of draconian anti-union legislation and rising affluence among unskilled workers allowed them to take part in the union movement as well. Self-help could also be found among cooperatives, who divided profits among their members.

The development of mutual assistance organisations to protect livelihoods, skills, working conditions and living standards was a very important aspect of the industrialisation process in Britain. Personal security against the vagaries of illness, accident, unemployment and the trade poverty cycles mattered a great deal to the nineteenth-century working class. Friendly societies, which provided mutual insurance against sickness and injury, and guaranteed a respectable funeral, became almost ubiquitous in the middle decades of the nineteenth century. This took place in the aftermath of the Poor Law Amendment Act of 1834, the most important effect of which was probably the stigmatisation of the recipients of poor relief, and thus an increase in the perceived need for voluntary provision of all kinds. The expenditure that the friendly societies allocated to conviviality and ceremonial helped make them attractive, but it compromised their respectability in the eyes of social superiors, who found the combination of thrift and boozy enjoyment difficult to reconcile with their own values. Their coverage spread from their industrial heartlands in Lancashire and West Yorkshire, with rapid expansion in the mid-Victorian years in the low-wage

southern agricultural counties. Trade unions offered similar benefits, especially in the more prosperous trades, as an attraction to members, and there was a good deal of overlap in function between trade unions and friendly societies.

Friendly societies, trade unions and consumer cooperative societies, the most important of the predominantly working-class mutual assistance associations, are often presented as 'self-help' organisations; but they were as much about self-protection as self-advancement, and much more about solidarity than individualism. Their social side, indeed, was an important attraction. Trade unions, as the guardians of wages and a measure of autonomy and control at work (the 'formal' as opposed to the 'real' subordination of labour), and especially of the privileged positions of 'aristocrats of labour' (those who had served apprenticeships to attain recognised skills and had something to lose), looked after the interests of producers. Cooperatives, on the model associated with the Rochdale Pioneers of 1844, were identified with consumers. Each reflected the regional (and

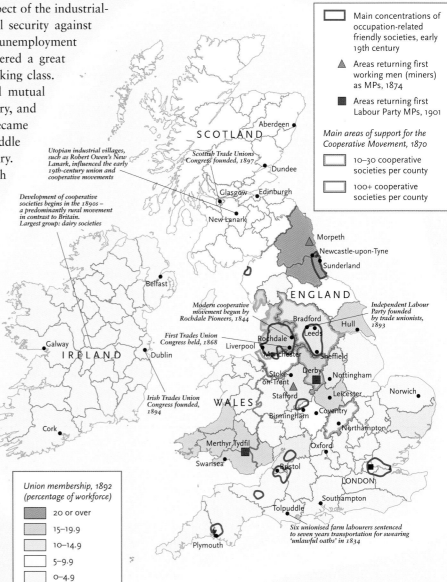

Main concentrations of occupation-related friendly societies, early 19th century

▲ Areas returning first working men (miners) as MPs, 1874

■ Areas returning first Labour Party MPs, 1901

Main areas of support for the Cooperative Movement, 1870

10–30 cooperative societies per county

100+ cooperative societies per county

Utopian industrial villages, such as Robert Owen's New Lanark, influenced the early 19th-century union and cooperative movements

Development of cooperative societies begins in the 1890s – a predominantly rural movement in contrast to Britain. Largest group: dairy societies

Modern cooperative movement begun by Rochdale Pioneers, 1844

First Trades Union Congress held, 1868

Independent Labour Party founded by trade unionists, 1893

Irish Trades Union Congress founded, 1894

Six unionised farm labourers sentenced to seven years transportation for swearing 'unlawful oaths' in 1834

Union membership, 1892
(percentage of workforce)

- 20 or over
- 15–19.9
- 10–14.9
- 5–9.9
- 0–4.9

local) distribution of working-class strengths and circumstances.

The spread of trade unions, as they became increasingly formally organised and visible after the repeal of the Combination Acts in 1824, and especially as trade picked up and government and employers became less implacably hostile towards mid-century, followed the rise of the workshop and factory trades. Growth was particularly strong across the coalfields of the industrial North, although the miners themselves were slow to sustain effective organisation. Skilled workers led the way, as they were better able to pay regular subscriptions and use their literacy to organise beyond the workplace, and their jobs and conditions were often threatened by technological innovation in the 1830s and 1840s. Their insecurity, coupled with angry reactions to government threats to union organisation in the mid-1830s, helped to push many trade unionists into active involvement in Chartism, the great campaign for male democracy between 1838 and the 1850s.

OLD AND NEW UNIONS

A well-developed example of an early Victorian trade union (although untypical in its centralised organisation) was the Amalgamated Society of Engineers, the classic so-called 'New Model Union' of skilled industrial workers, which ramified wherever the engineering industry had strongholds or outposts, and looked after its members wherever they travelled in search of work. But there were also older, locally based craft unions that were strongly and sometimes violently resistant to innovation, as in the Sheffield cutlery and metal trades. When the Trades Union Congress was founded in 1868, the main strongholds were the Lancashire and Yorkshire textile districts, the steel and cutlery trades of the Sheffield area, the mining, shipbuilding and metal-working industries of the northeastern coalfield, the mining and heavy industries of the South Wales valleys, and the wide range of industries (including shipbuilding as well as mining, metal-working and textiles) in the Scottish industrial lowlands between Glasgow and Edinburgh.

As legal restraints were lifted in the 1870s, it became less difficult for trade unions to spread to 'unskilled' groups, who were more vulnerable to substitution by 'blackleg' labour. The growth of waterfront and related unions in the great seaports helped to change the geography of the movement, although their strength ebbed and flowed spectacularly with the trade cycle. In 1891, on the crest of the cycle, officially recorded trade union membership had penetrated deepest in Northumberland, Durham, industrial Lancashire, Yorkshire and Derbyshire, and South Wales. It remained at a very low ebb across the Home Counties, southwest England, most of Wales and most of East Anglia, despite a rise in agricultural trade unions in the early 1870s.

The same geographical pattern applies to the development of consumer cooperatives. Cooperation originated as a movement based on the doctrines of the radical mill owner Robert Owen, and was an attempt to build virtuous alternative societies based on a fair distribution of the rewards of labour, whose superiority to corrupt competitive capitalism would gradually prevail. To raise funds for these Owenite communities, shops were established, with the surpluses going towards the next stages of cooperative manufacturing and agriculture. Dozens of such societies were established during the 1820s and 1830s, mainly in the industrial north of England.

The extra dimension that sparked a major movement was provided by Lancashire's Rochdale Equitable Pioneers in 1844. They decided that the profits from sales, after meeting expenses, including those necessary for the expansion of the business, should be divided among the members in proportion to their spending at the store. This 'dividend' enabled working-class consumers to save while they spent, and its attractions provided the basis for a tremendous expansion in consumer cooperation (extending to housing, manufacturing and insurance) through the second half of the nineteenth century. News of the success of early co-operative societies rippled through the textile towns, villages and even hamlets around Rochdale, on either side of the Lancashire–Yorkshire border, during the 1850s, and local societies began to multiply further afield. By 1870, Yorkshire had 121 societies of varying sizes, and Lancashire 112, followed by Durham (28), the Northamptonshire footwear district (21), Northumberland (18) and Cheshire and Derbyshire (17). At this stage there were only six societies within 20 kilometres (about 12 miles) of London.

Wherever the Chartist legacy was strong, and trade union commitment coexisted with hard-working, thrifty Nonconformity, there cooperation took early root. Falling prices and rising working-class living standards in late Victorian times made it compatible with popular pleasures like football and the seaside, as more people could afford to save and spend, or to save in order to spend. The community-building ideal, while it did not disappear, became the preserve of a committed minority as cooperation became a mass movement. By 1899, 1,531 cooperative societies in Great Britain had over 1.6 million members, and in heartlands like 'cotton Lancashire', practically every household included a cooperator. London, the great sea ports and even the popular resorts were catching up with the older industrial centres by this time, and cooperation and the trade unions marched in step (though they rarely collaborated, except when local societies offered special help to strikers). As a more widely supported movement that drew in women as well as men, and pulled in whole families as consumers, the cooperative (with its proto-feminist Women's Guild) had an even bigger impact than the better-documented trade unions. The geographical influence of the two movements is best understood if they are regarded as two sides of the same coin.   **JKW**

Certificate of union membership

The Amalgamated Society of Engineers was a union for skilled industrial workers, and was the third largest union in Britain by 1890. In 1897–8 it fought long, hard and unsuccessfully for an eight-hour day.

WORKING-CLASS HOUSING

Sunderland slum, c.1889

Squalor was all too often the fate of the industrial working class. By-laws might regulate new housing; clearing slums such as these was to take longer.

Leon Faucher and Friedrich Engels, both writing in 1844, identified in Manchester the process of social and residential segregation that was typical of so many towns and cities in mid-Victorian Britain. Faucher and Engels identified the 'Two Nations' of Britain, as captured in Disraeli's novel *Sybil* (1846), in which the poor were spatially separated from an emerging middle class increasingly housed in a rural or suburban idyll of villas and private gardens. With their strengthening purchasing power, the middle classes were able to move away from town centres to genteel suburbs with their domesticity and security.

Population growth on a scale never experienced before or since averaged 30 per cent per decade in English boroughs in the 1810s and 1820s; overall, the urban population doubled between 1801 and 1831, in an era when there were no building controls, planning or environmental policies. It was the equivalent of housing an additional 50 million people in present-day British towns and cities without any regulatory framework whatsoever. Bradford expanded by 66 per cent in the 1820s; Salford by 56 per cent; Leeds,

Liverpool and Manchester by 46 per cent each, and Sheffield and Birmingham by over 40 per cent. These were city-wide averages; sub-districts grew even faster.

A HOUSING CRISIS

In the first half of the nineteenth century, very few houses were purpose-built for the British urban working classes. Instead, the existing housing stock was 'made down' (subdivided into many rooms) as the wealthy quit the increasingly hostile physical and moral environment of the city centre for houses some distance away. Alternatively, outhouses and courtyards were adapted and back-to-back housing developed.

By the 1840s, 12 per cent of the population of Manchester lived underground in cellars; in Liverpool, 20 per cent lived in this way. In Leeds, in 1851, there were over 220 common lodging houses within a quarter-mile radius of the parish church and these provided shelter each night to about 2,500 people, at an average of 2.5 per bed and more than 4.5 to a room. Shelter in Leeds, London and other major urban centres was often not much more than sub-let floor space in a sub-culture of dens and brothels, shown

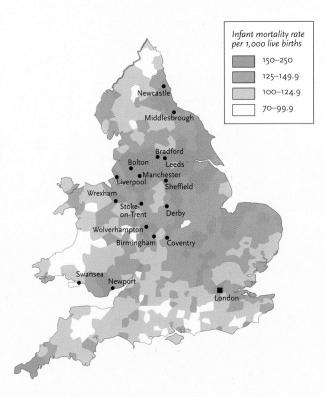

landowners any more likely to produce coherent housing development than a more fragmented pattern of land ownership. More important in determining housing quality was, on the supply side, the role of speculative builders, the extreme fluctuations in the house-building industry itself, and the zoning effect of mid-century railway developments. On the demand side, the stability of employment and the level of household incomes were crucial. In Leicester, for example, where female employment in the hosiery trade complemented a male workforce mainly occupied in the boot and shoe industry and in engineering, steady household incomes contributed to a housing stock that on the eve of World War I was superior in quality and amenities to that of over a hundred other English towns and cities.

A NEW VISION

Housing quality improved ultimately because of four linked developments in the final quarter of the nineteenth century: rising real wages, smaller family sizes, slum clearance, and compulsory building by-laws. Together, these resulted in improved dietary, sanitary and environmental conditions. The 'by-law' terrace house became an almost universal English working-class housing form, as housing around central courtyards was opened up, cellar-dwelling banned, and back-to-back house-building suspended.

The nature of twentieth-century housing was influenced by the block dwellings of the Peabody (London) and Guinness Trusts (London and Dublin), and by those by the newly formed London County Council in the 1890s, which were much criticised by their tenants. Company housing, though it achieved little in quantitative terms at Saltaire (Bradford), Port Sunlight (Cheshire), New Earswick (York) and Bournville (Birmingham), did emphasise perspectives, planted boulevards, curves and an explicitly traditional English cottage design, and was associated with an emerging concept of garden cities, as championed by Ebenezer Howard, and later by Raymond Unwin and Barry Parker at Letchworth. These design developments were an important legacy for twentieth-century housing. They offered an alternative vision of society to that of the nineteenth century, when speculative, mass-produced housing underpinned an urbanising society that depended on cheap labour to compete in world markets.   **RR**

memorably, for example, in Charles Dickens's 1837–8 novel *Oliver Twist*.

For many Victorians, housing conditions and morality were interconnected issues. This relationship was brought under closer scrutiny after 1837 (in England) and 1855 (in Scotland), when details of the causes of death began to be recorded in the Registrar General's annual reports on births, marriages and deaths. The correlation between poverty and housing conditions became widely publicised through Edwin Chadwick's *Report on the Sanitary Condition of the Labouring Classes* (1842).

The conditions in British cities contributed to the process of suburbanisation from about 1850, as the middle classes increasingly sought to distance themselves from the moral and physical degeneration identified with town centres. Infant mortality rates, a sensitive indicator of the relationship between poverty and death, show how, in the 1860s, this was closely associated with urban districts and, in London, with the central part of the city. Indeed, moving away from London to housing with more generous space significantly reduced infant mortality.

Though in Scotland a distinctive system of land tenure contributed to levels of overcrowding far more extreme than elsewhere in Britain, in England overcrowding was as likely in rented (leasehold) as in privately owned (freehold) property. Nor was the dominance of two or three major

Infant mortality, 1861–70
The map shows a fairly clear correlation between areas of intense industrialisation and high infant mortality. Rapid urban population growth caused intense pressure on existing housing. The entrepreneurial response, being free of any form of regulation, was to subdivide larger properties or construct cramped new housing for rent. Only slowly were steps taken to regulate the standards of housing built for the working class.

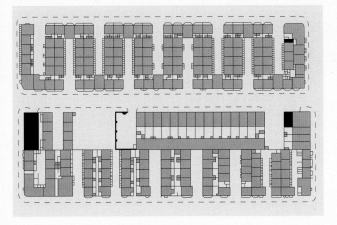

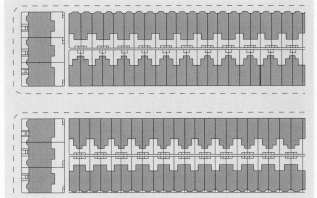

Working-class housing in Liverpool
Working-class houses (left) from the early 19th century, many back-to-back, generally overcrowded and with shared privies, were usually appalling slums. In comparison, the 'by-law' houses of the 1870s (right), built under local authority regulation, were larger, more pleasant and healthier.

BRITAIN'S OVERSEAS TRADE

From about 1780 Britain began the rapid economic and social transformation known as the Industrial Revolution. New technology employed by private entrepreneurs, aided by stable governments and sound public credit, stimulated rapid commercial growth. By about 1800, Britain's domestic market was no longer large enough to absorb the rising output of industry, and overseas markets had become essential to maintain economic growth. While the Napoleonic wars, and the dislocation that followed them, hampered the development of Britain's trade, it began to grow rapidly in the 1820s. Britain had a near monopoly on the production of cotton goods, which provided well over half of the nation's exports until the middle of the century. Cheap, washable and easily dyed, British cotton manufactures were in huge demand. Technological developments and falling costs of raw materials led to a steady fall in prices, but the volume of exports expanded so much that their value remained stable. Initially, Britain exported to Europe and North America, its traditional markets, but as these markets began to develop their own industries, the British sought new markets, in the Middle East, Africa, Australia, Latin America and especially India. The destruction of India's domestic handicrafts industry by cheap British imports appeared to guarantee a permanent mass market.

Britain's commercial might did not, however, depend purely on textiles. Through the nineteenth century there were steady developments in the metal industries. These did not involve dramatic technological innovations, but small improvements involving simple machinery and, for example, better methods of refining and tinplating. There was a heavy demand for small metalwares and cutlery in America, where two-thirds of exports were sent in the first half of the century. The discovery of gold in Australia in the 1850s stimulated a new large-scale market. There was also a demand for the machinery and steam engines essential for industrialisation by Britain's emerging continental and American rivals which, by mid-century, accounted for about 10 per cent of British exports. Even more important,

> 'The English nation have a strength of individual character among them, which enables them to do for themselves by free choice, energy, and judgement, much that in other countries, except for the interference of public authority, would not be done at all.'
>
> William Gladstone, *Gleanings from Past Years*, Volume V (1879)

British overseas trade

In the course of the 19th century Britain developed and came to dominate a world economy. Based initially on textiles, British exports became increasingly diversified. Imports also expanded; indeed, food imports became essential to feed a quickly growing population. Eventually it would be the earnings from large-scale foreign investments and other 'invisible' earnings that would keep Britain financially afloat.

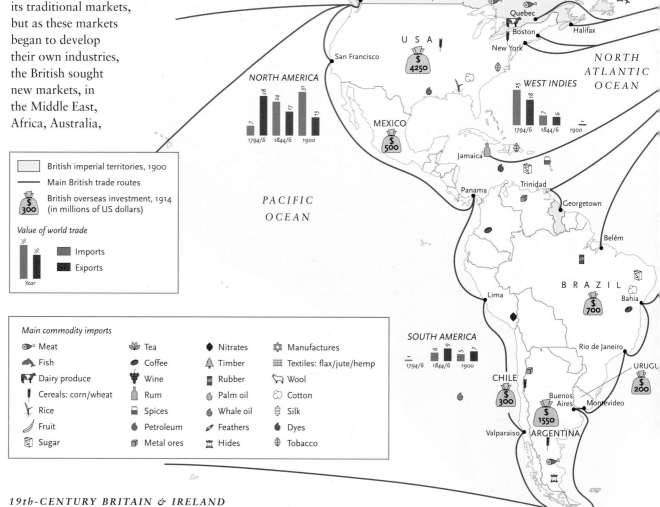

from the 1840s, was the huge demand for the simply made products such as rails, wheels and frames for rolling stock necessary to build railways. Initially, these were exported to Europe, but that demand was outstripped in the 1850s by the much greater needs of America. Australia and Asia also provided lesser, but still significant, markets.

As the century progressed, British exports became more diversified. Some were the products of industrialised and modernised processes. New industrial techniques helped the pottery industry to reach a worldwide market. But modernisation was not necessarily essential for an export industry. The leather and saddlery industry remained stubbornly old-fashioned and based on the work of independent craftsmen, yet it surpassed the pottery industry's contribution to the export market. With all these various industries taken together, Britain was providing perhaps 40 per cent of the world's manufactured goods by the middle of the nineteenth century. The spread of steam power, for both railways and shipping, also created a great demand for British coal – the only raw material Britain exported in significant quantities during the century.

In terms of imports, manufactured goods were almost totally absent through much of the century. What British industry demanded were raw materials in unprecedentedly large amounts. Cotton came from America, Brazil, Egypt and India, hides from Argentina, dyes from the West Indies and India, and wool from Australia, New Zealand and South Africa. An even heavier demand grew for foodstuffs. At the beginning of the nineteenth century, Britain was self-sufficient in basic foodstuffs, but developed a great demand for tropical and subtropical products such as tea, sugar and coffee. These had been expensive luxuries in the eighteenth century, but now they became cheap and available to all social classes. Home agriculture was protected by the Corn Law, which restricted imports of basics and kept

The Stock Exchange
Britain's ability to mobilise surplus wealth and invest it productively was crucial.

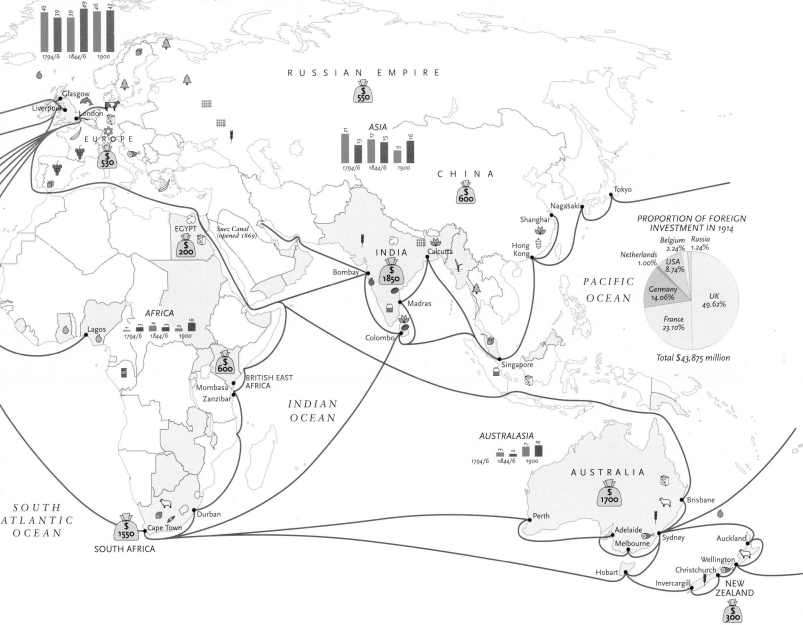

prices high, but by the middle of the nineteenth century, population growth had made basic food imports absolutely essential, and protection was abandoned for free trade. New technology aided food imports: for example, in the 1880s refrigeration made it possible for meat to be brought from Australia and New Zealand. With about a quarter of Britain's food needs being imported by the 1850s, it was essential for national security that the navy kept trade routes open. Another feature of British trade was the thriving entrepôt that was growing in Britain. British traders had the resources to import great quantities of goods, which they could then break down into smaller amounts to sell to foreign markets lacking those resources. This was another vital source of wealth, as imports regularly exceeded exports.

'Multitudes of goods are shipped; railway supplies, iron in all shapes, of all kinds and sizes, sheet, wire, bar, spring, etc.; bales, boxes, casks, wines, spirits, ales, for India, Madagascar, Asia, Persia, the Continent and America.'

Description of Liverpool docks in the 1870s, by an American visitor

OVERSEAS INVESTMENT

After 1870, the world's major nations began to base the value of their currencies on that of gold. The establishment of the gold standard did much to further the dominance of Sterling and of London as the centre of international finance – a process already well under way. The pegging of Sterling to a fixed value in gold made the currency literally 'as good as gold' and a preferred medium of international finance. From the 1850s, a new feature of the international economy, which was to have a profound impact throughout the world, began to develop. This was a huge rise in British foreign investment. From 1870 to 1914 about one-third of British national accumulations of income were exported –

a scale of investment overseas never seen before or since. Britain had ceased to be simply a manufacturer and trader: it had become the principal mobiliser of the resources of other nations, even whole continents, making vast investments in the world's agriculture, industry and commerce. A sudden halt in lending in London could cause recession as far away as Australia. With its vast money market, domination of industry and commerce, and the largest empire in history, it seemed impossible that British power could ever be challenged. Britain had come closer to achieving complete global hegemony than any one nation ever had in the past. So favoured were they that it seemed to many Victorians that God himself must be an Englishman. The British government was quite capable, however, of behaving unscrupulously and using threats or even force to expand or maintain trade – as the Chinese found in 1842, when they tried to halt the opium imports that had done much to ruin China's own economy. But British financial might, and the knowledge that only London could supply the credit that they needed, was usually sufficient to ensure that other nations respected Britain's interests.

British pre-eminence was, however, short lived. In the 1880s the first signs of approaching problems became apparent. Britain's virtual monopoly of industrial methods could only ever be temporary. In Europe and America, industrialisation, stimulated by British investment, soon challenged British market domination. In new technology, for example in the motor car and electrical goods industries, Britain began to lag behind its competitors. In absolute terms, Britain's output and trade steadily increased, but competitors, especially Germany and the USA, were catching up, and threatened to overtake British industry in many sectors. The reasons for this relative decline became the subject of a national debate, to this day not yet resolved. What is clear is that British imports began to outstrip exports by a formidable margin. Only the income from overseas investments, and other 'invisibles' such as shipping and insurance, enabled Britain to pay. By

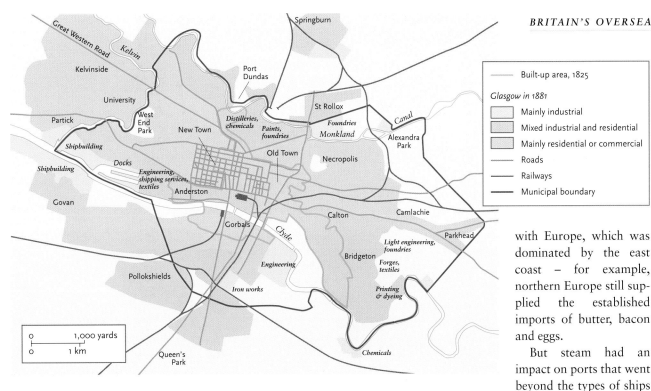

Glasgow in 1881

- Built-up area, 1825

Glasgow in 1881
- Mainly industrial
- Mixed industrial and residential
- Mainly residential or commercial
- Roads
- Railways
- Municipal boundary

0   1,000 yards
0   1 km

Glasgow in 1881

Deep-water docks made the ancient city of Glasgow one of Victorian Britain's greatest industrial cities. Shipbuilding and its associated industries quickly expanded after 1830. Other industries were attracted by low transport costs and a rapidly growing workforce. Textiles, chemicals and distilling were only part of the diversifying economy by 1881. By then, the city and its population were growing at a phenomenal rate.

the end of the century, there was in Britain a rising clamour to abandon free trade and to attempt to turn the empire into a closed economic zone for the benefit of Britain alone.

THE SHIPPING INDUSTRY

The development of a world economy in Britain naturally transformed the nation's shipping industry. Shipping had, of course, long been important – Europe, North America and the Far East were established destinations of British ships – but the tonnage of shipping entering British ports increased dramatically, from under half a million tonnes in 1790 to nearly 50 million tonnes in 1900.

Until the early twentieth century, Britain's tonnage in sailing ships grew steadily, and they remained profitable on many routes. But steam power soon drove sail from the North Atlantic, and with the opening of the Suez Canal in 1869, from the Far East route as well. By the 1870s, the tonnage of British sailing ships was being overtaken by that of British steamships. Britain maintained a dominant position in shipbuilding until at least the 1890s, when the German challenge became significant. Still, in 1914, 60 per cent of the world's tonnage remained British-built. Economies of scale meant that ships became larger, as well as faster and more reliable. Some reached up to 20,000 tonnes, which only the largest deep-water docks could accept. As a result, the oceanic shipping trade became ever more dominated by the largest ports, most notably Liverpool, Glasgow and London. Ownership of these facilities also became concentrated in the hands of a few companies based in these ports. Coastal trade remained important, as did traditional trade

with Europe, which was dominated by the east coast – for example, northern Europe still supplied the established imports of butter, bacon and eggs.

But steam had an impact on ports that went beyond the types of ships and amounts of produce passing through them: from the middle of the century, the railways encouraged the growth of industry in the areas around ports, for the processing of foods for re-export, for example. In addition to this, the need for bunker coal at the many ports of call on steamship routes, and the vast demands of foreign steam-powered equipment, meant that coal itself became a truly enormous export. Virtually all of the ships using Whitehaven, for example, carried coal to Ireland, and about half of the ships leaving British ports by 1900 carried coal. Coal exports rose from 1.6 million tonnes in 1840 to 44.1 million tonnes in 1900. As later events were to show, the entire shipping industry became excessively dependent on this single commodity. But in the last five years of the nineteenth century, shipping brought in £62 million, on average, contributing heavily to the 'invisibles' that prevented economic crisis due to the imbalance between imports and exports.   **JS**

St Katharine's Dock, London

London's elaborate system of docks made it the busiest port in the world in the 19th century.

THE SOUTH AFRICAN WAR

The South African War, also known as the Boer War, was fought between the British and the Afrikaner republics (the South African Republic, or Transvaal, and the Orange Free State) for the dominance of Southern Africa. The origins of the war lie deep in the white conflict over the subcontinent during the nineteenth century. The confirmation of British rule of the Cape, in place of the Dutch, at Vienna in 1815, had inaugurated a struggle that manifested itself in the desire of many of the Dutch Afrikaners, or Boers, to establish their independence. The Great Trek of the Boers from the Cape into the interior in 1835 and subsequent years was followed by repeated attempts on the part of the British to bring them back into the political and legal orbit of the imperial power, culminating in the British annexation of the Transvaal in 1877. Once the Zulu threat to the Boers had been eliminated in 1879, the Boers fought the British and defeated them at Majuba Hill in 1881, in what is often called the first Boer War.

The Pretoria and London conventions of 1881 and 1884 re-established Boer independence, although the British claimed a residual sovereignty, which the Boers disputed. The Jameson Raid of 1896, often described as the first shot of the second Boer War, was a clumsy attempt on the part of Cape Colony Prime Minister Cecil Rhodes, possibly with the complicity of the Colonial Office in London, to overthrow the Transvaal government. Since the discovery of massive gold resources in the Witwatersrand in 1886, the Boer government of Paul Kruger had maintained tight controls over mining activity, stimulating considerable grievances on the part of the mine magnates and their immigrant white workers, or *uitlanders*, many of whom came from Europe. The pretext for the war was the civil rights of the *uitlanders*, including the franchise, which they were denied in the Transvaal. Alfred Milner, the High Commissioner in South Africa, and Joseph Chamberlain, the Colonial Secretary, were probably pursuing imperial strategic goals while claiming to be acting for the *uitlanders*. The international dimension of Britain's involvement is revealed by a congratulatory telegram to Kruger from the German emperor after the failure of the Jameson Raid. A conference between Milner and Kruger at Bloemfontein broke down and Kruger realised that what was in fact at stake was nothing less than the independence of his country. He delivered an ultimatum to the British.

THE COURSE OF THE WAR

The war can be divided into three phases. In the first (October 1899 to January 1900), the Boers achieved a series of victories at Stormberg, Modderrivier, Magersfontein and

The Boer War

When the British provoked a war in South Africa, they never expected the Boers to take the initiative and launch a rapid offensive. Caught unprepared, the British suffered humiliating early defeats. It was only when they moved in heavy reinforcements that they were able to occupy the Boer republics. Even then, the Boers fought on in a protracted guerrilla war that was finally defeated by a ruthless occupation policy on the part of the British.

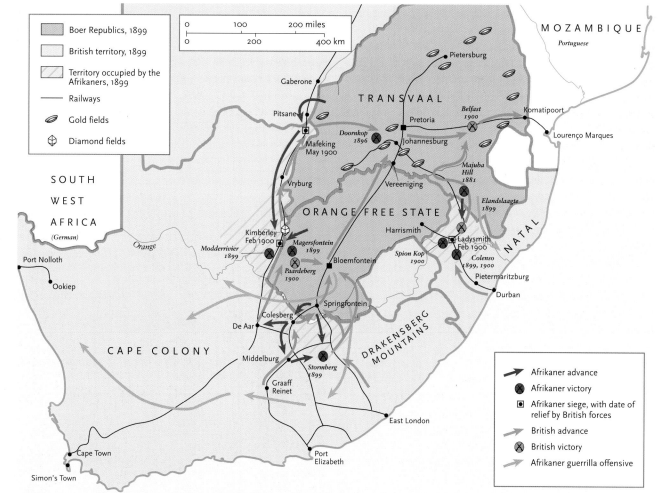

Colenso, as well as successfully laying siege to Ladysmith, Kimberley and Mafeking. British military power, regarded as virtually invincible in the imperial spirit of the time, was seriously shaken.

In the second phase (February to August 1900), Britain poured in huge numbers of troops and mounted a series of counter-offensives under the overall command of Frederick Roberts. The sieges were raised (that of Mafeking, relieved in mid-May 1900, being greeted with great celebration in Britain), a major victory was secured at Paardeberg, and Pretoria, the Transvaal capital, was captured. These British successes appeared to bring the war to an end. The Boers had proved to be a formidable enemy, well armed and having the advantage of knowing the country well. The performance of the British army had been less than satisfactory. British casualties in the war as a whole amounted to 5,774 killed and 22,829 injured – many more than those of their enemies.

The third phase (September 1900 to May 1902) saw extended guerrilla actions by the Boers. Herbert Kitchener, who had replaced Roberts, attempted to break Boer resistance using lines of block houses, a scorched-earth policy, farm burnings, and the concentration of Boer women and children into camps in which medical and sanitary arrangements were so rudimentary that death rates were high.

The conditions in the concentration camps were exposed by the campaigner Emily Hobhouse, among others, and were described by the Liberal leader, Sir Henry Campbell-Bannerman, as 'methods of barbarism'. The British government, which had secured electoral victory in the 'khaki election' of 1900, so called because it traded on sympathy for the British soldiers, sent a women's commission under the suffragist Millicent Fawcett to investigate these allegations. The commission reported that the situation had been considerably exaggerated and placed some of the blame for the conditions upon the Boer women themselves. The South African War was one of the first wars in which the direct agency of women was highly influential.

The war is usually seen as a war between whites, but black Africans were involved on both sides as auxiliaries, grooms, porters, intelligence agents, and in other capacities. Many were also caught up in the sieges. They were often

brutally treated and many died. The white deaths were commemorated through the activities of war graves commissions, but African war cemeteries have only recently come to light, as has the full scale of black involvement.

THE PEACE SETTLEMENT

The Boers won the peace, finally signed at Vereeniging in 1902. They largely maintained control of 'native affairs', and Kitchener conceded to them the right to decide on the African franchise only after they had secured responsible government within the British Empire. The two Boer republics won back representative government in 1907 and the four territories of South Africa – the Transvaal, the Orange Free State, Natal and the Cape – came together not as a federation, but as a Boer-dominated Union, in 1910. The Boers were able to impose their own racial views on the legislation of the Union, which grievously disadvantaged blacks. On the other hand, British economic and strategic interests in South Africa were protected and, despite internal strains, South Africa entered both world wars in the twentieth century on the Allied side.

For the British, nevertheless, the war constituted a considerable shock. The aggressive imperialism of the recent past was halted, at least temporarily, and the imperial authorities were forced to re-think their military arrangements. As a result of the numbers of men rejected for active service on health grounds, considerable attention was given to notions of physical deterioration and theories of eugenics. These suggested that a stronger and healthier 'race' could be created by careful breeding. The war also helped to lead to a long period of Liberal rule from late 1905, and stimulated the political activities of women.   **JM**

British troops in South Africa, 1899
Vast numbers of troops were needed to defeat the two Boer republics. Indeed, severe short-comings in British army training and organisation were exposed by the war, which were largely addressed by 1914.

Boer troops in the field, 1900
The Boers looked less 'professional' than the British, but they had modern weapons and were experts in their use. They were adept at guerrilla warfare, which was to cost the British dearly.

PART FIVE

MODERN BRITAIN & IRELAND

War, economic change and regionalism leading to devolution characterised British and Irish history in the twentieth century. The unified Great Britain of 1914 no longer existed by the end of it, although certain strands of a shared identity remained. The scars left by World Wars I and II were a powerful source of identity for many Britons, and even for some Irish. Both conflicts dealt a devastating blow to British confidence. The battles at the Somme and Passchendaele exposed British and Irish men to the great horrors of war, and questions about the competence of their leaders continue to excite controversy. The agony was repeated between 1939 and 1945. By the end of World War II, Britain had slipped from being the world's second largest creditor to its greatest debtor. Postwar reconstruction proved to be a Herculean task.

The century was also characterised by extensive political restructuring. The electoral franchise was extended, to include women and, from 1969, young people over the age of 18. Although franchise reform was radical, it was overshadowed by an even more dramatic series of political events, which led to the breaking up of Great Britain. The Act of Union, passed by Westminster and Dublin in 1800, was dissolved in 1921 under the Anglo-Irish treaty.

The treaty excluded the 'six counties', which became the province of Northern Ireland within the United Kingdom. This partition of Ireland, after 120 years as part of Great Britain, was a traumatic and bloody event, the ramifications of which are still being felt. More recently, self-government in domestic affairs was granted to Scotland, Wales and Northern Ireland. The principle of the sovereignty of the Westminster parliament was retained but a Scottish parliament was established, as were a Welsh national assembly in Cardiff and a Northern Ireland assembly in Belfast. English regions in the Northeast and Southwest are campaigning for further devolution to regional assemblies.

Economic restructuring accompanied these political shifts. Traditional industries declined, particularly in the 1920s and 1930s, because of a succession of international economic crises, and in the 1960s as a result of the reduction in military expenditure and the loss of the empire. Coal-mining, iron and steel manufacture and shipbuilding all but disappeared from the urban landscape, and the decline in manufacturing trades such as textiles had a devastating impact on levels of unemployment and poverty. Financial industries and services linked to consumption and leisure took over, employing progressively larger proportions of the population.

Some parts of the country were more affected by these economic shifts than others. Economically as well as politically, the north–south divide stayed in place. Privation remained high in Scotland, Wales and the north of England, while wage levels and employment soared in the South. Ireland's economic renaissance in the 1990s was exceptional and is attributed to substantial transfers of subsidies from the European Union.

Cultural changes have been just as radical. The population of the British Isles has always been a mobile one. Despite the stagnation of coastal transport, the expansion and subsequent contraction of the railway network, the dynamic road-building schemes of the 1960s and the appearance of airports transformed the way the British explored their own communities and those further afield. Although some innovative programmes of regeneration were introduced, inner cities decayed. Wales and Scotland were particularly prone to losing their residents. Garden suburbs, industrial estates and New Towns ate into agricultural land. The impact on rural as well as urban communities was immense.

Large numbers of people came into the country from the Indian subcontinent and the Caribbean. By the end of the century, over 5 per cent of the population of Britain was classified as 'ethnic minorities', the bulk living in the South, the Midlands and the industrial north of England.

Power relationships also underwent major shifts in generational terms. Youth politics and the anti-establishment values that burst onto the scene in the 1960s transformed relationships between young people and their elders, as well as between the State and its citizens. Issues of education, lifestyle and popular culture competed with class, ethnicity and politics in the way people saw themselves.

Finally, as Britain declined in influence internationally, it moved closer to Europe economically, politically and culturally. The opening of the Channel Tunnel between England and France signalled a new relationship between the two countries. No longer an 'island standing alone', the United Kingdom was transformed into a group of linked nations looking towards Europe in a way that it previously looked only towards its own centre.

JOANNA BOURKE

THE WAR IN EUROPE 1914–18

When Queen Victoria's long reign finally came to its end in 1901, it seemed, even without the benefit of hindsight, to mark the passing of an era. Under Victoria's elderly son Edward VII, Britain remained the world's leading commercial, colonial and naval power, but its industrial pre-eminence had already passed to Germany and the USA. The determination of Kaiser Wilhelm II to turn Germany into a major naval and colonial power led Britain to abandon its Victorian policy of 'splendid isolation' and to agree the *Entente Cordiale* with its old rival France in 1904. When Germany's provocative encouragement of Austro-Hungarian ambitions in the Balkans led to the outbreak of a general European war in August 1914, Britain, fearing the consequences of the establishment of German hegemony in Europe, did not hesitate to join in. All the participants expected the war to be short and glorious: in the event, it was long and grim.

The British experience of the 'Great War' – as it became known even before it was over – was dominated by the slaughter on the Western Front, where the bulk of the country's land forces were deployed in support of France and Belgium. 'Lions led by donkeys' is a commonplace summation of the British army's performance. That there were lions cannot be doubted – a visit to the Menin Gate at Ypres and the surrounding war graves is all the proof needed. But were they led by donkeys – incompetent generals with no understanding of the horrors their men endured attempting to perform impossible tasks, and whose only response to failure was to repeat their mistakes over and over again? This is a harder question to answer. It is certain that the static warfare that developed on the Western Front was entirely unexpected. All the armies involved struggled to adapt and learn how to gain victory. But the British did seem to be particularly slow learners.

THE STATIC FRONT

The Schlieffen Plan, named after the chief of the German general staff from 1892 to 1906, envisaged a rapid sweep through Belgium and around Paris to catch the French army in the rear and thus defeat France before Russia could fully mobilise, but it soon ran into trouble. The Germans could not advance quickly enough in the face of stubborn rearguard actions by the British (at Mons and Le Cateau), as well as by the Belgians and the French. They therefore took up strong defensive positions of their own choice, which placed them securely in control of much of Belgium and northern France. Soon a static front stretched from Switzerland to the Channel.

For much of the war, the Germans were prepared to stand on the defensive while they concentrated on defeating Russia. It was the British and the French who had to take the initiative. This was to prove remarkably difficult and horrifyingly costly. Given the numbers of troops that both sides concentrated in a comparatively small space, perhaps it is not surprising that neither side could advance. Trenches were, after all, effective: they provided protection from artillery and shelter from which to slaughter attackers struggling to force a way through barbed wire entanglements. No surprise could be gained beyond the first line of trenches, and there were generally three well-separated lines of parallel trenches: by the time the first line was secured, the second line was fully alerted. Frontal attack caused horrific losses. Even when breakthroughs occurred – and the British broke the German lines three times (at Neuve Chapelle and Loos in 1915 and at Cambrai in 1917) – the problems were only beginning. Using massed artillery to smash defences reduced the ground to an impassable morass. Getting reserves and supplies forward to exploit such successes was immensely difficult, and became more difficult and slower the further from their railheads troops advanced. The enemy, meanwhile, was falling back towards its own railheads, reserves and supplies – it was easy to re-establish defensive positions.

The British commanders Sir John French and Sir Douglas Haig believed, however, that the only way to break these defences was to press infantry attacks, whatever the cost. Haig, with powerful press and political friends, was free from government control. He was also a

Retreat from Mons

The shock of defeat and a gruelling retreat shows on the faces of British and Belgian troops in France in August and September 1914. The battles to halt the German advance all but destroyed Britain's small professional army, and a huge recruiting campaign was needed to replace them.

bullying commander who intimidated his subordinates. There was, therefore, no discussion of alternatives. He remained determined to win a glorious British victory.

THE GREAT OFFENSIVES

Haig chose to launch the large new armies raised after the failures of 1914 and 1915 on a decisive offensive on the Somme. The defences here were particularly strong, with three lines, the last two beyond the range of British guns, all incorporating fortified villages and with belts of barbed wire some 27 metres (about 90 feet) across. In order to prevent massive losses, British artillery needed to achieve three tasks: to cut the wire, to destroy the deep shelters

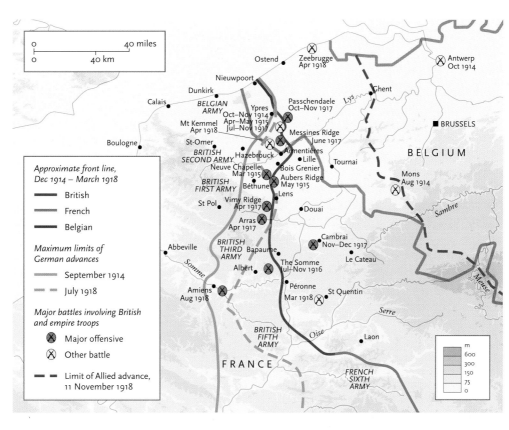

The Western Front
By December 1914 the war of movement was over and British forces had to adapt themselves to static warfare. Despite numerous offensives, breaking the strategic deadlock proved to be both difficult and costly. Only when the great German offensive of March 1918 ran out of steam did British forces finally prove effective in coordinating aircraft, tanks and artillery to win victory.

protecting the German troops, and to silence their artillery. Although the British artillery fired 1.5 million shells, most were shrapnel: the blithe assumption that the lead bullets in the shrapnel would cut barbed wire more effectively than high explosives proved to be tragically unfounded. The deep shelters were believed to have been destroyed and enemy artillery was ignored, as it was too difficult to identify their gun positions. When the British infantry advanced on 1 July 1916, at the walk so as not to break up their formations, it was in fact against positions that had suffered only superficial damage. The resulting massacre is well known. On the first day there were 60,000 casualties – no army in history had known such losses on a single day. They captured 8 square kilometres (about 3 square miles) of territory.

Haig refused to consider cancelling further operations. That would have been an admission of massive failure. Also, it was impossible for him to believe that, after such losses, the Germans were not on the brink of collapse. The battle was pressed until November 1916, by which time mounting British losses threatened to prevent any campaign being fought in 1917. The British attempted to use their new tanks, but they proved too slow and prone to breakdown. Besides, no one was sure how to use them effectively – they were not the decisive weapon that had been hoped for. The British suffered about 420,000 casualties, over 100,000 of them dead. German losses were comparable, but at no point were they in any danger of defeat. Many of the first day's objectives were never taken, and the defences the British faced were as strong as ever. There were in fact more Germans on the Western Front after the battle than there had been before.

To many, the Somme epitomises the futility of the slaughter on the Western Front. It was the bloodiest battle in British history. The losses were measured in thousands; the ground gained measured in yards. Yet perhaps Third Ypres (31 July–6 November 1917; ending with the Passchendaele offensive) was even more futile. Haig was still convinced that the Germans must be near collapse. Superficially, there was some sense in an offensive into Belgium. It was the base from which air raids and U-boat attacks were launched, which caused Britain intense anxiety. To eliminate this danger would indeed be a valuable victory. But attackers here would face a defence far more formidable than anything the Germans could construct – the nature of the land itself. The water table was very high and it was impossible to dig more than 45 centimetres (about 18 inches) without striking water. Two previous battles had already reduced the land to a quagmire. The next battle would render it an impassable sea of mud, into which dead, wounded and healthy alike would sink without trace. British soldiers would learn to fear the mud more than any German defences. It is an easy afternoon's stroll from Ypres to Passchendaele, but it was to take the British over three months to cover the distance. It was to cost them 300,000 casualties. There was never any chance of achieving a breakthrough. The subsequent breakthrough at Cambrai, where tanks were used properly – sent in large numbers in a surprise attack to batter a path through the German lines, unlike the penny-packets in which they had previously been deployed – was little compensation: it proved impossible to exploit and the Germans soon won back the ground they had lost.

It would seem that British military leadership was incapable of learning from its mistakes. Yet this is not the full

'The total casualties are estimated at over 40,000 to date. This cannot be considered severe in view of the numbers engaged and the situation is much more favourable than when we started today.'

Douglas Haig's diary, 2 July 1916

*Expecting to overwhelm
an enemy already
defeated by artillery,
British troops were
slaughtered in their
thousands on the first
day of the Somme
offensive. The 'New
Armies' proved tragically
unprepared for the sort
of war they faced.*

picture. There were minds in all armies grappling with the question of how to find a strategy that would win. The Germans approached this in the most systematic manner. They formed specially armed and trained assault units – 'storm troopers' – to develop new techniques and train others. They learned that small units, armed with a variety of weapons such as grenades, flame-throwers and mortars, could infiltrate and isolate enemy defences, and were highly effective in spearheading attacks. A more sophisticated use of artillery was also important, to silence enemy guns and provide a creeping barrage protecting advancing infantry until the last sec-

ond. Such techniques made their counter-attack at Cambrai successful. General Erich Ludendorff intended to turn the entire German army on the Western Front into storm troopers and smash the British and French in 1918, before the USA could send vast new armies to Europe.

THE DEFEAT OF GERMANY

Initially, the German offensive of March 1918 seemed to offer complete victory. The British, inexperienced in defence, were soon retreating rapidly. There was an air of panic in Allied councils. But while the British bent, they did not break. German supply problems became evident when their troops stopped to loot captured stores. Even more importantly, Allied divisional commanders (especially of the Dominion troops), lacking guidance from their own high command, had already initiated their own training programmes. They were applying in an ad hoc manner the tactical lessons that the Germans had learned more systematically. In coordinating aircraft and artillery and using tanks and aircraft to subdue strong points, the British proved devastatingly effective. Control of the air was decisive. Small assault units with mixed arms used the same tactics as the storm troopers. Also, reinforcements were released, and with French and American help, the German advance was halted. On 8 August the British went on the offensive and delivered what Ludendorff called 'the black day of the German Army', inflicting 75,000 casualties for little loss. Many German troops surrendered readily, realising that the failure of their offensive meant that no hope of victory remained. Using their artillery to blast paths through the wire, rather than attempting the impossible task of battering down all

The home front

The war placed
enormous burdens
on the British people.
Rationing and shortages
affected everybody, and
many civilians were
killed in Zeppelin bomb-
ing raids and German
naval raids on East
Coast towns. Women
were mobilised in large
numbers to meet the
demands of the war
industries. They were
given greater responsi-
bilities than ever before,
though many of these
slipped away after
the war.

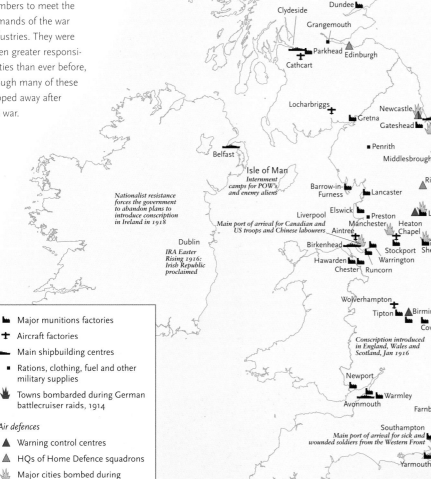

Major munitions factories

Aircraft factories

Main shipbuilding centres

Rations, clothing, fuel and other
military supplies

Towns bombarded during German
battlecruiser raids, 1914

Air defences

Warning control centres

HQs of Home Defence squadrons

Major cities bombed during
Zeppelin raids

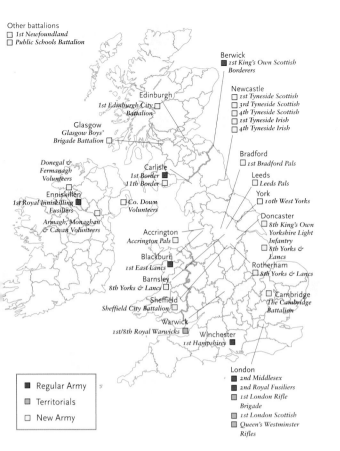

Other battalions
☐ *1st Newfoundland*
☐ *Public Schools Battalion*

Berwick
■ *1st King's Own Scottish Borderers*

Edinburgh
☐ *1st Edinburgh City Battalion*

Newcastle
☐ *1st Tyneside Scottish*
☐ *3rd Tyneside Scottish*
☐ *4th Tyneside Scottish*
☐ *1st Tyneside Irish*
☐ *4th Tyneside Irish*

Glasgow
☐ *Glasgow Boys' Brigade Battalion*

Bradford
☐ *1st Bradford Pals*

Donegal & Fermanagh Volunteers
☐

Carlisle
■ *1st Border*
☐ *11th Border*

Leeds
☐ *Leeds Pals*

Enniskillen
■ *1st Royal Inniskilling Fusiliers*

Co. Down Volunteers
☐

York
☐ *10th West Yorks*

Armagh, Monaghan & Cavan Volunteers
☐

Doncaster
☐ *8th King's Own Yorkshire Light Infantry*
☐ *8th Yorks & Lancs*

Accrington
☐ *Accrington Pals*

Rotherham
☐ *8th Yorks & Lancs*

Blackburn
☐ *1st East Lancs*

Barnsley
☐ *8th Yorks & Lancs*

Cambridge
☐ *The Cambridge Battalion*

Sheffield
☐ *Sheffield City Battalion*

Warwick
☐ *1st/8th Royal Warwicks*

Winchester
■ *1st Hampshires*

London
• *2nd Middlesex*
■ *2nd Royal Fusiliers*
☐ *1st London Rifle Brigade*
☐ *1st London Scottish*
☐ *Queen's Westminster Rifles*

■ Regular Army
■ Territorials
☐ New Army

defences, the British forces went on to break the hitherto impregnable Hindenberg Line in just six days. Germany had finally been defeated on the battlefield.

THE IMPACT IN BRITAIN

World War I committed Britain to the deployment of larger land forces than any previous war. Britain's small professional army, though well trained, was inadequate to the task – so a major recruiting effort was begun almost immediately. National romanticism and general ignorance of the nature of war initially ensured a flood of volunteers. The British Army encouraged volunteers to come forward by forming 'Pals' units, recruited from a single locality with the promise that they would serve together throughout the war. When such units were badly mauled, the impact on their home communities could be catastrophic, and the first day of the Somme came as a shattering blow to many parts of Britain. Illusions of a quick, glorious victory began to evaporate. The casualty lists lengthened, shortages grew more acute and the prospects of victory receded. The first measure for military conscription had to be presented in January 1916. Though it did not meet the mass resistance it encountered when it was threatened in Ireland in April 1918, there was strong opposition from a highly vocal minority. By 1917, there were definite signs of war-weariness and murmurings of dissent in Britain. Though never strong enough to threaten the war effort, they still caused the government intense anxiety, especially after the Bolshevik Revolution in Russia. The Western Front exacted a terrible price in Britain. There was a growing feeling that such a price warranted a matching reward – Britain surely must become a land fit for heroes to live in. When such expectations were not met after the war, bitterness set in, with profound consequences for the post-war years. **JS**

The impact of the Somme offensive

The British army had long had locally based recruitment patterns, especially obvious among the 'Pals' units. This map, which shows battalions that suffered over 500 dead on the first day of the battle of the Somme, demonstrates how devastating the war could be for many communities.

> 'As far as you could see there were all these bodies lying out there – literally thousands of them, just where they'd been caught on the First of July. A terrible sight.'
>
> **Cpl R. Weeber, describing the Somme battlefield**

British troops near Ypres, September 1917
The battle of Passchendaele was both bloody and miserable for the British. The flat land and high water table meant that the ground near the front line was reduced to an impassable sea of mud.

A world war

During World War I a massive coalition was formed to defeat the Central Powers, and British and Imperial forces fought on a worldwide scale. German colonies were seized and the British conquered desirable Ottoman territory. Limited commitments were also made in Italy and Russia. After an unexpected defeat at Coronel, battlecruisers were sent to destroy Admiral Maximilian Graf Von Spee's squadron in the Falklands. Not surprisingly, British resources were stretched very thin indeed.

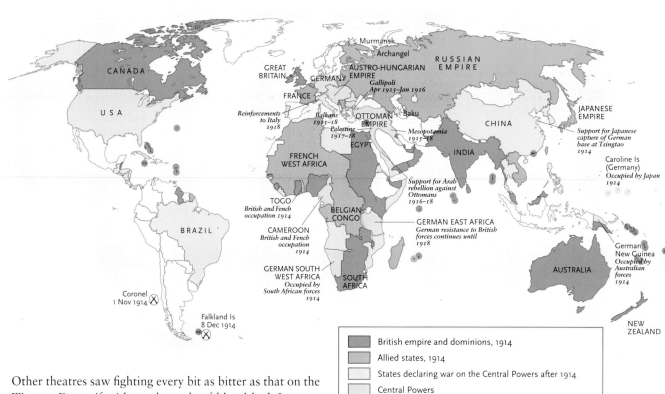

Salonika

British troops are shown arriving at Salonika in 1915. Because of limited resources, Allied soldiers were inactive for a long time and were jeeringly referred to as 'the gardeners of Salonika'.

	British empire and dominions, 1914
	Allied states, 1914
	States declaring war on the Central Powers after 1914
	Central Powers
⊗	Battle (naval)
☆	Anti-Bolshevik intervention in the Russian Civil War, 1918

Other theatres saw fighting every bit as bitter as that on the Western Front, if without the scale of bloodshed. In some theatres, Britain followed the familiar pattern of imperial warfare – keeping sea-lanes open, ensuring the security of British colonies and maintaining British supremacy where it had traditionally been exercised. In other areas, campaigns were initiated to ease problems on the Western Front.

There was much debate in Britain over the opening of new theatres of war against the Turks in Gallipoli, Palestine and Mesopotamia, and against the Bulgarians in Salonika. Germany's Turkish ally was ideally placed to cripple Russia by closing the Dardanelles, which were vital to the Russian economy. It was hoped that by forcing open this route, Britain could enhance the Russian war effort. Was it a useless diversion of resources away from the Western Front – the only place victory could be won? Or was it a sensible policy to seek victory without the futile slaughter seen in Europe? A study of the campaigns seems to suggest that imperial ambitions could have more influence in London than strategy. Indeed, the campaign in Salonika, where no imperial interests were involved and Britain's motive was simply to influence Greece and Serbia, was pursued in such a desultory fashion that the Germans referred to the whole theatre as an 'Allied internment camp'.

MESOPOTAMIA

Initially, the British campaign in Mesopotamia had limited objectives – to capture Basra and so secure Kuwait and the Persian oil fields, and provoke an Arab revolt against the Ottoman Turks. But capturing Basra proved easy, and even if there was no Arab revolt, the temptation to press ahead for further imperial conquests was irresistible. General Townshend's 6th Poona Division continued, aiming to capture Baghdad. Supply and transport problems were simply ignored. In November 1915, however, they met a larger Turkish force at Ctesiphon, and an indecisive battle left the British in a difficult position, lacking water and ammunition, and their wounded suffering terribly as a result of declining medical stores. They retreated to Kut al-Amara, determined to hold the town in expectation of an early relief. The Turks settled in to starve them into submission.

A relief expedition was, of course, ordered – imperial prestige in the Middle East was, after all, at stake. But a

Mesopotamia
The relief of Kut al-Amara was imperative if Britain was to maintain imperial prestige in the Middle East. Unfortunately, incompetent organisation only compounded the problems caused by inadequate roads and heavy rain. Here a British truck has become bogged down in the mud.

mixture of bad weather and incompetent organisation (which was to cause a scandal in Britain) led to it being bogged down only a few miles from the town. Costly attempts to break through all failed. On 25 April 1916, after a five-month siege, the garrison surrendered. Baghdad was not to fall to the British until March 1917.

GALLIPOLI

On the face of it, the Gallipoli campaign was a sensible strategic step. By forcing a passage through the Dardanelles, a vital supply route to Russia could be opened. The Eastern Front would be strengthened – perhaps even the eventual Russian collapse might have been averted. But whether it was ever a realistic aim is questionable. It is certain that initial attempts by the navy in February and March 1915 to batter a way through not only failed, but also alerted the Turks to Allied ambitions.

The defences were formidable, and a landing was an entirely predictable step for the British to take. The British plan was for two landings and a rapid advance inland, which would secure the peninsula before the Turks could react. But the British had no experience in combined operations, especially against heavily defended shores; this would prove tragically costly.

When the landings occurred on 25 April 1915, every-thing that could go wrong, did. The ANZACs (Australia and New Zealand Army Corps) were landed in the wrong place – instead of facing an easy slope, they landed against formidable hills, and were soon fighting desperately. The 29th Division ran into concealed defences on the beaches and suffered massive casualties. Where troops had landed unopposed, instead of moving quickly to outflank the Turks, they did nothing. The British were trapped in their beachheads and the same pattern of trench warfare developed as on the Western Front. Futile and bloody offensives were launched in the conviction that the enemy must be near cracking. Supply problems were so severe that treatment of the wounded was compared to that during the Crimean War at its worst. Casualties mounted at an appalling rate, while the Turks remained as tenacious as ever. Despite huge losses, Turkish morale always remained high.

It eventually became clear that only a further landing at Suvla to outflank the Turks might save the day. When IX Corps landed there, however, instead of rapid movement inland and victory, there was chaos on the beaches and complacency by the commander. The crucial high ground might still have been seized, but no orders were given. It was an utter fiasco and an astonishing display of military incompetence. Once again, the British were trapped in their beachhead. The chance to salvage the campaign was lost. The onset of winter caused immense suffering, and to press on with the campaign without huge reinforcements, which were simply not available, was clearly pointless. In December 1915 the evacuation began. Ironically, after so many failures and blunders, the evacuation itself was carried out with enormous skill and the Turks were astonished to realise that the British positions were empty. But this was small consola-

> *'Chahels is really a horrible spot, Where there isn't a drop of drink to be got, Yet here we're going to be left till we rot, In the Middle of Mesopotamia'*
>
> **BEF Times, 20 January 1917**

Gallipoli
British troops landing at Cape Helles faced formidable defences. Troops aboard the River Clyde, shown here landing on the beach in April 1915, suffered particularly heavy casualties: in many landing boats, every single man was killed or wounded.

tion. The British might have gained a great victory; instead, they suffered over 100,000 casualties for nothing. The scale of the tragedy is well illustrated by the fate of the Munster Fusiliers – 1,000 men landed at Gallipoli in April; when they were evacuated, only 86 men remained fit for duty.

PALESTINE

If the British at Gallipoli were acting to strengthen their hand on the Western Front, and in Mesopotamia for imperialist reasons, their motives in Palestine were more mixed. The defence of the Suez Canal from Turkish attack was vital if imperial communications were to be kept open. At the same time, the Canal area was a convenient place from which to launch an offensive against the Turks. In addition, there was clearly valuable territory to be won for the empire. Lloyd George ever after insisted that victory here knocked the props from under Germany, though as Germany was propping up Turkey here, this seems most unlikely.

The confrontation began with a half-hearted Turkish attack towards the Canal, which was easily defeated. But this pushed the British into making a serious attempt to secure it by driving the Turks out of Palestine. This was no easy task: water pipes and a railway had to be built across the Sinai. Early British offensives in 1917 were mishandled. A new commander, General Sir Edmund Allenby, was appointed. A cavalryman, he saw the value of mounted troops in this terrain and was able to coordinate his cavalry and infantry effectively. In October 1917 he launched a lightning offensive which, after hard fighting, captured Jerusalem in December. In September 1918 a similar assault led to a decisive victory at Megiddo that all but destroyed the Turkish forces. The capture of Damascus followed quickly afterwards.

The Turkish hold over their empire was broken by these campaigns, aided by a revolt the British had stirred up among the Arabs. T. E. Lawrence was to gain renown for his role in this. He later claimed that the Arabs, through their guerrilla warfare, had made a vital contribution to victory and had won their own independence, which should be recognised. Faisal, the son of the Sharif of Mecca, had

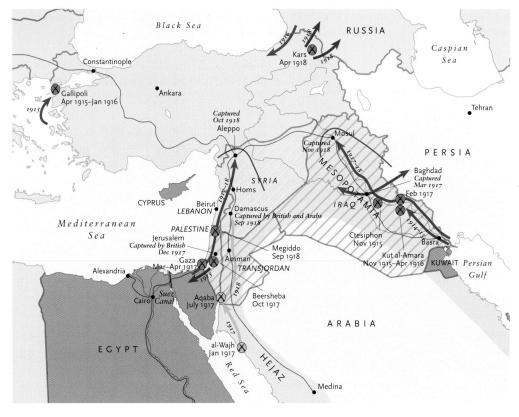

Controlled territory

- British, 1914
- Other Allied territory, 1916–18
- Ottoman empire, 1914
- Other Central power, 1916–18
- Railway

- ⊗ British victory
- ⊗ Arab victory
- ⊗ Turkish victory

Offensives

- → Allied
- → Arab
- → Turkish
- — Limit of Turkish advance, Feb 1915
- — Limit of British advance, Nov 1918

Postwar settlement

- British League of Nations mandate
- French League of Nations mandate

The war in the Middle East, 1914–18

British strategy in the Middle East combined strategic and imperial aims. A breakthrough at Gallipoli might have opened a sea-route to Russia and thus strengthened the Eastern Front. Offensives to drive the Turks back from both Kuwait and Suez had strategic value, but valuable territories could also be won for the empire.

hoped to win a united Arab kingdom with a capital at Damascus. In the event, his claims were ignored. The British and the French, in the Sykes–Picot agreement of May 1916, had already decided on an imperialist partition of the region. This would win Palestine for Britain, and with the Balfour Declaration – a deliberately vague statement of sympathy for a Jewish homeland there, made for propaganda purposes – would also create a political nightmare for the future. In short, imperial interests had once again been the real motive behind the campaign.

AFRICA

British and imperial forces in Africa undertook an imperialist land grab. There was considerable cooperation with the French in this, but also intense suspicion between the two. Most German colonies, like those in the Pacific, were poorly defended and fell easily enough; the major difficulties were the climate and disease. Only in German East Africa was there serious resistance. Here, Colonel Paul von Lettow-Vorbeck fought a brilliant guerrilla war, tying down great numbers of British troops. He did not surrender until the war was over.

THE SEA WAR

It had long been assumed that in a new war the Grand Fleet would play a central role. Indeed, a naval victory on the scale of Trafalgar was expected, if not demanded, by the public. Admiral Sir John Jellicoe certainly wanted to fight such a battle, but he had to bear in mind recent advances in torpedoes, mines and submarines, to which even his most modern Dreadnoughts were vulnerable. There was therefore no close blockade of the German coast and both the British and the Germans chose not to seek battle unless conditions seemed highly favourable. In short, no major naval battle was likely to be fought unless by chance. The German High Seas Fleet was able to venture out occasionally to shell British coastal towns, but did not attempt to challenge Britain's distant blockade, where they might not be able to evade a battle. On the occasions when there were major actions (Dogger Bank, 1915, and Jutland, 1916) a mixture of bad luck, bad leadership and human error prevented the British from using their superiority to the best advantage. There was no decisive victory. But then the British really did not need one – as long as the fleet remained in being and the blockade effective, they were winning the war. The Germans could not break the blockade, and though their attempts to blockade Britain through surface

raiders and, especially, U-boats did cause serious problems and much anxiety, they also brought the USA into the war. By February 1917 the Germans had adopted unrestricted submarine warfare in an effort to starve Britain into submission. Losses grew alarmingly and by April the 600,000 tons the Germans thought they needed to sink every month had been exceeded. The Royal Navy's eventual response was the convoy system. They had long been sceptical of the system, thinking they would simply gather targets for the U-boats together, but with such losses there really was no choice. Convoy protection was to be the most important task of the navy – hardly the glorious role expected, but utterly vital all the same. By summer the convoy system was proving an effective answer to the U-boat, and the war at sea had turned Britain's way. **JS**

> *'The Grand Fleet can never have any other objective than the High Sea Fleet, and until the High Sea Fleet emerges from its defences I regret to say that I do not see that any offensive against it is possible.'*
>
> **Admiral Sir John Jellicoe to First Lord of the Admiralty Arthur Balfour, 25 January 1916**

The war at sea, 1914–18

The British had long assumed that a war with Germany would quickly see a decisive naval battle and a resounding British victory. But in the event the major fleet actions which occurred did so almost by chance, and ended indecisively. The Royal Navy found a less glorious, but essential role in convoy protection and in their long-distance blockade of Germany. While the U-boats caused real alarm to the British, the German High Seas Fleet could never hope to win mastery of the seas. But by sinking American ships and killing American citizens, the Germans did drive the USA into the war, destroying any hope of victory.

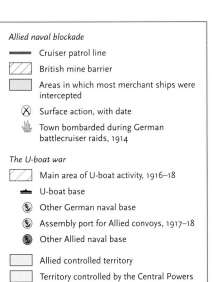

Allied naval blockade

— Cruiser patrol line
/// British mine barrier
▨ Areas in which most merchant ships were intercepted
⊗ Surface action, with date
🔥 Town bombarded during German battlecruiser raids, 1914

The U-boat war

/// Main area of U-boat activity, 1916–18
⚓ U-boat base
⚓ Other German naval base
⚓ Assembly port for Allied convoys, 1917–18
⚓ Other Allied naval base

▨ Allied controlled territory
▨ Territory controlled by the Central Powers
▨ Neutral territory

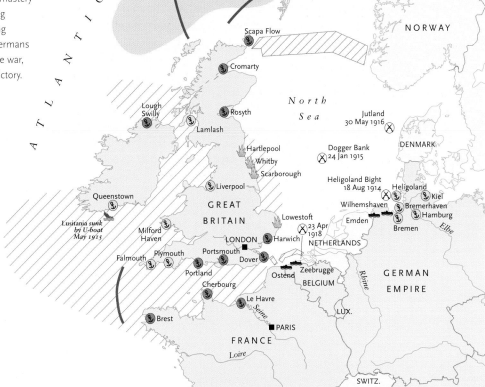

WOMEN'S SUFFRAGE

Public protest

A common form of protest for women was to chain themselves to railings. This ensured publicity, especially as the police found it time-consuming to remove them.

Women's suffrage

In 1913 suffragettes launched a terrorist campaign that saw attacks on property across much of Britain. It alienated many moderate sympathisers. Between 1914 and 1918, however, women made a major contribution to the war effort. The principle of extending the vote to at least some women at last came to be accepted.

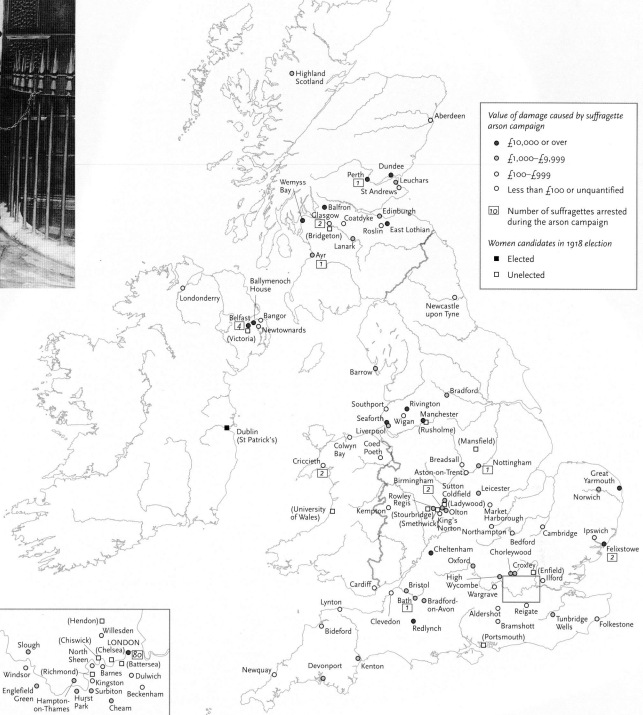

In January 1913 suffragettes in all parts of Great Britain began destroying property in an attempt to coerce the government into granting women the vote in parliamentary elections. They torched churches and cricket pavilions, set letter-boxes ablaze, slashed works of art and detonated bombs. Excluding property of 'incalculable value', the most conservative estimate suggests that property worth well over £500,000 was destroyed within 18 months. The 'arson campaign', as it was called, ceased only with the outbreak of World War I.

The campaign was the culmination of a long-standing demand for female suffrage. As early as 1832, Mary Smith had presented the first female suffrage petition to parliament. In 1867 the Manchester Women's Suffrage Committee was established, quickly followed by suffrage associations in London, Edinburgh and Bristol. By the 1870s suffrage societies existed all over Great Britain, from Orkney and Shetland to Brighton. In 1872, these local societies united to form a Central Committee of the National Society for Women's Suffrage, which became the National Union of Women's Suffrage Societies (NUWSS) in 1897. Presided over by Mrs Millicent Fawcett, this was the largest suffrage organisation in the United Kingdom.

On the declaration of war in 1914, the WSPU became overtly patriotic. Its paper, *The Suffragette*, was renamed *Britannia* and dedicated 'For King, For Country, For Freedom'. The 'hysterical, wild women' became 'indomitable war-workers' almost overnight. Active campaigning for the vote ceased with the war, but debates in 1917 about changing the law to re-enfranchise men who had served in the armed forces overseas for more than 12 months gave the NUWSS an opportunity to lobby again for female suffrage. Even Herbert Asquith (Liberal Prime Minister until 1916, and a strong opponent of female suffrage) could not deny that women had 'aided in the most effective way in the prosecution of the war'. The arson campaign had alienated many politicians, as it had women who disapproved of the suffragettes' rejection of conventional femininity or resented the upper-class and upper-middle-class domination of the suffragette movement. But broader changes in society, some hastened by the war, were decisive.

On 19 June 1917 the House of Commons accepted the female-suffrage clause in the Representation of the People Bill by 385 votes to 55. In the House of Lords, it was passed by a vote of 134 to 71. In the general election of 1918, 8.5 million women joined 12.9 million men in voting. Nonetheless, female suffrage remained restricted to women over the age of 30 years who were local government electors (or married to local government electors) – in short, those who met a property qualification.

The 1918 general election was also the first in which women could stand as MPs, and 17 of the 1,623 candidates were women. Only four were Labour candidates, even though this party supported female suffrage. The suspicion of many suffrage leaders of party politics was evident in the fact that of the 17 candidates, eight were independents. Only one woman won a seat: Constance Markievicz, the Sinn Féin candidate for a Dublin constituency. As an Irish nationalist, she refused to sit in the House of Commons and joined the parliament in Dublin. It was not until December 1919 that the first woman, Nancy Astor, took a seat in the Commons, after a by-election. She was neither a suffragist nor a political activist, but took the seat to replace her husband, who had entered the Lords. Nevertheless, she dedicated herself to the rights of women and children.

While the suffragettes ceased to exist after 1918, suffragists continued to fight for universal female suffrage. It was not until the Equal Franchise Act of 1928 that women won the vote on the same terms as men.   JB

The arson campaign, however, was organised by the Women's Social and Political Union (WSPU), formed in 1903 with Emmeline Pankhurst and her daughters, Christabel and Sylvia, at its head. Although they initially concerned themselves with lobbying for the vote for women, they soon became disillusioned by the slow progress being made. In contrast to the NUWSS, they proposed a violent approach. From 1909 onwards, the violence of their attacks grew progressively until, in 1913 and 1914, WSPU members began making serious attacks on property. In the words of Emmeline Pankhurst, speaking in the Albert Hall in October 1912, 'Those of you who can break windows – break them. Those of you who can still further attack property so as to make the government realise that property is as greatly endangered by Women Suffrage as it was by the Chartists of old – do so. And my last words to the government: I incite this meeting to rebellion.' In part, this escalation in violence was a response to frustration at the slow rate of progress and the increasingly violent response of the police and prison officials. This was particularly noticeable after the hunger strikes of imprisoned suffragettes led to force feeding and the passing of the Prisoners (Temporary Discharge for Ill Health) Act, better known as the Cat and Mouse Act, in April 1913. This allowed the release of prisoners weakened by hunger, but then allowed them to be re-arrested when they regained their strength. The arson campaign brought the suffragettes (the militant wing of the movement) to public attention, but alienated many politicians who had been broadly in favour of reform, and led to the barring of suffragists (the moderate, propagandist wing) from large halls and other public platforms. On 31 May 1913 the suffragettes gained their first martyr when Emily Wilding Davison threw herself in front of the king's horse during Derby Day and was trampled to death.

THE IMPACT OF THE CAMPAIGN

The geography of the campaign was remarkably wide, the exception being Ireland, which was scarcely affected outside Dublin and northeast Ulster. In Ireland, feminists faced a dilemma: should they support the campaign for national independence or the campaign for female suffrage? Most decided that the fight for national independence was their first priority. Wales had many active suffragettes, but saw little of the arson campaign. Nonetheless, the campaign spread throughout Great Britain, in part because it was largely carried out by a relatively small group of highly mobile women.

The suffragettes' first martyr
One of the most spectacular acts of protest occurred on Derby Day, 1913, when Emily Wilding Davison threw herself in front of the king's horse. She died from her injuries.

A campaigner in Whitehall, 1913
The police in general showed little sympathy to the women's cause. Indeed, it was the intolerance of protest shown by the authorities, and the government's refusal to listen to the suffragettes, that drove them to violence.

IRELAND'S INDEPENDENCE

The position of Ireland, after 120 years as an integrated part of the United Kingdom, changed dramatically in 1921, when the island was partitioned and the two parts received different degrees of autonomy. The six northeastern counties remained part of the United Kingdom but were given devolved government, while in the south the Irish Free State was established as a dominion within the British empire. These changes were a result of the events that took place between 1912 and 1921, which followed a long period of constitutional impasse.

In parliamentary elections between 1885 and 1912, constitutional nationalists, who stood for Home Rule, always took at least 80 of the 103 Irish seats, the remainder going to unionists mainly from the northern part of the island. Although the nationalists' demand was supported by the Liberal Party, which introduced Home Rule bills in 1886 and 1893, Conservative domination of the House of Lords made its acceptance impossible. The end of this constitutional impasse came in 1911, when the Liberal Party managed to curtail the Lords' veto after their rejection of the Finance Bill. The Liberal government was dependent on Irish nationalist support and consequently initiated the Third Home Rule Bill in 1912, which could then only be delayed by the Lords for three parliamentary sessions. The now seemingly unstoppable introduction of Home Rule caused great alarm among unionists, who received wholehearted support from the Conservative Party. The reduction of the veto power of the Lords, combined with the loss of three general elections, caused a willingness in that party to back any type of opposition to the bill. The main expression of this opposition was the creation of the Ulster Volunteer Force, set up to prevent Home Rule by force. In response, nationalists established their own militia, the Irish Volunteers. With three opposing armies on the island, tension rose rapidly. Frantic attempts to find a constitutional compromise continued during 1913 and 1914, but civil war seemed inevitable when the Home Rule Bill approached its third reading in parliament. In the event, however, World War I intervened. Although the Home Rule Bill was passed, the government decided to postpone its introduction until after the war, and decided, too, that a special arrangement would then be made for Ulster.

THE ANGLO-IRISH WAR

Many assumed that the shared experience of fighting for a common cause would unite the Irish, but the unexpectedly long duration of World War I changed everything. Support for the war by constitutional nationalists, and their willingness to compromise in the preceding negotiations, exposed them to criticism from more extreme nationalists when the war dragged on. Dissatisfaction with the Irish Party – who sought Home Rule by constitutional means at Westminster – was galvanised by the events of Easter 1916,

Irish independence

Until 1914, the Irish Party, which called for Irish Home Rule, had the loyalty of most nationalists. The Easter Rising of 1916, the repression that followed it, and the threat of conscription in Ireland, swung the electorate towards the more radical, republican Sinn Féin. With de facto independence as a British dominion achieved, and partition an established fact, the tide of radicalism began to recede. The Irish Civil War proved disastrous for Sinn Féin: too many Irish voters preferred the freedom they had, and wanted stability rather than the all-Ireland republic Sinn Féin demanded.

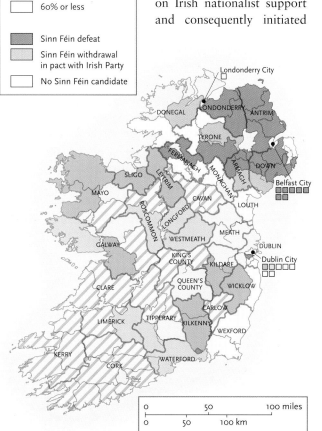

Sinn Féin victories, 1918
- No opposing candidate
- 80%
- 71–80%
- 61–70%
- 60% or less
- Sinn Féin defeat
- Sinn Féin withdrawal in pact with Irish Party
- No Sinn Féin candidate

First preference votes cast for Sinn Féin candidates, 1923
- Over 30%
- 21–30%
- 14–20%

when a small group of radical nationalists tried to take advantage of Britain's preoccupation with the war by staging a rebellion. The attempt to seize power failed within a week. Dissent within the ranks of the insurgents, and the strong counter-measures taken by the British government, doomed the rising. After five days of fighting, concentrated almost exclusively in Dublin, the leader of the rebels, Patrick Pearse, surrendered. In particular, the shelling of the rebels' headquarters in the General Post Office in Sackville (now O'Connell) Street from a gunboat in the Liffey caused enormous damage and many casualties among the civilian population. The heavy-handed reaction to the rebellion, and the 15 executions and thousands of arrests that followed it, appalled moderate Home Rulers. This, combined with the continued willingness of the Irish Party to compromise and the looming introduction of conscription in Ireland, turned the population away from the Irish Party to the more revolutionary objectives of Sinn Féin. This became apparent in by-elections in 1917, and in the increasingly daring nature of the actions of the reorganised Irish Volunteers, but was made absolutely clear in the 1918 general elections, in which Sinn Féin won 73 seats, against six for the constitutional nationalists.

The electoral success of Sinn Féin has subsequently been used to vindicate the republican fight for independence. Republicans claim that their campaign is justified by the support the Irish gave to the republic in the last election held free of threat and on an all-Ireland basis. Opponents argue that republicans actually took less than 48 per cent of the vote. However, the fact that constituencies in which there was no opposing candidate have been excluded from the count, and that in northern areas constituencies were divided between Sinn Féin and the Irish Party, suggests that a majority of voters probably did support Sinn Féin. Nonetheless, this did not constitute agreement with the means later used by republicans. The 1918 Sinn Féin man-

ifesto was very vague on the use of physical force, and strongly advocated passive resistance and an appeal to the Versailles Peace Conference.

Following the 1918 election, the members of Sinn Féin, who had been elected to the parliament in Westminster, set up their own Irish parliament, called Dáil Éireann, in Dublin. At the same time, the Irish Volunteers, who now called themselves the IRA (Irish Republican Army) became increasingly forceful. After the failure of the appeal to the Peace Conference in Versailles, and amid the growing repression of republicans, a more coherent campaign began in January 1920. The republican leadership allowed the IRA to attack police barracks and patrols, and violence escalated. The nature of the conflict in 1920–1 was very different from previous violent episodes in Anglo-Irish relations. The guerrilla warfare that established itself was largely determined by limited republican resources and calculations of where they could best be employed to make Ireland ungovernable, rather than constituting an attempt to challenge British might directly. As a result, wide discrepancies in the intensity of the violence emerged between various parts of the country. The southwestern counties,

Michael Collins

A veteran of the Easter Rising, General Michael Collins took command of the National Army fighting against the IRA. In reprisal, his former comrades murdered him.

Longford and Dublin City stood out as the main arenas of conflict. The exact causes of these differences are the subject of debate among historians, and attempts to link the levels of violence to socio-economic characteristics of individual counties have not yielded a satisfactory answer. A more comprehensive explanation for these differences can be found by tracing the individual experiences of the perpetrators of violence.

During this Anglo-Irish War, the British government attempted to ease a possible future settlement with the introduction of the Government of Ireland Act in 1920. This allowed for the creation of two Home Rule governments in Ireland: one for six of the nine Ulster counties, and one for the rest of the island. Although northern unionists had never wanted their own government and their comrades who formed a minority of the population in three Ulster counties were left in a state dominated by nationalists, they saw this as an opportunity to protect themselves against the whims of the British parliament. A Protestant parliament in Belfast might exercise a veto against any future British attempt to dragoon them into a united Ireland, and they therefore proceeded to form the new, devolved government of Northern Ireland. However, as expected, Sinn Féin did not accept partition and refused to participate in the setting up of state institutions of any sort for Southern Ireland. Consequently, the conflict raged on. Nonetheless, the de facto partition made it much more difficult for nationalists to demand a unitary Irish state in subsequent negotiations.

The growing severity of the conflict and the mounting casualties, particularly among the Crown forces, resulted in a desire on both sides to explore the possibility of a constitutional compromise. To allow for talks, a truce was called on 11 July 1921.

After five months of hard and ultimately unsuccessful negotiations, the British government finally lost patience. It forced a settlement on the Irish delegation by threatening immediate and all-out warfare. The Anglo-Irish Treaty that followed made the whole of Ireland a dominion of Britain, but allowed Northern Ireland, under certain conditions, to secede as an autonomous region of the United Kingdom. The treaty was narrowly accepted by the Dáil, but a majority of the IRA refused to accept it. The result was civil war.

THE IRISH CIVIL WAR

The Irish Civil War began on 28 June 1922 with an attack by Free State forces on the headquarters of die-hard republicans in the Four Courts and on other strongholds in Dublin that die-hard republicans had occupied. The result was a stand-up fight similar to that of 1916. The die-hards had no strategic plan behind the occupation of these buildings: their decision to make a stand was based on a calculation of its propaganda value – an appeal to the memory of the Easter Rising. However, as communications between the various positions taken up by the republicans were poor, the government forces were able to capture each in

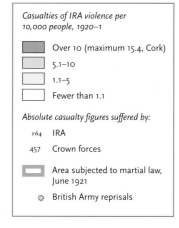

Casualties of IRA violence per 10,000 people, 1920–1

- Over 10 (maximum 15.4, Cork)
- 5.1–10
- 1.1–5
- Fewer than 1.1

Absolute casualty figures suffered by:

164   IRA

457   Crown forces

☐   Area subjected to martial law, June 1921

✿   British Army reprisals

The Anglo-Irish War

Fuelled by popular support for Sinn Féin, the IRA launched a guerrilla war against the British in 1920. They aimed to drive the British out by making Ireland ungovernable. This left British security forces floundering for a reply. The brutality of the countermeasures used shocked both British and international opinion.

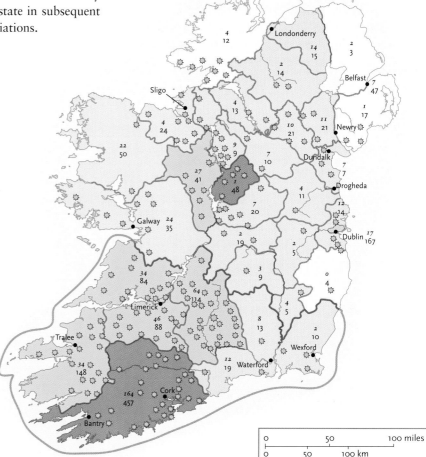

the British government and the backing of most institutions in Ireland. Among the tactical reasons for the government success was the hotly debated – and in some cases clearly illegal – execution of 77 republican prisoners. Together with other, unofficial killings, these executions sapped the will of much of the republican opposition.

The leaders of the new Irish state instituted what they called a conservative revolution. The violent opposition of republicans to the Free State's very existence quickly killed any inclination the Free State politicians might have had for genuinely revolutionary change. They effectively took over all the existing institutions, and made very few, if any, fundamental alterations to the way in which the country was run. Although the republicans continued their opposition to the treaty settlement, most of them eventually accepted the established constitutional framework and endeavoured to change it from within, by political means. Indeed, their political representatives, Fianna Fáil, won control of the Free State in the general election of 1932, and so helped to shape the present-day Republic of Ireland. **JA**

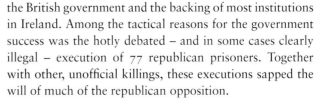

Eamon de Valera
Republican leader Eamon de Valera inspects an IRA unit. De Valera first fought for a republic, but went on to steer Ireland towards independence by constitutional means.

succession relatively easily; government troops were also much better equipped than the republican irregulars. Engagements of this type were repeated in many parts of the country with much the same results – and led to the death or capture of several prominent republicans. The conflict then again became a guerrilla war.

Contrary to popular impressions, it is now clear that the Irish Civil War was in fact less bloody than the Anglo-Irish War that had preceded it. Actual deaths numbered 1,872 between January 1920 and the truce, 470 in the truce period (from 11 July 1921 to 28 June 1922) and 927 in the ensuing civil war. As in the earlier conflict, a regional diversity in the intensity of violence emerged, with the Southwest and Dublin City again most affected.

The war was finally won by the Free State government. In April 1923 the republicans proclaimed a unilateral cease-fire and dumped their arms – but not their opposition to the new state, which they continued to regard as a puppet regime of the British. The Free State victory had been achieved with substantial material support from

> *We may make mistakes in the beginning and shoot the wrong people, but bloodshed is a cleansing and a sanctifying thing, and the nation which regards it as the final horror has lost its manhood.*
>
> **Patrick Pearse, Irish writer and nationalist, 1913**

The Irish Civil War

In the Irish Civil War the IRA found only limited public support. They were unable to make Ireland ungovernable, as they had in their fight against the British. The Free State government, meanwhile, responded ruthlessly. Though casualties were low, the war was still a savage one. The IRA proved no match for the National Army.

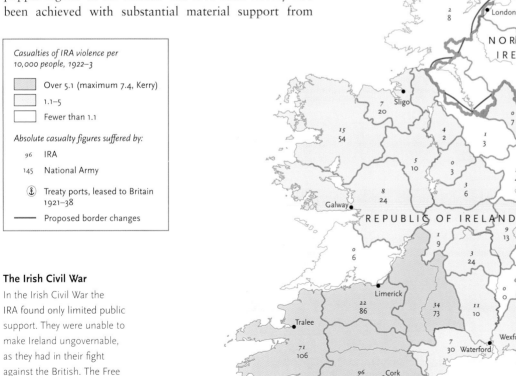

Casualties of IRA violence per 10,000 people, 1922–3

- Over 5.1 (maximum 7.4, Kerry)
- 1.1–5
- Fewer than 1.1

Absolute casualty figures suffered by:
- 96   IRA
- 145   National Army
- ⚓   Treaty ports, leased to Britain 1921–38
- ——   Proposed border changes

| 0 | 50 | 100 miles |
| 0 | 50 | 100 km |

The General Strike

An armoured car takes to the streets of London. During the General Strike of 1926 the government was prepared to take extreme measures to maintain law and order if it proved necessary.

The interwar years were difficult ones for the British economy. Britain had incurred a heavy burden of debt to the USA during World War I. In the winter of 1920, 1.5 million British workers were unemployed. Within six months, the number had reached over 2 million, and numbers fluctuated between 1 and 2 million throughout the decade. An international trade crisis was also growing. Between 1929 and 1934, world economies underwent a severe slump, sparked by the Wall Street Crash of October 1929. Its impact on Britain was immediate. Exports fell by half and unemployment soared. In the early 1930s unemployment peaked at 3 million; it did not drop below 1.5 million until the end of the decade. Employees in textiles, steel works, shipbuilding and coal-mining were hardest hit.

The government's response to unemployment was mixed. In November 1918 an Out of Work donation was started. This was a non-contributory benefit paid to unemployed ex-servicemen and unemployed civilians who had been employed for at least three months during the war. When unemployment escalated, insurance was extended to include all manual workers and all non-manual workers earning less than £250 a year. When the Poor Law Guardians were replaced by local Public Assistance Committees (PACs), people whose benefits had 'run out' were entitled to 'transitional benefits' from the local PACs. These benefits were means-tested and entitlements were gradually reduced, most notoriously with the 'genuinely seeking work' provision passed to exclude married women from the register, and the introduction of the Family Means Test in 1930. In 1934 a National Assistance Board was created, which set a uniform assistance rate throughout the country. In general, benefits to the unemployed were cut by about 10 per cent in the 1930s. In Wales and in northern industrial

areas, unemployed people were much more reliant on means-tested and discretionary benefits than insurance. This was because periods of unemployment in these areas were longer, forcing unemployed workers to turn to the 'dole' and locally funded poor relief (or public assistance). This fuelled the sense of shame and anger among the unemployed and their families.

PROTESTS AND STRIKES

The unemployed protested against their condition by marching, organising rallies and engaging in rent strikes. The Communist Party of Great Britain founded the National Unemployed Workers Movement (NUWM) in 1921. Led by Wal Hannington, it had around 20,000 members by 1932, with the active support of at least twice that number. Their most famous actions were the 'Hunger Marches' of 1922–3, 1929, 1932, 1934 and 1936. They also organised protest marches to London, particularly from South Wales and Scotland.

The Jarrow March of October 1936 was the most famous of the hunger marches. It involved 200 men and was led by the MP Ellen Wilkinson. One of the few marches not organised by the NUWM, it survived in public consciousness because it was an officially approved 'peaceful protest' and because Jarrow was widely regarded as one of the worst-hit areas (80 per cent of men in Jarrow were unemployed). The marchers carried over 80,000 signatures to parliament, asking the House to 'realise the urgent need that work should be provided without delay'. Neither this march nor those organised by the NUWM achieved much in economic terms, but they did draw widespread public attention to the plight of the unemployed. The NUWM was disbanded in 1939, partly due to the improved employment conditions as a result of the growth in the arms industry.

The interwar years were also characterised by major strikes. There were waves of strikes in 1919–23 and again in 1926. In contrast, the 1930s were generally calm, although there was a series of strikes in the textile industries between 1929 and 1932. The General Strike of 1926, which started on 3 May, was the climax to years of industrial unrest in interwar Britain. It began, and ended, with a miners' strike. When miners refused to accept wage cuts, they were locked out. Transport, metal, building, printing, electricity and gas workers came out in support of the miners. Of these groups, the most important were the railway workers, dockers and public transport workers. Transport workers turned what was a localised strike into a national one, increasing the number of workers involved to nearly 3 million. The government deployed the navy and some 80,000 troops, showing that they were prepared to use force if necessary to break the strike. By 12 May, the unions had called the strike off, without guarantees. In 1927 Stanley Baldwin's Conservative government passed the Trades Disputes Act, which made general strikes illegal.

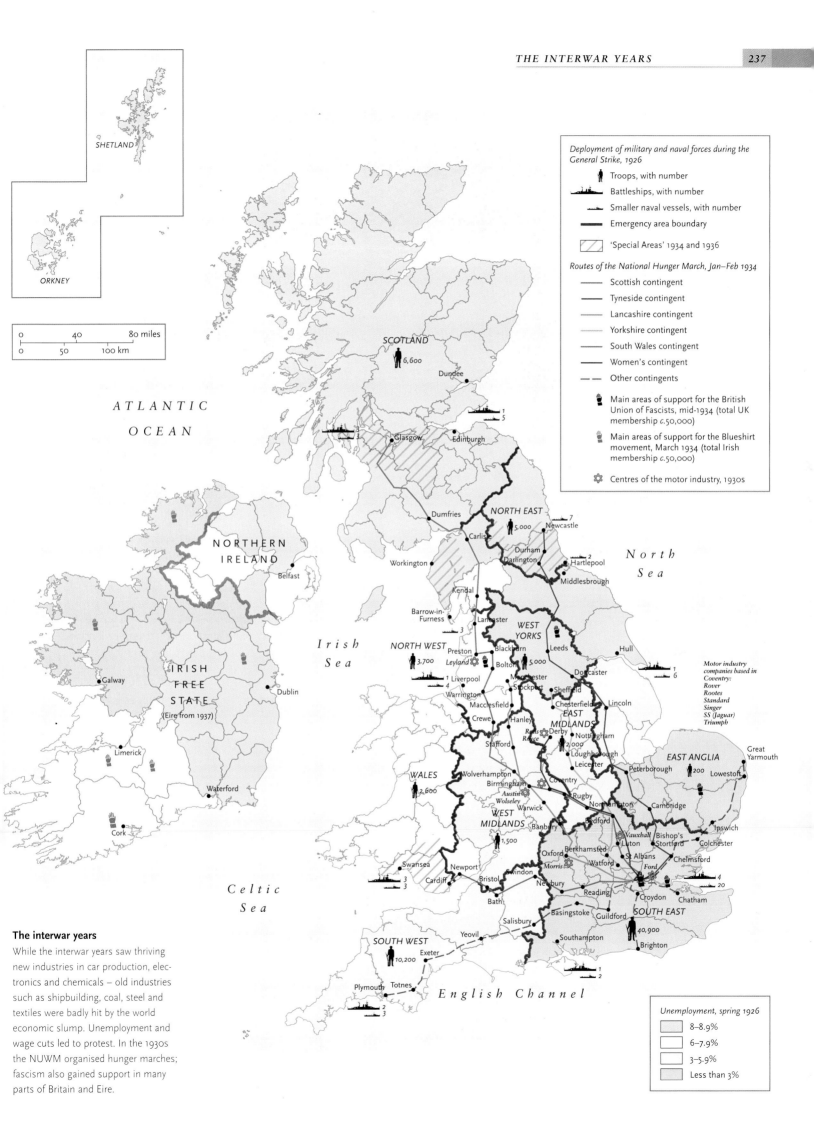

SHETLAND

ORKNEY

ATLANTIC OCEAN

Deployment of military and naval forces during the General Strike, 1926

- Troops, with number
- Battleships, with number
- Smaller naval vessels, with number
- Emergency area boundary
- 'Special Areas' 1934 and 1936

Routes of the National Hunger March, Jan–Feb 1934

- Scottish contingent
- Tyneside contingent
- Lancashire contingent
- Yorkshire contingent
- South Wales contingent
- Women's contingent
- Other contingents

- Main areas of support for the British Union of Fascists, mid-1934 (total UK membership c.50,000)
- Main areas of support for the Blueshirt movement, March 1934 (total Irish membership c.50,000)
- Centres of the motor industry, 1930s

SCOTLAND 6,600
Dundee

NORTH EAST 5,000 Newcastle
Dumfries
Carlisle
Durham
Darlington
Hartlepool
Workington
Middlesbrough
Kendal
Barrow-in-Furness
Lancaster
WEST YORKS
NORTH WEST
Preston 3,700
Leyland
Blackburn
Bolton 5,000
Leeds
Hull
Liverpool
Manchester
Stockport
Doncaster
Warrington
Sheffield
Macclesfield
Chesterfield
Lincoln
Crewe
Hanley
EAST MIDLANDS
Stafford
Rolls Royce
Derby
Nottingham
Loughborough
Leicester
Peterborough
EAST ANGLIA 200
Great Yarmouth
Lowestoft
WALES 2,600
Wolverhampton
Birmingham
Coventry
Rugby
Northampton
Cambridge
Austin Wolseley
Warwick
WEST MIDLANDS 1,500
Banbury
Bedford
Ipswich
Vauxhall
Luton
Bishop's Stortford
Colchester
Oxford
Berkhamsted
St Albans
Chelmsford
Morris
Watford
Ford
Swansea
Newport
Swindon
Croydon
Chatham
Cardiff
Bristol
Newbury
Reading
Bath
Basingstoke
Guildford
SOUTH EAST 40,900
Salisbury
Southampton
Brighton
SOUTH WEST 10,200
Yeovil
Exeter
Plymouth
Totnes

NORTHERN IRELAND
Belfast
IRISH FREE STATE (Eire from 1937)
Galway
Dublin
Limerick
Waterford
Cork

North Sea
Irish Sea
Celtic Sea
English Channel

Motor industry companies based in Coventry:
Rover
Rootes
Standard
Singer
SS (Jaguar)
Triumph

The interwar years

While the interwar years saw thriving new industries in car production, electronics and chemicals – old industries such as shipbuilding, coal, steel and textiles were badly hit by the world economic slump. Unemployment and wage cuts led to protest. In the 1930s the NUWM organised hunger marches; fascism also gained support in many parts of Britain and Eire.

Unemployment, spring 1926
- 8–8.9%
- 6–7.9%
- 3–5.9%
- Less than 3%

The Jarrow March

The Jarrow marchers, pictured at Lavendon in 1936, protested against unemployment. They received widespread public sympathy – but little from the government.

of the explanation was rising consumption. By the beginning of World War II, there were over 2 million privately owned cars in the United Kingdom and the number of commercial motor vehicles had exceeded the half-million mark. Improved production technologies and the concentration of producers through mergers and amalgamations also played an important part in the success of the industry.

As a consequence of these 'new industries', the living standards of people who remained in employment actually improved by about 16 per cent between the wars. Although the new industries were not sufficiently large to reverse the overall trend of economic decline, they were important in minimising the effect of the Depression for the employed.

POVERTY IN WALES

Wales was hit harder than any other region. The Welsh economy was heavily dependent on mining and shipbuilding, so the slump in world markets, combined with the lack of investment capital, had a severe impact. Average unemployment in Wales was 31 per cent, compared with 20 per cent in Scotland and 12 per cent in England. Within Wales, there were huge regional variations. In Taff Wells, for example, 82 per cent of the insured population was unemployed; in Pontycymmer this figure was 72 per cent, and in Merthyr and Abertillery over 66 per cent of the populations were unemployed. By the 1930s, Glamorgan and Monmouthshire had the highest proportion of people on poor relief in the United Kingdom, apart from Durham.

The economic crisis was particularly severe in the mining industry, which employed around 60 per cent of the men in

Not all parts of the United Kingdom experienced poverty in these years. Some sectors of the economy grew, particularly car manufacture, electrical engineering, the paper and publishing industries, and rayon production – all industries heavily concentrated in the Midlands. The share of these 'new industries' in total industrial output rose from 7 per cent in 1924 to 14 per cent in 1924, and then to 21 per cent by 1935. One of the great successes of the period was the motor car industry, which paid high wages. The output

Interwar South Wales

Wage cuts, lay-offs and the coercive use of troops and police during industrial disputes in the 1920s led to the development of strong traditions of union militancy, radical extra-parliamentary action and socialist internationalism in the South Wales coalfield. These traditions made the area a stronghold of anti-fascism in the 1930s, and, of around 165 Welsh volunteers for the International Brigades in the Spanish Civil War (1936–9), over 80% came from the coalfield.

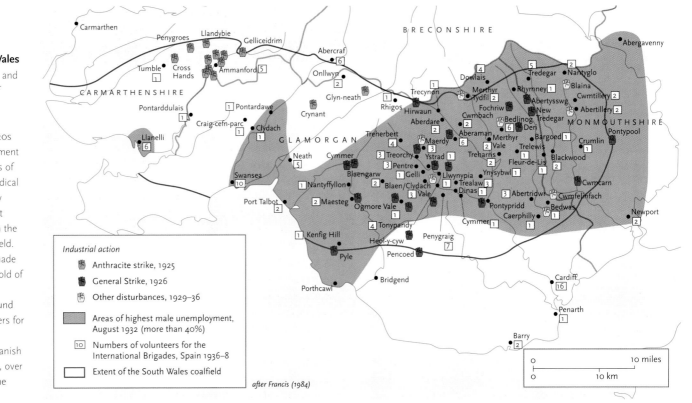

after Francis (1984)

of the UK motor industry increased from 71,000 vehicles in 1923 to over 390,000 by 1937, by which time Britain was second only to the USA in the export of motor vehicles. Part

southeast Wales. Welsh colliers suffered in the aftermath of the 1926 strike. Although the Trades Union Congress had ended the strike on 12 May, the Welsh colliers remained on strike until the end of the year. They lost the fight and, by 1931, the wages of miners were at starvation levels. Other areas of the Welsh economy also went into decline, particularly steel and iron works, transportation and shipping. Only people living in Cardiff, where there was a radio relay station, and Swansea, which had nickel that was required by car manufacturers, escaped extreme poverty.

To combat poverty, the government passed the Special Areas (Development) Act in 1934 and the Special Areas Reconstruction (Agreement) Act in 1936, which provided financial incentives to industry to move to four distressed areas in the United Kingdom. Most of Glamorgan and west Monmouthshire became one of the four 'Special Areas'. Other regions were Glasgow–Linlithgow–Kilmarnock, South Shields–Hartlepool, and Workington. A few new industries were established, but the effects were inadequate.

In Wales, the social effect of high levels of poverty was devastating. With poverty came disease and malnutrition. One-quarter of all South Welsh miners aged 25 to 34 had lost all their teeth. The incidence of scarlet fever and rickets soared, and the death rate from tuberculosis was 130 per cent above the average for the United Kingdom. Culturally, Wales also went into decline. The number of Welsh-speakers fell from 155,000 in 1921 to just 60,000 by 1939. Local services and shops became nonviable. Chapels found their congregations dwindling. Large numbers of people were forced to leave Wales, many moving to the 'new industries' of southeast England and the Midlands. Some of the migration was planned by the Ministry of Labour, which sponsored the transfer of workers to, for instance, the Morris motor car works at Cowley, the engineering works at Coventry, and the light industry at Watford and Slough. Between 1921 and 1940, over 440,000 people left Wales; 85 per cent from Glamorgan and Monmouthshire.

FASCISM

The interwar years are frequently regarded as radical years, characterised by popular support for the Labour Party, the founding of the Communist Party in 1920, and protest marches by the unemployed. Nevertheless, in five out of the seven general elections held between 1918 and 1939, the Conservatives formed or dominated governments. Despite soaring unemployment and the 1926 strike, the majority of the population continued to vote Conservative.

A wide range of right-wing extremist groups appeared during these years. These consisted largely of disaffected Conservatives demanding a renewed emphasis on imperial unity and tariff reform to protect British industry, while at the same time rejecting parliamentary democracy. The financial crisis of 1931 was seen as proof of the failings of the policies of the established political parties. The most notorious of the right-wing groups was the British Union of Fascists (BUF), established by Oswald Mosley on 1 October 1932. Although the BUF gained support in Manchester, Liverpool and Leeds, the East End (which was home to one-third of all Jews in Britain) remained its heartland. In the London County Council elections of March 1937, the BUF won 23 per cent of the vote in North East Bethnal Green, 19 per cent in Stepney (Limehouse) and 14 per cent in Shoreditch. Nonetheless, the fascists failed to win widespread support. Membership figures are unreliable, but total BUF membership probably rose from 17,000 in early 1934 to a peak of 50,000 by July. After dropping to 5,000 within a year, it recovered slowly to 15,500 during 1936, reaching 22,500 by the time war broke out.

Large numbers of people protested against the BUF's increasingly anti-Semitic stance, most famously during the riots at Cable Street, where anti-fascist demonstrators prevented 3,000 fascists from marching. In 1936 the government restricted BUF activities by passing a Public Order Act banning political uniforms and allowing the police to ban marches for three-month periods. More generally, the fascists were unable to win parliamentary seats. The voting system worked in favour of the two dominant parties. The Conservative Party remained attractive to the middle classes and the BUF was unable to compete with Labour and the trade unions for the support of the unemployed. As the

1930s anti-fascists in Limehouse, London

Wherever fascism was strongest, as it was in East London, opposition was also very strong, and could be violent. While Limehouse had a significant fascist vote, it was still the safe seat of Labour Party leader Clement Attlee.

economy improved in the late 1930s, the attraction of a political alternative diminished.

In Ireland, the Army Comrades Association, composed of Irish Army veterans, was formed in February 1932, with about 10,000 members. By 1934, they had become the 'Blueshirts', and had around 50,000 members, gaining the support of the influential Cumann na nGaedheal. The Blueshirts attracted people angry with the dramatic deterioration of the agricultural economy and those who were afraid of the spread of Communism and the IRA (which seemed too close to the Fianna Fail government). Clashes between the Blueshirts and IRA and Fianna Fail supporters grew particularly bloody in 1932, even threatening resumption of the civil war. The Blueshirts were strongly influenced by European fascists and were led by General Eoin O'Duffy, who had strong fascist beliefs; nevertheless, most of the members were concerned with local Irish issues.

Though fascism, for all the passions it aroused, had only limited influence on domestic politics, the rise of aggressive fascist dictatorships in Europe meant that it dominated British foreign policy in the late 1930s. The British government pursued a policy of appeasement towards fascist Italy and Nazi Germany in the hopes of avoiding a general European war. The German invasion of Poland on 1 September 1939 signalled the failure of this policy and led to a British declaration of war three days later. **JB**

METROLAND

Two contrasting images of 1930s urban England predominate. One is the depressed Northern city of George Orwell's *The Road to Wigan Pier*. The other is the Jazz Age southern suburb immortalised by John Betjeman as 'Metroland'. Suburbs are as old as cities, but between the wars they acquired a new meaning. Arterial roads, garden suburbs, industrial estates, the Green Belt, New Towns: these core elements of modern life came into being in the early twentieth century. The capital was on the move, extending its tentacles over virgin agricultural land.

LEAVE THIS AND

"I never had any other desire so strong and so like to covetousness as that one which I have had always, that I might be Master of a small House and a Large Garden, with moderate conveniences joined to them."
Abraham Cowley

MOVE TO EDGWARE

Greater London grew dramatically between the wars. Other centres, such as Manchester, Newcastle and Southampton, witnessed expansion, but not on the scale of the capital. Between 1925 and 1935, three-quarters of a million Britons, the equivalent of a large provincial town's population, moved to London annually, and needed homes. By 1935, a fifth of the nation's population, some 8.5 million, lived in this small area, a mere one one-hundred-and-twenty-seventh of the country's surface. No wonder that the fields and hedgerows of Middlesex vanished to make way.

These were largely economic migrants, drawn by the promise of employment in the new factories and offices that were rapidly opening in the commercially vibrant London area. Between 1923 and 1934 the population of insured workers in the southeast grew by 44 per cent; during the same period, that of Wales fell by 26 per cent. The rise of electricity freed industry from location near its power source; London, hub of the nation's transport network and with a pool of skilled workers, offered an attractive choice. Along with the 'semi', the factory on the arterial road became the canonical suburban building. Best-known of these is the Hoover Factory in Perivale, built in 1933. Industrial estates also began to open, starting with Slough's in 1920.

London's population was on the move, too. The aged housing stock within Inner London was emptying rapidly: some 450,000 Londoners migrated outwards before 1939, as new rail and road links enabled workers to commute, and to occupy brand-new houses. A revolution in private finances ushered in the age of the owner-occupier: from the early 1930s, building societies were making affordable mortgages available, thereby placing house-buying within the aspirations of a growing number of households. Large-scale developments of public-sector housing (such as the huge London County Council estate at Dagenham, with its 26,000 houses) did take place, but overwhelmingly it was private companies of house-builders that were at work.

Much of the nation's housing stock still dates from the interwar building boom: it witnessed the construction of 3,998,000 dwellings in England and Wales, and reached a peak in 1937. This was the golden age of the speculative builder. Houses came in a number of styles. A few were modernistic and white, with flat roofs and sharp edges. Much more common, however, was the vernacular look: houses of red brick with half-timbering, tile-hanging and pebble-dashing, all echoing the regional style of the London Basin. The more thrusting examples of this were dubbed 'Stockbroker Tudor' by the cartoonist and writer Osbert Lancaster. Set in broad, leafy streets, and served by regular and swift-running transport links, these modern houses, replete with modern domestic conveniences, represented a new high in living standards for many. As J. M. Richards wrote in his pioneering study of suburbia, *Castles on the Ground* (1946), they were 'each individual Englishman's idea of its home, except for the cosmopolitan rich, a minority of freaks and intellectuals and the very poor'. Once-rural Middlesex was now promoted as offering the charms of the country within reach of town. J. B. Priestley observed that 'the suburban villa enables the salesman or the clerk, out of hours, to be almost a country gentleman.'

MARKETING THE SUBURB

The suburban dream was made possible by developments in town planning. The Garden City ideal of spacious, healthy and planned new settlements had been promoted by the town planner Ebeneezer Howard in 1898, and first saw the light of day at Letchworth in Hertfordshire in 1903; Hampstead Garden Suburb followed in 1907 and Welwyn Garden City in 1920. The conventional suburb may have contributed to urban sprawl, but it, too, shared the dream of balancing town and country. The heirs to Howard's vision were the eight New Towns founded in the wake of a 1946 Act, such as Basildon and Stevenage, which shifted London's growth to well beyond its boundaries.

The image of suburban life was marketed intensively by interested parties such as house-builders and railway companies. The extended transport network spearheaded the growth of the suburbs: Edgware became the classic 'underground suburb'. 'Metroland' takes its name from the most energetic of these partnerships. The Metropolitan Railway ran from Baker Street to Amersham in Buckinghamshire, and brought the Chilterns within the reach of the London commuter. The company vehemently promoted the leafy allure of its routes, and private building firms developed areas along their length. The results could be dramatic: the station of Rayners Lane, for example, had 22,000 passengers in 1930, but 7 million passed through in 1937. Car ownership, too, was rising sharply, helping to conquer further the age-old restriction of distance on London's growth.

However, suburbia had its foes, and a reaction gathered pace: H. J. Massingham thought that suburban development 'destroyed the true England' and widespread alarm at London's unchecked expansion and the monotonous regularity of much of the development led to repeated calls for the securing of a 'Green Belt' around the capital. Calls to fasten it were first made in 1927 and a London Green Belt Act was passed in 1938, enabling the London County Council to acquire open space outside its boundaries. **RHB**

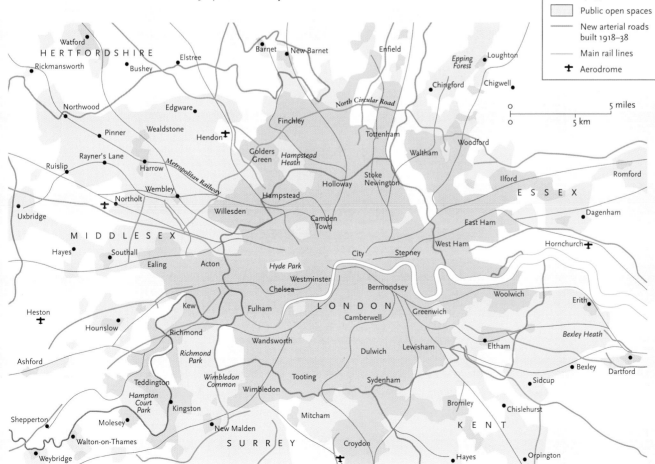

Built up area, *c.*1920
Urban expansion by 1938
Public open spaces
New arterial roads built 1918–38
Main rail lines
✝ Aerodrome

Greater London in 1938

In the interwar years Greater London underwent extremely rapid growth. New businesses sprang up, thanks to easy access to electricity, and employment opportunities grew as a result. Many people opted for a suburban lifestyle, and, in consequence, great tracts of rural farmland were rapidly built over to provide new housing.

During World War II, Britain's home front assumed an importance never seen before. The whole economy had to be mobilised in support of modern warfare. Essential industries and services were maintained, while other industries were converted to war production. At the same time, agricultural output had to be increased to make Britain self-sufficient in food, reducing the country's dependence on imports threatened by the German U-boat campaign. Enormous demands were therefore made of the population at large. The general willingness of the British people to meet these demands was a remarkable feature of the nation's experience of the war.

This economic mobilisation had to be achieved while several million men were in the services. To meet Britain's labour needs, therefore, over 7 million women were drawn into the workforce. Recruitment campaigns were mounted by the government to encourage women to enter the factories, but ultimately compulsion was used. This was a controversial step, given existing social values and the fact that women were paid far lower wages than men. It was made plain that female employment was a wartime expedient only: women were expected to return to domesticity once the war was over.

The scale of the restructuring task is best illustrated by the aircraft industry, in which the workforce increased from about 35,000 in 1935 to nearly 2 million in 1944 (some 40 per cent of whom were women). It became the largest industry in Britain, employing about 10 per cent of the total workforce. One typical company, De Havilland, builders of the Mosquito, had to expand rapidly from its Hatfield base into 'shadow factories' – plants built with government finance in anticipation of war – at Lostock and Leavesden. Parts of the company were further dispersed, to escape bombing and to create extra space, into hastily requisitioned and converted premises around the main plants. Other firms, in Luton, Coventry and Portsmouth, also built Mosquitoes, as did De Havilland's subsidiaries in Toronto and Sydney. In addition, work was subcontracted to some 400 other widely scattered firms that often had no prior experience in aircraft production, including several coach-builders and manufacturers of furniture and bicycles. Coordinating this complex arrangement was a major task. Yet the Mosquito was one of the most successful aircraft of the war, with nearly 7,000 produced and large numbers repaired.

> 'Every ton of household waste which can be salvaged saves vital shipping space... Last year British housewives saved 40 shiploads of paper and enough metal to build 16,000 tanks.'
>
> **Deputy Prime Minister Clement Attlee in a speech at Henham, 1941**

Women's work

Government campaigns brought over 7 million British women into the workforce to support the war effort.

A similar mix of planning and improvisation throughout the economy ensured – despite local breakdowns, bottlenecks and the damage caused by German bombing – that Britain achieved the most thoroughly mobilised economy of all the belligerent nations.

CIVIL MORALE

The creation of a war economy on this scale placed great pressure on the civilian population. The burden of war work, combined with wartime regulations, rationing and shortages was onerous enough – but civilians also faced physical danger from bombing. British wartime morale later assumed mythic qualities as the 'Dunkirk spirit', but at the time the government worried a great deal. The defeat of Germany in 1918 was believed to have been caused by a collapse in civilian morale, so maintaining British spirits was regarded as essential. Britain entered the war expecting immediate, devastating air raids, causing perhaps

The Home Front 1939–45

World War II had a far greater impact on the day-to-day life of Britain's civilian population than any war before or since. Apart from the enormous effort of mobilising an entire economy for war production, civilians in many parts of the country faced the prospect of devastating air attack. The distressing mass evacuations of the early war soon gave way to more measured government efforts to maintain civilian morale. A widespread 'business as usual' attitude ensured that neither politics nor industrial action was entirely set aside. Profound social changes were set in motion, though – not only by the mobilisation of women into the workforce, but also by the exposure of British people to the wealthier, alien culture of US service personnel.

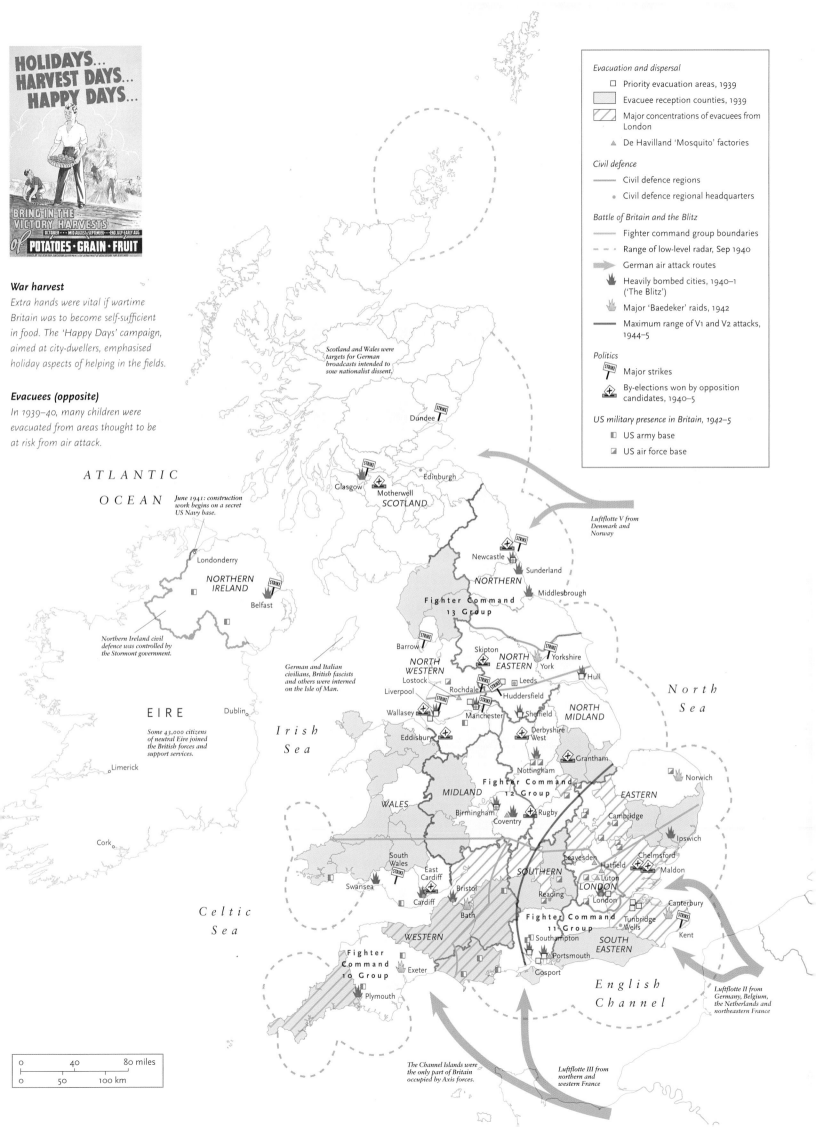

**HOLIDAYS...
HARVEST DAYS...
HAPPY DAYS...**

BRING IN THE VICTORY HARVESTS
OCTOBER • MID AUGUST & SEPTEMBER • END JULY-EARLY AUG
of **POTATOES · GRAIN · FRUIT**

War harvest

Extra hands were vital if wartime Britain was to become self-sufficient in food. The 'Happy Days' campaign, aimed at city-dwellers, emphasised holiday aspects of helping in the fields.

Evacuees (opposite)

In 1939–40, many children were evacuated from areas thought to be at risk from air attack.

Legend

Evacuation and dispersal
- ☐ Priority evacuation areas, 1939
- Evacuee reception counties, 1939
- Major concentrations of evacuees from London
- ▲ De Havilland 'Mosquito' factories

Civil defence
- Civil defence regions
- • Civil defence regional headquarters

Battle of Britain and the Blitz
- Fighter command group boundaries
- Range of low-level radar, Sep 1940
- German air attack routes
- Heavily bombed cities, 1940–1 ('The Blitz')
- Major 'Baedeker' raids, 1942
- Maximum range of V1 and V2 attacks, 1944–5

Politics
- Major strikes
- By-elections won by opposition candidates, 1940–5

US military presence in Britain, 1942–5
- ▣ US army base
- ▣ US air force base

Scotland and Wales were targets for German broadcasts intended to sow nationalist dissent.

ATLANTIC
OCEAN

June 1941: construction work begins on a secret US Navy base.

Londonderry

NORTHERN IRELAND

Belfast

Northern Ireland civil defence was controlled by the Stormont government.

EIRE

Dublin

German and Italian civilians, British fascists and others were interned on the Isle of Man.

Some 43,000 citizens of neutral Eire joined the British forces and support services.

Limerick

Irish Sea

Cork

Dundee

Glasgow · Motherwell
SCOTLAND
Edinburgh

Luftflotte V from Denmark and Norway

Newcastle · Sunderland
NORTHERN
Middlesbrough

Fighter Command 13 Group

Barrow
Skipton · **NORTH EASTERN** · Yorkshire
NORTH WESTERN · York
Lostock · Leeds · Hull
Liverpool · Rochdale · Huddersfield
Wallasey · Manchester · **NORTH MIDLAND**
Eddisbury · Sheffield

North Sea

Derbyshire West
Grantham
Nottingham

Fighter Command 12 Group

MIDLAND
WALES
Birmingham · Rugby
Coventry

EASTERN
Norwich
Cambridge
Ipswich

South Wales
East Cardiff
Swansea

Leavesden · Chelmsford
Hatfield · Maldon
Luton
SOUTHERN
Reading · **LONDON** · London

Fighter Command 11 Group

Bristol
Bath
Cardiff

Celtic Sea

WESTERN

Southampton
Portsmouth
Gosport
Tunbridge Wells
SOUTH EASTERN
Canterbury
Kent

Fighter Command 10 Group

Exeter

Plymouth

English Channel

Luftflotte II from Germany, Belgium, the Netherlands and northeastern France

Luftflotte III from northern and western France

The Channel Islands were the only part of Britain occupied by Axis forces.

0 — 40 — 80 miles
0 — 50 — 100 km

was transferred to Russia, smaller, culturally important targets such as York, Canterbury and Bath were attacked in the so-called 'Baedeker' raids, named for a famous German tourist handbook and aimed specifically at weakening British morale.

The government carefully monitored every site, and any sign of defeatism among the civilian population was observed with intense anxiety. Generally, in the immediate aftermath of a raid, there was an air of depression and gloom, especially among the bereaved and the homeless (who often found relief slow in arriving). One phenomenon that the government vehemently opposed was the common practice of 'trekking'. After raids, large numbers of city dwellers would decamp every night into the countryside (or into London's Underground stations), intent on escaping the danger and the noise as far as possible. The government feared that this would seriously undermine the war effort because it would result in absenteeism, and believed that it was a sign of defeatism, if not cowardice, but every effort to deter the practice was ignored. In fact, there was little cause for alarm. An initial sense of panic or despair generally subsided quite quickly.

On the whole, the British people proved to be adaptable to the burdens of war. They disliked restrictions on movement, rationing, interminable queuing, compulsory extra duties like fire-watching, and petty and irritating regulations, but there was a general perception of equality of sacrifice. Even severe rationing was largely considered bearable because food allowances were the same for everybody. In

Coventry Cathedral, November 1940

Not only homes and lives were lost to German bombing: much of Britain's cultural heritage was also destroyed.

500,000 casualties in the first six weeks of war, and the authorities had little faith in the ability of the civilian population – particularly the working class – to bear such a strain. The country was divided into 12 regions, each with an appointed commissioner who could assume dictatorial powers in case of invasion or a breakdown of order. In the event, no such catastrophe occurred, but every major industrial centre and port was attacked. Even neutral Dublin was twice bombed by stray German aircraft, although the name 'Eire' was painted in large letters on many headlands. When the bulk of the Luftwaffe

parts of Britain that had been depressed in the 1930s, many people were actually better fed under war rationing than they had been in peacetime.

Another source of irritation was the often condescending and hectoring propaganda of the early war – most people simply wanted reliable news and popular entertainment. As the war progressed, these became increasingly available. Other government initiatives, such as the 'Saucepans into Spitfires' campaign, were often intended more as a way of keeping people busy and giving them a sense of involvement in the war than for any intrinsic value. But some campaigns were very valuable – especially 'Dig for Victory', which encouraged people to supplement their food rations through their own efforts.

The billeting of evacuees and servicemen was resented by many. Although billeting is often seen as having awakened much of Britain for the first time to the grinding poverty endured by the urban poor, the experience in many cases simply reinforced existing class prejudices on both sides. A duty some people found more pleasant was welcoming US servicemen. Scattered across the country, with their high pay and access to luxuries long unseen, the Americans provided a touch of colour and glamour to a nation weary of austerity. Yet even they could be viewed as burdensome. British troops resented the difference in their pay, and that the Americans were able to compete with them for scarce goods and services. The racial tensions that the segregated US Army brought with it were also bewildering to many British observers. In July 1944, for example, the citizens of Bristol were dismayed by racial violence involving over 400 US troops, which left one dead and dozens injured.

In short, the British people put up with a great deal during the war. There were occasions when morale sagged, such as after the fall of France and the loss of Tobruk. The V1 and V2 attacks from 1944, coming after D-Day, when the war seemed nearly over, were also a serious blow and caused 1.25 million people to leave London. Despite such low moments, morale never came close to breaking.

THE POLITICAL LANDSCAPE

Despite the existence of an electoral truce intended to prevent divisive campaigning, political life did not come to a halt in wartime Britain. Strikes, though illegal under war regulations, were sometimes large-scale and damaging. Scotland had the most stoppages, while the mining and engineering industries as a whole accounted for the most working days lost. A number of by-elections were

Entertaining American troops

Among the American troops stationed in Britain were many African-Americans. The racial tensions within the segregated American forces bewildered many Britons, most of whom were then unfamiliar with multi-racial societies.

also contested, often by independent candidates or those representing the newly formed Common Wealth Party, who took a generally left-wing stance. As the burdens, shortages and irritations of wartime grew, these independents increasingly appealed to the electorate. Many Conservatives were annoyed by losing seats to what appeared to be thinly disguised Labour candidates at a time when both parties were members of the coalition government. This was not entirely unjustified: constituency Labour parties were often willing to defy their own leadership and support these independent candidates. But the Labour Party leadership itself was far from happy, since it appeared to be losing its grip on its supporters. This divided loyalty on the left meant that few doubted that Churchill's Conservatives would win a landslide victory in the next general election.   **JS**

Newcastle
Conspiracy to strike

Belfast
Defrauding the War Office

Bevin boy (young man conscripted to work as a miner) leaving mine
● York

Excessive use of a glasshouse for flowers
Failure to attend Home Guard
● Blackpool
Refusal to accept evacuees

Liverpool
● St Helens
Bevin boy leaving mine

● Chester
Refusal to accept evacuees

Bilston ●
Failure to perform fire watch

● Leicester
Theft of a collection for servicemen

Norwich ●
Black marketeering

Worcester
Forged ID card

Watford
Profiteering

Camden
Profiteering

Ruislip
Failure to perform fire watch

Forest Gate
Witchcraft

Chippenham
Theft of aviation fuel

Teddington
Passing seditious literature

Hatton Garden
Evading Excess Profit tax

Salisbury ●
Failure to attend Home Guard

Morden
Black marketeering

Croydon
Black marketeering

East Preston
Visiting prohibited beach

Lewes
Black marketeering

Refusal to accept evacuees
St Ives

Wartime offences

Offences reported in *The Times* between July and September 1944 suggest that the British did not become a nation of saints during the war. There were acts of defiance by civilians impatient with wartime regulations. These regulations, especially rationing, meant that new crimes for gain appeared. Even archaic witchcraft laws were used in one instance to silence a medium deemed to be preying on the recently bereaved.

OVERSEAS THEATRES 1939-45

Britain and France entered World War II in 1939 expecting the Western Front to be the decisive one, as it had been in World War I. The German attack of May 1940, Britain's summary expulsion from the Continent and the collapse of France were stunning and catastrophic. Attempts to aid Norway, which Germany invaded in April 1940, had ended in a fiasco that led to the fall of Prime Minister Neville Chamberlain. In October 1940 Italy invaded Greece; the

Europe and the Middle East 1940–5

Between the fall of France and the American entry into the war, Britain could not hope to launch an invasion of Europe. Instead, the British fought on the periphery of German and Italian power, hoping gradually to wear them down. Thus a major British commitment was made in North Africa. As American military might expanded, Britain's control of strategy faded. Eventually, the USA dictated when the invasion of Europe would occur.

Greeks proved capable of dealing with the attack, but a coup in Yugoslavia installed a pro-British government, and Hitler decided to intervene. German forces swept through both states very quickly. The British attempted to aid the Greeks, but were soon expelled, with heavy losses. Britain was left with the problem of how to defeat Germany and its new Italian partner without a major continental ally. The solution was to adopt a strategy of peripheralism: opera-

tions would be limited to the periphery of enemy power, and, combined with bombing, blockade and subversion, would, it was believed, gradually wear down the enemy until a continental invasion would precipitate the total collapse of Germany. This was an opportunist approach, realistic in view of Britain's limited resources. Apart from toppling some of the Vichy French colonial regimes (such as Syria), overturning pro-German governments (such as Iraq) in the Middle East and defeating the Italians in Abyssinia, there was only one place where Britain could hope to win a victory: North Africa.

THE MEDITERRANEAN

In December 1940 British imperial forces launched an offensive against a much larger but half-hearted Italian force that had crept into Egypt. It was an overwhelming success; 10 Italian divisions were destroyed and it seemed that the British could advance all the way to Tripoli. But events elsewhere intruded. When Italy attacked Greece, Churchill felt it politically impossible to leave the Greeks unaided. Forces were diverted from North Africa just as Rommel began to land a German armoured division in Tripoli. The result was defeat on two fronts: expelled from Greece and Crete with heavy losses in troops and equipment, the British were also driven from Benghazi all the way back to Egypt, leaving a largely Australian garrison besieged in Tobruk. This left Churchill clamouring for victory and prepared to commit an ever-increasing volume of resources to the theatre – arguably leaving Britain dangerously exposed in other areas, such as the Far East.

The result was a successful offensive launched in November 1941, which was disastrously defeated in a German-backed Italian counter-offensive in May 1942. British forces were driven back to Alamein before they had stabilised their position. Humiliatingly, Tobruk, whose defences had largely been dismantled, fell after the briefest of sieges.

Coinciding with the fall of Singapore, this defeat saw Britain's military prestige sink to its lowest level, and Churchill faced a political crisis at home. He easily won a vote of confidence in Parliament, but real unease about the conduct of the war was revealed.

The entry of the USA into the war following Japan's attack on Pearl Harbor (7 December 1941) was soon to alter the situation radically. Even before Pearl Harbor, Churchill had secured from Roosevelt an undertaking that if the USA intervened it would concentrate on defeating Germany first.

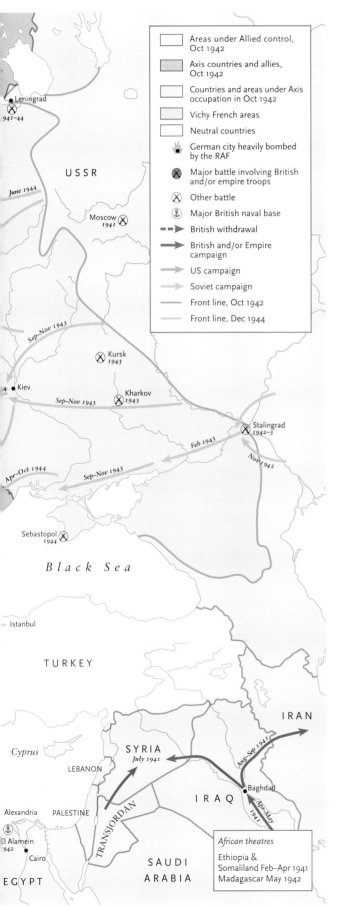

Liberating Athens

A British soldier gives a Union Jack armband to a Greek boy, as Greek partisans look on. Britain had committed considerable resources to arming such partisans.

Malaya 1941–2

Britain's defence of Malaya was one of the least successful military campaigns in its history. By late 1941, wartime commitments elsewhere meant that the resources necessary to defend Malaya – especially modern aircraft – simply did not exist. Nor did the fleet Britain was long committed to sending if needed. Well-trained Japanese forces overran successive defensive positions on the ground, while their aircraft delivered a stunning blow by sinking two of the Royal Navy's most powerful capital ships – the last major Allied warships in the Far East. The surrender of Singapore was a huge shock, both in Britain and worldwide.

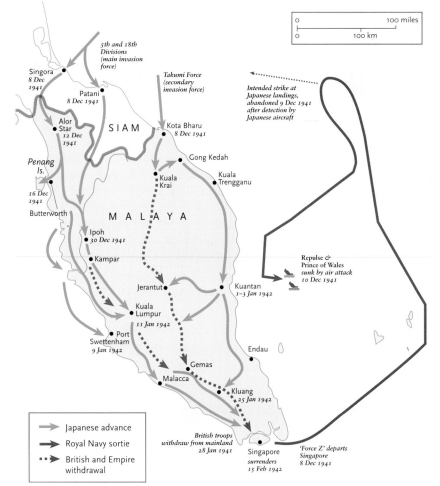

'Very gloomy. Japs have penetrated 5 miles into Singapore island. Our generals are no use, and do our men fight? As P.M. says, what will happen if Germans get a footing here? I shudder to think. Our army is the mockery of the world.'

Sir Alexander Cadogan, Under-Secretary of State to the Foreign Office, in his diary, 9 February 1942

Now Britain and the USA discussed how to achieve this. The American view was that peripheralism was wasteful and pointless: the way to defeat Germany was to land in overwhelming force in Europe and invade Germany itself. This would satisfy Stalin's repeated demands for a second front in Europe – which had considerable public support in Britain – and would bring the war to a swift end.

The US government went to great efforts to extract a British commitment to an invasion in 1943, if not in 1942, and believed they had secured one. The British, however, remained convinced that a precipitate invasion would be disastrous. In July 1942 Churchill informed Roosevelt that an invasion was impossible that year, but might be achieved in 1943. He persuaded Roosevelt to commit US forces to operations in North Africa – much to the disgust of his own military, who thought they were being used to protect Britain's empire – and Roosevelt agreed.

As a result, only days after the British had secured their decisive victory at Alamein, Allied forces landed in north-west Africa. As the Americans had feared, however, operations proved so protracted that an invasion of Europe in 1943 was rendered impossible, and they refused to accept anything but an absolute British commitment to the invasion in 1944.

The question remained, of course, what Allied forces should do after complete victory in Africa. Rather than have them stand idle while the Russians were fighting for their lives, US commanders had to accept Churchill's proposal for an invasion of Italy. In July 1943 Sicily was duly invaded; this operation was soon followed by landings on the mainland. Again there was no rapid victory. The invasion faced stiff German resistance and made slow progress, and the Americans, whose mobilisation was rapidly expanding while Britain's relative power in the alliance declined, refused to commit resources to a theatre that might undermine the D-Day operations.

EUROPE

Controversy between Britain and the USA was not confined to the timing of the invasion. There was also an argument over where in Germany their respective armies proposed to end up. The Americans wanted the northern zone, as they intended to remove their forces rapidly after the war. The British, however, feared facing a triumphant Russia astride central Europe alone. They wanted the northern zone precisely because it would render an American withdrawal more difficult. The British won the argument. While Roosevelt hesitated in naming the Supreme Allied Commander, the British appointed his chief-of-staff, Frederick Morgan, who positioned British invasion forces in southeast England and Americans in the southwest. Because it would be impossibly complicated to change those dispositions once made, and lunacy to have supply lines cross, simple geographic logic prescribed that the British were destined to arrive in northern Germany.

As a result of these strategic considerations, however, British forces were faced with a difficult advance along the north European coast, with several major river estuaries to cross: not for them the dramatic advances of the Americans. When Field Marshal Montgomery did try to win a spectacular victory by airborne landings at Arnhem, his over-ambitious plan ended in disaster.

The final advance into Germany met with comparatively light resistance. Most remaining German forces were trying to stem the Russian tide to their east. German civilians were relieved that Allied bombing was over. The British, especially, had devoted vast resources to the bombing campaign, in the hope of bringing Germany to its knees without an invasion. But the bomber proved to be no war-winning weapon on its own. Nevertheless, the Allied air forces – despite heavy casualties – had wrought utter devastation on most German cities. With Allied troops on German soil, and the massive wreckage around them, there could be no repeat of the mythology Germany developed after 1918: there was no doubt that their defeat was absolute.

THE FAR EAST

Given Britain's need for home defence, its commitment in North Africa, and the necessity of supplying Russia, it was perhaps unavoidable that defences in the Far East were given low priority. In Malaya, however, Britain showed a degree of complacency that would prove disastrously expensive. Britain's position in the region was based largely on bluff – it was assumed that a fleet could be sent at need – and on the myth of a mighty fortress of Singapore. In the event, no fleet was available in 1941, and Singapore's defences were flimsy, being designed to resist seaborne attack rather than a land assault from the north. The forces available for the defence of Malaya were desperately short of modern aircraft, tanks and anti-tank guns.

The fall of France spelled doom for Malaya. It allowed the Japanese to intimidate the colonial administration in French Indo-China into allowing a Japanese occupation, which made an invasion of the Malay peninsula from the north possible. In December 1941 the Japanese quickly established supremacy in the air, because of which they were able to destroy Britain's hastily assembled naval strike force, the battlecruiser *Repulse* and battleship *Prince of Wales*. The loss of these two capital ships was a serious shock in Malaya and Britain alike. On land, British units were outflanked and forced into a series of retreats. They attempted a stand in central Malaya, around Kampar, but the area was overrun on 2 January 1942, just before reinforcements arrived in Singapore. The troops who arrived after the fall of Kampar merely added to the scale of the disaster: the attempt to hold Singapore proved hopeless – there were no landward defences worthy of the name. British forces in Malaya finally surrendered, to a much smaller Japanese force that had suffered trivial casualties, after a campaign of just 55 days.

It was in Burma, from which they had been ejected after a gruelling fighting retreat from January to May 1942, that British and empire forces could hope to regain the initiative. First, however, they had to regain their badly shaken confidence, and receive realistic training and adequate resources. This was slowly achieved, largely under the direction of General William Slim. A limited offensive in Arakan in December 1942 was unsuccessful, but operations by the 'Chindit' special forces behind Japanese lines in February to April 1943 showed at least that Allied forces could master jungle fighting as effectively as their enemies. When Japanese forces at last launched a major offensive against Kohima and Imphal from April to June 1944, intending to create a defensive position in the Naga Hills on the Assam border, British and Indian forces were able to reply with a crippling counter-attack. After hard fighting, the offensive brought the recapture of Mandalay in March 1945 and Rangoon in May, and the annihilation of three Japanese armies as they tried to escape into Siam.

The British high command had intended to recapture Malaya by sea, but the Japanese surrender in August 1945 robbed them of their chance to avenge the events of 1941–2. While Churchill was eager to contribute towards the final assault on Japan, the Americans, confident of their ability to defeat Japan alone, had no intention of allowing Britain a say in the future of what was seen as an American preserve; British naval forces were given only a minor role in the war's final campaigns.   **JS**

Recapturing Burma

British troops advance towards Mandalay in March 1945. The recapture of Burma saw savage fighting, but, with adequate training and resources, the British proved a match for the Japanese in jungle warfare.

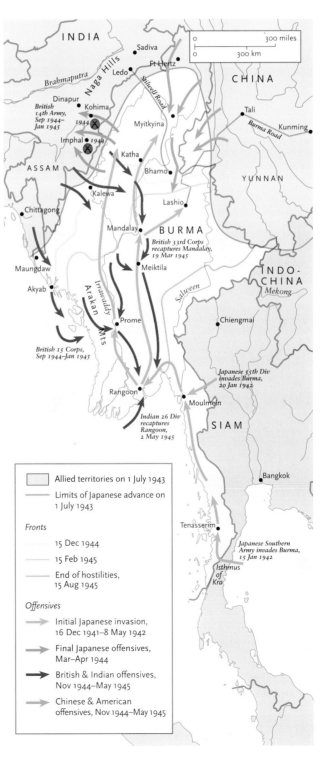

Burma 1942–5

Like British forces in Malaya, the defenders of Burma lacked the resources to withstand the Japanese onslaught. They could at least retreat into India, and prepare to return in force. It took considerable time to gather the resources and ready the troops to undertake a major offensive. But when it came, following a failed Japanese offensive into India, it was to prove devastatingly effective.

Convoy with escorts

A convoy with Royal Navy escorts seen at sunset in the Atlantic in July 1942. The adoption of the convoy system was a key element in defeating the U-boat threat.

For Britain, the battle of the Atlantic was the longest and most critical of World War II; defeat would have forced Britain out of the war and made US intervention in Europe impossible. In September 1939 neither the British nor the Germans could ignore the lessons of the 1914–18 sea war: the German High Seas Fleet had remained largely inactive, while German U-boats had brought Britain perilously close to catastrophe. In the U-boat, Germany had deployed a potentially war-winning weapon, and there was no reason not to attempt to use it more decisively in a second war. While Germany had entered the war in 1939 with a number of particularly formidable capital ships, including three purpose-built 'pocket battleship' commerce raiders and two powerful modern battleships (with two even more powerful units, *Bismarck* and *Tirpitz*, launched early in the war), there were always too few to challenge the Royal Navy directly. Instead, Germany was once again to use its limited naval resources to attack Britain's sea communications. The capital ships were used as raiders against British commerce. Tracking down and destroying these threats severely stretched British resources. The pocket battleship *Graf Spee* enjoyed considerable success at the beginning of the war, until outfought by three British cruisers at the battle of the River Plate and scuttled off Montevideo in December 1939, while *Bismarck* made a spectacular but brief voyage in May 1941. It took virtually the entire Home Fleet, as well as Coastal Command aircraft and warships from the Mediterranean Fleet, to ensure that the ship that sank the battlecruiser *Hood* never returned to port.

Just as in the previous war, however, it was the U-boat that was to prove the greatest danger. The threat to Britain's supply lines caused Churchill and others intense anxiety: the U-boat appeared to be proving a decisive weapon. To Karl Dönitz, commander of the U-boat fleet, it was a simple question of arithmetic: Britain depended on supplies that were carried by a fleet of about 3,000 ocean-going merchant ships, and these could carry about 17 million tonnes. If he could keep sufficient U-boats at sea and sink enough of this tonnage, Britain would be forced to capitulate. He had devised tactics to overcome convoys, based on the simple concept of overwhelming the escorts. His boats would attack in groups, on the surface and at night at close range.

THE U-BOAT CAMPAIGN DEVELOPS

Neither side was prepared for war in 1939. Dönitz simply did not have the boats to launch attacks in groups and the British had made very few preparations. ASDIC (the British equivalent of the US Sonar system for detecting submarines by sound) had been developed, and was initially seen as a complete solution to the U-boat threat, but it proved less than perfect. It was only effective at ranges of 200–1,000 metres (220–1,100 yards), when most U-boats were operating on the surface in any case. Britain's escort fleet had been allowed to run down to such an extent that Churchill was prepared to trade valuable bases in Britain's possessions in the West Indies and Newfoundland for 50 obsolete American destroyers. Perhaps even more damaging was the misuse of resources: the Royal Navy insisted on largely futile attempts to hunt down U-boats instead of concentrating on escorting convoys. RAF Coastal Command was left critically short of aircraft because of the priority given

> '...the spectacle of all these splendid ships being...sunk – three or four every day – torments me day and night.'
>
> **Winston Churchill, in a letter to Franklin D. Roosevelt, 31 October 1942**

The battle of the Atlantic, 1939–45

Air power was crucial in the battle of the Atlantic. German spotter aircraft could locate convoys and guide U-boats to their targets, while land-based Allied air patrols – and fighters launched by catapult from convoy ships or (later) escort carriers – provided essential protection. The U-boats had limited underwater range, and spent most of their time on the surface, where they were vulnerable to Coastal Command bombers or carrier-based aircraft. U-boat tactics and operational areas changed regularly in response to improvements in Allied air cover and escort technology, and until late 1941 convoy losses were alarming. Thereafter, the Allies slowly gained the upper hand, maintaining the critical flow of war supplies from the USA to Britain.

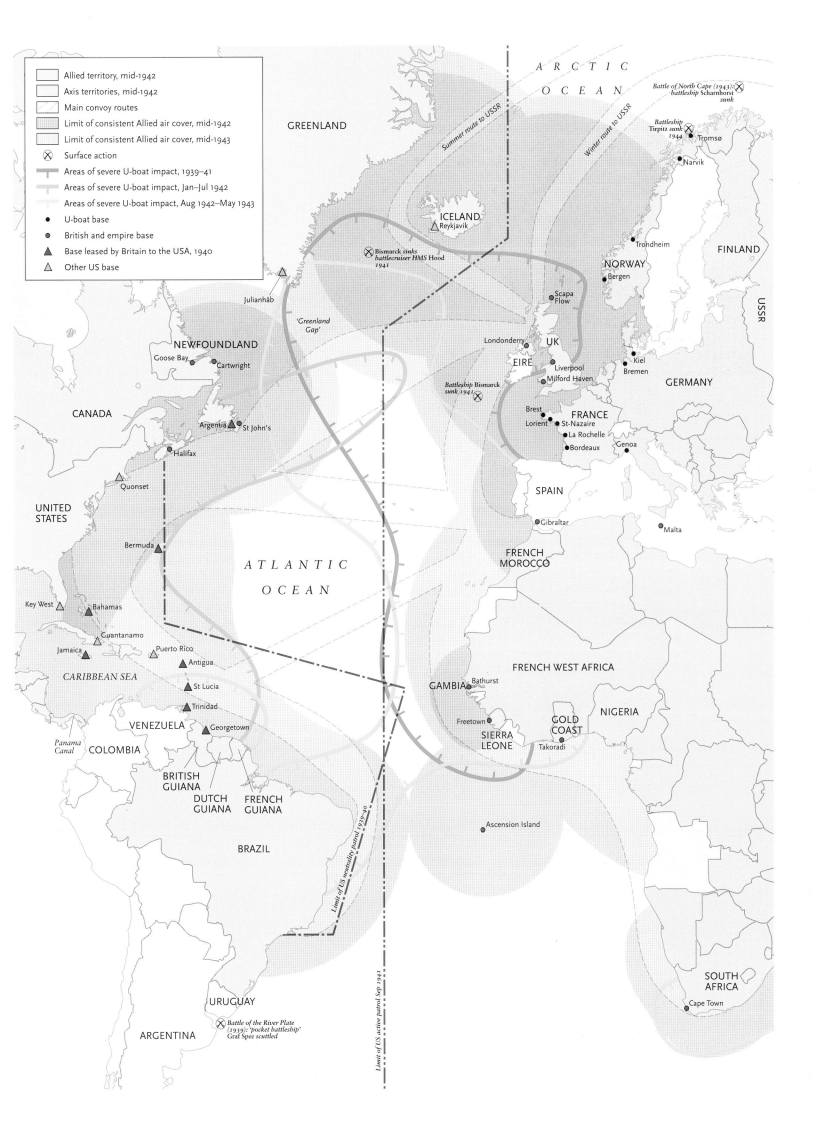

Allied territory, mid-1942

Axis territories, mid-1942

Main convoy routes

Limit of consistent Allied air cover, mid-1942

Limit of consistent Allied air cover, mid-1943

⊗ Surface action

Areas of severe U-boat impact, 1939–41

Areas of severe U-boat impact, Jan–Jul 1942

Areas of severe U-boat impact, Aug 1942–May 1943

● U-boat base

● British and empire base

▲ Base leased by Britain to the USA, 1940

△ Other US base

ARCTIC OCEAN

Battle of North Cape (1943): ⊗
battleship Scharnhorst sunk

Battleship Tirpitz sunk ⊗
1944 Tromsø

● Narvik

GREENLAND

Summer route to USSR

Winter route to USSR

FINLAND

ICELAND
△ Reykjavik

● Trondheim

NORWAY

● Bergen

Julianhåb △

'Greenland Gap'

⊗ *Bismarck sinks battlecruiser HMS Hood 1941*

Scapa Flow

USSR

NEWFOUNDLAND

Londonderry ●

UK

EIRE

● Kiel

Goose Bay ● ● Cartwright

Liverpool ●

● Bremen

Milford Haven ●

GERMANY

CANADA

Argentia △ △ St John's

Battleship Bismarck sunk 1941 ⊗

Brest ● FRANCE

Halifax ●

Lorient ● ● St-Nazaire

● La Rochelle

● Genoa

Quonset △

● Bordeaux

UNITED STATES

SPAIN

Bermuda △

ATLANTIC OCEAN

Gibraltar ●

● Malta

FRENCH MOROCCO

Key West △ ● Bahamas

Jamaica ● ▲ Guantanamo

FRENCH WEST AFRICA

Puerto Rico △ ▲ Antigua

CARIBBEAN SEA

GAMBIA ● Bathurst

▲ St Lucia

NIGERIA

▲ Trinidad

Freetown ●

GOLD COAST

VENEZUELA ▲ Georgetown

SIERRA LEONE

Takoradi ●

Panama Canal COLOMBIA

BRITISH GUIANA

DUTCH GUIANA

FRENCH GUIANA

Ascension Island ●

BRAZIL

Limit of US neutrality patrol 1939–40

Limit of US active patrol Sep 1941

SOUTH AFRICA

URUGUAY

Cape Town ● ⊗

⊗ *Battle of the River Plate (1939): 'pocket battleship' Graf Spee scuttled*

ARGENTINA

to Bomber Command, and the flying boats it received did not have enough range – there remained a gap in the central Atlantic where no air patrols were possible: the 'Greenland gap', where U-boats could concentrate in relative safety. This was the period known to the Germans as the 'happy time', when their losses were slight and successes high. The fall of France proved a serious disaster for Britain, as the operational range of Atlantic U-boats was considerably extended by new bases in western France. In a desperate attempt to extend the range of Britain's air patrols, Churchill offered the Irish government unification with Northern Ireland in exchange for the use of bases in Lough Swilly, Cobh and Berehaven – but Ireland's government insisted on maintaining its strict neutrality in the war.

The British did have some advantages. Decryption of coded German radio signals by British Intelligence at Bletchley Park was of great value. It was not a decisive advantage, as it could take too long to decrypt signals for them to be of use, and on a number of occasions there were periods when decryption proved impossible. Radio direction-finding could be more useful – Dönitz required frequent radio reports from his captains, which betrayed their positions and allowed convoys to avoid U-boat concentrations. Far more significant for Britain was the attitude of the USA, which quickly established a neutrality zone far out into the Atlantic, limiting U-boat operations. Once President Roosevelt had decided that it was in US interests to support the British war effort, the vast economic power of the United States began to be mobilised in Britain's favour. US-built merchant ships did much to replenish British losses in the Atlantic.

Having taken the decision to supply Britain's needs via Lend-Lease, the Americans quickly accepted that supplies without assured delivery were of little value. The USA thus became increasingly involved in foiling the U-boats. During 1941 the US Navy began escorting convoys to the mid-Atlantic, and by October 1941 to within 650 kilometres (400 miles) of Ireland. Not surprisingly, this led to a series of incidents between U-boats and US warships, which stung Roosevelt into issuing an order to sink U-boats on sight. The Germans concluded that the USA was doing as much harm to them as a neutral as it could as an active enemy. Once Germany had declared war on the United States, U-boats were quick to flock to the relatively unprotected waters off the US coast, where they enjoyed a second 'happy time', before moving into the Caribbean when the US Navy belatedly began organising its own convoy system.

CLIMAX OF THE BATTLE

In April 1942 the U-boats again concentrated in the central Atlantic. Dönitz now had enough boats to keep 50 on station at any time: enough, he calculated, to clinch victory. Up to 20 boats could be launched against a single convoy. In March 1943, 67 out of 85 ships in convoy were lost. The Allies were appalled, but could see no alternative to convoys. Dönitz scented victory. Yet by May he had lost the battle. This was due partly to improved Allied tactics and partly to improved technology, but the most significant factor was simply the diversion of sufficient resources to meet the threat. At the Casablanca conference in January 1943, Churchill and Roosevelt had agreed that losses in the Atlantic were no longer bearable and that absolute priority must be given to defeating the U-boats. Coastal Command then received adequate aircraft, and escort carriers were made available to close the 'Greenland gap'.

WINNING THE BATTLE: CONVOYS ON 202 AND ONS 18

In September 1943 two convoys left Britain for North America, part of the regular shuttle of merchant ships to collect war materials from the USA and Canada. Their experience is typical of the mid- to late-war convoys, when the battle was finally turning Britain's way. Between them, convoys ON 202 and ONS 18 included 69 merchant vessels and 14 escorts, including an escort carrier – a small aircraft carrier built specifically for convoy escort duties. They were to run the gauntlet of a concerted U-boat attack in mid-Atlantic. The U-boats were newly equipped with snorkels (extended air intakes for their diesel engines that allowed them to travel beneath the surface for long periods, rather

Depth charge

A depth charge explodes astern of a Royal Navy ship hunting for a submerged U-boat. Dropped from surface ships, depth charges could cause fatal damage to a submarine, but they had a limited effective range.

than the usual pattern of long, vulnerable periods on the surface interspersed with brief submerged attacking runs using their electric motors) and, for the first time, with

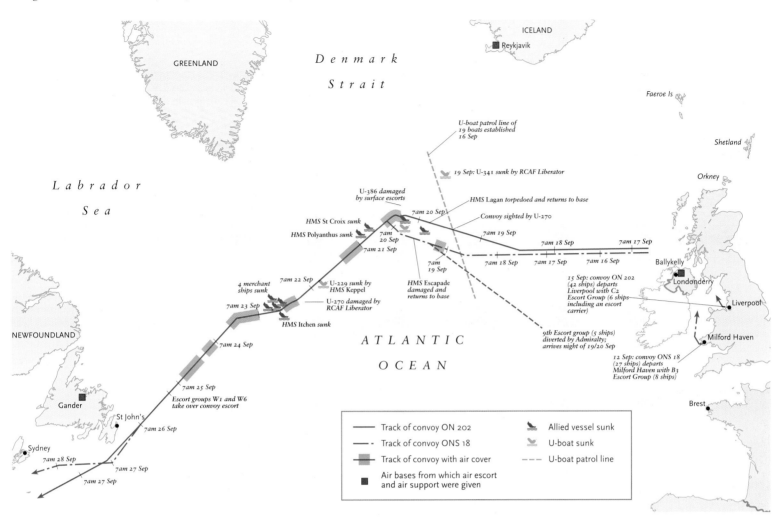

ICELAND
Reykjavik

GREENLAND

Denmark Strait

Faeroe Is

Labrador Sea

Shetland

Orkney

U-boat patrol line of
19 boats established
16 Sep

19 Sep: U-341 sunk by RCAF Liberator

U-386 damaged
by surface escorts

HMS Lagan torpedoed and returns to base

HMS St Croix sunk

7am 20 Sep

Convoy sighted by U-270

HMS Polyanthus sunk

7am 20 Sep

7am 19 Sep

7am 18 Sep   7am 17 Sep

7am 21 Sep

Ballykelly

7am 22 Sep

7am 19 Sep

7am 18 Sep   7am 17 Sep   7am 16 Sep

Londonderry

4 merchant ships sunk

U-229 sunk by HMS Keppel

HMS Escapade damaged and returns to base

15 Sep: convoy ON 202
(42 ships) departs
Liverpool with C2
Escort Group (6 ships
including an escort
carrier)

Liverpool

7am 23 Sep

U-270 damaged by
RCAF Liberator

ATLANTIC OCEAN

Milford Haven

HMS Itchen sunk

9th Escort group (5 ships)
diverted by Admiralty;
arrives night of 19/20 Sep

NEWFOUNDLAND

7am 24 Sep

12 Sep: convoy ONS 18
(27 ships) departs
Milford Haven with B3
Escort Group (8 ships)

7am 25 Sep

Gander

Escort groups W1 and W6
take over convoy escort

Brest

St John's

7am 26 Sep

Sydney

7am 28 Sep

7am 27 Sep

7am 27 Sep

---- Track of convoy ON 202   Allied vessel sunk

---- Track of convoy ONS 18   U-boat sunk

▨ Track of convoy with air cover   ---- U-boat patrol line

■ Air bases from which air escort
and air support were given

improved T5 acoustic torpedoes (detonated by the sound of a ship's engines in near proximity, rather than by contact with the ship's hull).

When signals intelligence alerted the Admiralty to the danger, immediate and decisive steps were taken. The two convoys were ordered to combine and were reinforced by a further escort group of five ships. Only two merchant vessels were lost before convoys reached their rendezvous. In addition, Liberator bombers in Britain and Iceland were sent to provide the closest air cover possible.

The escort groups, now long practised in working together, were by this time also being equipped with new technology, such as the HF/DF radio direction finder, with which they could locate U-boats from their radio signals, and the ASV III radar, which the Germans were unable to detect. They were able to provide a screen so effective that, despite repeated attacks over five days, the escort screen was penetrated only once, and then only four merchant ships were sunk. The U-boats achieved nothing whenever the Liberators were providing close cover – attacking at these times would have been suicidal.

The Germans lost three boats, with a further two badly damaged, out of a force of 19 – unsustainable losses for a trivial return in merchant ships sunk. The heaviest Allied losses were to the escorts; the acoustic torpedo proved particularly deadly against warships, and three escorts were sunk and two badly damaged. For the Allies, the convoy battle was therefore an expensive success, which showed

that immense resources were still vital to keep supply lines open. Partly as a result of experience gained in the battles for convoys ON 202 and ONS 18, the Allies quickly developed a trailed noise-maker – the 'foxer' – which foiled the acoustic torpedo by causing it to detonate a safe distance away from the target ship.

STRATEGIC VICTORY

In fact, the strategic balance of the battle of the Atlantic had begun to turn decisively toward the Allies from about May 1943, when most of the U-boats began moving to supposedly easier hunting grounds around the Azores. At about the same time, British aircraft diverted from Bomber Command launched a highly effective campaign in the Bay of Biscay, sinking many U-boats. Germany was never again able to launch a serious challenge in the Atlantic. It is worth remembering that Dönitz sought only to sink tonnage, not to close vital routes that the Allies were determined to keep open. Nor did he seek to concentrate on valuable ships, such as tankers or American troop ships. For all of the terrible losses suffered by the merchant seamen, he did not come close to sinking enough tonnage to win a decisive victory. Allied, and especially US, industrial might was so great that while the British merchant fleet suffered severely, total Allied tonnage actually grew during the war, and while 30,000 merchant seamen died, Germany lost 781 of 1,175 U-boats and 28,000 of 41,000 crewmen.   **JS**

Convoys ON 202 and ONS 18, 1943

The experience of the combined outward convoys ON 202 and ONS 18 in September 1943 was typical of the later stages of the U-boat war. Air patrols provided cover at crucial points along the route, and the Royal Navy was able to reinforce the convoy escort groups in time to defeat a major concentration of U-boats. Of 69 merchantmen, 63 made the crossing successfully, to return with vital war supplies for Britain.

A Liberal party rally in 1906

Though they were often rowdy, rallies were vital in mobilising votes. As the 20th century progressed, political parties made increasing use of new forms of mass media: radio, newsreel and, ultimately, television.

In Britain, voting behaviour and the electoral system underwent profound changes over the course of the twentieth century. In 1900, only seven out of 10 adult men (and no women) were qualified to vote. Four million men were excluded from the franchise and there were nearly half a million plural voters (including around 2,000 men with four or more votes). Universal male suffrage was achieved in 1918. After a long struggle, women over the age of 30 were permitted to vote in 1918, and in 1928 the age limit was lowered to 21, the same as that for men. However, the ideal of 'one person, one vote' was not reached until 1948, when plural voting and the anomalous 'university' seats were abolished. British youth was enfranchised in 1969, when the age of voting was reduced to 18.

In practice, however, the ideal of universal suffrage is yet to be reached. Apart from the peers, criminals and the mentally ill legitimately excluded from the franchise, failings in the electoral register mean that some groups (especially the young, certain ethnic groups and those living in inner cities) remain disproportionately unable to vote.

Voter turnout for general elections has also been subject to change, and may be in decline. The overall turnout for 2001, for example, was the lowest since universal male suffrage was introduced, even including the 1918 election, which was affected by the aftermath of World War I. Declines in other indicators of political engagement, such as party membership, active canvassing and attendance at political meetings,

support the view that the public are increasingly indifferent to parliamentary politics. However, the average turnout for the period 1950–92 was actually higher than the average for 1922–45, so evidence of an overall decline is not yet conclusive.

SEAT DISTRIBUTION

The principle of single-member, equal-sized constituencies was accepted in 1885, though it was not completely achieved until 1948. The creation of Boundary Commissions in 1944 established a mechanism for reviewing the distribution of voters, but anomalies in the system still remain. Historically, Scotland and Wales have been over-represented at Westminster, although the devolution of certain powers to the Scottish and Welsh assemblies in 1999 may yet mark the end of that privilege. Over the century, inner-city constituencies tended to depopulate, while suburban seats expanded. One Manchester constituency, for example, declined from over 55,000 voters to 18,000 during a 15-year period in the 1950s and 1960s. More recently, there has been a tendency for suburbs to depopulate, too, with the result, for example, that in 1997 Bromley and Croydon's representation was reduced from four constituencies to three. A drift of population to the countryside has resulted in increased representation for shire counties such as Oxfordshire, which had five seats at the last election, up from three in 1974, reversing the trend

Parties	
■	Conservative
▨ ■	Labour
□	Liberal
■	SNP
□	Unionist
■	Sinn Féin

1918

servatives held a third of the seats in northern England, while Labour penetrated the cities of southern England in 1997. The decline of class-based voting has been attributed to increased affluence, changing occupational structures following the collapse of heavy industries, and the fragmentation of traditional communities. Until the 1960s, most voters remained loyal to the party they had voted for in previous elections – and even to the party their parents had supported. At the end of the century, party choice was increasingly determined by voter perceptions of the overall competence of the main parties. This trend has led to increased importance of the media in elections. Newspapers have maintained their influential voice, both in reporting elections and, to some extent, in setting the agenda for campaigns, but it is the evolution of political broadcasting that has revolutionised elections since the 1950s. Television has provided voters with their main source of information on campaigns since the 1960s. As a result, politicians have modified their language and their message for television and its audience.

The fears of opponents of women's suffrage that gender would play a major role in voting behaviour have proven unfounded. Women MPs, for their part, remained unable to challenge the male dominance of parliament for much of the century. In 1993, however, the Labour party decided to select women candidates for winnable parliamentary seats, and 120 women MPs were elected in 1997. Although early expectations of dramatic change were not realised, increased numbers of women MPs are but one indication of the changing nature of parliamentary politics as Britain enters the twenty-first century.   **SR**

Bethnal Green by-election, 1914

Door-to-door canvassing was, and remains, an important aspect of electioneering. Though women did not get the vote until 1918, this candidate seeks support on the doorstep from a female shopkeeper. His attention is an early sign of the growing political importance of women.

established by the 19th-century Reform Acts for rural representation to decline. The Boundary Commissions, which sit periodically, have not been able to keep up with the country's demographic changes. The distribution of seats remains an imprecise science and it is unlikely that the ideal of equal constituencies will ever be achieved.

VOTER BEHAVIOUR

Voting behaviour also changed dramatically. Most obviously, Labour replaced the Liberals as one of the two major political parties after 1918 (though increased volatility in the electorate has led to a Liberal revival and the rise of Scottish and Welsh nationalist parties since the 1960s). The first half of the century witnessed class-based voting at its height. Labour was concentrated in areas of heavy industry and the North, while the Conservatives held a near monopoly of seats in the rural South. Even in 1987, Labour won only three seats in the south of England outside London.

The north–south divide began to be less significant in the second half of the century. For example, in 1992 the Con-

1955

1997

British regional voting patterns

Though simplified maps of seats won per region (shown here for three elections) do not provide an accurate picture of electoral results, they do reveal major voting trends. In 1918 the Conservatives were dominant, though Liberal support remained strong. By 1955, Labour had replaced the Liberals almost everywhere, but the Conservatives remained comfortably in control. In 1997, a Labour resurgence and Liberal and SNP gains reduced Conservative strength largely to the Southeast.

The general election of 1945 produced a landslide victory for the Labour Party. As the brutality of warfare gave way to visions of a fairer society, the electorate turned its back on Churchill, and on foreign adventures and imperial glory. Better housing and a welfare state topped the new agenda. Many believed that Labour would be in power for a generation. Instead, Clement Attlee's ministers had only six years to build their New Jerusalem.

Britain had larger debts by the end of the war than any other nation in history and was precariously dependent on American aid – and these two factors ultimately crippled the new government. Nonetheless, Labour's achievements were substantial. India became independent, and the Commonwealth became a multiracial institution. Over a million new houses were built, a comprehensive social insurance scheme was begun and the National Health Service was inaugurated. Surveys suggested that, by 1951, poverty had been all but eliminated. In addition, Labour nationalised a number of industries and services, including coal, the railways, gas and electricity. The postwar years also generally saw full employment, and the government established special 'development areas', in which half the new buildings of the late 1940s were sited, in an attempt to avoid a return to the 'depressed areas' of the previous decade. A dozen new towns were constructed – the first of an eventual 27 – designed to draw population from over-crowded cities like London and Glasgow and to create balanced urban communities.

Labour lost the election of 1951 in part because its achievements in the postwar years had been accompanied by continued – and indeed intensified – austerity for Britain's people. Wartime rationing was tightened, and now extended to bread and potatoes. There were signs, for instance in the Festival of Britain celebrations, that the drabness of the period was coming to an end, but memories of the winter of January and February 1947 were still acute: temperatures had been at their lowest for over 100 years, unemployment had

Bread queue, Streatham, July 1946
Shortages persisted after the war and the British soon wearied of austerity. Bread rationing, unseen during the war but introduced in February 1947, proved deeply unpopular and very damaging to the new Labour government.

'*There was a new society to be built; and we had the power to build it. There was exhilaration among us, joy and hope, determination and confidence. We felt exalted, dedicated, walking on air, walking with destiny.*'

Hugh Dalton, recalling the atmosphere among Labour colleagues in 1945

briefly touched 2.5 million, and the floods that came with the thaw wrought destruction on the nation's agriculture. 'We work or we want', proclaimed government posters. Many worked hard, and industrial production increased by a third between 1946 and 1951, but what people wanted was more consumer goods.

Furthermore, the government's foreign policy initiatives had also encountered serious difficulties. Foreign Secretary Ernest Bevin negotiated Marshall Aid for Britain from the USA in 1949, and in the same year he helped organise the North Atlantic Treaty Organisation. But the price of such security – and the maintenance of a place at the top table of international politics – was high. Not only were American B-29 bombers stationed in East Anglia from 1948 (and from 1950 they had a nuclear capacity), but in 1951 Britain followed the Americans into the Korean War. The government had to accept inflated defence estimates that not only produced cuts in welfare spending (and the resignation of Aneurin Bevan, the founder of the NHS) but helped fuel a balance of payments crisis. It was a temporary deficit, but by the time balance had been restored, in 1953, Labour was out of office.

AFFLUENCE AND AFTER

It took longer for the Conservatives to remove rationing than they had hoped, but even so the years from 1951 are generally considered a period of affluence. Commentators even spoke of a 'new Elizabethan age'. Broadly speaking, the new government continued the policies of the old and built upon their achievements. Substantial economic growth continued, with industrial production rising by a third in the decade after 1951. By sacrificing a certain degree of quality, the government was able to build 300,000 new houses a year. The programme of creating new towns was continued, with Cumbernauld appearing in 1956,

From austerity to affluence

The immediate postwar years were a drab time for Britain. Rationing continued and even tightened. But a period of unprecedented affluence followed the achievements of Attlee's governments. With the development of new universities, television, motorways, nuclear power stations and national parks, Britain seemed to be entering a new age of wealth and social and technological progress by the end of the 1950s. For Ireland, it was a period of economic stagnation and continuous emigration, much of it to Britain, where there was a labour shortage.

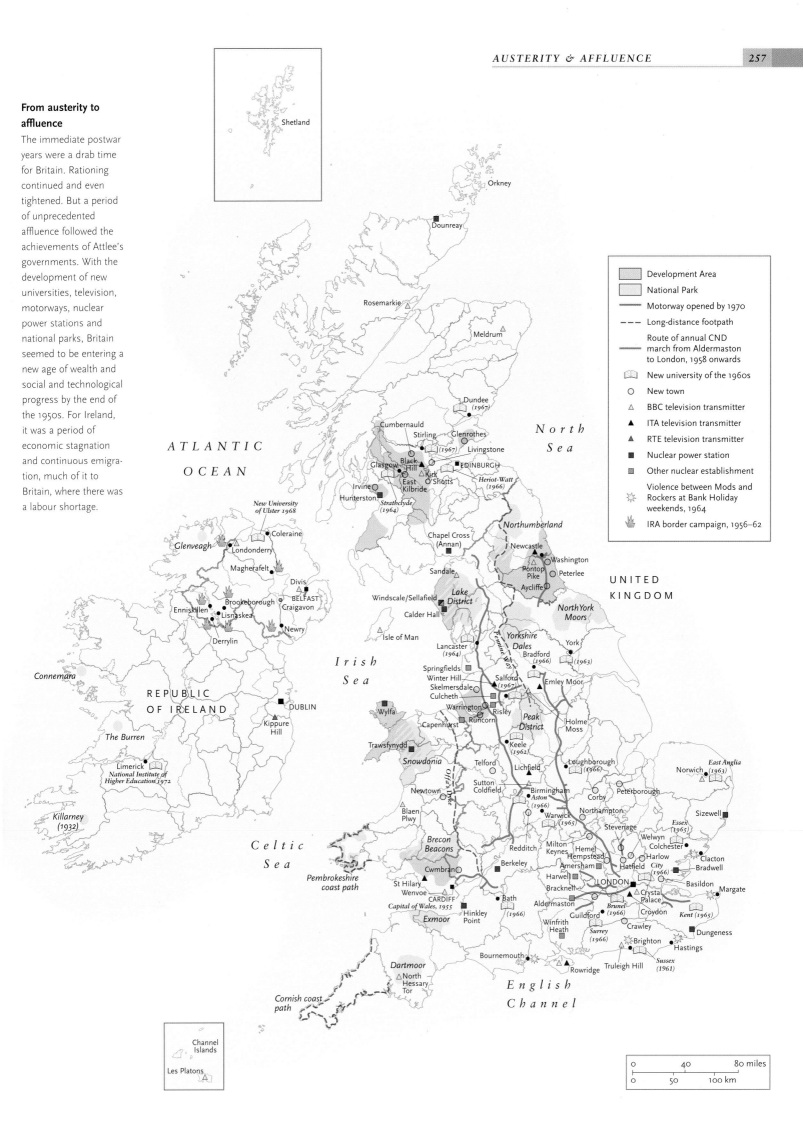

Development Area
National Park
Motorway opened by 1970
Long-distance footpath
Route of annual CND march from Aldermaston to London, 1958 onwards
New university of the 1960s
New town
BBC television transmitter
ITA television transmitter
RTE television transmitter
Nuclear power station
Other nuclear establishment
Violence between Mods and Rockers at Bank Holiday weekends, 1964
IRA border campaign, 1956–62

though market forces were allowed to override the previous government's regional policy. Achievements in the electricity industry were particularly marked. Most of the country's electrical power was produced by coal-fired stations (though hydroelectric schemes were also important in Scotland); but Attlee had made the decision to build the atomic bomb, which was successfully tested in 1952, so a reactor was set up at Windscale to produce the necessary plutoni-

um. In October 1956 Calder Hall became Britain's first nuclear power station. Despite a major fire in 1957 at Windscale (later renamed Sellafield), which produced widespread contamination, a series of Magnox power stations was built throughout the country. The road system was also improved. In December 1958 the Prime Minister, Harold Macmillan, opened the Preston bypass, the first 13 kilometres (8 miles) of motorway in Britain, and the following month the M1 was opened. By 1967 motorways totalled 845 kilometres (525 miles) in length, at a cost of considerable environmental damage. Bridges were built over the Forth and the Severn between 1964 and 1966. The railways were also to be made more efficient, with the closure of almost 10,000 kilometres (6,000 miles) of track and 2,000 stations after the Beeching report in 1963. The least utilised third of track had previously carried little more than 1 per cent of passengers and freight; henceforth, the railways were to concentrate on fast intercity services and bulk-freight transportation. The docks also began to be modernised, with container ports like Tilbury and Felixstowe hastening the decline of ports like London, which could not handle containerised freight.

Real wages grew, on average, by 50 per cent between 1951 and 1964, and the *Financial Times* index of industrial shares rose from 103 in 1952 to 366 in 1961. Many British people were at last able to experience the affluence that they felt was their due. By 1963, three out of four households had a vacuum cleaner, one in three had a fridge, and one in five a washing machine. Most significant of all, four out of five had a television set. BBC TV had begun in 1936, though it had been suspended during the war. Now it went from strength to strength. In 1955 commercial televi-

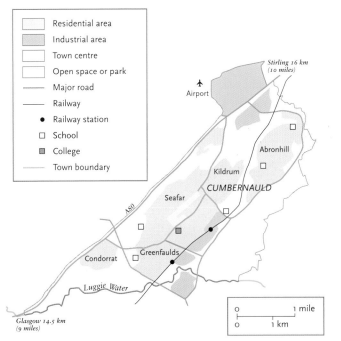

Cumbernauld New Town

Designed to house the overspill population of nearby Glasgow, Cumbernauld was intended as a well-balanced community of 50,000 people. The communications and education provisions were good, and industry was attracted there. Unfortunately the population density was high and the construction uncompromisingly concrete. Though it won awards for its original designs, the community was left with all the problems of social alienation subsequently associated with other postwar new towns.

sion began, and by 1959 new transmitters allowed over 90 per cent of the population to receive pictures, by which time three-quarters of the population had access to a set. In 1964, BBC2 started, with a brief to provide more 'highbrow' programmes, and in 1969 colour sets were introduced. Watching television was the most popular leisure activity in the country (while cinema attendances declined from 26.8 million in 1950 to 3.7 million in 1970). For those who preferred more physically healthy pursuits, 10 National Parks had been designated between 1951 and 1957, and hence protected from many forms of industrial and commercial development. There was also a significant expansion of education. The school-leaving age was raised to 15 in 1947 and 16 in 1973, and higher education saw particular expansion. In 1938 there had been 20,000 students, a figure that rose to 118,000 in 1962, but the real spurt in numbers came thereafter, as new 'plateglass' universities were formed and former colleges of advanced technology received university status. By 1972 there were 45 universities, compared with 17 in 1945.

In October 1963 Harold Wilson, Labour leader of the opposition (and prime minister from 1964 to 1970), predicted that Britain would be forged in the 'white heat of the technological revolution'. Certainly, living standards continued to rise, aided by the discovery in the North Sea of natural gas in 1965 and oil in 1969, and consumer goods became ever more common. But there were disquieting signs that Britain was approaching an as yet undefined crisis – cultural as well as financial. British economic growth rates did not match those of competitor states, and it was partly for this reason that Britain applied to join the European Economic Community, in 1961 and 1967 – entry both times being vetoed by France. In addition, television programmes like 'Cathy Come Home' made the public aware of the poverty that remained in the midst of Britain's affluence. In foreign affairs, the nation became ever more dependent on the Americans. After the Korean War, the US Air Force was allowed eight airfields in Britain. In 1957 (after the fiasco of the Anglo-French invasion of Egypt in the Suez Crisis, when American financial pressure alone was sufficient to force a humiliating British climb-down) there were 60 US Thor missiles in East Anglia. Indeed, in 1960 the Americans were allowed to build a Polaris nuclear submarine base at Holy Loch in Scotland. Violence also began to increase in British society, not only in terms of more crime than before but also riots by teenage 'Teddy Boys' in the late 1950s and by 'Mods and Rockers' in the 1960s – their social alienation perhaps being fuelled by a new vogue for high-rise flats. 'The Troubles' began again in Northern Ireland in 1968. Britain was a more secular and iconoclastic, as well as a more affluent, society. The 1950s saw the 'Angry Young Men', in 1958 the Campaign for Nuclear Disarmament began, and in the 1960s there were anti-Vietnam and students 'demos'. 'Sexual intercourse began in 1963,' wrote the poet Philip Larkin, with some exaggeration. While many insisted that the new 'permissive' society was essentially civilised and liberating, prophets of doom believed that Britain had progressed from austerity to affluence and, finally, to decadence. **RDP**

> *'Let's be frank about it: most of our people have never had it so good. Go around the country, go to the industrial areas, go to the farms, and you will see a state of prosperity such as we have never had in my lifetime.'*
>
> **Harold Macmillan, in a speech, 20 July 1957**

Aldermaston march, 1958

The first march from London to the Atomic Weapons Research Establishment at Aldermaston. The marchers argued that Britain had no need for nuclear weapons, and that British unilateral nuclear disarmament would be followed by other nations.

THE AFTERMATH OF EMPIRE

Although it is possible to trace the British retreat from empire back to World War I, it was not until after World War II that Britain began formally to relinquish political sovereignty of its Asian and African colonial possessions. The dissolution of the British Empire was accomplished in two main waves. The first, presided over by the Labour Party in the 1940s, centred in Asia, which incorporated India, Pakistan, Ceylon, Burma and Palestine. The second phase took place in Africa in the late 1950s and early 1960s, under the direction of the Conservative Party, and was followed by withdrawal from Aden, the Gulf States, the Far East and Pacific possessions. In the 1970s and 1980s, smaller Caribbean Islands and Zimbabwe left the Empire, and just a handful of islands and the disputed territories of Gibraltar, the Falkland Islands and Hong Kong (finally returned to China in accordance with the 100-year lease agreement on the New Territories in 1997) remained.

> *'The wind of change is blowing through this continent and whether we like it or not, this growth of national consciousness is a political fact.'*
>
> **Harold Macmillan in a speech in Cape Town, South Africa, 1960**

In 1947 India became the first British colony to achieve independence. World War II had weakened the British imperial state, both economically and militarily, and this forced the government, under the leadership of Clement Atlee, to concede to Indian nationalist demands. Britain had neither the will nor the capacity to continue to hold an increasingly ungovernable and violent subcontinent to the empire. A decade after the decolonisation process was initiated in Asia, the 'wind of change' began to sweep through Africa, hastened by the Suez crisis in 1956. The Gold Coast was the first African colony to gain independence, under the new name Ghana. This set in motion British disengagement from other colonies in West Africa. In contrast to the rich and relatively well-developed colonies in the west, transfer of power in the central and eastern African colonies was complicated by the competing claims of impoverished black populations and privileged, entrenched European minority settler communities. Yet, despite these difficulties, a combination of African nationalism and the British desire to relinquish costly imperial commitments in the region resulted in independence and black majority rule in most African colonies, with the notable exception of Southern Rhodesia, which did not achieve similar status until 1980.

Despite some ideological differences within and between the two main political parties on colonial policy, both the Conservatives, under Harold Macmillan, and Labour, led by Harold Wilson, entered government determined to retain Britain's remaining imperial and military possessions. However, both administrations succumbed to economic, political and international pressures, resulting first in Macmillan's retreat from Africa, and then in Wilson's

Retreat from empire

Britain's disengagement from empire was not entirely voluntary. After World War II, Britain's comparative international weakness required it to grant independence to territories in Asia that were rapidly becoming ungovernable.

Further retreats were forced on successive governments by Britain's inability to sustain a world role. Despite hopes to the contrary, the Commonwealth never allowed Britain to retain any real influence.

Legend:
- Countries gaining independence from Britain before 1945
- Countries gaining independence from Britain 1945–73, with dates
- Remaining British dependencies, 1973
- Members of the Commonwealth, 1973

withdrawal from 'East of Suez'. The East of Suez policy was precipitated by a combination of escalating defence costs, the devaluation crisis and the impact of Europe and the USA on British foreign policy, resulting in the scaling down and termination of military commitments in the Middle and Far East.

The spread and character of decolonisation was determined by a mixture of international cold war politics, British imperial interests and local nationalist movements, which varied from region to region. In India, Palestine, Egypt, Malaya, Kenya and Cyprus, for example, nationalism took on radical, populist and violent forms, culminating in 'state of emergency' declarations by British governments. Withdrawal was also impaired by communal and ethnic tensions. In contrast, the transfer of power was comparatively peaceful in the Gold Coast and throughout the West Indies.

Despite the speed at which the British Empire was liquidated in the second half of the twentieth century, Britain had no intention of severing all links with former colonial possessions. On the contrary, the British Commonwealth of Nations, or 'Commonwealth', as it was more popularly known, was seen as a natural successor to the Empire. Although politicians trumpeted the ideal of an association of states, sharing a common past, democracy and racial partnership, many of them in fact viewed the Commonwealth as a means of preserving – and perhaps even expanding – British spheres of influence in Asia and Africa. But Britain's leaders soon discovered they were unable to exercise the level of economic and political control that they had hoped to retain.

COMMONWEALTH IMMIGRATION

Paradoxically, just as Britain was retreating from its formal imperial commitments, Commonwealth immigration into Britain, principally from the West Indies and South Asia, was becoming an increasingly salient issue in British domestic politics. During the 1950s, the number of West Indians entering Britain reached annual rates of 30,000. Immigration from the Indian subcontinent began to escalate from the 1960s onwards. The census of 1951 recorded 74,000 New Commonwealth immigrants; 10 years later the figure had increased to 336,000, climbing to 2.2 million by 1981.

Immigration from the New Commonwealth was driven by a combination of 'push' and 'pull' factors. Partition of the Indian subcontinent and the construction of the Mangla Dam in Pakistan had displaced large numbers of people, many of whom had close links with Britain through the colonial connection. In Britain, postwar reconstruction, declining birth rates and labour shortages resulted in the introduction of government schemes to encourage Commonwealth workers, particularly from the West Indies, to seek employment in Britain. Jamaicans and Trinidadians were recruited directly by agents to fill vacancies in the British transport network and the newly created National Health Service. Private companies also recruited labour in India and Pakistan for factories and foundries in Britain. As more Caribbeans and South Asians settled in Britain, patterns of chain migration developed, in which pioneer migrants aided friends and relatives to settle. Despite the influx of immigrants after the war, however, migration from Britain continued to outpace immigration.

The 1948 Nationality Act reaffirmed the right of British citizenship and free entry to the United Kingdom to all Commonwealth citizens and colonial subjects, without restrictions. But as growing numbers of Caribbeans and South Asians began to take up their right of abode, the British authorities became increasingly alarmed. The importance assigned to the Commonwealth in the 1950s prevented the imposition of immigration controls on New Commonwealth citizens. However, by the 1960s, Britain's retreat from the Commonwealth in favour of Europe and events such as the Notting Hill race riots in 1958 heralded a policy of restriction, which gradually whittled away the right of New Commonwealth citizens to automatic British citizenship. Although the 1962 Immigration Act was intended to reduce the inflow of blacks and Asians into Britain, it had the opposite effect: fearful of losing the right of free entry, immigrants came to Britain in greater numbers. In the 18 months before the restrictions were introduced, the volume of newcomers equalled the total for the previous five years.

Starting a new life

A Jamaican immigrant seeking work and lodgings in Birmingham in 1955. Many West Indian immigrants encountered considerable racial prejudice when seeking accommodation.

'As I look ahead, I am filled with foreboding. Like the Roman, I seem to see "the river Tiber foaming with much blood".'

Enoch Powell, speech in Birmingham, 1968

The 1968 Immigration Act was specifically targeted at restricting Kenyan Asians with British passports. The notorious 'Rivers of Blood' speech by Conservative MP Enoch Powell, in which he prophesied violent racial war if black immigration continued, formed the backdrop to the legislation. Legislative momentum continued with the 1971 Immigration Act, which effectively restricted citizenship on racial grounds by enacting the 'Grandfather Clause', by which a Commonwealth citizen who could prove that one of his or her grandparents was born in the UK was entitled to immediate entry clearance. This operated to disadvantage Black and Asian applicants, while favouring citizens of the 'old Commonwealth' – the descendants of (white) British settlers from Australia, New Zealand, Canada and South Africa. Thus immigration control had moved away from primary immigration to restricting the entry of dependants, or secondary immigration.

The 1991 census provided the first detailed breakdown of Britain's ethnic minorities, which by then had reached

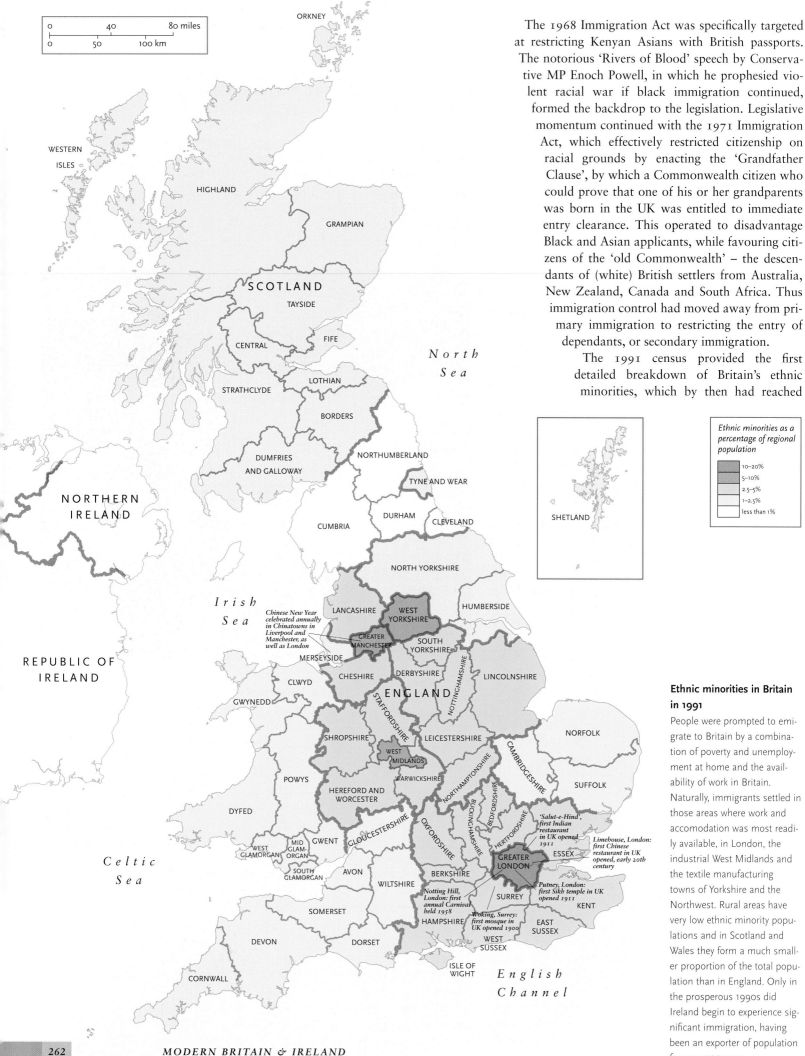

Ethnic minorities as a percentage of regional population

- 10–20%
- 5–10%
- 2.5–5%
- 1–2.5%
- less than 1%

Ethnic minorities in Britain in 1991

People were prompted to emigrate to Britain by a combination of poverty and unemployment at home and the availability of work in Britain. Naturally, immigrants settled in those areas where work and accomodation was most readily available, in London, the industrial West Midlands and the textile manufacturing towns of Yorkshire and the Northwest. Rural areas have very low ethnic minority populations and in Scotland and Wales they form a much smaller proportion of the total population than in England. Only in the prosperous 1990s did Ireland begin to experience significant immigration, having been an exporter of population for over 200 years.

Chinese New Year celebrated annually in Chinatowns in Liverpool and Manchester, as well as London

'Salut-e-Hind', first Indian restaurant in UK opened 1911

Limehouse, London: first Chinese restaurant in UK opened, early 20th century

Putney, London: first Sikh temple in UK opened 1911

Notting Hill, London: first annual Carnival held 1958

Woking, Surrey: first mosque in UK opened 1900

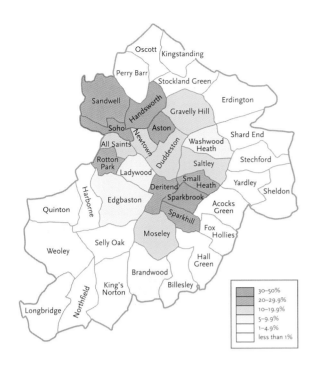

Ethnic minorities in Birmingham in 1971

The employment available to new immigrants was poorly paid. Also, faced with prejudice in finding private rented accommodation, and more subtly discrimi- nated against in residency requirements for council housing, immigrants tended to concentrate in poor inner city areas, as can be seen in Birmingham.

3 million, or 5.5 per cent of the population. Nearly half were of South Asian origin, including Indians, Pakistanis and Bangladeshis. West Indians numbered only 500,000, making up approximately 15 per cent of the non-European population. Descendants of the New Commonwealth population who were born in Britain had grown to form approximately half of the total ethnic minority population by 1991. Original settlement patterns remain static, with most blacks and Asians concentrated in the major connurbations of the South, the Midlands and northern England. Greater London houses 60 per cent of the Caribbean population, and the overwhelming majority of the Bangladeshi and Indian communities also reside in and around the capital. Pakistani demographic patterns, however, reflect the influence of historic links with the former textile towns of the North and the Midlands.

THE BIRMINGHAM EXPERIENCE

As in other parts of Britain, a small West Indian and Asian presence was already established in Birmingham prior to the 1950s. In 1939, for example, the were 100 South Asians living in Birmingham, and this figure rose to 1,000 by 1945. These included students and ex-seamen who had married local women and settled, and those recruited by the Ministry of Labour to work in munitions factories.

Birmingham's booming postwar economy attracted West Indian settlers from Jamaica, Barbados and St Kitts in the 1950s, followed by South Asians from Gujarat and the Punjab in India and West and East Pakistan (Bangladesh) from the 1960s onwards. By 1971, the South Asian and West Indian populations were equal in size and concentrated in the inner city wards of North Central Birmingham,

particularly Handsworth, Newtown, Sandwell and Sparkbrook. Labour shortages had developed in Birmingham as a result of an overall movement towards skilled and white-collar employment among the native population, which created vacancies in less attractive, poorly paid, unskilled and semi-skilled jobs in manufacturing, particularly in metal foundries and factories, and in the transport and health care sectors of the public services. These jobs were filled by newcomers from the Commonwealth. In the 1970s, poor pay and working conditions caused some black and Asian workers to resort to industrial action.

By 1991, Pakistanis had overtaken West Indians and Indians to become the largest single ethnic minority in Birmingham. The concentration of Caribbeans and South Asians in the inner city areas of Birmingham has shown surprisingly little change, though there is evidence of a flight to the suburbs among some groups, notably Indians.

Hostility to Commonwealth immigrants was pronounced in some sections of the local white population. One manifestation of this hostility was the establishment of the Birmingham Immigration Control Association, founded in the early 1960s by a group of Tory MPs.

As New Commonwealth immigrants began to become established in postwar Birmingham, community infrastructures, including places of worship, ethnic groceries, butchers and, most significantly, restaurants, began to develop. Birmingham and the West Midlands have in recent years become closely associated with the phenomenal rise of the ubiquitous 'curry house' selling primarily North Indian cuisine adapted for a British palate, and the city and the region boast an unrivalled number of 'balti' restaurants. This is one example among many of how settlers from the New Commonwealth have materially changed the cultural and social life of a British city.   **SL**

Factory work

An Asian immigrant employed in a Bradford textile factory. While work was available to immigrants in the 1950s and 1960s, it was often poorly paid and unskilled. The decline of the textile industry in the 1970s and 80s led to high long-term unemployment in the Asian communities.

LANGUAGE & DIALECT

For as long as it is possible to determine, the British Isles have been characterised by linguistic diversity. When the language that was to become known as English first came to these isles, in the mid-fifth century AD, it arrived in a land of Celtic dialects. Both English (as it became) and Celtic had been in contact with the language of the Romans, Latin, and when languages are in contact, change invariably occurs to at least one of them. Even in its earliest years, therefore, English – the language that dominates modern Britain – contained 'loanwords' taken in from Latin and Celtic and added to its existing Germanic word-stock. Throughout the Middle Ages, English continued to borrow words from Latin, Old Norse and, after the Norman Conquest, also from French. Even today, French maintains a toe-hold in Britain, in the Channel Islands.

The pattern of diversity and contact with other languages has continued throughout the period of Modern English, and with ever-increasing intensity. Through the British Empire, English received words from a great number of languages and itself spread across the globe, leading to the creation of new national varieties until, in the twentieth century, the USA helped establish English as a global language.

A counter-trend can also be observed, however: since the advent of the printing-press in England at the end of the fifteenth century, pressure has existed for the standardisation of English, particularly in writing, which has seen the evolution of a 'prestigious' variety of the language in Britain – known as Standard English.

But English worldwide, and certainly in Britain, remains a language of regional variation. The major dialect regions – despite massive urbanisation – have their basis in the

Language and dialect

In modern Britain and Ireland, English is without doubt the dominant language. While standardisation has taken place in written English, however, the spoken language is still subject to wide regional variations. Attempts to preserve or even revive Celtic languages have enjoyed some success, though English tends to remain people's first language. Another source of linguistic diversity in many cities has come through Commonwealth immigration.

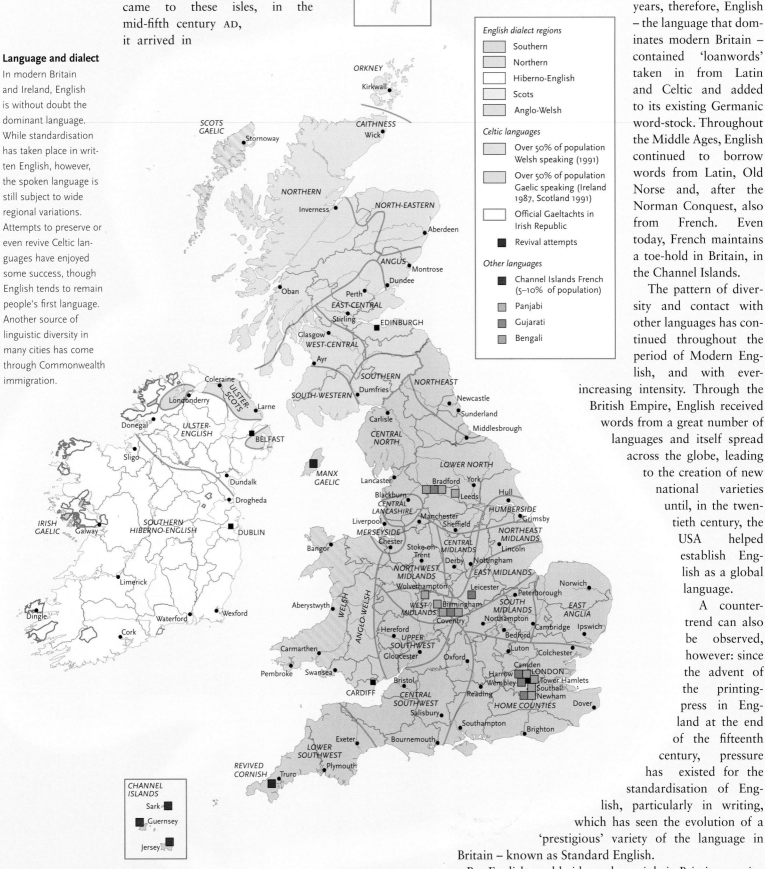

English dialect regions
- Southern
- Northern
- Hiberno-English
- Scots
- Anglo-Welsh

Celtic languages
- Over 50% of population Welsh speaking (1991)
- Over 50% of population Gaelic speaking (Ireland 1987, Scotland 1991)
- Official Gaeltachts in Irish Republic
- Revival attempts

Other languages
- Channel Islands French (5–10% of population)
- Panjabi
- Gujarati
- Bengali

English has been and continues to be a threat to the survival of the Celtic languages of Britain. Two, Cornish and Manx, have all but gone, their last native speakers dying in 1891 and 1974 respectively. There have been attempts to revive Cornish and Manx, though the number of speakers is very small. In recent decades, official measures (for example, in education and broadcasting) have been taken to protect and promote the surviving Celtic languages of Britain. Census statistics have tended to produce inflated estimates of the numbers of speakers of these languages but, officially at least, there are currently half-a-million Welsh speakers – that is, around 19 per cent of the resident population of Wales. In Scotland, the Scottish Gaelic speech community totals around 66,000 – just over 1 per cent of the population. In the Republic of Ireland, the official figure is 1.4 million Irish speakers, nearly 40 per cent of the population, but Reg Hindley, an expert on minority languages, estimated in 1990 that only 0.25 per cent of the population were habitual speakers of Irish living in habitually Irish-speaking communities. This discrepancy between official statistics and estimates of habitual speakers is a symptom of the lack of monoglot speakers of Welsh, Scottish Gaelic and Irish – the languages survive, but not as the sole languages of their speakers, whether habitual or not, and it is difficult to gauge what counts as habitual use.

The multilingual setting in which English exists has become more diverse since World War II, owing to immigration from, for example, the Indian subcontinent, the Caribbean, the Far East, and West and East Africa. The largest of these so-called 'community languages', in terms of number of speakers, is Panjabi, with over 500,000 speakers, but there are also substantial communities of Gujarati speakers (perhaps a third of a million) and Bengali speakers (up to 100,000).   **RP**

Road sign in Powys

The equality accorded to English and Welsh on road signs symbolises a victory for Welsh nationalists. They campaigned long and hard to gain recognition of their language by the State, and also to ensure its survival.

Road sign in East London

Various languages, such as Bengali, have entered Britain, and in some areas, such as East London, public notices recognise this. A new level of linguistic and cultural diversity has been introduced by Commonwealth immigration.

major dialect regions of Old English and, in the case of the Celtic countries, in the effects of the historical mingling of English with the Celtic languages of the British Isles. The modern dialect regions of English in England were distinguished by the sociolinguist Peter Trudgill in *The Dialects of England* (1990). His diagnosis is actually based on the distribution of a number of accent (that is, pronunciation) features, such as the vowel sound in the words 'but' and 'up'. Northerners typically say 'boott' and 'oopp', while southerners use a more 'standard' vowel. This feature suggests that the northern dialect region extends as far south as Birmingham and Lincoln; another feature, the vowel sound in 'gate', enables Trudgill to distinguish northern and central ('Midlands') sub-regions within the North. In the case of 'gate', the typical far northern pronunciation is something like 'geht' (a monophthong), while the central and indeed the southern pronunciation is the more standard 'gayt' (a diphthong). In his analysis, Trudgill sees both a continuity with old accent boundaries of English, as for example in the north/south split of 'but', and some change, as for example in the spread of features of London speech (such as the loss of 'l' in words like 'hill' and 'milk') into the surrounding regions.

THE CELTIC LANGUAGES

The Celtic regions also have their own Celtic-influenced brands of English, each of which can be subdivided into further localised varieties. For example, Welsh English, or Anglo-Welsh, has differing northern and southern varieties, with parts of the south, specifically south Pembroke and the Gower Peninsula, having had English-speaking colonies, influenced by the dialects of southwest England, since the twelfth century. The traditional dialect (language, some would argue) in Scotland is Scots, an unusual 'English' dialect in having a long-standing and surviving literary tradition. And in the north of the island of Ireland we have Ulster Scots, which originated in immigration from southwest Scotland. As for the future, some traditional features may fall out of use, but innovations, regional and social, will always continue. A uniform spoken English in England and in the British Isles is a very unlikely prospect.

20th-CENTURY TRANSPORT

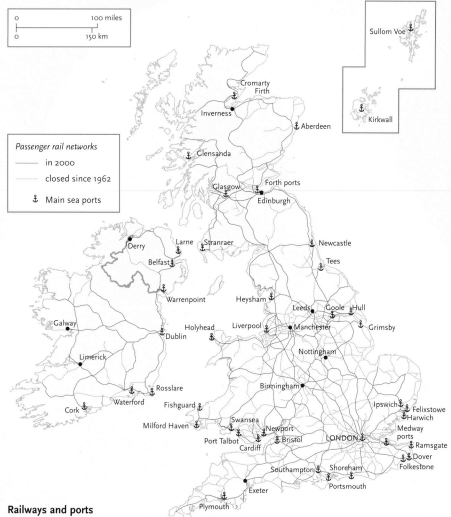

Railways and ports

At the beginning of the 20th century, Britain's inland transport was dominated by the railways. But increasingly cheap and flexible motor transport took an ever-greater share of passengers and freight. By 1970 half of British and one-third of Irish railway track had closed. Coastal traffic and ports suffered a similar loss of business.

The M1 at Luton Spur

Britain's second stretch of motorway opened in November 1959. Motorways were meant to ease congestion on the roads; the planners never envisaged that car ownership would reach 20 million by 1990.

In twentieth-century Britain and Ireland, trends in surface transport reversed the nineteenth-century pattern, when railways had overwhelmed road transport. Airports appeared for the first time, their importance growing with relentless increases in air traffic. Domestic coastal traffic and seaports became less significant, while inland waterways enjoyed a late renaissance as a leisure facility.

In 1900 some 40,000 kilometres (24,000 miles) of railway track was open for traffic. By mid-century, the figure was slightly smaller, as wartime economising had slightly reduced line length. Amalgamation of railway companies in the early 1920s, which aimed to combat competition from war-surplus road vehicles, put small branch lines and services under pressure. Centralisation of decision-making on the railways broke up established locally specific rail haulage arrangements and thus strengthened small, independent road transport businesses.

Railways lost traffic share during the Depression of the 1930s. Facing rapidly expanding road motor competition, British and Irish railways began to acquire and operate road services in the 1920s (and domestic air transport services in Britain from 1934). In the 1930s, motor licence duties and petrol tax favoured rail over road transport, but the fixed freight rates of the common carriers ensured that the most lucrative traffic was transported by road.

Road transport blossomed, owing to the reduced operating costs of lorries, and their increasing geographical range and flexibility. Their number increased eightfold in Britain between 1923 and 1939, while the number of passenger buses and coaches doubled. There was also an eightfold rise in the number of licensed motor vehicles in Ireland between 1910 and 1939. In Britain, the number of licensed motor vehicles trebled between 1914 and 1930, and then doubled again to reach 3 million by 1939. The growth of road traffic was, however, not matched by expansion of road infrastructure. In 1936 Britain's road network was barely longer than it had been in 1899, and most road improvement was confined to building bypasses and ring roads. By 1938 only 43 kilometres (27 miles) of the 7,160 kilometres (4,450 miles) of trunk road were dual carriageway. Road improvement in Ireland involved mostly realignment and extension, using unskilled labour as part of a drive towards unemployment relief.

POSTWAR DEVELOPMENTS

Reinvesting in exhausted railways was not a priority after World War II. Railway nationalisation was followed by rail closures. By 1953, nearly 2,000 kilometres (over 1,200 miles) of railway had been closed to passenger traffic in Britain. Industrial change brought the

As the car replaced the railway as Britain's preferred form of transport in the late 20th century, it became increasingly difficult for the road system to cope with the increase in traffic. A motorway system became imperative.

Airports also increased in number to meet an ever-growing demand. Environmental concerns, however, have become an important factor in limiting further expansion of roads and runways.

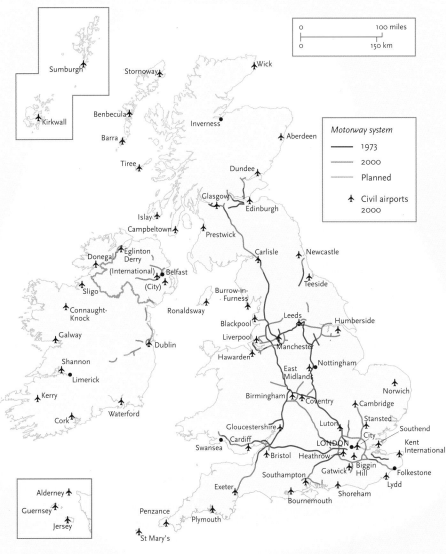

loss of staple coal and textile traffic. Britain's compact industrial geography also diminished any long-haul advantages that railways had over modern road transport. Comparatively low-cost rural bus services damaged the railways further. Ireland's low population density, short travel distances and port-dominated geography of trade only ever generated thin rail traffic.

Road transport recovered slowly from vehicle and fuel shortages during and after World War II. Road haulage was assisted by a succession of regulations, including, in Britain, the lifting of the 25-mile (40-kilometre) limit on road freight consignments. By the 1960s, British road transport had eclipsed railways as the dominant carrier of freight. Yet, even though private car ownership and use expanded to 3 million, between 1939 and 1952 there was practically no major road improvement or new road construction.

In 1958 Britain got its first stretch of dedicated, high-speed, limited-access motorway, and by the early 1960s, traffic flow had been eased by a total of 160 kilometres (100 miles) of motorway. Between 1953 and 1963, vehicle numbers more than doubled: motorways allowed fast, convenient commercial and social travel, household incomes were rising, and the real cost of private motoring was falling. Workplace, retail and residential decentralisation encouraged the desertion of trains and car dependency.

The start of Britain's largest-ever road-building programme in the 1960s coincided with an increase in the tempo of contraction of the railways. Roughly half of Britain's branch-line railways and stations had become uneconomic. By 1970, when asset reduction in the railways (involving the loss of rolling stock, locomotives, workforce, 2,000 stations, 280 lines and 250 services) had finally slowed, the railway network in Britain had been reduced to half its 1900 length. Ireland had lost more than 200 stations and 1,600 kilometres (1,000 miles), or one-

third, of rail track by the mid-1960s. By then, flight frequencies and passenger loads on intercity air routes were increasing vigorously. Rail passenger mileage in Britain was stable for most of the second half of the century, but in 1990, when the number of cars reached 20 million, railway's share of total passenger miles collapsed from its 1952 level of 20 per cent to 6 per cent. Railway's share of freight ton-miles in 1990 was 8 per cent, one-eighth that of road.

Oil and fuel price rises, and recession, cut back expenditure on British motorway construction and motor vehicle use during the 1970s. Plans to triple the 1,060 kilometres (660 miles) of motorway in use by 1970 were also frustrated by environmental protest. By 1980 there were 2,300 kilometres (1,430 miles) of motorway in Britain. In the last 20 years of the century, the stretching of the congested motorway network to just over 3,200 kilometres (nearly 2,000 miles) mostly involved linking existing sections. Motorway building, and airport development, was disrupted by lengthy public inquiries, well-organised public protest and less benign government policy. **GP**

'The motorway/trunk road programme with all its ramifications poses a consummate evil, and constitutes the greatest threat to the interests of this nation in all its history.'

John Tyme, English anti-motorway campaigner, 1978

SOCIETY IN THE 1960s

The 1960s were dramatic years in Britain: demographic trends, especially the increase in the proportion of teenagers in the population, coincided with economic affluence and ideological experimentation to reconfigure social mores to a revolutionary extent. In 1964 the Labour Party, under Harold Wilson, came into power, promising economic and social modernisation. In an attempt to tackle the problem of poverty, public expenditure on social services was expanded considerably, resulting in a small degree of redistribution of income. Economically, the main problems of the decade arose from the devaluation of the currency in November 1967, and the increase in industrial action. Employment in manufacturing declined throughout the period, until it accounted for less than one-third of the workforce by 1973. In contrast, employment in the service sector rose. By 1973, over half of all workers were employed in providing services.

Young people were most affected by the changes of the 1960s. Education gained new prominence in government circles and student numbers soared. By 1966, seven new universities had opened (Sussex, East Anglia, Warwick, Essex, York, Lancaster and Kent) and some technical colleges had been awarded university status. More importantly, students throughout the country were becoming increasingly radicalised as a response to a growing hostility towards capitalism and what they perceived as the political and social complacency of the older generation. They protested loudly against exorbitant fees for overseas students, poor student accommodation, the unfairness of the examination system, restrictions on their freedom of expression, dictatorial university decision-making, apartheid in South Africa, and the Vietnam War. The latter conflict not only angered the young of Britain, but also placed immense strain on relations between the US and British governments. Although protests against the Vietnam War and other issues were less violent than those in the United States (due, in part, to more moderate policing in Britain), there were major demonstrations all over the country; some, such as that which took place in London's Grosvenor Square in 1968, involved 100,000 protesters.

A CULTURAL REVOLUTION

Anti-establishment values spread much wider than the student population. The cultural revolution had a profound effect on sexual behaviour and on women. An unexpurgated *Lady Chatterley's Lover*, banned as pornography since the 1920s, was released. Sex before marriage became slightly less taboo (one-third of young women were pregnant when they married), and there was a general feeling of 'sexual freedom' in some circles. It was in the 1960s that women's liberation really took off, its first major victory being the 1970 Equal Pay Act. The family also underwent important changes. From the 1950s, the household had begun to be transformed, affected by smaller family sizes (helped by the spread of abortion and effective contraception) and increased domestic technology. In 1956 only 7 per cent of households had refrigerators; by 1971, this had increased to 70 per cent. By this time, 64 per cent of households also possessed a washing machine. In addition, the real earnings of young manual workers had grown rapidly, creating a generation who had money to spend on leisure and luxury. By 1960, the average British teenager was spending £8 a week on clothes, cosmetics, records and cigarettes. In London, King's Road, and then Carnaby Street, became the haunt of this generation. Their attitude is summed up by the designer Mary Quant, whose shop, Bazaar, in King's Road, provided clothes 'that allowed people to run, to jump, to leap, to retain their precious freedom'. Clothes became a symbol of the 'Chelsea set'.

Another symbol was music. No band was more important than the Beatles. They expressed both youth deviance and commercialism, and provided British teenagers with an identity that cut across the barriers of class, accent and region. The Beatles (or the Quarrymen, as they were first known) were formed in July 1957 and in October 1962 'Love Me Do' reached Number Seventeen; in April 1963 'From Me to You' became their first Number One single. Between 1957 and 1970 they performed live in 84 dif-

Sixties fashion

Fashion in the 1960s was marked by a self-confident – and often highly experimental – break with the past.

Alexandra Palace, April 1967

Young people sleeping after a 14-hour concert, dubbed 'the psychedelic happening of happenings'. It was held in support of an anarchist newspaper, the International Times, *which had been raided by the police earlier in the year.*

The 'Swinging Sixties'

The 1960s was a decade of social upheaval, especially for the young. Teenagers enjoyed greater freedom and affluence than ever before, and developed their own distinctive youth culture. Beatlemania swept the country. When the BBC failed to supply the music that people demanded, pirate radio stations filled the gap.

ferent venues in England, 15 in Scotland, six in Wales, and two in Ireland). A national and a global phenomenon, they played all over Europe, as well as in countries as far afield as Australia, Japan and the USA.

Many people in the establishment regarded popular music with disdain. The BBC held a monopoly over the radio waves and, in a deal with the Musicians' Union and record manufacturers, ensured that popular music was not given air time. Anyone wanting to listen to popular musicians had to tune in to Radio Luxembourg, where the reception was very poor. At Easter 1964, however, the first illegal 'pirate' radio station, Radio Caroline, began broadcasting from a ship just off the Sussex coast. Within months, millions of young people were listening to Radio Caroline North, Caroline South, Radio London and the other pirate stations that sprang up. Not only did they broadcast popular music, but they also reminded their listeners that any attempt to silence them would constitute a direct 'attack on youth'. Eventually, the Government acted. The BBC set up Radio One, a popular music station and, in August 1967, the Marine Offences Act outlawed the pirate ships.

Despite the dramatic increase in wealth – coupled with the emergence of distinctive subcultures, technological advances (including television and, from 1962, the contraceptive pill), and unprecedented shifts in popular culture – by the end of the 1960s, there was a general feeling of disillusionment with Labour's policies. In the 1970 election, the Conservative Party, under Edward Heath, was returned to power. By the time of the 1973–4 oil crisis, Britain's 'golden age' had come to an end.   JB

	Location and number of Beatles concerts
4	
⚡	Pirate radio station
🎸	Major music venue

Merseyside/Wirral area

SCOTLAND

NORTHERN
IRELAND

Radio Scotland 1966

Radio Caroline (North) 1964

IRELAND

Radio 270 1966

WALES

ENGLAND

Wembley

Hyde Park

Radio London 1964

Radio England/ Britain Radio 1966

Radio Caroline (South) 1964

Radio 390 1965

Radio City 1964

Britain's Better Music Station 1965

Isle of Wight Rock Festival

National Jazz & Blues Festival Richmond

Channel Islands

1982
17 killed in
I RA bombing
1993
'Grey Steel' shootings
by Loyalists

Ballycastle

Coleraine

Ballykelly

Derry

LONDONDERRY

ANTRIM

1968
Civil rights marchers
clash with police
1972
'Bloody Sunday'

Ballymena

Larne

DONEGAL

Strabane

1992
8 killed in
IRA bombing

1972
'Bloody Friday'
1993
Shankill Road
bombing

TYRONE

Teebane
Cross

Bangor

Omagh

1998
37 killed by dissident
republican 'Real IRA'
car bomb

Belfast

Dungannon

Maze/Long Kesh

1979
Lord Mountbatten
assassinated by IRA

Lurgan

Portadown

DOWN

Hillsborough

Mullaghmore

Loughall

1987
8 IRA members killed
by security forces

Armagh

Downpatrick

1987
11 killed by IRA
in war memorial
bombing

ARMAGH

1976
10 Protestant workmen
shot dead by IRA

Enniskillen

FERMANAGH

Sligo

Monaghan

1974
Loyalist car bomb

Kingsmills

1979
18 paratroopers killed
in IRA bus bombing

Newry

Warrenpoint

SLIGO

MONAGHAN

Crossmaglen

LEITRIM

CAVAN

Dundalk

| 0 | 10 | 20 miles |
| 0 | 10 | 20 km |

The Troubles

In the 1960s civil rights demonstrations sparked off a wave of political violence in Northern Ireland. Most violence has been concentrated in relatively small areas: Derry in the 1970s and South Armagh and parts of Belfast throughout the period. In only one year of the Troubles (1972) have more people in Northern Ireland been killed by political violence than in road accidents.

Peace rally

US president Bill Clinton addressing a peace rally in Belfast during his visit in 1995. Clinton played a significant role as a 'peace broker' in negotiations leading up to the Good Friday Agreement.

In 1963 Terence O'Neill became prime minister of Northern Ireland. His government's policies of economic modernisation coincided with and encouraged a growing self-confidence among the Catholic middle classes, who were willing to accept the partition of Ireland provided that they were given equal status as citizens within Northern Ireland. This confidence found expression in the civil rights groups of the mid-1960s, which campaigned in particular on issues of discrimination against the Catholic minority in housing and electoral gerrymandering. O'Neill's Catholic-friendly rhetoric began to alienate the more conservative fringes of unionism, but it was the emergence of the radical People's Democracy movement and its socialist anti-state wing that made the prime minister's standing within his own party increasingly difficult.

By the late 1960s politics had moved onto the streets, where demonstrations and counter-demonstrations frequently led to riots. The radicals may only have wanted a fully democratic society, but the majority of the province's population increasingly saw this as a return to the ancient power fight between unionism and nationalism. While the last unionist governments from 1969 to 1972 were trying to create a consensus by granting most of the civil rights demands, the revival of the latent violent sectarianism made the province ungovernable. Westminster deployed troops in the province in 1969 and then, in 1972, the most violent year of the 'Troubles', took over government of Northern Ireland through Direct Rule. In that year, over 400 people in the province lost their lives as a result of political violence.

The British government had only reluctantly become involved. Its subsequent policies were aimed at finding a political solution by creating a middle ground where the liberal wings of nationalism and unionism could find a consensus that would eventually make the militants of both sides redundant. This strategy proved unsuccessful – not least because of the nature of Direct Rule. Because they were denied direct access to power, both sides could attack British policies as inappropriate and for failing to deliver their respective demands. At the same time, paramilitaries of both sides could drive the point home by violence that was – at least in part – justifiable in the eyes of their respective communities. Nonetheless, the level of political violence subsided considerably after 1972; in most subsequent years considerably more people died in road accidents.

All British initiatives encountered similar problems: one side or the other, and sometimes both, was unwilling to accept what was proposed. The Sunningdale power-sharing agreement of 1973 failed because the majority of unionists would not accept an 'Irish dimension' in the form of the proposed Council of Ireland that nationalists demanded. While the British government's approach became subtler with regard to unionist concerns, a formula that was acceptable to both sides remained elusive.

With hindsight, the emergence of Sinn Féin, the political wing of the Provisional IRA, as a political party in the early 1980s can be seen as one element in the rethinking of British policies. Another was the belated interest that Irish governments began to take in Northern Ireland during the same period. The fear that the disturbances in the North might spread south and destabilise their state lay behind the Dublin government's decision to start talking directly to Downing Street from 1980 onwards. This led to the Anglo-Irish Agreement of 1985 – which essentially represented a reiteration of

Sectarian divisions in Belfast c.1985

- ▨ Predominantly Catholic
- ☐ Predominantly Protestant
- ▨ Mixed or non-residential
- ▨ City centre security zone
- ▬ Confrontation line
- ── Railway line

British policy aims in the province, but now with an added all-Ireland dimension, which the unionists continued to find very difficult to accept. It was in the wake of this agreement that an entirely new approach emerged. Sinn Féin's strategy of 'ballot box as well as bullet', and its realisation that 'the war' could not be won militarily, led it to conduct secret discussions with both Dublin and London in the late 1980s in pursuit of a way into active participation in politics. Britain's recognition that if the extremists could be brought into the search for a political solution then the mainstream Northern Ireland political parties would follow suit was a complete reversal of its previous approach. Once the IRA had accepted the need for a ceasefire, the remaining difficulty was to persuade unionists that the reformed ex-paramilitaries could be trusted.

The willingness of some unionists to give up previous policies – which in essence had consisted of trying to get back the power they had lost in 1972 – sprang from their pragmatic realisation that only sharing power with nationalists would guarantee unionists some say in the future government of Northern Ireland. After long negotiations, and with the help of the American ex-senator George Mitchell, the Good Friday Agreement was signed in 1998. This sought to establish a power-sharing government in Northern Ireland, as well as acknowledging both British and Irish interest in the future of the province. Despite recurrent crises and accusations of bad faith, the peace survived more or less intact. Whether a long-term solution will be found remains to be seen. **SW**

Rioters in Belfast
Rioters, in this case unionists, pelt police with stones after Orangemen were prevented from marching through nationalist Drumcree, near Portadown, in July 1996.

A divided city
Political violence in Belfast has largely been confined to the confrontation lines where working-class unionist districts, such as the Shankill, and working-class nationalist areas, such as the Falls, Ardoyne and New Lodge, border directly on one another. The mixed middle-class districts of the city have not experienced political violence.

DEINDUSTRIALISATION

'If this pit closed down, the whole village would close down because of the number of men working there. This shop and a lot of other shops would have to close down.'

Armthorpe dress shop sales assistant, 1984

The decline of manufacturing

Employment in manufacturing reached a peak of 9 million in 1966. It thereafter fell rapidly, reaching 4 million by 1994. The resulting mass unemployment hurt the old industries of the Northwest badly. But the losses in employment were proportionally as high in the Southeast, reflecting the location of newer, but still declining, manufacturing industry.

Deindustrialisation – the decline of manufacturing industry, in particular as an employer – raised its head in Britain in the 1970s. This was to become a phenomenon common to all mature industrial nations. Theorists argued that it was perhaps the natural outcome of the industrialisation process. The so-called 'maturity thesis' suggested that, as industry developed and became more technologically sophisticated, it required less labour. At the same time, rising living standards meant that more wealth was available, beyond what would normally be spent on basic necessities and consumer goods, giving rise to a growing demand for services such as travel and entertainment. By 1976, services had become the largest area of employment in all regions of Britain.

Another problem faced by the manufacturing sector was a long-standing British taste for imports. Many observers noted that not only was Britain failing to compete internationally, but British industry was also failing to compete with foreign imports in the domestic market. The problem of deindustrialisation was perceived to be particularly acute, as it became entangled with the debate over Britain's long decline – at least a century old – as the world's leading industrial power. It was taken by some, in short, to be further evidence of national failure.

Employment in manufacturing industry reached a peak of about 9 million in 1966, and thereafter declined, falling to about 4 million in 1998, with three periods of severe recession, in 1973–5, 1979–83 and 1990–3. British indus-

try's share of world trade fell dramatically, from over 20 per cent in the 1950s to about 10 per cent by 1975, and continued to fall. Nor could it maintain its hold on the domestic market. A particularly extreme example of this was the car industry: in 1965 only one car in 20 was imported, yet by 1978 about half were. Many of the staple industries of the nineteenth century, such as coal and shipbuilding, which had been in serious difficulty in the interwar years, continued to decline as employers, surviving only through nationalisation. In addition, many of the 'new industries' of the 1930s, such as the car industry, were themselves declining by the 1970s. Thus, deindustrialisation was not simply a

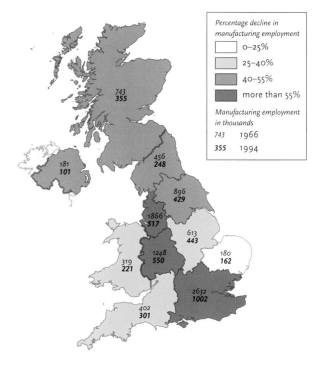

Percentage decline in manufacturing employment

- ☐ 0–25%
- ☐ 25–40%
- ☐ 40–55%
- ■ more than 55%

Manufacturing employment in thousands
743 1966
355 1994

Number employed

Area of employment

Agriculture

Mining

Manufacturing

Services

million

after Law

Changing patterns of employment

A comparison of employment patterns in 1921 (left) and 1976 (right) shows the scale of deindustrialisation. Everywhere, employment in mining and agriculture declined. In most places employment in manufacturing also declined. The service sector, however, expanded to the point where it became the major employer in every region of Britain. Further general deindustrialisation occurred in the 1980s.

regional problem of the old industrial North. In fact, the decline in manufacturing was proportionally as great in the Southeast, where many of these newer industries had been established, as it was in the Northwest; in terms of the numbers leaving manufacturing, the loss in the Southeast was actually much greater. The decline was lowest in East Anglia, simply because there was comparatively little manufacturing there to decline. Nonetheless, long-standing regional disadvantages in terms of employment opportunities and incomes were increased – the north–south divide was growing.

POLITICAL RESPONSES

A great variety of explanations for the decline in British industrial competitiveness has been put forward. None has proved satisfactory. One explanation suggests that the problem is cultural: that the British have been conditioned to despise industry. There is also the argument that it is a matter of choice: that the British are not sufficiently materialistic to work hard for the rewards associated with improved productivity. Complacency from generations of national success has also been blamed, as has the welfare state's 'cosseting' of the workforce. Alternatively, the government's failure adequately to support research and development is blamed. The Civil Service has also been held at fault for its 'exclusive' cultural and educational background, which has left it ignorant of, and indifferent to, the needs of industry. Obstructionist trade unions are a favourite target for many, as is incompetent management.

Punk rockers

Punk rock was in part a reaction to growing youth unemployment and came to symbolise rejection of commercialism. Ironically, this new youth culture soon became highly commercialised.

The Durham coalfield

The mining industry contracted sharply during the 1980s. In the Durham coalfield, for example, two-thirds of the pits were closed. In many areas, pits were the only real source of employment to local communities, and the economic and social impact of closures could be devastating. The year-long miners' strike of 1984–5 was an attempt to force a reversal of the decline, but the government resisted miners' demands.

Britain's falling competitiveness was, by the 1970s, making it increasingly difficult for governments to maintain high employment by intervening in the economy. Since 1945 successive governments had followed the tenets of the economist John Maynard Keynes, and borrowed in order to create jobs if unemployment approached a figure deemed as unacceptable (in the 1970s about 600,000). During the 1970s this became increasingly difficult to do. Edward Heath's government (1970–4) struggled to follow such policies in the face of the world recession associated with the 1973 OPEC oil price rise. OPEC, an international cartel of oil producers, retaliated against the West after the USA gave Israel strong support during the Yom Kippur war of 1973, by trebling the price of oil. This caused immediate recession and fuelled international inflation.

The following Labour governments, facing huge balance-of-payments crises and the tumbling value of the pound, could do less – they were more at the mercy of the International Monetary Fund, which insisted on severe spending cuts. The contraction of manufacturing began to accelerate. Inflation was also increasing alarmingly, reaching 24 per cent by 1975, and came to be seen as a far more urgent problem than unemployment. There was a national, and indeed international, political swing to the right as a reaction against perceived high-taxing and high-spending governments. Demands were being made that governments cease propping up 'lame duck' industries with public money. Attacks on trade union power were becoming popular, owing to a growing perception that they had become too powerful and disruptive. This came to a head during the miners' strike of 1974, which led to a three-day working week, and the so-called 'Winter of Discontent' of 1978–9, when there was an explosion of resentment, largely by poorly paid public employees, against a government incomes policy they felt was discriminatory.

Succeeding Conservative governments were to follow policies designed first and foremost to reduce inflation, and mass unemployment was now deemed politically acceptable – inflation, not unemployment, was now public enemy number one, and harsh measures seemed justified. Indeed, as wage-rises were believed to be the main source of inflation, heavy unemployment, it was sometimes argued, would weaken trade unions and was a price worth paying. An economic squeeze was introduced, involving heavy tax increases and a reduction in public borrowing to deflate the economy, thus reducing demand and employment. In the 1980s, 2 million manufacturing jobs disappeared, most of them by 1982. The government took a more confrontational attitude towards trade unions, especially after the 1983 election. A year-long miners' strike (1984–5) was defeated, amid scenes of mass picketing and some violence, from both police and miners.

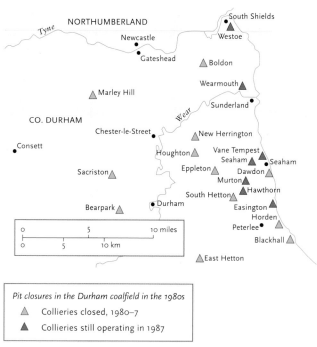

Pit closures in the Durham coalfield in the 1980s
△ Collieries closed, 1980–7
▲ Collieries still operating in 1987

THE COLLAPSE OF OLD INDUSTRIES

The severe contraction of the mining industry continued: it vanished in Kent, while in Durham two-thirds of the pits were closed. The government had little interest in ensuring the survival of the industry, with its troublesome and well-organised union. The social cost, especially in places in which mining was the single major employer, as in many pit villages in Durham, could be devastating. The entire local economy could be crippled.

In Tyneside and Merseyside a more general deindustrialisation occurred. Whole sections of industry, including coal, steel and shipbuilding, virtually vanished from many of their traditional areas. Of all areas of Britain, it was Northern Ireland that suffered the highest level of unemployment. This was largely because sectarian violence discouraged investment.

In February 1986 there were officially over 3.4 million unemployed, although statistics were manipulated for political reasons and the real figure is a matter of speculation. The socially corrosive effects were felt nationally, manifested, for example, in the inner-city rioting that broke out in 1981 and 1985. London was just as vulnerable as Liverpool, and a crucial contributory factor was the number of young men of Asian and Afro-Caribbean origin who saw no hope of ever entering employment: opportunities were minimal and they felt particularly discriminated against. The term 'underclass' was increasingly used to describe those who felt themselves to be completely excluded from the benefits of prosperity.

Service industries certainly offered alternative employment. Indeed, between 1983 and 1987, about 1.5 million new jobs were created. Most of these were for women, and part-time vacancies predominated. The total number of men in full-time employment fell still further. The unhappy fact was that many who left manufacturing for the service sector earned much-reduced incomes. Thus, for example, by the end of the century more people were employed in Indian restaurants than in the steel and coal industries combined, but for much lower pay. The economic recovery that led to the growth of this new employment was based mainly on finance, banking and credit. Little was invested in British manufacturing. Far more was invested overseas – British foreign investments rose from £2.7 billion in 1975 to a staggering £90 billion in 1985.

At the same time, there was also a degree of reindustrialisation, especially in the Southeast, where new industries employing the most advanced technology grew. In fact, many industries shed a large proportion of their workforce but, using new technology, maintained or improved their output. These new industries were certainly not confined to the Southeast: Nissan built the most productive car plant in Europe at Sunderland, while Siemens established a microchip plant at Wallsend. But such industries tended not to be large-scale employers of local workers. Siemens invested £1.1 billion, but only employed about 1,800. There was, nevertheless, intense competition across Europe as governments bid to attract such investment.

The closure of the Swan Hunter shipyard on the Tyne in May 1993 is an illuminating example of the impact of deindustrialisation. Swan Hunter was the last working shipyard in the region, but had failed to secure a warship contract. An old, established firm, which had launched the *Mauritania* in 1906, it was suffering the same long-term decline that reduced shipbuilding nationally from an employer of 200,000 in 1914 to an employer of a mere 26,000 by the end of the century. This devastated the local economy, especially as a bitter legal wrangle over redundancy payments left many former workers with no compensation whatever for the loss of what they had believed was employment for life.

The effects, however, were not confined to the Northeast. According to Keynes, the result of spreading employment is multiplied through the economy as the newly re-employed spend part of their higher incomes on services and goods, and the recipients spend part of this new income on goods and services themselves, and so on. By this argument, the effects of rising unemployment are also multiplied as the demand for services and goods declines. The closure of Swan Hunter was certainly to have a widespread impact. In Tyne and Wear alone, 240 suppliers lost contracts. But the crucial factor is that the fall-out was national: 45 Swan Hunter suppliers in Greater London also lost business. From the closure of a single concern, unemployment resulted in even the most prosperous regions in the country. The growing North Sea oil industry was to benefit the region, with its demands for drilling platforms and support ships, and this benefit was, of course, also felt nationally. But this did little to soften the impact of job losses. **RM/JS**

The miners' strike 1984–5
Striking Yorkshire miners barrack moderate union leaders in Sheffield. The miners' strike was long and bitter, but ultimately the government proved equally determined and had the resources to withstand miners' demands.

Number of Swan Hunter suppliers per county:	
☐	17–30
☐	31–45
☐	50 or more

after Bazen & Thirlwell

Swan Hunter shipyard

Swan Hunter's suppliers in 1993
The effects of deindustrialisation could spread much further than local communities. The closure of the Swan Hunter shipyard in 1993 certainly hurt the Tyneside area, but the failure of the firm also had a 'knock-on' effect as suppliers as far afield as London and Glasgow lost valuable orders and, as a result, jobs.

In the late 1980s, the north–south divide in Britain seemed as intractable as it had all century, with high unemployment (peaking at over 3 million in 1986) particularly concentrated in the declining manufacturing areas of the North and West. In the Irish Republic growth remained slow.

That the north–south divide increasingly had a political as well as an economic complexion seemed borne out by the outcome of the British 1987 general election. While Margaret Thatcher was swept back to power for the third time, her healthy Conservative majority was largely based on the votes of the South and East of England. North of a line roughly between the Severn and the Humber, the long decline of the Tories, especially in Scotland – where they were reduced to 10 seats – was increasingly apparent. At the same time, the national two-party system seemed to be breaking down. South of the Severn–Humber line, where Labour seats were now very rare outside London, the Liberal–SDP Alliance were the main challengers to the Conservatives in many constituencies.

ECONOMIC CHANGE

Regionally based industries suffered a dramatic decline during this period. Coal-mining, for example, was decimated in the decade following the 1984–5 miners' strike, not least because of the shift of the electricity generation industry towards alternative energy sources, especially gas. The economic effect on local communities could be devastating, as the 1996 film *Brassed Off* acutely shows, with its memorable depiction of the social impact on the Yorkshire pit vil-

Albert Dock

The Albert Dock in Liverpool is an example of a redundant industrial relic that has taken on a multitude of other uses. Its 19th-century buildings now house a maritime museum, an art gallery, shopping centre and television studio, and it has become a major tourist attraction.

lage of Grimethorpe of the 1992 closure programme, a programme that sparked protests and demonstrations as far afield as Cheltenham. During the period 1984–7 the coal industry shed 170,000 workers. A further net loss of employment in traditional coalfields (with the exception of north Warwickshire and south Derbyshire) took place in the 1990s, even though this decade otherwise saw general and long-sustained economic expansion. The social impact of this decline was, however, to some extent mitigated by inward investment initiatives and by some people's decision to move to areas where jobs were more readily available.

Across most of Britain and Ireland, there was also a decline in the number of manufacturing jobs in the 1980s and 90s. The service sector, however, expanded, and general levels of unemployment, especially in Britain, fell dramatically in the 1990s. Financial services saw strong growth, particularly in such places as London's Docklands and Edinburgh. Indeed, by the end of the 1990s, the financial industry was the largest employer in northern manufacturing towns like Leeds. Leeds grew rapidly in the 1990s, aided by its ability to offer a range of cultural facilities that helped to attract an array of UK company headquarters. Manchester, similarly, enjoyed a renaissance, particularly in the spheres of music and football. Manchester United's commercial successes have led it to become by far the largest sports franchise in existence.

NEW INDUSTRIES

Other areas were helped by their ability to attract high-technology industry. 'Silicon Glen' in central Scotland, for instance, was by the end of the 1990s the largest producer of computing equipment in Europe. Computing and software design was also one of the main engines of growth along the so-called 'silicon highway' of the M4 corridor west from London. But areas of vigorous expansion were not necessarily dominated by new technologies. East Anglia – and Cambridgeshire, in particular – grew rapidly in the 1980s and 1990s. But while Cambridge, aided by the university-related science parks, fostered high-technology companies, especially in biotechnology and pharmaceuticals, expansion in Peterborough, for instance, was largely in the low-tech areas of business services and distribution.

Economic change was most dramatic in the Irish Republic, which enjoyed the highest growth rates in Europe in the 1990s. The so-called 'Celtic tiger' economy boomed, aided by inward investment, so that by the end of the decade Gross Domestic Product (GDP) per capita had passed that of the UK. Dublin, which remained if anything even more dominant than London as a capital city, flourished as a result of strong growth in the service industries. Growth rates for 'new economy' industries such as information and communication technology were among the highest in the world. Generous tax arrangements and the city's growing reputation as a cultural centre meanwhile helped to encourage the development of Dublin's 'rockbroker belt'.

Agriculture in the Irish Republic was in decline during the 1990s but still contributed 9 per cent of Ireland's GDP, three times the European average. In the west of Ireland it was increasingly supplemented by the growth of tourism. Nevertheless, while the expansion of Ireland's prosperity lessened the traditional east–west divide, it did not eliminate it. In Britain, the old north–south divide seemed to be eroding during the recession of the early 1990s, which hit southeast England relatively hard, but it reasserted itself with a vengeance later in the decade as people moved south in search of jobs and property prices rose. Even though the shift towards service industries was reducing regional economic diversity, the geographical distribution of regions eligible for European structural funds for economic improvement confirmed the continuing north–south divide.

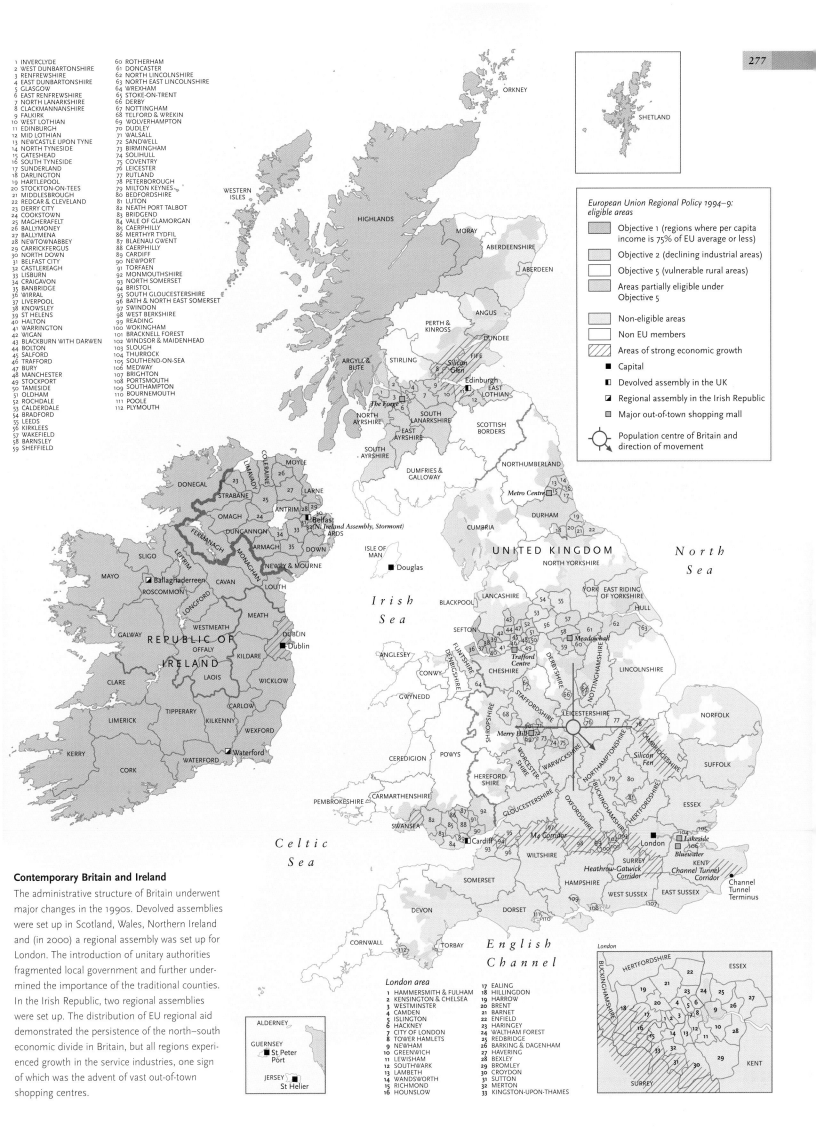

1 INVERCLYDE
2 WEST DUNBARTONSHIRE
3 RENFREWSHIRE
4 EAST DUNBARTONSHIRE
5 GLASGOW
6 EAST RENFREWSHIRE
7 NORTH LANARKSHIRE
8 CLACKMANNANSHIRE
9 FALKIRK
10 WEST LOTHIAN
11 EDINBURGH
12 MID LOTHIAN
13 NEWCASTLE UPON TYNE
14 NORTH TYNESIDE
15 GATESHEAD
16 SOUTH TYNESIDE
17 SUNDERLAND
18 DARLINGTON
19 HARTLEPOOL
20 STOCKTON-ON-TEES
21 MIDDLESBROUGH
22 REDCAR & CLEVELAND
23 DERRY CITY
24 COOKSTOWN
25 MAGHERAFELT
26 BALLYMONEY
27 BALLYMENA
28 NEWTOWNABBEY
29 CARRICKFERGUS
30 NORTH DOWN
31 BELFAST CITY
32 CASTLEREAGH
33 LISBURN
34 CRAIGAVON
35 BANBRIDGE
36 WIRRAL
37 LIVERPOOL
38 KNOWSLEY
39 ST HELENS
40 HALTON
41 WARRINGTON
42 WIGAN
43 BLACKBURN WITH DARWEN
44 BOLTON
45 SALFORD
46 TRAFFORD
47 BURY
48 MANCHESTER
49 STOCKPORT
50 TAMESIDE
51 OLDHAM
52 ROCHDALE
53 CALDERDALE
54 BRADFORD
55 LEEDS
56 KIRKLEES
57 WAKEFIELD
58 BARNSLEY
59 SHEFFIELD
60 ROTHERHAM
61 DONCASTER
62 NORTH LINCOLNSHIRE
63 NORTH EAST LINCOLNSHIRE
64 WREXHAM
65 STOKE-ON-TRENT
66 DERBY
67 NOTTINGHAM
68 TELFORD & WREKIN
69 WOLVERHAMPTON
70 DUDLEY
71 WALSALL
72 SANDWELL
73 BIRMINGHAM
74 SOLIHULL
75 COVENTRY
76 LEICESTER
77 RUTLAND
78 PETERBOROUGH
79 MILTON KEYNES
80 BEDFORDSHIRE
81 LUTON
82 NEATH PORT TALBOT
83 BRIDGEND
84 VALE OF GLAMORGAN
85 CAERPHILLY
86 MERTHYR TYDFIL
87 BLAENAU GWENT
88 CAERPHILLY
89 CARDIFF
90 NEWPORT
91 TORFAEN
92 MONMOUTHSHIRE
93 NORTH SOMERSET
94 BRISTOL
95 SOUTH GLOUCESTERSHIRE
96 BATH & NORTH EAST SOMERSET
97 SWINDON
98 WEST BERKSHIRE
99 READING
100 WOKINGHAM
101 BRACKNELL FOREST
102 WINDSOR & MAIDENHEAD
103 SLOUGH
104 THURROCK
105 SOUTHEND-ON-SEA
106 MEDWAY
107 BRIGHTON
108 PORTSMOUTH
109 SOUTHAMPTON
110 BOURNEMOUTH
111 POOLE
112 PLYMOUTH

European Union Regional Policy 1994–9: eligible areas

Objective 1 (regions where per capita income is 75% of EU average or less)

Objective 2 (declining industrial areas)

Objective 5 (vulnerable rural areas)

Areas partially eligible under Objective 5

Non-eligible areas

Non EU members

Areas of strong economic growth

■ Capital

▫ Devolved assembly in the UK

◪ Regional assembly in the Irish Republic

▪ Major out-of-town shopping mall

⊕ Population centre of Britain and direction of movement

London area

1 HAMMERSMITH & FULHAM
2 KENSINGTON & CHELSEA
3 WESTMINSTER
4 CAMDEN
5 ISLINGTON
6 HACKNEY
7 CITY OF LONDON
8 TOWER HAMLETS
9 NEWHAM
10 GREENWICH
11 LEWISHAM
12 SOUTHWARK
13 LAMBETH
14 WANDSWORTH
15 RICHMOND
16 HOUNSLOW
17 EALING
18 HILLINGDON
19 HARROW
20 BRENT
21 BARNET
22 ENFIELD
23 HARINGEY
24 WALTHAM FOREST
25 REDBRIDGE
26 BARKING & DAGENHAM
27 HAVERING
28 BEXLEY
29 BROMLEY
30 CROYDON
31 SUTTON
32 MERTON
33 KINGSTON-UPON-THAMES

Contemporary Britain and Ireland

The administrative structure of Britain underwent major changes in the 1990s. Devolved assemblies were set up in Scotland, Wales, Northern Ireland and (in 2000) a regional assembly was set up for London. The introduction of unitary authorities fragmented local government and further undermined the importance of the traditional counties. In the Irish Republic, two regional assemblies were set up. The distribution of EU regional aid demonstrated the persistence of the north–south economic divide in Britain, but all regions experienced growth in the service industries, one sign of which was the advent of vast out-of-town shopping centres.

The Channel Tunnel

The Channel Tunnel is highly symbolic of Britain's commitment to Europe. Millions of people and vehicles have now travelled from London to Paris in a mere three hours.

POLITICAL CHANGE

Politics were transformed in the course of the 1990s by nationalism and (to a lesser extent) by regionalism. In Scotland, a minor Tory recovery in 1992 was wiped out in the Labour landslide of 1997, when all the Conservative seats in Scotland were lost (as they also were in Wales). Only one Scottish seat was regained in 2001. The Tories, who had successfully played the Scottish card against centralising opponents in the 1950s, had themselves become labelled as a centralising and purely English party. Nationalist political sentiment grew in Scotland and to a lesser extent in Wales. Local government had already been reorganised in Britain and Northern Ireland in the early 1990s with the introduction of unitary authorities. Now, in 1999, devolved governments, with varying powers, were introduced in Scotland, Wales and Northern Ireland. The Republic of Ireland simi-

Ashford, Kent

Like many other parts of Kent, Ashford has been heavily affected by the opening of the Channel Tunnel. Today it even has its own international railway station. Like other towns, it has seen the construction of new ring roads, which in turn have attracted the construction of out-of-town shopping malls.

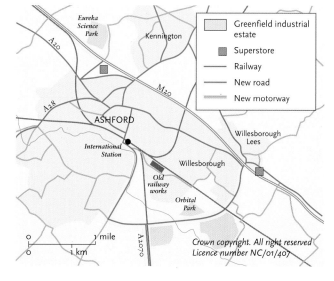

larly was divided between two regional assemblies but unlike the assemblies in the UK, these were not directly elected.

In 2000, a mayor and regional assembly with powers over local planning and transport were introduced in London. This new authority in part replaced the Greater London Council abolished by the Thatcher government in 1986. However, there were no signs that the authorities in the other English conurbations, which had been abolished at the same time, would be similarly restored. Elsewhere in England, except in the Northeast and Cornwall, there was only limited interest in regionalisation. The creation of nine Regional Development Agencies in England in 1998–9 did not seek to meet a regionalist agenda. In fact, these new bodies to a large extent matched the existing structures set up from the 1960s onwards for administrative convenience and to encourage inward investment.

TRANSPORT IN BRITAIN

Improving transport links was seen as an important means of stimulating regional development and combating congestion. Major road developments in the 1990s included the completion of the M25 orbital motorway round London, the Skye bridge and the M40 link between London and Birmingham. However, despite this construction programme, congestion remained a problem: the M25, for example, became the butt of jokes labelling it the largest car park on the planet, while average traffic speeds in central London continued to fall, reaching 15 kilometres per hour (about 10 miles per hour) by 1997, about the same as they had been at the beginning of the century. Congestion was not the only problem. Environmental issues also came to the fore as protesters tried to disrupt the Conservatives' ambitious roads programme, most notably at the Newbury bypass and the extensions of the M3 across Twyford Down and the M11 in East London. Such protest, combined with growing concern about greenhouse gas emissions, of which motor vehicles contribute about one-quarter, led to much of the roads programme being shelved after 1997.

As far as public transport networks were concerned, improvements tended to be largely confined to urban centres, such as the light rail networks developed in Manchester, Sheffield and Croydon. At the same time, the migration of some financial services and much of the national press to major new developments in London's Docklands prompted the development of the Docklands Light Railway and the Jubilee line extension, as well as some of the most expensive urban motorway in Europe. Undoubtedly the most important transport development, however, was the Channel Tunnel rail link to France, completed in 1994.

A SUCCESS STORY: ASHFORD

Ashford is a historic town with a market dating from the thirteenth century. Its development in the 1990s, following the opening of the Channel Tunnel rail link, provides a good example of the interrelationship between transport links and general economic development. Growth in the nineteenth century had been stimulated by the coming of the railway in 1842; the closure of the town's railway works between 1981 and 1993 did not, however, undermine the local economy. Instead, Ashford benefited from the Chan-

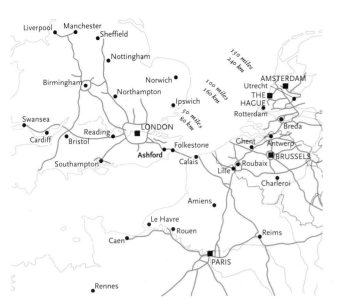

nel Tunnel rail link, which made use of railway lines running through the town, and its population actually grew by over 10 per cent in the 1990s. The completion of the Channel Tunnel and, in 1987, the M25 London orbital motorway, gave the town an international catchment area of some 85 million people within a single day's journey. This and the opening of Ashford International railway station – a main terminal for the rail link to Europe – attracted a range of engineering, financial, distribution and manufacturing companies. In addition to the 14 business parks that were opened in the town itself, four greenfield sites were opened on the outskirts, including a science park owned by Trinity College, Cambridge, which had opened the first UK science park in Cambridge in 1970. Even the historic market relocated to Orbital Park to the south of the town, reflecting in microcosm a national trend towards siting not only industrial but also retail parks on the edge of towns.

TRANSPORT IN IRELAND

In Ireland, low population density and a dispersed pattern of settlement were felt to make rail developments unsuitable. Consequently, Ireland's first integrated transport programme, the Operational Programme for Peripherality, introduced in 1989, and its successors, concentrated on improving the road network. Four strategic corridors, in particular, were identified for improvement: the routes from Belfast to Cork; Dublin and the Southwest; east–west routes across the Republic; and routes from the west of Ireland to the ferry port of Rosslare. Many of these improvements benefited from European Union (EU) funding. The EU has also aided, via its peace programme, the development of transport infrastructure in Northern Ireland, and it is also having an impact upon transport planning in Britain, with infrastructure projects in, for example, the Highlands and Islands. In 1993 the EU decided to create a European combined transport network. Of the 14 priority projects associated with this aim, three are based in Britain and Ireland – a rail link from Cork to Northern Ireland and the

ferry port for Scotland; a road link from the Low Countries across England and Wales to Ireland; and the West Coast mainline rail route in Britain.

THE IMPACT OF EUROPE

Transport policy is only one way in which the EU increasingly came to shape the geography of the British Isles in the 1990s. It was, for example, a key factor in the creation of the new administrative regions of Britain and Ireland in 1999. At the same time, a number of British local authorities opened offices in Brussels for lobbying purposes. Indeed, attempts to maximise receipts from European structural funds also encouraged the articulation of regionalism. Cornwall, for instance, 'closed' the border with Devon briefly in 1998 in protest at its non-receipt of certain EU social funds, while the enthusiasm the Scottish National Party discovered in the late 1980s for the supposed economic benefits that would result from 'independence in Europe' may help to explain its subsequent political revival.

The European connection has proved less welcome in other quarters. Fishermen, particularly in Cornwall and on the east coast of England, have felt themselves the victims of the Common Fisheries Policy quota system. There is also a strong sense of Euroscepticism in England, fuelled by a mixture of concerns about sovereignty and economic policy. Even the most enthusiastic Europeans, the Irish, have rejected developments that they felt were not in their interest, as the 2001 referendum on the Treaty of Nice demonstrated. Nevertheless, links with Europe are growing, whether via the Channel Tunnel, or the connections between the French and British electricity grids, or airline policy, as are the number of policy decisions shaped by the EU. This pace of change has quickened since the 1987 Single European Act and it is now clear that Britain and Ireland are, both in economic and administrative terms, increasingly becoming integrated with Europe. **PPC**

Ashford and Europe
The Channel Tunnel has transformed the economy of Kent. Ashford is closer to Paris and Brussels than it is to Manchester and Liverpool. The town, with its international rail link and position at the hub of a huge motorway network (shown here), is now in a position to be part of a truly international economy.

A contemporary shopping mall
Modern-day affluence is reflected in the variety of goods and services concentrated in shopping malls. They are now often built on major roads outside cities to make them accessible to the maximum number of people.

20th-CENTURY LONDON

Unilever House, built 1930–1 as a commercial headquarters

St Paul's Cathedral, rebuilt 1675–1711 and a survivor of the Blitz that destroyed neighbouring Paternoster Square

River Thames

Cannon Street station (1866), remodelled in the 1960s

London Bridge (1831), replaced in 1967–72 and re-erected in Arizona, USA

Billingsgate Fish Market, closed in 1982 and refurbished as offices

The 'London Eye'

Built as a temporary structure to celebrate the Millennium, the giant wheel occupies part of the site used in 1951 for the Festival of Britain, and is next to County Hall, the former home of London government.

London in the year 1900 was the capital of the British empire and the world's most powerful metropolis. By the end of the twentieth century, with a population of about 7 million people, it still ranked among the world's largest cities, but no longer dominated world trade and commerce, though it remained a significant force in global finance. The twentieth century brought enormous changes to Britain's capital.

An agent of traumatic change, particularly in central London, was the devastation visited on the city by German bombers in the Blitz of September to November 1940, and subsequent raids. One third of the City of London was rebuilt between 1945 and 1972, largely because of bomb damage.

Some 20,000 tons of bombs fell on London during the Blitz. Miraculously, St Paul's Cathedral and the Tower of London survived, symbols of national resilience. The task of reconstruction began during the war years; the 1943 Abercrombie Plan for the County of London laid down the blueprint for London's future as a more rational, cleaner city where industry would be confined to zones and cars accommodated through new road schemes. These principles informed the Barbican development of 2,000 flats with an integrated Arts Centre. Begun in the 1950s, the Barbican was Europe's largest reconstruction project of the period and included Europe's tallest residential tower block.

What postwar planners failed to predict was the disappearance from the city's heart of centuries-old activities such as commercial warehousing and the docks. London's docks achieved record levels of activity in the 1950s, but trade fell away rapidly thereafter. St Katharine's Dock was among the first wave of dock closures in 1967–8. By 1982 all of London's working docks had migrated down river to

Site of the Barbican scheme, which gave the city a new residential quarter

The Bank of England, brought into public ownership in 1946

a new container port at Tilbury. Billingsgate Fish Market moved from the site it had occupied under licence since the seventeenth century.

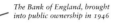

Canary Wharf

Construction of the vast Canary Wharf office precinct on the Isle of Dogs (seen here looking east towards the Millennium Dome) began in 1988. Canada Tower, the landmark building, was the tallest in Europe at the time.

By contrast, demand for office space in central London grew throughout the century. Between the wars, a new breed of large headquarters buildings marked the emergence of international corporations such as Unilever. After the war, the increasing dominance in London's economy of the banking, finance and insurance sector was marked by the rising prominence of its modernistic buildings, including such landmarks as the Natwest Tower and the Lloyds Building. Only the Bank of England retained a traditional appearance.

The late twentieth century also saw the transformation of former docks areas into offices and fashionable modern residential developments – with a new focus around the huge Canary Wharf scheme, to the east of the City on the previously isolated Isle of Dogs. **CR**

The Tower of London, which has become a major tourist attraction, with over 2 million visitors annually by the 1990s

The Blitzed City

The City of London in late 1945, devastated by the aerial bombing of the 1939–45 war but yet to experience the mammoth office blocks that have transformed London's skyline.

St Katharine's Dock, closed as a working dock in 1968 and redeveloped as a hotel and marina

Bermondsey, a traditional industrialised area heavily dependent on the docks

Bermondsey, a district still based around Victorian industry, was hit by the loss not just of the docks but also of many dependent factories in the area. In London as a whole, manufacturing jobs declined by almost a half in the 1970s.

British troops in Saudi Arabia

Britain sent 43,000 troops to support US forces in the Gulf War in 1991. The American alliance, more than direct national interest, decided the policy.

Britain, Ireland and the world

By 1970, Britain's disengagement from empire was nearly complete. The European Union, the Cold War and the American alliance were Britain's main foreign concerns until 1990, while Ireland pursued a policy of neutrality. With the end of the Cold War, Britain took a more active role for the UN in Iraq, Bosnia and Kosovo, a practice followed by Ireland in Cyprus and Lebanon.

In the final 30 years of the twentieth century, Britain's status as a world power continued to decline; the country remained a major global economy, but its foreign relations became increasingly tied to those of its neighbours in Europe. In the Cold War, which lasted until 1990, Britain was a nuclear power, a member of the transatlantic NATO alliance and other regional defence pacts, and US bases in Britain contained nuclear missiles. By contrast, Ireland maintained its traditional policy of neutrality. It remained outside the Commonwealth, but was an active member of the United Nations and various European organisations.

By 1970, Britain had abandoned overseas defence commitments 'east of Suez'. The defence of western Europe and meeting any Soviet threat was now the main concern. The army was also increasingly involved in counter-insurgency operations in Northern Ireland. Small military detachments helped to guard remaining outposts of empire such as Belize. Argentine claims to the Falkland Islands were not taken seriously, and naval vessels were withdrawn from the South Atlantic in 1981. In April 1982, though, Argentina launched a surprise attack on the Falklands and occupied the islands. Despite the logistical problems, a naval task force set sail, and with US intelligence support, the islands were regained after fierce fighting.

The end of the Cold War altered British defence strategies and commitments. In the 'New World Order' post-1990, US missiles were withdrawn from Britain, but alliance with the United States remained a key aspect of British foreign policy. British armed forces began to play a more active role in international policing and peace-keeping. In 1991 Britain contributed forces to the Gulf War, when the UN expelled Iraq from Kuwait; the following year, British forces served as peace-keepers in Bosnia, and again in Kosovo in 1998. Britain participated in the NATO bombing raids in 1998 to seek to end Serbian repression in Kosovo. A further peace-keeping role involved military intervention in support of the elected government of the troubled West African state of Sierra Leone. While acting in this role as peace-keeper Britain, ironically, remained a major exporter of arms to countries throughout the world. Since 1970, Irish military forces have primarily been involved in peace-keeping roles, mainly in cooperation with the British to secure the frontier with Northern Ireland, but also serving with the United Nations, primarily in Cyprus and south Lebanon.

Britain and Ireland became members of the European Economic Community (subsequently the European Union) in 1973. The rise in international oil prices that year served to stimulate the search for new sources in British and Irish waters. Ireland benefited greatly from the EU budget, and

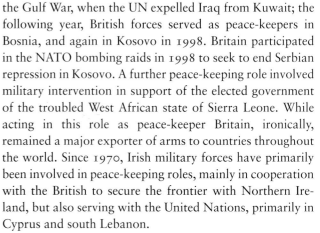

by the 1990s, with new investment from the United States, the Irish economy was expanding rapidly and the long-term pattern of Irish emigration was being reversed. British and Irish trade with Europe increased, and Ireland's economy became less dependent on Britain. In 1991 both countries signed the Maastricht Treaty for closer political and economic unity in Europe. Irish political leaders eagerly embraced the idea of European integration, although a closer relationship was rejected in a referendum in 2001, while British political parties were deeply divided over greater involvement and the adoption of the euro as a currency.

VESTIGES OF EMPIRE

Britain had retreated from most of the empire by 1970. Immigration from the 'old empire' continued but, following restrictive legislation by Britain, at greatly reduced levels. The major remaining colony was Rhodesia, which had been illegally ruled by a white minority government since 1967. Britain resumed nominal control in 1980 and the territory became independent as Zimbabwe later that year. Various smaller island colonies in the Caribbean and the Pacific were granted independence in the 1970s and 1980s. Hong Kong and the adjacent New Territories became an autonomous region of China in 1997, on the expiry of the agreed 100-year lease. The removal of that colony, with its large population, cleared the way for the British government to offer citizenship to the peoples of the remaining small colonies that formed the British Overseas Territories.

Relations between Ireland and Britain since 1970 have been focused primarily on the crisis in Northern Ireland. Both states have an interest in the suppression of violence there, although it was not until the late 1990s, when the Irish constitution was amended, that Dublin recognised British sovereignty over Northern Ireland. Lengthy diplomatic discussions between London and Dublin, often bitterly opposed by Ulster Unionists, have led haltingly to cross-border agreements and a measure of power-sharing in the North. The Northern Ireland question has also involved the United States, where an influential pro-Irish lobby provides financial aid to the IRA. In the 1990s, US President Clinton acted as a peace broker, which contributed towards an uneasy cease-fire in the North from 1994 onwards. **DK**

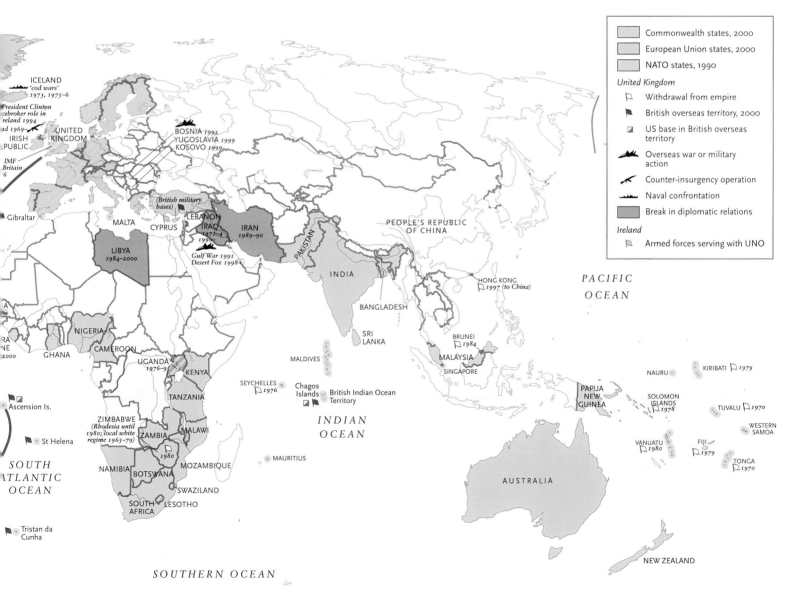

CHRONOLOGICAL TABLE

c.8000 BC–AD 300	EVENTS IN BRITAIN & IRELAND	SOCIETY, ECONOMY & TECHNOLOGY	ARTS & SCIENCE	OTHER EVENTS
c.8000 BC	*c.*8000 BC End of the last glaciation			
	*c.*5000 BC Rising sea levels cut Britain off from the rest of Europe	*c.*4000–3500 BC Farming spreads throughout Britain and Ireland		*c.*3500 BC The first cities and states develop in Mesopotamia
	*c.*3000 BC Construction of Newgrange passage tomb in Ireland	*c.*2500 BC Copper mining begins, in SW Ireland		*c.*2550 BC The Great Pyramid of Khufu is built at Giza
	*c.*2000 BC The main stage of Stonehenge is completed	*c.*2000 BC Bronze tools and weapons in use in Britain and Ireland		
		*c.*1000 BC Earliest use of iron in Britain		
			*c.*550 BC Hallstatt ornamental style reaches Britain	753 BC Traditional date for the foundation of Rome
	*c.*320 BC Greek navigator Pytheas of Massalia visits Britain		*c.*400 BC Influence of the La Tène ornamental style reaches Britain	
	55–4 BC Julius Caesar's raids on Britain	*c.*70 BC First native coinage produced, in southeastern Britain		58–52 BC Roman conquest of Gaul
				27 BC Augustus becomes the first emperor of Rome
				*c.*6 BC Probable date of the birth of Jesus of Nazareth
AD 1	43 Beginning of the Roman conquest of Britain			
	*c.*50 Foundation of London (Londinium)			
	60 The Iceni rebel under Boudica			
	71 Foundation of York (Eburacum)	*c.*70 The palace at Fishbourne (Sussex) is built		
	79–84 Agricola campaigns in Scotland			
AD 100		*c.*100 British *civitas* capitals established		
	122–33 Construction of Hadrian's Wall			117 Roman empire reaches its greatest extent under Trajan
	142–3 Construction of the Antonine Wall			
	163–4 Final abandonment of the Antonine Wall			
	*c.*197 Roman Britain is divided into two provinces	198–211 Temple of Mithras built at Carrawburgh on Hadrian's Wall		
AD 200	210 Emperor Severus campaigns against the Maeatae			212 Citizenship is granted to all free inhabitants of the Roman empire
	259–73 Britain is part of the independent Gallic empire of Postumus			
	286–96 Britain is independent under the usurpers Carausius and Allectus			
	*c.*296 Roman Britain is divided into four provinces			
AD 300		297 Earliest reference to the Picts		

EVENTS IN BRITAIN & IRELAND	SOCIETY, ECONOMY & TECHNOLOGY	ARTS & SCIENCE	OTHER EVENTS	AD **300–800**
				AD 300
306 Constantine proclaimed Roman emperor at York	301 Diocletian's Prices Edict fixes the prices of British woollens and beer	**4th century** Development of the Irish ogham alphabet	313 Edict of Milan: Constantine introduces toleration for Christians	
	314 Three British bishops attend a church council at Arles			
367 The 'Barbarian Conspiracy': Britain ravaged by barbarian raids		**first half of the 4th century** Schools of mosaicists flourish in Britain		
383–8 Rebellion of Magnus Maximus				
	*c.*397 St Ninian founds the monastery of Candida Casa at Whithorn in Galloway		395 The Roman empire is permanently divided into eastern and western halves, each with its own emperor	
				AD 400
*c.*400 Niall Noígiallach raids Britain	402 Last issue of Roman coinage to reach Britain	**5th century** First Pictish symbol stones erected		
409 Britain becomes independent of Rome	**early 5th century** Decline of urban life and trade		410 The Visigoths sack Rome	
*c.*430 Beginning of Anglo-Saxon settlement in Britain	*c.*435 Start of St Patrick's mission in Ireland		*c.*450 Many British Celts migrate to Brittany to escape the Anglo-Saxon invasions	
*c.*440 Cunedda defeats Irish invaders in Wales			476 The last Roman emperor of the West is deposed	
				AD 500
*c.*500 British victory at Mt Badon halts Anglo-Saxon expansion		**early 6th century** Gildas, *On the Ruin of Britain*		
500 Irish Dál Riata dynasty wins control of Argyll				
577 Battle of Dyrham: Anglo-Saxons capture Bath, Cirencester and Gloucester	563 St Columba founds the monastery of Iona			
	597 St Augustine's mission arrives in Kent		591 Columbanus of Bangor begins missionary work on the Continent	
				AD 600
*c.*600 The Gododdin defeated by the Anglo-Saxons at Catterick	601 Augustine becomes the first archbishop of Canterbury	*c.*600 Aneurin composes the heroic Welsh poem *Y Gododdin*		
627 King Edwin of Northumbria is converted to Christianity	*c.*625 Sutton Hoo ship burial		622 The hejira: Muhammad's flight from Mecca marks the beginning of the Muslim era	
	*c.*630 First English coinage struck			
664 Synod of Whitby	635 Aidan founds the monastery of Lindisfarne		635–711 Period of the Islamic Arab conquests of the Middle East, North Africa and Spain	
		670–700 Northumbrian crosses at Bewcastle and Ruthwell erected		
685 Battle of Nechtansmere: Northumbrian attempt to conquer the Picts is defeated	688–726 King Ine of Wessex issues the earliest known English laws	*c.*680 Caedmon composes the earliest surviving English poetry		
		late 7th century The *Book of Durrow*, the earliest surviving insular gospel book		
				AD 700
	by 700 London, Southampton, Ipswich and York develop as major ports: the first renewal of urban life since Roman times	**8th century** *Beowulf*	716–54 St Boniface's missions in Saxony and Frisia	
716–57 Mercia becomes the leading Anglo-Saxon kingdom under King Aethelbald		731 Bede, *Ecclesiastical History of the English People*		
*c.*790 Offa's Dyke constructed to defend Mercia's Welsh frontier			781–2 Alcuin of York becomes an advisor to the Frankish king Charlemagne	
793 Vikings sack the monastery of Lindisfarne				
795 First recorded Viking raids on Scotland and Ireland		*c.*796 Nennius, *Historia Brittonum* ('History of the Britons')		
				AD 800

	EVENTS IN BRITAIN & IRELAND	SOCIETY, ECONOMY & TECHNOLOGY	ARTS & SCIENCE	OTHER EVENTS
800			c.800 The *Book of Kells* is made, probably at Iona	800 Charlemagne is crowned Roman emperor by Pope Leo III
	825 Battle of Ellendun: Wessex overthrows the Mercian hegemony			c.800 Irish monks become the first visitors to the Faeroe Islands and Iceland
	841 Dublin is founded as a Viking raiding base			
	843 Kenneth MacAlpin, king of the Scots of Dál Riata, conquers the Picts			843 Treaty of Verdun partitions the Carolingian empire between Charlemagne's grandsons
	844–78 Rhodri Mawr of Gwynedd dominates Wales			
	865 The Danish 'Great Army' arrives in England			
	c.870 Foundation of the Norse earldom of Orkney		c.870 John Scotus Erigena, *On the Division of Nature*	c.870 Norse settlement of Iceland begins: the settlers include many Irish slaves
	876 Beginning of Danish settlement in England			
	878 Battle of Edington: Alfred the Great, king of Wessex, defeats the Danes			
	878 Death of Doniert, last independent king of Cornwall			
	889 Donald II is the first to use the title 'king of Scotland'	890s Alfred creates his system of burhs (fortified towns) in Wessex	c.890 King Alfred translates Boethius' *Consolation of Philosophy* into English	
			893 *Anglo-Saxon Chronicle* begun	
900	912 King Edward of Wessex begins the conquest of the Danelaw			911 Viking leader Rollo is made count of Rouen, founding Normandy
	927 Hywel Dda and other Welsh kings recognise Aethelstan of Wessex as overlord			
	937 Battle of Brunanburh: Aethelstan defeats the Vikings and Scots	940s St Dunstan leads monastic revival in England		
	954 Erik Bloodaxe, last Viking king of York, is killed. All of England is now firmly controlled by the Wessex dynasty			962 King Otto I of Germany is crowned Holy Roman Emperor by Pope John XII
	973 King Edgar of England cedes Lothian to Scotland	c.973 *Regularis Concordia* (monastic rule) compiled	c.970 Flourishing of the Winchester School art style	986 Erik the Red leads the Norse settlement of Greenland
				988 Prince Vladimir of Kiev is converted to Christianity
	991 The English pay 'Danegeld' after their defeat by Vikings at Maldon	997 Sihtric Silkbeard of Dublin issues the first coinage in Ireland		
1000	1002 Brian Boru becomes High King of Ireland			c.1000 Leif Eriksson becomes the first European to land in the Americas
	1013 The English submit to Svein Forkbeard of Denmark			
	1014 Battle of Clontarf: Brian Boru killed defeating Viking-Leinster alliance			
	1016 Danish conquest of England: Cnut becomes king			
	1018 Owain the Bald, last British king of Strathclyde, is killed at the battle of Carham			1018 On the death of his brother, Cnut becomes king of Denmark
				1028 Cnut conquers Norway
	1035 Following his death, Cnut's Anglo-Scandinavian empire collapses		late 1040s Edward the Confessor begins the construction of Westminster Abbey in the Romanesque style	1035 William the Conqueror, aged 7, becomes duke of Normandy
	1042 Edward the Confessor restores the Wessex dynasty in England			
1050				

EVENTS IN BRITAIN & IRELAND	SOCIETY, ECONOMY & TECHNOLOGY	ARTS & SCIENCE	OTHER EVENTS	1050–1200
				1050
1057 Macbeth is killed by Malcolm Canmore who becomes king of Scotland			1054 The Great Schism between the Latin (western) and Greek churches	
1066 Battle of Hastings: the Normans, under William the Conqueror, invade England			1059–72 The Normans conquer southern Italy and Sicily	
1069 The Normans defeat English rebellions				
			1071 Battle of Manzikert: Byzantine empire loses control of Asia Minor to the Turks	
1075 Last Danish invasion of England			1075–1122 The Investiture Contest between the papacy and German emperors	
1079 Godred Crovan becomes king of Man and the Isles				
1085 King William orders the compilation of the *Domesday Book*	1086 *Domesday Book* records 5,624 watermills in England			
1092 William Rufus captures Carlisle from Scotland				
1093 Beginning of the Anglo-Norman conquest of Wales		1093 Construction of Durham Cathedral begins		
1098 Magnus Barelegs establishes Norwegian sovereignty over Man and the Hebrides			1099 The First Crusade captures Jerusalem	
				1100
	1102 Council of London: priests forbidden to marry	12th century Earliest manuscript of the Irish epic *Táin Bó Cuailnge* ('The Cattle Raid of Cooley')	1106 Battle of Tinchebrai, Henry I captures Normandy from his brother Robert	
1110 English and Flemish settlement begins in Pembrokeshire, South Wales				
1120 William the Atheling, Henry I's heir, drowns in the Channel				
1124–53 David I invites Norman and English settlers to Scotland	1128 Foundation of the first Cistercian monastery in England at Waverley			
1135–54 Reign of Stephen: period of civil wars in England		*c.*1136 Geoffrey of Monmouth, *History of the Kings of Britain*		
	1142 The first Cistercian monastery in Ireland is founded at Mellifont	1142–4 Adelard of Bath writes a treatise on the astrolabe	1147–9 The Second Crusade	
			1147 English and Flemish crusaders capture Lisbon from the Muslims	
	1152 Synod of Kells begins reform of the Irish church			*1150*
1154 Henry II becomes king of England				
1169 Anglo-Norman mercenaries recruited by Diarmit Mac Murchada, king of Leinster				
1170 'Strongbow' captures Waterford and Dublin		*c.*1170 John of Salisbury, *Policraticus*		
1170 Murder of Archbishop Thomas Becket				
1171 Irish kings submit to Henry II of England		*c.*1175 The choir of Canterbury Cathedral is rebuilt in the Gothic style		
1173–4 Henry II defeats a baronial rebellion		1176 First recorded eisteddfod held in Wales		
1177 Prince John is made Lord of Ireland	*c.*1176 Richard Fitznigel, *Dialogue of the Exchequer*			
	1180 Ranulf Glanville, *Treatise on the Laws and Customs of England*			
1183 Rory O'Connor, last High King of Ireland, abdicates	*c.*1185 Foundation of Oxford University		1187 Saladin recaptures Jerusalem	
		late 12th century Layamon, *Brut*, a verse history of England: first major work in English since the Norman conquest	1189–92 Richard I in the Holy Land on the Third Crusade	
1194 Llewelyn the Great becomes king of Gwynedd	1199 Start of the English chancery rolls			
				1200

1200–1300	EVENTS IN BRITAIN & IRELAND	SOCIETY, ECONOMY & TECHNOLOGY	ARTS & SCIENCE	OTHER EVENTS
1200	1203–4 King John loses his French lands to Philip Augustus 1208–13 England placed under papal interdict 1215 King John accepts Magna Carta 1216–7 Prince Louis of France invades England	1209 Foundation of Cambridge University 1215 English Court of Common Pleas established		1204 The Fourth Crusade captures Constantinople 1214 King John's plan to recover his French lands collapses after his German allies are defeated at the battle of Bouvines
1220		1224 First Franciscan friars arrive in England c.1230 Franciscan friars arrive in Ireland	1220 Construction of Salisbury Cathedral is begun	
1240	1258 Baronial rebellion against Henry III	c.1250 Walter of Henley, *Hosebondrie*, a manual of estate management; Roger Bacon invents the magnifying glass	1242 Roger Bacon describes the manufacture of gunpowder 1245 Henry III begins the rebuilding of Westminster Abbey in a French Gothic style c.1250 The song *Sumer is icumen in* is composed 1252 Roger of Wendover writes a treatise on anatomy	1241 The Mongols invade eastern Europe
1260	1263 Battle of Largs: Scots defeat a Norwegian invasion 1264–5 Simon de Montfort leads a baronial revolt in England 1266 Norway cedes the Hebrides and Man to Scotland 1267 Treaty of Montgomery: Henry III recognises Llewelyn ap Gruffudd as prince of Wales 1276–83 Edward I conquers Wales		1272 Roger Bacon advocates study of nature by observation and exact measurement	1271–2 Prince Edward of England crusades in the Holy Land
1280 **1300**	1284 Statute of Wales establishes the Principality of Wales 1290 Edward I intervenes in a Scottish succession crisis; the Isle of Man comes under the English crown 1295 Scotland and France conclude the 'Auld Alliance' 1296 Beginning of the Scottish wars for independence 1298 Wallace defeats the English at Falkirk Bridge	1290 The Jews are expelled from England	c.1295 *The Harrowing of Hell*: earliest surviving English miracle play	1291 The last Christian states in the Holy Land are recaptured by the Muslims

CHRONOLOGICAL TABLE

EVENTS IN BRITAIN & IRELAND	SOCIETY, ECONOMY & TECHNOLOGY	ARTS & SCIENCE	OTHER EVENTS	**1300–1400**
1301 Edward I gives his son and heir the title 'Prince of Wales' **1306** Robert Bruce crowned king of Scotland **1314** Scots defeat the English at the battle of Bannockburn **1315–8** The English defeat Edward Bruce's invasion of Ireland	**early 14th century** Hanseatic League kontor established at the Steelyard, London	**1303** Robert Mannyng, *Handlynge Synne* **1318** The scholastic philosopher William of Ockham begins teaching at Oxford		*1300*
1327 Edward II is deposed and murdered **1328** Edward III recognises Scottish independence		**1322–42** Lantern tower of Ely Cathedral	**1324–5** Anglo-French war over Gascony **1337** Outbreak of the Hundred Years War	*1320*
1346 Scottish invasion of England defeated at Neville's Cross **1348–50** The Black Death **1354** John of Islay adopts the title 'Lord of the Isles'	**1351** The Statute of Labourers attempts to fix wages in England	*c.*1340 Richard Rolle writing lyrics and prose in Latin and English	**1340** Battle of Sluys: English destroy French invasion fleet **1346** English defeat the French at Crécy **1347** Calais is captured by Edward III **1356** English defeat the French at Poitiers	*1340*
1371 Accession of Robert II, first Stuart king of Scotland	**1366** Statutes of Kilkenny forbid English settlers to adopt Irish customs	**1362** William Langland, *Piers Plowman* **1375** John Barbour, *The Bruce* *c.*1375 *Sir Gawain and the Green Knight* **1376** First known performance of the Corpus Christi mystery play cycle at York	**1360** Treaty of Brétigny settles peace between England and France **1367** Black Prince's victory over Castile at Nájera **1369** Hundred Years War renewed by Edward III **1378–1417** Great Schism of the Papacy	*1360*
1381 English Peasants' Revolt **1386** Treaty of Windsor agrees Anglo-Portuguese alliance **1388** Battle of Otterburn **1399** Henry Bolingbroke deposes Richard II and becomes king	**1382** Winchester College founded **1392** Date of the oldest surviving clock in Britain (Wells Cathedral)	**1387–92** Geoffrey Chaucer, *Canterbury Tales* **1390** Lollards produce the first English translation of the Bible **1391–2** Chaucer, *Treatise on the Astrolabe*: the earliest scientific work in English *c.*1393 Julian of Norwich, *Revelations of Divine Love* *c.*1395 The Wilton Diptych (painting)	**1385** Anglo-Portuguese victory over Castile at Aljubarrota **1396** Anglo-French 28-year truce agreed	*1380*
				1400

1400–1500	EVENTS IN BRITAIN & IRELAND	SOCIETY, ECONOMY & TECHNOLOGY	ARTS & SCIENCE	OTHER EVENTS
1400	1400–10 Owain Glyndwr's revolt in Wales 1403 Rebellion of the Percies	1401 *De heretico comburendo*: legislation against Lollard heretics 1410 Foundation of the first Scottish university (St Andrews)	1412–21 John Lydgate, *The Troy Book*	1414 Henry V renews the Hundred Years War 1415 Battle of Agincourt
1420			*c.*1423 John Dunstable introduces counterpoint polyphony into music; James I of Scotland, *The King's Quair* 1430 40 shilling freehold franchise introduced for English county elections *c.*1432–6 *The Book of Margery Kempe*	1420 Treaty of Troyes: Henry V becomes heir to the French throne 1429 Joan of Arc breaks the siege of Orleans
1440	1450–5 Civil war in Scotland 1455 Battle of St Albans begins the Wars of the Roses	1441 Eton College is founded	1446–1515 King's College chapel, Cambridge, built in the Perpendicular style	1449 French recapture Normandy 1453 French victory at Castillon effectively ends the Hundred Years War; fall of the Byzantine empire: Ottoman Turks capture Constantinople
1460	1461 Lancastrians defeated by Yorkists at the battle of Towton 1469 Denmark cedes Orkney and Shetland to Scotland	1468 Statutes against livery and maintenance	1469–70 Thomas Malory, *Le Morte Darthur* 1476 William Caxton establishes the first printing press in England, at Westminster	1474 Edward IV invades France
1480	1485 Battle of Bosworth Field: Richard III killed; Henry Tudor becomes king 1493 The Lordship of the Isles is abolished 1497 A Cornish rebel army is defeated outside London	1481 Thomas Littleton, *Of Tenures*	late 15th century Robert Henryson, *Testament of Cresseid* *c.*1495 *Everyman* (morality play) 1499 Oxford University introduces a music degree	1492 Columbus's first voyage to the Americas 1497 John Cabot discovers Newfoundland and claims it for England 1498 Vasco da Gama sails to India
1500				

EVENTS IN BRITAIN & IRELAND	SOCIETY, ECONOMY & TECHNOLOGY	ARTS & SCIENCE	OTHER EVENTS	1500–1560
				1500
1503 James IV of Scotland and Margaret Tudor marry; William Warham becomes last pre-Reformation archbishop of Canterbury	**1504** English guilds and trade companies placed under Crown supervision **1505** Christ's College, Cambridge, founded	**1503–19** Henry VII's chapel in Westminster Abbey built		
		1507 First printing press in Scotland		
1509 Henry VIII and Catherine of Aragon marry	**1511** Henry VIII begins reform of Royal Navy			
1513 Battle of Flodden	**1512** Royal Navy builds 70-gun warships			
		1516 Thomas More, *Utopia*		
	1518 Royal College of Physicians founded		**1517** Martin Luther begins Protestant Reformation	
			1520 Henry VIII and Francis I meet at the 'Field of Cloth of Gold'	*1520*
	1523 Anthony Fitzherbert, *Book of Husbandry*			
		1525 Cardinal Wolsey gives Hampton Court to Henry VIII		
1529 Fall of Cardinal Wolsey				
1533 Thomas Cranmer becomes archbishop of Canterbury; Marriage of Henry VIII and Catherine of Aragon declared annulled				
1534 Act of Supremacy				
1535 Thomas More executed		**1535** Hans Holbein, *Henry VIII*		
1536 Welsh Act of Union; Pilgrimage of Grace				
1537 Jane Seymour dies				
1539–40 Dissolution of larger monasteries		**1539** 'The Great Bible' (English translation)		
1541 Henry VIII made king of Ireland				*1540*
1542 Catherine Howard executed				
1542–3 War with Scotland; battle of Solway Moss				
	1546 First printed book in a Celtic language (Welsh), *Yn y Lhyvyr Hwnn*		**1545–63** Council of Trent launches the Counter-Reformation	
	1547 Poor Rate levied in London			
1549 Cornish rebellion against Anglican church services	**1550** First written reference to cricket			
1553 Lady Jane Grey queen for nine days			**1553** Richard Chancellor's expedition to Russia	
1554 Princess Elizabeth imprisoned in the Tower; Mary I and Philip of Spain marry; Catholic restoration in England; Lady Jane Grey executed	**1554** Christ's Hospital, London and St Andrews golf course, Scotland, founded			
1556 Thomas Cranmer burnt		**1556** Recorde, *The Castle of Knowledge* (manual of astronomy)	**1558** French take Calais	
1559 Restoration of Protestantism in England; outbreak of Shane O'Neill's rebellion in Ireland				
				1560

1560–1600	EVENTS IN BRITAIN & IRELAND	SOCIETY, ECONOMY & TECHNOLOGY	ARTS & SCIENCE	OTHER EVENTS
1560	1561 Mary, queen of Scots, returns to Scotland		1563 John Foxe, *The Book of Martyrs*	1562 English occupy Le Havre; John Hawkins makes first voyage to Americas and establishes slave trade
		1565 Royal Exchange founded; tobacco introduced to England		
	1567 Mary, queen of Scots, forced to abdicate	1567 Rugby School founded		
	1568 Mary, queen of Scots, flees to England			1568 Jesuits found English College at Douai
	1569–72 Fitzmaurice revolt in Ireland			
1570	1570 Pope excommunicates Elizabeth I	1570 Brass and wire foundries established at Tintern	1570 Nicholas Hilliard, *Elizabeth I* (portrait)	
		1571 Harrow School founded; Jesus College, Oxford, founded for the Welsh		
	1572 Parliament demands execution of Mary, queen of Scots		1572 Society of Antiquaries founded	1572 St Bartholomew's Day Massacre of French Huguenots; Dutch war of independence begins; Drake attacks Spanish harbours in Americas
	1573 Attempted plantation of Ulster		1575 Christopher Saxton, *County Atlas of England and Wales*	
			1576 Richard Burbage opens a theatre in London	
		1578 Levant Trading Company founded	1577–80 Francis Drake circumnavigates globe	
	1579–83 Desmond rebellion in Ireland			
1580		1582 University of Edinburgh founded		1582 First English colony in Newfoundland established
		1583 Queen's Company of Players formed		
				1585 Drake attacks Santo Domingo; attempt to establish colony at Roanoke Island, Virginia
	1586 Babington plot uncovered; Mary, queen of Scots, tried and sentenced to death			
	1587 Mary, queen of Scots, executed		1587 Thomas Kyd, *The Spanish Tragedy*	1587 Drake raids Cadiz; second attempt to found colony at Roanoke Island
	1588 Spanish Armada defeated			
	1589 English attempt to take Lisbon fails	1589 William Lee invents the first knitting machine		
1590		1590 First English paper mill established	1590 Philip Sidney, *Arcadia* (posthumously); Edmund Spenser, *The Faerie Queene*	
	1593 Five Puritans executed for denying Elizabeth I's supremacy	1591 Trinity College, Dublin, founded	1592 Shakespeare, *Richard III*	
	1594–1603 Tyrone's rebellion in Ireland (The Nine Years War)		1594 Shakespeare, *Romeo and Juliet*; Christopher Marlowe, *Edward the Second* (posthumously)	
	1595 Spanish raid Cornwall		1595 Shakespeare, *A Midsummer Night's Dream*	1595 Drake and Hawkins die on expedition to Panama
		1596 Tomato introduced to England; water closet installed in the Queen's Palace, Richmond	1596 Shakespeare, *The Merchant of Venice*	1596 English raid on Cadiz
			1597 Francis Bacon, *Essays, Civil and Moral*	
		1598 Poor Law Act: Hanseatic League's trading privileges in London are ended		1598 Edict of Nantes; Philip II of Spain dies
			1599 Erection of the Globe Theatre, Southwark	
1600				

EVENTS IN BRITAIN & IRELAND	SOCIETY, ECONOMY & TECHNOLOGY	ARTS & SCIENCE	OTHER EVENTS	1600–1650
	1600 East India Company founded	1600 Shakespeare, *Twelfth Night* and *Hamlet*		**1600**
1601 Execution of earl of Essex; Elizabeth I's 'Golden Speech' to Parliament; battle of Kinsale		1602 Bodleian Library opens		
1603 Union of Crowns: James VI of Scotland becomes king of England		1605 Francis Bacon, *The Advancement of Learning*	1604 Treaty of London ends war with Spain	
1605 Gunpowder Plot				
1607 Flight of the earls ends Gaelic Ireland	1607 Anti-enclosure rising in the Midlands	1607 Building begins of Hatfield House, Hertfordshire	1607 First successful English colony in North America at Jamestown	
1609 First Scottish plantations in Ireland; Articles of Plantation allow Irish to be confined in reservations	1609 Charterhouse School founded			
	1611 King James Bible published			**1610**
	1612 Pendle witch trial			
1614 Addled Parliament meets and refuses to discuss finance		1614 Ben Jonson, *Bartholomew Fair*		
		1615 Inigo Jones becomes England's leading architect		
1618 Raleigh executed			1618–48 Thirty Years War	
		1619 William Harvey announces discovery of blood circulation	1619 First Negro slaves arrive in Virginia	
	1622 First Turnpike Act; *Weekeley Newes* first issued		1620 Voyage of the *Mayflower*	**1620**
		1623 Patents law passed	1623 Amboina massacre	
	1624 Virginia Company fails	1624 John Donne, *Devotions upon Emergent Occasions*	1624 St Kitts the first English colony in Caribbean	
	1625 First fire engines in England; tobacco is taxed		1624–30 War with Spain	
1626 Charles I raises forced loan				
1627–9 War with France				
1628 Petition of Right; Oliver Cromwell enters parliament				
1629–40 No parliaments meet		1629 Thomas Hobbes's translation of Thucydides' *The Peloponnesian War*		
	1632 First coffee shop opens in London		1630 Boston, Massachusetts, founded	**1630**
1633 William Land becomes archbishop of Canterbury	1633 First Baptist Church founded in London	1633 John Ford, *Tis Pity She's a Whore*		
	1634 Covent Garden market opens			
1635 Ship money is levied throughout England	1635 First postal service established			
1638 National Covenant drawn up in Scotland; outbreak of first Anglo-Scottish Bishops' War	1639 First Puritan Congregation in Wales	1636 Anthony van Dyck, *Charles I on Horseback*	1639 English traders in Madras	
1640 Short Parliament meets; second Bishops' War; Scots occupy Newcastle		1640 Izaak Walton, *The Life of Donne*		**1640**
1641 Rebellion in Ireland; the Long Parliament elected; Earl of Strafford executed; ship money abolished	1641 First production of cotton goods in Manchester			
1642–6 First English Civil War	1642–60 Puritans close all theatres in England			
1642 Battle of Edgehill				
1643 Battle of Roundway Down		1643 Thomas Browne, *Religio Medici*		
1644 Battles of Marston Moor and Newbury				
1645 New Model Army formed; battles of Naseby and Langport				
1648–9 Second English Civil War	1648 Society of Friends (Quakers) founded		1648 Treaty of Westphalia ends the Thirty Years War	
1649 Execution of Charles I; England a republic; sieges of Drogheda and Wexford		1649 John Milton, *The Tenure of Kings and Magistrates*		
				1650

1650–1690	EVENTS IN BRITAIN & IRELAND	SOCIETY, ECONOMY & TECHNOLOGY	ARTS & SCIENCE	OTHER EVENTS
1650	1650 Battle of Dunbar: Cromwell defeats the Scots	1650 Tea first drunk in England; adultery made capital offence		
	1651 Charles Stuart defeated at Worcester and flees to France	1651 Navigation Act	1651 Thomas Hobbes, *Leviathan*	
			1652 Gerrard Winstanley, *The Law of Freedom* (Digger pamphlet)	1652–4 First Anglo-Dutch war
			1653 Peter Lely, *Oliver Cromwell*; Izaak Walton, *The Compleat Angler*	
	1655 Major-generals appointed to govern districts of England	1655 Jews readmitted into England		1655 Capture of Jamaica
			1656 First opera house in London opened	
	1658 Oliver Cromwell dies	1657 Drinking chocolate introduced to England		
1660	1660 Declaration of Breda; Charles II enters London; Long Parliament dissolves itself; Act of Indemnity		*c.*1660 Actresses appear on English stage	
			1660–9 Samuel Pepys keeps his diary	
	1662 Charles II and Catherine of Braganza marry; Act of Uniformity	1662–7 Acts passed to restrict Irish trade with England and its colonies	1662 Charles II awards charter to Royal Society	1662 Charles II sells Dunkirk to France
		1663 Hearth tax and turnpike tolls introduced		
				1664 English rename New Amsterdam as New York
		1665–6 Great Plague of London	1665 First scientific journal in England, *Philosophical Transactions*, published; Isaac Newton invents differential calculus	
		1666 Great Fire of London; first cheddar cheese produced		1666–7 War with France and the Dutch
	1667–73 The Cabal ministry		1667 John Milton, *Paradise Lost*	1668 East India Company in control of Bombay
1670	1670 Secret Treaty of Dover	1670 Hudson Bay Company founded		
				1671 Sir Henry Morgan appointed deputy governor of Jamaica
			1672 Milton, *Paradise Regained*	1672–4 War with the Dutch
	1673 Test Act excludes Catholics from office; James, duke of York, resigns offices and marries Mary of Modena			
	1675 Charles II agrees to accept a secret subsidy from Louis XIV of France		1675 Wren begins rebuilding St Paul's Cathedral; Greenwich Observatory established	1676 End of war between settlers and Indians in New England
			1677 John Dryden, *All for Love*	
	1678 Popish Plot alleged, followed by anti-Catholic hysteria		1678–84 John Bunyan, *The Pilgrim's Progress*	
	1679–81 Exclusion Crisis; Whig and Tory parties emerge		1679 Ashmolean Museum founded	
1680		1680 Penny post established in London		
	1683 Rye House Plot revealed			
			1684 Dublin Philosophical Society founded	
	1685 Monmouth's rebellion; battle of Sedgemoor; 'Bloody Assizes'	1685 Silk manufactured in Britain		1685 Edict of Nantes revoked: Huguenot emigration to Britain
	1687 Declaration of Indulgence		1687 Isaac Newton, *Philosophiae Naturalis Principia Mathematica*	
	1688 The Glorious Revolution; William of Orange lands at Torbay	1688 Regular meetings of Insurance Underwriters at Lloyd's Coffee House		1688–97 War of the League of Augsburg
	1689 Bill of Rights; siege of Londonderry		1689 John Locke, *Two Treatises of Government*; Henry Purcell, *Dido and Aeneas*	1689 Louis XIV declares war on England
1690				

EVENTS IN BRITAIN & IRELAND	SOCIETY, ECONOMY & TECHNOLOGY	ARTS & SCIENCE	OTHER EVENTS 1690–1730
			1690
1690 Battle of the Boyne			
1691 Battle of Aughrim; treaty of Limerick			
1692 Glencoe Massacre	**1693** National Debt established	**1693** William Congreve, *The Double Dealer*	**1692** Port Royal, Jamaica, destroyed by an earthquake
	1694 Bank of England founded		
	1695 Royal Bank of Scotland founded; window tax introduced		
	1696 *Lloyd's News* published	**1696** John Vanbrugh, *The Relapse*	**1697** Treaty of Ryswyck
1697 Parliament establishes a civil list of up to £700,000 per annum for William III	**1698** Thomas Savery builds the first practical steam pump; Society for Promoting Christian Knowledge founded		**1698–9** Scotland fails to found a colony at Darien
1699 Parliament demands drastic reduction in the size of the army	**1699** Market established at Billingsgate	**1699** Vanbrugh designs Castle Howard, Yorkshire	
			1700
1701 Act of Settlement to ensure Protestant succession		**1701** Daniel Defoe, *The True-Born Englishman*	**1701–14** War of the Spanish Succession
1702 Duke of Marlborough appointed Captain General of English forces	**1702** Earliest English pantomime performed; *The Daily Courant*, first London daily newspaper, published; royal approval given to horse racing	**1703** Isaac Newton President of the Royal Society	
		1704 Jonathan Swift, *A Tale of a Tub*	**1704** Battle of Blenheim; English capture Gibraltar
			1705 Royal Navy takes Barcelona
	1706 *The Evening Post*, first London evening newspaper, published		**1706** Battle of Ramillies; Marlborough conquers Spanish Netherlands
1707 Act of Union of England and Scotland as Great Britain		**1707** Edward Lhuyd, *Archaeologica Britannica* on Celtic languages	
1708 Abortive landing by James Edward Stuart in Scotland	**1708** Newcomen's steam engine		**1708** Battle of Oudenarde; British capture Sardinia and Minorca
			1709 Battle of Malplaquet
			1710
	1710 South Sea Company founded; Sacheverell riots in London against Nonconformists	**1710** George Frederick Handel, *Rinaldo*	**1710** Battle of Brihuega
1711 Marlborough dismissed	**1711** Ascot races established	**1711** London Academy of Arts founded	
	1712 Last witch executed in England	**1712** Alexander Pope, *The Rape of the Lock*	
		1713 Swift made dean of St Patrick's Cathedral, Dublin	**1713** Treaty of Utrecht
1714 George I lands in England; Schism Act allows only Anglicans to keep schools			
1715 Jacobite rebellion; battles of Sheriffmuir and Preston; Riot Act passed		**1715** Society of Ancient Britons formed	
	1717 First inoculations against smallpox in England; Order of Bards, Ovates and Druids founded	**1717** Handel's *Water Music* first performed	**1718–20** War with Spain
	1719 James Figg becomes first boxing champion of England	**1719** Daniel Defoe, *Robinson Crusoe*	
			1720
1721 Robert Walpole becomes Chancellor of the Exchequer	**1720** South Sea Bubble bursts, many investors ruined		
1722 Jacobite Atterbury plot uncovered	**1722** Guy's hospital founded	**1722** Defoe, *Moll Flanders*	**1723** Treaty of Charlottenburg with Prussia
	1725 Malt tax riots in Scotland	**1725** Alexander Pope's translation of Homer's *Odyssey*	
	1726 Lloyd's List published	**1726** Swift, *Gulliver's Travels*	**1727–8** Spanish besiege Gibraltar
		1728 John Gay, *The Beggar's Opera*	**1727–9** War with Spain
		1729 Pope, *Dunciad*	**1730**

	EVENTS IN BRITAIN & IRELAND	SOCIETY, ECONOMY & TECHNOLOGY	ARTS & SCIENCE	OTHER EVENTS
1730		1730 Methodism founded		
		1731 Dublin Society for Improving Husbandry, Manufacturing, and Other Useful Arts founded	1731 10 Downing Street built	
			1732 Covent Garden opera house opened; William Hogarth, *A Harlot's Progress*	
		1733 John Kay patents the 'flying shuttle'	1733 Pope, *Essay on Man*; Hogarth, *A Rake's Progress*	1733 War of the Polish Succession; Savannah, Georgia, founded
	1735 William Pitt becomes MP for Old Sarum			
	1737 Death of Queen Caroline	1736 Porteous riots in Edinburgh; Gin Acts taxing spirits passed		1737 Richmond, Virginia, founded
		1739 Highwayman Dick Turpin executed		1739 Anglo-Spanish War of Jenkins's Ear; British take Porto Bello
1740			1741 Handel, *Messiah*	1740–8 War of the Austrian Succession
		1742 Cotton factories built in Northampton and Birmingham		
		1743 East Indian yarns arrive in Lancashire; Methodist Association of Wales established		1743 Battle of Dettingen
		1744 First recorded cricket match		1744–8 War with France
	1745 Jacobite rebellion; Charles Edward Stuart lands in Scotland; battle of Prestonpans		1745 Hogarth, *Marriage à la Mode*	1745 Battle of Fontenoy; British take Louisburg, Canada
	1746 Battles of Falkirk and Culloden; Charles Edward Stuart flees to France; acts to prohibit wearing tartans and to disarm the Highlands passed		1747 Samuel Johnson, *Plan of a Dictionary of the English Language*	
			1748 Tobias Smollett, *The Adventures of Roderick Random*	
			1749 Henry Fielding, *The History of Tom Jones, A Foundling*	
1750		1750 English Jockey Club founded		
			1751 Cymmrodorian Society founded; Thomas Gray, *Elegy Written in a Country Churchyard*	
		1752 Britain adopts Gregorian calendar		
		1753 Permanent racetrack founded at Newmarket; Marriage Act brings marriage under state control		
		1754 Royal and Ancient Golf Club at St Andrews founded; first British iron-rolling mill founded at Fareham	1754 Thomas Chippendale, *The Gentleman and Cabinet Maker's Director*	1756–63 Seven Years War
				1756 120 die in 'Black Hole of Calcutta'; loss of Minorca
	1757 Admiral Byng executed, having failed to prevent the French capturing Minorca			1757 Robert Clive retakes Calcutta
		1758–61 Construction of Bridgwater Canal		1758 Clive becomes governor of Bengal
			1759 British Museum opened	1759 British take Quebec; battles of Minden, Lagos and Quiberon
1760	1760 French force lands at Carrickfergus	1760 First school for deaf and dumb in Britain founded at Edinburgh; Josiah Wedgwood founds pottery works	1760 Laurence Sterne, *Tristram Shandy*; Kew Botanical Gardens opened	1760 British take Montreal
			1762 George Stubbs, *Mares and Foals*	1762 War with Spain; British take Grenada, Martinique, Havana and Manila
		1764 First houses in London numbered; Anglesey copper industry begins		
1765	1765 Stamp Act passed to tax American colonies			1765 Virginia Assembly challenges Britain's right to collect stamp tax

EVENTS IN BRITAIN & IRELAND	SOCIETY, ECONOMY & TECHNOLOGY	ARTS & SCIENCE	OTHER EVENTS	**1765–1790**
				1765
1767–8 Series of industrial disputes involving London tradesmen		1766 Oliver Goldsmith, *The Vicar of Wakefield*	1767–9 First Mysore War; New York Assembly suspended for resisting quartering of troops; taxes on several imports leads to protests and boycotts in America	
1768–9 John Wilkes elected to parliament and is expelled; widespread petitioning for parliamentary reform; Society of the Supporters of the Bill of Rights formed	1769 James Watt invents the condensing steam engine	1768 Joseph Wright of Derby, *Experiment with an Air Pump* 1768–71 James Cook's first circumnavigation of the globe	1768 Massachusetts Assembly dissolved for resisting taxes; Boston refuses to quarter British troops	
		1770 Edmund Burke, *Thoughts on the Cause of the Present Discontents*; Thomas Gainsborough, *The Blue Boy*	1770 Brawl between civilians and troops labelled the 'Boston Massacre'; many taxes repealed by Britain, but not the tax on tea; James Bruce discovers source of Blue Nile; James Cook discovers Botany Bay	*1770*
1772 Royal Marriages Act	1771 Sir Richard Arkwright opens first spinning mill in England 1772 Somerset case determines that a slave is free upon entering England	1771 First Edition of the *Encyclopaedia Britannica* 1772–5 Cook's second voyage		
1774 *Hansard* first printed	1773 First cast-iron bridge at Coalbrookdale		1773 Boston Tea Party 1774 Coercive Acts against Massachusetts; Continental Congress calls for boycott of British goods	
1775 Sailors' strike in Liverpool			1775–83 American Revolution 1775 Battles of Lexington and Bunker Hill; British hire 29,000 German mercenaries for war	
	1776 Adam Smith, *The Wealth of Nations*; St Leger horse race established 1777 Last monoglot Cornish speaker dies	1776–88 Edward Gibbon, *Decline and Fall of the Roman Empire*	1776 American Declaration of Independence; battle of Trenton 1777 Battles of Princeton, Brandywine, Germantown and Saratoga	
		1778–9 Cook's third voyage	1778–83 War with France 1778 Battle of Monmouth	
1779–80 Widespread petitioning for reform of parliament; Association Movement for Parliamentary Reform founded	1779 First children's clinic in London; the Derby horse race established		1779–83 Spain declares war and besieges Gibraltar 1779–82 Mahratta war	
1780 Home Rule demanded by Grattan and the Irish Volunteers	1780 Gordon anti-Catholic riots in London		1780 Battles of Camden and King's Mountain 1780–4 Second Mysore War	*1780*
	1781 First building society founded	1781 William Herschel discovers Uranus 1782 Royal Irish Academy founded	1781 Battle of Cowpens; British army surrenders at Yorktown 1782 Battle of The Saintes	
1783–1881 The Highland Clearances	1783 Bank of Ireland founded 1784 Andrew Meikle invents threshing machine 1785 James Watt and Matthew Boulton install a steam engine in a cotton-spinning factory; *Daily Universal Register*, from 1788 *The Times*, published		1783 Peace of Versailles establishes American independence	
1787 Warren Hastings impeached	1787 Marylebone Cricket Club founded; steam engines introduced in Manchester cotton mills			
1788–9 Regency crisis with George III's first bout of mental illness		1788 James Hutton, *Theory of the Earth*, first work of modern geology	1789 French Revolution	
				1790

1790–1830	EVENTS IN BRITAIN & IRELAND	SOCIETY, ECONOMY & TECHNOLOGY	ARTS & SCIENCE	OTHER EVENTS
1790			1790 Edmund Burke, *Reflections on the Revolution in France*	1790–2 Third Mysore War
	1791 Theobald Wolfe Tone forms Society of United Irishmen	1791 *English Stud Book* first published	1791 Robert Burns, *Tam o'Shanter*	
	1792 Libel Act passed		1792 Mary Wollstonecraft, *Vindication of the Rights of Women*	
	1793 British Convention assembles at Edinburgh and is dispersed			1793–1814 Wars with France
	1794 *Habeas Corpus* suspended; leaders of reform societies arrested	1795 Widespread food rioting and anti-war demonstrations	1795 Royal College of St Patrick, Maynooth, opened	1795 British take Ceylon and occupy Cape of Good Hope
		1797 England exporting iron; first copper pennies and pound notes issued		1797 Battles of Cape St Vincent and Camperdown; mutiny at Spithead and the Nore; abortive French landing in Pembrokeshire
	1798 Income tax introduced; rebellion in Ireland; battle of Vinegar Hill; capture of Wolfe Tone		1798 T. R. Malthus, *Essay on the Principle of Population*; William Wordsworth and Samuel Coleridge, *Lyrical Ballads*	1798 Battle of the Nile; abortive French landing in Ireland
	1799 Combination Act passed; trials by courts martial in Ireland			
1800	1801 Act of Union of Britain and Ireland		1800 Royal College of Surgeons founded	1800 British take Malta
				1801 Battle of Copenhagen; British enter Cairo
		1802 John Debrett's *Peerage* published; London's West India Docks built	1802 John Dalton proposes atomic theory	1802 Peace of Amiens
				1803 Second Mahratta War; renewed war with France
				1805 Battle of Trafalgar
	1807 Slave trade prohibited	1807 Gas lighting introduced in London streets		1809 Battles of Oporto and Talavera; British take Cayenne and Martinique; Walcheren expedition fails
1810				1810 British take Guadaloupe
	1811 Prince of Wales becomes Prince Regent due to George III's insanity	1811 Luddites destroy machinery in the North and Midlands; separation of Welsh Methodists from Church of England	1812 Elgin Marbles in England	1812 War with United States; Wellington takes Madrid; battle of Salamanca
	1812 Prime Minister Spencer Percival assassinated		1812–18 Lord Byron, *Childe Harold*	
			1813 Jane Austen, *Pride and Prejudice*; London Philharmonic Society founded	1813 Battle of Vitoria
		1814 The Year of the Burnings in Scotland		1814 British burn Washington
	1815 Corn Law passed, causing widespread protest; income tax ended	1815 Humphrey Davy invents miner's safety lamp		1815 Napoleon's 'Hundred Days'; battles of New Orleans and Waterloo
		1816 *Blackwood's Magazine* published in Edinburgh	1816 Austen, *Emma*	
	1817 Attempted assassination of Prince Regent; rioting in Derbyshire against low wages	1817 *The Scotsman* founded		
		1818 General Union of Trades formed in Lancashire	1818 Mary Shelley, *Frankenstein*	
	1819 'Peterloo' Massacre			
1820	1820 Cato Street conspiracy uncovered	1820 Culrain riots; evictions in Strath Oykel	1820 Walter Scott, *Ivanhoe*; John Keats, *Ode to a Nightingale*	
	1822 Suicide of Foreign Secretary, Lord Castlereagh	1823 Mechanics Institute founded; Rugby Football invented	1821 John Constable, *The Hay Wain*; Thomas de Quincey, *Confessions of an English Opium Eater*	
	1824 Combination Act repealed		1824 National Gallery founded	1824–6 First Burmese War
	1825 New Combination Act	1825 Stockton and Darlington railway opened		
			1826 Royal Zoological Society and University College, London, founded	
	1829 Catholic Emancipation; Birmingham Political Union founded	1829 Metropolitan Police formed; George Stephenson's steam locomotive *The Rocket* runs		
1830				

EVENTS IN BRITAIN & IRELAND	SOCIETY, ECONOMY & TECHNOLOGY	ARTS & SCIENCE	OTHER EVENTS	**1830–1865**
				1830
			1830 British annexe Mysore	
		1831 Faraday discovers electromagnetic induction		
1832 First Reform Act	1832 Cholera epidemic		1832 Britain occupies the Falkland Islands	
			1833 Slavery abolished in the British Empire	
1834 Poor Law Amendment Act; parliament burns down	1834 'Tolpuddle Martyrs' deported to Australia; Hansom cabs introduced in London			
1835 Municipal Corporations Act		1835 William Wordsworth publishes best-selling collection of poems	1835 Melbourne, Australia, founded; 'Great Trek' begins in southern Africa	
1836 Marriage Act; enforced registration of marriages, births and deaths		1837 Charles Dickens, *Pickwick Papers*	1837–8 Rebellion in Canada; Lord Durham's report favours introduction of responsible self-government	
1838 People's Charter drawn up by Working Men's Associations; Richard Cobden forms Anti-Corn Law League		1838 Elizabeth Barrett Browning, *The Seraphim and Other Poems*; Dickens, *Oliver Twist*	1838–42 First Afghan War	
1839–44 The Rebecca Riots	1839 First Aintree Grand National horse race		1839–42 Opium War with China	
				1840
1840 Queen Victoria and Prince Albert marry	1840 Penny Post introduced	1840 Present Houses of Parliament begun	1840 New Zealand becomes a British colony	
	1841 *Punch* published	1841 Robert Browning, *Pippa Passes*		
1842 Pro-Chartist 'Plug Plot'	1843 Brunel's *Great Western* (ship)	1843 *The Economist* published	1843–7 First Maori War; Natal annexed	
	1844 Cooperative Society founded			
1845–6 Potato blight causes famine in Ireland (perhaps 1 million die), the Highlands of Scotland and the Isle of Man	1845 Glencalvie cleared	1845 Benjamin Disraeli, *Sybil*	1845–6 First Sikh War	
1846 Corn Laws repealed	1846 Destitute Relief Boards in Edinburgh and Glasgow			
1847 Factory Act restricts working hours of women and children		1847 Charlotte Brontë, *Jane Eyre*; Emily Brontë, *Wuthering Heights*		
1848 Public Health Act		1848 William Thackeray, *Vanity Fair*	1848–9 Second Sikh War; Punjab annexed	
	1849 Glen Elg evictions			
				1850
		1850 Dickens, *David Copperfield*		
1851 Great Exhibition held	1851 Amalgamated Society of Engineers formed; Skye Emigration Society formed		1851–3 Basuto War	
			1852–3 Second Burmese War	
		1853 Queen Victoria uses chloroform during childbirth; smallpox vaccination compulsory	1853 Nagpur annexed	
		1854 Alfred, Lord Tennyson, *Charge of the Light Brigade*; University College, Dublin, founded	1854–6 Crimean War; battles of Balaklava and Inkerman	
	1856 Henry Bessemer introduces new steel-making process; Welsh national anthem composed		1856–8 Anglo-Chinese War	
1857–82 Matrimonial Causes Act and Married Women's Property Acts		1857 Victoria and Albert Museum opened; Thomas Hughes, *Tom Brown's Schooldays*	1857–8 Indian Mutiny	
1858 Irish Republican Brotherhood (the Fenians) founded		1859 Charles Darwin, *The Origin of Species*; Dickens, *A Tale of Two Cities*; J. S. Mill, *On Liberty*	1858 Richard Burton and John Speke discover Lake Tanganyika	
				1860
			1860–70 Second Maori War	
1861 Abortion a criminal offence; Prince Albert dies	1861 First National Eisteddfod held	1861 George Eliot, *Silas Marner*; Dickens, *Great Expectations*	1861–5 American Civil War	
1862–70 Contagious Diseases Act	1862 First English cricket tour of Australia			
	1863 Football Association founded			
1864 Reform Union founded	1864 Schools Enquiry Commission calls for high schools for girls			
1865 Reform League founded		1865 Lewis Carroll, *Alice's Adventures in Wonderland*	1865 Welsh colonists arrive in Patagonia	
				1865

1865–1900	EVENTS IN BRITAIN & IRELAND	SOCIETY, ECONOMY & TECHNOLOGY	ARTS & SCIENCE	OTHER EVENTS
1865		1866 'Sheffield outrages' attacks on non-union labour; Dr Barnardo's first home opened		1867 Dominion of Canada established; discovery of diamonds in South Africa
	1867 Second Reform Act; first women's suffrage committee formed; Fenian unrest in Ireland and England; National Union of Conservative Associations formed	1868 First Trade Union Congress; the game badminton invented	1868 Wilkie Collins, *The Moonstone*	1868 British expedition to Ethiopia
	1869 Women rate-payers allowed to vote in municipal elections			1869–70 Red River rebellion in Canada
1870	1871 Trade Union Act gives unions legal recognition	1871 Bank Holidays introduced; Newnham College, Cambridge, founded for women; F A Cup established	1871 George Eliot, *Middlemarch*	1871 Griqualand West in South Africa annexed following discovery of diamonds
	1872 Ballot Act establishes voting by secret ballot	1873–86 Severn Tunnel built	1872 University College of Wales opens	1873 Ashanti War
			1874 Thomas Hardy, *Far from the Madding Crowd*	
	1876 Queen Victoria made empress of India	1875 Matthew Webb swims the English Channel	1875 Gilbert and Sullivan, *Trial by Jury*	1875 Britain buys major interest in the Suez Canal
		1878 Electric street lighting introduced to London; Bicycle Touring Club formed	1877 Oxford Professorship of Celtic established	1877 Transvaal annexed
	1879 Irish National Land League founded	1879 First London telephone exchange opened		1879 Zulu War; battle of Isandhlwana
1880	1880 Captain Boycott 'boycotted' in Ireland	1880 Trades Union Congress adopt principle of equal pay for women	1880 Gilbert and Sullivan, *Pirates of Penzance*	1880–1 First Anglo-Boer War; battle of Majuba Hill
	1882 Phoenix Park Murders; Kilmainham Agreement		1881 Natural History Museum opened	1882 British occupy Egypt
	1882–6 Highland Land War (Crofters' War)	1883 Age of consent raised to 16 years; Fabian Society founded		
	1884 Third Reform Act		1884 First part of *Oxford English Dictionary* published; Gaelic Athletic Association founded	1884–5 General Charles Gordon besieged and killed at Khartoum by Mahdists
	1885 Single member constituencies created	1885 Electric trams introduced in Blackpool	1885 H. Rider Haggard, *King Solomon's Mines*; Gilbert and Sullivan, *The Mikado*	1885 Indian National Congress formed
	1886 Irish Home Rule Bill defeated; Liberal Party badly divided			1886 Gold discovered in Transvaal
	1887 National Union of Women's Suffrage Societies a nationwide group; Queen Victoria's Golden Jubilee	1888 Football League formed; 'Jack the Ripper' murders	1889 J. K. Jerome, *Three Men in a Boat*; Robert Louis Stevenson, *The Master of Ballantrae*	
	1889 London dock strike			
1890			1892 Arthur Conan Doyle, *The Adventures of Sherlock Holmes*	1890 Cecil Rhodes prime minister of Cape Colony
	1892 Kier Hardie enters House of Commons			
	1893 Second Irish Home Rule Bill defeated in House of Lords	1893 Gaelic League and Independent Labour Party both formed; Manchester Ship Canal opened		
	1894 Death duties introduced		1894 Rudyard Kipling, *The Jungle Book*	
			1895 First Promenade Concerts conducted by Henry Wood; H. G. Wells, *The Time Machine*; Oscar Wilde, *The Importance of Being Earnest*	1895–6 Jameson Raid fails to provoke revolt in Transvaal; resignation of Cecil Rhodes
				1896 British campaign against Mahdists launched; Klondike gold rush begins
	1897 Queen Victoria's Diamond Jubilee	1897 Royal Automobile Club founded		1898 Battle of Omdurman; Fashoda Incident
			1899 Edward Elgar, *Enigma Variations*	1899–1902 Second Anglo-Boer War
1900				

CHRONOLOGICAL TABLE

EVENTS IN BRITAIN & IRELAND	SOCIETY, ECONOMY & TECHNOLOGY	ARTS & SCIENCE	OTHER EVENTS	**1900–1930**
				1900
1901 Taff Vale case over union recognition	1900 Celebrations of summer solstice at Stonehenge by neo-Druids begins	1901 Seebohm Rowntree, *Poverty: A Study of Town Life*; George Bernard Shaw, *Three Plays for Puritans*	1900 Australia becomes a Dominion	
1903 Women's Social and Political Union founded			1902 Anglo-Japanese alliance	
1905–14 Militant suffragette campaign	1904 Rolls Royce founded		1904 Anglo-French entente	
1905 Sinn Féin and Ulster Unionist Council founded	1906 HMS *Dreadnought* launched			
	1907 Boy Scouts founded	1907 J. M. Synge, *The Playboy of the Western World*	1907 Anglo-Russian entente; New Zealand becomes a Dominion	
	1908 Olympic Games held in London	1908 William Butler Yeats, *Collected Works*	1908 South Africa becomes a Dominion	
1909 Osbourne judgement; Labour Exchange Act; House of Lords reject Lloyd George's 'People's Budget'	1909 Girl Guides founded			
				1910
	1910 Tonypandy riots			
1911 National Insurance Act; Parliament Act		1911 Ernest Rutherford formulates theory of atomic structure		
1912 Irish Home Rule Bill introduced	1913 Stainless steel first cast, at Sheffield	1913 D. H. Lawrence, *Sons and Lovers*		
1914 Curragh mutiny; Anglican Church in Wales disestablished; Defence of the Realm Act; declaration of war on Germany	1914 'Treasury Agreement' between unions and government	1914 Vaughan Williams, *A London Symphony*	1914–8 World War I	
			1914 Battles of Mons and first battle of Ypres	
	1915 Rent controls introduced		1915 Battle of Neuve Chapelle; second battle of Ypres; Edith Cavell executed; SS *Lusitania* sunk	
1916 Easter Rising in Dublin; Roger Casement executed	1916 British summertime and conscription introduced	1916 Marie Stopes, *Married Love*	1916 Battles of the Somme and Jutland	
	1917 Bread rationing introduced; growing industrial unrest	1917 Imperial War Museum founded; T. S. Eliot, *Prufrock*	1917 Battle of Passchendaele; Balfour Declaration; British take Jerusalem; Russian Revolution; USA enters World War I	
1918 Women householders over 30 given the vote	1918 Rationing of meat and butter; school leaving age raised to 14 years		1918 German offensive on Western Front fails; the Armistice	
1919 Nancy Astor the first woman to sit in the House of Commons; Ministry of Health formed	1919–20 Widespread industrial unrest	1919 Rutherford conducts the first artificial nuclear reactions	1919 Treaty of Versailles; Amritsar Massacre	
	1919 John Maynard Keynes, *The Economic Consequences of the Peace*			
				1920
1920 Unemployment Insurance Act; Black and Tans in Ireland; 'Bloody Sunday'		1920 University College, Swansea, opened; Wilfred Owen, *War Poems* (posthumously)		
1921 Anglo-Irish Treaty	1921 British Legion founded			
1922–3 Irish civil war	1922 British Broadcasting Company (BBC) founded	1922 James Joyce, *Ulysses*	1922 Gandhi imprisoned in India for civil disobedience; Chanak crisis	
1922 Erskine Childers executed; Sir Henry Wilson assassinated; 'Geddes Axe'; Honours scandal; Carlton Club meeting to end coalition government	1923 First FA Cup final at Wembley Stadium			
1924 First minority Labour government; Zinoviev letter		1924 P. G. Wodehouse, *The Inimitable Jeeves*		
1925 Plaid Cymru founded; Britain rejoins Gold Standard	1926 General Strike; Central Electricity Board and Imperial Chemical Industries founded	1926 A. A. Milne, *Winnie the Pooh*; T. E. Lawrence, *The Seven Pillars of Wisdom*; John Logie Baird demonstrates television	1925 Treaty of Locarno	
1927 Kevin O'Higgins assassinated	1927 Greyhound racing at White City	1927 Virginia Woolf, *To the Lighthouse*		
1928 All women over 21 given the vote		1928 D. H. Lawrence, *Lady Chatterley's Lover*; Alexander Fleming discovers penicillin		
		1929 Henry Moore, *Reclining Figure*		*1930*

1930–1960	EVENTS IN BRITAIN & IRELAND	SOCIETY, ECONOMY & TECHNOLOGY	ARTS & SCIENCE	OTHER EVENTS
1930		1930 First Empire Games held		
	1931 National Government formed; Invergordon mutiny; Britain leaves Gold Standard	1931 Unemployment benefits cut by 10%; household means test introduced		
	1932–8 Anglo-Irish trade war		1932 Aldous Huxley, *Brave New World*	1932 Indian National Congress banned; Gandhi arrested; Ottawa conference
	1932 Tariffs imposed by Britain			
		1933 3 million unemployed; MCC 'bodyline' tour of Australia		1933 Hitler German Chancellor
		1934 Driving tests introduced; SS *Queen Mary* launched; hunger marches on London		
	1935 Peace Ballot		1935 Sidney and Beatrice Webb, *Soviet Communism: a New Civilisation?*; Robert Watson Watt develops radar; Alfred Hitchcock, *The Thirty-nine Steps* (film)	1935 Hoare-Laval Pact
	1936 Edward VIII abdicates	1936 First Butlin's holiday camp at Skegness; Jarrow Crusade		1936–9 Spanish Civil War
	1937 New constitution for Ireland	1937 Frank Whittle invents the jet engine		
	1938 Ireland regains 'Treaty Ports'	1938 SS *Queen Elizabeth* launched; *Picture Post* published	1938 Graham Greene, *Brighton Rock*	1938 Munich crisis
	1939 Britain declares war on Germany; conscription introduced; Ireland declares neutrality	1939 Large-scale evacuation of children from London	1939 Sutton Hoo excavation; Dylan Thomas, *The Map of Love*	1939–45 World War II
				1939 Battle of the River Plate
1940	1940 Churchill forms coalition; battle of Britain; the Blitz	1940 Internment of fascist sympathisers		1940 Dunkirk evacuation
	1941 House of Commons bombed	1941 Household means-testing ended		1941 Lend-Lease introduced; *Bismarck* sunk; Crete evacuated
		1942 Beveridge Report		1942 Fall of Singapore, Rangoon and Tobruk; Dieppe raid; battle of El Alamein
	1943 Pay-as-you-earn scheme for income tax introduced		1943 Alan Turing builds the first electronic computer, 'Colossus'	1943 Dambusters raid; Sicily landings
	1944 White Papers on employment, health and social insurance; V1 and V2 attacks	1944 Butler Education Act provides free secondary education		1944 Normandy landings; battle of Arnhem
	1945 Labour landslide in the first postwar election	1945–9 c.20% of industry nationalised	1945 George Orwell, *Animal Farm*; J. B. Priestley, *An Inspector Calls*	1945 Rangoon retaken; Germany and Japan surrender
		1945 Family Allowances introduced		
	1946 National Insurance Act	1946–8 Bread rationing		
		1946 Royal Commission on equal pay; Heathrow airport opened	1947 First Edinburgh Festival of Arts	1947 India, Pakistan and Burma independent; Marshall Aid received
	1948 Ireland becomes a republic	1948 National Health Service established; Olympic Games in London; first large-scale immigration of Afro-Caribbeans to Britain	1948 Cambridge awards degrees to women	1948 Israel and Ceylon independent
	1949 Ireland Act severs last legal ties with Britain; Britain becomes a founder member of NATO		1949 George Orwell, *Nineteen Eighty-four*; Carol Reed, *The Third Man* (film)	1949 NATO formed
1950			1950 Ray Bradbury, *The Martian Chronicles*	1950–3 Korean War
	1951 Ministry for Welsh Affairs formed	1951 Festival of Britain	1951 Benjamin Britten, *Billy Budd*	
		1952 Smog kills 4,000 in London; the DH Comet, the first passenger jet airliner, enters service	1952 First British atomic bomb	
			1953 Watson and Crick announce the discovery of the DNA double helix	1953 Hillary and Tenzing climb Mount Everest
		1954 Independent Television Authority founded; rationing ended	1954 Kingsley Amis, *Lucky Jim*; William Golding, *Lord of the Flies*	
	1955 Cardiff officially capital of Wales	1955 Duke of Edinburgh Awards founded	1954–5 J.R.R. Tolkien, *The Lord of the Rings*	
	1956–62 IRA bombing campaign in Northern Ireland	1956 First Aldermaston march by CND	1956 Calder Hall nuclear power station opened; John Osborne, *Look Back in Anger*	1956 Suez Crisis
	1956 Clean Air Act to control air pollution			1957 European Economic Community formed; Ghana and Malaya independent
	1957 Harold Macmillan's 'never had it so good' speech	1958 First parking meters in London; race riots in Notting Hill		
1960				

CHRONOLOGICAL TABLE

EVENTS IN BRITAIN & IRELAND	SOCIETY, ECONOMY & TECHNOLOGY	ARTS & SCIENCE	OTHER EVENTS	**1960–2000**
				1960
1960 Conscription ends			1960 Cyprus and Nigeria independent	
	1961 First betting shop opened; *Private Eye* founded	1961 Benjamin Britten, *War Requiem*; The Beatles are formed	1961 South Africa leaves the Commonwealth	
1962 'Night of the Long Knives' as Macmillan fires 7 Cabinet Ministers; Commonwealth Immigrants Act	1962 Welsh Language Society founded	1962 Anthony Burgess, *A Clockwork Orange*; David Lean, *Lawrence of Arabia* (film)	1962 Jamaica, Trinidad and Tobago and Uganda independent	
1963 Profumo scandal; Beeching Report recommends large-scale railway closures; Great Train Robbery		1963 John Le Carré, *The Spy Who Came in from the Cold*	1963 French veto Britain's entry into EEC; Kenya, Tanzania and Singapore independent	
1964–9 Civil Rights protests lead to 'the troubles' in Northern Ireland	1964 Licences granted to drill for oil in North Sea; Mods and Rockers riot in seaside towns		1964 Malawi, Malta and Zambia independent	
1965 First Race Relations Act; death penalty abolished		1965 Harold Pinter, *The Homecoming*	1965 Unilateral Declaration of Independence by Rhodesia; Gambia independent	
	1966 England wins World Cup		1966 Guyana, Botswana, Lesotho and Barbados independent	
1967 Sterling devalued; abortion legalised	1967 Colour television introduced	1967 Tom Stoppard, *Rosencrantz and Guildenstern are Dead*	1967–84 Over 20 British colonies granted independence	
1968 Enoch Powell's 'rivers of blood' speech	1968 Widespread student unrest			
1969 Voting age lowered to 18 years	1969 Open University founded; maiden flight of Concorde			
				1970
1971 First British soldier killed in Northern Ireland	1971 Free milk for schoolchildren abolished			
1972 'Bloody Sunday'; British Embassy in Dublin burned during protests	1972 Miners' strike leads to power cuts; *Cosmopolitan* and *Spare Rib* published	1972 Frederick Forsyth, *The Day of the Jackal*; Ted Hughes, *Crow*	1972 Expulsion of Ugandan Asians	
1973 Britain joins the EEC	1973 School leaving age raised to 16 years; VAT introduced		1973 OPEC raises price of oil, causing recession in West	
1974 Direct rule over Northern Ireland imposed	1974 Last native Manx speaker dies; miners' strike leads to three-day week	1974 Philip Larkin, *High Windows*		
1975 Sex Discrimination and Equal Pay Acts; referendum on membership of EEC			1975–6 British 'Cod War' with Iceland over fishing limits	
1979 The 'Winter of Discontent' strikewave by public employees; Margaret Thatcher becomes Britain's first woman prime minister		1978 The world's first test-tube baby is born in Britain		
				1980
1980 Trade Union rights strictly curtailed	1980 Rioting in Bristol; over 2 million unemployed		1980 Rhodesia becomes legally independent as Zimbabwe	
	1981 Rioting in Toxteth and Brixton			
	1982 Welsh language television channel opened		1982 Falklands War	
1984–5 Miners' strike	1984–91 Large-scale privatisations of nationalised industries			
1984–90 Further restrictions on Trade Union rights				
1985 Anglo-Irish agreement	1985 Rioting in London and Birmingham	1985 British Antarctic Expedition discovers a hole in the ozone layer	1989 Fall of the Berlin Wall	
				1990
1990 Mary Robinson becomes the first woman president of the Irish Republic		1990 Glasgow made the 'Cultural Capital of Europe'		
1991 Rape within marriage prosecutable	1992 Church of England allows ordination of women	1993 Damien Hurst, *Mother and Child Divided*	1991 Persian Gulf War	
1994 Paramilitaries declare cease-fire in Northern Ireland	1994 Coal mines privatised	1994 Channel Tunnel opened		
		1995 Seamus Heaney wins the Nobel Prize for Literature	1995 NATO intervention in Bosnia	
		1997 Dolly the sheep cloned in Scotland	1997 Hong Kong returned to China	
1998 Good Friday peace agreement in Northern Ireland			1999 NATO intervention in Kosovo	
1999 Devolution establishes Welsh assembly and Scottish parliament		2000 US–British human genome project announces preliminary results		
				2000

RULERS OF BRITAIN & IRELAND

KINGDOM OF KENT

455–88	Hengest (legendary)
488–512	Oisc
512–22	Octa
522–60	Eormenric
560–616	Aethelbert I
616–40	Eadbald
640–64	Earconbert
664–73	Egbert
673–85	Hlothere
685–6	Eadric
688–90	Oswine
689–94	Swaefhard
690–725	Wihtred
725–48	Aethelbert II
748–62	Eadberht
762–4	Sigered
764–70	Heaberht
765–84	Egbert II
784–5	Ealhmund
796–8	Eadberht II
798–807	Cuthred
807–23	under Mercian rule
823–5	Baldred

KINGDOM OF WESSEX

519–34	Cerdic
534–60	Cynric
560–91	Ceawlin
591–7	Ceol
597–611	Ceolwulf
611–42	Cynegils
642–72	Cenwalh
672–4	Seaxburh
674–6	Aescwine
676–85	Centwine
685–8	Caedwalla
688–726	Ine
726–40	Aethelheard
740–56	Cuthred
756–7	Sigeberht
757–86	Cynewulf
786–802	Berhtric
802–39	Egbert
839–58	Aethelwulf
856–60	Aethelbald
858–65	Aethelbert
865–71	Aethelred I

KINGDOM OF BERNICIA

547–59	Ida
559–60	Glappa
560–8	Adda
568–72	Aethelric
572–9	Theoderic
579–85	Frithuwald
585–92	Hussa

KINGDOM OF DEIRA

569–99	Aelle
599–604	Aethelric

KINGDOM OF NORTHUMBRIA

592–616	Aethelfrith
616–33	Edwin
633–4	Osric and Eanfrith
634–42	Oswald
642–70	Oswiu
644–51	Oswine
651–5	Aethelwald
670–85	Ecgfrith
686–705	Aldfrith
705–6	Eadwulf I
706–16	Osred
716–18	Cenred
718–29	Osric
729–37	Ceolwulf
737–58	Eadberht
758–9	Oswulf
759–65	Aethelwald
765–74	Alhred
774–9	Aethelred I (deposed)
779–88	Aelfwald
788–90	Osred II
790–6	Aethelred I (restored)
796	Osbald
796–808	Eardwulf (deposed)
808	Aelfwald
808–9	Eardwulf (restored)
809–41	Eanred
841–4	Aethelred II (deposed)
844	Redwulf
844–8	Aethelred II (restored)
848–66	Osbert
866–7	Aelle
867–73	Egbert I
873–6	Ricsige
876–8	Egbert II
878–913	Eadwulf
913–27	Aldred

KINGDOM OF MERCIA

633–55	Penda
658–75	Wulfhere
675–704	Aethelred I
704–9	Cenred
709–16	Ceolred
716–57	Aethelbald
757	Beornred
757–96	Offa
796	Ecgfrith
796–821	Cenwulf
821–3	Ceolwulf I
823–5	Beornwulf
825–7	Ludeca
827–840	Wiglaf
840–52	Berhtwulf
852–74	Burgred
874–9	Ceolwulf II
879–911	Aethelred II
911–18	Aethelflaed
918–19	Aelfwyn

KINGDOM OF GWYNEDD

825–44	Merfyn Frych
844–78	Rhodri Mawr (the Great)
878–916	Anarawd
916–42	Idwal Foel
942–50	Hywel Dda
950–79	Iago I
979–85	Hywel II
985–86	Cadwallon
986–99	Maredudd
999–1005	Cynan I
1005–23	Llewelyn I
1023–39	Iago II
1039–63	Gruffudd I
1081–1137	Gruffudd II
1137–70	Owain
1170–4	Cynan II
1174–94	Dafydd I
1174–95	Rhodri II
1194–1200	Gruffudd III
1194–1240	Llewelyn Fawr (the Great)
1240–6	Dafydd ap Llewelyn
1246–82	Llewelyn ap Gruffudd
1282–3	Dafydd ap Gruffudd

KINGDOM OF MAN AND THE ISLES (to 1266)

c.971	Magnus mac Arailt
d.989	Gofraid mac Arailt
d.1004–5	Ragnall
1052–64	Echmarcach mac Ragnaill
c.1066–75	Godred Sihtricsson
c.1075–9	Fingal Godredsson (deposed)
1079–95	Godred Crovan
1095–6	Lagmann Godredsson
1096–8	Domnall mac Muirchertaig úa Briain
1098	Magnus Barelegs (king of Norway 1093–1103)
1099–1102	Sigurd Magnusson (king of Norway 1103–30)
c.1103–53	Olaf I
1153–8	Godred II
1158–64	Sumerled
1164	Reginald I
1187–1226	Reginald II (deposed)
1226–8	Olaf II (deposed)
1228–9	Reginald II (restored)
1229–37	Olaf II (restored)
1237–48	Harald I
1249	Reginald III
1249–52	Harald II
1252–65	Magnus Olafsson

KINGDOM OF SCOTLAND
House of Alpin

842–58	Kenneth I
858–62	Donald I
862–76	Constantine I
876–8	Aed
878–9	Giric
889–900	Donald II
900–43	Constantine II
943–54	Malcolm I
954–62	Indulf
962–6	Duf
966–71	Culén
971–95	Kenneth II
995–7	Constantine III
997–1005	Kenneth III
1005–34	Malcolm II

House of Dunkeld

1034–40	Duncan I

House of Moray

1040–57	Macbeth
1057–8	Lulach

House of Dunkeld

1058–93	Malcolm III, Canmore
1093–4	Donald III (deposed)
1094	Duncan II
1094–7	Donald III (restored)
1097–1107	Edgar
1107–24	Alexander I
1124–53	David I
1153–65	Malcolm IV, the Maiden
1165–1214	William the Lion
1214–49	Alexander II
1249–86	Alexander III

House of Norway

1286–90	Margaret

House of Balliol

1292–6	John

House of Bruce

1306–29	Robert I
1329–71	David II

House of Balliol

1332–56	Edward

House of Stewart
(Stuart from mid-16th century)

1371–90	Robert II
1390–1406	Robert III
1406–37	James I
1437–60	James II
1460–88	James III
1488–1513	James IV
1513–42	James V
1542–67	Mary
1567–1625	James VI
1625–49	Charles I
1649–51	Charles II

Commonwealth and Protectorate

1651–3	Commonwealth
1653–8	Oliver Cromwell, Lord Protector
1658–9	Richard Cromwell, Lord Protector
1659–60	Commonwealth

House of Stuart

1660–85	Charles II (restored)
1685–8	James VII

House of Orange

1689–94	William of Orange and Mary
1695–1702	William of Orange

House of Stuart

1702–7	Anne

HIGH KINGSHIP OF IRELAND

N = Kings of the Northern Uí Néill

S = Kings of the Southern Uí Néill

?–453?	Niall Noígiallach (Niall of the Nine Hostages) (King of Tara)
454/6–61/3	Lóegaire
?–482	Ailill Molt
?–507	Lugaid
507–34/6	Muirchertach (**N**)
534/6–44	Tuathal Máelgarb
544–64/5	Diarmait I
564/5–6	Forggus (**N**) and Domnall Ilchelgach (**N**)
566–9	Ainmire (**N**)
569–72	Báetáin I (**N**) and Eochaid (**N**)
572–86	Báetáin II (**N**)
586–98	Áed (**N**)
598–604	Áed Slaine (**S**) and Colmán Rímid (**N**)
604–12	Áed Uaridnach (**N**)
612–15	Máel Cobo (**N**)
615–28	Suibne Menn (**N**)
628–42/3	Domnall (**N**)
642/3–54	Conall Cáel (**N**)
642/3–56/8	Cellach (**N**)
656/8–65/6	Diarmait II (**S**) and Blathmac (**S**)
665/6–71	Sechnussach (**S**)
671–5	Cennfáelad (**S**)
675–95	Finsnechta Fledach (**S**)
695–704	Loingsech (**N**)
704–10	Congal Cennmagair (**N**)
710–22	Fergal (**N**)
722–4	Fogartach (**S**)
724–8	Cináed (**S**)
728–34	Flaithbertach (**N**)
734–43	Áed Allán (**N**)
743–63	Domnall Midi (**S**)
763–70	Niall Frossach (**N**)
770–97	Donnchad Midi (**S**)
797–819	Áed Oirdnide (**N**)
819–33	Conchobar (**S**)
833–46	Niall Caille (**N**)
846–62	Máel Sechnaill I (**S**)
862/3–79	Áed Findliath (**N**)
879–916	Flann Sinna (**S**)
916–19	Niall Glúndub (**N**)
919–44	Donnchad Donn (**S**)
944–56	Congalach Cnogba (**S**)
956–80	Domnall ua Néill (**N**)
980–1002	Máel Sechnaill II (**S**) (deposed)

1002–14	Brian Bóruma (Brian Boru) (Dál Cais; king of Munster)
1014–22	Máel Sechnaill II (**S**) (restored)
1063–86	Toirrdelbach Ua Briain (Munster)
1083–1121	Muirchertach Ua Briain (Munster)
1086–1119	Domnall Mac Lochlainn (**N**)
1106–56	Toirrdelbach Ua Conchobair (Connacht)
1136–66	Muirchertach Mac Lochlainn (**N**)
1156–83	Ruaidrí Ua Conchobair (Rory O'Connor) (Connacht)

KINGDOM OF ENGLAND

House of Wessex

871–99	Alfred the Great
899–924	Edward the Elder
924	Aelfweard
924–39	Aethelstan
939–46	Edmund I
946–55	Eadred
955–9	Eadwig
957–75	Edgar the Peaceful
975–8	Edward the Martyr
978–1016	Aethelred II, the Unready
1016	Edmund II, Ironside

House of Denmark

1016–35	Cnut the Great
1037–40	Harold I, Harefoot
1040–2	Harthacnut

House of Wessex

1042–66	Edward the Confessor
1066	Harold II

House of Normandy

1066–87	William I, the Conqueror
1087–1100	William II, Rufus
1100–35	Henry I

House of Blois

1135–54	Stephen

House of Anjou

1154–89	Henry II
1189–99	Richard I, Coeur-de-Lion
1199–1216	John

House of Plantagenet

1216–72	Henry III
1272–1307	Edward I
1307–27	Edward II
1327–77	Edward III
1377–99	Richard II

House of Lancaster

1399–1413	Henry IV
1413–22	Henry V
1422–61	Henry VI (deposed)
1470–1	Henry VI (restored, deposed)

House of York

1461–70	Edward IV (deposed)
1471–83	Edward IV (restored)
1483	Edward V
1483–5	Richard III

House of Tudor

1485–1509	Henry VII
1509–47	Henry VIII
1547–53	Edward VI

House of Suffolk

1553	Jane

House of Tudor

1553–8	Mary I
1588–1603	Elizabeth I

House of Stuart

1603–25	James I
1625–49	Charles I

Commonwealth and Protectorate

1649–53	Commonwealth
1653–8	Oliver Cromwell, Lord Protector
1658–9	Richard Cromwell, Lord Protector
1659–60	Commonwealth

House of Stuart

1660–85	Charles II
1685–8	James II

House of Orange

1689–94	William III and Mary II
1695–1702	William III

House of Stuart

1702–7	Anne

KINGDOM OF GREAT BRITAIN
House of Stuart
1707–14   Anne

House of Hanover
1714–27   George I
1727–60   George II
1760–1820 George III
1820–30   George IV
1830–7   William IV
1837–1901 Victoria

House of Saxe-Coburg-Gotha
(Windsor from 1917)
1901–10   Edward VII
1910–36   George V
1936   Edward VIII
1936–52   George VI
1952–   Elizabeth II

PRESIDENTS OF IRELAND
1938–45   Douglas Hyde
1945–59   Seán Thomas O'Kelly
1959–73   Eamon de Valera
1973–74   Erskine Hamilton
           Childers
1974–76   Cearbhall Ó Dálaigh
1976–90   Patrick John Hillery
1990–97   Mary Robinson
1997–   Mary McAleese

BRITISH PRIME MINISTERS 1721–2001

W = Whig   c = coalition   P = Peelite
T = Tory   Li = Liberal   C = Conservative
L = Labour   nc = national coalition

1721–42   Robert Walpole (**W**)
1742–3   Earl of Wilmington (**W**)
1743–54   Henry Pelham (**W**)
1754–6   Duke of Newcastle (**W**)
1756–7   Duke of Devonshire (**W**)
1757–62   Duke of Newcastle (**W**)
1762–3   Earl of Bute (**T**)
1763–5   George Grenville (**W**)
1765–6   Marquess of
           Rockingham (**W**)
1767–70   Duke of Grafton (**W**)
1770–82   Lord North (**T**)
1782–3   Earl of Shelburne (**W**)
1783   Duke of Portland (**c**)
1783–1801 William Pitt the
           Younger (**T**)
1801–4   Henry Addington (**T**)

1804–6   William Pitt the
           Younger (**T**)
1806–7   Lord Grenville (**c**)
1807–9   Duke of Portland (**T**)
1809–12   Spencer Perceval (**T**)
1812–27   Earl of Liverpool (**T**)
1827   George Canning (**c**)
1827–9   Viscount Goderich (**T**)
1828–30   Duke of Wellington (**T**)
1830–4   Earl Grey (**W**)
1834   Viscount Melbourne (**W**)
1834–5   Robert Peel (**T**)
1835–41   Viscount Melbourne (**W**)
1841–6   Robert Peel (**C**)
1846–52   Lord Russell (**Li**)
1852   Earl of Derby (**C**)
1852–5   Lord Aberdeen (**P**)
1855–8   Viscount Palmerston (**Li**)
1858–9   Earl of Derby (**C**)
1859–65   Viscount Palmerston (**Li**)
1865–6   Lord Russell (**Li**)
1866–8   Earl of Derby (**C**)
1868   Benjamin Disraeli (**C**)
1868–74   William Ewart
           Gladstone (**Li**)
1874–80   Benjamin Disraeli (**C**)
1880–5   William Ewart
           Gladstone (**Li**)
1885–6   Marquess of Salisbury (**C**)
1886   William Ewart
           Gladstone (**Li**)
1886–92   Marquess of Salisbury (**C**)
1892–4   William Ewart
           Gladstone (**Li**)
1894–5   Earl of Roseberry (**Li**)
1895–1902 Marquess of Salisbury (**C**)
1902–5   Arthur J. Balfour (**C**)
1905–8   Henry Campbell-
           Bannerman (**Li**)
1908–16   Herbert H. Asquith
           (**Li/c** 1915–16)
1916–22   David Lloyd George (**Li/c**)
1922–3   Andrew Bonar Law (**C**)
1923–4   Stanley Baldwin (**C**)
1924   Ramsay MacDonald (**L**)
1924–9   Stanley Baldwin (**C**)
1929–35   Ramsay MacDonald
           (**L/nc** 1931–5)
1935–7   Stanley Baldwin (**C/nc**)
1937–40   Neville Chamberlain
           (**C/nc**)
1940–5   Winston S. Churchill
           (**C/c**)
1945–51   Clement Attlee (**L**)
1951–5   Winston S. Churchill (**C**)

1955–7   Anthony Eden (**C**)
1957–63   Harold Macmillan (**C**)
1963–4   Alec Douglas-Home (**C**)
1964–70   Harold Wilson (**L**)
1970–4   Edward Heath (**C**)
1974–6   Harold Wilson (**L**)
1976–9   James Callaghan (**L**)
1979–90   Margaret Thatcher (**C**)
1990–7   John Major (**C**)
1997–   Tony Blair (**L**)

PRIME MINISTERS OF IRELAND
1922–2001

SF = Sinn Féin   FG = Fine Gael
FF = Fianna Fáil

1922   Michael Collins (**SF**)
1922–32   William T. Cosgrave (**FG**)
1932–48   Eamon de Valera (**FF**)
1948–51   John A. Costello (**FG**)
1951–4   Eamon de Valera (**FF**)
1954–7   John A. Costello (**FG**)
1957–9   Eamon de Valera (**FF**)
1959–66   Sean Lemass (**FF**)
1966–73   Jack Lynch (**FF**)
1973–7   Liam Cosgrave (**FG**)
1977–9   Jack Lynch (**FF**)
1979–81   Charles Haughey (**FF**)
1981–2   Garrett Fitzgerald (**FG**)
1982   Charles Haughey (**FF**)
1982–7   Garrett Fitzgerald (**FG**)
1987–92   Charles Haughey (**FF**)
1992–4   Albert Reynolds (**FF**)
1994–7   John Bruton (**FG**)
1997–   Bertie Ahern (**FF**)

BIBLIOGRAPHY

PART 1: ANCIENT BRITAIN & IRELAND

BRITAIN'S EARLIEST HUMANS
Barton, N., *Stone Age Britain* (London, 2000)
Bell, M., Caseldine, A. & Neuman, H., *Prehistoric Intertidal Archaeology in the Welsh Severn Estuary* (York, 2000)
Roberts, M.B. & Parfitt, S.A., *Boxgrove: A Middle Pleistocene Hominid Site at Eartham Quarry, Boxgrove, West Sussex* (London, 1999)

THE NEOLITHIC AGE
Bewley, R., *Prehistoric Settlements* (London, 1994)
Darvill, T., *Prehistoric Britain* (London, 1987)
Manley, J., *Atlas of Prehistoric Britain* (Oxford & New York, 1989)
Thomas, J., *Understanding the Neolithic* (London, 1999)

THE RITUAL LANDSCAPE
Bradley, R., *The Significance of Monuments* (London, 1998)
Cooney, G., *Landscapes of Neolithic Ireland* (London, 2000)
Eogan, G., *Knowth and the Passage-tombs of Ireland* (London, 1986)
Gibson, A., *Stonehenge and Timber Circles* (Stroud, 1998)

THE BRONZE AGE
Burgess, C., *The Age of Stonehenge* (London, 1980)
Parker Pearson, M., *Bronze Age Britain* (London, 1993)
Waddell, J., *The Prehistoric Archaeology of Ireland* (Galway, 1998)
Wainwright, G., *The Henge Monuments* (London, 1989)

THE IRON AGE
Cunliffe, B., *Iron Age Britain* (London, 1995)
Cunliffe, B., *Iron Age Communities in Britain* (London, 1991)
de Jersey, P., *Celtic Coinage in Britain* (Princes Risborough, 1996)
Raftery, B., *Pagan Celtic Ireland* (London, 1994)
Ritchie, J.N.G., *Brochs of Scotland* (Princes Risborough, 1988)

HILL-FORTS & OPPIDA
Cunliffe, B., *Danebury* (London, 1993)
Hogg, A.H.A., *Hill-forts of Britain* (London, 1975)
Sharples, N.M., *Maiden Castle* (London, 1991)

THE ROMAN CONQUEST
Cunliffe, B., *Fishbourne Roman Palace* (Stroud, 1998)
Frere, S.S., *Britannia* (3rd edn., London, 1997)
Webster, G., *The Roman Invasion of Britain* (London, 1980)
Welfare, H. & Swan, V., *Roman Camps in England: The Field Archaeology* (London, 1995)

ROME'S NORTHERN FRONTIER
Breeze, D.J., *Hadrian's Wall* (3rd edn., London, 1987)
Breeze, D.J., *The Northern Frontiers of Roman Britain* (London, 1982)
Maxwell, G., *The Romans in Scotland* (Edinburgh, 1989)
Shotter, D.C.A., *The Roman Frontier in Britain* (Preston, 1996)

ROMAN ECONOMY & SOCIETY
Birley, A.R., *The People of Roman Britain* (London, 1979)
Hingley, R., *Rural Settlement in Roman Britain* (London, 1989)
Millett, M., *The Romanisation of Britain* (Cambridge, 1990)

Wacher, J.S., *The Towns of Roman Britain* (2nd edn., London, 1995)
Webster, G., *The British Celts and their Gods under Rome* (London, 1986)

LATE ROMAN BRITAIN
Dark, K.R., *External Contacts and the Economy of Late-Roman and Post-Roman Britain* (Woodbridge, 1996)
de la Bédoyère, G., *The Golden Age of Roman Britain* (Stroud, 1999)
Esmonde Cleary, A.S., *The Ending of Roman Britain* (London, 1989)
Faulkner, N., *The Decline and Fall of Roman Britain* (Stroud, 2000)
White, R. & Barker, P., *Wroxeter: Life and Death of a Roman City* (Stroud, 1998)

ROMAN LONDON
Bird, J. (ed.), *Interpreting Roman London* (Oxford, 1996)
Milne, G., *Roman London* (London, 1993)
Rowsome, P., *Heart of the City: Roman, Medieval and Modern London Revealed by Archaeology at 1 Poultry* (London, 2000)
Shepherd, J.D., *The Temple of Mithras, London* (London, 1998)
Webster, G., *Fortress into City* (London, 1998)

PART 2: MEDIEVAL BRITAIN & IRELAND

THE MIGRATION PERIOD
Alcock, L., *Arthur's Britain* (Harmondsworth, 1971)
Campbell, J. (ed.), *The Anglo-Saxons* (London, 1982)
Carver, M., *Sutton Hoo: Burial Place of Kings?* (London, 1998)
Clancy, T.O. (ed.), *The Triumph Tree: Scotland's Earliest Poetry AD 550–1350* (Edinburgh, 1999)
Edwards, N., *The Archaeology of Early Christian Ireland* (London, 1990)
Foster, S., *Picts, Gaels and Scots* (Edinburgh, 1996)

SAXONS & CELTS
Bede, *A History of the English Church and People*, Leo Sherley-Price (trans.) (Harmondsworth, 1955)
Davies, W., *Wales in the Early Middle Ages* (London & New York, 1982)
Lane, A. & Campbell, E., *Dunadd: An Early Dalriadic Capital* (Oxford, 2000)
Redknap, M., *The Christian Celts: Treasures of Late Celtic Wales* (Cardiff, 1991)
Thomas-Edwards, T., *Early Christian Ireland* (Oxford, 2000)
Webster, L. & Blackhouse, J. (eds), *The Making of England: Anglo-Saxon Art and Culture AD 600–900* (London, 1991)

THE VIKING AGE
Fell, C.E. et al, *The Viking Age in the Isle of Man* (London, 1983)
Graham-Campbell, J. & Batey, C.E., *Vikings in Scotland* (Edinburgh, 1998)
Haywood, J., *The Penguin Historical Atlas of the Vikings* (London, 1995)
Ó Cróinin, D., *Early Medieval Ireland 400–1200* (London, 1995)
Richards, J.D., *Viking Age England* (London, 1991)
Sawyer, P.H. (ed.), *The Oxford Illustrated History of the Vikings* (Oxford, 1997)

VIKING YORK

Clarke, H. & Ambrosiani, B., *Towns in the Viking Age* (2nd edn., Leicester, 1995)

Hall, R.A., *Viking Age York* (London, 1994)

Smyth, A.P., *Scandinavian York and Dublin* (2 vols, Dublin, 1975–9)

THE AGE OF UNIFICATION

Barrell, A.D.M., *Medieval Scotland* (Cambridge, 2000)

Hill, D., *An Atlas of Anglo-Saxon England* (Oxford, 1981)

Lapidge, M., Blair, J., Keynes, S. & Scragg, D. (eds), *The Blackwell Encyclopaedia of Anglo-Saxon England* (Oxford, 1999)

Ó Cróinin, D., *Early Medieval Ireland 400–1200* (London, 1995)

Walker, D., *Medieval Wales* (Cambridge, 1990)

THE NORMANS

Bartlett, R., *England under the Norman and Angevin Kings* (Oxford, 2000)

Chibnall, M., *The Debate on the Norman Conquest* (Manchester, 1999)

Rowley, T., *Norman England* (London, 1997)

Williams, A., *The English and the Norman Conquest* (Woodbridge, 1997)

THE MEDIEVAL CHURCH

Burton, J., *Monastic and Religious Orders in Britain 1000–1300* (Cambridge, 1994)

Hamilton, B., *Religion in the Medieval West* (London, 1986)

Knowles, D., *The Monastic Order in Britain* (2nd edn., Cambridge, 1963)

Lynch, J.H., *The Medieval Church* (London, 1992)

Thomson, J.A.F., *The Western Church in the Middle Ages* (London, 1998)

THE ANGEVIN EMPIRE

Davies, R.R., *Domination and Conquest: The Experience of Ireland, Scotland and Wales 1100–1300* (Cambridge, 1990)

Davies, R.R., *The First English Empire: Power and Identities in the British Isles 1093–1343* (Oxford, 2000)

Duffy, S., *Ireland in the Middle Ages* (Basingstoke, 1996)

Gillingham, J., *The Angevin Empire* (London, 2000)

BRITAIN & THE CRUSADES

Lloyd, S., *English Society and the Crusades 1216–1307* (Oxford, 1988)

Macquarrie, A., *Scotland and the Crusades* (Edinburgh, 1997)

Tyerman, C., *England and the Crusades 1095–1588* (Chicago, 1998)

CASTLES

King, D.J.C., *The Castle in England and Wales: An Interpretative History* (London, 1988)

McNeil, T.E., *Castles* (London, 1992)

McNeil, T.E., *Castles in Ireland* (London, 2000)

Mertes, K., *The English Noble Household 1250–1600* (Oxford, 1988)

Suppe, F., *Military Institutions on the Welsh Marches* (Woodbridge, 1993)

THE PLANTAGENET HEGEMONY

Barrow, G.W.S., *Robert Bruce and the Community of the Realm of Scotland* (3rd edn., Edinburgh, 1988)

Davies, R.R., *The Age of Conquest: Wales 1063–1415* (Oxford, 1991)

Frame, R., *Colonial Ireland, 1169–1369* (Dublin, 1981)

Frame, R., *The Political Development of the British Isles 1100–1400* (Oxford, 1990)

McNamee, C., *The Wars of the Bruces: Scotland, England and Ireland, 1306–28* (East Linton, 1997)

Prestwich, M., *The Three Edwards: War and State in England 1272–1377* (London, 1980)

MEDIEVAL LANDSCAPES

Ault, W.O., *Open-field Farming in Medieval England* (London & New York, 1972)

Barry, T., *A History of Settlement in Ireland* (London & New York, 2000)

Edwards, N. (ed.), *Landscape and Settlement in Medieval Wales* (Oxford, 1997)

Roberts, B.K. & Wrathmell, S., *An Atlas of Rural Settlement in England* (London, 2000)

Taylor, T., *Village and Farmstead: A History of Rural Settlement in England* (London, 1983)

Turnock, D., *The Making of the Scottish Landscape* (Aldershot, 1995)

THE HUNDRED YEARS WAR

Allmand, C.T., *The Hundred Years War* (Cambridge, 1988)

Allmand, C.T. (ed.), *Society at War* (new edn., Woodbridge, 1998)

Curry, A.E. & Hughes, M. (eds), *Arms, Armies and Fortifications in the Hundred Years War* (Woodbridge, 1994)

Curry, A.E., *The Hundred Years War* (Basingstoke, 1993)

Hooper, N. & Bennett, M., *The Cambridge Atlas of Warfare: The Middle Ages* (Cambridge, 1996)

Sumption, J., *The Hundred Years War: Trial by Battle* (London, 1990)

Sumption, J., *The Hundred Years War: Trial by Fire* (London, 1999)

THE MEDIEVAL ECONOMY

Campbell, B.M.S., Galloway, J.A., Keene, D.J. & Murphy, M., *A Medieval Capital and its Grain Supply: Agrarian Production and its Distribution in the London Region c.1300* (Historical Geography Research Series, 30, 1993)

Carus-Wilson, E.M. & Coleman, O., *England's Export Trade 1275–1547* (Oxford, 1963)

McNeill, P.G.B. & MacQueen, H.L. (eds), *Atlas of Scottish History to 1707* (Edinburgh, 1996)

Moore, E.W., *The Fairs of Medieval England: An Introductory Study* (Toronto, 1985)

Palliser, D.M. (ed.), *The Cambridge Urban History of Britain, I, 600–1540* (Cambridge, 2000)

THE BLACK DEATH

Horrox, R. (ed.), *The Black Death* (Manchester, 1994)

Lewis, C., Mitchell-Fox, P. & Dyer, C., *Village, Hamlet and Field: Changing Medieval Settlements in Central England* (Manchester, 1997)

Platt, P., *King Death* (London, 1996)

Ormrod, M. & Lindley, P. (eds), *The Black Death in England* (Stamford, 1996)

THE LATER MIDDLE AGES

Dobson, R.B. (ed.), *The Peasants' Revolt of 1381* (London, 1983)

Dyer, C., *Standards of Living in the Later Middle Ages: Social Change in England c.1200–1520* (Cambridge, 1989)

Grant, A., *Independence and Nationhood* (London, 1985)

Horrox, R. (ed.), *Fifteenth-century Attitudes: Perceptions of Society in Late Medieval England* (Cambridge, 1994)

Pollard, A.J., *Late Medieval England 1399–1509* (Harlow, 2000)

Swanson, R.N., *Church and Society in Late Medieval England* (Oxford, 1993)

MEDIEVAL NORWICH

Atkin, M.W., *Norwich: History and Guide* (Stroud, 1993)
Ayers, B.S., *Norwich* (London, 1994)
Campbell, J., 'Norwich' in Lobel, M.D. (ed.), *Historic Towns, II* (London, 1975)
Meeres, F., *A History of Norwich* (Chichester, 1998)
Rawcliffe, C., *The Hospitals of Medieval Norwich* (Norwich, 1995)

PART 3: EARLY MODERN BRITAIN & IRELAND

THE AGE OF THE REFORMATION

Bush, M.L., *The Pilgrimage of Grace* (Manchester, 1996)
Dickens, A.G., *The English Reformation* (2nd edn., London, 1989)
Duffy, E., *The Stripping of the Altars: Traditional Religion in England c.1400–c.1580* (London, 1992)
Ellis, S.G., *Ireland in the Age of the Tudors* (London, 1998)
Guy, J., *Tudor England* (Oxford, 1988)
Haigh, C., *English Reformations: Religion, Politics and Society under the Tudors* (Oxford, 1993)
Wormald, J., *Court, Kirk and Community: Scotland 1470–1625* (London, 1981)

WALES AFTER THE UNION

Bassett, T.M. & Davies, B.L., *Atlas of Caernarvonshire* (Caernarfon, 1986)
Jenkins, G.H., *The Foundations of Modern Wales 1642–1780* (Oxford, 1993)
Jenkins, P., *A History of Modern Wales 1536–1990* (Harlow, 1992)
Jones, J.G., *Early Modern Wales c.1525–1640* (Basingstoke & London, 1994)
Williams, G., *Recovery, Reorientation and Reformation: Wales c.1415–1642* (Oxford, 1987)

THE ANGLO-SCOTTISH BORDER

Ellis, S.G., *Tudor Frontiers and Noble Power: The Making of the British State* (Oxford, 1995)
MacDonald Fraser, G., *The Steel Bonnets* (London, 1971)
Neville, C.J., *Violence, Custom and Law: The Anglo-Scottish Border Lands in the Late Middle Ages* (Edinburgh, 1998)
Rae, T.I., *The Administration of the Scottish Frontier, 1513–1603* (Edinburgh, 1966)

PARLIAMENT & POLITICS

Ellis, S.G., *Tudor Ireland: Crown, Community and Conflict of Cultures, 1470–1603* (London, 1985)
Hayton, D.W. (ed.), *The Irish Parliament in the Eighteenth Century* (Edinburgh, 2001)
Jones, C. (ed.), *The Scots and Parliament* (Edinburgh, 1996)
Kelsey, S. (ed.), *Parliamentary Buildings and their Uses: Dublin, Edinburgh and Westminster* (Edinburgh, 2002)
Loach, J., *Parliament under the Tudors* (Oxford, 1991)

TUDOR LONDON

Prockter, A., *A to Z of Elizabethan London* (Lympne, 1979)

ROYAL PALACES

Colvin, H.M. et al, *The History of the King's Works, vols III–VI* (London, 1973–82)
Thurley, S., 'A Country Seat Fit for a King: Charles II, Greenwich and Winchester', in Cruikshanks, E. (ed.), *The Stuart Courts* (Stroud, 2000)

Thurley, S., *The Royal Palaces of Tudor England: Architecture and Court Life* (London, 1993)

THE FIRST CIVIL WAR

Carlton, C., *Going to the Wars: The Experience of the English British Civil Wars 1638–51* (London & New York, 1992)
Kenyon, J. & Ohlmeyer, J. (eds), *The Civil Wars: A Military History of England, Scotland and Ireland 1638–60* (Oxford, 1998)
Morrill, J., *The Nature of the English Revolution* (Harlow, 1993)
Warmington, A.R., *Civil War, Interregnum and Restoration in Gloucestershire, 1640–72* (Woodbridge, 1997)

THE BRITISH REPUBLIC

Barber, S., *Regicide and Republicanism: Politics and Ethics in the English Revolution* (Edinburgh, 1998)
Barnard, T., *The English Republic 1649–60* (Harlow, 1997)
Reilly, T., *Cromwell: An Honourable Enemy* (London, 2000)
Woolrych, A., *Commonwealth to Protectorate* (Oxford, 1982)

RESTORATION & UNION

Bradshaw, B. & Morrill, J. (eds), *The British Problem c.1534–1707: State Formation in the Atlantic Archipelago* (Basingstoke, 1996)
Ellis, S.G. & Barber, S. (eds), *Conquest and Union: Fashioning a British State 1485–1725* (Harlow, 1995)
Glassey, L.K.J. (ed.), *The Reigns of Charles II and James VII & II* (Basingstoke, 1997)
Jackson, C., 'Restoration to Revolution 1660–90' in Burgess, G. (ed.), *The New British History: Founding a Modern State 1603–1715* (London, 1999)

COLONIAL EXPANSION TO 1707

Andrews, K.R., *Trade, Plunder and Settlement: Maritime Enterprise and the Genesis of the British Empire, 1480–1630* (Cambridge, 1984)
Canny, N., *The Oxford History of the British Empire, Vol. 1: The Origins of Empire* (Oxford, 1998)
McFarlane, A., *The British in the Americas 1480–1815* (London, 1994)
Porter, A.N., *Atlas of British Overseas Expansion* (London, 1991)

18th-CENTURY DUBLIN

Arnold, B., *Swift: An Illustrated Life* (Dublin, 2000)
Cosgrove, A. (ed.), *Dublin Through the Ages* (Dublin, 1988)
Dickson, D. (ed.), *The Gorgeous Mask: Dublin 1700–1850* (Dublin, 1987)

THE JACOBITE REBELLIONS

Lenman, B., *The Jacobite Risings in Britain, 1689–1746* (London, 1980)
Macinnes, A., *Clanship Commerce and the House of Stuart, 1603–1788* (East Lothian, 1996)
Monod, P., *Jacobitism and the English People, 1688–1788* (Cambridge, 1992)
Ó Ciardha, É., *Ireland and the Jacobite Cause, 1685–1766: 'A Fatal Attachment'* (Dublin, 2001)
Szechi, D., *The Jacobites: Britain and Europe* (Manchester, 1994)

LANGUAGES 1500–1800

Price, G., *The Languages of Britain* (London, 1984)
Price, G. (ed.), *The Celtic Connection* (Gerrards Cross, 1992)
Williams, G., *Religion, Language and Nationality in Wales* (Cardiff, 1979)

AGRICULTURAL CHANGE

Beckett, J.V., *The Agricultural Revolution* (Oxford, 1990)
O'Flanagan et al (eds), *Rural Ireland 1600–1900* (Cork, 1987)

Overton, M., *The Agricultural Revolution in England* (Cambridge, 1996)
Whyte, I.D. & K., *The Changing Scottish Landscape 1500–1800* (London, 1991)

COUNTRY ESTATES
Clemenson, H.A., *English Country Houses and Landed Estates* (London, 1982)
Girouard, M., *Life in the English Country House* (Yale, 1993)
Wilson, R. & Mackley, A., *Creating Paradise: The Building of the English Country House, 1660–1880* (Hambledon & London, 2000)

ENLIGHTENMENT EDINBURGH
Gifford, J. et al, *Edinburgh* (Harmondsworth, 1984)
Houston, R.A., *Social Change in the Age of Enlightenment: Edinburgh 1660–1760* (Oxford, 1994)

THE 18th-CENTURY EMPIRE
Bayly, C.A., *Imperial Meridian: The British Empire and the World, 1780–1830* (London, 1989)
Bowen, H.V., *Elites, Enterprise, and the Making of the British Overseas Empire, 1688–1775* (London, 1996)
Lawson, P., *The East India Company: A History* (London, 1993)
McFarlane, A., *The British in the Americas 1480–1815* (London, 1994)
Marshall, P.J. (ed.), *The Oxford History of the British Empire, Vol. II: The Eighteenth Century* (Oxford, 1998)
Morgan, K., *Bristol and the Atlantic Trade in the Eighteenth Century* (Cambridge, 1993)

TURNPIKES & CANALS
Albert, W., *The Turnpike Road System in England, 1663–1840* (Cambridge, 1972)
Aldcroft, D.H. & Freeman, M.J. (eds), *Transport in the Industrial Revolution* (Manchester, 1983)
Pawson, E., *Transport and Economy: The Turnpike Roads of Eighteenth-century Britain* (London, 1977)

THE INDUSTRIAL REVOLUTION
Berg, M., *The Age of Manufactures, 1700–1820* (London, 1994)
Daunton, M., *Progress and Poverty* (Oxford, 1995)
Hudson, P., *The Industrial Revolution* (London, 1992)
King, S. & Timmins, G., *Making Sense of the Industrial Revolution* (Manchester, 2001)
O'Brien, P. & Quinault, R., *The Industrial Revolution and British Society* (Cambridge, 1993)
Timmins, G., *Made in Lancashire* (Manchester, 1998)

AMERICAN INDEPENDENCE
Black, J.M., *War for America: The Fight for Independence 1775–1783* (Stroud, 2001)
Conway, S., *The British Isles and the War of American Independence* (Oxford, 2000)
Dickinson, H.T. (ed.), *Britain and the American Revolution* (Harlow, 1998)

PART 4: 19th-CENTURY BRITAIN & IRELAND

THE NAPOLEONIC WARS
Chandler, D., *On the Napoleonic Wars* (London, 1999)
Emsley, C., *Britain and the French Revolution* (Harlow, 2000)
Hall, C.D., *British Strategy During the Napoleonic Wars* (Manchester, 1992)
Rothenburg, G., *The Napoleonic Wars* (London, 1997)

THE AGE OF REFORM
Briggs, A., *The Age of Improvement 1783–1867* (2nd edn., Harlow, 1999)
Clark, A. & Richardson, S. (eds), *History of Suffrage* (London, 2000)
Evans, E.J., *Parliamentary Reform in Britain c.1770–1918* (Harlow, 1999)
Hanham, H.J., *The Reformed Electoral System in Great Britain, 1832–1914* (London, 1968)
Royle, E., *Chartism* (3rd edn., Harlow, 1996)

INDUSTRIAL MANCHESTER
Engels, F., *The Condition of the Working-class in England*, edited with an introduction by Eric Hobsbawm (London, 1969)
Hewitt, M., *The Emergence of Stability in the Industrial City: Manchester, 1832–67* (Aldershot, 1996)
Lloyd-Jones, R. & Lewis, M.J., *Manchester and the Age of the Factory* (London, 1988)
Messinger, G., *Manchester in the Victorian Age: The Half-Known City* (Manchester, 1985)

THE 19th-CENTURY EMPIRE
Chamberlain, M.E., *'Pax Britannica?'* (Harlow, 1989)
McDonough, F., *The British Empire 1815–1914* (London, 1994)
MacKenzie, J.M., *Imperialism and Popular Culture* (Manchester, 1989)
Porter, A. (ed.), *The Oxford History of the British Empire, Vol. III: The Nineteenth Century* (Oxford, 1999)

THE RAILWAY AGE
Freeman, M.J., *Railways and the Victorian Imagination* (New Haven, 1999)
Freeman, M.J. & Aldcroft, D.H. (eds), *Transport in Victorian Britain* (Manchester, 1988)
Robbins, M., *The Railway Age* (3rd edn., London, 1998)
Simmons, S., *The Victorian Railway* (London, 1991)

VICTORIAN BRITAIN
Briggs, A., *Victorian Cities* (London, 1963)
Langton, J. & Morris, R.J., *Atlas of Industrializing Britain 1780–1914* (London & New York, 1986)
MacKenzie, J.M. (ed.), *The Victorian Vision: Inventing New Britain* (London, 2001)
Marsden, G., *Victorian Values* (Harlow, 1998)

EDUCATION & LITERACY
Bryant, M., *The Unexpected Revolution: A Study in the History of the Education of Women and Girls* (London, 1979)
Marsden, W.E., *Unequal Education Provision in England and Wales: The Nineteenth Century* (London, 1987)
Stephens, W.B., *Education, Literacy and Society, 1830–70* (Manchester, 1987)

PUBLIC LEISURE: SPORT
Hill, J. & Williams, J. (eds), *Sport and Identity in Northern England* (Keele, 1996)
Holt, R., *Sport and the British* (Oxford, 1989)
Lowerson, J., *Sport and the English Middle Classes* (Manchester, 1993)
Russell, D., *Football and the English* (Preston, 1997)

SEASIDE RESORTS
Pearson, L.F., *The People's Palaces: The Story of the Seaside Pleasure Buildings of 1870–1914* (Buckingham, 1991)
Pimlott, J.A.R., *The Englishman's Holiday: A Social History* (1947, reprinted Brighton, 1976)

Walton, J.K., *The English Seaside Resort: A Social History 1750–1914* (Leicester, 1983)

Walvin, J., *Beside the Seaside* (London, 1978)

MIGRATION & EMIGRATION

Baines, D., *Migration in a Mature Economy: Emigration and Internal Migration in England and Wales 1861–1950* (Cambridge, 1985)

Erickson, C., *Leaving England: Essays on British Emigration in the Nineteenth Century* (Ithaca and London, 1994)

Hammerton, A.J., *Emigrant Gentlewomen: Genteel Poverty and Female Emigration 1830–1914* (London and Totowa, New Jersey, 1979)

Sherington, G., *Australia's Immigrants* (Sydney, 1990)

Wagner, G., *Children of the Empire* (London, 1982)

IRISH NATIONALISM

Boyce, D.G. (ed.), *The Revolution in Ireland 1879–1923* (London, 1988)

Comerford, R.V., *The Fenians in Context: Irish Politics and Society 1848–82* (Dublin, 1985)

Gailey, A., *Ireland and the Death of Kindness: The Experience of Constructive Unionism 1890–1905* (Cork, 1987)

Hoppen, K.T., *Elections, Politics and Society in Ireland 1832–85* (Oxford, 1984)

MacDonagh, O., *O'Connell: The Life of Daniel O'Connell 1775–1847* (London, 1991)

Vaughan, W.E., *Landlords and Tenants in Mid-Victorian Ireland* (Oxford, 1994)

THE LABOUR/CO-OP MOVEMENTS

Gosden, P.H.J.H., *Self-help* (London, 1973)

Gurney, P., *Co-operative Culture and the Politics of Consumption in England, 1870–1930* (Manchester, 1996)

Lancaster, B. & McGuire, P. (eds), *Towards the Co-operative Commonwealth: Essays in the History of Co-operation* (Manchester, 1996)

Price, R., *Labour in British Society* (London, 1986)

WORKING-CLASS HOUSING

Muthesius, S., *The English Terraced House* (New Haven, 1982)

Rodger, R., *Housing in Urban Britain 1780–1914* (Basingstoke, 1989)

BRITISH OVERSEAS TRADE

Cain, P.J. & Hopkins, A.G., *British Imperialism: Innovation and Expansion, 1688–1914* (London, 1993)

Checkland, S.G., *The Upas Tree: Glasgow 1875–1975* (Glasgow, 1981)

Cottrell, P.L., *British Overseas Investment* (Basingstoke, 1975)

Davis, R., *The Industrial Revolution and British Overseas Trade* (Leicester, 1979)

Ville, S., *English Shipbuilding During the Industrial Revolution* (Manchester, 1987)

THE SOUTH AFRICAN WAR

Pakenham, T., *The Boer War* (London, 1992)

Wilson, K. (ed.), *The International Impact of the Boer War* (London, 2001)

PART 5: MODERN BRITAIN & IRELAND

THE WAR IN EUROPE 1914–18

Chickering, R. (ed.), *Great War, Total War: Combat and Mobilization on the Western Front, 1914–18* (Cambridge, 2000)

Griffith, P., *British Fighting Methods in the Great War* (London, 1998)

Millman, B., *Pessimism and British War Policy, 1914–18* (London, 2000)

Terraine, J., *White Heat: The New Warfare, 1914–18* (London, 1992)

Travers, T., *The Killing Ground: The British Army, the Western Front and the Emergence of Modern Warfare, 1900–18* (London, 1990)

OTHER WAR THEATRES 1914–18

Halpern, P.G., *A Naval History of World War I* (London, 1994)

Hickey, M., *Gallipoli: A Study in Failure* (London, 1998)

Hughes, M., *Allenby and British Strategy in the Middle East, 1917–19* (London, 1999)

Millar, R., *Kut: The Death of an Army* (London, 1969)

Travers, T.H.E., 'Command and Leadership Styles in the British Army: The 1915 Gallipoli Model' in *Journal of Contemporary History*, 28 (1994)

WOMEN'S SUFFRAGE

Holton, S.S., *Suffrage Days: Stories from the Women's Suffrage Movement* (London, 1996)

Joannou, M. & Purvis, J., *The Women's Suffrage Movement: New Feminist Perspectives* (Manchester, 1998)

Liddington, J., *One Hand Tied Behind Us: The Rise of the Women's Suffrage Movement* (London, 2000)

Pugh, M., *Women and the Women's Movement in Britain 1914–59* (Basingstoke, 1992)

Van Wingerden, S.A., *The Women's Suffrage Movement in Britain, 1928–88* (Basingstoke, 1999)

IRELAND'S INDEPENDENCE

Augusteijn, J., *From Public Defiance to Guerrilla Warfare: The Experience of Ordinary Volunteers in the Irish War of Independence* (Dublin, 1996)

Hart, P., 'The Geography of Revolution in Ireland' in *Past and Present*, 155 (1997)

Hart, P., *The I.R.A. and its Enemies: Violence and Community in Cork, 1916–23* (Oxford, 1998)

Hopkinson, M., *Green against Green: The Irish Civil War* (Dublin, 1988)

Laffan, M., *The Resurrection of Ireland: the Sinn Féin Party, 1916–23* (Cambridge, 1999)

O'Day, A., *Irish Home Rule 1867–1921* (Manchester, 1998)

THE INTERWAR YEARS

Burnett, J., *Idle Hands: The Experience of Unemployment, 1790–1990* (London, 1994)

Constantine, S., *Unemployment in Britain Between the Wars* (London, 1980)

Francis, F., *Miners against Fascism* (London, 1984)

McKibbin, R., *Classes and Cultures: England 1918–51* (Oxford, 2000)

Stevenson, J. & Cook, C., *Britain in the Depression* (Harlow, 1994)

METROLAND

Jackson, A.A., *Semi-detached London* (rev. edn., Didcot, 1991)

Oliver, P. et al, *Dunroamin: The Suburban Semi and its Enemies* (rev. edn., London, 1984)

Saint, A. et al, *London Suburbs* (London, 1999)

THE HOME FRONT 1939–45

Calder, A., *The Myth of the Blitz* (Oxford, 1991)

McLaine, I., *Ministry of Morale: Home Front Morale and the Ministry of Information in World War II* (London, 1979)

Sheridan, D. (ed.), *Wartime Women: An Anthology of Women's Wartime Writing for Mass-observation, 1937–45* (London, 1991)

Smith, H.L. (ed.), *War and Social Change: British Society in the Second World War* (Manchester, 1986)

OVERSEAS THEATRES 1939–45
Allen, L., *Singapore, 1941–2* (London, 1993)

Ceva, L., 'The North Africa Campaign, 1940–3: A Reconsideration' in *Journal of Strategic Studies*, 13 (1990)

Cox, S., *The Strategic Air War against Germany, 1939–45* (London, 1998)

Ellis, J., *Brute Force: Allied Strategy and Tactics in the Second World War* (London, 1990)

Levine, A.J., 'Was World War II a Near Run Thing?' in *Journal of Strategic Studies*, 8 (1985)

THE ATLANTIC WAR 1939–45
Buckley, J., 'Air Power in the Battle of the Atlantic' in *Journal of Contemporary History*, 28 (1993)

Doughty, M., *Merchant Shipping at War* (London, 1982)

Milner, M., 'The Battle of the Atlantic' in *Journal of Strategic Studies*, 13 (1990)

Padfield, P., *War Beneath the Sea: Submarine Conflict, 1939–45* (London, 1997)

20th-CENTURY ELECTIONS
Butler, D., *British General Elections since 1945* (Oxford, 1995)

Craig, F.W.S., *British Parliamentary Election Statistics, 1918–68* (Glasgow, 1968)

Denver, D., *Elections and Voting Behaviour in Britain* (London, 1994)

Rallings, C. (ed.), *British Electoral Facts, 1832–1999* (Aldershot, 2000)

AUSTERITY & AFFLUENCE
Hennessy, P., *Never Again: Britain 1945–51* (London, 1992)

Jefferys, K., *Retreat from New Jerusalem: British Politics, 1951–64* (Basingstoke, 1997)

Morgan, K.O., *Labour in Power 1945–51* (Oxford, 1984)

Thompson, A., *The Day Before Yesterday* (London, 1971)

Tirstsoo, N. (ed.), *From Blitz to Blair: A New History of Britain since 1939* (London, 1997)

THE AFTERMATH OF EMPIRE
Darwin, J., *Britain and Decolonisation: The Retreat from Empire in the Post-war World* (Basingstoke, 1988)

Lahiri, S., 'South Asians in Post-imperial Britain: Decolonisation and Imperial Legacy' in S. Ward (ed.), *British Culture and the End of Empire* (Manchester, 2001)

Layton-Henry, Z., *The Politics of Immigration: Immigration, Race and Race Relations in Post-war Britain* (Oxford, 1992)

Paul, K., *White-washing Britain: Race and Citizenship in the Post-war Era* (London, 1997)

LANGUAGE & DIALECT
Hindley, R., *The Death of the Irish Language: A Qualified Obituary* (London, 1990)

Penhallurick, R. (ed.), *Debating Dialect: Essays on the Philosophy of Dialect Study* (Cardiff, 2000)

Price, G. (ed.), *Languages in Britain & Ireland* (Oxford, 2000)

Tristram, H.L.C. (ed.), *The Celtic Englishes* and *The Celtic Englishes II* (Heidelberg, 1997 and 2000)

Trudgill, P., *The Dialects of England* (Oxford, 1990)

Upton, C. & Widdowson, J.D.A., *An Atlas of English Dialects* (Oxford, 1996)

20th-CENTURY TRANSPORT
Bonavia, M.R., *Railway Policy between the Wars* (Manchester, 1981)

Frater, A., *Stopping Train Britain* (London, 1983)

Gourvish, T.R., *British Railways 1948–73* (Cambridge, 1987)

Starkie, D., *The Motorway Age* (Oxford, 1982)

Tyme, J., *Motorways versus Democracy* (London, 1978)

SOCIETY IN THE 1960s
Humphries, S. & Taylor, J., *The Making of Modern London* (London, 1986)

Johnson, P. (ed.), *Twentieth-century Britain: Economic, Social and Cultural Change* (London, 1994)

McKie, D. & Cook, C. (eds), *The Decade of Disillusion: British Politics in the Sixties* (London, 1972)

Marwick, A., *The Sixties: Cultural Revolution in Britain, France, Italy, and the United States, c.1958–c.1974* (Oxford, 1998)

Osgerby, B., *Youth in Britain since 1945* (Oxford, 1997)

THE TROUBLES
Hennessy, T., *A History of Northern Ireland, 1920–96* (Dublin, 1997)

Mallie, E. & McKittrick, D., *The Fight for Peace: The Secret Story Behind the Irish Peace Process* (London, 1997)

Mulholland, M., *Northern Ireland at the Crossroads: Ulster Unionism in the O'Neill Years* (Basingstoke, 2000)

O'Doherty, M., *The Trouble with Guns: Republican Strategy and the Provisional IRA* (Belfast, 1998)

Wichert, S., *Northern Ireland since 1945* (2nd edn., London & New York, 1999)

DEINDUSTRIALISATION
Bazen, S. & Thirlwall, A.P., *UK Industrialization and Deindustrialization* (London, 1997)

Middleton, R., *The British Economy since 1945* (London, 2000)

Pope, R., *The British Economy since 1914: A Study in Decline?* (Harlow, 1999)

THE BRITISH ISLES TODAY
Crotty, W. et al, *Ireland and the Politics of Change* (Harlow, 1999)

Dorling, D., *A New Social Atlas of Britain* (Chichester, 1995)

Moore, L., *Britain's Trade and Economic Structure* (London, 1999)

Robbins, K., *Great Britain: Identities, Institutions and the Idea of Britishness* (Harlow, 1997)

Warde, A. et al, *Contemporary British Society* (London, 2000)

20th-CENTURY LONDON
Humphries, S. & Taylor, J., *The Making of Modern London* (London, 1986)

BRITAIN, IRELAND & THE WORLD
Darwin, J., *The End of the British Empire: The Historical Debate* (Oxford, 1991)

Dodge, J. & Barrington, R. (eds), *A Vital National Interest: Ireland in Europe 1973–98* (Dublin, 1999)

Gowland, D., *Reluctant Europeans: Britain and European Integration 1945–98* (Harlow, 1999)

Reynolds, D., *Britannia Overruled* (2nd edn., Harlow, 2000)

INDEX

A

PICTURE SOURCES

t top; b bottom; l left; c centre; r right

Page 16 British Museum; 17bl, 17c Natural History Museum; 17t Bridgeman Art Library/Oxford University Museum of Natural History; 18 Skyscan Balloon Photography; 20tr Mick Sharp Photography; 21tl John Haywood; 22–23 Image Bank/Alvis Ulpitis; 24t, 24–25c, 25b John Haywood; 26cr, 26bl, 28bl, 28br The Art Archive; 29t, 29b Mick Sharp Photography/Jean Williamson; 30br Werner Forman Archives; 31tr John Haywood; 32tl Werner Forman Archives/ National Museum of Ireland; 32c The Art Archive/British Museum; 34 Mick Sharp Photography; 35b Skyscan Photolibrary; 36t Professor Barry Cunliffe; 37b, 38 Mick Sharp Photography; 40 CM Dixon; 43t Leslie Garland; 44tl CM Dixon; 44c British Museum; 47 CM Dixon; 48 Fortean Picture Library; 49 CM Dixon; 51tl, 51br Museum of London; 54 Crown Copyright: Royal Commission for Ancient and Historical Monuments, Scotland; 56tr CM Dixon; 57 The Art Archive/British Museum; 59 Mick Sharp Photography; 60 John Haywood; 62 Michael Holford; 65t Bridgeman Art Library; 65b Skyscan Photolibrary; 66tl, 66bl, 67br York Archaeological Trust; 68 Corpus Christi College: The Master & Fellows of Corpus Christi College, Cambridge; 69tl John Haywood; 70 Werner Forman Archives; 71b Bridgeman Art Library/British Library; 72 The Art Archive; 75cl Mick Sharp Photography; 76 Bridgeman Art Library; 78 John Haywood; 79b English Heritage; 80, 82t Bridgeman Art Library; 83b Bridgeman Art Library/Archives Nationales, Paris; 85cl Peter Newark's Pictures; 86t Bridgeman Art Library/John Bethell; 87b Bridgeman Art Library/John Bethell; 88 Skyscan Photolibrary; 91 Peter Newark's Pictures; 92t, 93b Skyscan Photolibrary; 94t English Heritage Photo Library; 96, 98 The Art Archive; 100 AKG London/British Library; 103 AF Kersting; 104b Church graffiti photographed by Peter John Gates, courtesy of Ashwell Church; 105tr The Art Archive; 106t Bridgeman Art Library; 108tl, 108cr Geoffrey Wheeler; 110tl Mick Sharp Photography; 110b Mick Sharp Photography; 111br Brian Ayers; 114 The Art Archive; 117tl Bridgeman Art Library; 118b Fortean Picture Library; 119t Bridgeman Art Library; 121t Peter Reynolds; 121b Leslie Garland; 122 The Art Archive/Sir John Soane's Museum; 125 John Haywood; 126bl Bridgeman Art Library/Hatfield House; 127cr The Bridgeman Art Library/Hatfield House; 128t AKG London; 130 Bridgeman Art Library; 132t Peter Newark's Pictures; 132b Bridgeman Art Library/British Library; 134 Hulton Getty; 136cr, 136bl Bridgeman Art Library; 138, 141 Peter Newark's Pictures; 143 The Art Archive/Musée de la Marine, Paris; 144 Bridgeman Art Library/British Library; 145t, 146b The Art Archive; 148 Bridgeman Art Library/Scottish National Portrait Gallery, Edinburgh; 151 Bridgeman Art Library/Coram Foundation, Foundling Museum, London; 152tc, 152tr Cambridge University Library; 152b Bridgeman Art Library; 154 The Art Archive/ Lincoln Museum & Art Galleries; 157b Hulton Getty; 158t Bridgeman Art Library/John Bethell; 159b Bridgeman Art Library/Yale Centre for British Art, Paul Mellon Collection; 161t Bridgeman Art Library/Guildhall Art Gallery, Corporation of London; 162t Peter Newark's Pictures; 164–165 Bridgeman Art Library; 166t Bridgeman Art Library/Guildhall Library, Corporation of London; 167b Ann Ronan Picture Library; 168t Peter Newark's Pictures; 170t Bridgeman Art Library; 171 The Art Archive; 173t Peter Newark's Pictures; 176tr Mick Sharp Photography/Jean Williamson; 176b Peter Newark's Pictures; 179t Art Archive/Parker Gallery, London; 179b Bridgeman Art Library/Christie's Image; 180 Mary Evans Picture Library; 183t The Art Archive; 183b Peter Newark's Pictures; 185cr Leslie Garland Picture Library; 186cl Mary Evans Picture Library; 188 Popperfoto; 190–191bl Peter Newark's Pictures; 191bl Bridgeman Art Library/National Railway Museum; 192t, 192b The Art Archive; 195b Hulton Getty; 196b Bridgeman Art Library/Penlee House Gallery & Museum, Cornwall; 198t Bridgeman Art Library; 199bl Mary Evans Picture Library; 200c, 201 Hulton Getty; 203t Bridgeman Art Library/Christopher Wood Gallery, London; 203b Peter Newark's Pictures; 205br with the kind permission of Victoria University Press, Wellington, New Zealand and the Alexander Turnbull Library; 207 Hulton Getty; 208tr Dr Caitriona Clear; 209b Mary Evans Picture Library; 210 Hulton Getty; 211 The Art Archive; 212 Hulton Getty; 215t The Art Archive; 216, 217b, 219t Peter Newark's Pictures; 219b The Art Archive; 222, 224t Hulton Getty; 225b Topham Picture Source; 226b, 227t, 227b Hulton Getty; 230tl Mary Evans Picture Library/Fawcett Library; 231t Hulton Getty; 231b Peter Newark's Pictures; 233t Popperfoto; 233b, 234t Peter Newark's Pictures; 235t Topham Picture Source; 236 Mary Evans Picture Library; 238t Hulton Getty; 239 Topham Picture Source; 240b London Transport Museum; 242tr Hulton Getty; 242bl Peter Newark's Pictures; 243tl The Art Archive; 244, 245, 247, 249, 250 Hulton Getty; 252 AKG London; 254t, 255t, 256 Hulton Getty; 258t, 258b, 259b Mary Evans Picture Library; 261, 263c Hulton Getty; 265t David Noble Photography; 265b Photofusion/Ray Roberts; 266–267 Hulton Getty; 268 Rex Features; 269, 270b Topham Picture Source; 271t Associated Press/Alistair Grant; 272t, 273b Topham Picture Source; 274tl, 275tr Press Association; 276 Sylvia Cordaiy Photo Library/Geoffrey Taunton; 278t Skyscan Photo Library; 279b Sylvia Cordaiy Photo Library/Chris Parkes; 280bl David Noble/Laurie Noble; 281tr Skyscan Photolibrary/ Quick UK Ltd; 282 Topham Picture Source/Associated Press